ISBN 978-0-331-94763-2
PIBN 11032426

CENTENNIAL HISTORY

OF THE CITY OF

WASHINGTON, D.C.

WIH FULL OUTLINE

OF THE

NATURAL ADVANTAGES A   UNTS OF THE INDIAN TRIBES, SELECTION OF THE SITE
FOUNDING OF TH   PIONEER LIFE, MUNICIPAL, MILITARY, MERCAN-
TILE, MANUF   ING. AND TRANSPORTATION INTERESTS, THE
PRES   LS, CHURCHES, SOCIETIES, PUBLIC
B   S. ETC. ETC., TO THE PRESENT TIME.

LLUSTRATED.

DAYTON, OHIO:
PUBLISHED FOR H. W. CREW BY THE
UNITED BRETHREN PUBLISHING HOUSE,
W. J. SHUEY, PUBLISHER.
1892.

CENTENNIAL HISTORY

OF THE CITY OF

WASHINGTON, D.C.

WITH FULL OUTLINE

OF THE

NATURAL ADVANTAGES, ACCOUNTS OF THE INDIAN TRIBES, SELECTION OF THE SITE
FOUNDING OF THE CITY, PIONEER LIFE, MUNICIPAL, MILITARY, MERCAN-
TILE, MANUFACTURING, AND TRANSPORTATION INTERESTS, THE
PRESS, SCHOOLS, CHURCHES, SOCIETIES, PUBLIC
BUILDINGS, ETC., ETC., TO THE PRESENT TIME.

ILLUSTRATED.

DAYTON, OHIO:
PUBLISHED FOR H. W. CREW BY THE
UNITED BRETHREN PUBLISHING HOUSE,
W. J. SHUEY, PUBLISHER.
1892.

G
9
W

1254261

PREFACE.

THIS CENTENNIAL HISTORY OF WASHINGTON has been written almost exclusively by Hon. William B. Webb, of Washington, District of Columbia, and J. Wooldridge, of Cleveland, Ohio, although assistance has been received by each writer from numerous individuals in Washington who have taken an interest in the work. The chapters written by Mr. Webb are Chapter III., "Washington Becomes the Capital"; Chapter IV., "Permanent Capital Site Selected"; Chapter V., "Pioneer Life"; Chapter VII., "Growth and Improvement of the City"; and Chapter XXII., "The Bench and Bar." He also rendered valuable assistance in connection with Chapter XXIII., "The Prosecution of Claims Against the Government.' The other chapters in the work were written by Mr. Wooldridge, assisted to some extent, especially in Chapter XIV. and Chapter XVI., by a gentleman of considerable experience in this kind of writing. But in all of his other chapters, as well as in these, he was assisted in many ways by numerous citizens of Washington, who, from their relations to certain institutions or enterprises, or special features of the history of the city, were better qualified than others to supply the data necessary to write these particular portions of the history. This was also, to a greater or less extent, the case with Mr. Webb. No one can write even a local history without numerous consultations with many of the citizens of the place. And it has been the experience of both writers of this HISTORY OF WASHINGTON that the great majority of those whom it was necessary to call upon for assistance in this way were more than usually courteous and obliging, and perfectly willing to aid to any extent in their power in the preparation of a work which they hoped would be at least creditable to those concerned in its compilation and its publication, as well as to the city of Washington itself. And inasmuch as the individuals who have given assistance in the ways referred to in the above sentences have been so numerous, it is believed that they will be satisfied if only the smallest possible number are named in this preface. Of those whom it would be impossible to omit with any degree of justice, the first is Dr. J. M. Toner, whose advice and assistance were always cheerfully and freely given, and always as freely and cheerfully accepted. The only regret in this connection, on the part of

either of the writers, is that it was found impracticable, on account of the peculiar exigencies of the enterprise, to consult with him as fully with reference to several of the chapters as it was earnestly desired to do; and it is also proper to say that wherever such omission was unavoidable, the work has suffered to that extent. The other gentleman whom it is also not only a duty, but at the same time a pleasure, to recognize in this way, is Mr. David Hutcheson, assistant librarian in the Congressional Library. Mr. Hutcheson was, during the whole time of the writer's labors in that library, always courteous and obliging, going beyond the requirements of his position in making valuable suggestions and referring to newspapers and books containing necessary information; his extensive knowledge of the contents of the library peculiarly qualifying him for the performance of these acceptable services.

That the work is without mistakes is not to be expected. Even Mr. Bancroft's great "History of the United States" is sometimes referred to as "merely an exhibition of the idiosyncrasies of its author"; and if such a criticism can be passed upon the greatest of American historians, how can the least hope to escape, even when writing under the most favorable auspices, which was far from being the case in the preparation of this work? But it is not designed or desired to dwell upon this particular, further than to say that a great deal of matter of greater or less value was prepared which was necessarily excluded from the work in order to avoid the production of an exceedingly unwieldly volume. But even as it is, it is believed to possess some merit; how much, must be left to the kind and considerate judgment of the reader.

While upon this subject of value, it may not be inappropriate to call attention to a few of the errors in standard works corrected in this work; for it is well known to all intelligent readers of history that even standard histories contain numerous errors, and that one of the objects of a careful writer is to correct the errors of his predecessors. In Barnes's "School History of the United States" it is stated that the first public messages sent over the telegraph wires between Washington and Baltimore in 1844 were in reference to the nomination of James K. Polk for the Presidency. On page 466 of this work this is shown to be an error, the first public messages passing on the 25th of May, 1844, while the announcement of the nomination of Mr. Polk for the Presidency was not made until the 29th of that month. In "The Story of Washington," by Charles Burr Todd, it is stated on page 38 that "This account is taken from the Washington letters in the State Department, and settles the much controverted point as to the authorship of the plan of the Capitol." By this, Mr. Todd means that in the text of his work he has established the fact that Mr. Hallett's plan of the Capitol was selected instead of Dr. Thornton's. In this supposition Mr. Todd is in error, and his assumption proves that he did not read all the correspondence on file in the State Department between President Washington and the commissioners, for that correspondence shows that while at one stage thereof it was thought best to adopt Mr. Hallett's plan, yet, after further consideration, Dr. Thornton's plan was in the main adopted, but modified somewhat by Mr. Hallett's ideas. Other papers and documents established the same point. Accordingly, in the chapter on "Government Buildings," this fact is so stated. To what extent, if to any extent, Dr. Thornton appropriated Mr. Hallett's ideas, is not discussed, that part of the controversy between those two architects being left to some future historian. These two instances are mentioned merely as illustrations of the effort made to write with accuracy.

H. W. CREW,

Publisher.

ILLUSTRATIONS.

CONTENTS.

CHAPTER IV.

PERMANENT CAPITAL SITE SELECTED.

CHAPTER V.

PIONEER LIFE.

CHAPTER VI.

MUNICIPAL.

CHAPTER VII.

GROWTH AND IMPROVEMENT OF THE CITY.

CHAPTER VIII.

MILITARY HISTORY.

CHAPTER IX.

TRANSPORTATION.

CHAPTER X.

HISTORY OF BANKING.

CHAPTER XI.

MERCANTILE HISTORY.

CHAPTER XII.

MANUFACTURING.

CHAPTER XIII.

HISTORY OF THE PRESS.

CHAPTER XIV.

EDUCATIONAL HISTORY.

CHAPTER XV.

LITERATURE AND ART.

CHAPTER XVI.

CHURCH HISTORY.

CHAPTER XVII.

MEDICAL HISTORY.

CHAPTER XVIII.

PUBLIC AND CHARITABLE INSTITUTIONS.

CHAPTER XIX.

GOVERNMENT BUILDINGS AND PUBLIC MONUMENTS.

CHAPTER XX.

CEMETERIES.

CHAPTER XXI.

SOCIETIES.

CHAPTER XXII.

THE BENCH AND BAR.

CHAPTER XXIII.

CLAIMS.

HISTORY OF WASHINGTON.

CHAPTER I.

NATURAL ADVANTAGES.

Situation and Natural Surroundings of the City—The District of Columbia—Prime
Meridians of the World—Design of Making and Attempts to Make the Merid-
ian of Washington a Prime Meridian—History of the Efforts to Determine the
Latitude and Longitude of Washington—Efforts to Establish an Astronomical
Observatory at Washington—William Lambert's Work—Andrew Ellicott's Work
—Errors in Mr. Lambert's Work—R. T. Paine's Work—Sears C. Walker's Work
—Latitude and Longitude of the Four Corners of the District of Columbia, of the
Washington Monument, and of the Naval Observatory—Ellicott's Azimuth Mark
—Other Original Landmarks—The Center Stone—The Center of the District of
Columbia—The Climate of Washington—Thermometrical and Barometrical Eleva-
tions—The Potomac River—Jefferson's Description of the Confluence of the
Potomac and Shenandoah Rivers—The Great Falls—Captain John Smith's Explo-
ration of the Potomac—The Potomac Fisheries—Theoretic Geology of the Vicinity
of Washington—Economic Geology—The Botany of the District of Columbia.

THE first question to be asked about a place is as to its situation; and
usually this has reference to its latitude, longitude, elevation above
the sea, and natural surroundings. In answering such questions as
these with regard to Washington, the Capital of the United States, it
is proper to begin with its latitude and longitude, and the history of
the determination thereof, although these were not determined even
approximately until some years after its selection as the site of
the Capital of the Nation. However, it may be briefly stated that
Washington is situated on the north side of the Potomac River, about
one hundred and sixty miles from its mouth. It is within the District
of Columbia, which, as originally laid out, was in the form of a
square, ten miles in length on each side, and hence containing one
hundred square miles of territory. The sides of this square extended
at an angle of forty-five degrees with the meridian line, so that the
several corners of the square pointed respectively to the north, east,

south, and west. The south corner, or point, was at the north cape of Hunting Creek, was known otherwise as Jones's Point, and was on the right bank of the Potomac River, just below Alexandria. The north corner is about a mile from Rock Creek, in Maryland. The west corner was near the Four-mile Road, in Virginia, and the east corner is about two miles east of the Eastern Branch, near Bladensburg, Maryland.

Inasmuch as it is necessary to introduce an account of the establishment of the meridian of longitude passing through Washington, it is deemed appropriate to present in the same connection brief mention of the various first meridians of the world. The earliest astronomer to determine longitude by astronomy was Hipparchus, of Rhodes, who chose for his first meridian that of Rhodes, where he observed. This island is on the dividing line between the Ægean and the eastern part of the Mediterranean Sea. Ptolemy adopted a meridian running through the *Insulæ Fortunatæ*, as being the farthest known land toward the west; while the Arabs adopted the meridian of the Straits of Gibraltar. In the eleventh century, Alphonso X., of Castile, adopted the meridian of Toledo. After the discovery of America by Columbus, and the voyages of the Portuguese navigators, Pope Calixtus caused the adoption of the meridian thirty-five degrees west of Lisbon; but later on, the first meridian was set back two degrees toward the east. Meanwhile, Protestant nations remained refractory to any action in this respect taken by Rome. The Dutch adhered to the meridian of Ptolemy until they changed it to that of the peak of Teneriffe; but a scientific congress, assembled by Richelieu, at Paris, in 1630, selected the meridian passing through the island of Ferro — one of the Canary Islands — for this purpose. Other famous first meridians have been that of Uraniemberg, and that of San Miguel, one of the Azores, twenty-nine degrees and twenty-five minutes west of Paris. These continued to be used for a long time, yet the meridian of Ferro, authorized by Louis XIII., April 25, 1634, gradually superseded all the others. In 1724, the longitude of Paris from the west coast of Ferro was found by Louis Feuillee, sent there by the Paris Academy, to be twenty degrees, one minute, and forty-five seconds; but upon the proposition of Guillaume de Lisle, the meridian of Ferro was assumed to be precisely twenty degrees west of the Paris observatory. The English held to the meridian of London, and added that of Jamaica, which island they had just conquered. During the first half of the seventeenth century, Mercator traced his first meridian through the Azores, his choice being determined by the circumstance that, in his time, at that longitude, the magnetic needle invariably pointed to the north. Mercator, however, was unaware of the fact that the magnetic meridian undergoes a constant but imperceptible oscillation, and that its extreme positions vary by many degrees.

Since the establishment of the meridian passing through the island of Ferro by Louis XIII., in 1634, each nation has held to the meridian passing through its principal metropolis, the three most in use since that time being that of this island, that of Paris, and that of Greenwich. The proceedings of the Washington Meridian Conference, held in 1884, with the view of establishing a first meridian of the world, will be detailed in their proper place.

The history of the determination of the longitude and latitude of the city, or rather of the Capitol building, is briefly as follows:

On October 20, 1804, Mr. William Lambert made observations on the occultation of Alcyone, one of the Pleiades, by the moon, from a position near the President's House. This was on Saturday evening. On Tuesday, November 14, 1809, Mr. Lambert prepared an abstract of calculations made for the purpose of determining the longitude of Washington from the observatory at Greenwich, England. In the introduction to this abstract of calculations he said:

"By the plan of the city of Washington, in the Territory of Columbia, the Capitol in that city is intended as a first meridian for the United States of America; but in order to establish it as such, the distance between it and some known meridian in Europe or elsewhere, measured or estimated on a parallel to the equator, and referred to the center of the earth under the respective meridians for which the computations may be made, should be ascertained on correct principles and with due precision. As many of our navigators and geographers are in the habit of taking their departure, or reckoning their longitude, from Greenwich Observatory, England, it will not, it is hoped, be considered as an instance of unpardonable presumption for attempting to extricate ourselves from a sort of deprecating and unnecessary dependence on a foreign nation, by laying a foundation for fixing a first meridian of our own."

Thus, from the first, it is evident that besides the object of finding the longitude of the city of Washington, another object was likewise entertained, namely, that of establishing a first meridian for the United States, in order that this country might be independent of other nations astronomically as well as politically. Of course it will be expected by no one that the details of Mr. Lambert's calculations will be presented here. The reader will desire to be instructed mainly as to the results of those observations and calculations. After presenting the rules for obtaining most of the elements necessary in the computation, Mr. Lambert collected and arranged the results obtained as follows: "Latitude of the Capitol in Washington by observation, thirty-eight degrees, fifty-two minutes, and thirty-seven seconds; latitude of the Capitol, reduced (334 to 333), thirty-eight degrees, forty-two minutes, and fifty-two and nine hundred and thirty-nine thousandths seconds; latitude of the Capitol, reduced (230 to 229), thirty-eight degrees, thirty-eight minutes, and nineteen and four hundred and sixty-five thousandths seconds; estimated longitude from Greenwich, five hours, seven minutes, and thirty-six seconds, or seventy-six degrees and fifty-four minutes west." But with reference to the longitude, Mr. Lambert closes as follows: "Supposing the error of the watch and the apparent times of immersion and emersion to have been exactly as they are here stated, the longitude of the Capitol in the city of Washington from Greenwich Observatory, by actual calculation, is determined as follows: Without reduction of latitude with the moon's horizontal parallax, seventy-six degrees, fifty-six minutes, and eleven and seventy-seven hundredths seconds; reduced (334 to 333), seventy-six degrees, fifty-four minutes, and four and one hundred and twenty-five thousandths seconds; reduced (230 to 229), seventy-six degrees, fifty-three minutes, and six and ninety-three hundredths seconds."

By the first process above, the form of the earth was assumed to be a perfect sphere; and in the second and third, it was assumed to be an oblate spheroid, with the ratio in the second between the equatorial and polar diameters of 334 to 333, and in the third, with a ratio of 230 to 229. Upon the assumption of a ratio of 282 to 281, the longitude of the Capitol was found to be seventy-six degrees, fifty-three minutes, and thirty-five and five hundred and twenty-seven thousandths seconds.

On March 9, and April 2, 1810, Mr. Lambert submitted other calculations. On March 28, Mr. Pitkin, from the committee on Mr. Lambert's memorial, submitted to the House of Representatives a report closing as follows:

"*Resolved*, That it is expedient to make provision by law authorizing the President of the United States to cause the longitude of the Capitol in the city of Washington from the observatory at Greenwich, in England, to be ascertained with the greatest degree of accuracy, and also authorize him, for that purpose, to procure the necessary instruments."

July 3, 1812, President Monroe submitted to Congress the report of his Secretary of State approving the project of establishing a first meridian for the United States, and on January 20, 1813, Hon. Samuel L. Mitchill, M. D., reported in favor of the establishment of an astronomical observatory at the city of Washington. Some time in 1815 Mr. Lambert revised his original calculation by another method of computation, assuming the ratio between the equatorial and polar diameters of the earth to be 320 to 319. Afterward he obtained observations founded on an occultation of Aldebaran, which occurred in January, 1793, the result being that the longitude of the Capitol was seventy-six degrees, forty-six minutes, and seventeen and fifty-five hundredths seconds, and by the observations of October 20, 1804, it was seventy-six degrees, fifty-four minutes, and twenty-seven and seventy-three hundredths seconds. From observations on an eclipse of the sun, September 17, 1811, the longitude was found to be seventy-seven degrees, five minutes, and twenty-three and seventy-seven hundredths seconds. From observations on the occultation of Gamma (γ) Tauri, which occurred January 12, 1813, the longitude was found to be seventy-six degrees, fifty-five minutes, and fifty-two and fifty-five hundredths seconds, and from the solar eclipse of August 27, 1821, it was seventy-six degrees, fifty-five minutes, and twenty-eight and sixty-five hundredths seconds.

Collecting all these results in the form of a table, we have the following:

	Stated in report.	As corrected.
From occultation, January 21, 1793	76° 46′ 17.85″	76° 46′ 17.55″
From occultation, October 20, 1804	76° 54′ 26.97″	76° 54′ 27.73″
From solar eclipse, September 17, 1811	77° 5′ 23.88″	77° 5′ 23.77″
Occultation of January 12, 1813	76° 55′ 52.85″	76° 55′ 52.55″
Solar eclipse, August 27, 1821	76° 55′ 28.20″	76° 55′ 28.65″
Mean result	76° 55′ 29.99″	76° 55′ 30.05″

The variance between the stated and corrected results was, therefore, six hundredths of a second, or about five feet, nine inches of linear measurement.

A joint resolution was adopted by the two Houses of Congress March 3, 1821, authorizing the President of the United States to cause to have astronomical observations made by methods which, according to his judgment, might be best adapted to insure a correct determination of the longitude of the Capitol in Washington from Greenwich, or from any other known meridian in Europe. Under authority of this resolution, on the 10th of April following he selected Mr. Lambert to make the necessary observation, by lunar observations, observations of lunar occultations of fixed stars, by observations of solar eclipses, or any other approved method adapted to ascertain the longitude of the Capitol in the city of Washington from Greenwich, and requiring him to return the data, with accurate calculations founded thereon, to the President to be laid before Congress at its next session. Mr. Lambert thereupon resigned the inferior clerkship which he then held in the Pension Office of the War Department, on the 30th of April, moved to the vicinity of the Capitol, and selected Mr. William Elliot, a well-known teacher of mathematics in Washington, to make the transit and other necessary observations. The instruments required were obtained from the Government, consisting of a transit instrument, a circle of reflection, an astronomical clock, and a chronometer. A true meridian was first established by means of concentric circles on a large platform nineteen feet west of the original line through the center of the Capitol, marked by Andrew Ellicott in the earlier history of the city. The daily rate of the chronometer was ascertained with due precision.

Some years before, Mr. Andrew Ellicott had obtained the latitude of Washington, to the nearest minute of a degree, to be thirty-eight degrees and fifty-three minutes north. The method of obtaining the latitude of the Capitol by Mr. Lambert was by altitudes of the sun on the passage of his eastern limb over the meridian at the south wing of the Capitol, sixty yards from the center of the building, and it was found to be thirty-eight degrees, fifty-two minutes, and forty-five seconds. On June 6, 7, and 8, 1821, the longitude of the Capitol was again sought for, and found to be west from Paris seventy-nine degrees, fifteen minutes, and twenty-seven and twenty-four hundredths seconds, from which, by deducting the longitude of Paris east from Greenwich, two degrees, twenty minutes, and eleven and fifteen hundredths seconds, the longitude of Washington west from Greenwich was found to be seventy-six degrees, fifty-five minutes, and sixteen and nine hundredths seconds. On the 22d of June, the longitude of Washington was found to be seventy-six degrees, fifty-five minutes, and nineteen and eighty-four hundredths seconds. Numerous other observations were made during the summer and autumn of that year with the view of securing the greatest possible accuracy, with a minimum result of seventy-six degrees, fifty-five minutes, and fourteen and eighty-one hundredths seconds, and a maximum result of seventy-six degrees, fifty-five minutes, and forty-three and thirty nine hundredths seconds. The result of all the observations may be summed up as follows:

	From Paris.	From Greenwich.
From observations prior to March 3, 1821..	79° 15′ 41.46″	76° 55′ 30.31″
Transit observations	79° 15′ 42 ″	76° 55′ 30.85″
Solar eclipse of August 27, 1821	79° 15′ 41.60″	76° 55′ 30.45″
Mean result	79° 15′ 41.69″	76° 55′ 30.54″

The President's House is north seventy degrees west, one and a half miles and fifty feet, or seven thousand nine hundred and seventy feet, from the center of the Capitol, and hence the longitude of the President's House is as follows:

	From Paris.	From Greenwich.
Longitude of the Capitol	79° 15′ 41.69″	76° 55′ 30.54″
Difference of longitude	1′ 34.79″	1′ 34.79″
Longitude of the President's House	79° 17′ 16.48″	76° 57′ 05.33″

In concluding his report, Mr. Lambert said: "The greatest variance in the result, allowing ninety-four thousand eight hundred and six yards to a degree of longitude in our latitude, was fourteen yards and eight inches, from which, if nineteen feet be deducted,— the distance of the transit from the Capitol center,— there are left seven yards, two feet, and eight inches. If we compare the mean result of all the observations with that which has been recorded in the abstracts of calculations heretofore furnished the two Houses of Congress, and allow the same deduction, the variance nearly vanishes, and does not amount to eleven inches of our admeasurement. If we admit the difference in the meridians of Paris and Greenwich to be two degrees, twenty minutes, and fifteen seconds, as stated in *Connaissance des Temps* for the present year, instead of two degrees, twenty minutes, and eleven and fifteen hundredths seconds, applied to the results of the transit observations which have been made, the variance would still be less than the length of the Capitol; namely, one hundred and twenty yards. Under all the circumstances in which the foregoing result can be viewed, allowing a small error to have been made in ascertaining the reduction of longitude from a sphere to a spheroid according to the ratio of three hundred and twenty to three hundred and nineteen, and to the distance of the meridians of Paris and Washington, it is not believed that it differs one-fourth of a minute of longitude from the truth."

Mr. Lambert then added, that it was in his opinion the duty of Congress to establish an astronomical observatory at Washington, in order that the right ascension, declination, longitude, and latitude of the moon, planets, etc., might be ascertained with sufficient accuracy, and thus it would be possible to compute a nautical almanac or astronomical ephemeris for ourselves, and then, but not before, we should be independent of the labors of European men of science.

With reference to the accuracy of the results as obtained up to this time (1821), it should be observed that Mr. Lambert used, all the way through, the lunar tables of Bürg, which contained errors sufficient to throw the longitude of the Capitol to the eastward too far by about twenty-five seconds of arc, or about five statute miles. These errors had been pointed out by Dr. Bowditch, but Mr. Lambert had omitted to make the necessary correction of his work. Some time afterward, a German mathematician named Wurm, by using Mr. Lambert's observations, arrived at the same result as that of Dr. Bowditch. Then, too, with reference to the accuracy of the longitude of the Capitol as determined by Mr. Lambert, D. B. Warden, in his "Chorographical and Statistical Description of the District of Columbia," published in 1816, makes the following observation:

"A celebrated astronomer, the Baron Lindenau, to whom we communicated this calculation, was pleased to favor us with the following observations concerning it:

"'On the 20th of October, 1804, the immersion of Eta (η) Pleiades was observed at Washington at nine hours, twenty-two minutes, and thirty-six and thirty-two hundredths seconds [true time]. From this the calculator deduces the conjunction of the moon and star at ten hours, forty-two minutes, and fifty-nine and two hundred and seventy-seven thousandths seconds. Calculating the place of the moon by tables, he finds this δ or conjunction for Greenwich at fifteen hours, five minutes, and thirty-five and five hundred and fifty-six thousandths seconds; and hence the western longitude of Washington equal to five hours, seven minutes, and thirty-six and two hundred and seventy-nine thousandths seconds. This calculation is perfectly just; nevertheless, the longitude which results from it remains uncertain, and may be defective by several minutes of the arc.

"'1. The calculator supposes the right ascension of Eta (η) Pleiades fifty-three degrees, fifty-nine minutes, and six and twenty-seven hundredths seconds, the declination twenty-three degrees, twenty-nine minutes, and forty-five and fourteen hundredths seconds; whereas the catalogue of Piazzi, generally considered as the best, gives the right ascension fifty-three degrees, fifty-eight minutes, and thirty and nine-tenths seconds, and the declination twenty-three degrees, twenty-nine minutes, and thirty-four and five-tenths seconds.

"'2. The conjunction for Greenwich having been calculated, not by real observations, but by the places of the moon, taken from the tables of Mason, perhaps incorrect by from ten to fifteen minutes, an error may result, from twenty to thirty-six minutes, in the time of this conjunction, and also in the longitude of Washington. Unfortunately, I have not been able to find an observation in Europe corresponding with this, which would have enabled me to repeat the calculation and establish the longitude of Washington above mentioned.

"'From the observatory of Lieberg, October 10, 1812.

"'B. LINDENAU.'"

The solar eclipse of February 12, 1831, was observed at Washington by F. R. Hassler. His observations were reduced by Robert T. Paine, and the difference of time between Greenwich and Washington found to be five hours, eight minutes, and seven and two-tenths seconds. This difference of time gives for the longitude of Washington seventy-seven degrees, one minute, and forty-eight seconds, which is six minutes and seventeen and forty-six hundredths seconds of longitude more than Mr. Lambert's average result.

It was on account of the errors in Mr. Lambert's calculations that, in December, 1841, a memorial was presented to Congress, signed by Peter S. Du Ponceau and forty-three other citizens of Philadelphia, and a similar one signed by W. A. Duer, president of Columbia College, and eighteen other citizens of New York, among them Theodore Frelinghuysen, John W. Draper, and Charles Anthon, praying that measures be taken for ascertaining the precise longitude of the Capitol. These memorials were presented to Congress by Hon. W. W. Boardman, of Connecticut, May 12, 1842.

Retracing our steps a little, it may be said that, in 1838, Mr. R. T. Paine, editor of the "American Almanac," determined the position of the Capitol from observations upon the eclipse of the sun, which was nearly central there. In coming to Washington, three chronometers made the difference between the meridian of the Capitol and that of the statehouse in Philadelphia, seven minutes and twenty-five and four-tenths seconds, and in returning to Philadelphia, seven minutes and twenty-six and five-tenths seconds. The mean of these two, added to the longitude of Philadelphia, five hours and thirty-nine and six-tenths seconds, gave for the longitude of the Capitol at Washington, five hours, eight minutes, and five seconds. By observations upon the annular eclipses of 1791, 1811, 1831, and 1838, the longitude was five hours, eight minutes, and six and five-tenths seconds. An error, therefore, of two or three seconds in this determination, Mr. Paine thought, was an improbability, and there being but little doubt that there was an error of six miles in those maps of this country in the construction of which the longitude of the Capitol was supposed to be five hours, seven minutes, and forty-two seconds, the quantity reported by an individual[1] acting under the authority of a resolution of Congress.

In the annual report of the Coast Survey for 1851, the latitude of the Capitol was given as thirty-eight degrees, fifty-three minutes, and nineteen and eighty-nine hundredths seconds, and the longitude, seventy-seven degrees and fifteen seconds, a value derived geodetically through the triangulation connected with Cambridge, Massachusetts, the longitude of Cambridge being assumed as correctly ascertained, four hours, forty-four minutes, twenty-nine and five-tenths seconds. This same value is given in the "American Almanac" for 1861. In an important paper, Mr. Sears C. Walker, assistant in the Coast Survey to the superintendent, gives the longitude of the Capitol at Washington as five hours, eight minutes, and eight hundred and fifty-three thousandths seconds, which in angular distance is seventy-seven degrees and one and two thousand seven hundred and ninety-five ten-thousandths seconds.

When the transatlantic cables were utilized for the determination of longitude, a new value for longitude was introduced. Again, in 1880, a change was made by substituting Clarke's spheroid[2] for that of Bessel,[3] previously employed for the development of the triangulations. By these operations the observed differences of longitude between Cambridge, Massachusetts, and Washington, District of Columbia, was twenty-three minutes and forty-one and forty-one thousandths seconds, which, added to the longitude of Cambridge, above given, gives five hours, eight minutes, and ten and five hundred and forty-one thousandths seconds for the longitude of the Capitol, which, expressed in angular distance, is seventy-seven degrees, two minutes, and thirty-eight and one hundred and fifteen thousandths seconds; or for the dome of the United States Naval Observatory, as given in the United States Coast Report for 1884, page 423, five hours, eight minutes, and

[1] William Lambert.
[2] Equatorial radius, 6,378,206.4 meters, equal 20,926,062 feet; Polar radius, 6,356,503.8 meters, equal 20,855,121 feet.
[3] Equatorial radius, 6,377,397.15 meters, equal 20,923,404.61 feet; Polar radius, 6,356,079.11 meters, equal 20,853,462.91 feet.

twelve and thirty - eight thousandths seconds, equal in degrees to seventy-seven degrees, three minutes, and fifty-seven seconds.

"The following table contains the positions of some prominent objects in the District, according to the latest geodetic data of the survey.

"United States Capitol, head of the Statue of Liberty.......................................38° 53′ 23.25″	77°		33.54″
Old monument, supposed meridian stone[1].38° 54′ 44.45″	77°		35.25″
Washington Monument, apex of obelisk...38° 53′ 22.02″	77°	2′	7.78″
District of Columbia south corner stone, Jones's Point...38° 47′ 25.15″	77°	2′	27.01″
District of Columbia north corner stone..38° 59′ 45.38″	77°	2′	28.48″
District of Columbia east corner stone....38° 53′ 34.23″	76°	54′	33.94″
District of Columbia west corner stone.. 38° 53′ 35.60″	77°	10′	21.19″
United States Naval Observatory, center of small dome, main building...........38° 53′ 42.27″	77°	3′	6.10″

"From these positions it will be seen that the boundary lines of the District are somewhat longer than ten statute miles; also, that the southwest line (and its parallel) is somewhat longer than the southeast line (and its parallel), which inequalities throw the north corner slightly to the west of the south corner, and the west corner slightly more north than the east corner."[2]

In connection with this valuable information furnished by the gentlemen named, through the kindness of Dr. T. C. Mendenhall

[1] This is "Ellicott's Azimuth Mark," or what is otherwise sometimes called the "North Meridian Stone." It is located, according to Mr. C. H. Sinclair, assistant in the United States Coast and Geodetic Survey, "to the west of the prolongation of North Capitol Street, just beyond Boundary Street, and near the beginning of Lincoln Avenue. The monument consists of six blocks of sandstone placed on top of each other; the two bottom stones are twenty-eight by twenty-eight inches, and extend to the height of forty inches. The next stone has a base of twenty-four by twenty-four inches, and tapers, as do all the others, to the top of the monument. The monument is fifteen and five-tenths feet above the ground. In the top stone, south face, are three vertical lines about one-half an inch deep and one-half an inch wide, the center one terminated by a horizontal line. Near the top of the fifth stone is a horizontal line, cut deeply like the others. This bench mark (?) is on the south face of the bottom stone. The stone next to the bottom has a similar piece of iron on the east face, about four inches below its top (or three feet above the ground). The monument leans slightly to the north.

"While in Salt Lake City in July, 1890, I met Major Wilkes, son of Admiral Wilkes, who told me that this stone was placed by his father in the meridian of the transit of the old observatory that stood on the north side of Capitol Hill." The date of this monument is about 1838.

[2] From a letter to the writer by Assistant Charles A. Schott, in charge of Computing Division, Coast and Geodetic Survey.

Superintendent of the United States Coast and Geodetic Survey, it may not be without both interest and value to note briefly a few facts about other original landmarks, established by the early surveys of the District of Columbia. In another chapter may be found an account of the setting of the corner stone of the District, at Jones's Point. The initial stone, at this point, was about two feet high and one foot square. It stood isolated until the United States built the wall enclosing the lighthouse, and it now forms part of this wall on the south. From this initial stone the meridional center line of the District was located by Andrew Ellicott. This meridian center line extended through the President's House, north along the center of Sixteenth Street, and thence over Peter's Hill, afterward called Meridian Hill, to the intersection of the diagonal lines at the north point of the District of Columbia, about one mile due west from Silver Springs, Maryland. Upon this line, about eighty yards south of the present unsightly and unutilized standpipe, near the brow of the hill, Commodore David Porter had a mansion, the entrance door of which was due north of the center door of the President's House. The farm upon which this mansion stood, was long known as the "Meridian Hill Farm." On the edge of the south lawn, in close proximity to the mansion, was placed the "Meridian Stone." This meridian stone was nearly two feet across and two feet high. The north edge of it was circular, and upon it was afterward placed a brass sundial. From this stone "Meridian Hill" received its name, and hence "Meridian Hill Farm." This stone remained in its original position until about the time of the opening of Sixteenth Street extended, when it was removed to its present place, at the southwest corner of Fourteenth and R streets, where it is used as a carriage step.

The line crossing this meridian line at a right angle near the Washington Monument, extends west across the Potomac, passes near old Fort Corcoran, and on to the intersection of the diagonals at the west corner of the District of Columbia, near the village of Falls Church, in Virginia. Eastward, it extends through the rotunda of the Capitol, and on to the intersection of the diagonals at the east point of the District, about three miles east of Bennings Bridge.

At the crossing of these lines, near the Washington Monument, should be found the precise center of the District, and at this intersection was placed, in 1792, a stone to mark the center of the District. It was called the Jefferson Stone, or Center Stone. Its precise position is not now visible, but it was about one hundred and fifty yards northwest from the present Washington Monument, on the bank of the old Tiber Creek. It had a blue rock foundation, which was six feet high on the creek side. It was covered by a huge sandstone cap, about five feet square and eight inches thick. This cap stone and part of the foundation were removed in 1872, by order of General Babcock, the Commissioner of Public Buildings and Grounds, through a mistake as to its identity, and what remained was covered up by earth several feet deep when the roadway was made. It is on the east side of the road, between the lakes and the intersection of Virginia Avenue.

There is still one other stone a remembrance of the location of which should be preserved. This was called the "Capitol Stone," and stood a little south of the Washington Monument, and about eighty-five yards to the west. This was a rough-hewn freestone, projecting about three feet above the surrounding earth, and one foot in diameter on the earth line and eight inches across on the top. The distance between this and the Center Stone corresponded with half the length of the old part of the Capitol building. These three objects, therefore, the Monument, the Center Stone, and the Capitol Stone, would, if all were visible, mark a triangle, two sides of which would be of the lengths given above, and the other perhaps about one hundred and seven yards. But for all practical purposes the Washington Monument may be considered the center of the District of Columbia.

The longitude and latitude of a place, especially the latitude, have much to do with its climate. And it may be naturally inferred from the low latitude of Washington, when coupled with its slight elevation above the level of the sea, that its climate in the summer time is very warm. Actual observation and experience prove the correctness of the inference. The winters, too, are found to be much milder than those of more northern cities, and even milder than some winters in earlier times. In January, 1772, the snow, in what is now the District of Columbia, was nearly three feet deep on the level, and in places it drifted to from ten to twelve feet in depth. In 1780, according to Mr. Jefferson, the Chesapeake Bay was frozen solid from its head to the mouth of the Potomac, and at Annapolis, where it is five and a fourth miles between the nearest points of land, the ice was from five to seven inches thick, so that loaded carriages went across. But in later years, as the country became more thickly settled, cleared, and better cultivated, the climate of winter became much milder. But mollification of the climate by the clearing away of the forests and better draining of the land is not unique in the United States. In the times of Julius Cæsar neither the olive nor the vine was grown upon the Rhine.

Now, with rare exceptions, one of these exceptions being the winter of 1890-91, which was a most remarkable winter in Europe, the winters of France are both mild and pleasant. The improvement in the climate of Rome, the mountains near which city were, in the days of Horace, covered with snow, and the great change in the climate of Germany from settlement, clearing away of the forests, drainage and cultivation of the land, and the great changes in our own Western States, all tend to show the natural results of civilized man's occupation upon the land which he inhabits. Heretofore, and now, the vicissitudes of temperature are often distressing, mainly, perhaps, because of the suddenness of the changes which occur. However, even if there should be a gradual and steady mollification of the weather, extremely cold winters and hot summers will occasionally come. In the United States, the winter of 1855-56 was like that of 1890-91 in France, excessively severe.

The following table shows the temperature of the city of Washington for each month of the five years, 1823, 1824, 1825, 1828, and 1829, the data for the first three years being extracted from *The Washington Gazette*, published by S. A. Elliott in 1826, and those of the other two years from other sources:

MONTH.	1823.			1824.			1825.			1828.			1829.		
	Maximum.	Minimum.	Mean.	Maximum.	Minimum.	Mean.	Maximum.	Minimum.	Mean.	Maximum.	Minimum.	Mean.	Maximum.	Minimum.	Mean.
January ...	57	28	42	66	20	38	50	19	35	66	10	38	55	10	32
February ..	62	29	35	69	11	34	57	16	39	66	22	44	50	10	30
March	67	29	47	62	28	33	66	34	48	78	20	49	66	22	44
April........	76	43	59	76	34	55	77	35	56	69	30	49	85	32	58
May	90	50	66	80	49	65	82	46	65	84	36	60	85	42	63
June	93	58	74	88	52	73	93	54	76	94	60	77	90	60	75
July	91	65	78	90	67	79	95	64	79	94	58	76	90	57	73
August.....	92	63	76	84	63	75	94	62	76	97	60	77	90	62	76
September	87	42	68	80	58	69	85	46	68	92	47	69	86	47	66
October....	76	34	54	71	31	57	87	34	60	80	29	54	70	35	52
November	60	24	41	61	27	43	69	25	44	70	30	50	62	28	45
December	59	26	37	62	24	40	54	10	36	62	10	39	62	27	44

. . The following table shows the barometric elevations for the years 1828 and 1829:

MONTH.	1828.			1829.		
	Maximum.	Minimum.	Mean.	Maximum.	Minimum.	Mean.
January	31.03	29.75	30.39	30.93	29.66	30.29
February	30.81	29.37	30.09	30.61	29.33	30.17
March	30.63	29.63	30.18	30.45	29.35	30.10
April	30.42	29.62	30.02	30.52	29.35	29.93
May	30.45	29.56	30.00	30.38	29.65	30.01
June	30.21	29.77	29.99	30.20	29.24	29.72
July	30.65	29.65	30.15	29.90	29.05	29.47
August	30.90	29.72	30.31	29.83	29.39	29.61
September	30.25	29.10	29.07	30.15	29.16	29.65
October	30.75	29.70	30.25	30.95	29.43	30.19
November	30.72	29.90	30.31	30.33	29.50	29.91
December	30.89	29.87	30.38	30.80	29.30	30.05

With reference to the healthfulness of the climate, early writers have made numerous comments. Warden, in his "District of Columbia," elsewhere quoted from, in connection with his remarks on the longitude of the city, says, "It is scarcely possible to imagine a situation more beautiful, healthy, and convenient than that of Washington." In another place he says: "It is a prevailing opinion throughout the United States that the climate of the District of Washington is unhealthy; but the opinion is formed on prejudice, for it is certain that in no season is it visited by habitual or endemic diseases. The best proof of the salubrity of the place is the longevity of its inhabitants; and we recollect to have seen several natives, always residents of this District, whose features and general appearance indicate a very advanced age. Mr. Blodgett has, we know not from what data, estimated the annual deaths in Washington City at one to 48 to 50 persons; in New York, at one to 44 to 50; at Baltimore, at one to 43 to 49; at Charleston, at one to 35 to 40; from which it results that of all these places Washington is the healthiest. And in this respect it has evidently an advantage over the great cities of

Europe, where the annual deaths are one to 23, and in towns as one to 28. . . . It may be remarked that during autumn bilious fever sometimes prevails; but at this season it is common to other parts of the United States."

In the "History of the Ten Miles Square," published in 1830, by Jonathan Elliott, the following table of deaths for the ten years preceding was given: In 1820, 327; 1821, 335; 1822, 296; 1823, 356; 1824, 290; 1825, 225; 1826, 283; 1827, 252; 1828, 254; 1829, 304; which was an average of one death to every 53 of the inhabitants, or, as the ratio would now be stated, of 19 to each 1,000, which, if it were intended to include the black race, was a very low ratio indeed. Further remarks will be made about the health of the city in another chapter.

The Potomac River forms the greater part of the boundary line between Maryland and Virginia. It rises near the Back Bone Mountain, and in its descent to the Chesapeake Bay, passes the District of Columbia about three hundred miles from the Atlantic Ocean. Tide water in the Potomac reaches a point about three miles above Washington, the rise and fall of the water in the river being about four feet. In its course from its source to the sea it receives the waters of several minor streams on either side, the largest of these being the Shenandoah River, which rises in Augusta County, Virginia, two hundred and fifty miles above its junction with the Potomac at Harper's Ferry, where the latter passes through the Blue Ridge.

In this connection, although perhaps not strictly within the scope of this volume, it may not be amiss to introduce Mr. Jefferson's description of the confluence of these two streams, in which description may be clearly seen the play of his imagination. "The passage of the Patowmac through the Blue Ridge is, perhaps, one of the most stupendous scenes in nature. You stand on a very high point of land. On your right, comes up the Shenandoah, having ranged along the foot of the mountains an hundred miles, to seek a vent. On your left, approaches the Patowmac in quest of a passage also. In the moment of their junction they rush together against the mountain, rend it asunder and pass off to the east. The first glance of this scene hurries our senses into the opinion that this earth has been created in time, that the mountains were formed first, that the rivers began to flow afterward, that in this place particularly they have been damned up by the Blue Ridge of mountains, and have formed an ocean which filled the whole valley; that continuing to rise, they at length broke over at this spot, and have torn the mountain down from its summit to its base. The piles of rock on each hand, but particularly on the

Shenandoah, the evident marks of their disrupture and avulsion from their beds by the most powerful agents of nature, corroborate the impression. But the distant finishing which nature has given to the picture is of a very different character. It is as placid and delightful as that is wild and tremendous. For the mountain being cloven asunder, she presents to your eye, through the cleft, a small catch of smooth blue horizon at an infinite distance in the plain country, inviting you, as it were, from the riot and tumult roaring around, to pass through the gulf and participate in the calm below. Here the eye ultimately composes itself, and then away to the road happens actually to lead. You cross the Patowmac above the junction, pass along its side through the base of the mountain for three miles, its terrible precipices hanging in fragments over you, and within about twenty miles reach Fredericktown and the fine country around that place. This scene is worthy of a voyage across the Atlantic. Yet here, as in the neighborhood of the Natural Bridge, are people who have passed their lives within half a dozen miles, and have never been to survey these monuments of a war between rivers and mountains, which must have shaken the earth itself to its center."

Volney, the celebrated traveler, visited Harper's Ferry in 1796, and wrote a description of this same chasm. Volney was much more of a scientist than was Mr. Jefferson, and his description has much more interest from a geological standpoint, but we must content ourselves with referring the reader to Volney himself.

Forty-seven miles below Harper's Ferry are the Great Falls of the Potomac, where the river breaks through a granite ridge which stretches across its pathway. Here the river gradually narrows itself, until it approaches the shute, to about one hundred yards in width, when the entire mass of water is precipitated over a fall of about forty feet in height. It then sweeps along with great velocity for three or four miles, when it subsides into a gentle, placid stream. About ten miles below the Great Falls are the Little Falls, which are, in fact, but rapids. Their descent is about twenty feet, and below the falls is a bridge across the river. From this point to Georgetown is two and a half miles, the fall of the river in this distance being about thirty-seven feet.

The Eastern Branch, or Anacostia, is the main branch of the Potomac River, and enters the latter at Greenleaf's Point. This stream was formerly navigable for good-sized vessels to the once flourishing town of Bladensburg. In later years, the navigation of the river has been impeded by the washings from the adjacent soil and sand banks,

3

and vessels now ascend it only a short distance above the Navy Yard. Tiber Creek, which in ancient times wound through the heart of the city, entered the Potomac near where stood the Van Ness mansion, and was navigable for boats carrying lumber and firewood to the Central Market, and thence by the canal to the Eastern Branch.

Fifty miles above Washington, the Monocacy, which is navigable for about thirty miles, enters the Potomac. Conogocheague and Patterson creeks enter the Potomac about forty miles above Washington; Opequon Creek, about twenty-five miles above; Cape Copeon Creek, about twenty miles above; and Rock Creek, between Washington and Georgetown.

Jefferson, in his notes on Virginia, gives the breadth and depth of the Potomac at different points as follows: At its mouth, the breadth is seven and a half miles; at Nomony Bay, four and a half miles; at Acquia, three miles; at Hallooing Point, one and a half miles; and at Alexandria, one and a fourth miles. At the mouth, he gives the depth at seven fathoms; at St. George's Island, five fathoms; at Lower Matchodie, four and a half fathoms; at Swan's Point and at Alexandria, three fathoms; thence to the falls,—thirteen miles above,—ten feet.

Bancroft, in his account of Captain John Smith's exploration of the Potomac, says: "The Patapsco was discovered and explored, and Smith probably entered the harbor at Baltimore. The majestic Potomac, which at its mouth is seven miles wide, especially invited curiosity; and passing beyond the heights of Vernon and the city of Washington, he ascended to the falls above Georgetown. Nor did he merely explore the river and inlets. He penetrated the territories, established friendly relations with the native tribes, and laid the foundations for future beneficent intercourse. The map which he prepared and sent to the company in London is still extant, and delineates correctly the great outlines of nature. The expedition was worthy the romantic ages of American History." General Washington's first exploration of the Potomac will be narrated in another chapter.

It will be seen, therefore, that the Potomac is navigable for vessels of a large size, and would be utilized for that purpose to a greater extent than it is, were Washington, like New York, Philadelphia, and Baltimore, a commercial city. As it is, the river has always been used, for the most part, by different kinds of passenger steamboats, plying between this city and the various other cities on the Chesapeake and on the rivers running into it. Further mention of the river steamboats will be made in the chapter devoted to the transportation facilities of this region.

The shad, herring, and other fisheries of the Potomac and its tributaries were, in former days, of greater value than at present, though they are by no means valueless now. It was recognized very early in the history of both Virginia and Maryland that laws were necessary to protect the fish in the streams, and hence, in 1768, an act was passed by the Legislature of Maryland prohibiting the destruction of young fish by weirs or dams, the penalty for a violation of this law being £20. This law became a permanent one in 1798. In 1796, an act was passed to prevent persons from visiting the Patuxent River with cords or poles from the commencement of February to the beginning of June, the penalty being £100 for a white person, and, if a slave, it was ten lashes on the bare back, unless the slave were redeemed by his master's payment of £10.

In the early days, many thousands of fish were taken each season, and sometimes extremely large hauls were made. This season usually lasted from five to seven weeks, beginning about the last of March and ending early in May. Early writers on this subject say that a million barrels of herring was not too high an estimate for the number of that kind of fish taken in a season. Also, with reference to the flavor of the fish taken in the Potomac, these same writers say that next to the small and delicate Nova Scotia herring, the herring of the Potomac was by far more nutritious than any others in the waters of the United States. The shad, rockfish, and sturgeon, according to epicures, also had a flavor superior to any others in the Union. In 1830, when Jonathan Elliott wrote the "Ten Miles Square," fine shad were worth $5 per hundred; Falls shad, $12 per hundred; herring, $1 per thousand; rockfish, from $3 to $4 per thousand; and sturgeon, 3 cents per pound. The weight of each kind of fish found in the Potomac River was given by him as follows:

Sturgeon, 40 to 120 pounds; rockfish, 1 to 75 pounds; shad—*Clupea alosa*, 6 pounds; white, ——; tailor, 3 pounds; gar, 6 pounds; eel—fresh water, 3 pounds; common, 1½ pounds; carp, 3 pounds; herring, 2 pounds; pike, 2 pounds; perch—white, 1 pound; yellow, 1 pound; mullet—fine scaled, 1 pound; coarse scaled, ½ pound; smelt, ——.

About thirty miles below Washington was located the noted fishery of General Mason, called Sycamore Landing. At this fishery, in perhaps the year 1825, at one draught of the seine, four hundred and fifty rockfish were taken, the average weight of each fish being sixty pounds. It was then, and is now, of course, a habit of many species of fish to annually ascend the Potomac and other Atlantic rivers to fresh water, to deposit their eggs, thus providing at the same time for the continuation of their species and an abundant supply of nutritious food for man. The principal kinds of these migratory fish thus ascending the Potomac and other rivers were, and are, the shad, herring, and sturgeon, the first two kinds ascending the rivers to fresh water annually, and the latter kind making two visits, one in May and the other in August. The sturgeon, in early days, was taken in great quantities between Georgetown and the Little Falls. He is sometimes of very large size, weighing from seventy-five to one hundred and fifty pounds. One remarkable fact about this fish, according to the early writers, was that while it was considered a great delicacy in the James, the Potomac, and the Hudson, yet in the Delaware it was considered of but little value, and was scarcely eaten. The sturgeon was caught with floating nets with large meshes, or with an ingeniously contrived hook, not provided with bait for the fish to swallow, but by a curious device prepared in such a way as to pierce him in the body so deeply as to surely hold him and bring him in. This method of fishing for sturgeon was at one time peculiar to the Potomac fisheries.

The great fisheries for herring, in earlier times, were situated between the city of Washington and the mouth of Acquia Creek, fifty miles below the city. The principal fisheries for shad were confined to yet stricter limits — between the mouth of the Occoquan River on the right bank of the Potomac and the shores just above Fort Washington on the left bank of the river; that is, say, from fifteen to thirty-five miles below Washington. Many herring, it is true, are caught both above and below these limits, but not nearly so many as within them. Some of the finest shad are caught in drop nets,— two or three at a time,— at the foot of Little Falls, which, on account of its remarkable agility, this fish sometimes contrives to ascend, the fall of the water here being only about thirty feet in three miles, and the fish, having surmounted the falls, are then found up to the Great Falls.

Herring, however, do not get above the Little Falls. Of this kind of fish from one hundred to three hundred thousand were often taken at a single haul of the seine, and of shad, according to later writers, from ten thousand to fifteen thousand were occasionally drawn at a time. The seines, however, were very large, being from six hundred to twelve hundred yards long, and were hauled in by means of long, stout ropes and capstans fixed on shore. The seines used at the best shad landings were constructed of such large meshes that the herring escaped, thus saving time and expense by separating the two kinds of fish.

Herring are not generally eaten when fresh, but when cured they keep remarkably well, and are most highly flavored when two years in salt. While the Potomac River can boast of the largest and best shad fisheries in the country, the herring fishing is participated in by other Southern rivers, and there is an equal amount of herring taken in the Susquehanna River.

Referring to statements found in older writers about the shad and herring fisheries of the Potomac, the publications of the Fish Commission of the Government, which are prepared by experts, say that this river has always been celebrated for the excellency and value of its shad and herring fisheries. Reports of their magnitude have come down to us from early days, and from them we must gather that the productions then, as compared with our own day, have been simply fabulous. The fisheries of this river annually decreased in value and production up to the time of the War. The intermission which then ensued in fishing operations, on account of those of a martial character, allowed the fisheries to recuperate, so that, in the years immediately subsequent to the War, it was found that they had, in a measure, recovered from their former depletion. In 1878, the minimum of production was attained, during which season less than two hundred thousand shad were taken in the entire river. In 1879, the result of artificial propagation first manifested itself, and there was a considerable increase in the run of shad, from which time up to 1880 there were taken nearly six hundred thousand shad.

The early fisheries on the Potomac were prosecuted almost entirely by means of haul nets, but in 1835 gill nets were introduced from the North, which steadily grew in favor, and up to about 1875 were almost exclusively employed. In this latter year, pound nets were introduced, and these rapidly superseded the gill nets, as the gill nets had previously superseded the haul nets or seines.

According to the Government report above referred to, the Potomac fisheries, in 1880, employed 1,208 men; 230 boats, valued at $30,750, and having an aggregate of apparatus and fishing houses worth $209,550. The products of these fisheries that year were as follows: Shad, 2,040,052 pounds, worth $60,201; herring, 6,291,252 pounds, worth $62,912; sturgeon, 288,000 pounds, worth $2,880; miscellaneous, 1,317,-030 pounds, worth $39,510.

In 1886, Gwynn Harris made a report of the shad and herring fisheries of the Potomac as follows: Number of shad landed at Washington from March 19, 1886, to June 10, 1886, 180,175; number at Alexandria, Virginia, 34,847; number shipped by steamer *Sue* to Bal-

timore, 48,000; number shipped by steamer *W. W. Corcoran*, 5,600; sold
on the different shores, 6,800; total [number of shad taken, 275,422.
The number of herring landed at Washington was 7,315,473; the
number landed at Alexandria was 3,979,324; the number shipped by
steamer *Sue* to Baltimore was 850,000; the number sold on the different shores and at the trap nets was 1,400,000; total number of herring
taken, 13,544,797.

About June 10, 1885, an Atlantic salmon was caught in the Potomac River, which was probably the first that was ever seen in the river.

According to the report of Colonel Marshal McDonald, Commissioner of Fish and Fisheries, there were planted in the Potomac
River from November 4, 1885, to January 5, 1886, 5,500 German
carp. The number of shad planted in the same river for 1886 was
1,282,000. The number of vessels employed in the Potomac fisheries
from March 31, to May 31, 1886, was 31, with 78 men, and an aggregate tonnage of 457.7. The number of shad sold at Alexandria during
the season of 1886 was 34,847, and the number of herring, 3,979,324.

The crawfish of the Potomac are in great abundance, in front of
and below the city of Washington, but they are not taken to supply
the markets of the city, as they find no ready sale. The business, in
1880, was entirely in the hands of a few parties who fished during a
short period in the spring, and sent nearly all their catch to New
York, where they brought about $2 per hundred, whereas in previous
years they had sold as high as from $4 to $6 per hundred.

Oysters from the Potomac are troublesome, because they are mixed
with numerous obnoxious mussels, and in addition to this they do not
grow well in this river. During the spring of 1879, Captain Samuel
M. Travers, of the oyster police force, directed his deputy commanders
to board all vessels loading plants for Northern markets, and obtain
the number of bushels taken. Through them he found that the total
number of bushels was 2,178,750, of which 625,000 bushels were from
the Potomac River and its tributaries.

The Potomac fisheries are prosecuted by citizens of Maryland,
Virginia, and the District of Columbia. The average number of men
employed in recent years has been about 3,700; the capital invested,
about $270,000, while the product reaches an average yield of more
than half a million dollars. The fish trade of the District of Columbia during the four years ending in 1890, averaged nearly 6,000,000
pounds of fish, received from the river and bay, besides oysters,
crabs, clams, and turtles. In 1890, it amounted to 6,393,974 pounds
of fish, 6,182,700 clams in number, 779,300 crabs, 376,875 bushels of

oysters, and **107** turtles. The shad and herring are the most important of the fish brought to this market.

The nature of the Potomac fisheries has greatly changed within
the past twenty years. So long ago as the beginning of this period,
the catch of shad and herring by haul seines was not made at the
spawning grounds of the fish, the entire run of both kinds reaching
their spawning grounds in the river. Under these conditions, fishing
in the river was prosperous. With the introduction of the pound net,
the site of the fisheries was transferred to the Chesapeake Bay, the
capture of shad beginning at the capes, all the shad reaching the river
having to run the gauntlet of the pound nets, which are set all the
way up the river, from its mouth to the District of Columbia, across
their path. The result is that eighty per cent of all the shad are taken
outside of the rivers and in the Chesapeake, or in the river's lower
estuaries. Under these conditions, it will readily be seen that a decline in
the river fisheries has been unavoidable, and the opportunities afforded
for natural production are entirely inadequate to keep up the supply.
The fisheries are now under conditions mainly artificial, and their maintenance to this extent is dependent upon artificial propagation.

In connection with artificial propagation, it must be borne in mind
that fish planted in the Potomac remain therein a few months and
then descend to salt water, and only a small porportion of those which
survive and mature can run the gauntlet of the pound nets and find
their way back into the river. The effect of artificial propagation
upon the fisheries of the Potomac cannot, therefore, be properly measured or estimated by the actual production of the fisheries of this river
from year to year, for the reason that the larger proportion of the
fish which would enter the Potomac, and be taken by the seines and
gill nets in the river, are captured in the bay and at the mouth of the
river by the pound nets. Hence it is, that to get a fair estimate of
the results of artificial propagation, the Chesapeake basin must be
dealt with as a whole.

The following table shows the production of the shad fisheries of
the Chesapeake Bay and its tributaries for the years given:

YEAR.	No. of Fish.	Value of Fish.	YEAR.	No. of Fish.	Value of Fish.
1880	1,500,100	$201,900	1887	2,860,235	$411,874
1885	1,632,800	228,592	1888	3,960,305	580,185
1886	2,009,742	281,364			

The following is a statement of the deposits of shad fry in the Chesapeake Bay and its tributaries by the United States Fish Commission, from 1880 to 1891, both years inclusive:

YEAR.	DEPOSIT.	YEAR.	DEPOSIT.	YEAR.	DEPOSIT.
1880	23,428,000	1885	19,632,000	1889	52,225,000
1881	53,755,000	1886	52,835,000	1890	22,627,000
1882	14,885,000	1887	70,199,000	1891	24,777,000
1883	5,948,000	1888	84,136,000	Total	432,716,000
1884	8,219,000				

The following numbers of shad were confined in the carp grounds until they were seven months old, and then released into the Potomac River: In 1888, 750,000; in 1890, 1,750,000; in 1891, 800,000; total number, 3,300,000.[1]

The various geologic formations east of the Appalachian Mountains are thus classified in a rare and valuable pamphlet prepared by Professor W. J. McGee for the "International Congress of Geologists," which convened in Washington in 1891. Of the Pleistocene period, there are two formations, the alluvium and the Columbia, the latter being from 5 to 40 feet; of the Neocene period, there are two formations, the Lafayette, from 5 to 50 feet thick, and the Chesapeake, from 10 to 125 feet thick; of the Eocene period, there is but one formation, the Pamunkey, which is from 3 to 100 feet thick. These all belong to Cenozoic time, or to the Mammalian age, and the Neocene and Eocene belong to the Tertiary period. Below these is the Cretaceous period, to which belong the Severn and the Potomac formations, the former being from 2 to 25 feet thick, and the latter from 5 to 500 feet. The Cretaceous period belongs to the Reptilian age, or Mesozoic time, as also do the Jurassic and Triassic periods. But it is doubtful whether any portion of even the Jurassic period is exposed in this section of the country. Still beneath the Mesozoic are the Paleozoic and Azoic times; the former comprising the Reptilian, Devonian, and Silurian ages; from which it appears that the exposures of the earth's crust in the vicinity of Washington consist of a very meager portion of geologic formations, and represent a very brief period of geologic history.

[1] Statistics kindly supplied by Colonel M. McDonald, United States Fish Commissioner.

Pursuing the description of these formations from the Potomac upward, the Severn "consists of fine black, micaceous and carbonaceous sands, sometimes glauconite, and rather poorly fossiliferous." Southward from the city, this formation gradually becomes thinner, and finally fails altogether; northward, it increases in thickness and expands.

The Pamunkey formation consists of a homogeneous sheet of sand and clay, with occasional calcareous layers. It commonly abounds in characteristic Eocene fossils. It lies in a gentle anticlinal, the great body inclining toward the sea.

The Chesapeake formation is separated from the Pamunkey below and from the Lafayette above, by strong unconformities. It consists of a heavy bed of fine sand and clay, sometimes containing more or less abundant glauconite and infusorial remains and characteristic Miocene fossils. This formation extends eastward to the ocean, and northward and southward for perhaps hundreds of miles.

The Lafayette formation consists of well-rounded, quartzite gravel, and a red or orange-tinted loam. The gravel predominates in the northwestern exposures, and the loam toward the interior of the Coastal plain. The pebbles are derived from the earlier members of the clastics, and the loam from the residua of the Piedmont crystallines. The deposits of the Lafayette formation may be distinguished from those of the younger Columbia by having finer pebbles, more completely water-worn, and more largely quartzite; and they may be discriminated from the older Potomac deposits by the smaller size and better rounding of the pebbles, by the dearth of arkose, etc. Despite its local diversity, it is remarkably uniform throughout the two hundred thousand square miles over which it has been recognized; "indeed, though the youngest member of the clastic series, this formation is at the same time more extensive and more constant in aspect than any other American formation." ·

"The Lafayette formation overlaps unconformably all the older members of the Coastal plain series in such a manner as to indicate that all were extensively degraded anterior to its deposition; yet the floor on which the formation rests is more uniform than its own upper surface, indicating that, while the antecedent erosion period was long, the land stood low, so that it was planed nearly to base level, and seldom deeply trenched. During the Post-Lafayette elevation, on the contrary, the land was deeply trenched and not planed, indicating a higher altitude than during the earlier one, but a shorter period of stream work. This record, within the Coastal plain proper, coincides with a geomorphic record found in the Peidmont and Appalachian zones. Throughout these zones the major and most of the minor rivers flow in broad and deep yet steep-sided gorges, excavated in a base-level plain. The Potomac gorge belonging to this category extends from Washington well toward the sources of the river. It is within this gorge that the newer Washington Great Falls Cañon is excavated. The same ancient gorge is admirably displayed at Great Falls, and again at the confluence of the Shenandoah, at Harper's Ferry. Moreover, the ancient gorges of this category are best developed in the northern part of the Middle Atlantic, where the Lafayette formation is most extensively degraded. Now, by the concordance of history thus recorded in plain and plateau, the degradation epochs of the adjacent provinces may be correlated, and the ancient gorges of the Piedmont plateau and of the Appalachian zone as well may be referred to the period of high level immediately following deposition. While the positive evidence for this correlation is hardly conclusive, the negative evidence is more decisive: the Coastal plain deposits yield no other record of continent movement of sufficient amplitude and extent to account for this wide-spread topographic feature."

The Columbia formation consists of brown loam or brick clay, grading downward into a bed of gravel or bowlders. Toward the mouths of the large rivers the loam generally becomes thinner, and the bowlder bed thicker, and in the several parts of the formation its constituents vary greatly in quantity. As a general thing, the deposit represents littoral and estuarine deposition. The materials differ from those of the alluvium in the greater size of the bowlders, in greater coarseness of sediments in general, and in the less complete trituration and lixiviation of the elements. These differences indicate long, cold winters, with, of course, heavy snow fall and thick ice, but do not indicate glaciation during this period.

"Traced northward, the formation is found to pass under the terminal moraine and the drift-sheet it fringes; at the same time, the size of the bowlders and other indications of contemporaneous cold multiply, and an element of ice-ground rock flour occurs in the upper member, from which it was long inferred to represent an early episode of glaciation, and during the present summer Salisbury has found it to pass into a premorainal drift-sheet in Northern New Jersey. From the relative extent of erosion and degree of oxidation, the Columbia formation and the corresponding drift-sheet are inferred to be five to fifty times as old as the later glacial deposit, and a rude but useful measure of the duration of the Pleistocene is thus obtained."

The Middle Atlantic slope is to a great extent destitute of alluvium.

What is called the "fall line" is the common boundary of two strongly distinguished provinces. To the west of this "fall line," the land is rising so rapidly that the rivers are unable to cut their channels down to base level; while to the eastward of it, the land is sinking so rapidly that deposition does not keep pace with the sinking.

"Anterior to the vaguely limited period which may be assigned to alluvium deposition, the land stood higher than now, for the antecedent formations are deeply trenched by the Potomac, the Anacostia, and other Coastal plain rivers; but whether it was the entire region, or only the now sinking Coastal plain that formerly stood higher, is not certainly known. It seems probable, however, that both Peidmont and Coastal provinces were elevated after Columbia deposition; that both were subsequently depressed to some extent, and that, while the downward movement of the Coastal plain continues, the movement of the Piedmont plateau was long since reversed."

The following extract from the "Guide to Washington and its Scientific Institutions," shows the latest estimates as to the length of time which has elapsed since the Potomac formation, and also since the Carboniferous era:

"This Sub-Potomac unconformity gives some indication of the relative position of the Potomac formation in the Mesozoic period, as well as of the relative duration of the several Coastal plain periods of deposition and degradation. Let Post-Columbia erosion represent unity; then Post-Lafayette degradation may be represented by 1,000, and the Post-Potomac and Pre-Lafayette base-level period may be represented by 100,000; then, using the same scale, the Post-Newark and Pre-Potomac erosion must be measured by something like 10,-000,000, and the Post-Carboniferous and Pre-Newark degradation by 20,000,000 or 50,000,000. These figures are but rude approximations; they are, moreover, in one sense, misleading, since degradation undoubtedly proceeded much more rapidly during the earlier eons, yet they give some conception of the relative importance of a long series of episodes in continent growth, and indicate definitely the wide separation of the Newark and Potomac periods."

The following extract from Mr. McGee's article, already quoted from, clearly shows the chronological relation borne by prehistoric to historic times:

"In the later geology of the Middle Atlantic slope, three episodes stand out so strongly as to overshadow all others. The first is that represented by the Potomac formation; the second is that of the first ice invasion and the deposition of the Columbia formation; the third is the shorter ice invasion, during which the earliest known relics of men were entombed in aqueo-glacial deposits; and then follows the present, by which these episodes of the past are interpreted and measured. In the archæology of the Potomac Valley, there are three salient and distinct stages, the first nearly coinciding in time with the last geologic episode. The first stage is that of the origin and development of the unknown ancestor of the race; the second stage is that of the human prototype, who manufactured and used rude implements in an unknown way and for unknown purposes; the third stage is that of the dominance of savage races, whose homes, habits, and implements and weapons are known; and there is the present stage of multifarious characteristics, one of which is the desire to interpret and elucidate the earlier stages. The common ground of the archæologist and geologist lies about where the series of stages in the development of man overlaps upon the series of episodes in the development of the earth."

Following is a description of the economic geology of Washington and vicinity, prepared especially for this work, at the request of the writer of this chapter, by Professor W. J. McGee, of the United States Geological Survey.

"There are in the District of Columbia and immediately adjacent territory eight formations or groups of rocks, each of which yields materials of economic value. The formations and the more important resources found within each are as follows:

Age.	Formation.	Economic Materials
Pleistocene	Columbia	Brick clays, building sand, gravel, and cobbles.
Neocene	Lafayette	Gravel and cobbles.
	Chesapeake	Infusorial earth.
Eocene	Pamunkey	Green sand or glauconitic marl.
Cretaceous	Severn	Building sand and molding sand.
	Potomac	Brick clays, pottery clays, building sand, gravel, cobbles, building stone, and iron ores.
Archæan	Piedmont gneiss	Building material, macadam, gold, and steatite.
Jura-Trias	Newark	Brown stone, Potomac marble.

"The Columbia formation is a sheet of brick clay, or loam, with a bed of sand, gravel, or bowlders at the base. It lies on both sides of the Potomac River below Georgetown up to altitudes of one hundred and forty or one hundred and fifty feet above tide, practically the whole of the city being founded upon it. Over the eastern part of the area occupied by the city, particularly between the Capitol and the city jail, and between Graceland Cemetery and the Pennsylvania Railway, the upper portion of the deposit is a valuable brick clay. South of the river the brick clay layer is even more extensive, stretching from Jackson City westward to Arlington Cemetery and southward to Alexandria, and in this tract the brick clay is quite thick, often reaching from ten to fifteen feet. The clay makes an excellent red brick, from which most of the buildings of the city have been constructed. It is also used to some extent for pressed brick. The deposit is similar, not only geologically but in composition and in the character of the product, to that of the well-known 'Philadelphia brick clay.'

"South of the Potomac, a bed of excellent building sand is found beneath the brick clay, and a corresponding sand bed is sometimes found in the eastern part of the city of Washington. In the western part of the city, a bed of gravel or of cobble stones and bowlders, which are largely used for guttering, for the foundation of asphalt pavements, and for other purposes, is frequently found below the brick clay or loamy member in a position corresponding to that of the sand bed.

"The Lafayette formation, as developed in the vicinity of Washington, consists of a bed of well-rounded quartz gravel, imbedded in a matrix of red sand. The gravel is coarsest and most abundant west and northwest of a line passing through the Capitol, and on some of the eminences in the direction of Tenallytown the deposit consists almost wholly of gravel, the sandy matrix being quite scant. Southeast of that line, the gravel is finer and less abundant, and toward Marlborough becomes inconspicuous, the formation consisting almost wholly of the sandy element. This gravel has been largely used as a foundation for asphalt pavements and as macadam, but its value for these purposes is not fully appreciated. It is within limits to say that no better material for road making exists in the world than this quartz gravel of the Lafayette formation. Considered as a geologic deposit, this formation once extended continuously from a line passing through Tenallytown and somewhat east of Falls Church eastward to Chesapeake Bay, and also extended northward and southward for hundreds of miles; but the greater part of this ancient deposit has been washed away by the rivers and streamlets, so that it now exists only in the form of remnants, generally crowning the higher lands back from the rivers. The most valuable deposits are found in the vicinity of the Soldiers' Home, about Silver Springs, in the neighborhood of Tenallytown, over Wesley Heights, and along the upland scarp stretching from Fort Myer to beyond Alexandria.

"The Chesapeake formation consists of fine materials, mainly sand with some clays, together with layers of a fine mealy substance which, under the microscope, is found to consist of the siliceous shells of minute organisms known as Infusoria. The infusorial earth of this formation has long been known at Richmond, and recent investigations by the Geological Survey indicate that the Washington beds are quite as extensive and valuable as those of Virginia. The material is used as a polishing powder (sometimes under the name tripoli) and for various mechanical purposes. It crops out in almost all of the roads of the eastern part of the District and contiguous portions of Maryland.

"The Pamunkey formation is composed of fine green sand mixed with varying amounts of organic matter and clay, and usually containing a considerable proportion of the mineral glauconite. In certain parts of the formation, the glauconite is so abundant as to give the deposit the character of the well-known natural fertilizer of this and other countries usually called green sand or green-sand marl. At Upper Marlborough, at Fort Washington, and indeed generally on the portion of the western shore of Maryland contiguous to the District of Columbia, the principal green-sand bed is fifteen to thirty feet in thickness, while the other beds of which the formation is composed are also glauconitic to a greater or less extent. Green sand has been mined and shipped for use as a fertilizer in a small way; but the value of the material is not yet adequately appreciated. In New Jersey a similar natural fertilizer, derived from the same formation, has been extensively employed, with the result of transforming the barren wastes of early days into the splendid fields and vegetable gardens from which the metropolis of New York is supplied. There is no doubt that eventually the sterile fields and naked hillsides sometimes seen in the vicinity of Washington will be similarly transformed by the use of this material.

"The Severn formation is commonly a thin bed of black micaceous sands found in the eastern part of the District and in contiguous portions of Maryland. The quartz sand of this formation is commonly sharp, and when found in sufficient purity, as is the case in several localities in Maryland, forms an excellent building sand. Some of the finer parts of the formation are used to a slight extent as molding sand.

"The Potomac formation consists of a variety of materials, including various kinds of clays and several grades of sand, besides beds of gravel and cobble stones. The finest clays are suitable for the manufacture of pottery, but have not been utilized for this purpose in the

vicinity of Washington, except at Terra Cotta. There the material is
employed in the manufacture of the so-called terra cotta or pottery
tubing used largely in the city for sewers, drain pipes, culverts, etc.
In New Jersey, the pottery clays of the same formation are extensively
used in the manufacture of fire brick, and other varieties are used for
the finer grades of porcelain for which this country is now becoming
famous.

"Another variety of clay sometimes found in the Potomac formation
is of too low grade for pottery use, yet is suitable f·r the manufacture
of common or pressed brick. This material has thus far been extensively used only at the Columbia Brick Works, but other works using
the same material might well be established in sufficient number to
supply local and other demands.

"Some of the sand beds of the formation yield an excellent grade
of sharp sand, the best building sand, indeed, of the District. In grading the northern part of the city, it has long been a common practice
to remove the entire thickness of the Columbia formation (using the
upper part for brick making, screening the lower part for sand and
for gravel, and removing the bowlders and cobbles for street making)
and then carry the excavation several feet or yards beneath the grade
level for the purpose of extracting the valuable building sands of the
Potomac formation, and finally filling these sand pits with the refuse
from both formations.

"West of a line passing through the Capitol and the town of
Laurel, the Potomac formation contains considerable quantities of well-
rounded quartzite pebbles and cobblestones, which are often accumu-
lated in considerable beds. These, like the similar materials of the
Lafayette formation, form the best of road material, and have been
largely used for that purpose. The roadside gutters of the Soldiers'
Home, Arlington, and other public parks and reservations, and of many
suburban streets and country roads, are lined with cobblestones taken
from this formation.

"In the early history of Washington, the formation now known as
the Potomac was well known as a source of building stone. The
principal quarries lie beyond the limits of the District, near the mouth
of Acquia Creek, a tributary of the Potomac from the Virginia side.
The formation here consists of a peculiar sand consisting of quartz
crystals, feldspar crystals, scales of mica, and other minerals derived
from the disintegration of granitoid rocks, the whole forming the material which geologists call arkose; this arkose being locally cemented
or lithified in such manner as to form a firm tough rock known

commercially as the Acquia Creek sandstone. The central portion of
the Capitol and many others among the older buildings of Washington
are built of this material. Of recent years it has not been extensively
used, partly by reason of the development of the brick industry and
partly by reason of increased transportation facilities, but it remains
a valuable resource. In some other localities within and near the
District, the sands and gravels of the Potomac formation are cemented
by ferruginous solutions so as to form sand ironstone, sometimes of
considerable extent and of sufficient firmness to form a strong and
durable building stone. The greater part of the wall surrounding the
grounds of St. Elizabeth's Asylum is built from the sand ironstone of
this character; and the same material is extensively used in the eastern
part of the District and contiguous portions of Maryland for foundations, bridge abutments, etc.

"In the neighborhood of Baltimore, the clays of the Potomac formation have long been known as the source of the famous iron carbonate
ores of Maryland. These 'ore banks,' as they are locally known, have
long been wrought, and workings extend almost to the District line,
and, recently, prospecting has been commenced in the. southern extension of the formation, below Washington, in Virginia. This ore is one
of the finest in the world, but hitherto has generally been extracted
only in limited quantities, for the purpose of mixing with lower grade
ores from other parts of the country.

"The Newark formation, or Triassic red sandstone, occupies a considerable area in Maryland and Virginia a few miles west of the
District boundary. It is the same formation as that yielding the
brown stone so extensively used in New York, Philadelphia, and
other Northern metropoles, and the quality of the rock in this latitude
is fully equal to that of the New Jersey and Connecticut brown stone.
The largest quarries thus far opened are at Seneca, nine miles above
Great Falls. The material is unlimited in quantity. Within the past
decade it has been largely used in Washington, and might easily be
shipped to Baltimore and other cities of Eastern Maryland and
Virginia.

"A few miles further westward the same formation contains great
beds of peculiar limestone conglomerate known as 'Potomac marble,'
which forms an effective building material, particularly for interior
decorative work. The columns in the rotunda of the Capitol are made
from it. The same material is also extensively used about Leesburg, in
Virginia, and Barnesville, Maryland, as a source of lime; for it is often
of sufficient purity for burning into lime, and yields a superior product.

"The eastern part of the District and contiguous parts of Maryland and Virginia are underlain by the crystalline rock known as the Piedmont gneiss. This formation usually consists of micaceous schists, sometimes running into steatite (or soapstone) on the one hand, or granite on the other; and, in addition, it contains dykes of the peculiarly hard and tough rock known as gabbro, and numerous veins of crystalline quartz. The formation extends southward through Virginia and the Carolinas into Georgia and Alabama, and northward through Maryland, and Pennsylvania, and Northern New Jersey into New York.

"The granitic portions of the formation yield granites which have been recently worked in a small way near Cabin John Bridge, just beyond the District limits. Thus far the workings here and elsewhere in the vicinity are not sufficiently extensive to fully indicate the quality and quantity of the material. Further southward, the formation yields the well-known Richmond granite.

"Within the District, as well as beyond its limits, the steatites (or soapstones) of the formation were wrought by the aborigines, and, to some extent, by the early white settlers; but of recent years the material has not been largely worked. The most extensive opening is on the line of Connecticut Avenue extended, in the northwestern part of the District. There are others in the National Zoölogical Park, and other openings, as well as unwrought veins, are known to occur.

"The common phase of the Peidmont gneiss, known to the trade as blue stone, is extensively quarried, particularly along the southern bank of the Potomac, between Georgetown and Little Falls, for use as rubble, etc. The harder variety, known as gabbro, is also used for common masonry. It forms an exceedingly strong and durable rock, but, by reason of its hardness, is expensive to work.

"The crystalline quartz, found in veins intersecting the Piedmont gneiss in great number, has long been worked for macadam and for other road-making purposes. It is one of the most durable of materials, and, unlike the softer rocks, is not ground or disintegrated into dust, but remains clean and firm for years. In Pennsylvania, this material is ground for use in the manufacture of flint ware or delf. It has not yet been thus utilized in the vicinity of the National Capital.

"In certain portions of the piedmont gneiss the vein quartz is auriferous. The gold mines of Alabama, Georgia, North Carolina, and Virginia, are in the quartz veins of this formation, and it seems probable that one of the richest parts of the entire belt is that crossing the Potomac River near Great Falls. In the early history of the country, this belt was partially prospected, and many workings were begun; but the discovery of gold in California and in the Rocky Mountains diverted attention from the eastern mines, and they were abandoned. Recently they have begun to again attract attention, and several mines have been opened, and works erected near Great Falls."

What is written in this volume in reference to the flora of the vicinity of Washington, is derived mainly from that excellent work of Professor Lester F. Ward, entitled, "Flora of Washington and Vicinity," published in 1881 as a "Bulletin of the United States National Museum." To this book the reader is referred for fuller details upon this subject. The territory included is limited by the Great Falls of the Potomac on the north; by the Mount Vernon estate on the south; and the east and west limits extend only a few miles in each direction.

In the early day, there was an organization known as the Washington Botanical Society, which was dissolved in 1825, and was followed by the Botanic Club, organized the same year. The Botanic Club left a catalogue, entitled, "Floræ Columbianæ Prodromus." The "Prodromus" contained a description of 919 distinct names of species and varieties of plants in the vicinity. Of these names, 59 are mere synonyms for the same plant, leaving 860 distinct plants. Of these 860 plants, Professor Ward had, at the time of the publication of the bulletin, succeeded in identifying 708 as among those now found, and he thought six others probably belonged among them, leaving 146 enumerated in the "Prodromus" not found in recent investigations.

Of these 146 species, it is not to be inferred that all had disappeared or become extinct, but, instead, were accounted for as follows:

1. The early botanists made mistakes in naming plants to the number of 43.

2. There were introduced into the catalogue the names of 12 plants not belonging to the flora of this vicinity.

3. The range was so unduly extended as to include 10 plants not belonging to this vicinity, and,

4. There were 81 indigenous plants actually extinguished.

Belonging to the fourth class are the following plants: The white baneberry, the cucumber tree, the American barberry, the water chinquapin, the Mexican poppy, whitlow-grass, the sweet white violet, milkwort, catchfly, corn spurrey, the knawel, herb Robert, indigo plant, the vetch, trefoil, butterfly pea, hawthorn, alum root, mitrewort, stonecrop, *Diamorpha pusilla*, deergrass, wild sarsaparilla, sunflower, tickseed, groundsel, plumeless thistle, *Lobelia Nuttallii*, bellflower, black ash, Indian hemp, poke-milkweed, Maryland pink-root, American century plant, American columbo, heliotrope, gromwell, false gromwell, hedge hyssop, *Gerardia quercifolia* and *auriculata*, blue curls, mountain mint, horse-mint, skullcap, false dragon-head, wild ginger, strawberry blite, glasswort or saltwort, knotweed of the Buckwheat family, red bay, spurgewort, three-seeded mercury, sugar berry, American aspen, downy poplar, *Calla palustris* or water arum, pondweed, arrowhead, *Arethusa bulbosa* (named for the nymph Arethusa), *Pogonia pendula* and *divaricata* of the Orchis family, lady's slipper, flower-de-luce, *Allium striatum* of the Onion family, birthroot, yellow-eyed grass, *pæpalanthus* or dust flower, galingale, nut-grass, *Arundinaria macrosperma* (a large reed or cane), joint grass, a species of millet, the white cedar, club-moss, and a certain water plant.

The extinction of this large number of plants is due, in part at least, to the fact that, in 1880, previously and after, a considerable extent of country was under cultivation which in 1830 belonged to the primeval forest. However, the "Prodromus" was not a complete record of the flora of its time, which, according to Professor Ward, must have reached as high as fourteen or fifteen hundred vascular plants. "It would appear, therefore, that only a little over half the plants actually existing were discovered by the early botanists. If the proportion of disappearance could be assumed to be the same for species not described as for those described by them, this would raise the aggregate number to considerably above one hundred — perhaps to one hundred and twenty-five.

"The great number of present known species not enumerated in the 'Prodromus,' some of them among our commonest plants, and amounting, in the aggregate, to five hundred and thirty-five species, is another point of interest, since, after due allowance has been made for mistakes in naming them, it remains clear on the one hand that their researches must have been, compared with recent ones, very superficial, and on the other that, not to speak of fresh introductions, many plants now common must have then been very rare; otherwise they would have proven too obtrusive to be thus overlooked."

The places around Washington which are of botanic interest are as follows: The Rock Creek region, the Upper Potomac region, the Lower Potomac region, the Terra Cotta region, the Reform School region, and the Holmead Swamp region.

Rock Creek Valley, forming the boundary between Washington and Georgetown, is still finely wooded for some distance back from the creek, and thus affords a rich field for botanical research. This region is divided into six sections, the first embracing the series of groves between Georgetown and Woodley Park, including several ravines. Many plants are found here that are rare elsewhere, as the *Chamælirium Carolinianum* or blazing-star, the *Cypripedium pubescens* or the large yellow lady's slipper, the *Hesperis matronalis* or rocket or dame's violet, the *Liparis Lœsellii* or twayblade, an orchidaceous plant. There is here also a grove of *Aralia spinosa*, angelica tree or Hercules' club. On the the left bank of the creek lie the Kalorama Heights and some fine open woodland. Several interesting plants are to be found in Woodley Park, including the *Obolaria Virginica* (so named from the Greek word όβολός, a small coin,) or pennywort, and the *Spiræa Aruncus* or goatsbeard. At the head of one of the ravines above this is a magnolia and sphagnum swamp, where may be found the following species of plants: The *Veratrum viride* or American white hellebore, a plant containing veratrine, an acrid and poisonous principle; *Symplocarpus fœtidus* or skunk cabbage, so named for its odor; the *Gonolobus obliquus*, a twining plant with a greenish flower; the *Polemonium reptans*, a blue ornamental water plant. Near Pierce's mill may be found the *Aralia spinosa* mentioned above, *Xanthoxylum Americanum,* Northern prickly-ash or toothache-tree, a shrub with yellowish-green flowers appearing in spring before the leaves; the *Acer saccharinum* or sugar or rock maple, the *Pinus Strobus* or white pine, the *Carya alba* or shellbark or shagbark hickory. Below the mill may be found the *Populus alba* or white poplar, the *Acer dasycarpum* or white or silver maple.

From Broad Branch to the Military Road is the fifth, and perhaps the most interesting, section in this region. Here are found the *Ophioglossum vulgatum* or adder's-tongue, *Anychia dichotoma* or forked chickweed, the *Perilla ocimoides*, which appears to have no English equivalent, and the *Tipularia discolor* or the crane-fly orchis. On a bluff above Blagden's mill grows the *Gaultheria procumbens* or creeping wintergreen, and half a mile farther up stand a few of the *Pinus pungens* or table-mountain pine.

In the sixth section, extending from the Brightwood Road to the north corner of the District of Columbia, the low hills are covered with a second growth of the *Pinus inops* or scrub pine, and *Quercus nigra* or black-jack. Above the Claggett estate lies the largest forest in the vicinity, and this was the first extensive tract found for the *Lycopodium complanatum* or ground pine, a long, creeping, evergreen plant with a resinous odor. The fame of this forest, however, now rests mainly upon its hybrid oaks. Here, also, are found *Pyrola elliptica* or shin-leaf, and the *Pyrola secunda*, another member of the Heath family; and the *Microstylis ophioglossoides* or adder's-mouth.

Above Georgetown is a broad and low strip of country, formerly known as the Carberry Meadows, between the canal and the river, about three and a half miles long. Conspicuous among the plants of this locality are the following: The *Polygonum amphibium* or knot-weed, the "hindering knotgrass" of Shakespeare, so-called because it was once thought that an infusion of it would stop the growth of an animal; the *Isanthus cœruleus* or false pennyroyal; the *Herpestis nigres-cens*, a creeping plant, apparently without an English name; the *Brasenia peltata* or water-shield, a plant having floating, shield-shaped leaves; the *Cyperus virens* or galingale, and the *Nesœa verticillata* or swamp loosestrife.

Below Ead's mills are found the following: The *Ammannia humilis*, the *Salix cordata* or heart-leafed willow, and the *Salix longi-folia*, another species of willow; *Spiranthes latifolia* or ladies'-tresses; the *Samolus Valerandi*, American variety, or water pimpernel. Between Ead's mills and the chain bridge are the following: The *Paronychia dichotoma* or whitlowwort, the *Œnothera fruticosa* or evening-primrose, the *Ceanothus ovatus* or red-root or New Jersey tea, the *Ranunculus pusillus*, a plant of the Crowfoot family; the *Utricularia gibba*, a plant of the Bladderwort family.

High Island is, however, much richer in varieties than the low lands, and here are to be found the *Jeffersonia diphylla* (named in honor of President Jefferson) or twin-leaf, and in some places called rheuma-tism-root; the *Caulophyllum thalictroides*, sometimes called pappoose-root; the *Erigenia bulbosa* or harbinger-of-spring, the *Silene nivea* or catchfly, the *Valeriana pauciflora* or valerian, named either after an illustrious Roman named Valerius or derived from the Latin word *valere*, to be strong; the *Erythronium albidum* or white dog-tooth-vio-let, and the *Iris cristata* or crested dwarf-iris.

Above the feeder of the canal is a series of islands, as Feeder Dam Island, Box Elder Island, Larkspur Island, Sugar Maple Island, etc., the names of which are suggested by the principal plants that are found upon them. On the Virginia side of the Potomac, the flora, though less rich and varied, is yet interesting, and includes the *Rhodo-dendron maximum* or great laurel, which is very common on the Atlantic slope from New York to Georgia; the *Iris cristata* mentioned above, the *Scutellaria saxatillis* of the Mint family, the *Pycnanthemum Torreyi* or mountain mint, the *Solidago rupestris*, a variety of golden-rod; the *Solidago virgata*, another variety of the golden-rod. On the Maryland side of the river, above the uppermost point thus men-tioned, is Cabin John Run, which is celebrated more by the botanist for the walking-fern or *Camptosorus rhizophyllus*, than for its world-renowned arch that spans the run.

In the Lower Potomac region, the localities of special interest are: First, Curtis Run, opposite the Arlington estate, where are found the following: *Sagittaria pusilla* or arrowhead, the *Discopleura capillacea* or mock bishop-weed, the *Cyperus arythrorhizos* or galingale, a species of the Sedge family. Second, Roach's Run, where are found *Scrophularia nodosa*, a member of the Figwort family; *Tripsacum dactyloides* or sesame grass, the *Pycnanthemum lanceolatum*, a species of mountain mint. Third, Four Mile Run, where are found the *Clematis ochroleuca*, a member of the Crowfoot family; *Asclepias quadrifolia*, a species of milkweed or Virginia silkweed. Fourth, Hunting Creek and its tributaries, where are found the *Clematis ochroleuca*, the *Gonolobus hirsutus*, a member of the Milkweed family; the *Itea Virginica*, *Itea* being the Greek name of the willow; the *Geranium columbinum* or long-stalked cranesbill, the *Micranthemum Nuttallii*, a minute flower; the *Habenaria virescens*, a member of the Orchis family; the *Quercus macrocarpa* or burr-oak, the *Carex*, a member of the Sedge family; the *Geum strictum*, a member of the Rose family; the *Galium asprellum* or rough bedstraw, a member of the Madder family, and also many others. On the left bank of the lower Potomac River, below the Government Hospital, is a rich botanical field, which yields the *Carex pubescens* and *tetanica*, members of the Sedge family; *Gonolobus hirsutus* mentioned above, *Silene arenaria*, a member of the Pink family; the *Parietaria Pennsylvania*, a wall plant; the *Myosotis arvensis* or forget-me-not, the *Scutellaria nervosa* or skullcap, a member of the Mint family. At Marshall Hall is found the *Asplenium angustifolium*, a fern; opposite Fort Foote, *Myriophyllum spicatum* or water-milfoil; and opposite Alexandria, the *Plantago cordata* or ribwort, a member of the Plantain family.

The Terra Cotta region surrounding Terra Cotta Station, three miles from Washington, on the Metropolitan Branch of the Baltimore & Ohio Railroad, furnishes the following on the dry ground: The *Onosmodium Virginianum* or false gromwell, the *Clitoria Mariana* or butterfly-pea, and the *Habenaria lacera* or ragged fringed orchis; while in the swamp are found the *Aster œstivus*, oraster, the *Solidago stricta* or golden-rod, the *Woodwardia Virginica* or chain fern, the *Asclepias rubra*, a milkweed; and the *Poterium Canadense* or Canadian burnet, a member of the Rose family.

In the region of the Reform School have been found the *Phlox maculata* or wild sweet-william, the *Melanthium Virginicum* or bunchflower, a member of the Lily family; the *Bartonia tenella* or screw-stem, the *Lespedeza Stuvei* or bush-clover, the *Desmodium Mariland-icum* or tick-trefoil, a member of the Pulse family; the *Buchnera Americana* or blue-hearts, the *Fimbristylis capillaris*, a member of the Sedge family; the *Quercus prinoides* or chestnut oak, the *Carex bullata*, a member of the Sedge family; the *Habenaria ciliaris* or the yellow fringed orchis, and the *Gentiana ochroleuca* or gentian.

In the Holmead Swamp region, which occupies the ravine leading to Piney Branch from the east, at the point where the continuation of Fourteenth Street crosses the stream, may be found the *Ludwigia hirsuta* or bastard loosestrife, the *Drosera rotundifolia* or round-leaved sundew, the *Asclepias rubra*, a milkweed; *Xyris flexuosa* or yellow-eyed grass, the *Fuirena squarrosa* or umbrella grass, the *Rhynchospora alba* or beak rush, the *Coreopsis discordia* or tickseed, and the *Calopogon pulchellus* or grass pink, the Greek and Latin name meaning a beautiful little beard.

There are other regions where are many rare and beautiful plants, but want of space forbids further detail.

CHAPTER II.

INDIAN HISTORY.

First Exploration of Chesapeake Bay and its Tributaries—Tribes of Indians upon the Bay—The Powhatans, the Manahoacs, and the Monacons—The Moyaones, the Nacotchtants, and the Toags—The Shawanese—The Susquehannocks, the Tockwocks, and the Nanticokes—The Delawares—Indian Fishing Ground—Indian Tradition as to Greenleaf's Point—Formation of the Indian Names of Rivers—Fate of the Delaware Indians—Resemblance between Indians of Maryland and Virginia—Massacres of and by Indians—Marriage of Pocahontas—The All-Conquering Iroquois—The Changing Fortunes of the Aborigines—The Descendants of the Powhatans Embrace Mormonism.

THE Indian history of the city of Washington, and indeed of the District of Columbia, if confined rigidly to the city or to the District as such, would be very brief indeed. In fact, it might be comprised in a paraphrase of that famous chapter "Concerning Snakes," in "The Natural History of Iceland," by Niels Horrebov, reading, "No snakes of any kind are to be met with throughout the whole island"; but, inasmuch as this work carries the reader back many years beyond the legal formation of the District, or the establishment of the city of Washington, in other chapters,—notably that on the settlement of this region,—it would seem at least proper, even if it be not required by the scope of this work, to notice briefly the various tribes of red men that inhabited the southern part of Maryland and the northern part of the State of Virginia, in the vicinity of the District of Columbia.

The first exploration of the Chesapeake and its tributary streams was made by Captain John Smith, accompanied by fourteen companions,—a physician, six gentlemen, and seven laborers,—on a June day in 1608. Upon entering the bay, they crossed to the eastern side, and there saw two stout and grim savages upon Cape Charles, with long poles, like javelins, headed with bone, who boldly demanded who they were, and what they were about. Having satisfied these fierce warriors of their peaceful intentions, they continued some distance up the bay, and, returning along the western shore, they ascended the Potomac River. But the great Chief Powhatan was opposed to this exploration, and so ordered the little band of explorers to be cut off; and in consequence of this opposition, they found themselves generally the objects of marked hostility at several points as they ascended the river. Their explorations were continued, notwithstanding, as far up the river as Little Falls,—about five miles above the present site of the city of Washington,—and then, unable to proceed farther, the river at that point being impassable for boats, they retraced their steps to Jamestown.

At the time of this exploration, there were about thirty tribes, principal and subordinate, living upon the shores of the bay in Maryland and Virginia. The chief of these principal tribes were the Powhatans, the Manahoacs, and the Monacons. The Powhatans inhabited the shores of the Chesapeake Bay as far north as the Patuxent, in Maryland, and the other tribes mentioned lived on the territory contiguous to the York and the Potomac rivers. The Manahoacs and the Monacans, who were continuously at war with the Powhatans in Virginia, inhabited the present District of Columbia. The former of these two tribes, after being greatly decimated by war, pestilence, and spirituous liquors, deserted their country in Virginia, about 1712, and migrated to the West, joining either the Iroquois or the Tuscaroras.

Some of the smaller tribes which had settlements at the time of Captain Smith's exploration mentioned above were the Moyaones, the Nacotchtants, and the Toags. These showed Smith and his companions all possible friendship. Each was a distinct tribe, and had a settlement of its own named after itself. The settlement of the Toags was at, or near, Mount Vernon, appears on Smith's map of Virginia as "Tauxenent," and was about seventeen miles below the present city of Washington. The settlement of the Moyaones appears, from the same map, to have been directly opposite, in Maryland, just below the mouth of the Piscataway, while Nacotchtant, or Nacochtank, was on the same side with the Moyaones, just below the Eastern Branch, and within the present limits· of the District.

The Shawnees, or Shawanese, as they were called at an earlier time, are believed to have inhabited that part of Maryland between the Patuxent and Patapsco rivers, and the Chesapeake Bay and the Allegheny Mountains. The Susquehannocks, or Susquehannas, lived on the banks of the Susquehanna River, in Maryland, toward the west, extending considerably into Pennsylvania. The Tockwocks and the Nanticokes lived in Kent, Queene Anne, and Talbot counties, from the Sassafras River to the Choptank; the Nanticokes also inhabited Dorchester and Somerset counties.

According to Heckewelder, the Lenai Lenape, or Delaware, Indians covered all that part of the seacoast from the "Potowmack" River to the Hudson, and Mr. Bozman, in his excellent history of Maryland, says: "There is indeed strong presumption, from the great extent of the Lenape language, together with the traditions of that nation, that their territory might formerly have extended from the tide water on the Hudson, near Albany, to those of the Patomack and Patuxent; and if the Nanticokes were one of the tribes of the Lenapes, and their language a dialect of the language of that nation, the Lenape territory might also have comprehended all the eastern shore of Maryland, and the several tribes thereof. It is stated in Smith's 'History of Virginia,' that the part of the peninsula of the eastern shore which was then deemed, and is still, as a part of Virginia, formed also a part of Powhatan's territories, and that the Accomacks and the Accohannocks, the two tribes who occupied the present counties of Northampton and Accomac, were of the Powhatan nation, and spoke that language."

And again: "As to the extent of the Lenape territory on the western shore of Maryland, being bounded by the tide water of the Patowmack, as stated by Mr. Heckewelder, this receives some confirmation from the circumstance mentioned in Pory's travels as hereinbefore stated. When Pory went, in 1820, to settle the secretary's lands on the eastern shore of Virginia, he there met with Namenacus, king of a large tribe on the Patuxent River, in Maryland, called Powtuxants. Namenacus had come to the eastern shore in order to meet one Thomas Salvage, an Englishman, who, when a boy, having been presented to the Emperor Powhatan in exchange for Nomentacke, an Indian boy, had long lived with the Powhatans, and having completely learned their language, was in the habit of occasionally acting as interpreter between the Indians and the English. Meeting with Pory and Salvage at Accomack, Namenacus invited them to visit him at Patuxent. Pory accordingly went, and was attended by Salvage, who acted on all necessary occasions as interpreter. If, then, the Indian language which this interpreter had learned when a boy with the Indians was the Powhatan language, as we must necessarily suppose it to have been, from his learning it with and under the Emperor Powhatan, it seems to follow that the several tribes of Indians on the Patuxent, with whose language Salvage, the interpreter, seems to have been familiar, spoke the Powhatan language, and might, therefore, be considered as among the confederate tribes who belonged to Powhatan's empire."

Mr. Bozman presents other correspondences and confirmations, which appear to strengthen this position, but it is not deemed necessary to follow them further in this work.

It is stated, on the authority of the early settlers of Maryland, that the valley at the foot of Capitol Hill, in the city of Washington, formerly drained by the Tiber Creek, the Potomac, and the Eastern Branch, was for some years periodically visited by the Indians, who named it their "fishing ground," to distinguish it from their hunting ground, and that in the spring of the year especially did they assemble there in great numbers to procure fish. The principal camp of the Indians and the residence of their chief were at Greenleaf's Point, and their councils were held among the various tribes thus gathered together. This, if not strictly historical, is at least traditional, and it is supposed by some writers that General Washington was informed of this tradition, and the inference is intimated that this fact had something to do with his determination to locate the Capitol of the Nation he was establishing on the same spot of ground.

According to Schoolcraft, the Indian tribes, in most cases, dwelt on the banks of the rivers, and the Indian geographical names are at once appropriate and euphonic. The rivers were denoted by an inflection to the root form of the name; as, *annah, annock, any, hany, ghany,* etc. Thus came the names Alle-*ghany,* Rappah-*annock,* Susqueh-*annock,* etc. In different languages there were of course different terminal inflections. The Delawares, or Lenapes, used the term *ittuk* for the same purpose; hence, in their language, Lenapeh-*ittuk* meant the Lenape River, or the Delaware River. In the fifth volume, however, Schoolcraft says: "This term, 'Lenapeh-*ittuk,*' is composed of *Lenape,* the name given themselves, and *ittuk,* which geographical term is equivalent to the English word *domain* or *territory,* and is inclusive of the specific *sepu,* their name for river. After the successful planting of the colony in Virginia, the coasts became more subject to observation than at prior periods by vessels bound to Jamestown with supplies. On one of these voyages, Lord De la Ware put into the capes of the river, and hence the present name of this river and the tribe."

According to the same authority, the name "Lenape" was probably used nationally in the sense of "men"; for these Indians had regarded themselves as having held an eminent position for antiquity, valor, and wisdom. This claim appeared to be recognized by other tribes of this region, who applied to them the term "grandfather," while to the Iroquois they applied the term "uncle," which was reciprocated by the latter by the term "nephew." The other tribes of the Algonquin lineage the Delawares called "brother," or "younger brother."

But the fate of the Delawares, like that of most of the tribes of red men that once inhabited this fair land, was a melancholy one. Like the Mohicans, the Algonquins, the Eries, the Andastes, and the Susquehannas, the Delawares were compelled to leave the country which had for many years been their home. About the year 1744, by the command of Canassatego, the chief of the powerful and relentless Iroquois, they were ordered to leave this section of the country and remove to the banks of the Susquehanna. They accordingly quitted forever the banks of their native and beautiful Delaware, the scene of many memories and the resting place of the bones of their ancestors, turning their faces, with emotions that may be imagined, to the west.

Mr. James Mooney lent the writer of this brief chapter valuable assistance. According to him, "on the Virginia side, directly across the Long Bridge, opposite Washington, was another settlement, called Nameroughquena, and between it and Tauxenent (Mount Vernon) were two others, known respectively as Assaomeck (about Alexandria) and Namassingakent (below Alexandria). Several other small settlements existed about the mouth of the Piscataway on the Maryland side. . . . Nacochtank, which was the residence of a chief and contained eighty warriors, was the principal settlement within or adjoining the District. The Jesuits, who came out later with Lord Baltimore, Latinized the name as *Anacostan*, whence we get *Anacostia*, the modern name of the Eastern Branch at Washington, and of the post office at Uniontown on its southeastern bank, and perhaps also *Analostan*, the name of the island opposite Georgetown."

The Indians of Maryland and those of Virginia closely resembled each other. Those of the former State were descendants of the same race with the Powhatans, and spoke dialects of the great Algonquin language. Powhatan himself claimed jurisdiction over the Patuxent, but it is doubtful as to whether he ever enforced his claim. The name of Chesapeake Bay is, in all probability, of Algonquin origin. As a general thing, the accounts of the Maryland Indians represent them as a simple, open, appreciative, and confiding people, filled with wonder at the appearance of their European visitors. Father White, who accompanied Calvert, says they were endowed with an ingenious and liberal disposition, and an acuteness of sight, and smell, and taste that even surpassed the Europeans, and that they lived mostly on an article of food which they called "pone," or hominy, etc.

The Susquehannas claimed the territory between the Potomac and the Susquehanna rivers, when Jamestown was settled, as their hunting ground, and it marked the boundary between their lands and the

Powhatanic kingdom. Subsequently they moved their council fire down the western shore to the Patuxent to avoid conflicts with the Iroquois; but, on the other hand, they came in contact with a class of white people from whom they contracted the habit of using alcoholic liquors, which proved a more powerful, even if a more insidious, enemy than the Iroquois. Like the coast tribes of Virginia, they exchanged all the available products of their streams and forests for the means of indulgence, and when they were gone they sold their lands; and besides, they sometimes engaged in war with neighboring tribes, so that it was not long before they were without the power of self-defense. The white people of Virginia, in order to avenge a supposed murder of one of their number, made war upon them and killed a good many of the Susquehannas, who accused the Senecas of having committed the murder; but who the perpetrators were, was never known. Other massacres followed, however, and the people of Maryland, raising a force of one thousand men, marched against the Susquehannas, under the command of Colonel John Washington, great-grandfather of General George Washington; and afterward, by other wars upon them, the Susquehannas were driven to the necessity of uniting with the Canastogas, an original Oneida tribe of Indians. Thus were the Susquehannas reduced from the proud position of a leading and conquering tribe to a subordinate one within another tribe, to be ultimately swallowed up and entirely obscured.

Besides the Powhatans in Virginia, there were the Iroquois and the Chickahominies. The Powhatans were won over to the English especially by the marriage of Pocahontas to Mr. Rolfe, and the powerful Chickahominies themselves desired the friendship of the English; but the marriage, though a remarkable event in history, was nothing more. The blending of the English and Indian races, which some fondly hoped and believed they saw foreshadowed by this marriage, was, in reality, an impossibility. In social affairs, and more particularly in marriage, there must, from necessity, be a community of thought, and feeling, and taste, much of which comes from heredity, which cannot be found in individuals of races differing so widely in habit of thought and feeling as do the white and Indian, or white and negro. This important fact, which is the essential basis of happiness in the married relation, was entirely unknown to those honest people who opposed the abolition of slavery on the ground that such abolition must soon be followed by an indiscriminate marriage of whites and blacks. It is now everywhere recognized that no argument against justice was ever more absurd.

In closing this brief mention of the Indian races that lived in this region up to and during a portion of the time since the country has been occupied by the white race, it is believed that we cannot do better than to introduce the following extract from Mr. Mooney's article on the same subject heretofore quoted from:

"The Susquehannocks continued their inroads upon Indians and whites alike until 1652, in which year a treaty was made, only to be broken in 1676, when the pressure of the terrible Iroquois on the north drove the Susquehannocks themselves from their ancient homes, and forced them down upon the frontiers of Maryland and Virginia, which they ravaged from the Patuxent to the James, until defeated and almost exterminated by Nathaniel Bacon in a decisive battle at the present site of Richmond. The result was a treaty of peace in 1677, by which all the Indians as far as the head of Chesapeake Bay were brought under tribute to the whites.

"Between the upper and nether millstones, the original proprietors of the Potomac region had been well-nigh ground out of existence, and the miserable remnant was still pursued with unrelenting hatred by the conquering Iroquois. The Tauxenents joined the few survivors of the Virginia Powhatans, who retired to the Pamunkey River, where about fifty mixed bloods still remain, about twenty miles east of Richmond. The Maryland tribes gradually consolidated under the name of the Piscataways, and removed about the year 1700 to a new settlement on the lower Susquehanna, near Bainbridge, Pennsylvania. Here they became known as the Conoys, and under this designation they afterward moved higher up the river and settled at Chenango, under the protection of the Iroquois, about 1740. In 1765, they numbered only about one hundred and fifty souls. Still later they removed to the Ohio Valley, where they joined their kindred, the Delawares. They made their last appearance as a separate tribe at a council held at Detroit in 1793.

"While on a visit to the Cherokee Reservation in North Carolina in the summer of 1887, the writer accidentally obtained some additional information which has never before appeared in print, and which illustrates, in a striking manner, the shifting fortunes of the aboriginal tribes. A young Cherokee, named Samuel Owl, had married a woman of the Catawbas—once a powerful tribe, but now reduced to a feeble remnant of about a dozen families, living on the river of the same name in South Carolina. In talking one day with this woman about her own people, she mentioned that a number of Indians formerly lived with them who were different from the Catawbas, and were called

'Pamunks.' On further questioning, she stated that they were all descendants of, or related to, an Indian named John Mush, who had come from Virginia about fifty years before. They were unquestionably some of the Pamunkeys, already mentioned as still existing near Richmond. On asking her what had become of them, she said that they were constantly quarreling with the Catawbas,—for the old tribe hatred still lives on,—until some Mormon missionaries from the West arrived in that vicinity a few years ago, when the 'Pamunks,' glad of an opportunity to escape from their persecutors, embraced the new doctrines, and followed their deliverers to the far-distant land of Utah, where the last descendants of the lordly Powhatans now read their lonely destiny in the waters of the Great Salt Lake."

CHAPTER III.

WASHINGTON BECOMES THE CAPITAL.

The First American Congress—Circular Letter to the Colonies—The Spirit of Independence—The Necessity of a Permanent Seat of Government—The Attack upon Congress in Philadelphia—Its Effect—Offers from States for a Site for a Permanent Residence—Views of Individuals—Discussions on the Subject in Congress—The Plan of Two Federal Towns—The Convention of 1787—The Nature of Control over the Seat of Government Sought by Congress—History of the Movement to Settle the Question of a Permanent Seat of Government—The Question Finally Set at Rest—The Act of July, 1790, Authorizing the President to Locate the Federal District—The Removal of the Federal Offices to the City of Washington.

IT is evident, from a study of the early history of our country, that the stability of its government was dependent upon no one circumstance more than the permanency of the seat of that government. The first American Congress, or rather Convention of the Colonies, for the purpose of organized opposition to the measures adopted by the parent country deemed oppressive to the colonies, was held in New York. Delegates were present from nearly all of the colonies, and the matters considered were the Stamp Act and other grievances, from which the colonies considered that they suffered great wrong and oppression. The call for this Congress—the reason for which it was assembled—was "to consult together on the present circumstances of the colonies, and the difficulties to which they are, and must be, subjected by the operation of the acts of Parliament for levying duties and taxes on the colonies, and to consider a general and united, dutiful and humble, representation of their condition to his Majesty and the Parliament, and to implore relief." This Congress was not without some good results. The Stamp Act, the principal ground of grievance, was repealed. Other causes of grievance, however, continued, and a second Congress was called, to meet at Philadelphia. The only known result of this Congress, which sat with closed doors, was that it was resolved that another Congress should be called, unless redress of grievances from which the colonies suffered should be first obtained. It was recommended that the session should also be held at Philadelphia. This Congress was opposed by the King and his advisers, and the secretary for the colonies sent to all the governors of the colonies a circular letter, as follows:

"Certain persons, styling themselves delegates of his Majesty's colonies in America, having presumed, without his Majesty's authority or consent, to assemble together at Philadelphia, in the months of September and October last [1774], and having thought fit, among other unwarrantable proceedings, to resolve that it will be necessary that another Congress should be held in the same place in May next, unless redress for certain pretended grievances be obtained before that time, and to recommend that all the colonies in North America should choose deputies to attend such Congress; I am commanded by the King to signify to you his Majesty's pleasure that you do use all your utmost endeavors to prevent any such appointment of deputies within the country under your government, and that you do exhort all persons to desist from such unwarrantable proceedings, which cannot but be highly displeasing to the King."

This proclamation, however, had but little or no effect. The spirit of independence had already taken root. In May, 1775, the third American Congress met at Philadelphia, and from that time America has never been without a Congress. The Declaration of Independence soon followed, and after the adoption of the Articles of Confederation, annual sessions of Congress were, by its provisions, held at such times and places as were determined upon.

The members of the Congress thus assembled were designated, in the credentials issued to them, as members of the "American Congress," and the "General Congress." Its meetings were held in Philadelphia during the whole period of the War of the Revolution, except when prevented by the exigencies of that war, or when that city was held and threatened by the enemy, at which times it met at Baltimore, from December 20, 1776, to February 27, 1777; at Lancaster, Pennsylvania, on the 27th of September, 1777, and at Yorktown, Pennsylvania, from September 27, 1777, to June 27, 1778.

During all this time it does not seem that any attempt or suggestion even was made toward the establishment of a permanent seat of government, or fixed residence of Congress. This may have been owing somewhat to the unstable and weak character of the government of the Confederation, or it may have been due to other circumstances. However this may have been, it became apparent that unless some fixed and determinate habitation was decided upon for the residence of Congress, it would be idle to hope for anything like a permanent government. It was when matters were in this condition, after the cessation of hostilities with the mother country, and after her colonies, which had declared themselves independent States, had assumed authority to treat for peace and a recognized nationality, that the Congress then sitting in Philadelphia was threatened by a mob of dissatisfied soldiers.

This event took place in June, 1783, and was the cause of great excitement and controversy. Its importance in the history of the country is great, for from it may be dated the first decided intimation of a fixed and permanent seat of government; in other words, the necessity of a National Capital City, under the sole and exclusive control of the Congress, and independent of all State government and influence. Its immediate effect was the removal of Congress from the city of Philadelphia; and though the Confederation continued to exist for five years longer, and every effort was made by the authorities of Pennsylvania to induce it to resume its sessions within her domain, Congress persistently refused to return to that city. Sessions were held at Princeton, Annapolis, Trenton, and New York, but never again in Philadelphia during the continuance of the Confederation. It is true that before the occurrence of the events detailed above the idea of the establishment of a permanent seat of government had been suggested. A motion was made that Congress should hold open sessions, the postponement of the consideration of which was urged until Congress "shall have fixed upon some place where it may be proper to continue its residence, and where it may have some kind of jurisdiction without being exposed to the influence of any particular State." New York offered to cede the town of Kingston, and Maryland the city of Annapolis, as places for the seat of government, and upon the report of a committee these offers of the two States mentioned were transmitted to the other States, and a day was assigned for their consideration. By these means the subject of a "permanent residence" for Congress was brought to the attention of all the States, and four months were allowed for reflection, examination, and offers before any action was proposed to be taken. But it must be evident, notwithstanding all this, that nothing so clearly presented the necessity of the determination of a place of permanent residence for Congress, and likewise the necessity of an exclusive jurisdiction over the place so selected, as the events which drove the Congress from the city of Philadelphia, and made that city and other cities which could be controlled by mob influence unsafe as a place for such permanent residence as Congress was seeking. It may be interesting in this connection to note some of the reasons urged, not only in Congress, but by citizens of different sections of the country, for the location of the seat of government in the places of their special selection.

A gentleman, writing from Philadelphia June 3, 1783, says: "The Legislature of Maryland has passed a resolution in which they bid · high for the residence of Congress. They offer the city of Annapolis and its precincts, to be solely and exclusively under the jurisdiction of Congress; the statehouse and all other public buildings for their use and the use of the diplomatic corps; the Governor's house for the residence of his Excellency, the President of Congress; and to build houses for the delegates of each State, for which purpose they appropriate a sum not exceeding £30,000 specie (dollars at six shillings each). This offer is for the permanent residence of Congress. Maryland has far exceeded the proposals of New York. What think you of this kind of auctioneering?"

The following article in favor of Williamsburg, Virginia, is from the newspapers of that day:

"Overtures have been made to Congress by the States of New York and Maryland, by which the former has offered to cede the township of Kingston in said State as the future seat of Congress, together with an exclusive jurisdiction therein and the establishment of such jurisdiction as Congress shall think proper. The State of Maryland has offered the city of Annapolis (with the unanimous concurrence of the inhabitants to subject themselves to the jurisdiction of Congress), the assembly house for the session of Congress, the Governor's house for the President, and to build a hotel for each State at the expense of Maryland, provided it does not exceed £30,000, together with a jurisdiction of whatever nature and extent Congress may deem necessary, over the city and three hundred acres of the adjoining land. The advantages which will accrue to any State in which Congress shall establish the seat of their future sessions will, we doubt not, be fully weighed by the legislature of the State, and the convenience which at first view presents itself in favor of the city of Williamsburg for that purpose, in which there are large, elegant, commodious public buildings now vacant, and a considerable tract of public lands thereto adjoining, when added to the superior advantages of its central situation to all America, will certainly counterbalance the liberal offers of the States of New York and Maryland, or any other State."

The following is an extract from a letter from a gentleman in New Jersey, where Congress was then sitting, to his friend in Providence, Rhode Island, dated August 26, 1783, recommending a western location for the seat of government:

"Where will Congress establish their residence? is a question much agitated. It is a question of great importance, no less to the United States in general, than to the particular State that may obtain the -honor. It seems the general voice of the people that large cities are to be avoided; for this opinion a variety of reasons are assigned, too obvious to need enumeration. A small State, nearly central, ought to be preferred to an opulent State, either northward or southward, which might hazard a competition of interest. On this account New Jersey has many voices. Whatever disadvantages hereafter mingle themselves with the emoluments attending the permanent residence of Congress, it is not to be doubted that the real estate in the vicinity, and even throughout the State, will instantaneously receive a great additional value.

"For these reasons I submit to you a proposition entirely new, and which cannot fail to be acceptable to your State, as you are largely interested in the public credit and can entertain little or no hope of seeing Congress established in your island, however delightful and commodious that situation might be. By the treaty of peace and by the cessions of the claims of some of the States made and to be made, the United States are and will be in possession of an immense extent of territory lying southward of the lakes, eastward of the Mississippi, and westward of the Allegheny Mountains.

"A late calculator in a Boston paper scruples not to assert that these lands at sixpence an acre would extinguish the whole of our national debt. On the proposition, therefore, that Congress should establish their residence (suppose for a term of only thirteen years) at some of those commodious and young settlements, as Detroit, Louisville, Kaskaskia, St. Vincent's, Sandusky, etc., etc., what an amazing value would be added to that important territory! how incredulously would it accelerate the rapidity of its settlement and population! Lest at first view you should sneer at the proposal, or condemn it at once as chimerical, I pray you to consider the subject for a moment in a serious light. Is not the establishment of a national credit an object of first magnitude? Ought any practicable means to obtain it (consistent with our liberties) to be left unattempted? But you will ask, Has Congress moneys to expend for buildings, etc.? I answer, Perhaps one quarter of the lands in the compass of twenty miles square fixed on for the residence of Congress, whereby they would be amazingly appreciated, would be amply sufficient to erect buildings suitable for a republican court. But you will, in fine, demand a security against the inconvenience of savage insurrections, etc., etc. To this I answer,

Congress may there assume plenary jurisdiction, or model their government on the most perfect plan of modern refinement, and lands in their vicinity being allotted to those brave officers and men who have served in the late glorious war, in lieu of their certificates, they would plant themselves around their patrons as an impregnable bulwark against the natives, and Congress would be safe as they ever were in the city of Philadelphia."

By a resolution of Congress then in session at Yorktown, Pennsylvania, passed June 4, 1783, it was resolved "that copies of the act of the Legislature of Maryland, relative to the cession of Annapolis to Congress for their permanent residence, and also copies of the act of the Legislature of New York, relative to the cession of Kingston for the same purpose, together with the papers which accompanied both acts, be transmitted to the executives of the respective States, and that they be informed that Congress have assigned the first Monday in October next for taking said offers into consideration." This resolution brought the whole subject before Congress for consideration. It was evident that the matter was deemed in every way of the first importance. The great State of New York generously offered one of its most thriving towns, beautifully situated on the romantic Hudson, and Maryland offered its capital, already distinguished for the charm of its climate and the culture and elegance of its inhabitants, as places fit for the permanent residence of Congress. These offers were coupled with the further grant to Congress of the exclusive, unlimited authority of the General Government over such places. This was all that could be required, and it seemed an easy matter for Congress to determine upon one or the other as the future residence of the infant government. Indeed, Congress went so far as to appoint a committee "to consider what jurisdiction may be proper for Congress in the place of its permanent residence." The importance of this had been rendered manifest by the condition of affairs at Philadelphia at the time of the mutiny, to which reference has already been made. This committee recommended in its report, made on the 5th of September, that Congress "ought to enjoy an exclusive jurisdiction over the district which may be ceded and accepted for its permanent residence, and that the district so ceded ought not to exceed the contents of six miles square, nor to be less than three miles square."

Subsequently this report was considered, but no conclusion reached. When the time fixed for the formal consideration of the subject by the resolution of June arrived, offers had been made by several other States, and it was determined to consider the whole matter in the

order of the thirteen States then composing the government of
the United States. This was in October, 1783. By a resolution passed
on the 6th of this month, it was ordered that the question be taken,
in which State buildings shall be provided and erected for the residence
of Congress, beginning with New Hampshire, and proceeding in the
order in which they stand; and it was finally determined "that buildings for the use of Congress be erected on or near the banks of the
Delaware, provided a suitable district can be secured on or near
the banks of said river for a Federal town; and that the right of soil
and an exclusive or such other jurisdiction as Congress may direct,
shall be vested in the United States." It was further determined that
the place should be near the falls of the Delaware, and that a committee should repair to that place, view the situation, and report a
proper district for carrying out the design of the resolution. An
effort was made to reconsider this action of the Congress with the view
to change the location so selected, but it proved fruitless. Thus as
early as October, 1783, Congress had apparently settled the question
of the location of the Capital City, and nothing seemed to be needed
but the execution of the details to that end to secure a final determination of this much mooted question. Subsequent events, however,
prove how fallacious such conclusions were.

While the location of the permanent residence of Congress was
apparently thus early and easily decided, the fact was soon manifested
that this action of Congress, instead of settling the matter, was but
the introduction to a long and exceedingly difficult contest. It is interesting, particularly in view of the final determination of the question
of the selection and establishment of the Capital of the Nation, to
follow the Continental Congress in its varied and ever-changing legislation on this subject. While we know now of how little import
that legislation was; how weak and indefinite was every action of
a government that was without a single essential of sovereignty, the
men who controlled the counsels of the Nation in those days were so
distinguished in every way, and their discussions manifest so surely
what was meant by the establishment of the seat of government, what
was the significance in the minds of those early legislators of the final
conclusion to build a capital,—not to make one of a city already constructed,—that a history of the city of Washington cannot be complete
without a review of this legislation, cursory and incomplete as it may
be, but sufficient to show what was done. The discussion was long, and
the projects offered and considered various. It commenced immediately. Resolutions were offered declaring that the retention of the

territory near the falls of the Delaware was not satisfactory to a large number of the citizens of the States; that the purposes of the government would be better effected by the providing of buildings for the accommodation of Congress in two places, in which alternate sessions could be held. This proposition was deliberately considered, and with some immaterial amendment was adopted. It was determined that the alternate places of residence of Congress should be on the banks of the Delaware, as already provided, and on the banks of the Potomac, near the lower falls of that river, and that until buildings suitable for their residence should be erected at the places designated, such residence should be temporarily, alternately, at equal periods of not more than one year and not less than six months, at Trenton and Annapolis. It is interesting to remark how speedily this proposition for alternate residences of Congress followed upon the adoption of the resolutions fixing that residence on the banks of the Delaware. Nothing is needed more than this to show how unstable any determination of the question was. Fortunately, the experiment of holding temporary sessions of Congress at Trenton and at Annapolis soon proved a failure, and the impracticable scheme of having two permanent seats of government was not carried into effect. No effort was made to erect buildings either at the falls of the Delaware or on the Potomac.

Mr. Force, in his history of the permanent seat of government for the United States, from which much of what is here written is derived, says:

"Much sport was made in the newspapers of the plan of having two Federal towns. One writer, in alluding to the resolution of Congress of the 7th of August, to erect 'an equestrian statue of General Washington at the place where the residence of Congress should be established,' remarks, that some persons suppose there may be difficulty in carrying out this resolution if two seats of government should be established. But he suggests, that so far from there being any difficulty, it is easy, 'not only to comply with the spirit of the resolve respecting the equestrian statue, but to make that very resolve conducive to the scheme of the two Federal towns.' And in a lengthy communication he describes how this may be done. 'The spirit and intention of the resolve respecting the equestrian statue,' he observed, 'was nothing more than this: that the said statue should always be where the House should sit. To effect which, nothing was necessary but to adjourn the statue whenever and wherever they should adjourn the House, which might easily be done by mounting it upon wheels. But this was not all; for if the horse should be constructed of a large size, and framed

with timbers like the hull of a ship, it would become a most convenient and proper vehicle to transport the members themselves, with
their books, papers, etc., from one Federal town to another.'"

He alluded, also, to the enormous expense of building two Federal
towns, where one might be sufficient for the purpose. To obviate this,
he proposed "that there should be two permanent places of alternate
residence, agreeably to the late resolve, and but one Federal town;
which town should be built upon a large platform mounted on a great
number of wheels, and be drawn by a great number of horses."

This fun of the olden times has been repeated in more modern
days, and the project of an enterprising citizen who proposed the
removal of our proud Capital City has been caricatured in very much
the same spirit that is exhibited in the extract from the newspaper of
1783. A procession of the Capitol and the several department buildings, mounted upon wheels, and drawn by horses over the mountains
in a journey to the far West, illustrated the derision with which a
project to remove the Capital from its present residence was regarded
by the people of to-day.

This failure of the project to establish alternate residences of Congress resulted finally in an abandonment of all such schemes. But
before this was effected, Congress, in response to resolutions to that
effect, appointed commissioners to visit the falls of the Delaware and
the Potomac, and to report suitable places for the erection of the
contemplated Federal buildings. These commissioners made report, but
nothing more was done under the resolutions referred to. It may not
be out of place to remark here, that the commissioners appointed
to examine and report upon the site near the falls of the Potomac,
in their report use the following language: "At Georgetown, however, a little to the northward of the buildings, is a rising ground
somewhat broken, but pleasantly situated, and commanding good water
as well as other prospects. At Funkstown, about a mile and a half
below Georgetown on the river, there is also a district which commands fine prospects. Some part of this is low, but the residue is
high and pleasant. The committee have ordered a plan of each of
these districts to be taken and transmitted to Congress." This is very
nearly what afterward became, and to-day is occupied as, the site of
the National Capital.

Again, Congress, by an ordinance of December, 1784, determined
upon the selection of a place upon the Delaware River for the permanent
residence of Congress, and commissioners were appointed to make a
selection. This seems to have been all that was done, and the question

of the permanent seat of government was left still undetermined. It is not worth while to deal any further with the many motions made toward the settlement of this much mooted question. No one matter seems to have occupied so much of the attention of Congress, nor to have been the subject of so much discussion. Nothing was so often submitted to the members of Congress for their votes, so often decided, and so often reconsidered. There was no subject about which so many plans were devised and abandoned, and about which the separate States developed so many conflicting interests, as the single subject of the permanent residence of Congress. It is not deemed necessary, in these pages, to go into the details of the legislation of which we have records on this subject, because such legislation is not of itself important, and because the results were for the most part of so little consequence. What has been said on this subject gives the only important measures that reached anything like a conclusion, while the unending motions, discussions, and votes upon the subject are left unnoticed because they are of little or no consequence.

After the ordinance of December, 1785, nothing was done of any importance. Matters remained undisturbed, except by a few spasmodic efforts to direct the attention of Congress to a matter of which it had evidently become tired, and the whole subject was postponed to the care of the government that was to have charge of affairs under the new Constitution. What has been said will serve to show that, throughout the whole of the history of this Congress of the Confederation, or the "Continental Congress" as it is frequently called, it was manifest, that great consequence was attached to the question of the selection of a permanent seat for the government—a Capital City, and that over such place or territory, which should be ample for the purposes for which it was designed, Congress should have and exercise exclusive jurisdiction, entirely exempt from the authority of any State ceding such territory. The matter of exclusive jurisdiction was always insisted upon, and no project was considered that did not involve the concession of such jurisdiction. Though there was no provision on this subject in the Articles of Confederation, there can be no doubt that, had a permanent seat of government been then established, Congress would have assumed exclusive jurisdiction. It was offered by the several States, and the proceedings of Congress show clearly that it would have been accepted. All this tends to show what was uppermost in the minds of the men of that day upon this subject of a Capital City, and as we proceed to the time when the various details of our free government found their consummation in our Constitution, it is interesting to observe what were the evident intention and meaning of the men who framed that Constitution, with respect to this particular matter. The idea of a great central Capital City was early developed, and its consummation was certain, and in keeping with the grandeur of the Nation.

In 1787, the Federal Convention, called "for the express purpose of revising the Articles of Confederation, and reporting such alterations and provisions as shall render the Federal Constitution adequate to the exigencies of government and the preservation of the Union," met at Philadelphia. This convention was composed largely of the men who had before served in the Continental Congress, and it was therefore not surprising that early in its deliberations we find this matter of a permanent Capital the subject of earnest consideration and discussion. Nor is it to be wondered at that men who had so long had the subject under discussion should find little difficulty in reaching a conclusion about it. We find that in the draft of a federal government submitted by Mr. Pinckney, of South Carolina, provision is made that the legislature of the United States shall have power "to provide for the establishment of a seat of government for the United States not exceeding ten miles square, in which they shall have exclusive jurisdiction." Again, in a proposition referred to a standing committee of eleven members was a proposition to confer upon Congress "the exclusive right of soil and jurisdiction over the seat of government," and finally a report from that committee as among the powers of Congress, "to exercise exclusive legislation in all cases whatsoever over such district (not exceeding ten miles square) as may by cession of particular States, and the acceptance of the legislature, become the seat of government of the United States." This last proposition of the committee was accepted by the Convention and passed without dissent, and is found in the final revision of the Constitution, as it was referred to the States, and by them ratified and confirmed. The exact language of the Constitution, as finally adopted, and ratified by the States, is found in Article I., Section 8, of that instrument, and is in the following words:

"The Congress shall have power to exercise exclusive legislation in all cases whatsoever over such district (not exceeding ten miles square) as may, by the cession of particular States and the acceptance of Congress, become the seat of government of the United States, and to exercise like authority over all places purchased, by the consent of the legislature of the State in which the same shall be, for the erection of forts, magazines, arsenals, dock yards, and other needful buildings;

and to enact all laws which shall be necessary and proper for carrying into execution the foregoing powers and all other powers vested by this Constitution in the government of the United States, or in any department or officer thereof."

Having thus determined, as part of the Constitution, in this positive manner, that there should be a permanent seat for the government, over which Congress should have exclusive jurisdiction, the only question remaining before Congress was where this seat of government should be located. This was a very grave question, and gave rise to much and very serious debate. Some difficulty was at first experienced in determining where the Congress of the new government should hold its first meetings. This was, however, soon determined, and on the first Wednesday in March (the 4th), 1789, the day appointed for "commencing proceedings" under the Constitution, several members of both Houses assembled in New York; but there was no quorum until the 8th of April, when the votes for President and Vice-President were counted. On the 21st of April, Vice-President Adams took his seat as President of the Senate, and on the 30th of April General Washington was inaugurated the first President of the United States. Thus the government under the new Constitution was established upon a firm and certain basis.

It was feared by many that the convening of the Congress at New York and the inauguration of the President at that city, which had offered for the accommodation of the government most commodious, convenient, and elegant accommodations for the various Federal offices, would result in the permanent establishment of the seat of government in that city. This was to be deplored, because a very large preponderance of opinion was opposed to the selection of a large city as the seat of government, but of New York particularly, as too remote from the center of the then existing Union. Early in the session, however, one of the Representatives from Virginia presented to the House a resolution of the legislature of that State, passed in December, 1788, offering for the acceptance of the Federal Government ten miles square of territory, or any lesser quantity, in any part of that State which Congress might choose, to be occupied by the United States as the seat of the Federal Government. About the same time an act of the Legislature of Maryland was presented, in which the State offered for the acceptance of Congress ten miles square of territory, anywhere within its limits, for the seat of government. Before the close of the session, memorials were presented from the inhabitants of Trenton, in New Jersey, and Lancaster and Yorktown, in Pennsylvania, praying that the seat of government might be established in those towns. These several acts and memorials were ordered to lie on the table for future consideration. It was evident that the selection of a site for the permanent seat of government had lost none of its interest and importance, and it soon became apparent that it was the intention of the new Congress to bring the matter to a speedy and satisfactory determination. When the question was finally presented to Congress as to which of the many places suggested should be determined on, a debate full of interest ensued, and many and various projects were offered and submitted to the votes of the members of the Senate and House. This whole matter is of so great interest, and is so important as showing how the final selection of the present site of the Capital City was brought about, that it cannot be amiss to spread at large on these pages a summary of the debates upon it, even at the risk of proving tedious.

On the 27th of August, 1789, in the House of Representatives, Mr. Scott, of Pennsylvania, moved "that a permanent residence ought to be fixed for the General Government of the United States at some convenient place, as near the center of wealth, population, and extent of territory as may be consistent with the convenience to the navigation of the Atlantic Ocean, and having due regard to the particular situation of the western country"; and moved to make this motion the order of the day for the 3d of September. This was warmly debated, a number of members urging the postponement of the subject till the next session. After full discussion, during which it was said that no question could have a greater tendency to produce broil and dissensions, and that the government, ill-cemented and feeble as it was, might not withstand the shock of such a measure, the motion was agreed to by a vote of 27 to 23, and on the 3d of September the question was taken up, and the whole subject of fixing upon a place for the seat of government was thrown open for debate. On the 7th, three resolutions were adopted by the House: the first, the one offered by Mr. Scott, and already given; the second, offered by Mr. Goodhue, of Maine, "that the permanent seat of government of the United States ought to be at some convenient place on the banks of the Susquehanna, in the State of Pennsylvania"; and the third, offered by Mr. Fitzsimmons, of Pennsylvania, authorizing the President to appoint three commissioners to select and purchase the site on the Susquehanna, and to erect, within four years, suitable buildings, and also authorizing a loan of $100,000 for the purpose; and on the 22d of September, a bill pursuant to these resolutions was passed by a vote of 31 to 17.

On the same day the bill was taken up in the Senate, and amendments were afterward made which radically altered its nature. On the 24th, the location on the Susquehanna was stricken out, and by the casting vote of the Vice-President, the following words were inserted: "In the counties of Philadelphia, Chester, and Bucks, and State of Pennsylvania, including within it the town of Germantown and such part of the northern liberties of the city of Philadelphia as are not excepted by the act of cession passed by the Legislature of Pennsylvania." On the 26th, the bill passed (yeas, 10; nays, 7), and was returned, as amended, to the House of Representatives.

In the House the contest had been almost wholly between the Susquehanna and the Potomac, and when the bill came back from the Senate so thoroughly altered, and only three days remaining till the time set for adjourning, strong efforts were made to postpone it to the next session. It was said that in all the long arguments which the question had drawn out, the place fixed on by the Senate had never been mentioned, and that the question the House was now called upon to consider was entirely new. The reasons which influenced the Senate to decide in favor of the Delaware do not appear, as that body sat with closed doors. The House proceeded with the bill, and the amendments of the Senate were agreed to on the 28th by a vote of 31 to 24, with a proviso, added on the motion of Mr. Madison, that the laws of Pennsylvania should continue in operation in the ceded district until otherwise provided by Congress. This proviso defeated the bill. It made action on it by the Senate again necessary, and when taken up the same day in that body its further consideration was postponed till the next session. The next day (29th) Congress adjourned.

Before Congress met again, the Assembly of Virginia passed an act, ceding to the United States ten miles square of her territory, and reciting the advantages of a location on the River Potomac above tide water, in which the States of Pennsylvania and Virginia might participate. The Legislature of the State of Maryland had passed an act nearly a year before, instructing the Representatives of that State in the Congress of the United States, appointed to assemble at New York, to cede to the Congress of the United States any district in that State of ten miles square which might be selected for the seat of government. Virginia offered to advance $120,000 and Maryland $72,000 for the purposes of the Federal City, in case it should be established on the banks of the Potomac.

At the second session of Congress, proceedings for establishing the seat of government originated in the Senate. The bill left unfinished at the preceding session was not again taken up, but a new one was introduced on the 31st of May, 1790, by Mr. Butler, of South Carolina, in which the place was left blank. On the 2d of June, this bill was referred to a committee, consisting of Mr. Butler, of South Carolina; Johnston, of North Carolina; Henry, of Maryland; Lee, of Virginia; and Dalton, of Massachusetts. On the 8th, the committee made the following report:

"That in their opinion, taking a combination of circumstances into consideration, the present session is a proper time for fixing upon the permanent residence of Congress and the government of the United States; and after due consideration, recommend that it be placed on the eastern or northeastern bank of the Potomac.

"Your committee further recommend that such sums of money as may be offered by the States for carrying this bill into effect may be accepted of; then the bill will read thus: 'And to accept grants of money or lands.' Your committee were of the opinion that Congress can best determine the time to be allowed for completing the buildings.

" With respect to the temporary residence of Congress, your committee, after weighing all the circumstances, considered the ground of choice to be so narrowed as to be fully in view of the Senate.

"Your committee recommend that the Senate should agree with all the other parts of the bill."

The opinion of the Senate was taken, whether it be expedient, at this time, to determine upon any place for the permanent seat of government, and it was decided in the negative by the casting vote of the Vice-President. It was then ordered that the consideration of the bill be resumed, the report of the committee being rejected.

A motion to insert "the easterly bank of the Potomac" was negatived by a vote of 9 to 15. "Baltimore" was proposed and lost — yeas, 7; nays, 17. "Wilmington, in the State of Delaware," was also moved and disagreed to. Several motions to postpone were made, also a motion to reject the first enacting clause, but none were agreed to. Without coming to any decision, a motion to adjourn was carried.

The subject was not resumed until the 28th of June. On that day, the Senate having under consideration a resolve of the House of Representatives of the 11th of June, "That when the two Houses shall adjourn, the President of the Senate and Speaker of the House of Representatives do adjourn their respective Houses to meet and hold their next session at the town of Baltimore," a motion was made and carried to postpone the consideration thereof to take up the "bill to determine the permanent seat of government of the United States." The Senate then resumed the second reading of the bill.

The representation of John O'Donnell, in behalf of himself and others, citizens of Baltimore town, stating that town to be exceedingly commodious and eligible for the permanent seat of the government of the United States, and the representation of Robert Peter, in behalf of himself and other freeholders and other inhabitants of George-town, for the same purpose, were severally read. A motion to insert "Baltimore" in the bill was again made and rejected — yeas, 10; nays, 15. It was then moved to insert the following words:

"On the River Potomac, at some place between the mouths of the Eastern Branch and the Connogocheague, be, and the same is hereby, accepted for the permanent seat of the government of the United States: *Provided, nevertheless,* that the operation of the laws of the State within such district shall not be affected by this acceptance until the time fixed for the removal of the government thereto, and until Congress shall otherwise by law provide."

This was passed by a vote of 16 yeas, 9 nays. The members voting in the negative were Messrs. Wingate, of New Hampshire; Dalton and Strong, of Massachusetts; Stanton, of Rhode Island; Ellsworth and Johnson, of Connecticut; King and Schuyler, of New York; and Patterson, of New Jersey. "The place" was now determined upon, and this clause formed a part of the act finally adopted by both Houses of Congress and approved by the President, and after further amendment and an ineffectual effort to strike out the words, "between the mouths of the Eastern Branch and the Connogocheague," and insert "within thirty miles of Hancock town," the bill passed on the 31st day of July by a majority of only two, fourteen voting in the affirmative and twelve in the negative.

July 2, 1790, the bill "for establishing the temporary and permanent seat of government," which had passed the Senate, was read twice in the House and committed.

July 6, in Committee of the Whole, Mr. Sherman, of Connecticut, moved that the word "Potomac" should be struck out and "a district to include the town of Baltimore" be inserted; seconded by Mr. Burke. The subject was again fully debated with regard to the "temporary" as well as "permanent" seat of government. Mr. White, of Virginia, observed that, if this House was alone to be consulted, on the principle of accommodation, Baltimore might answer; but when it was considered that this bill originated in the Senate, in which this place has been repeatedly rejected, it is evident that, if the clause is struck out, the bill will be lost. Mr. Lee, of Virginia, insisted that Baltimore is as far south as the place proposed, besides being exposed by its frontier position on the sea. "We are not confined by the bill," said he, "to a particular spot on the Potomac, but may fix upon a spot as far north as the gentleman from Connecticut wishes." Mr. Burke, of South Carolina, said there was no political necessity for removing the temporary seat of government from New York to Philadelphia. The measure would excite the most turbulent passions in the minds of the citizens. He thought it a very extraordinary measure. It is calculated to arrest the funding system, and throw everything into confusion. If the bill is passed in its present form, Congress will never leave Philadelphia.

Mr. Lawrence, of New York, wished the motion might succeed. He objected to the place proposed for the permanent residence. By the bill it is conceded that the place is not at present a suitable situation. By what magic can it be made to appear it will be more proper at the end of ten years? He adverted to the funding business and other important matters which remained to be decided upon, and very strongly intimated that these questions were to be determined agreeably to the fate of this bill.

Mr. Stone, of Maryland, said all the question of difference seemed to be whether Baltimore or the Potomac shall be the seat of government. If the amendment now proposed should take place, nothing would be done, and the business will be left in a very inauspicious state. He was therefore resolved not to be drawn off by any motion, amendment, or modification of the bill whatever. As a Marylander, if he saw a prospect of success, he would vote for the town of Baltimore; but as it respects the United States, he should vote for the Potomac. He considered the subject as one of the most painful and disagreeable that could be agitated, and he wished to have the business finally and unalterably fixed.

Mr. Seney, of Maryland, said the interests of Maryland were to be sacrificed to those of the two adjoining States, and however flattering it may seem to Maryland to fix the seat of government on her side of the Potomac, the real advantages were, in a great measure, nugatory, as it would be but a very small portion of that State that would reap any benefit therefrom; the real advantages would undoubtedly result to Pennsylvania. Besides, after the government shall have remained ten years in Philadelphia, the probability of quitting it for the Potomac appeared to be very slight indeed.

Mr. Scott, of Pennsylvania, observed, that from the town of Baltimore there was no water conveyance to the interior; but from the proposed site on the Potomac there are two hundred miles of navigation directly into the heart of the country.

Mr. Madison, of Virginia, said, if any argument could be brought against the proposed place on the Potomac, it was its being too far northward; for the mileage south of the Potomac is twelve thousand seven hundred and eighty-two miles, and to the north of it twelve thousand four hundred and twenty-two miles. If to this Rhode Island is added, it will be not more than equal. We have it now in our power to procure a southern position. We should hazard nothing. If the Potomac is struck out, are you sure of getting Baltimore? May no other place be proposed? Instead of Baltimore, is it not probable Susquehanna may be inserted? perhaps the Delaware? Make any amendment, and the bill will go back to the Senate. He urged not to consent to any alteration, lest the bill be wholly defeated, and the prospect of obtaining a southern position vanish forever.

Mr. Gerry, of Massachusetts, regretted that the subject of establishing the permanent seat of government had been brought forward, for it is very evident that it has had a very pernicious influence on the great business of funding the public debt. If the present bill is carried into execution, a very great uneasiness will ensue. Those States who think that they shall be injured, it cannot be expected will then acquiesce. He adverted to the sacrifices which the Northern States are ready to make in consenting to go so far south as Baltimore, and contended that their explicit consent ought to be obtained before they are dragged still farther south. He ridiculed the idea of fixing the Government at Connogocheague, and did not think there was any serious intention of going to this Indian place. He considered the whole business as a mere maneuver. Baltimore holds out the only prospect of a permanent seat of government.

Mr. Vining, of Delaware, attributed the embarrassments of public business to the assumption of State debts, and not to the subject of residence.

The committee rose and reported progress.

The bill was again debated in Committee of the Whole the next day, July 7. Mr. White, of Virginia, adverted to the situation of the proposed place on the Potomac, and said that a line drawn from the Atlantic east and west to the extreme point mentioned in the bill would intersect the State of New Jersey and include the whole of Delaware and Maryland. He observed that, after the present ferment is subsided, the position will be considered as a permanent bond of union, and the Eastern States will find their most essential interests promoted by the measure. He adverted to the trade of Massachusetts, which, he said, was greater to Virginia than to the whole Union besides.

The question being put for striking out "Potomac" and inserting "Baltimore," it was negatived, 23 to 37.

Several other amendments were offered and negatived without a division. Mr. Burke, of South Carolina, then made the following motion: "That the seat of government shall remain in New York two years from last May; and from the expiration of that time to the year 1800, that the seat of government shall remain in Philadelphia." Before the question was taken, the committee rose.

July 8, 1790, Mr. Burke's motion, after debate, was negatived, as also was a motion offered by Mr. Smith, of South Carolina, to erase the words, "at which place the ensuing session of Congress shall be held." The committee then rose and reported the bill without any amendment.

July 9, the bill was taken up in the House, and a variety of amendments were offered, but none were agreed to, a majority of the members being in favor of the bill, and not willing to jeopard its passage by any amendment whatever. Mr. Boudinot, of New Jersey, moved to strike out "Potomac" and insert "Delaware"—yeas, 22; nays, 39. Mr. Ames, of Massachusetts, moved to strike out "Potomac" and insert "Germantown"—yeas, 22; nays, 39. Mr. Smith, of Maryland, moved to strike out "Potomac" and insert "between the Potomac and the Susquehanna"—yeas, 25; nays, 36. Mr. Lawrence, of New York, moved to strike out "Potomac" and insert "Baltimore"—yeas, 26; nays, 34. Mr. Gerry, of Massachusetts, moved to strike out "Potomac" and insert the words, "purchase or,"—yeas, 26; nays, 35. Mr. Gerry moved to insert a clause which should limit the commissioners in the expense to the sum appropriated in the bill—yeas, 26; nays, 33. Mr. Lawrence moved to add these words: "*Provided* the buildings shall not exceed the sum of ———— dollars,"—yeas, 26; nays, 32. Mr. Gerry moved that the words, "three commissioners, or any two of them," be struck out—yeas and nays not given. Mr. Tucker, of South Carolina, moved that the whole of the fifth section be struck out—yeas, 28; nays, 33. Mr. Burke, of South Carolina, moved to strike out "the first Monday in December next," and to insert "the first Monday in May, 1792,"—yeas, 28; nays, 32. Mr. Sherman, of Connecticut, moved that "December" be struck out before the word "next" and "May" inserted—yeas, 28; nays, 33. Mr. Smith, of South Carolina, moved that the words, "at which place the next session of Congress shall be held," be struck out—yeas, 26; nays, 33. Mr. Smith, of Maryland, moved an amendment by which the public offices should be removed to the Potomac previous to the year 1800, provided the buildings should be prepared for their reception before that time—yeas, 13; nays, 48. Successive motions were then made, that the bill be read a third time on Monday next; that it be read a third time to-morrow; that the House now adjourn,—all of which were negatived. Every effort, either to defeat or postpone the bill being found unavailing, a direct vote was now taken, and it was carried by 32 yeas to 29 nays. The vote was as follows:

Yeas—Messrs. Cadwalader and Sinnickson, of New Jersey; Clymer, Fitzsimmons, Hartley, Heister, Muhlenberg, Scott, and Wyncoop, of Pennsylvania; Vining, of Delaware; Carroll, Contee, Gale, and Stone, of Maryland; Brown, Coles, Griffin, Lee, Madison, Moore, Page, Parker, and White, of Virginia; Ashe, Bloodworth, Sevier, Steele, and Williamson, of North Carolina; Sumter, of South Carolina; Baldwin, Jackson, and Matthews, of Georgia.

Nays—Messrs. Foster, Gilmer, and Livermore, of New Hampshire; Ames, Gerry, Goodhue, Grout, Leonard, Partidge, Sedgwick, and Thatcher, of Massachusetts; Huntington, Sherman, Sturgis, Trumbull, and Wadsworth, of Connecticut; Benson, Floyd, Hathorn, Lawrence, Sylvester, and Van Rensselaer, of New York; Boudinot and Schureman, of New Jersey; Seney and Smith, of Maryland; Burke, Smith, and Tucker, of South Carolina.

The bill was approved by President Washington on the 16th of July, 1790, and thus ended the seven years' struggle for the seat of government. The following is a copy of the act:

"AN ACT for Establishing the Temporary and Permanent Seat of the Government of the United States:

"SECTION 1. *Be it enacted by the Senate and House of Representatives of the United States of America, in Congress assembled,* That a district of territory, not exceeding ten miles square, to be located, as hereafter directed, on the River Potomac, at some place between the mouths of the Eastern Branch and Connogocheague, be, and the same is hereby, accepted for the permanent seat of government of the United States: *Provided, nevertheless,* that the operation of the laws of the State within such district shall not be affected by this acceptance until the time fixed for the removal of the Government thereto, and until Congress shall otherwise by law provide.

"SEC. 2. *And be it further enacted*, That the President of the United States be authorized to appoint, and by supplying vacancies happening from refusals to act or other causes, to keep in appointment as long as may be necessary, three commissioners,- who, or any two of whom, shall, under the direction of the President, survey, and by proper metes and bounds define and limit, a district of territory under the limitations above mentioned; and the district so defined, limited, and located shall be deemed the district accepted by this act for the permanent seat of government of the United States.

"SEC. 3. *And be it enacted*, That the said commissioners, or any two of them, shall have power to purchase or accept such quantity of land on the eastern side of said river within the said district as the President shall deem proper for the use of the United States, and according to such plans as the President shall approve, the said commissioners, or any two of them, shall, prior to the first Monday in December in the year one thousand eight hundred, provide suitable buildings for the accommodations of Congress and of the President, and for the public offices of the Government of the United States.

"SEC. 4. *And be it enacted*, That for defraying the expenses of such purchases and buildings, the President of the United States be authorized and requested to accept grants of money.

"SEC. 5. *And be it enacted*, That prior to the first Monday in December next, all offices attached to the seat of government of the United States shall be removed to; and until the said first Monday in December in the year one thousand eight hundred shall remain at, the city of Philadelphia, in the State of Pennsylvania, at which place the session of Congress next ensuing the present shall be held.

"SEC. 6. *And be it enacted*, That on the said first Monday in December in the year one thousand eight hundred, the seat of government of the United States shall, by virtue of this act, be transferred to the district and place aforesaid. And all offices attached to the said seat of government shall accordingly be removed thereto by their respective holders, and shall, after that day, cease to be exercised elsewhere, and that the necessary expense of such removal shall be defrayed out of the duties on imposts and tonnage, of which a sufficient sum is hereby appropriated.   GEORGE WASHINGTON,

"President of the United States.

"Approved July 16, 1790."

The section in the foregoing act of Congress by which it is provided that the offices of the Government were to be removed to and remain in Philadelphia until the first Monday in December, 1800, caused much discussion, and was only passed after a great struggle. It was feared by some that if the Capital remained in Philadelphia for ten years, it would never be removed; but their fears were unwarranted by the event.

In June, 1800, the public offices were transferred to the city of Washington, and opened there on the 15th of that month. On the 22d of November, 1800, the President, John Adams, in his speech at the opening of Congress, said:

"I congratulate the people of the United States on the assembling of Congress at the permanent seat of their Government, and I congratulate you, gentlemen, on the prospect of a residence not to be changed. It is with you, gentlemen, to consider whether the local powers over the District of Columbia, vested by the Constitution in the Congress of the United States, shall be immediately exercised. If, in your opinion, this important trust ought now to be executed, you cannot fail, while performing it, to take into view the future probable situation of the Territory for the happiness of which you are about to provide. You will consider it as the capital of a great nation, advancing with unexampled rapidity in arts, in commerce, in wealth, and in population; and possessing within itself those resources which, if not thrown away or lamentably misdirected, will secure to it a long course of prosperity and self-government."

The House of Representatives, in their answer to the speech of President Adams, said:

"The final establishment of the seat of National Government which has now taken place in the District of Columbia, is an event of no small importance in the political transactions of the country. A consideration of those powers which have been vested in Congress over the District of Columbia, will not escape our attention; nor shall we forget that in exercising these powers a regard must be had to those events which will necessarily attend the Capital of America."

Time has shown that our ancestors were not wrong in the estimate they placed upon the importance of a Capital City, nor in their anticipations of what that city was destined to become. Speaking of the provision by which Congress is clothed with exclusive legislative powers in the District of Columbia, Mr. Curtis, in his "History of the Constitution," says:

"This provision has made the Congress of the United States the exclusive sovereign of the District of Columbia, which it governs in its capacity of the legislature of the Union. It enabled Washington to found the city which bears his name, toward which, whatever may be the claims of local attachment, every American who can discern the connection between the honor, the renown, and the welfare of his country, and the dignity, safety, and convenience of its Government, must turn with affection and pride."

CHAPTER IV.

PERMANENT CAPITAL SITE SELECTED.

The Act of Congress Approved July 16, 1790—Appointment of Commissioners—President Washington's Proclamation—Location and Surroundings of the District Chosen under Above Act—Description of the Site by John Cotton Smith—Extract from the *Herald*—Carrollsburgh and Hamburgh—The Agreement with the Proprietors—The Act of Maryland—Conveyance of Lands to Trustees—Major Pierre Charles L'Enfant Selected to Prepare a Plan of the City—His Plan Approved—Thomas Jefferson's Part in This Matter—The Name, "City of Washington," Conferred—The Plan of the City Discussed—Major L'Enfant's Dismissal—Act of Congress Compensating L'Enfant for His Services—Andrew Ellicott Succeeds L'Enfant—Completes the Survey of the District of Columbia—Close of the Rule of the Commissioners—Difficulties with the Original Proprietors—Washington's Letter in Reference Thereto—David Burns Still Obstinate—Finally Yields—Extracts from New York *Daily Advertiser*—Estimate of the Value of the Work of Those Who Selected the Site of the National Capital.

THE organic act of Congress, approved by President Washington July 16, 1790, ordained that a district of territory not exceeding ten miles square, to be located on the River Potomac, at some place between the mouth of the Eastern Branch of that river and of the Connogocheague, should be accepted for the permanent seat of government of the United States. The President was to appoint three commissioners, who, under his direction, were to survey and by proper metes and bounds define and limit the territory or district required under and for the purposes of the foregoing organic act. All powers necessary to the purchase or acceptance of the quantity of land within the territory prescribed, on the eastern bank of the Potomac, required according to plans to be approved by the President, were given to the commissioners mentioned, to the extent that such land was needed by the United States, for the provision of suitable buildings for the accommodation of Congress, and of the President, and the public offices of the Government.

The letters patent appointing said commissioners read as follows:

"*George Washington, President of the United States, to all who shall see these presents, Greeting:*

"Know ye, that reposing special trust and confidence in the integrity, skill, and diligence of Thomas Johnson and Daniel Carroll, of

Maryland, and David Stuart, of Virginia, I do, in pursuance of the powers vested in me by the act entitled, 'An Act for Establishing the Temporary and Permanent Seat of the Government of the United States,' approved July 16, 1790, hereby appoint them, the said Thomas Johnson, Daniel Carroll, and David Stuart, commissioners for surveying the district of territory accepted by the said act for the permanent seat of government of the United States, and for performing such other offices as by law are directed, with full authority for them, or any two of them, to proceed therein according to law, and to have and hold the said offices, with all the privileges and authorities to the same of right appertaining, each of them during the pleasure of the President of the United States for the time being.

"In testimony whereof, I have caused these letters to be made patent, and the seal of the United States thereto affixed.

"Given under my hand at the city of Philadelphia, the 22d day of January in the year of our Lord one thousand seven hundred and ninety-one, and of the independence of the United States the fifteenth.

"By the President,

"George Washington.

"Thomas Jefferson."

In further pursuance of the act of Congress, approved July 16, 1790, the President issued a proclamation designating the experimental boundary lines of the district to be accepted for the permanent seat of government, and directing the commissioners to run the lines and survey the proper metes and bounds of said district.

In this proclamation, after reciting the acts of the States of Maryland and Virginia and the act of Congress, he says:

"Now, therefore, in pursuance of the powers to me confided, and after duly examining and weighing the advantages and disadvantages of the several situations, within the limits aforesaid, I do hereby declare and make known that the location of one part of said district of ten miles square shall be found by running four lines of experiment in the following manner: Running from the courthouse in Alexandria in Virginia, due southwest half a mile, and then a due southeast course till it shall strike Hunting Creek, and fix the beginning of the said four lines of experiment:

"Then begin the first four lines of experiment at the point on Hunting Creek where the said southeast course shall have struck the same, and running the said first line due northwest ten miles; thence the second line into Maryland due northeast ten miles; thence .the third line due southeast ten miles; and thence the fourth line due southwest ten miles, to the beginning on Hunting Creek.

"And the said four lines of experiment being so run, I do hereby declare and make known that all that part within the said four lines of experiment which shall be within the State of Maryland, and above the Eastern Branch; and all that part within the same four lines of experiment which shall be within the Commonwealth of Virginia, and above the line to be run from the point of land forming the upper cape of the mouth of Eastern Branch due southwest, and no more, is now fixed upon and directed to be surveyed, defined, limited, and located for a part of the said district accepted by the said act of Congress for the permanent seat of the Government of the United States; hereby expressly reserving the survey and location of the remaining part of the said district, to be made hereafter contiguous to such part or parts of the present location as is or shall be agreeable to law.

"And I do accordingly direct the said commissioners appointed agreeably to the tenor of the said act, to proceed forthwith to run the said lines of experiment; and the same being run, to survey and by proper metes and bounds to define and limit the part within the same which is hereinbefore directed for immediate location and acceptance; and thereof to make due report to me, under their hands and seals."

It will be seen that the district was, by the act mentioned, confined within the limits bounded by the mouths of the Eastern Branch of the Potomac and a stream known as the Connogocheague, which emptied into the Potomac in Washington County, in the State of Maryland, about forty miles above the Eastern Branch. This legislation confined the district to be located to the territory north of the Potomac, and by its very terms excluded any selection within the State of Virginia. That State had, by the act of her legislature, ceded to the Government a territory ten miles square for the purposes of the General Government, all of which territory was of course situated south of the Potomac. President Washington does not seem to have regarded the restriction as binding upon those entrusted with the selection of the territory for the seat of government. It will be seen by his proclamation, issued on the 22d of January, 1791, that he includes within the boundaries determined upon by the district of ten miles square to be dedicated to the uses of the Government, a portion of the territory of the Commonwealth of Virginia lying south of the Potomac River. This selection was afterward approved by Congress. That body, by an act approved March 3, 1791, repealed all the provisions of the preceding act which limited the selection of the territory within which was to be established the seat of government to a district above or north of the Eastern Branch of the Potomac, and ordained that it should be lawful for the President to make as part of the said district "a convenient part of the Eastern Branch and of the lands lying on the lower side thereof, and also the town of Alexandria."

The President had already, as will be seen, under the powers conferred upon him, appointed Thomas Johnson, Daniel Carroll, and David Stuart commissioners for surveying the district of territory accepted by the act of July 16, 1790, for the permanent seat of the Government of the United States, and performing such other offices as by law were directed. Daniel Carroll, one of the aforesaid commissioners, being at the time one of the delegates appointed by the State of Maryland in the House of Representatives of the Congress of the United States, refused to act as commissioner; and hence there were only two commissioners on duty from that time until March 4, 1791, when Mr. Carroll's term of service in Congress having expired, a new commission was issued to him, and he agreed to serve as commissioner. As soon as convenient after this, the President proceeded in person to the point designated for the seat of government, there to take an active part in what was to him the dearest project of the latter years of his life. In a letter to Daniel Carroll, dated March 11, 1791, he says:

"I write to you by this post in conformity with my promise so to do; but it is not yet in my power to determine whether I can set out on Monday or not. If I find the roads do not mend much between this time and that, I shall not be anxious about beginning on that day, even if business should permit. As my fixing the day for meeting the commissioners at Georgetown must depend upon my departure from this place [Philadelphia], I cannot determine upon the former until the latter is decided. I shall write you again by Monday's post, and in that letter shall be able to say with certainty when I leave this city."

Soon after this, that is to say, on the 28th of March, President Washington reached Georgetown, and on the 29th rode over the entire new district, in company with the three commissioners and the two surveyors, Major Pierre Charles L'Enfant and Andrew Ellicott.

It will be interesting to accompany this distinguished party in their survey of the site selected by the wisdom of Congress for the future Capital of the yet infant Republic. To most of them the scene was not new, but to one or two of them at least we can suppose that this was their first view of its beauties. We can imagine the heights above Georgetown to be the point from which they first gazed upon the territory from which they were to select a site for the future seat of government. At their feet was the already thriving town of Georgetown, than which no town in this or any other country is more beautifully situated. Rising from the River Potomac, which formed the base of the town, it already partly occupied, and was destined in its gradual growth and improvement to occupy entirely, the heights that skirted and adorned that beautiful river.

On their right was the river itself. Rising in the distant Alleghenies and running for many miles between the States of Maryland and Virginia with comparative placidity until joined by the Shenandoah at Harper's Ferry, it bursts through the chain of mountains that has hitherto confined it, tearing the mountain from its summit to its base and hurrying away to the sea. For a while after this apparent declaration of its freedom from the restraint which the mountains had imposed upon its waters, its course is smooth. Again it encounters difficulties, and leaping over a steep, it forms what is known as the Great Falls of the Potomac. It rushes along, with rapids and cascades, amid grand and picturesque banks that are the admiration of all who view them, until finally reaching the town of Georgetown, it washes the shores of that town with waters so calm and deep that ships bring to its wharfs the commerce of the remotest regions of the earth. Flowing on, the river turns to the east, and widening as it goes till it assumes the appearance of a lake, describes a curve that forms a beautiful boundary to the lap of land that is finally selected as the abiding place of the National Capital.

Here again it is met by the Eastern Branch, or Anacostia, then a navigable stream and one of the commercial highways of the new Republic; and so calmly and peacefully that it seems incredible that it has a short while ago been a tumultuous stream, full of wild leaps and grand cascades, it flows away by the town of Alexandria and Mount Vernon, the home of Washington, and is finally lost in the waters of the Chesapeake Bay.

Looking across the river, the heights of Arlington rise in view, commanding a most comprehensive view of the river, in themselves forming a beautiful boundary to the scene now gazed upon by the august party with so much interest. Far away to the south was the city of Alexandria, then a port of considerable importance, at whose wharves lay ships from all parts of the world, and destined —at least so thought President Washington—to be the great tidewater doorway to that immense western country which had already given evidence of its future importance. President Washington was not out of his reckoning; for this city, being the nearest and most convenient port to the Northwestern Territory, would undoubtedly have furnished to that Territory the most important outlet for its wealth, had not the application of steam to internal commerce brought about a revolution that no human wisdom could foresee.

Turning from the river and looking toward the east, their gaze encounters as the eastern boundary of Georgetown a considerable stream, flowing between romantic banks and adding greatly to the beauty of the landscape, known as Rock Creek. Beyond this extends an extensive plateau, bounded by the waters of the Potomac and the Eastern Branch, nearly level throughout its whole extent, save as it is diversified by gentle elevations, nowhere of any great height, but still sufficient to provide commanding eminences for the future public buildings of the Capital City. Through this plateau at that day ran a considerable stream known as the Tiber, with low marshy banks. This stream ran from east to west, and had its mouth in the Potomac River near what is now the foot of Seventeenth Street. South of this, extending to the bank of the river, was a plain, level nearly throughout its entire extent and divided in those early days into fields for agricultural purposes. Through this plain ran a branch of the larger stream known as the Tiber, and called St. James's Creek, having its mouth in the Eastern Branch at or near its confluence with the main stream or river. North again of the Tiber the land was rolling in its character, covered with trees and low undergrowth, and finally rising into high lands that formed a beautiful background to the beauties of the rural landscape. Far away to the east ran the Eastern Branch or Anacostia, forming with the Potomac a magnificent frame for what was then selected by these commissioners as the site for the seat of the new Government, and which was destined to be the location of a capital city so grand that the wildest dreams of the enthusiast failed to realize its splendors. The commissioners seem to have had no hesitation in adopting the site described, as the result of their labors under the act of Congress, and their descendants of to-day recognize and appreciate the wisdom that guided and controlled their deliberations. It is safe to say that nowhere, now that natural obstacles principally in the way of complete drainage are nearly, if not entirely, overcome, can there be found a site better adapted to the development of the grand idea conceived by the distinguished engineer selected by President Washington to prepare the plans of the Capital City of the United States.

It is interesting in this connection to read what was said of the site of the city by a distinguished member of Congress from Connecticut in the Sixth Congress, the first that held its sessions in the city of Washington. It is true this is written several years after the selection of the site and when some progress had been made in the erection of the public buildings, but so little had been done that the description fits in many respects the condition of things at the date about which we have been writing.

"Our approach to the city [says Mr. John Cotton Smith] was accompanied with sensations not easily described. One wing of the Capitol only had been erected, which with the President's House, a mile distant, both constructed with white sandstone, were shining objects in dismal contrast with the scene around them. Instead of recognizing the avenues and streets portrayed in the plan of the city, not one was visible, unless we except a road with two buildings on each side of it, called the New Jersey Avenue. The Pennsylvania Avenue, leading, as laid down on paper, from the Capitol to the President's Mansion, was then nearly the whole distance a deep morass, covered with alder bushes, which were cut through the width of the intended avenue during the then ensuing winter. Between the President's House and Georgetown a block of houses had been erected which then bore (and do now) the name of the Six Buildings. There were also two other blocks, consisting of two or three dwelling houses in different directions, and now and then an isolated wooden habitation; the intervening spaces, and indeed the surface of the city generally, being covered with shrub oak bushes on the higher grounds, and on the marshy soil with either trees or some sort of shrubbery. Nor was the desolate aspect of the place a little augmented by a number of unfinished edifices at Greenleaf's Point, and on an eminence a short distance from it; commenced by an individual whose name they bore, but the state of whose funds compelled him to abandon them not only unfinished, but in a ruinous condition. There appeared to be but two really comfortable habitations in all respects within the bounds of the city, one of which belonged to Daniel Carroll, and the other to Notley Young, who were the former proprietors of a large portion of the land appropriated to the city, but who reserved for their own accommodations ground sufficient for gardens and other useful appurtenances. The roads in every direction were muddy and unimproved. A sidewalk was attempted in one instance by a covering formed of the chips of the stones which had been hewed for the Capitol. It extended but a little way, and was of little value; for in dry weather the sharp fragments cut our shoes and in wet weather covered them with mortar. In short, it was a 'new settlement.'

* * * * * * * * *

"Notwithstanding the unfavorable aspect which Washington presented on our arrival, I cannot sufficiently express my admiration of its local position. From the Capitol you have a distant view of its fine undulating surface, situated at the confluence of the Potomac and its Eastern Branch, the wide expanse of that majestic river to the bend at Mount Vernon, the cities of Alexandria and Georgetown, and the cultivated fields and blue hills of Maryland and Virginia on either side of the river, the whole constituting a prospect of surpassing beauty and grandeur. The city has also the inestimable advantage of delightful water, in many instances from copious springs, and always attainable by digging a moderate depth; to which may be added the singular fact that such is the due admixture of clay and loam in the soil of a great portion of the city, that a house may be built of brick made of the earth dug from the cellars; hence it was not unusual to see the remains of a brick kiln near the newly erected dwelling house or other edifice. In short, when we consider not only these advantages, but what in a national point of view is of supreme importance, the location on a fine navigable river, accessible to the whole maritime frontiers of the United States, and yet rendered easily defensible against foreign invasion, and that by the facilities of internal navigation it may be approached by the population of the Western States, and indeed of the whole Nation, with less inconvenience than any conceivable situation, we must acknowledge that its selection by Washington as the permanent seat of the Federal Government affords a striking exhibition of the discernment, wisdom, and forecast which characterized that illustrious man. Under this impression, whenever, during the six years of my connection with Congress, the question of removing the seat of government to some other place was agitated,—and the proposition was frequently made,—I stood almost alone as a Northern man in giving my vote in the negative."

In an article published in a newspaper, the *Herald*, in Philadelphia, under date of January 4, 1795, we find the following:

"To found a city in the center of the United States for the purpose of making it the depository of the acts of the Union and the sanctuary of the laws which must one day rule all North America, is a grand and comprehensive idea, which has already become with propriety the object of public respect. In reflecting on the importance of the Union, and on the advantages which it secures to all the inhabitants of the United States collectively, or to individuals, where is there an American who does not see in the establishment of a Federal town a national means for confirming forever that valuable connection to which the Nation is indebted for liberation from the British yoke? The Federal City, situated in the center of the United States, is a temple erected to liberty; and toward this edifice will the wishes and expectations of all true friends of their country be incessantly directed. The city of Washington, considered under such important points of view, could not be calculated on a small scale; its extent, the disposition of its avenues and public squares, should all correspond with the magnitude of the object for which it was intended; and we need only cast our eyes upon the situation and plan of the city to recognize in them the comprehensive genius of the President, to whom the direction of the business has been committed by Congress."

Within the limits of the territory so selected by the commissioners were two tracts that had been laid off for towns into squares and streets. They were called Carrollsburgh and Hamburgh. It does not appear that there were any improvements of importance on these projected town sites, except that, in the rates of fare prescribed by the early laws of the corporation of Washington for the government of hacks, such vehicles are allowed to charge for the conveyance of passengers from Greenleaf's Point to Hamburgh wharf twenty-five cents. Suffice it to say, that Hamburgh was in the western part of the city, and was laid out in lots and streets in the latter part of 1771; and that Carrollsburgh, which was in the eastern part of the city, on the banks of the Anacostia and James Creek, was subdivided in the year 1770.

The commissioners seem to have been perfectly satisfied with the survey made by them of the site selected for the permanent seat of the Government. On the evening of the day when they, in company with the President, rode over the district submitted to them, a meeting was held for the purpose of effecting a friendly agreement between the property holders in the new district and the United States commissioners. Washington's counsel on that occasion was of so great effect that the general features of an agreement were settled, and the signatures of nineteen of the proprietors of the soil were appended to it the next day. By this means it may be said the rights and titles to property within the District and the city of Washington were determined, and the great fact of a permanent seat of government finally settled. The agreement is in the language following:

"We, the subscribers, in consideration of the great benefits we expect to derive from having the Federal City laid off on our lands, do hereby agree and bind ourselves, our heirs, executors, and administrators, to convey in trust to the President of the United States, or commissioners, or such persons as he shall appoint, by good and sufficient deeds in fee simple, the whole of our respective lands which he may think proper to include within the lines of the Federal City, for the purposes and on the conditions following:

"The President shall have the sole power and directing of the Federal City, to be laid off in what manner he pleases. He may retain any number of squares he may think proper for public improvement, or other public uses, and the lots only which shall be laid off shall be a joint property between the trustees on behalf of the public and each present proprietor, and the same shall be fairly and equally divided between the public and the individuals as soon as may be after the city shall be laid off.

"For the streets the proprietors shall receive no compensation; but for the squares, or lands in any form which shall be taken for public buildings, or any kind of public improvements or uses, the proprietors whose lands shall be so taken, shall receive at the rate of £25 per acre, to be paid by the public.

"The whole wood on the lands shall be the property of the proprietors; but should any be desired by the President to be reserved or left standing, the same shall be paid for by the public at a just and reasonable valuation, exclusive of the £25 per acre to be paid for the land on which the same shall remain.

"Each proprietor shall retain the full possession and use of his land until the same shall be sold and occupied by the purchasers of the lots laid out thereupon, and in all cases where the public arrangements, as the streets, lots, etc., will admit of it, each proprietor shall possess his buildings and other improvements, and graveyards, paying to the public only one-half the present estimated value of the lands on which the same shall be, or £12 10s. per acre. But in cases where the arrangements of the streets, lots, squares, etc., will not admit of this, and it shall become necessary to remove the buildings, improvements, etc., the proprietors of the same shall be paid the reasonable value by the public.

"Nothing in this agreement shall affect the lots which any of the proprietors, parties to this agreement, may hold in the towns of Carrollsburgh or Hamburgh.

"IN WITNESS WHEREOF, we have hereunto set our hands and seals this 30th day of March, 1791."

This agreement was signed by Robert Peter, David Burns, James M. Lingan, Uriah Forrest, Benjamin Stoddert, Notley Young, Daniel Carroll of Duddington, Overton Carr, Thomas Beall of George, Charles Beatty, Anthony Holmead, William Young, Edward Pierce, Abraham Young, James Pierce, William Prout, Eliphas Douglas, John Warring (the last two by their attorneys), and William King.

The Legislature of the State of Maryland, by an act dated December 19, 1791, ratified her cession of land to the United States for a Federal District, and after reciting the boundaries as given above, and stating that the territory has been called the "Territory of Columbia," proceeds as follows:

"AND WHEREAS, Notley Young, Daniel Carroll, of Duddington, and many others, proprietors of the greater part of the land hereinafter mentioned to have been laid out into a city, came into an agreement and have conveyed their lands in trust to Thomas Beall, son of George, and John Mackall Gantt, whereby they have subjected their lands to be laid out as a city, giving up part to the United States, and subjecting other parts to be sold to raise money as a donation, to be employed according to the act of Congress for establishing the temporary and permanent seat of government of the United States, under and upon the terms and conditions contained in each of said deeds; and many of the proprietors of lots in Carrollsburgh and Hamburgh having also come into an agreement, subjecting their lots to be laid out anew, giving up one-half of the quantity of their lots to be sold, and the money thence arising to be applied as a donation aforesaid, and then to be reinstated in one-half the quantity of their lots in the new location, or otherwise compensated in lands in a different situation within the city, by agreement between the commissioners and them; and in case of disagreement, that then a just and full compensation shall be made in money; yet some of the proprietors of lots in Carrollsburgh and Hamburgh, as well as some of the proprietors of other lands, have not, from imbecility and other causes, come into any agreement concerning their lands within the limits hereafter mentioned, but a very great proportion of the landholders having agreed on the same terms, the President of the United States directed a city to be laid out, comprehending all the land beginning on the east side of Rock Creek, at a stone standing in the middle of the road leading from Georgetown to Bladensburg; thence along the middle of the said road to a stone standing on the east side of Reedy Branch of Goose Creek; thence southeasterly, making an angle of sixty-one degrees and twenty minutes with the meridian, to a stone standing in the road leading from Bladensburg to the Eastern Branch ferry; thence south to a stone eighty poles north of the east and west line already drawn from the mouth of Goose Creek to the Eastern Branch; thence east parallel to the said east and west line to the Eastern Branch; thence with the waters of the Eastern Branch, and Potomac River, and Rock Creek to the beginning, which has since been called the city of Washington.;

"AND WHEREAS, It appears to this General Assembly highly just and expedient that all the lands within said city should contribute, in due proportion, in the means which have already very greatly enhanced the value of the whole; and an incontrovertible title ought to be made to the purchasers, under public sanction; that allowing foreigners to hold land within said Territory will greatly contribute to the improvement and population thereof; and that many temporary provisions will be necessary till Congress exercises the jurisdiction and government over the said Territory; and, whereas, in the cession of this State heretofore made of territory for the Government of the United States, the line of such cession could not be particularly designated, and it being expedient and proper that the same should be recognized in the acts of the State;

"*Be it enacted by the General Assembly of Maryland,* That all that part of the said Territory, called Columbia, which lies within the limits of this State shall be, and the same is hereby acknowledged to be, forever ceded to the Congress and Government of the United States, in full and absolute right and exclusive jurisdiction, as well of soil as of persons residing or to reside thereon, pursuant to the tenor and effect of the eighth section of the first article of the Constitution of the Government of the United States: *Provided,* that nothing herein contained shall be construed to vest in the United States any right of property in the soil so as to affect the rights of individuals therein, otherwise than as the same shall or may be transferred by such individuals to the United States: *And provided, also,* that the jurisdiction of the laws of the State over the persons and property of individuals residing within the limits of the cession aforesaid shall not cease or determine until Congress shall by law provide for the government thereof under the jurisdiction in manner provided by the article of the Constitution before recited."

May 9, 1791, John M. Gantt accepted the appointment of secretary to the board of commissioners, to be paid according to the judgment of the President, and on June 30, the same year, William Deakins was appointed treasurer.

On or about the 29th of June, 1791, the original proprietors of the greater part of the lands which now constitute the city of Washington made conveyance of them to trustees, to hold for the purposes of the Government. These trustees were Thomas Beall, of George, and John M. Gantt. By the deeds the lands belonging to said proprietors within the Federal Territory are conveyed, in consideration of five shillings, to the trustees mentioned, to be by them taken and held in certain trusts in the deeds mentioned. These trusts are, that all such lands, or such parts thereof as may be thought necessary or proper, be laid out, together with other lands within the Federal City, with such streets, squares, parcels, and lots as the President of the United States for the time being shall approve, and by said trustees to be conveyed to the commissioners appointed under the act of Congress for establishing the temporary and permanent seat of the Government of the United States, for the use of the United States forever, all the streets and squares, parcels and lots, as the President shall deem proper for that purpose, to belong forever to the said United States; that, as to the residue of the said lots into which said lands shall have been laid off and divided, a fair and equal division shall be made, to be agreed upon, or, if a fair division cannot be obtained by agreement, then such residue shall be divided by giving to the owners of said lands every alternate lot. Having thus provided how these lands are to be divided between the proprietors of them and the trustees on the part of the Government, provision is made for the lands taken by the United States, and the disposition of the funds arising from such sales; first, for the payment to the original proprietors at a fixed sum per acre for the lands taken for the use of the United States, not including the streets and avenues, and next, to the purpose and according to the act of Congress establishing the temporary and permanent seat of government, such disposition to be subject to such terms and conditions as shall be thought reasonable by the President for regulating the materials, and buildings, and improvements on the lots generally in the city, or in particular parts thereof, for common convenience, safety, and order, such conditions to be declared before any sale of said lots.

There were other provisions in the conveyance of these lands, with respect to the trees and wood growing thereon, and to the portion thereof occupied by the proprietors for their private residences and graveyards, having reference always to the public use and convenience.

When President Washington returned from his famous tour of one thousand nine hundred miles through the South in his cream-colored chariot, during the progress of which a part of the letters above quoted were written, he found awaiting him at Mount Vernon that skillful French engineer, Major Pierre Charles L'Enfant. He was an educated soldier who had distinguished himself while serving as major of engineers in the Revolutionary War, and had been selected to lay out the plan of the new Federal City. Major L'Enfant was warmly' received by the President, and remained with him at Mount Vernon nearly a week, during which time the plan of the city was completely matured. Major L'Enfant's plan was very elaborate, and was fully set forth upon a map finely executed. He followed the work of Le Notre in Versailles, the seat of the French Government buildings. His plan comprised broad transverse streets and avenues, numerous open squares, circles, and triangular reservations and parks, all of which were designed to be so drawn that from the intersection of any two or more streets and avenues the horizon would be visible. The locations of the public buildings were indicated, and everything was designed upon a most spacious scale.

L'Enfant's design meeting with the approval of President Washington and Mr. Jefferson, it was formally adopted, and L'Enfant was engaged to superintend its execution. He had as assistant a young Pennsylvanian named Andrew Ellicott, who, together with his brother, had established the town of Ellicott's Mills in Maryland. He was remarkably intelligent and a competent surveyor, and by him the streets and squares were laid out. Before the erection of any building was permitted, an accurate survey was made and properly recorded, and to this survey all subsequent building operations had to conform.

Mr. Jefferson, the Secretary of State under President Washington, took an active interest in the plan of the new city; and indeed in everything that related to it. In a letter to a friend, that distinguished statesman says:

"I received last night from Major L'Enfant a request to furnish him any plans of towns I could for his examination. I accordingly send him by this post plans of Frankfort on the Main, Carlsruhe, Amsterdam, Strasburg, Paris, Orleans, Bordeaux, Lyons, Montpelier, Marseilles, Turin, and Milan, on large and accurate scales, which I procured while in those towns respectively. They are none of them comparable to the old Babylon, revived in Philadelphia and exemplified. While in Europe, I selected about a dozen or two of the handsomest parts of private buildings, of which I have the plates. Perhaps it might decide the taste of the new town, were they to be engraved and distributed gratis among the inhabitants of Georgetown. The expense would be trifling."

On April 30, 1791, President Washington, in his proclamation, referred to the city of Washington as the "Federal City." The name "City of Washington" was conferred upon it in September, 1791, as appears from the following letter from the commissioners of the District to Major L'Enfant:

"GEORGETOWN, September 9, 1791.

"SIR: We have agreed that the Federal District shall be called 'The Territory of Columbia,' and the Federal City the 'City of Washington.' The title of the map will therefore be, 'A Map of the City of Washington in the Territory of Columbia.'

"We have also agreed that the streets be named alphabetically one way and numerically the other, the former to be divided into north and south, and the latter into east and west numbers from the Capitol. Major Ellicott, with proper assistance, will immediately take, and soon furnish you with, the soundings of the Eastern Branch, to be inserted in the map. We expect he will also furnish you with the proposed post road, which we wish to be noticed in the map.

"We are respectfully yours,

"THOMAS JOHNSON.
"DAVID STUART.
"DANIEL CARROLL."

The plan of the Capital City is most undoubtedly the result of the talent, industry, and zealous interest of Major L'Enfant He was evidently a man of great accomplishments, and it is marvelous, now that time has developed his grand plans, that he could have conceived the erection of so magnificent a capital in what was then apparently a hopeless wilderness. But Major L'Enfant seems to have been as eccentric and impracticable in some respects as he was talented and capable in others. These qualities soon made his intercourse with the commissioners and others interested in the city unbearable, and his connection with its plans and progress terminated abruptly in March, 1792, almost at the outset of his work.

General Washington wrote of him, January 17, 1792, that he might be a useful man, if he could be brought to reduce himself within those limits which the commissioners, under their responsibility, were obliged to prescribe; but that at that time he did not appear to be in that temper. "Perhaps," he said, "when Mr. Johnson shall arrive here, he may be able to let him see that nothing will be required of him but what is perfectly reconcilable to reason and to a degree of liberty on his part."

March 2, 1792, Mr. Jefferson, Secretary of State, wrote to the commissioners:

"It having been found impracticable to employ Major L'Enfant about the Federal City, in that degree of subordination which was lawful and proper, he has been notified that his services are at an end. It is proper that he should receive the reward of his past services, and the wish that he should have no just cause of discontent suggests that it should be liberal. The President thinks of $2,500 or $3,000, but leaves the determination with you. Ellicott is to go on and finish laying off the plan of the ground and surveying and plotting the district."

Major L'Enfant's dismissal caused apprehension in certain quarters that he and his friends would use what influence they possessed to injure the prospects of the new Capital, even Washington writing that "the enemies of the enterprise will take advantage of the retirement of L'Enfant to trumpet the whole as an abortion." But the Major was loyal to the Government and to the city, and lived on the site and in the vicinity the rest of his days. G. A. Townsend, in his "Washington Outside and Inside," says of him that "he several times afterwards came under the notice of the Executive, and was a baffled petitioner before Congress." However this may be, an act of Congress was approved May 1, 1810, which was as follows:

"AN ACT for the Relief of P. C. L'Enfant:

"*Be it enacted by the Senate and House of Representatives of the United States of America, in Congress assembled,* That the Secretary of the Treasury be authorized and directed to pay P. C. L'Enfant, out of any money in the treasury not otherwise appropriated, the sum of $666.66, with interest from the 1st day of March, 1792, as a compensation for his services in laying out the plan of the city of Washington."

At this late date and in the presence of the fruition of his great plan, it is not difficult to draw a veil over the weaknesses and foibles of this brilliant and enthusiastic Frenchman. He had manifested his gallantry on the battlefields of the Revolution. He showed to the world how great was his faith in the stability of our institutions and the future progress of his adopted country in the plan he devised for its future Capital, and his loyalty never flagged under the pressure of what must have seemed to him ingratitude and neglect. Somewhere in our beautiful city there will some day arise a proper monument to the man who deserves so much at the hand of every true American.

During the year 1792, the commissioners employed Andrew Ellicott to survey the boundary lines of the Federal District, and on January 1, 1793, he made the following report of the survey to them:

"It is with singular satisfaction that I announce to you the completion of the survey of the four lines comprehending the Territory of Columbia. These lines are opened and cleared forty feet wide; that is, twenty feet on each side of the lines limiting the Territory; and in order to perpetuate the work, I have set up square milestones, marked progressively with the number of miles from the beginning on Jones's Point to the west corner; thence from the west corner; thence from the north corner to the east corner, and thence to the place of beginning on Jones's Point, except as to a few cases where the miles terminated on a declivity or in water; in such cases the stones are placed on the nearest firm ground, and their true distances in miles and poles marked on them. On the sides facing the Territory is inscribed, 'Jurisdiction of the United States'; on the opposite sides of those placed in the State of Virginia is inscribed 'Virginia,' and of those in the State of Maryland is inscribed 'Maryland.' On the fourth side is inscribed the year and the present position of the magnetic needle at the place. With this you will receive a map of the four lines, with a half mile on each side, to which is added a survey of the waters in the Territory and a plan of the city of Washington."

The rule of the District commissioners over the city of Washington came to a close by the abolishment of the board in 1802, and the appointment of a superintendent. In the meantime, the Government of the United States was removed to Washington, Congress first convening there November 22, 1800, during the presidency of John Adams. Legal jurisdiction over the District of Columbia was assumed by Congress February 27, 1801, and the laws of Maryland and Virginia were declared in force. The city of Washington was incorporated by a Congressional enactment passed May 3, 1802, by which act the appointment of the mayor was vested in the President of the United States, and there were established two branches of the City Council, the members of which were elected by the people on a general ticket.

By this act the city of Washington was definitely established as a city, and was clothed with powers of municipal government. Its progress to this point had been slow, and attended with many and very serious difficulties; so many, indeed, that nothing but the great faith of the men who assisted in its foundation, in the future growth and development of the country, would have insured success. These

difficulties were to be found in embarrassments growing out of national
legislation, to obstacles thrown in the way of the city's progress by
movements in Congress, and by the ceaseless opposition, in some
quarters, of the public press. In this account of these matters we
have principally to do with the difficulties presented by the persons
who were proprietors of the lands to be occupied, and we shall find
that these, notwithstanding the early acquiescence of the proprietors
in the proposed plans, were in some instances of a serious character,
and were calculated to discourage, and, indeed, did for a while
dishearten, the commissioners who had the work in charge.

Almost immediately after the meeting at Georgetown, which
resulted in the agreement with the original proprietors of the lands
to be occupied by the Federal City, General Washington took steps to
procure from the State authorities of Virginia the funds voted by
that State to aid in the erecting of the city. It appears from a letter
written by him as early as May 7, 1791, to the commissioners, that
difficulties were already obstructing the progress of those gentlemen;
for he says, writing from Charleston: "I have received your letter
of the 13th of last month. It is an unfortunate circumstance in the
present stage of the business relating to the Federal City, that difficulties unforeseen and unexpected should arise to darken, perhaps to
destroy, the fair prospect which it presented when I left Georgetown,
and which the instrument then signed by the combined interest [as it
was termed] of Georgetown and Carrollsburgh so plainly describes.
The pain which this occurrence occasions me is the more sensibly felt,
as I had taken pleasure during my journey throughout the several
States to relate the agreement, and to speak of it on every occasion
in terms which applauded the conduct of the parties, as being alike
conducive to the public welfare and to the interests of individuals.
. . . When the instrument was presented, I found no occasion to add
a word with respect to the boundary, because the whole was surrendered upon the conditions which were expressed. Had I discovered
a disposition in the subscribers to contract my views, I should then
have pointed out the inconveniences and impolicy of the measure.
Upon the whole, I shall hope and expect that the business will be
suffered to proceed, and the more so as they cannot be ignorant that
the further consideration of a certain measure in a neighboring State
[alluding to the payment of the funds voted by Virginia] stands
postponed; for what reason, is left to their own information and
conjecture."

He alludes in this connection by name to Messrs. Young, Peter,

Lingan, Forrest, and Stoddert as the discontented proprietors. However, it appears that after the difficulties had been overcome, negotiations
were effected with tolerable ease with all the proprietors except David
Burns. With him the commissioners failed to effect any arrangements
for the surrender of his property, and the President was told that he
alone could bring him to terms. The farm of Mr. Burns lay directly
south of where the President's House now stands, and extended east
as far as the Patent Office. It contained six hundred acres, and was
patented to William Langworthy by an instrument dated July 5, 1681.

Upon the failure of the commissioners, President Washington made
his way to the Burns cottage, and causing Uncle David to sit down
on a rustic seat under a clump of trees, used all his powers of
persuasion to bring about a sale. But "obstinate Mr. Burns," as
President Washington often called him afterward, yielded not a jot.
Washington's efforts appear to have been repeated several times, and
upon one of these occasions, when Washington was trying to convince
him of the great advantage it would be to him, Uncle Davy testily
replied:

"I suppose you think that people here are going to take every
grist that comes from you as pure grain; but what would you have
been if you had not married the rich Widow Custis?"

At length, after frequent interviews, Washington lost his patience.
He gave Mr. Burns to understand that he had been authorized to
select the location of the National Capital, and said: "I have selected
your farm as a part of it, and the Government will take it; and I
trust you will, under the circumstances, enter into an amicable agreement."

When the President asked again, "Upon what terms will you
surrender your plantation?" Mr. Burns replied, "Upon any terms that
your Excellency may choose to name."

In the New York *Daily Advertiser*, a newspaper of that day, under
date of February 24, 1789, appeared a communication from Baltimore,
which was as follows:

"There are already subscribed for the erecting of buildings in this
town for the use of Congress, TWENTY THOUSAND POUNDS. When we
reflect on the present state of population in the United States, nothing
can be more preposterous and absurd than the idea of fixing the seat
of Congress in a village, or the raising a new city in a wilderness for
their residence. Before we give in to such fancies, we should consider
whether we have such a surplus of people and trade as is necessary
for the erection and maintenance of a new city. If we have not, the

new city must necessarily draw from our present towns their wealth, trade, and people to compose its greatness. I believe no considerate man will venture to say that a new city can be established by any other means than by attracting the wealth, trade, and inhabitants of the old ones; or that it is consistent with the interests of the United States to adopt a measure so pregnant with injury and desolation. The contest for the seat of Congress will, therefore, and must necessarily, be between New York and Baltimore."

The following piece of doggerel from one of the papers of the day exhibits the feeling which pervaded the many communications with which the city papers were then flooded, in relation to the removal of the Government from New York, where the Council had gone to considerable expense in fitting up the City Hall for the reception of Congress. It stood in Wall Street, at the head of Broad, the site of the present Custom House.

"THE WAITING-GIRL IN NEW YORK, TO HER FRIEND IN PHILADELPHIA.

"Well, Nanny, I'm sorry to say, since you writ us
The Congress and court have determined to quit us.
And for us, my dear Nanny, we're much in a pet,
And hundreds of houses will be to be let.
Our streets, that were quite in a way to look clever,
Will now be neglected, and nasty as ever.
Again we must fret at the Dutchified gutters,
And pebble-stone pavements, which wear out our trotters.
My master looks dull, and his spirits are sinking;
From morning till night he is smoking and thinking,
Laments the expense of destroying the fort,
And says your great people are all of a sort.
He hopes and he prays they may die in a stall,
If they leave us in debt for Federal Hall.
In fact, he would rather saw timber, or dig,
Than see them removing to Connogocheague,
Where the houses and kitchens are yet to be framed,
The trees to be felled, and the streets to be named."

It will be remembered that General Washington himself, when the insubordination and intolerable conduct of Major L'Enfant had rendered that officer's dismissal imperative, expressed his fears that the friends of the discharged engineer would trumpet the whole plan as an abortion, and do all they could to hinder the successful completion of his design in regard to the Capital City. These were only a few of the occurrences that combined to dampen the ardor and chill the enthusiasm of the men who had undertaken the work of building up a great city in a forbidding wilderness. It was a gigantic undertaking; and when we consider the circumstances that surrounded the project, the conditions with respect to all the appliances that entered into the successful erection of such a city at that early day, while we are amazed at the conception of the idea, we are more amazed at the spirit and energy which carried that idea into practical effect. It must be remembered that two of the States, at least, had offered towns — one its State capital, with such concessions as to jurisdiction as Congress might deem essential — as places in which might be arranged the permanent residence of the Government; and it is reasonable to conclude, from what we know of the actions of other States and cities, that no difficulty would have been encountered, had Congress manifested a desire in that direction, to have found not only a fit residence prepared to hand, but also commodious and fitting buildings for the accommodation of the Federal offices. But Congress feared most of all things the unbridled license of a mob. A lesson had been taught by those mutinous soldiers at Philadelphia, and by the timid, irresolute action of the authorities of that city and the State of which it was a part, that could not be erased from the minds of the men who had the affairs of the Nation in their hands. No argument, no persuasion, could induce them to subject themselves again to that peril. These and other motives were so controlling in their effects that, turning a deaf ear to harsh criticism, doleful predictions, and public ridicule, they persisted in their work, and upon that beautiful lap of earth on the banks of the Potomac, in the midst of forbidding swamps, country brooks, thriving cornfields, and all the desolation we can imagine must have marked the spot in those days, they planned the city, of which more need not be said than that it is worthy of the name it bears. We who live to-day cannot fail to have our pride as Americans amply gratified as we gaze on the beauty and grandeur of our country's Capital. Here has Congress completed nearly a century of its deliberations, free from interruption save only when a band of ruthless invaders destroyed the public buildings, disturbed for a short time the peace of the community, and sent their own names down to posterity with a heritage of unending disgrace.

CHAPTER V.

PIONEER LIFE.

The Early Settlers of the District of Columbia—Daniel Carroll, of Duddington—David Burns—Marcia Burns—John P. Van Ness—Notley Young—Benjamin Oden—Robert Peter—The Removal of the Government to Washington—Officers Who Came Here at That Time—Samuel Meredith—Thomas Tudor Tucker—Joseph Nourse—Richard Harrison—Peter Hagner—John Steele—Gabriel Duval—William Simmons—Thomas Turner—Abraham Bradley, Jr.—Thomas Munroe—Roger C. Weightman—Stephen L. Hallett—Dr. William Thornton—George Hadfield—Benjamin Henry Latrobe—Pierre Charles L'Enfant—Samuel Harrison Smith—Andrew Ellicott—Benjamin Bannecker.

IN our last chapter, we have shown how the site upon which the Capital City was to be erected was finally determined upon, and how the Government was established in what was to be its future residence. Before proceeding further in the history of the city, it appears appropriate to dwell for a few moments upon the history of those men who were the proprietors of the plantations selected for the proposed site of the city. The entire area selected for this site of the seat of government belonged apparently to a few proprietors — we mean the entire area north of the Potomac; for, inasmuch as that portion in Virginia which, for about half a century, belonged to the Federal District was, in 1846, ceded back to that State, it is not deemed necessary in this connection to make special mention of the original proprietors of the lands once included in the District south of the Potomac River.

First among the men owning the lands originally forming a part of and still constituting the District of Columbia, was Daniel Carroll, of Duddington. He was a fine specimen of the gentleman of the régime —pure, patriotic, hospitable, and kind. He was a delegate from Maryland to the Continental Congress from 1780 to 1784, being first elected when only thirty years of age, and was a signer of the Articles of Confederation, and also of the Constitution of the United States. From 1789 to 1791, he was a Representative in Congress from Maryland, and was appointed by General Washington one of the commissioners for surveying and limiting the site of the Federal District, and entered upon the duties of that office immediately upon the expiration of his term as Representative. He was the owner of a considerable tract of land within the limits of the territory selected by General Washington for the Federal District, which was allotted to him in the partition of a larger tract belonging to the historical Carroll family, and known as Carroll Manor. He resided upon his farm in a substantial, and for those days, elegant residence. His mansion is spoken of by those who were first among the officials of the General Government to come to the new Capital from Philadelphia as being really comfortable in all respects, surrounded by a garden and other useful appurtenances. He was the owner of all that portion of the District bordering upon the Anacostia or Eastern Branch of the Potomac, and embracing within its limits the hill upon which the Capitol building was subsequently erected, and stretching out to and beyond the boundary of the city in an easterly direction. His possessions included the town of Carrollsburgh, so named from a project of forming a town in the neighborhood, but which project was of course swallowed up in the far greater project of the establishment of a city, which was to be at the same time the capital of a nation; though so far as our information goes, this town site was improved by the erection thereon of some few dwelling houses. But if this statement should hereafter be proved slightly incorrect, the fact will still remain that the town itself was projected as early as 1770, and it is a matter of record among the ancient land records of Prince George's County, Maryland, that at that early day the town was subdivided into village lots, and the owners of the town site were authorized by said deeds to establish a town thereon, to be named Carrollsburgh, they themselves being known as grantees of Duddington Manor and Duddington Pasture. These grantees were Charles Carroll, Jr., Henry Rozer, Daniel Carroll, and Notley Young.

The land of Daniel Carroll, of Duddington, was beautifully situated upon the high table land that skirted the low grounds between Georgetown and the Anacostia. They included, as has been said, the hill upon which the Capitol building was afterward erected, and were evidently selected for the site of that building because they offered the most eligible location for that purpose, and perhaps because they were above the malarial influences of the marshy lands upon either bank of the Tiber. The fact that the Capitol building has for its eastern front its most imposing presentation, would seem to indicate that its designers anticipated that the city would first extend in that direction. In addition to this, the fact that the Anacostia or Eastern Branch was a stream navigable for many miles of its course, and that upon this stream at that early day was selected a site for a navy yard and an arsenal, both of which were expected to be of very considerable importance in the future growth of the city, also points to the existence of the same anticipation.

All these things combined to give to the lands of Daniel Carroll, of Duddington, the very greatest importance in connection with the future development of the city, and it is not singular that all these circumstances combined should invest this tract of land with great speculative value in the estimation of its proprietor. It is not to be wondered at, then, that this worthy gentleman, trusting to what he considered the superiority of his lands over those of others, should have placed so high a price upon them that parties seeking building sites within the influence of the Federal Government were driven to seek other portions of the city upon which to build. The result was, that Mr. Carroll failed to make sales of his lands so beautifully situated, and the city was driven away from his property, to seek a permanent location on lands that were considered of little or of no possible value, far away to the westward. This was Mr. Carroll's great mistake; for the taxes levied upon his unimproved property involved him in difficulties which he never entirely overcame.

Another of the original proprietors of the lands within the limits of the Federal District was David Burns, to whom reference has been made in the preceding chapter. So far as is known, he was a humble Scotchman, who had inherited a considerable tract of land from his ancestors, and who lived the life of a simple farmer, tilling the soil for his daily bread, with the assistance of his slaves. Attaching to him was little or nothing of the prestige which dignified his neighbor of whom we have been speaking. He was evidently a man of but little consideration at the time of the selection of this location for the Federal District. However, he held on to his possessions with such obstinacy as to yield only when he became convinced that the power of the Government of the United States would be used to dispossess him, unless he should voluntarily agree to part with them on reasonable terms. His lands were very considerable in extent, embracing the site of the President's House and, in fact, a very large portion of the future Capital which lies nearest to Georgetown. The several department buildings now stand on what was once David Burns's estate or patrimony. They also included the grounds south of the President's House, bordering on the Potomac and the Mall, as it afterward came to be called. The southern border of the Burns plantation was south of Tiber Creek and included that stream, and it extended northward beyond Pennsylvania Avenue. This became, within a short time, the most important part of the city of Washington. Besides being a planter and owning numerous slaves, David Burns was a justice of the peace. He lived in a small cottage, which stood a little back from the river, on the square now lying between Seventeenth and Eighteenth streets. When President Washington came to select David Burns's patrimony for a portion of the seat of National Government, Mrs. Burns had but recently died, and Mr. Burns was bringing up his two children, a son and a daughter just approaching manhood and womanhood. The young man was intended for the law, but his health failing, he died soon after his mother, leaving young Marcia Burns the wealthiest as well as one of the most beautiful women in the land. The precise period of the death of David Burns is not now known, but it must have been in the early spring of 1802. Of the many suitors for his daughter's hand was John P. Van Ness, then a member of Congress from New York, a member of that aristocratic family occupying the magnificent country seat of Lindenwald, subsequently owned by President Martin Van Buren, to whom she was married on the 9th of May, 1802, shortly after her father's death, which it is believed hastened her decision.

One of the first acts of General John P. Van Ness, as he afterward came to be known, after his marriage with the beautiful heiress of David Burns, was to erect a most elegant mansion on or near the site of the ancient cottage, paying therefor out of the sales of lands to individuals and to the Nation. In its day, it was the most beautiful mansion in the United States, and was at the same time the most expensive and the most hospitable. It was the first in which both hot and cold water were carried to all the chambers. Its cost was $75,000. Latrobe, the architect of the Capitol, drew the plans and superintended its erection. Beneath its' spacious basements are the largest and coolest wine vaults in the country, and it was in these dark recesses that it was rumored that it was the original intention of the conspirators who assassinated President Lincoln to conceal him, had they succeeded in their original plan of capturing him alive. Thus, for more reasons than one, the memory of this elegant and hospitable mansion is indissolubly connected with the progress, preferment, and history of the city of Washington.

It is matter of regret that we know so little of Notley Young, whose lands embraced that portion of the city south and southeast of those of David Burns. They bordered on the Potomac, extending down to the point where the Potomac and Anacostia meet, otherwise known as Greenleaf's Point. All that appears to be known of Mr. Young is, that, at the time of the selection of his estate as a portion of the Federal City, he lived in a handsome residence, surrounded by the most elegant grounds in this region. This residence is referred to by Mr. John Cotton Smith, one of the members of the first Congress that assembled in Washington, as one of the most comfortable residences of the locality. Mr. Young, like Daniel Carroll, had some difficulty with the autocratic and irascible Frenchman, Pierre Charles L'Enfant, arising out of the fact that his residence occupied one of the streets of the city, as laid out by that great engineer.

Of the other original proprietors of the lands forming the Federal District, Samuel Davidson, of whom we know but little, resided at Georgetown. The lands belonging to him embraced that portion of the city now lying between Ninth and Seventeenth streets north of Pennsylvania Avenue — at this time the site of many magnificent private residences.

About Benjamin Oden, whose property was bounded by what was known as Goose Creek, a continuation of the Tiber, and embraced the property upon which is now situated the Baltimore & Ohio Railroad Depot, and several adjacent squares, we know almost nothing.

Conspicuous among the owners of property within the District was Robert Peter, who resided in Georgetown, and who was one of the men who offered to the Continental Congress the town of Georgetown as the site for the Capital City. The lands belonging to him embraced a large portion of that now beautiful quarter of the city intersected by Massachusetts and Connecticut avenues, where are found many of the finest modern residences.

It is unfortunate that we have so little information of a reliable nature, and that is of interest to the general reader, concerning the men who were the original proprietors of the lands from which the District of Columbia was selected. There were also a number of other proprietors of whom we have comparatively no knowledge. Their holdings were, however, comparatively small, and it is not deemed essential to attempt any further account of them.

The first duty imposed upon those who selected the site for a Federal District was the preparation of it for the residence of the Government. The legislation of Congress with reference to this matter required that such public buildings should be erected as were necessary for the accommodation of Congress and the President, his cabinet, and the other officers of the Government, and it was determined that the Government of the United States should occupy these new buildings as early as June, 1800. At this time, John Adams was President, John Marshall Secretary of State, Samuel Dexter Secretary of War, Benjamin Stoddard Secretary of the Navy.

It is thought worthy of record as a part of this history that some notice should be taken of those men who accompanied the Government in its removal to the Federal City, many of whom afterward became permanent citizens of the Capital, and whose descendents are still inhabitants of that city.

Of these we proceed to give such an account as is now possible from the biographical data they have left.

Samuél Meredith was appointed by President Washington Treasurer of the United States at the organization of the Federal Government, and held the office until 1801, when he resigned. He was one of the first to espouse the cause of the Revolution, distinguished himself at the battles of Trenton and Princeton, served in the Colonial Legislature of Pennsylvania, and was a delegate to the Continental Congress in 1787 and 1789.

Thomas Tudor Tucker was Treasurer of the United States from 1801 to the time of his death, in 1828. He had formerly been a delegate to the Continental Congress in 1787 and 1788, and was a Representative from South Carolina in Congress in 1789 and 1793.

Joseph Nourse was the first Register of the Treasury of the United States, and held that office from 1789 to 1829. He was born in London, England, and emigrating to Virginia, entered the Revolutionary army in 1776. He was clerk and auditor of the Board of War from 1777 to 1781, when he was appointed Assistant Auditor-General.

Richard Harrison was First Auditor of the Treasury from 1791 to 1836, a period of forty-five years, and died in Washington in 1841.

Peter Hagner was the son of Valentine Hagner, who served with credit in the War of the Revolution. He was graduated from the University of Pennsylvania, and in 1792 received from President Washington the appointment of accountant of war. He accompanied the Government to the city of Washington, and in 1817 was appointed by President Monroe Third Auditor of the Treasury Department, which position he continued to hold until the date of his death in 1850, under every President from Monroe to Taylor. He erected for himself a handsome residence in the city of Washington, and it is worthy of note that at this day this residence is occupied by one of his sons, who is a leading physician of the city, and that adjoining it are the residences of two other sons, one a retired general officer of the army,

8

and the other one of the judges of the Supreme Court of the District of Columbia.

. John Steele was First Comptroller of the Treasury under Presidents Washington and Adams. He was a member of Congress from 1790 to 1793, and was a commissioner to adjust the boundary between the States of North and South Carolina. He was elected to the Legislature of North Carolina in 1814, and died on the day of his election.

Gabriel Duval succeeded John Steele as First Comptroller of the Treasury, and served in that capacity from 1802 to 1811. He was a clerk of the Legislature of Maryland before the Declaration of Independence, and was a member of Congress from 1794 to 1796. In 1811, he was appointed a judge of the Supreme Court of the United States, and held that office twenty-four years. He died in Prince George's County, Maryland, in 1844.

William Simmons was appointed accountant of the War Department and came to this city with the Government when it removed here from Philadelphia.

Thomas Turner was appointed in 1800 accountant of the Navy Department, the office being subsequently known as the Fourth Auditorship. He continued its occupant until 1810.

Abraham Bradley, Jr., was appointed Assistant Postmaster-General in 1817, holding the office for about one year. His descendants have continued citizens of the District to this time, and have, many of them, held positions of importance and responsibility, always with great credit.

Thomas Munroe came to Washington with the Government in 1800, and in 1802 was appointed Superintendent of the Public Buildings for the District of Columbia. He was appointed postmaster of the city of Washington in 1799, and retained that office until removed by President Jackson. He continued to reside in the city until his death. He acquired considerable property, and was identified with the progress of the city in every way in which he could be useful. Members of his family still continue to reside in the city.

Roger C. Weightman was one of the early residents of Washington, but was not connected in any way with the Government. He held a prominent position among the citizens of his adopted city, was Mayor of the city several terms, and was afterward cashier of the Bank of Washington. During his entire life, which was quite extended, he was held in the highest regard by citizens of all classes.

Altogether the most important incident connected with the establishment of the permanent residence of the Government at the Capital

City, was the erection of the buildings intended for the accommodation of the Federal officers. As early as 1784, when the subject of the selection of the site for the Government residence was under discussion in the Continental Congress, a motion was made to select a parcel of land upon the banks of the Delaware. This motion prevailed, but was never acted upon. By the terms of this motion commissioners were selected whose duty it was to purchase the soil and enter into negotiations for the erection and completion of elegant buildings for the Federal House, a President's House, and houses for the Secretaries of Foreign Affairs, of War, Marine, and Treasury; and that in devising the situation of such buildings due regard should be had to the accommodation of the States for the use of their delegates respectively. It will thus be apparent that the erection of these buildings was considered at the outset a matter of great importance. When the site upon the Potomac was finally decided upon, this same subject was carefully considered, and steps were taken for the procurement of plans for the Capitol and other public buildings. The men who were principally engaged in the erection of these buildings are entitled to a prominent place in the history of the Capital City. That they were remarkable men is shown by the stability and grandeur of the buildings erected under their guidance. Under all these circumstances it will not be amiss if a few short sketches of the lives of these men are here inserted.

Stephen L. Hallett was a cultivated French architect residing in New York City in 1792. In that year the following advertisement appeared in the principal newspapers of the country:

"WASHINGTON, IN THE TERRITORY OF COLUMBIA.

"A premium of a lot in this city, to be designated by impartial judges, and $500, or a medal of that value, at the option of the party, will be given by the Commissioners of the Federal Buildings to the person who, before the 15th of July, 1792, shall produce to them the most approved plan for a capitol, to be erected in this city; and $250, or a gold medal, for the plan deemed next in merit to the one they shall adopt. The building to be of brick, and to contain the following apartments, to wit: A conference room and a room for the Representatives, sufficient to accommodate three hundred persons each; a lobby, or anteroom, to the latter; a Senate room of twelve hundred square feet area; an antechamber; twelve rooms of six hundred square feet each, for committee rooms and clerks' offices. It will be a recommendation of any plan if the central part of it may be detached and erected for the present with the appearance of a complete whole, and be capable of admitting the additional parts in future, if they shall be wanted. Drawings will be expected of the ground plots, elevations of each front, and sections through the building in such directions as may be necessary to explain the internal structure; and an estimate of the cubic feet of brick work composing the whole mass of the walls."

Architect Hallett offered a plan for a capitol building, and singularly enough his principal contestant was an Englishman named Dr. William Thornton, who, it is said, was a man of fine natural abilities, but unskilled as an architect. On many accounts the plan presented by Dr. Thornton was considered the best, and as may be seen by reference to the chapter on Public Buildings, was in the main adopted, although not without considerable modifications, these modifications being in the direction of the plan submitted by Mr. Hallett. The result was that Mr. Hallett was made supervising architect of the Capitol, but remained in office only a short time, when he resigned. But little is known of Mr. Hallett beyond what is here expressed.

George Hadfield succeeded Mr. Hallett, and continued on the work until 1798, when he resigned, having had as his associate a portion of that time James Hoban, who in 1799 or 1800 finished the north wing of the Capitol. Mr. Hoban, in response to an advertisement for plans for the President's House, submitted the plans that were accepted by the commissioners, and was the supervising architect in its construction. Mr. Hoban was an Irishman by birth, and a man of great activity and vigor. He made the city of Washington his home, and some of his descendants are now living in the Capital. His son, James Hoban, was a lawyer of considerable prominence, serving for some years as attorney for the District of Columbia.

Benjamin Henry Latrobe, born in Yorkshire, England, May 1, 1764, succeeded Mr. Hoban as architect of the Capitol. He was descended from Boneval de la Trobe, who emigrated from France to Holland after the revocation of the Edict of Nantes, and who, while in the service of the Prince of Orange, was severely wounded in the battle of the Boyne. Benjamin H. Latrobe, in 1785, entered the Prussian army as a cornet of Hussars. Resigning his commission in 1788 and returning to England, he was made engineer of London in 1789. Declining a crown surveyorship, he came to the United States, landing at Norfolk, Virginia, May 20, 1796. In 1798, he removed to Philadelphia, where he designed the Bank of Pennsylvania, the old

Academy of Art, and the Bank of the United States, besides other buildings. He was the first to supply water to Philadelphia, pumping it by steam from the Schuylkill in 1800. He was appointed surveyor of the public buildings in Washington by President Jefferson in 1803, following Thornton, Hadfield, and Hoban as architect of the Capitol. He perfected Dr. Thornton's designs, and altered those for the interior construction of the south wing of the Capitol, with the approval of the President.

In the reconstruction of the north wing of the Capitol, Mr. Latrobe planned the vestibule in which are six columns, each of which is composed of cornstalks bound together, the joints forming a spiral effect, while the capitals are modeled from the ears of corn. He also designed the tobacco-plant capitals of columns in the circular colonnade in the north wing, and left drawings of a capital whose ornamentation is designed for the cotton plant. In 1812, he became interested with Robert Fulton in the introduction of steamboats on the Western rivers, and built the *Buffalo*, at Pittsburg, the fourth steamboat to descend the Ohio River. While at work on this boat, Mr. Latrobe was called to Washington to repair the Capitol after its partial destruction by the British in 1814. Resigning his position at the Capital, he was succeeded by Charles Bullfinch, who executed his predecessor's designs of changing the oblong hall of the old Capitol into a semi-circular form. At the time of his death, September 3, 1820, he was engaged in erecting waterworks to supply water to New Orleans.

It happened very fortunately, when Congress had finally, after years of struggle, determined to venture upon the experiment of erecting a capital city in the wilderness upon the banks of the Potomac, that such an engineer as Pierre Charles L'Enfant was found. He was unquestionably at that time the first engineer and architect of any consequence in the United States. His genius was equal to the occasion. He had already distinguished himself by the work he had performed in transforming an old public building in the city of New York into a Federal Hall, in which Congress held its sessions with great comfort and convenience; and he had made manifest his taste and patriotism by completing a design for the insignia of the Society of the Cincinnati. In addition to this, he had planned a house for Robert Morris, the great financier of the Revolution, which was not completed at that time. It was the first instance ever seen on the Western Continent of the mansard roof, which a century afterward was so generally used.

General Washington did not hesitate to place in the hands of L'Enfant the execution of the great design of a Federal City for the Government's official residence. Time has shown how wise the first President was in this respect, as in all things else he did in relation to our national existence. For years people ridiculed the extravagant plan of the erratic Frenchman. Not only our own citizens but also visitors from other lands laughed at the idea of "squares in morasses, obelisks in trees," and every American felt mortified when taunted with the charge that the Capital of his Nation was a city of only "magnificent distances." It took no little of the bravery of genius to plan amid the swamps and creeks of the lands lying between the Potomac and Anacostia, in those early days, a city that time was to develop into the model capital of the world. And yet such is the result. L'Enfant did not hesitate to enter upon the duty to which he had been assigned, and it is remarkable that from the first his design was to plan a city, not for the day in which he lived, nor for the population of a country such as that of the new Republic then promised to be, but a capital for all time, a nation of more millions than the population of any country in the world of that day numbered. Writing about this matter years afterward, one says: "Although the site of Washington looked very engaging to the eye of the traveler from the opposite hill, who imagined that its flatness would dispense with costly grades and engineering, yet it was in reality a mere gully,—the alluvial overflow from the hills of Maryland brought down by the heavy rainfall and creeks. Much of it was swamp, and the engineers were persecuted with insects and malaria, with mud and extortion, with foolish questions and more insolent criticisms."

L'Enfant was assisted by Ellicott, a surveyor; the negro almanac maker, Bannecker; and Roberdieu, a young Frenchman full of impetuosity and reckless of what he said. Many men regarded the great engineer as a mere subordinate, working out the plans of the commissioners in charge of the Federal Territory, and sought to influence him as such, to the end that they might accomplish their own views of profit and self-aggrandizement. The men of those days were like their sons of to-day, and it is not surprising, therefore, that the conscientious Frenchman who refused to expose his plans for the benefit of those who wished to find out where to purchase lots with the greatest assurance of profit, was made the subject of unfair criticism, and was finally discharged from his office.

Little is known of L'Enfant after his retirement from the office of engineer of the plan of Washington. President Monroe offered him the place of professor at West Point, but he did not accept the offer. He was afterward selected to prepare a design for, and to superintend the erection of, Fort Washington, on the Potomac, in the neighborhood of Mount Vernon. It seems, however, that his old spirit of impatience and insubordination followed him into this work, and he was soon mustered out of service. From this time, through several years of comparative obscurity and seeming neglect, we trace him to the home of a gentleman named William Dudley Digges, in the neighborhood of Washington, known as Green Hill, and for many years the country residence of Mr. George Riggs, the banker. Here he spent the evening of his days, amusing himself with books and designs that were confined to the arrangement of the flower garden of his tract. In 1825, he died, and was buried on the grounds near his last residence. His grave is not marked by a memorial of any kind; indeed, it is doubtful if its exact site can be ascertained. And this is all that is known of a man who, at some future day, will be the subject of a public statue in one of the squares of the magnificent city the plan of which is now recognized as the offspring of his genius.

Samuel Harrison Smith was the son of Jonathan Bayard Smith, of Philadelphia, a distinguished Revolutionary patriot. During the greater part of that war he filled with honor and reputation the responsible trust of a member of the Committee of Safety. Samuel H. Smith was born in 1772. In 1796, he opened a printing office on Chestnut Street, Philadelphia, between the western corner of Carpenter Street and Fourth Street, from which he issued, in August and September of that year, a newspaper twice a day, morning and evening, under the name of the *New World*. This enterprise was in all probability original with him, and never afterward imitated by anyone. It was not long before he discovered that zeal and talent were not the only prerequisites to success in the newspaper business, and learning from his experience that the people did not wish to receive a paper more than once a day, he changed his paper to a daily, the first number of which appeared October 24, 1796, and was marked No. 122 in the series. A few months further experiment induced him to abandon the daily paper, there being really but little demand for a fifth daily paper in Philadelphia at that time.

Another paper, however, began to be called for by the party then springing into consequence in Congress and the country under the leadership of Mr. Jefferson, Vice-President of the United States. This new party was known by the name of the Republican Party, and the paper demanded was a weekly, that it might be fit for distribution through the mails, which at that time were, as a general thing, transmitted but once a week. Mr. Smith was urged to undertake this new enterprise. There was then published in Philadelphia a paper by Joseph Gales, purchased by him about a year before from Colonel John Oswald, a Revolutionary hero, the name of the paper being the *Independent Gazetteer.* Mr. Smith bought this paper and changed its name to the *Universal Gazette*, and issued the first number of it under this new name November 16, 1797. He continued to publish it weekly until he relinquished the printing business in Philadelphia.

Upon the removal of the Capital of the United States to Washington, in 1800, Mr. Smith also removed to Washington, and began the publication of a tri-weekly paper named the *National Intelligencer*, the first number of which was issued October 31, 1800. From the first, this paper received the support of the leading men of its own side of politics. It sustained Mr. Jefferson's administration, and ·was sustained by him in return, as was also the case with the administration of Mr. Madison. Mr. Smith, however, having partially engaged in rural pursuits, longed to devote his life to those labors which were more of a literary and philosophical nature, and hence, in September, 1810, he sold the *Intelligencer* to Joseph Gales, Jr., who had been connected with it about three years.

Mr. Smith, therefore, at the age of thirty-eight years, was a retired gentleman, having a farm of about two hundred acres, upon which was a delightful "country seat," and he also had a comfortable competency in money. He now became exclusively devoted to the rearing and education of his children, to the cares of a farm and garden, and to the pursuit of deferred studies with a view to certain literary enterprises. But these literary undertakings were never fully carried out, because of the persistent intervention of other duties. In 1813, he accepted from President Madison the responsible office of Commissioner of the Revenue, and performed its duties, until it was abolished, with scrupulous exactness and faithfulness. He then became president of the Bank of Washington, and still later, president of the Branch Bank of the United States, located in Washington. He was for many years a member of the corporate body of the city of Washington, and for a time president of one of the branches of the Council. He was for a long time registrar for the county of Washington and a member of its levy court. He was influential in the establishment of the public schools of the city and of the Washington City Library, and for many years previous to his death he was one of the vice-presidents of the American Colonization Society. He was an active member and treasurer of the Washington National Monument Society.

The distinguished characteristics of Mr. Smith were his public spirit and his personal independence, and all through his life he lived with the blameless simplicity and purity of a philosopher. His death occurred November 18, 1845.

Andrew Ellicott was born in Bucks County, Pennsylvania, January 24, 1754; was a civil engineer; founded Ellicott's Mills, in Maryland; was a personal friend of Franklin and Washington; in 1790, was appointed by the General Government to survey and lay out the site of the city of Washington; in 1792, was appointed Surveyor-General of the United States; and in 1812, became a professor of mathematics at West Point, where he died August 29, 1820.

Benjamin Bannecker, the mulatto mathematician and astronomer, assisted Ellicott in his survey. He was born in 1751, and died in 1804. The Maryland Historical Society has published a sketch of his life. Condorcet, secretary of the French Academy of Sciences, wrote him a complimentary letter concerning his almanac, which had been sent him by President Jefferson. One of the public school buildings in Washington is named after him, the Bannecker School.

CHAPTER VI.

MUNICIPAL.

THE history of the government of the city of Washington may well begin with the history of the formation of the District of Columbia. The formation of the District was provided for in the cession by the States of Maryland and Virginia of portions of their territory lying north and south respectively of the Potomac River, sufficient to constitute a tract of land ten miles square. The act of Maryland, passed December 23, 1788, was as follows:

"AN ACT to Cede to Congress a District of Ten Miles Square in this State for the Seat of Government of the United States:

"*Be it enacted by the General Assembly of Maryland,* That the Representatives of this State in the House of Representatives of the United States appointed to assemble at New York on the first Wednesday of March next, be and they are hereby authorized, on the behalf of this State, to cede to Congress of the United States any district in this State not exceeding ten miles square which the Congress may fix upon for the seat of government of the United States."

The Virginia cession act was as follows:

"WHEREAS, The equal and common benefit resulting from the administration of the General Government will be best diffused, and its operations become more prompt and certain, by establishing such a situation for the site of the seat of government as will be the most central and convenient to the citizens of the United States at large, having regard as well to the population, extent, territory, and the free navigation to the Atlantic Ocean through the Chesapeake Bay, as to the most direct and ready communication with our fellow citizens on the western frontier; and

"WHEREAS, It appears to this Assembly that a situation combining all these considerations and advantages before recited may be had on the banks of the Potomac, above tide water, in a country rich and fertile in soil, healthy and salubrious in climate, and abounding in all the necessities and conveniences of life; where, in a location of ten miles square, if the wisdom of Congress shall so direct, the States of Pennsylvania, Maryland, and Virginia may participate in such location;

"*Be it therefore enacted by the General Assembly*, That a tract of country not to exceed ten miles square, or any lesser quantity, to be located within the limits of this State, and in any part thereof, as Congress may by law direct, shall be and the same is hereby forever ceded and relinquished to the Congress and Government of the United States, in full and absolute right and jurisdiction, as well of soil as of persons residing therein, pursuant to the tenor and effect of the eighth section of the first article of the Constitution of the Government of the United States: *Provided*, that nothing herein contained shall be construed to vest in the United States any right of property in the soil, or to affect the rights of individuals therein, otherwise than the same shall or may be transferred by such individuals to the United States: *And provided, also*, that the jurisdiction of the laws of this Commonwealth over the persons and property of individuals residing within the limits of the cession aforesaid shall not cease or determine until Congress, having accepted the said cession, shall by law provide for the government thereof under their jurisdiction in the manner provided by the article of the Constitution before recited."

The selection of a location for the seat of government was discussed in the convention held in Philadelphia in 1787 to revise the Federal system of government, but it was not then decided. But at the second session of the First Congress, held in New York in the summer of 1790, an act was passed (recited in Chapter III.) which finally decided its location. The discussion was, as has been in that chapter clearly indicated, long and earnest. New York, Philadelphia, Baltimore, Trenton, Harrisburg, and other places pressed their claims upon Congress to be made the Capital City of the new Nation. For a time it seemed as if no selection was possible. Maryland and Virginia, as may be seen by reading the acts of those States recited above, by ceding territory to the United States, had each done its part toward a solution of the question; but at length, in much the same manner that legislation is effected even down to the present day, a compromise was arrived at in the passage of the act of Congress above mentioned. This act was introduced first into the Senate, and passed by that body, June 1, 1790, by the following vote:

Yeas — Bassett, Butler, Charles Carroll, Elmer, Gunn, Hawkins, Henry, Johnston, Langdon, Lee, Maclay, Morris, Read, and Walker — 14.

Nays — Dalton, Ellsworth, Few, Foster, Johnson, Izard, King, Patterson, Schuyler, Stanton, Strong, and Wingate — 12.

The history of the struggle in the House of Representatives has been presented in Chapter III.

If the interior history of the passage of this act could be accurately and fully ascertained, it would doubtless be much more interesting and instructive than anything that can now be written upon the subject. However, enough is known to establish the fact of a compromise between the friends of this measure and the friends of another measure which was radically different in every way from this one. The other measure was one favoring the assumption of the debts incurred by the respective States in establishing the independence of the United States. With reference to this assumption, Mr. Madison, then a member of the House, wrote on the 13th of April, 1790, as follows: "The last vote was taken yesterday, and it passed in the negative by 31 against 29. The minority do not abandon hope, however; and 't is impossible to foretell the final destiny of the measure. Massachusetts and South Carolina, with their allies from Connecticut and New York, are too zealous to be arrested in their project unless by the force of an adverse majority."

May 24, 1790, while the debate upon the public debt was in progress in the House of Representatives, Mr. Gerry, of Massachusetts, moved to insert a clause providing for the assumption of the State debts by the United States, thus bringing the subject again before that body, which led to considerable earnest debate, by Mr. Sherman, Mr. Boudinot, Mr. Ames, and Mr. Madison. Mr. Madison, with most of the Southern members, was opposed to the proposed assumption, as they were generally favorable to the location of the

Federal District on the Potomac, "in the woods at the Indian town of Connogocheague," as it was expressed by some of those favoring a more northern location. June 22, 1790, Mr. Madison wrote to Edmund Randolph: "We are endeavoring to keep the pretensions of the Potomac in view, and to give to all the circumstances that occur a turn favorable to it. If any arrangement should be made that will answer our wishes, it will be the effect of a coincidence of causes as fortuitous as it will be propitious."

It is, from this extract, evident that there was but little hope existing then for the success of the Potomac site. But the fortuitous coincidence of causes, which was Mr. Madison's only hope, did in a short time afterward occur. How it occurred, is related in a most interesting manner by Mr. Jefferson in the ninth volume of his works, commencing on page 93. Mr. Jefferson says:

"This measure [the assumption of the State debts] produced the most bitter and angry contest ever known in Congress before or since the union of the States. I arrived in the midst of it [from his mission in Paris]. But a stranger to the ground, a stranger to the actors on it, so long absent as to have lost all familiarity with the subject, and as yet unaware of its objects, I took no concern in it. The great and trying question however was lost in the House of Representatives. So high were the feuds excited by the subject that on its rejection business was suspended. Congress met and adjourned from day to day without doing anything, the parties being too much out of temper to do business together. The Eastern members particularly, who, with Smith, of South Carolina, were the principal gamblers in these scenes, threatened a secession and a disunion. Hamilton was in despair. As I was going to the President's House, one day I met him in the street. He walked me backwards and forwards before the President's door for half an hour. He painted pathetically the temper in which the legislators had been wrought; the danger of the secession of their members, and the separation of the States. He observed that the members of the administration ought to act in concert; that the President was the center on which all administrations ultimately rested, and that all of us should rally around him and support with joint efforts measures approved by him, and that the question having been lost by a small majority only, it was probable that an appeal from me to the judgment and discretion of some of my friends might effect a change in the votes, and the machinery of the Government, now suspended, might be again set in motion.

"I told him that I was really a stranger to the whole subject; that not yet having informed myself of the system of finance adopted, I knew not how far this was a necessary sequence; that undoubtedly, if a rejection threatened a dissolution of our Union at this incipient stage, I should deem that the most unfortunate of all consequences, to avert which all partial and temporary evils should be yielded. I proposed to him, however, to dine with me next day, and I would invite another friend or two, bringing them into conference together; and I thought it impossible that reasonable men, consulting together fully, could fail, by some mutual sacrifices of opinion, to form a compromise which would save the Union. The discussion took place. I could take no part in it save an exhortatory one, because I was a stranger to the circumstances which should govern it. But it was finally agreed that whatever importance had been attached to the rejection of this proposition, the preservation of the Union and of concord among the States was more important, and that therefore it would be better that the vote of rejection should be reconsidered, to effect which some members should change their votes. But it was observed that this pill would be exceeding bitter to the Southern States, and that some concomitant measure should be adopted to sweeten it a little to them. There had before been propositions to fix the seat of government either at Philadelphia or at Georgetown, and it was thought that by giving it to Philadelphia for ten years and to Georgetown permanently afterwards, this might act as an anodyne, and calm in some degree the ferment which might be excited by the other measure alone. So two of the Potomac members (White and Lee, but White with a revulsion of stomach almost convulsive) agreed to change their votes; and Hamilton undertook to carry the other point.

"In doing this, the influence he had established over the Eastern members, with the agency of Robert Morris with those of the Middle States, effected his side of the engagement, and so assumption was passed, and twenty millions of stock divided among favored States, and thrown in as a pabulum to the stock-jobbing herd. This added to the number of votaries to the treasury, and made its chief the master of every vote in the legislature which might give to the Government the direction suited to his political views."

The debate on the assumption of the debts of the States was long and earnest, frequently "bitter," as Mr. Jefferson says; but it is evident that it is unnecessary to give a summary or further description of it in this connection, except to say that the proposition to assume was as strongly supported by Hon. Elbridge Gerry, of Massachusetts, as it was by Mr. Smith, of South Carolina; and that according to these gentlemen's opinion it was a duty the General Government owed to the States, because these debts had been assumed by the States at the request of the General Government when that Government could not meet its obligations. Upon such representations as these the bill for the assumption passed the House of Representatives August 4, 1790, three weeks and five days after the passage of the bill locating the seat of government on the Potomac River.

The act of Congress, as first passed, directed that the district of ten miles square should be located "on the River Potomac, at some place between the mouths of the Eastern Branch and Connogocheague." President Washington, not being fully satisfied with the limitations prescribed by this act, in his proclamation of January 24, 1791, provided for the location of a part only of the district, in the following language: "I do hereby declare and make known that the location of one part of said district of ten miles square shall be found by running four lines of experiment in the following manner:" etc., trusting to Congress to grant him the authority to locate a part of the district below the mouth of the Eastern Branch. President Washington preferred the location as it was at length determined upon, because it was the most suitable for the public buildings, and Congress, perceiving the propriety of his suggestions, passed an amendatory act, March 3, 1791, which enacted "that it shall be lawful for the President to make any part of the territory below the said limit and above the mouth of Hunting Creek a part of the said district, so as to include a convenient part of the Eastern Branch, and the lands lying on the lower side thereof, and also the town of Alexandria." Then, on March 30, 1791, the President issued his proclamation for the purpose of amending and completing the location of the whole of the said territory of ten miles square, in conformity with the said supplemental act, in which he recited all of the previously related official matters connected with the project of locating the Federal District, and then went on to say:

"Now, therefore, for the purpose of amending and completing the location of the whole of said territory of ten miles square, in conformity with the said amendatory act of Congress, I do hereby declare and make known that the whole of said territory shall be located and included within the following lines: that is to say,—

"Beginning at Jones's Point, being the upper cape of Hunting Creek, in Virginia, and at an angle in the outside of forty-five degrees west of north, and running in a direct line ten miles from the first line; then beginning again at the same Jones's Point, and running another direct line, at a right angle from the first, across the Potomac ten miles for the second line; then, from the determinations of the first and second lines, running two other direct lines of ten miles each, the one crossing the Eastern Branch aforesaid, and the other the Potomac, and meeting each other in a point.

"And I do, accordingly, direct the commissioners named under the authority of the said first act of Congress, to proceed forthwith to have the said four lines run, and by proper metes and bounds defined and limited; and thereof to make due report under their hands and seals; and the territory so to be located, defined, and limited, shall be the whole territory accepted by the said act of Congress as the district for the permanent seat of the Government of the United States."

April 3, 1791, President Washington wrote to the commissioners from Mount Vernon with reference to the form of deed, etc., that should be used in transferring the lots to the public, saying:

"As the instrument which was subscribed at Georgetown by the landholders in the vicinity of that place and Carrollsburgh was not given to me, I presume it was deposited with you. It is of the greatest moment to close this business with the proprietors of the lands on which the Federal City is to be, that arrangements may be made without more delay than can be avoided.

"To accomplish this matter so that the sales of the lots around the public buildings, etc., may commence with as much facility as the nature of the case will admit, would be, I conceive, advisable under any circumstances. Perhaps the friends of the measure may think it materially so from the following extract of a letter from Mr. Jefferson to me, of the 27th *ultimo:*

"'A bill was yesterday ordered to be brought into the House of Representatives here for granting a sum of money for building a Federal Hall, house for the President, etc.'

"This (though I do not want any sentiment of mine promulgated with respect to it) marks unequivocally in my mind the designs of the State, and the necessity of exertion to carry the residence law into effect agreeably thereto."

April 13, 1791, President Washington wrote: "It having been intimated to me that the proprietors of Georgetown are desirous of being comprehended within the limits of the Federal City, I see no objection to the measure, provided the landholders adjoining to it, included within the red lines of Messrs. Beatty & Orme's survey, referred to in the first offer from Georgetown, agree to cede to the public on the same terms with those under the last or combined agreement; and if those within the blue lines are likewise desirous of being comprehended on the same terms, it may be so,—the doing of which could only place them on the same footing with the rest of the subscribers, at the same time that it would render the plan more comprehensive, beneficial, and promising, drawing the center of the Federal City nearer to the present town.

"If this measure is seriously contemplated, the present is the fit moment for carrying it into effect; because in that case it will become part of the original plan, and the old and new towns would be blended and assimilated as nearly as circumstances will admit—and Major L'Enfant might be instructed to lay out the whole accordingly."

The commissioners appointed by President Washington, January 22, 1791, to locate, define, and limit the Federal District, were Governor Thomas Johnson, of Maryland; Hon. Daniel Carroll, of Maryland, and Dr. David Stuart, of Virginia. At the time of his appointment Daniel Carroll was a member of Congress, and for this reason refused to serve; but after the termination of the Congress, March 4, 1791, he consented to serve, and a new commission was issued to him. The first meeting of these commissioners was held at Georgetown, April 12, 1791, and on April 15 the corner stone was laid near Jones's Point, in the vicinity of Alexandria, on the Virginia side of the Potomac River. The ceremony in laying this corner stone was under the supervision of Hon. Daniel Carroll and Dr. David Stuart, and was in accordance with Masonic customs. An address was delivered by Rev. James Muir, and was as follows:

"Amiable it is for brethren to dwell together in unity; it is more fragrant than the perfumes of Aaron's garment; it is more refreshing than the dews on Hermon's Hill. May this stone long commemorate the goodness of God, in those uncommon events which have given America a place among nations. Under this stone may jealousy and selfishness be forever buried. From this stone may a superstructure arise whose glory, whose magnificence, whose stability, unequaled hitherto, shall astonish the world, and invite even the savage of the wilderness to a shelter under its roof."

Difficulties having arisen with reference to the boundaries of the District, President Washington wrote to the commissioners from Charleston, South Carolina, May 7, 1791, as follows:

"It is an unfortunate circumstance in the present state of the business relating to the Federal City, that difficulties unforeseen and unexpected should arise to darken, perhaps to destroy, the fair prospect which it presented when I left Georgetown, and which the instrument

9

then signed by the combined interest [as it was termed] of Georgetown and Carrollsburgh so plainly describes. The pain which this occurrence occasions me is the more sensibly felt, as I had taken pleasure during my journey through the several States to relate the agreement, and to speak of it on every occasion in terms which applauded the conduct of the parties, as being alike conducive to the public welfare and to the interests of individuals, which last, it was generally understood, would be most benefitted by the amazing increase of the property reserved to the landholders.

"The words cited by Notley Young, Peter, Lingan, Forrest, and Stoddert may be nearly what I expressed; but will these gentlemen say this was given as the precise boundary? or will they, detaching these words, take them in a sense unconnected with the general explanation of my ideas and views upon that occasion, or without the qualifications which, if I am not much mistaken, were added, of running about so and so, for I had no map before me for direction? Will they not recollect that Philadelphia stood upon an area of three by two miles? and that if the metropolis of one State occupied so much ground, what ought that of the United States to occupy? Did I not, moreover, observe that before the city should be laid out and the spot for the public buildings be precisely fixed upon, the water courses were to be leveled, the heights taken, etc.? Let the whole of my declaration be taken together, and not a part only, and being compared with the instrument then subscribed, together with some other circumstances that might be alluded to, let any impartial man judge whether I had reason to expect that difficulties would arise in the conveyances. When the instrument was presented, I found no occasion to add a word with respect to the boundary, because the whole was surrendered upon the conditions which were expressed. Had I discovered a disposition in the subscribers to contract my views, I should then have pointed out the inconveniences and the impolicy of the measure. Upon the whole, I shall hope and expect that the business will be permitted to proceed, and the more so as they cannot be ignorant that the further consideration of a certain measure in a neighboring State stands postponed; for what reason, is left to their own information and conjecture."

The agreement alluded to by President Washington, about which some trouble had arisen, was signed by nineteen of the principal proprietors of the lands constituting the present site of Washington, March 30, 1791, and presented to the commissioners, and by them accepted April 12. It has been given in full in Chapter IV.

September 24, 1791, the following resolution was passed by the commissioners:

"*Resolved*, That Major L'Enfant be instructed to employ, on the first Monday of October next, one hundred and fifty laborers to throw up clay at the President's House and the house of Congress, and in doing such other work connected with the post road and the public buildings as he shall think most proper to have immediately executed.

"*Resolved*, That Major L'Enfant be instructed to direct three hundred copies of the plan of the Federal City to be transmitted to such parts in the Northern States as he shall think proper, and that he keep the remainder subject to the direction of the commissioners."

On November 18, 1791, Pierre Charles L'Enfant presented to the commissioners the following agreement between himself and John Gibson, of Dumfries, merchant:

"The said Pierre Charles L'Enfant, on behalf of the public, hath rented from the said John Gibson, for ten years, to commence on the 1st day of next month, all the quarries of freestone on the land on Acquia Creek sold on the 14th of this present month by the trustees of Robert Brent, deceased, to James Reid, and by him bought for the said John Gibson, at the rent of £20 current money, to be paid to the said John Gibson, or his assigns, on the 1st day of December of every year, the first rent to become due and payable on the 1st day of December, 1792. And it is further agreed by the said Pierre Charles L'Enfant, that full and free use and occupation of the soil of the lands, woods, and all appurtenances to the land belonging or in any wise appertaining, shall be and remain the property and at the sole disposal of him, the said John Gibson, or his assigns, during the term aforesaid, except only the quarries aforesaid, four acres of land adjoining for buildings, with reasonable right of egress and ingress from and to the same; and the said John Gibson doth hereby agree to let the said quarries with the right aforesaid to the said Pierre Charles L'Enfant for public use at the yearly rent before mentioned, £20 current money for the term of ten years as in the former part of this agreement, and both parties bind themselves each to the other in the penalty of £200 for the true performance of this agreement and to execute any other or further article or writing for the better perfection of the same."

A full account of the proprietors of the land at the time of the location of the Capital of the country, may be found in another chapter; but it is necessary to mention briefly, in this connection, one of them who was quite unfortunate in more ways than one. This

one was "Daniel Carroll, of Duddington," whose estate, known as
the "Duddington Manor," covered nearly the whole of what has since
been known as "Capitol Hill." Daniel Carroll was a man of culture
and of high social standing in Maryland. He belonged to the famous
Carroll family, which embraced among its members the Rt. Rev.
John Carroll, first Bishop of Baltimore, who founded the college of
Jesuits at Georgetown, and the venerable Charles Carroll, of Carrollton. Daniel Carroll was a brother of the former and a cousin of the
latter. His residence was known as the "Duddington House," and
shortly after the streets had been marked out, in accordance with
Major L'Enfant's plan, Mr. Carroll, who was one of the commissioners,
assumed and asserted the right to erect his house in the middle of
New Jersey Avenue, near the Capitol grounds. Against this proceeding Major L'Enfant vigorously protested, as it would close up the
avenue and destroy the symmetry of the plan he had marked out.
Mr. Carroll paying no attention to the protests of the Major, he, one
morning, gave orders to his assistants to demolish the structure, and
himself went down to Acquia Creek. The work of demolition had
not proceeded far, when Mr. Carroll hastened to a magistrate, procured a warrant, and put a stop to it. That night, when the Major
returned from Acquia Creek, he found his orders unfulfilled, and so he
organized a gang of laborers, took them quietly up the hill in the
darkness, and set them to work on the demolition of the house. By
sunrise next morning not one brick of the obnoxious building was left
upon another. Mr. Carroll was, of course, very indignant at this high-
handed proceeding, and made application to the President for redress;
and Major L'Enfant, on December 8, 1791, wrote a letter to the commissioners in explanation of the reasons for his course. This matter
was under consideration by the commissioners for some time, and
considerable interest was taken in it by the other proprietors. December 21, a memorandum was received from some of them as follows:

"GENTS: Understanding that Daniel Carroll, Esq., of Duddington, has lodged a claim with you for the full value of his house
lately taken down by order of Major L'Enfant, we hope and request
that you will not apply any money granted for the improvement of
the city of Washington to the payment thereof.

"By this, however, we do not mean to reflect on Major L'Enfant's
conduct; but, on the contrary, we are of opinion that his zeal, activity,
and good judgment in the affairs of the city merit the thanks of the
proprietors and well deserve the approbation of the public," etc.

This memorandum was signed by Robert Peter, Overton Carr,

William King, for himself, and also for William Prout; George Walker, Uriah Forrest, for himself and for P. R. Fendall; Samuel Davidson, and David Burns.

In order to settle the matter, President Washington sought the advice of the Attorney-General, and at length ordered the reconstruction of the "Duddington House" precisely as it was before, but not in the same location. December 22, 1791, Major L'Enfant informed the commissioners that Notley Young's house was in the middle of a street, and made suggestions for the conduct of the commissioners in connection with the fact. December 27, President Washington wrote the commissioners in reference to both these houses, saying that he hoped the Major did not mean to proceed to the demolition of the house of Mr. Young also, unless properly authorized and instructed.

April 11, 1792, the commissioners received a letter from Andrew Ellicott with respect to the plan of the city, and on the same day they requested Mr. Harbaugh, Mr. Carlisle, and Mr. Mahan to act as arbitrators with respect to the amount that should be paid to Daniel Carroll, of Duddington, for the demolition of the house. The next day these arbitrators reported that in their opinion £310 6s. 3d. was the value of the materials destroyed.

July 5, 1792, the commissioners adopted a resolution that they would pay the passage of any number not exceeding one hundred of Scotch passengers, at Georgetown, on their arrival there, on the terms of their working out the money; mechanics at 20 shillings, and laborers at 12 shillings sterling per month, twenty-six working days to the month, and clothing found, to be repaid in work or in money at the option of the person; provisions to be found by the commissioners, besides the allowance for wages. These advantageous terms were proposed to able-bodied, single men only, and the payment for passage money was limited to ten guineas for each person.

The government of the District by commissioners was continued from 1791 until 1802, in which year the city of Washington was incorporated, the act of Congress granting the charter to the city having been passed May 3, 1802. The first commissioners have already been given. Those serving in 1801 were William Thornton, Alexander White, and Tristam Dalton; and those in office in 1802, the last ones of the early commissioners, being William Thornton, Alexander White, and William Cranch. Under the charter of the city the Mayor was appointed by the President, and the city Council was elected by the people. The first Mayor appointed in accordance with the provisions of the charter was Robert Brent, who continued to be reappointed annually until June, 1811, when he declined to serve the city longer in that capacity. All of this history is sufficiently set forth in the succeeding pages.

A meeting was held November 12, 1802, for the purpose of putting in nomination six persons to serve in the Council of the city, of which meeting Dr. Cornelius Conyngham was chosen chairman, and Nicholas King secretary. These six persons were to represent that part of the city west of Sixth Street. The following were the nominees: Nicholas King, Cornelius Conyngham, Thomas Herty, Thomas Carpenter, James Hoban, and W. M. Duncanson. Another meeting was held about the same time by other persons, to nominate six persons to represent the western part of the city in the Council. This meeting nominated James Hoban, John Kearney, William Brent, Thomas Peter, William Thornton, and Augustus Woodward.

It appears that at the time when the people were selecting their first Council, there was considerable feeling aroused. A writer in the *National Intelligencer*, under the name of "Philanthropos," a native of the city, warned his fellow citizens against letting their angry feelings cloud their judgment, and thus prevent the election of a good Council for the first one. He presented a ticket of his own, by the election of which he thought every interest of the young city would be conserved. This ticket was as follows: Daniel Carroll, of Dudding-ton, James Barry, Henry Ingle, George Blagden, Robert Brent, Samuel H. Smith, Robert W. Peacock, Thomas Munroe, John Jack, James Hoban, William Brent, and Nicholas King.

The election was held on Monday, June 7, 1802, resulting as follows:

CANDIDATE.	First and Second Wards.	Third and Fourth Wards.	Fifth Ward.	Total Vote.	CANDIDATE.	First and Second Wards.	Third and Fourth Wards.	Fifth Ward.	Total Vote.
Daniel Carroll	36	102	66	204	Nicholas King	29	60	35	124
George Blagden	37	100	65	202	A. B. Woodward	27	45	51	123
James Barry	27	87	55	169	Samuel H. Smith	26	55	40	121
William Brent	35	57	65	157	William Prout	13	61	46	120
Benjamin Moore	24	70	35	129	Thomas Peter	23	45	47	115
James Hoban	23	46	55	124	John Hewitt	23	45	30	98

On Monday, June 14, 1802, the Council convened at the Capitol. Daniel Carroll, of Duddington, was chosen chairman, and John Hewitt secretary. Then, agreeably to the act of incorporation, a ballot was taken for five members to constitute the second chamber, resulting in the election of Daniel Carroll, Benjamin Moore, William Prout, John Hewitt, and James Hoban. The first chamber then elected James Barry president, and Nicholas King secretary; and the second chamber elected Daniel Carroll president, and John Hewitt secretary. Committees were appointed and the Council adjourned until the 21st of the month.

On this day there was a partial reorganization of the two chambers, John T. Frost being elected secretary of the first chamber, and Thomas Herty of the second. The joint committee of the two chambers which had been appointed to examine the ground over which Maryland Avenue passed from the Capitol to the line eastward of the city toward Bladensburg, and also the situation and nature of the ground over which Tenth and Eleventh streets passed from Pennsylvania Avenue to the north line of the city, or any other street which had been calculated for opening the most direct communication from said avenue to the road then leading from Fredericktown to Montgomery County Courthouse by Rock Creek to Georgetown, and to make an estimate of the probable cost of clearing and making the same passable for wagons, etc., reported substantially as follows: That they were of the opinion that Fourteenth Street West was the proper street to open and to make passable for wagons and carriages from Pennsylvania Avenue to the boundary of the city, and continued thence to intersect the Montgomery road at the south end of what was chiefly called Boucher's Lane. It would benefit the western part of the city especially with respect to the marketing, and the entire city chiefly by opening a more direct and better road to Montgomery, Fredericktown, and the upper counties of Maryland. Maryland Avenue was, in the opinion of the committee, the most direct and proper street for the principal post road toward Bladensburg and Baltimore. The committee making this report was composed of Benjamin Moore, John Hoban, and Nicholas King.

Under the first charter of the city, the Mayor was appointed by the President of the United States, and the first Mayor thus appointed was Robert Brent. Washington Boyd was the first treasurer and Thomas Herty the first register.

Among the first acts passed by the above-named Council was one on October 6, 1802, to regulate the size of bricks. It provided, that after the first day of January, 1803, bricks sold in the city should be eight and three-quarter inches long, four and one-fourth inches wide, and two and three-eighth inches thick, and that they should be well burned. None should be made in the city smaller than the size given, under a penalty of $1 for every one thousand so made, sold, or offered for sale.

Another of their early acts was one providing that all hay, straw, or fodder brought to the city and sold after the 1st of November, 1802, east of the Tiber, should be sold by weight, and should be weighed on the machine erected for that purpose by John McCarty, who was granted the exclusive privilege of weighing all such hay, straw, and fodder, and who was required to keep his scales in perfect order.

Under an ordinance of the two chambers of the Council of the corporation, the Mayor appointed as trustees of the poor, early in November, 1802, Joseph Hodgson, John Kearney, and Griffith Coombes, and as overseer of the poor, Benjamin Burch.

November 19, 1802, Robert Brent, Mayor, advertised for bids to open West Fourteenth Street from North F Street to its extremity, the bids all to be in by December 1, 1802.

On this same day an act was passed by the Council to regulate weights and measures, which authorized the Mayor to procure complete sets of weights and measures according to the statute then in operation on this same subject in Maryland. The act also provided for the appointment of a sealer of weights and measures, and that all weights and measures in use should be rectified and branded before the 1st of February, 1803.

January 7, 1803, a meeting of citizens of Washington and of Washington County was held for the purpose of petitioning Congress for a legislature for the Territory of Columbia, the committee appointed to present the petition to Congress being composed of Robert Brent, Benjamin Moore, Nicholas King, Samuel H. Smith, and Augustus B. Woodward. The election for members of the Council, held on Monday, June 6, 1803, resulted in the return of William Brent, John P. Van Ness, John Hewitt, Samuel H. Smith, Nicholas King, Charles Menifee, Benjamin Moore, Daniel Rapine, Joel Brown, George Hadfield, Daniel Carroll, and Joseph Hodgson, all Republicans but the last two. The election passed off "with unsullied decorum and tranquillity." The President of the United States appointed Robert Brent to a second term as Mayor. Upon the organization of the Council John P. Van Ness was elected president of the first chamber, and

Thomas Herty secretary, and Daniel Carroll president of the second chamber.

Early in the history of the city a fire company was organized, the precise day, however, not being obtainable; but an act was passed by the corporation Council in June, 1803, extending the time for procuring fire buckets to the first of the following October. In July, 1803, an act was passed for the enumeration of the population of the city, and also one for the reassessment of the property of the city. In August an act was passed appropriating $600 toward erecting and repairing lamps in the city, and the Mayor was authorized to require such individual contributions as he might see fit. In accordance with this act the Mayor did require that lamps should be on some of the public streets in front of an improved lot, and that persons applying for the digging of wells and the erection of lamps should contribute one-half the sum necessary to complete the work.

In September, 1803, the trustees of the poor appointed were Peter Lenox, Joseph Mechlin, Griffith Coombes, George Blagden, and William Brent. In the same month an act was passed creating the office of superintendent of police. In November, 1803, an act was passed authorizing the Mayor to appoint two members of the board of appeal, since there had been no election of such board, in accordance with an act entitled, "An Act Supplementary to the Act Directing a New Assessment of Property and an Enumeration of the Inhabitants of the City," and the Mayor was empowered to extend the time for the performance of the duties enjoined by said acts for a period not to exceed two months.

February 24, 1804, an act was passed by Congress supplementary to the act incorporating the inhabitants of Washington, in which it was provided that the provisions of the former act should be enforced for fifteen years after the end of that session of Congress, and also that the two chambers of Council should be composed of nine members, a majority of each being sufficient to transact business. Powers of inspection were given them, and to superintend the health of the city, to preserve the navigation of the River Potomac and the Anacostia River, and providing that the levy court of the county of Washington should not thereafter possess the power to impose any tax on the inhabitants of the city of Washington.

The result of the enumeration of the inhabitants of Washington as provided for by act of the Council, and published May 9, 1804, was found to be as follows: Total number of people, 4,352. Whites, males, 1,902; females, 1,510. Slaves, males, 338; females, 379. Free blacks, males, 103; females, 120. Whites, 3,412; slaves, 717; free blacks, 223. In 1800, the population was 3,210.

At the first election held under the supplementary charter, the following gentlemen were chosen members of the two chambers of the Council: First chamber, George Blagden, Samuel H. Smith, Joseph Bromley, S. N. Smallwood, Henry Herford, Daniel Rapine, Robert Alexander, Cornelius Conyngham, and Thomas Carpenter; of the second chamber, William Brent, William Woodward, Alexander McCormick, Charles Jones, Nicholas King, James C. King, Joseph Hodgson, John Sinclair, and George Andrews.

July 24, 1804, an act was passed by the corporation of Washington to establish fire wards and fire companies, as follows: Ward one, all that part of the city which lies west of Sixteenth Street West; ward two, bounded on the west by Sixteenth Street West, on the south by South G Street until it intersects West Third, and by said street from said intersection to the northern extremity thereof; ward three, all that part of the city which lies southward of South G Street; ward four, the rest of the city. The Mayor was required, by August 1, to appoint a suitable person in each of the above wards who should call the citizens together, and those assembled were to organize themselves into fire companies. Each person so appointed was to be a member of the board of fire directors, who were required to make an annual report.

The trustees of the poor for 1805 were Peter Lenox, Henry Ingle, George Gollard, John Woodside, and William Brent.

The result of the election for members of Council, which was held June 2, was as follows: First chamber, John Dempsie, Samuel N. Smallwood, Jeremiah Booth, Frederick May, William Prout, Robert Alexander, Samuel H. Smith, James Hoban, and Thomas II. Gilliss. The second chamber was composed of John Sinclair, Matthew Wright, Alexander McCormick, Peter Lenox, Henry Herford, Phineas Bradley, Joseph Bromley, Nicholas King, and Henry Ingle. T. H. Gilliss was chosen president of the first chamber, and Alexander McCormick of the second. Robert Brent was continued as Mayor, and Thomas Herty as register.

November 26, 1806, an act was passed establishing the eastern branch market at the market house on Market Square, the market to be held on Mondays, Wednesdays, and Fridays, the Mayor being required to provide the necessary stalls, benches, scales, weights, and measures.

On March 19, 1807, the rules with regard to the size of bricks were changed by an act of the corporation. The molds for brick making were by this act required to be nine and one-eighth inches long in the clear, four and three-eighths inches broad, and two and five-eighths inches deep. This rule was to go into effect April 20, 1807.

On the same day as above the city corporation made regulations regarding the sweeping of chimneys, substantially as follows: The Mayor was authorized to make a contract with such person as he might deem a proper one, and to give to him the exclusive right to sweep the chimneys in Washington for a term not to exceed three years. The chimneys were to be swept once in each three months from the 1st day of April to the 1st day of October, and once in each two months the rest of the year, between five and seven o'clock in the morning, or at such time as the chimney sweep and the householder could agree upon. The chimney sweep was entitled to receive from the person so contracting with him the sum of ten cents for each story of each flue or chimney swept; and if any chimney or flue should take fire from the presence of soot in the chimney within two months from the last sweeping, then the chimney sweep should pay a fine of $5, and if any chimney should take fire that had not been swept, then the owner of the house should pay a fine of $5. As required to do, the Mayor, Robert Brent, gave notice to the citizens that he had made a contract for the sweeping of the chimneys with Job Haight, who would commence June 10, 1807.

On Monday, June 1, 1807, an election was held for councilmen, and afterward Frederick May was made president of the first chamber, and Charles Menifee of the second. Robert Brent was again appointed Mayor by the President of the United States, and Washington Boyd was made treasurer. During this year an act was passed by the Council to provide for the appointment by the Mayor of one commissioner from each ward, whose duty it should be to superintend the execution of all the laws of the Council, and to direct prosecutions for their infraction; to superintend the expenditure of all moneys appropriated by the Council for the opening or repair of streets, wharves, bridges, pumps, wells, springs, rivers, and creeks, and all appropriations not otherwise provided for by law. In June, 1807, under this act the Mayor appointed from the First Ward, Michael Nourse; from the Second Ward, Thomas H. Gilliss; from the Third Ward, Daniel Rapine; and from the Fourth Ward, George Gollard.

In the early history of the city, the Council made a monthly "assize of bread." For January, 1808, loaves of bread were required to be of the following sizes: From flour worth $5 per barrel, single loaf, 27 ounces; double loaf, 54 ounces. For September, 1808, a single loaf was required to weigh 30 ounces, and a double loaf 60 ounces, from flour worth from $4.50 to $5 per barrel. In March, 1810, from flour worth $7.25 per barrel, a single loaf was required to weigh 19 ounces, and a double loaf 38 ounces. In November, 1812, from flour worth from $10 to $11 per barrel, a single loaf was required to weigh 12 ounces, and a double one 24 ounces.

For August, 1813, from flour worth from $5.50 to $6 per barrel, a single loaf was required to weigh 23 ounces, and a double loaf 46 ounces. For January, 1820, from flour worth from $5.50 to $6 per barrel, a single loaf was required to weigh 23 ounces, and a double loaf 46 ounces.

A census of the city taken about the last part of the year 1807 and the beginning of 1808 gave the following results: Whites, males, 2,139; females, 2,009. Slaves, males, 409; females, 479. Free blacks, males, 126; females, 153. Free mulattoes, males, 95; females, 126. Slaves owned by non-residents, males, 55; females, 61. Total population of the city, 5,652. By wards the population was as follows: First Ward, 1,108; Second Ward, 1,447; Third Ward, 1,751; Fourth Ward, 1,346.

After the election of councilmen, on Monday, June 5, 1809, Robert Brent was again appointed Mayor. He was again appointed after the election for councilmen held on Monday, June 4, 1810. In June, 1811, Mr. Brent peremptorily declined to serve longer as Mayor of the city. Whatever were the reasons that influenced Mr. Brent to refuse longer to serve in this capacity, it is certain that the citizens of Washington were not satisfied with their city's form of government, and especially with that feature of it which required the President of the United States to appoint their Mayor; for being thus appointed, he was not responsible to them in the exercise of his powers and duties. They would much have preferred to be able to elect their own Mayor, and it was suggested that inasmuch as they could not do this, it would perhaps be well for them to indicate to the President whom they would prefer by having a kind of *quasi* election. After the election of councilmen held on Monday, June 3, 1811, the President appointed as Mayor Daniel Rapine.

On October 31 and November 2, 1811, meetings were held, which were quite generally attended by the citizens, to take into consideration the propriety of making application to Congress to amend the act of incorporation. Dr. James H. Blake was chairman of the latter meeting, and George Sweeney secretary. The following resolutions were adopted:

"WHEREAS, Experience having shown that various provisions of the act of incorporation are extremely defective, and particularly the present mode of electing the city Council on a general ticket, as prescribed by that instrument, having been productive of very injurious consequences to the interests of the city; therefore,

"*Resolved,* That the chairman of this meeting, together with two citizens to be chosen by each ward, be a committee to prepare a memorial to Congress, praying that such alteration and amendments may be made in the act of incorporation as they may deem necessary."

The committee as chosen was as follows: James Hoban, John Hewitt, Phineas Bradley, Henry Herford, Elias B. Caldwell, John Coyle, Buller Cocke, and Joseph Cassin. The following resolution was then adopted: "That the above named committee be authorized to receive the signatures of the citizens of Washington to the memorial which shall be prepared."

In obedience to the request of the committee, a supplementary act was passed by Congress, May 4, 1812, by which the corporation was made to consist of a Mayor, a Board of Aldermen and a Common Council. The Board of Aldermen consisted of eight members elected for two years, and were required to be chosen from the wards in which they resided. The Common Council consisted of twelve members, three from each ward, and the Mayor was elected by the joint ballot of the members of the boards to serve for one year.

Under the charter as amended in accordance with this petition, the first election was held on Monday, June 1, 1812, resulting as follows:

Aldermen — First Ward, John Davidson and James Hoban; Second Ward, Andrew Way, Jr., and Peter Lenox; Third Ward, Alexander McCormick and Daniel Rapine; Fourth Ward, Joseph Cassin and James S. Stevenson.

Councilmen — First Ward, W. Worthington, Jr., Toppan Webster, and James Hoban; Second Ward, William James, James Hewitt, and R. C. Weightman; Third Ward, Edmund Law, George Blagden, and Benjamin G. Orr; Fourth Ward, John W. Brashear, Matthew Wright, and John Dobbyn.

Alexander McCormick was elected president of the Board of Aldermen, and James Hewitt of the Board of Common Council.

At this same time Daniel Rapine was elected Mayor.

A census of the city was taken in 1810, resulting as follows: Whites, males, 2,895; females, 3,009. Slaves, 1,437. All other persons,

867. Total population, 8,208. The total population of Georgetown was then 4,948; of Washington County outside of Washington and Georgetown, 2,315; of Alexandria, 7,227; of Alexandria County outside of Alexandria, 1,325. Total population of the District of Columbia, 24,023.

Dr. James H. Blake was elected Mayor of the city, June 12, 1813; June 6, 1814; June 12, 1815; June 3, 1816; and in June, 1817.

Benjamin G. Orr was elected Mayor by the councils in June, 1818; Samuel N. Smallwood in June, 1819, and Mr. Smallwood held over in 1820, under a new charter just granted.

The new charter granted the city by Congress, May 15, 1820, provided that the Mayor should be elected by the people, to serve for two years from the second Monday in June. The Board of Aldermen was required to be composed of two members from each ward, to serve for two years, and were *ex officio* justices of the peace for the entire county. The Board of Common Council was to consist of three members from each ward, to serve for one year. Every free white male citizen of the United States of lawful age, having resided within the city one year previous to the election, and being a resident of the ward in which he offered to vote, having been assessed on the books of the corporation for the year on the 31st of December preceding the election, and having paid all taxes due on personal property when legally required to pay the same, was entitled to vote for Mayor and members of the two boards.

By this act the city was divided into six wards. All that part of the city to the westward of Fifteenth Street West constituted the First Ward. The Second Ward contained all that part eastward of Fifteenth Street and westward of Tenth Street West. The Third Ward contained all that part east of Tenth Street West, west of First Street West, and north of E Street South; the Fourth Ward, all that part to the eastward of First Street West, westward of Eighth Street East, and north of E Street South; the Fifth Ward, all that part east of Tenth Street West, west of Fourth Street East, and south of E Street South. The Sixth Ward contained all the rest of the city.

Section 1 of this act provided that all the officers in office at the time of its passage should continue in office until the expiration of their respective terms, and that all their acts done in pursuance of former acts of incorporation, and not inconsistent with the new charter, should be valid.

Section 2 provided that the name of the corporation should be

"The Mayor, Board of Aldermen, and Board of Common Council of the City of Washington."

Section 3 provided that the Mayor should be elected biennially, commencing on the first Monday in June, 1820, and that in case of a tie in the popular vote the Boards of Aldermen and Common Council should determine by joint ballot which should serve.

By this charter the city was divided into six wards, two aldermen being chosen to represent each ward, and three common councilmen. Under this charter the government of the city was a very complicated piece of machinery, as may be seen by the following list of aldermen, councilmen, etc.

Aldermen — First Ward, James H. Handy and J. W. Moulder; Second Ward, James Hoban and Thomas H. Gilliss; Third Ward, R. C. Weightman and W. W. Seaton; Fourth Ward, Henry Tims and Nicholas L. Queen; Fifth Ward, Daniel Carroll, of Duddington, and Thomas Dougherty; Sixth Ward, William Prout and Israel Little.

Common Councilmen — First Ward, Thomas Carberry, Josiah Taylor, and Satterlee Clark; Second Ward, John McClelland, Henry Smith, and John Strother; Third Ward, Hanson Gassaway, Samuel Burch, and George Sweeney; Fourth Ward, Dr. Andrew Hunter, John Ingle, and Benjamin Burch; Fifth Ward, Richmond Johnston, Dr. C. B. Hamilton, and James Middleton; Sixth Ward, Gustavus Higdon, Adam Lindsay, and Benjamin Bryan.

Register, William Hewitt; health officer, Dr. Henry Hunt; surveyor, Joseph Elgar; inspector of tobacco, Samuel P. Lowe; sealer of weights and measures, Jacob Leonard; inspectors of flour, Samuel McIntire and William A. Scott; members of the board of appeal, John Davidson, Peter Lenox, Frederick May, and Matthew Wright; commissioners of wards: First Ward, Samuel Harkness; Second Ward, Edward G. Handy; Third Ward, Joseph Dougherty; Fourth Ward, Henry Ingle; Fifth Ward, John Van Riswick; Sixth Ward, John B. Forrest; inspectors of lumber, Thomas Sandiford, Jr., Thomas Wilson, Leonard Harbaugh, Benjamin Bryan, and William H. Barnes; wood corders and coal measurers, Thomas Taylor, Jr., Thomas Burch, George Sanford, William Wise, Benjamin Bryan, and John B. Ferguson; gaugers, Samuel McIntire and William H. Barnes; commissioners of the West Burial Ground, David Easton, Robert King, and Benjamin M. Belt; commissioners of the East Burial Ground, John Crabb, John Chalmers, and Daniel Rapine; sexton of the West Burial Ground, Alexander Watson; sexton of the East Burial Ground, Benson McCormick; clerk of the West Market

House, Philip Williams; clerk of the Center Market House, John Waters; clerk of the Capitol Hill Market House, Benson McCormick; clerk of the Eastern Branch Market House, Peter Little.

Under this charter the Mayor served two years, as also did the members of the Board of Aldermen, after the rotation was established. In 1822, Thomas Carberry was elected Mayor to succeed Mr. Smallwood, and in 1824 R. C. Weightman was elected to succeed Mr. Carberry.

In March, 1824, the citizens of Alexandria, becoming tired of being in the District of Columbia, made an attempt to have Alexandria retroceded to Virginia. A meeting was held on the 9th of that month for the purpose of preparing a memorial to Congress on the subject. Thomson F. Mason was chairman of the meeting, and P. R. Fendall secretary. The memorial as drawn up set forth that the citizens of Alexandria County were deprived of their constitutional rights without the existence or assumption of authority of the people of the United States to do so; but by what seemed to them to be an oversight of the framers of the Constitution of the United States. The citizens of Alexandria could not presume that the framers of the Constitution, who had just previously been engaged in a struggle for liberty for themselves, would designedly deprive others of that precious boon, which they had done in the case of the inhabitants of the District of Columbia, by the imposition of taxes upon an unrepresented community, for this was the very grievance which produced the Revolution, etc.

An adverse meeting was held March 11, over which Phineas Janney presided, and of which Nathaniel S. Wise was the secretary. The object of the meeting was fully stated by Robert I. Taylor, who explained what disadvantages the citizens of Alexandria County would labor under if the proposed retrocession of the county should become an accomplished fact. A memorial against the movement was drawn up and a committee appointed to present it to Congress.

The proposed retrocession was defeated at that time by a vote of the people of 404 against it to 286 for it, but at length, in 1846, another movement for the same purpose was inaugurated, and was successful.

Mayor R. C. Weightman was reëlected in June, 1826, and on July 20, 1827, Mayor Weightman was elected cashier of the Bank of Washington, and resigned his position, to be succeeded by Joseph Gales, Jr. In June, 1828, Mr. Gales was elected to the position for two years, and was reëlected in 1830 for two years more.

On June 4, 1832, John P. Van Ness was elected Mayor; on June 2, 1834, William A. Bradley was elected to the position, and in June, 1836, Peter Force was elected by a vote of 570, to 337 cast for H. M. Morfit.

Mr. Force, in his inaugural, congratulated the citizens upon having been relieved of a heavy burden. In 1828, the city had made a large subscription to the stock of the Chesapeake and Ohio Canal Company, to which subscription that great work owed its existence. The subscription carried with it obligations greater than the city could carry. The responsibilities growing out of this subscription were rendered greater than they would otherwise have been by the hostile proceedings of a rival company, which interrupted the prosecution of the work for years, and for each year that the work was delayed Washington City, the wealthiest of all the parties connected with the subscription to the stock of the company, though one of the largest contributors, lost in the aggregate about $50,000 per year. But now the United States had assumed the payment of the interest of this subscription on the pledge and deposit of its stock in the company; still the corporation owed on its subscription about $450,000, and at the same time it was possible that by a change in circumstances the city might derive no benefit from the canal, and Mr. Force advised the most rigid economy and the limiting of expenditures to the smallest possible amount.

On Monday, June 1, 1840, W. W. Seaton was elected Mayor of the city. Previously to this election there had been great excitement in political circles, in the District of Columbia as elsewhere in the United States. The financial measures of President Jackson's two administrations, and the practical continuation of the same destructive policy by Mr. Van Buren's administration, aroused the people to such an extent that they were determined to throw off the incubus of a "democratic" government, which was, in fact, a democratic government only in name, being in reality a monarchy in disguise. In the city of Washington, this feeling succeeded in electing Mr. Seaton Mayor, he being a determined and outspoken Whig. With reference to this election, Hon. William Cost Johnson, of Maryland, in an address to the people of the District of Columbia, quoted from elsewhere, with reference to the powers of Congress with regard to the banking institutions of the District of Columbia, said, under date of July 22, 1840:

"But not satisfied with destroying the banking institutions of the District, in punishment of the people, the administration Senate really passed to a third reading a bill to abolish the present charter of the city of Washington, and to cause a new election for Mayor of the

10

city to be held in October next, because the people had selected only a few weeks ago a Whig Mayor to serve for two years from the day of election; and containing, besides, features virtually depriving every master of control over his servant, which no one but an abolitionist could have urged, or a Southern Jacobin have supported," etc.

Another, a citizen of the District, called for a convention of the people, from the corporations within the District, for the purpose of expressing their indignation at the treatment they had received from Congress, and a writer in the public press said: "Till 1829, the people of the District, and especially of Washington, had always been friendly to the administration of the Government, and the administration had always been friendly to the people, regarding them with a kind of parental attachment. Jefferson, Madison, Monroe, and Adams did what they could to give an impetus to its improvements; but the Hun, Attila, came, and swept like a destructive avalanche over the fair face of the land under the plea of democracy, and clothed with the power which popularity gave him, he 'played such fantastic tricks before high heaven as made the angels weep.' Almost every family was more or less affected by his wild and reckless despotism. He was followed by the Northern man with Southern principles, who professed to follow in the footsteps of his illustrious predecessor, and who has brought the country and the District, as well as the Government, to bankruptcy and ruin by the folly of his measures, and his profligate and useless extravagance in the expenditure of the public money," etc.

A public meeting of the citizens of the District of Columbia who were over twenty-one years of age, and who were opposed to the then recent ruinous legislation of Congress toward this District, by which the business, trade, and industry of the community had been prostrated, was held on Monday, July 27, 1840, in front of the City Hall, to give voice to their wrongs, and to endeavor peacefully to devise a remedy for them. Of this meeting W. W. Seaton was made chairman and Walter Lenox secretary. Samuel H. Smith submitted a series of resolutions, which were in substance as follows: That the course pursued by the late Congress toward the District of Columbia was insulting to the character of the people of the District, derogatory to their rights, and subversive of their prosperity; that in it the meeting beheld a total disregard of the principles of justice and the calls of humanity, connected with a stern purpose to punish sixty thousand people for the exercise of their undoubted right to think and to speak freely of public men and public measures; and that the meeting would appoint five delegates from each ward of the city, to attend a convention of delegates to assemble in Washington on the second Monday (10th) of August, and invited the citizens of Georgetown and Alexandria to appoint delegates to the said convention, for the purpose of adopting such measures as the alarming crisis in the affairs of the District seemed to render expedient.

A committee of one from each ward was then appointed to name a list of delegates to attend the proposed convention, the delegates as named by this committee being as follows: First Ward, Samuel H. Smith, Benjamin O. Taylor, William Easby, Alexander McIntire, and Thomas Munroe; Second Ward, John McClelland, Anthony Preston, William H. Gunnell, Wallace Kirkwood, and William M. McCauley; Third Ward, Walter Jones, Joseph H. Bradley, John C. Harkness, Jacob A. Bender, and John C. McKelden; Fourth Ward, Dr. Frederick May, Henry J. Brent, George Watterston, John Kedgely, and W. McGill; Fifth Ward, Daniel Carroll, of Duddington, Thomas Blagden, John W. Martin, Griffith Coombes, and Thomas R. Riley; Sixth Ward, Noble Young, James Marshall, Dr. Alexander McWins, Robert Clarke, and Robert Coombs.

The chairman and secretary of the meeting were then added to the list of delegates, and then, by resolution, the grateful thanks of the meeting were tendered to Hon. William D. Merrick, chairman of the District Committee of the Senate, and to Hon. William Cost Johnson, chairman of the District Committee of the House of Representatives, and their zealous friends of both Houses of Congress, for their generous and manly resistance to the aggressive measures attempted to be adopted with reference to the District.

The citizens of Georgetown held a meeting, July 21, for the purpose of giving expression to their sentiments as to the course of Congress. Their meeting was held in front of the Mayor's office, and in obedience to a call issued on the 18th of the month. At this meeting a committee on resolutions was appointed, and instructed to report to an adjourned meeting to be held in the Lancasterian Schoolhouse, July 23. This committee was composed of Samuel McKenny, John Marbury, William Laird, Henry Addison, and Judson Mitchell. The resolutions reported by this committee were as follows:

"1. That the surrender of the rights of self-government by the people of the District of Columbia to the people of the United States, to enable them to carry into practical operation the principles of the Government devised by the Constitution of the United States, was a great personal and political sacrifice, and merited a kind, liberal, and generous consideration in return; but has been paid by the majority of the present Congress with indignity, insults, wrong, and oppression, of which it becomes us to speak with temperate, but at the same time with indignant, reprehension, and to which no citizen of the District of Columbia having any interest in its prosperity can patiently submit.

"2. That the people of the District, in common with the people of the States, are of right free, and equally with the latter entitled to the benefits of the laws suited to promote their happiness and welfare; that the Congress of the United States has refused to the people laws by them deemed absolutely necessary to their happiness and prosperity, and such as exist in every State in the Union, and have thereby failed to discharge their solemn duty, wantonly and wickedly exposing the people of this District to ruinous embarrassment and distress.

"3. That we trace the whole of the wrongs and evils of which. we complain to the subjection of the people of this District to the exclusive legislation of Congress, the members of which, being chosen by strangers, are without the knowledge of our wants or in sympathy with our condition; and we are confident that we cannot be contented and prosperous so long as so unjust and intolerable a mode of government is allowed to continue.

"4. That the only remedy from the evils which we now suffer, and the only mode of securing permanent and general prosperity to our town, is retrocession to Maryland; and with a view to effect a measure so indispensable to our interests, the following address to the citizens of the United States at large, and to Maryland in particular, be adopted at this meeting, and signed by the president and secretary, and printed under their direction; and that a copy be forwarded to the governor of each State, with a request that he will lay the same before the legislature of his State at the next meeting."

"An Address to Our Countrymen Throughout the Twenty-six States of the Union, and to Maryland, in Particular," was then read by William Laird, Esq., and was afterward published, together with the above resolutions. The address was as follows:

"We, the citizens of Georgetown, in the District of Columbia, in town meeting assembled on this 23d day of July, 1840, have resolved to address you in the following terms:

"A provision in the Constitution grants to Congress the power 'to exercise exclusive legislation in all classes whatsoever over such district not exceeding ten miles square as may, by cession of particular States and the acceptance of Congress, become the seat of government of the United States.' We are thus left entirely at the mercy of the Legislature of the Union, without a representative on the floor, without a voice in their counsels,—dependent altogether on their will and pleasure, on their wisdom and justice, for action, beneficial or otherwise, operating on our interests and immediately affecting our prosperity and happiness.

"We, a trading and commercial community, have for a long time had banks among us, those indispensable prerequisites for mercantile operations and facilities. The law chartering the one we now have was signed by James Madison; the laws rechartering it were signed by James Monroe, and twice by Andrew Jackson. Previously to the expiration of the charter of this bank a memorial numerously signed by the citizens was presented to Congress, praying in the most respectful manner for a recharter, and stating the fact that the institution was perfectly able and willing to resume the payment of specie on its notes as soon as the neighboring banks of Virginia and Maryland paid the same on theirs. A petition was also presented by the bank for a recharter, to include as a feature of it the immediate resumption of specie payments on all its notes. Nevertheless, our prayer for a recharter, as well as the prayer of every one of the other five banks of the District for the same, was rejected, and nothing whatever granted to the banks but the privilege of having a specified time wherein to close up their concerns; and this through the votes and influence of members of the Senate, who insist on the destruction of all banks as a policy of the administration."

The above is only a part of the address, which was very long.

But perhaps the most remarkable thing connected with the attitude of Congress toward the people of the District of Columbia during the remarkable session of 1839–40, which has heretofore been adverted to in an extract from an address by Hon. William Cost Johnson, was the attempt, which came near succeeding, to grant a new charter to the city of Washington. The charter under which the city was then operating was granted to it May 15, 1820, and by its terms was to continue in force for and during the term of twenty years, and until Congress by law should determine otherwise. Here, then, was a fine opportunity for a few of its citizens, the population being then about twenty-five thousand, to memorialize Congress for a new charter, and accordingly, such a memorial was presented to Congress, signed by about four hundred of the citizens. This memorial, or petition, instead of being referred to the standing committee on the District of Columbia, as was the usual and proper course with such petitions, was referred to a select committee, with Mr. Norvell, of Michigan, as its chairman.

The bill reported by the committee was very elaborate and voluminous, containing five or six sections more than the charter which it was designed to supersede. The section which declared the continuance of the charter for twenty years, or indefinitely without Congressional action, was inserted in the new bill and altered to ten years, with a reservation to Congress to alter or repeal it at any time; and thus, while the new act was entitled, "An Act to Amend and Continue in Force the Act to Incorporate the Inhabitants of Washington," yet, in fact, it was one merely to amend, and not to continue in force.

But the most amazing and mischievous feature of the bill, and the one which aroused the inhabitants of the city of Washington, as had perhaps nothing ever done or attempted to be done before, to a realizing sense of the danger which they had so narrowly escaped,—for the friends of the bill did not succeed in getting it through Congress,— was that with reference to slaves in the city of Washington. The people of the city were then almost universally opposed to the abolition of slavery in the District. In the old bill or charter careful discrimination was made as to the different modes in which slaves and free persons were to be dealt with or punished. The corporation was empowered to prohibit the nightly or other disorderly meetings of slaves, free negroes, or mulattoes, and to punish the slaves by whipping and imprisonment, and the free negroes by pecuniary fines; and such slaves as should commit offenses against municipal ordinances as would impose fines upon others might be subject to corporal punishment, unless the masters should come forward and pay the fines.

In the proposed new charter of the city, every provision relating to slaves was expunged! Every clause and part of a clause in which the word *slave* occurred was carefully picked out, here and there through the section, and it was impossible to believe otherwise than that these omissions were from design. This course would have resulted in the practical abolition of slavery within the District. It would have amounted to a renunciation on the part of Congress of the recognition by that body of any such thing as slavery, or of any such property as slave property, and would have amounted to a declaration that slavery could not in the nature of things be established or permitted by any human institution, and that human laws yield to the paramount force of the natural or divine law.

The bill was passed to a third reading by the unanimous vote of the Democratic Party in the Senate, and among those who thus voted were several Senators from slave States, who, it seemed to the people of the District most natural to infer, were not in the dark as to the effect of the proposed charter upon slave property. However, the next day after the passage of the bill to a third reading, a Southern Senator who had voted for the bill renewed a motion to lay it on the table, previously made by one of the minority without success, and it was laid on the table accordingly. But for this motion it would have passed. But yet during the recess of Congress for the summer of 1840, this proposed new charter, with its clause abolishing slavery in the city of Washington, still, like the sword of Dionysius over the neck of Damocles, hung over their devoted heads, and they might well, as they did, feel considerable anxiety as to the fate of this obnoxious measure when Congress should again convene. Though upon reflection it should have occurred to them, and doubtless would have occurred to them but for the excess of their injured party feelings, that before the next session of Congress should commence the Senators from the Southern States would find out how nearly they had been trapped into voting for a bill which would have accomplished at one sweep the very thing which they had been voting against for years, and which they could not have sanctioned without going back on their own record, and without at the same time injuring to a greater or less extent the safety of slave property in the States.[1]

The people of the District took great interest in the politics of the time, being as a general thing in favor of the election of Harrison and Tyler, as President and Vice-President respectively. One of the clubs organized was named the "Washington City Tippecanoe Club," organized September 18, 1840. John Tyler, in passing through the city on his way to Columbus, Ohio, was invited to address the club, and accepting the invitation, spoke fully and feelingly of the troubles of the District, and joined his voice with the voices of others in various parts of the country who had greeted and cheered the independent spirit of the people of the District in the assertion of and demand for their rights. Of this club John A. Blake was president; Robert W. Bates, H. W. Queen, Jacob Gideon, Jr., and Richard H. Stewart, vice-presidents; J. L. Henshaw, corresponding secretary; and Wallace Kirkwood, treasurer. There was in addition to these officers an executive committee of thirteen.

---

[1] The history of emancipation in the District of Columbia, which was effected some twenty years later, will be presented in a subsequent chapter.

On Saturday, October 3, this club raised a spacious log cabin and a handsome liberty pole on the vacant ground between the Center Market and Pennsylvania Avenue. The cabin was forty feet front by fifty feet in depth, fronting on Pennsylvania Avenue, and built in regular log-cabin style, with a platform in front for public speaking. The liberty pole was one hundred and seven feet high, and it was surmounted by a streamer bearing the inscription, "Harrison and Tyler." The stars and stripes were afterward elevated above the streamer. The cabin was used as a meeting room for the club, and as a reading and intelligence room for the Whigs generally throughout the presidential contest. The first meeting which took place in this cabin was on Saturday evening after the raising of it, upon which occasion speeches were made by General Walter Jones, Richard S. Coxe, and Robert Ould.

On Saturday morning, November 7, 1840, it was finally ascertained that William Henry Harrison was elected President of the United States, and the rejoicing of the people of this District knew no bounds; for, having suffered from the effects of President Jackson's policy toward them, they fully realized from what they had escaped.

John W. Maury served as Mayor of the city from June, 1852, to June, 1854. John T. Towers was elected Mayor in 1854. In June, 1856, W. B. Magruder was elected Mayor, by a vote of 2,936, over Silas B. Hill, who received but 2,904 votes. At the election which occurred on Monday, June 1, 1857, there was a serious riot, resulting in the death of several citizens and the wounding of others. The principal cause of the unusual excitement preceding this election and of the riot while it was in progress, arose from the heated discussion of the question as to whether naturalized citizens should exercise their right of suffrage, the Know-nothing Party being to a considerable extent bitterly opposed to such exercise. Trouble was anticipated for some days prior to the election, and everything that could be done was done to prevent any outbreak and to calm the excitement, especially by the press. These papers, however, did not know that arrangements had been made to introduce "bands of intrusive strangers" from abroad to interfere with the elections in this city. By the earliest train, however, and on subsequent trains, bands of ill-looking men, mostly a year or two under age, with the generic and suggestive title of "Plug Uglies," arrived from Baltimore, crowding the sidewalks, and giving every indication of being able and willing to carry out any instructions they might have received, or might receive, from headquarters. About 9:30 A. M., at the first precinct of the Fourth Ward, a sudden attack was made upon a naturalized citizen in the ranks of the voters, and an effort was made to drive all such voters from the polls. In this onslaught, and in the defense which it rendered necessary, several citizens were wounded, natives as well as naturalized. Richard Owens, commissioner of the ward, was badly shot in the arm and wounded in the head; F. A. Klopfer was struck in the forehead by a slung-shot; George D. Spencer was seriously bruised by a stone; Justice Goddard was struck in several places with bricks; Justice Donn was similarly wounded with stones; Officer H. Degges, Policeman Birckhead, and Chief of Police Baggott were all more or less severely wounded and driven from the field. The result of all this was that naturalized citizens became badly demoralized and generally retired from the scene.

About 10:30 A. M., the imported rowdies appeared at the lower precinct of the Second Ward, where they fired about a dozen pistol shots, one of them taking effect in the forehead of a bystander. Representations being about this time made to the Mayor that it was impossible to keep the polls open at the first precinct of the Fourth Ward, that official made application to the President of the United States for the services of the company of marines then in the city, to maintain the peace. This request of Mayor Magruder was referred to the Secretary of the Navy, who promptly ordered out one hundred and ten of the marines, under the command of Major Tyler and Captain Maddox, and placed them at the disposal of the Mayor. The marines were marched to the precinct in question, accompanied by General Henderson in citizen's clothes. As soon as it became known that the marines had been ordered out, a number of young men secured possession of a six-pound brass swivel gun, and hitching a long cord to it, dragged it along Seventh Street, with the avowed object of resisting the marines. Upon arriving at the polling place in the first precinct of the Fourth Ward, the marines, who were accompanied by the Mayor, the corporation attorney, Marshal Hoover, Ex-Marshal Wallach, Captain Baggott, and several other policemen, found the swivel party on the ground, with their gun on the sidewalk, under the shed of the Northern Liberties Market House. The Mayor ordered the polling place to be opened, and was informed by the opponents of naturalized citizens voting that that should not take place. About one thousand five hundred persons were present, whom the Mayor then addressed; but his address, instead of quieting them and calming the disturbance, only served to excite the angry crowd the more. Soon the order was given to capture the swivel gun, and a section of the marines, under Major Tyler, advanced for this purpose with fixed bayonets, which induced the abandonment of the cannon and the retirement of the party in charge. This party, however, in retiring, hurled volleys of stones, and fired upon the marines with revolvers, one of them being shot in the jaw. The order was then given to the marines to fire upon the crowd, which order being obeyed, two persons immediately fell on Massachusetts Avenue, and in other directions many were shot, and several of them mortally wounded. The crowd thereupon took to flight in all directions, and the marines were marched back to the City Hall.

There were killed in this riot and its suppression the following persons: A Mr. Allison, aged fifty-five years; F. M. Deems, a clerk in the General Land Office; Archibald Dalrymple, baggage-master on the Baltimore and Ohio Railroad; a colored man named Neale, from the northern liberties; another colored man from Georgetown, named Redding; an infant child was killed on English Hill, and several were severely wounded. The polls at the first precinct were reopened about three o'clock in the afternoon, and remained open until the legal hour for closing arrived. The "Plug Uglies," finding themselves so unwelcome in the city and their disinterested services in the cause of "Americanism" so disappointingly unappreciated, silently and slyly stole away, some of them walking to Bladensburg and others jumping upon the cars just as the train was starting from the depot for Baltimore. In order to insure the safety of the citizens from further attack, many of whom had been personally threatened with violence, a strong body of Major French's flying artillery was brought down from Fort McHenry, arriving here in the evening of election day. No further trouble was experienced however from the Baltimore immigrants at that time.

But the Know-nothing sentiment had not expired when the election for Mayor occurred in June, 1858. The opposing candidates for the mayoralty at that time were the then late postmaster of Washington, James G. Berrett, Anti-Know-nothing candidate, and Ex-Marshal Richard Wallach, of the District of Columbia, the Republican candidate. The result of the election was that Mr. Berrett was elected by a vote of 3,688 to Mr. Wallach's 3,117.

In June, 1860, the same contest was waged over again, between the same candidates for Mayor, James G. Berrett receiving 3,434 votes to 3,410 for Richard Wallach. William B. Magruder, as an independent candidate, received 147 votes. Mr. Wallach then gave notice that he would contest the election of Mr. Berrett on the ground of fraud. This promised or threatened contest, however, never came to trial, because Mayor Berrett, on Saturday, August 24, 1861, was arrested at his residence by a portion of the Provost Marshal's guard, and taken to Fort Lafayette, he having several days previously refused to take the oath prescribed by act of Congress for members of the board of police commissioners. Both branches of the city Council were thereupon convened in special session to perform the duties devolving upon them in consequence of the Mayor's arrest. The residence of the Mayor, though searched, furnished no evidence of complicity with the Rebellion. Mr. Berrett also said that he was a strong Union man. But it being necessary that there should be a Mayor to execute the laws of the corporation, the two boards, on the 26th of the month, elected Richard Wallach to fill that office until the regular Mayor's return. James M. Carlisle, corporation attorney, resigned his position and Joseph H. Bradley was appointed to the place, September 1, 1861. Mayor Berrett was released from prison. He resigned the mayoralty on the 14th, and returned to Washington on the 16th. The Mayor's resignation did not reach the city until the 23d, and then the question arose as to whether the city had a Mayor. The corporation attorney decided, however, that Mr. Wallach was Mayor according to law, because Mayor Berrett had resigned, and hence had no claim to the office. Notwithstanding this opinion of the attorney, the two councils, in order to make assurance doubly sure, on October 17, 1861, elected Mr. Wallach to the office, to fill out the unexpired term of Mayor Berrett.

At the election held in June, 1862, Mr. Wallach was elected by the popular vote to the office, receiving 3,850 votes to 958 cast for James F. Halliday. On June 6, 1864, Mayor Wallach was again reëlected to the office by a vote of 3,347 to 2,373 cast for John H. Semmes. June 4, 1866, Mr. Wallach was once more reëlected Mayor of Washington by a vote of 3,621 to 1,345 for Mr. Easby.

It is altogether likely that in 1868 greater interest was attached to the election of Mayor than at any other such election. The reason for this was that the negroes voted that year for the first time. The registration showed the following state of things as to the number of negroes having the right to vote: In the First Ward the negro majority was 218; in the Second Ward the white majority was 176; in the Third Ward, 1,031; in the Fourth Ward, 1,310; in the Fifth Ward, 593; in the Sixth Ward, 1,076, and in the Seventh Ward, 263. Total white majority, 4,231. It therefore appeared clear that if the white voters chose to do so they could defeat any candidate the negroes favored. The two candidates for Mayor were, on the part of the Democrats, John T. Given, and on the part of the Republicans, Sayles J. Bowen. On the face of the returns Mr. Bowen was elected by a majority of 83; the vote being 1,230 to 1,147. The Council, however, was Democratic by a small majority, and they had to appoint a joint committee to count the ballots. The *National Intelligencer* said, "It is to be hoped they will perform their duty, as there may have been mistakes made by the judges." While the count of the vote was in progress the Republican members of the Boards of Aldermen and Common Council declared Mr. Bowen Mayor *pro tempore*, and the Democratic members similarly declared W. W. Moore Mayor *pro tempore*, each protesting against the illegality of the other's action. Mr. Bowen obtained possession of the Mayor's office and proceeded to act as Mayor.

On account of the difficulty thus existing, the councils, in joint convention, on June 11, elected a Mayor *ad interim*, in the person of Thomas E. Lloyd. On Saturday, June 13, Mr. Lloyd, as Mayor *ad interim*, waited upon Mr. Bowen as Mayor *de facto*, and handed him a communication demanding of him the possession of the office, which Mr. Bowen refused to grant. Mr. Lloyd then called upon Major A. C. Richards, chief of police, and protested against the presence of metropolitan policemen as guards at the City Hall, to which Major Richards replied that the board of police commissioners would be in session on the 18th, and that he would lay the communication before them. On the 18th the city councils deposed Frederick A. Boswell from his office as register of the city, for failure to perform his duties in connection with the election of June 1, 1868, in that he did not notify certain individuals of their election as he was required by law to do, and a committee on the part of the Boards of Aldermen and Common Council submitted charges against Major Richards for unlawful acts in connection with the performance of his duties. The result of the struggle between the parties was that Mr. Bowen served as Mayor from that time to June, 1870.

Early in January, 1870, the movement directed toward a change in the form of the government of the District of Columbia received an impetus which carried it forward to success. A meeting of citizens was held, January 12, for the purpose of securing this reorganization, at which there were present S. P. Brown, Dr. Lindsley, W. H. Phillips, A. R. Shepherd, Hallet Kilbourn, William B. Todd, William H. Tenney, J. A. Magruder, Esau Pickrell, and Dr. Charles H. Nichols. A committee of five persons was appointed at this meeting to draft a bill providing that the District of Columbia should be provided with a Territorial form of government, similar to that of the several Territories of the United States, consolidating the three municipal governments then existing into this one government, except that the governor and the upper branch of the legislature should be appointed by the President of the United States and confirmed by the Senate, and the lower branch of the legislature and a delegate to Congress should be elected by the people. Meetings were held by different classes of citizens, some in favor of the change in the form of government, and others in opposition thereto. At length, about February 1, at a mass meeting held in Lincoln Hall, a committee of one hundred and fifty persons was appointed to take general charge of the matter, which committee appointed a subcommittee to draft a suitable bill, which was approved at a large meeting held at Metzerott Hall, March 3, 1870, in several very able speeches, especially one by Hon. A. G. Riddle. This bill passed the Senate May 27.

In the meantime there was held a highly interesting and important election for Mayor of the city of Washington, the Mayor, Sayles J. Bowen, and M. G. Emery being the respective candidates. The result of the election was that Mr. Emery was elected by a vote of 10,096 votes to 6,877 for Mayor Bowen. Mr. Emery was the last Mayor of Washington, his term expiring in June, 1871, when what is called the Territorial government went into operation.

This Territorial form of government, as has been intimated, consisted of a Governor and other executive officers, and a Legislature composed of a Legislative Assembly and a House of Delegates. It was established under an act of Congress passed February 21, 1871. The first officers appointed under this act were Henry D. Cooke, formerly of Sandusky, Ohio, Governor; and a board of public works consisting of Alexander R. Shepherd, S. P. Brown, James A. Magruder, and A. B. Mullett. Governor Cooke received his commission February 28, and assumed the duties of his office May 15, 1871, although the Territorial government did not get into operation until June 1 following. The Legislative Assembly of this Territorial government consisted of seventeen members, and the House of Delegates of forty-six members. The delegate in Congress was Hon. Norton P. Chipman. The delegate in Congress and the forty-six members of the House of Delegates were elected by the people. Governor Cooke resigned his position September 13, 1873, and was succeeded by Alexander R. Shepherd, who served until June 20, 1874, when by reason of an investigation by Congress into the operations of the Territorial government, made at the instance of certain citizens of the District, who could not then, but who can now, appreciate the great work that was being accomplished in the way of improving the city, which had ever since it came into existence rested with more or less complacency in a quagmire of lethargy and general dilapidation, the Territorial form of government was abolished and a government by commissioners established in its place; though to the impetus given to the improvement of the city during the brief period of the Territorial government by the large brain, splendid executive ability, correct appreciation of the necessities of the District, and the indomitable energy of Alexander R. Shepherd, do the inhabitants of the city owe its present beauty and magnificence, and the world-wide reputation it now enjoys as one of the finest capital cities of the world. This enviable reputation is now and must continue to be inseparable from the name of the city of Washington so long as it shall remain the Nation's Capital. But the improvements brought about through the impetus thus given to the work by Governor Shepherd will be more fully and appreciatively treated in another chapter by a more competent hand.

The following are the names of the officers of the District of Columbia under its Territorial form of government:

Delegate to Congress — Norton P. Chipman, from April 21, 1871, to March 4, 1875.

Secretaries — Norton P. Chipman, from March 2, 1871, to April 21, 1871; Edwin L. Stanton, from May 19, 1871, to September 22, 1873; Richard Harrington, from September 22, 1873, to June 20, 1874.

Board of Public Works — Henry D. Cooke, while Governor; Alexander R. Shepherd, from March 16, 1871, to September 13, 1873; S. P. Brown, from March 16, 1871, to September 13, 1873; A. B. Mullett, from March 16, 1871, to June 2, 1873; James A. Magruder, from March 16, 1871, to June 20, 1874; Adolph Cluss, from January 2, 1873, to June 20, 1874; Henry A. Willard, from May 22, 1873, to June 20, 1874; John B. Blake, from September 13, 1873, to June 20, 1874.

Board of Health — N. S. Lincoln, from March 15, 1871, to March 22, 1871; T. S. Verdi, from March 15, 1871, to July 1, 1878; H. A. Willard, March 15, 1871; John M. Langston, from March 15, 1871, to November 10, 1877; John Marbury, Jr., from March 15, 1871, to July 1, 1878; D. Willard Bliss, from May 23, 1872, to July 1, 1878; Robert B. Warden, from November 10, 1877, to July 1, 1878; Christopher C. Cox, from April 3, 1871, to July 1, 1878.

By the act of Congress of June 20, 1874, which abolished the Territorial form of government for the District, the executive municipal authority was vested temporarily in three commissioners, appointed by the President of the United States. These commissioners were Hon. William Dennison, of Ohio; Henry T. Blow, of Missouri; and John H. Ketcham, of New York. The first of these served from July 1, 1874, to July 1, 1878; the second, from July 1, 1874, to December 31, 1874; and the third, from July 3, 1874, to June 30, 1877. Seth L. Ledyard was commissioner from January 18, 1875, to June 30, 1878; Thomas B. Bryan from June 30, 1877, to July 1, 1878; and Captain Richard L. Hoxie from July 2, 1874, to July 1, 1878.

The temporary form of government gave way at this time to a permanent form of government provided for by an act of Congress passed June 11, 1878. This government is administered by a board of three commissioners, two of whom are appointed from civil life by the President of the United States and confirmed by the United States Senate, and the third is detailed from time to time by the President from the Engineer Corps of the army. These commissioners control, either directly or indirectly, the appointments to and removals from office in the District, except in case of teachers and janitors in the public schools. The commissioners under the permanent form of government have been as follows

Josiah Dent, from July 1, 1878, to July 17, 1882; Seth L. Phelps, July 1, 1878, to November 29, 1879; Major William J. Twining, June 29, 1878, to May 5, 1882; Thomas P. Morgan, November, 29, 1879, to March 8, 1883; Major Garrett J. Lydecker, May 11, 1882, to April 1, 1886; Joseph R. West, July 14, 1882, to July 22, 1885; James B. Edmunds, March 3, 1883, to April 1, 1886; William B. Webb, July 20, 1885, to May 21, 1889; S. E. Wheatley, March 8, 1886, to May 21, 1889; Colonel William Ludlow, April 1, 1886, to January 26, 1888; Major Charles W. Raymond, January 26, 1888, to February 14, 1890; Henry M. Robert, February 14, 1890, to October 14, 1891; Lemon G. Hine, May 21, 1889, to October 1, 1890; John W. Douglass, May 21, 1889, to the present time; John W. Ross,[1] October 1, 1890, to the

---

[1] John W. Ross, commissioner of the District of Columbia, was born in Lewistown, Illinois, June 23, 1841. He attended private schools in Lewistown, and took a four years' course at the Illinois College, and one year at the Harvard Law School. He was admitted to the bar, upon examination in open Supreme Court, at Springfield, in 1866, and was elected as a Democrat to the Illinois Legislature in 1868, and again in 1870. He removed to Washington in 1873, and since that time has resided here, and has been engaged most of the time in the practice of the law. In 1883, he was appointed lec-

present time; Captain William T. Rossell, October 14, 1891, to the present time.

Dr. William Tindall has been secretary to the commissioners since July 1, 1878. Dr. Smith Townsend was health officer from 1878 to 1891. The attorneys of the District have been Edwin L. Stanton, William Birney, Alfred G. Riddle, and George C. Hazleton.

On a preceding page has been given the date of the appointment of the first police force. By an act of Congress passed in 1842, an auxiliary guard, or watch, was established for the protection of public and private property against incendiaries, and the enforcement of police regulations in the city of Washington was also provided for. This auxiliary guard was made to consist of a captain, appointed by the Mayor, at a salary of $1,000 per year, and fifteen other persons, to be employed by the captain, five of them at a salary of $35 per month and the other ten at a salary of $30 per month. They were to occupy such building as might be furnished by the United States or by the corporation of Washington, and which might be approved of by the President of the United States. They were to be subject to such rules and regulations as might be prescribed by a board to consist of the Mayor of Washington, the United States attorney of the District of Columbia, and the attorney for the corporation of Washington, with the approval of the President of the United States; and the sum of $7,000 was appropriated by the act for the purchase of the necessary implements to be used in the discharge of the duties of the police. Annual appropriations were made of the same amount for the next ten years.

An act was passed March 3, 1851, authorizing an additional force of fifteen men, and the bill placed in the hands of the Mayor the authority to appoint them. The compensation of half this force was fixed at $500 per annum, and that of the other half at $400 per annum. The annual appropriation under this legislation was $15,000.

August 4, 1854, an act was passed increasing the appropriation, and making the salaries of the private members of the force all $500 per year. On January 3, 1855, the salary was again increased to $600 per year.

turer in the law school of the Georgetown University, and served in that capacity until 1888. He was appointed trustee of the public schools of the District of Columbia in 1886, and served three years as president of the school board, and until appointed commissioner of the District of Columbia. He was appointed postmaster of the city of Washington by President Cleveland, and qualified February 1, 1888, and served in that capacity until October 1, 1890, when he was appointed by President Harrison commissioner of the District of Columbia.

March 3, 1859, Congress passed an act appropriating $12,530.52, "to repay to the corporation the compensation of twenty policemen from July 13, 1858, to June 30, 1859," and continuing the force of twenty policemen, and on June 20, 1860, an appropriation for the year was made of $32,400.

By the act of August 6, 1861, the Metropolitan Police District of the District of Columbia was created, comprising the corporations of Washington and Georgetown, and the county outside of the cities' limits. By this act the President was authorized to appoint, by and with the advice and consent of the Senate, five commissioners,—three from Washington, one from Georgetown, and one from the county,— who, together with the Mayors of the two cities, were to constitute a board of police, selecting a president and treasurer from among themselves, the treasurer to give bonds in the sum of $10,000. The board was empowered to appoint a police force, to consist of a super-intendent, ten sergeants, and a patrol force not to exceed one hundred and fifty men for the regular service.

The board was authorized to divide the District into precincts, not to exceed ten in number; to establish stations; to detail and change sergeants and patrolmen to such part of the District as they might deem advisable; and to appoint and swear in any number of additional patrolmen for special service. The superintendent of police was to receive a salary of $1,500 per year, each sergeant $600, and each patrolman $480. All rewards or fees, and all moneys arising from the sale of unclaimed goods, were to constitute the "Policemen's Fund," which was to be used to defray the necessary expenses of any member of the police force disabled in the discharge of his duty.

The board of metropolitan police was declared to possess powers of general police supervision and inspection over all licensed venders, hackmen, cartmen, dealers in second-hand merchandise, intelligence offices, auctioneers of watches and jewelry, suspected private banking houses, and other doubtful establishments within the District of Columbia. It was also authorized to prepare and publish all the laws and ordinances in force in the District of Columbia having relation and being applicable to police and health matters, as the police code of the District, which was constituted the law upon such matters as it contained.

June 25, 1864, an act was passed authorizing an increase of fifty per cent. in the compensation of the entire police force, to commence July 1, 1864, such increase to be borne by the cities of the District and the county in proportion to the number of patrolmen allowed to each, and a special tax not exceeding one-fourth of one per cent. An act was passed July 23, 1866, authorizing a large additional force and prescribing the titles of the members, — major, captains, lieutenants, sergeants, and privates. Each member was to provide a uniform at his own expense. Private detectives were prohibited, except upon special authority, and these private detectives were required to give bonds in the sum of $10,000 for the faithful performance of their duties, and to be subject to the control of the board of police.

By an act of March 2, 1867, no one could serve as policeman or watchman who had not served in the army or navy of the United States and received an honorable discharge. By an act of July 20, 1868, an appropriation was made of $211,050 for salaries and other necessary expenses. The corporate authorities of the two cities and the county were authorized to levy a special tax of one-third of one per cent., to pay their proportionate expenses. The appropriations made by Congress for the support of the police force of the District from August 23, 1842, to the close of the year 1877, were $2,890,350 21.

By an act of March 3, 1875, it was provided that the duties devolved upon and the authority conveyed to the board of metropolitan police by law for police purposes should extend to and include all public squares and places.

By an act of June 11, 1878, a permanent form of government for the District of Columbia was established, which provided that from and after July 1, 1878, the board of metropolitan police should be abolished, and all the powers and duties exercised by them should be transferred to the commissioners of the District, who were granted authority to employ such officers and agents and to adopt such provisions as might be necessary to carry into effect the powers and duties devolved upon them by the act; and they were empowered to fix the salaries to be paid to the officers and privates of the metropolitan police until otherwise provided by law; and all expenses previously incurred by the General Government for the metropolitan police were afterward to be paid by the Government of the District, according to the act of June 20, 1878.

A question afterward arose as to whether the District commissioners, under the above legislation, could legally appoint upon the police force men who had not served in the army or navy of the United States. The matter was brought to a legal test by a suit for salary by a driver of an ambulance who had not so served. The decision of the Supreme Court of the District of Columbia was in favor of the driver, and the District commissioners were willing to accept the decision as settling the question, but the First Comptroller of the Treasury refused to pay the account, and appealed the case to the Supreme Court of the United States. The decision of this court, rendered February 1, 1892, was to the effect that the law of June 11, 1878, repealed the army and navy limitation, and gave the commissioners full power to employ on the police force whomsoever they thought suitable to serve thereon.

The police force of the District of Columbia at the present time is as follows: One major and superintendent, William G. Moore; 2 captains, 39 lieutenants, 1 chief and property clerk, 3 clerks, 4 surgeons, 32 sergeants, 415 privates, 20 station keepers, 10 laborers, 2 messengers, 1 van driver, 1 ambulance driver, 2 assistant ambulance drivers, 13 drivers of patrol wagons, and 3 police matrons. The total annual cost of maintaining this force is about $500,000. During the year ending in 1891, although there was in certain instances a slight increase in the number of crimes committed, as in disorderly conduct and drunkenness, yet on the whole there was a general decrease in the amount of crime. In this connection it is deemed proper to state that the police force of the city of Washington is noted for its efficiency, as well as for its orderly and gentlemanly conduct.

The ancient springs of the District of Columbia in the early day were as follows: The most important one was that on Smith's farm, at the head of North Capitol Street, above Boundary Street. It had a great flow of water. From it there were two mains—one down North Capitol Street to the Capitol grounds, which still supplies the grotto with its constant flow of water, and the other going down Pennsylvania Avenue nearly to Fifteenth Street. Then there was a spring in the City Hall lot, about fifty feet west of the building, which supplied pumps on Second Street as far as the Lafayette House, and another line of pipe went down Louisiana Avenue to Seventh Street. South of the City Hall, on C Street, between Four and a Half and Sixth streets, was another famous spring. It was on a lot owned by the corporation, and upon which the building first used for a police court stood afterward.

There was also a spring under where the Masonic Temple stands [in 1884], which was tapped by pipes running along F Street and down Ninth and Tenth streets. There was a spring in Franklin Square, and another just outside the square. The old Carroll Spring on Capitol Hill, located at the intersection of New Jersey and New York avenues, had a most copious flow, and the water was both cool and of excellent quality. The best spring in the northwestern part of the city was on P Street, near the Georgetown bridge, which for many years supplied the Metropolitan street-car stables, in Georgetown, by a pipe under the bridge. There is a splendid spring on Virginia Avenue, between Twenty-sixth and Twenty-seventh streets, near the gas works.

The springs above described supplied the necessities of the inhabitants for several years, but at length they of course became inadequate. In 1831, Congress appropriated $12,000 to bring to the Capitol the waters from one of the springs of the Tiber, rising on the farm of J. A. Smith, about a mile away. The water was conducted in iron pipes from the reservoir at the head of the stream, and supplied the marble fountain at the foot of the terrace on the west front of the Capitol, the surplus being discharged into basins, one on the east and one on the west front of the building. The one on the west contained seventy-eight thousand eight hundred and twenty-seven gallons, and that on the east one hundred and eleven thousand two hundred and forty-one gallons. In 1849, the yield of the fountain was thirty-two gallons per minute.

It was about this time that the necessity for a larger supply of water began to attract serious attention. Robert Mills, engineer and architect of the city of Washington, wrote and had published a series of able articles on the entire subject of water supply, giving a succinct history of waterworks from the most ancient times down to the then present. The rare gift of nature to the city of Washington in the form of underground springs, which rose up wherever a well was dug, and which in several instances overflowed their margins, and which, ever since the settlement of the place, had satisfied the inhabitants, was a remarkable circumstance. The founders of the city, when they laid it out, especially noticed the abundant supply of pure water in the springs of the Tiber, and in others in various parts of the city and outside thereof. After the fire which destroyed the Treasury building, and the General Post Office and Patent Office buildings, Mr. Mills, as architect of the city, recommended that a supply of water should be conducted from the basins at the Capitol to those buildings, where, being under a head of sixty feet, the water might be conducted to their top by means of hose. It was in this connection that Congress appropriated the money above mentioned to carry the suggestion into execution, and in order to benefit that portion of the city through which the pipe passed, fire plugs were stationed at proper distances, which were accessible in case of need.

On March 30, 1830, Mr. Mills addressed a letter to Hon. G. C. Verplanck, chairman of the Committee on Public Buildings, upon the subject of supplying the city of Washington with water, the sources being, first, the Tiber, and second, Rock Creek. With reference to the Tiber, it was the nearer to the Capitol, and its waters could be brought there at the least expense; but the supply was limited, and it was not certain that its yield would be permanent. The main head springs of this creek were three in number, and from them the water flowed in quantity as follows: From No. 1, 7 gallons per minute; from No. 2, 3 gallons per minute; and from No. 3, 4½ gallons per minute. Total flow, 14½ gallons per minute. The expense of bringing the water from these springs to the Capitol would be $43,710.50, exclusive of the purchase of the springs. The water of Rock Creek was looked upon by Mr. Mills very favorably as a source of supply, not only for the then present, but for the future, and the high grounds were suitable for the formation of a reservoir from which to supply the entire city; and the conduit pipes, before reaching the Capitol, would pass through the city, instead of passing through vacant territory, as in case of drawing water from the head springs of the Tiber. The entire cost of conducting the water from Rock Creek, he thought, would not exceed $50,000.

On February 14, 1853, Brigadier-General Joseph G. Totten made a report to the Secretary of War on the subject of supplying water to the cities of Washington and Georgetown, embodying in his report that to himself of Montgomery C. Meigs, a synopsis of which is here introduced. The aqueduct from Rock Creek, complete, to the Capitol and Navy Yard, and public buildings, would cost $1,258,863. The supply of water in winter and spring would be 26,732,300 gallons, and would run down in summer to 9,860,000 gallons. The Little Falls work, complete, would cost $1,597,415, and the supply would be steadily 12,000,000 gallons. The Great Falls project would cost $1,-921,244, and the constant daily supply would be 36,000,000 gallons. This latter project had numerous and great advantages over every other. The work of constructing the Washington aqueduct, which was to supply the citizens of Washington and Georgetown with water, was assigned to the Engineering Department, and General Totten, with the approval of the Secretary of War, placed Captain Montgomery C. Meigs in charge.

But this work, so much needed by the two cities of Washington and Georgetown, received a backset in April, 1853, by the refusal of the Legislature of Maryland to permit the Washington aqueduct to convey the water from the Great Falls to these cities. This was a great surprise and a great disappointment. The construction of this aqueduct was looked upon as a more important measure than the extension of the Capitol, which was then going on. There would be expended nearly a million dollars between the District of Columbia and the Great Falls, and nearly another million within the limits of the District itself. It would make the city a far more desirable place of residence, increasing the comfort and health of all the citizens, and cheapening insurance, besides increasing the safety of all the buildings, public and private, from fires. Better counsel, however, soon prevailed in the legislature, and on May 3, 1853, an act was passed consenting to the draft of water from the Potomac and its conveyance to the District of Columbia.

Preparations, therefore, went on for the beginning of work on the proposed aqueduct. November 8, 1853, was a memorable day in the history of Washington and Georgetown; for on that day work was at length commenced upon the great aqueduct that was to bring in to them the waters of the Potomac. The President of the United States and a portion of his cabinet, with the municipal authorities of Washington, went by steamboat and pack horses from Georgetown up the Chesapeake and Ohio Canal to Crommelin, near the Great Falls of the Potomac, in the vicinity of which the aqueduct commenced. The spot having been designated by a flag erected upon a pole, the President approached it, and surrounded by a large concourse of people, the exercises were opened with a prayer from Rev. Dr. Pyne, of St. John's Episcopal Church, Washington, after which Captain M. C. Meigs made a short address. President Pierce then broke ground with the spade presented to him for that purpose. Hon. Jefferson Davis followed the example of the President; Senator Douglas, of Illinois, did the same, and then John W. Maury, Mayor of Washington, W. W. Seaton, the late Mayor, and others, among them being Thomas Ritchie, Mr. Walter, and Captain William Easby, followed the same example.

Passing over the Rock Creek aqueduct, as it would have been had it been constructed, and confining ourselves to the Potomac aqueduct, we have from Captain Meigs's report the following synopsis: That while from a casual survey of the route necessary to be followed it would appear almost impossible to construct an aqueduct along the Potomac River, on account of the jagged and vertical precipices, etc., that would have to be overcome; yet upon a careful and mathematical survey, there were really but few difficulties that an engineer would not delight in overcoming; because the rocky precipices and difficult passages were really below the level which would naturally be selected for the conduit. There were indeed necessary several tunnels, of an average length of 220 feet, and but three bridges, only one of these being large enough to make its erection an object of ambition to an engineer. The distance in a right line from the beginning of the conduit to the north end of the Georgetown aqueduct was 11¾ miles, and the length of the conduit 14 miles to the same point. The elevation of the water in the Potomac River opposite the fifteenth milestone on the canal, which is somewhat less than three-fourths of a mile above Collins's Great Falls House, is at low water 147 feet above high tide at Washington; and there was an average depth of water in the river of 5 feet. As the water was not high enough to allow the conduit to be constructed above the canal, it was necessary to convey the water under the canal in large iron pipes to the gate house on the opposite side, where regulating gates, worked by screws, controlled the quantity of water admitted. From this gate house the water was to be conducted in a circular brick conduit, 7 feet in diameter, afterward changed to 9 feet in diameter, because while the expense of constructing the conduit would be increased by about one-sixth, yet the capacity of the conduit would be doubled. With a slope of .792 feet to the mile, the water running at a depth of 6 feet, the 7-foot conduit would discharge 36,000,000 gallons per day, while the 9-foot conduit would discharge 67,596,000 gallons per day.

After leaving the river, there are two tunnels near the pipe chamber, one 215 feet long, the other 272 feet long. Then the line is principally in rock, but soon crossing a ravine and small brook by an arch of 24-foot span. It then passes through two tunnels, one 115 feet, the other 61 feet in length. At 5¾ miles from the dam, it crosses Mountain Spring Brook by an arch of 50-foot span; and thence proceeds in easy cuttings, until at the end of 7 miles it comes to the valley of the Cabin John Branch, the only serious obstacle in the way. Over this branch it was proposed to construct an aqueduct of the following description: Length, 482 feet; greatest height, 101 feet; width, 20 feet; six semi-circular arches, each of 60-foot span, resting upon piers 7 feet thick by 20 feet long at the top and varying in height, the highest being 32½ feet. Its estimated cost was $72,400. This plan was, however, changed, as will be seen later on. Near the end of the tenth mile the line reaches the valley of Little Falls Branch, a dam across which — 41 feet in height and 200 feet long — floods a little more than 50 acres of land, which makes a fine receiving reservoir of an irregular shape, 140 feet above high tide, and having a capacity of 163,000,000 gallons.

The objects proposed to be accomplished in the construction of this receiving reservoir were to furnish storage capacity and to secure a large area in which the water might have opportunity to deposit its impurities. The first object was accomplished, but the second object, after an experience of four years, from 1860 to 1864, was found to be impracticable, for the reason that four or five streams were constantly discharging into the basin, each draining a hilly country, and consequently swollen and muddied by every rain; and besides, the hillsides discharged their surface water into the reservoir. The water for the most part was shallow, the area compared with the shore line was small, and the banks were unprotected from the wash of the waves.

Just before reaching this receiving reservoir the conduit passes through a tunnel of more than one thousand two hundred feet in length, but after leaving it there is no further tunneling. Below this reservoir there is a distributing reservoir, near Drover's Rest, above Georgetown. This distributing reservoir is on the thirteenth mile from the upper end of the aqueduct.

The first appropriation made for the prosecution of this work, by Congress, was on September 30, 1850, the amount being $500. The next appropriation was $5,000, made April 30, 1852. This appropriation was made to enable the President of the United States to have the survey of the route made. The next appropriation was made in 1853, of $100,000, for the purpose of beginning the work. The date of breaking ground has already been given, as has also the date of Maryland's consent to the construction of the aqueduct. Virginia, on March 3, 1854, gave her consent to the purchase of a tract of land for the Virginia abutment of the dam at Great Falls. A tract of land for this purpose, also a tract of several acres containing the quarries necessary for the construction of the dam, were purchased of Virginia, and also the lands along the line of the aqueduct in Maryland from the Great Falls to the District of Columbia.

Contracts were entered into for the several portions of the aqueduct with Degges & Smith, of Washington, District of Columbia, and of Baltimore, Maryland, respectively, January 23, 1854, for the delivery of from twenty-five millions to forty millions of brick along the line of the canal, at $8.75 per thousand; May 28, 1854, with Felix Duffin, of Ohio, for the graduation and culverts, including the 1-foot culverts; May 19, 1855, with N. H. Decker, of Albany, New York, for graduation and culverts; June 16, 1855, with Patrick Crowley, for tunnels; and November 24, 1855, with Hugh L. Gallaher, of Virginia, to take up and complete the work contracted to be done by Felix Duffin, Mr. Duffin having failed to carry out his contract.

During the fall of 1853 and the year 1854, the work was prosecuted with diligence. Connection with the Potomac River under the canal was made, and tunnels Nos. 1, 2, and 3 were commenced, about four hundred and fifty feet being pierced, and a small portion of the brick conduit built. No appropriation having been made in 1854, work was suspended until after March 4, 1855, when Congress made an appropriation of $250,000. With this sum most of the lands in Maryland were purchased, 827 feet of tunnels pierced, 1,800 feet of conduit built, 13 culverts nearly completed, together with the embankments over them, and most of the other tunnels in Maryland begun. The crossing under the canal at the Great Falls was completed, and the canal itself restored to its full dimensions.

In 1856, the work was again suspended for want of an appropriation. March 3, 1857, an appropriation of $1,000,000 was made, most of the lands in the District of Columbia purchased, contracts made for the great conduit, the receiving reservoir made, the arch stones at Cabin John Bridge, 12 inch pipes, and bridges Nos. 1 and 2 nearly completed, Nos. 3 and 5 commenced, 6,104 feet of conduit built, 2,034½ feet of tunnels pierced, and the Potomac dam commenced. During the winter of 1857–58 a large quantity of stone was quarried and deposited along the line of the aqueduct, and preparations made for the work of 1858. June 12, 1858, an appropriation was made of $800,000, the remainder of the lands in the District of Columbia purchased, all the culverts completed, the conduit nearly finished, bridges Nos. 3 and 5 completed, bridge No. 4 (Cabin John) commenced, and the granite arch cut, and part of the rubble arch was built. In the spring of 1859, the Rock. Creek Bridge was well advanced, the tunnels, except No. 1, finished, waste weirs Nos. 1 and 3 completed and No. 2 sufficiently so for use, the 12-inch main pipe laid, and the 30-inch pipe commenced. September 27, 1858, the receiving reservoir being finished, the sluice gate was closed. December 8, the water rose to the bottom of the conduit, and on January 3, 1859, it was introduced into the pipes supplying the cities.

In the spring of 1859, the work was again suspended for want of funds. In June, 1860, an appropriation was made of $500,000, "to be expended according to the plans and estimates of Captain Meigs, and under his superintendence." This provision caused some official comment, President Buchanan, in a message, calling attention to the fact that if strictly construed it, in effect, took away from the President the power of appointing officers of the army, and was therefore a usurpation of executive authority, hence unconstitutional. He, however, could not think it possible that Congress intended to encroach upon his powers, and so construed the law as he supposed Congress intended to enact it.

Upon July 17, 1860, Captain W. H. Benham was appointed chief engineer, and in December following he was succeeded by Lieutenant Morton. February 22, 1861, General M. C. Meigs again resumed charge of the aqueduct. Work on the aqueduct was resumed in the fall of 1860, under Captain Benham, who expended while in charge $98,345.11; Lieutenant Morton expended while in charge $55,441.40; and General Meigs in 1861 spent $81,802.61.

Up to June 17, 1862, the total appropriations had been $2,900,000, and the total expenditures $2,675,832.53. February 22, 1864, S. Seymour, engineer of the aqueduct, reported that an ample supply of water for the cities of Washington and Georgetown could be obtained from the Potomac by the erection of a tight dam from the Maryland side of the Potomac to Conn's Island, which would give a height of six feet of water in the aqueduct, and yield a daily supply of 65,000,-000 gallons, which was more by one-third than was used in the city of New York in 1861, when its population was over 800,000. The engineer, at the same time, estimated that the amount necessary to complete the work was $546,433.62, making the entire cost of the aqueduct $3,446,433.62, or, in round numbers, $3,500,000. And upon making a comparison with twenty other large cities in this country, this would be less than half the average cost of their waterworks, and the capacity of the Washington aqueduct would be more than double the average capacity of theirs.

Washington and Georgetown were no exception to the rule that cities waste a vast amount of water distributed to their inhabitants by means of waterworks. In 1870, this subject began to attract attention here, General N. Michler saying that the two cities consumed about 12,000,000 gallons per day. A large portion of this amount was consumed in the Government departments, especially in the Navy Yard and at the Treasury. On Capitol Hill and other high points, the supply was not equal to the demand, because of the reckless and wasteful use of the water in the lower portions of the city. To remedy this waste, the General recommended the adoption of the meter system.

According to Colonel Casey, who had charge of the aqueduct in 1879, there had been expended in the construction and maintenance of the waterworks, prior to June 30, 1879, by the United States, $3,784,546.72, by the corporation of Washington, $1,313,351.17, and by Georgetown, about $40,000, though the precise amount spent by Georgetown could not be ascertained, because her accounts had been so poorly kept. The aggregate expenditure had been $5,137,897.89. The total receipts had been $1,104,956.56.

The first mention of water rents, in legislation referring to this system, was in the third section of an act of Congress entitled, "An Act to Provide for the Care and Preservation of the Works Constructed by the United States for Bringing the Potomac Water into the Cities of Washington and Georgetown, for the Supply of said Water for all Governmental Purposes, and for the Use and Benefit of the Inhabitants of said Cities." This act was passed March 3, 1859. By this act the corporations of the two cities were authorized to establish a scale of annual rates for the supply of water, apportioned to the different classes of buildings, and to the uses for dwellings, manufactories, etc., and their exposure to fire; and to alter or amend their ordinances relating to the supply of water, so as to increase or reduce the rates, and generally to enact such laws as might be necessary to secure a supply of pure and wholesome water to the inhabitants of the two cities. The corporate authorities of the two cities were also, by this act, authorized to borrow money not to exceed $150,000 for Washington and $50,000 for Georgetown, redeemable within ten years, out of water rents.

The next legislation of Congress on the subject of water rents was on March 3, 1863, when an act was passed, authorizing the corporation of Washington to levy and collect a water tax on all real property within the corporate limits of the city, "which binds on or touches on any avenue, street, or alley, in which a main water pipe has been laid, or hereafter may be laid, by the United States, or by the corporation of Washington." This same act also provided for the "erection, maintenance, and efficiency of fire plugs throughout the city," and authorized the corporation of Washington to "levy and collect a special annual tax on all buildings within five hundred feet of any water pipe, into which, or the premises connected therewith, the water has not been introduced, and the owner or occupiers of which do not pay any annual water rate, etc., and which tax shall not be more than $5, nor less than $1." The same act also provided that the water tax collected under it should be constituted a fund, to be used exclusively to defray the cost of distributing the water, etc.

Georgetown, in carrying out the provisions of this act, assessed the property owners the full cost of laying the water pipes in that city, and thus relieved themselves of the necessity of establishing a water rent.

An ordinance of the city of Washington, passed June 2, 1859, provided for the appointment of a water registrar, and imposed upon him the duty of assessing water rates, according to the tariff established by the ordinances of the city, and of making out and presenting to the Mayor annually a full report of all his proceedings in connection with the duties of his office. It was also made the duty of the Mayor to appoint four suitable citizens of Washington, who, together with the Mayor, should constitute the water board of the city.

By a law passed July 14, 1870, the engineer of the Washington aqueduct was required to lay from the distributing reservoir to Capitol Hill an iron pipe, or main, thirty-six inches in diameter, the entire cost of which was to be borne proportionately by the corporations of Washington and Georgetown, the water rates to be increased to such an amount as might be necessary.

By 1879 the question of an increased water supply became one of great importance. The daily supply for the past six years had been as follows: In 1874, 17,554,848 gallons; in 1875, 21,000,000 gallons; in 1876, 24,177,797 gallons; in 1877, 23,252,932 gallons; in 1878, 24,885,945 gallons; in 1879, 25,947,642 gallons. When the proper deduction was made by the United States, viz., 2,626,188 gallons, there were left 23,321,454 gallons, which amount was consumed by the inhabitants of the two cities. This was an average of 155½ gallons per head for each person, while in twenty other cities of the United States the average number of gallons used by each inhabitant ranged from 25 in Providence, Rhode Island, to 119 in Chicago, the average in these twenty large cities being 58½ gallons per head, a little more than one-third as much as was used in Washington and Georgetown.

An increased supply of water was therefore an apparent necessity, and the commissioners of the District of Columbia recommended the extension of the conduit from the distributing reservoir to a point north of the city and east of Seventh Street, and the building there of a large reservoir, to be connected by a four-foot main along New Jersey Avenue with the principal mains then maintained from the vicinity of L and G streets. The total cost of the extension of the conduit was estimated at $554,731.41; the cost of the four-foot main was estimated at $91,298; and the cost of completing the dam at Great Falls was estimated at $200,000, making the total cost of these three items $846,029.41. The commissioners also recommended the building of an additional reservoir, which would cost $462,512.50, making a total expenditure needed of $1,308,541.91. General Meigs was opposed to the reservoir north of the city, because in his opinion it would be a constant menace to the lives and property of the citizens.

One of the most remarkable structures in the world is "Cabin John Bridge," erected by General Meigs over Cabin John Run, at a distance of seven miles from Washington on the line of the aqueduct, for the purpose of carrying the aqueduct over the run. It is a stone structure, 584 feet in extreme length, and 101 feet high, above the stream. The arch proper is 200 feet wide at the base, and 50 feet high, and is believed to be the largest stone arch in the world. The thickness of the bridge above the arch is 14½ feet, and it is 20 feet wide.

Ever since the Potomac River water has been introduced into the District, there has been great interest taken by scientific men in the question as to the reasons for the impurities that at regular periods are noticeable therein, as well as by those who are compelled to use the water thus affected. In addition to its roiled and muddy appearance, there has been detected a fishy odor which is anything but pleasant. The chemist of the Engineer Department, in 1886, in referring to this odor, which is noticeable only occasionally, stated that all scientific men believed it to be due to the formation of microscopic *algæ*, such as *confervæ, oscillatoria*, and *protococci;* but there was no evidence, he said, to warrant the suspicion that the water would produce deleterious effects upon the health. He also explained the periodicity of the phenomenon of the muddy water by saying it was more noticeable during that portion of the year when most moisture falls, and said that the same thing was remarkable more or less in all parts of the world.

During the fiscal year ending June 30, 1890, a 48-inch main was constructed. It was begun in August, 1889, and so far completed by March 20, 1890, that the water was turned on, and the protracted famine of water at the Capitol building then came to an end. The meter system was introduced in 1888, and by June 30, 1890, there were 90 of them in operation, varying in size from ¾ of an inch to 6 inches in diameter. The prevailing sizes, however, were 1, 1½, and 2 inches, of which sizes there were 70 in all. The 48-inch main, in the relief it gave to the city, was a very gratifying improvement for the area supplied by the gravity system. The average quantity of water drawn daily from the gravity supply and delivered into the standpipe was in 1891

376,130 gallons, and the entire average daily amount of water used in the two cities of Georgetown and Washington at the present time is 38,000,000 gallons. In the latter part of 1891, there were 1,157 fire hydrants in service, and 287 public hydrants, the latter being largely used by the poorer people, who cannot afford to have the Potomac water introduced into their houses. There were, also, at that time (December 1, 1891), 264 public pumps in the District, the cool water supplied by which in the summer time is very acceptable to such as cannot afford the use of ice. The total number of houses in Georgetown and Washington which are supplied with Potomac water was at this same time 32,074, and the number of miscellaneous water takers was 5,174.

One of the first fires that occurred in the city of Washington was that which destroyed the building occupied by the War Department, and the one adjoining, November 8, 1800. The building in which the department was situated was owned by Joseph Hodgson, and upon the repeated petition of his widow, his legal representatives received $6,000 for the loss thus occasioned, in accordance with an act passed by Congress, May 7, 1822. Another extensive fire occurred January 20, 1801, in the Treasury Department, which was extinguished by the citizens with water buckets; but not until after several valuable books had been destroyed The necessity thus becoming apparent for organized protection against the ravages of fire led to the enactment of a law by the city authorities, January 10, 1803, which provided that every proprietor of a dwelling or business house should, prior to March 1 ensuing, provide at his own expense as many fire buckets of leather, containing two and a half gallons, as there were stories to his house, under a penalty of $1 for each bucket he did not provide as required by law; and all were required to keep these buckets in a conspicuous place, and send them to fires that might break out.

On July 24, 1804, the city was divided into fire wards, and fire companies provided for. All that part of the city west of Sixteenth Street constituted the first ward; that part bounded by Sixteenth Street on the west, by G Street on the south, and by Third Street on the east, constituted the second ward; that portion south of G Street constituted the third ward, and the rest of the city the fourth ward. Under this act, one individual in each ward was appointed to call the citizens together for the purpose of organizing themselves into fire companies, one in each ward. Each company was to elect annually one of its members as a member of a board of fire directors, which board should have general charge of the extinguishing of fires. Meetings were held then to organize companies, in accordance with the law. Union Fire Company was organized September 8, 1804. On December 31, 1814, this company had the engines of the Treasury Department placed in its charge. The apparatus of the companies then consisted of ordinary hand engines. The Union Fire Company was in existence until 1864, when, on account of many of its members having enlisted in the army of the Union, its organization ceased.

On December 18, 1837, a meeting was held at the Franklin Fire Company's Hall, to organize a regular fire department, and on January 4, 1838, the following officers were elected: Rev. French S. Evans, president; E. Hanley, vice-president; Charles Calvert, secretary; S. Stott, treasurer; and S. Drury, captain of engineers. Rev. Evans resigned his position February 13, and was succeeded by Mr. Hanley. The Perseverance Fire Company was also in existence at this time, and the Northern Liberties Fire Company was organized in 1840. The Columbia Fire Company was organized soon afterward.

In 1856, there were in existence the Union Fire Company, the Franklin Fire Company, the Perseverance Fire Company, the Northern Liberties Fire Company, the Columbia Fire Company, the Anacostia Fire Company, the American Hook and Ladder Company, and the Metropolitan Hook and Ladder Company.

September 15, 1859, the steam fire engine of the American Fire Company, of Philadelphia, was publicly exhibited near the corner of Pennsylvania Avenue and Tenth Street. A stream was thrown 110 feet in perpendicular height through a nozzle $1\frac{1}{8}$ inches in diameter, and a horizontal stream was thrown 198 feet. The stream thrown was equal in extinguishing power to at least three of those thrown by the most efficient hand engines in the city. The cost of the steam engine was $3,200.

January 21, 1860, the steam fire engine "Maryland," built by Poole & Hunt, of Baltimore, was tried in front of the Bank of Washington, and its efficiency conclusively established. The engine was attached to a street hydrant and the boiler filled directly from the street main. Steam was raised from this water and the engine put in operation in nine minutes from the lighting of the torch. The greatest distance played from the cistern was 241 feet horizontally, through a nozzle $1\frac{1}{4}$ inches in diameter. The weight of the engine was 6,000 pounds.

Under an act passed October 6, 1862, the fire department was reorganized, and named the Washington Fire Department. It was made to consist of five delegates from each of the companies then in

12

existence, the Columbia, the Union, the Franklin, the Anacostia, and the Perseverance Engine companies, and the Western Hose Company, the Metropolitan Hook and Ladder Company, and the American Hook and Ladder Company, and from such other companies as should afterward be organized. The department as thus organized was given power to make all by-laws and regulations needful for their own government, and to make nominations for a chief engineer on the last Monday in May in each year. An act for the purchase of one steam fire engine was introduced at the same time, which was afterward changed so as to provide for the purchase of three steam fire engines. On Monday, November 17, 1862, nominations were made for a chief engineer, and J. J. Peabody was chosen. Early in 1865, the first steam fire engine was received in the city, and it was tested March 31, that year. This engine threw a large stream of water from the corner of Eighth and E streets to the center of Seventh Street. Steamer No. 2 was also received early in the same year. This was a second-class engine with a double-acting plunger pump, and ten feet long, exclusive of the pole. At fair working speed it was capable of throwing four hundred gallons of water per minute, and of throwing the stream over two hundred feet. Engine No. 3 was tried March 14, and threw a stream through a one-inch nozzle two hundred and twenty feet. By April 1, 1865, the steam fire department was completed. These three steamers were located as follows: No. 1, at the Union Engine House, in the first ward; No. 2, at the Franklin Engine House, on D Street, between Twelfth and Thirteenth streets; and No. 3, on Capitol Hill. The Metropolitan Truck House was on Massachusetts Avenue, between Fourth and Fifth streets. Besides these, the Government steamers acted with the city fire department. The names of the Government steamers were the "General Meigs," the "Hibernia," and the "Rucker." J. H. Sessford was then chief engineer of the fire department. All the steamers in the city at that time were manufactured by the Amoskeag Company, of New Hampshire. On April 4, they were tested at the corner of Indiana Avenue and Four and a Half Street, to the satisfaction of all concerned.

In 1864, the Government disbanded its fire department, and in 1867 the city added two more steam engines to its number. In 1874, it was recommended to the city government that two additional engines be introduced, so as to bring the department up to the efficiency it had eight or ten years before, before the fire brigade of the Government was dispensed with. In 1891, on account of the steadily increasing extent of territory to be protected and of the increase in the number and size of the buildings within the territory thus increasing in extent, a movement was started to increase the capacity of the department by the organization of a new company in the northern section of the city. According to the report of Joseph Parris, chief engineer of the department, for June 30, 1891, there were then 8 engine houses and 2 truck houses in use. The engines in active use were as follows: 3 second size engines, 700 gallons per minute; 1 third size, 650 gallons per minute; 1 third size, 500 gallons per minute; and 3 fourth size, 450 gallons. Besides these, there were two engines in reserve. The force consisted of 1 chief engineer, 2 assistant engineers, 1 fire marshal, 1 clerk, 8 engine companies of 10 men each, 2 truck companies of 12 men each, 1 truck company of 11 men, 1 chemical company of 3 men, and 6 watchmen,—129 in all. The department had 53 horses. From this statement it is clear that the department is far too small for the extent of territory—72 square miles, containing nearly 50,000 houses, and a population of 235,000 — which it is required to protect. To meet possible exigencies, which it is only the part of a wise precaution to provide for, the number of engines should now be fifteen, with other apparatus in proportion.

In 1877, an improved fire alarm telegraph was introduced, and the expense incurred in its erection was much more than saved by its celerity and certainty in operation, enabling the firemen, as it did, to get almost immediate information of the breaking out of fires. In 1879, there were 80 automatic signal boxes, and in addition several of the police stations were used as fire alarm stations. During the year ending June 30, 1885, 46 new fire alarm signal boxes were added, of the latest improved Gamewell system. In the latter part of 1891, the fire alarm telegraph consisted of 7 signal and 4 alarm circuits, all metallic. There were 150 alarm boxes on the 7 signal circuits,—precisely twice as many as when the system was first introduced in 1877, but the number of circuits remained the same. On the 4 alarm circuits are the gongs and bells upon which are sounded the alarms for fires and the hours of the day. In all there were then 19 gongs and 4 bells. In addition to these, the department was using 233 sets of exchange telephones.

The city post office of Washington was established in 1795, with Thomas Johnson as postmaster, who was appointed September 1, that year. Prior to that time, the nearest post office was in Georgetown, mails being received there three times each week. Mr. Johnson kept the post office in his own residence on Pennsylvania Avenue, just west of Seventeenth Street. He served as postmaster until January 1, 1796, when Christopher Richmond was appointed. Mr. Richmond served until the 1st of the following October, when Lund Washington was appointed, and served until April 1, 1799. During Mr. Washington's time the post office was on New Jersey Avenue. Thomas Munroe was appointed postmaster April 1, 1799, and served continuously until April 29, 1829. Early in Mr. Munroe's term, the post office was removed to the west executive building, west of the White House. Subsequently, the room thus occupied by the post office being needed, a room was rented still further to the westward on Pennsylvania Avenue, to which the post office was removed. "Indeed, the officials generally of that day, like their successors, could not be convinced that the center of the city was to be found anywhere but in one end of it; and it was apprehended by many that our post office would at last be located in Georgetown, by way of promoting the public good of the citizens of Washington." Other removals occurred, and for a time the office was in a building on the north side of F Street, between Fourteenth and Fifteenth streets, and still later on a square further to the east.

At length Congress took up the question, and purchased Blodgett's or the Great Hotel for the use of the Post Office Department, on E Street, between Eighth and Ninth streets, for $15,000. This hotel was situated on the southwest portion of the present site of the Post Office Department. To this building the city post office was removed in 1812. Still later, a building was erected at the east end of the hotel building for the accommodation of the city post office, and both the General Post Office and the city post office remained here until the fire of 1835 destroyed the buildings.

April 29, 1829, Dr. William Jones was appointed to succeed Mr. Munroe. He served until March 23, 1839. It was during his incumbency that the fire mentioned above occurred. After this disaster, the post office was opened in the lower part of Mr. Seaver's brick house on Seventh Street, near the office of the *National Intelligencer*. It was afterward moved to the Masonic Hall building, where it remained until 1839, in which year Dr. Jones was succeeded by James S. Gunnell, who proposed to remove it to the westward. This proposition brought out several remonstrances from the people in the eastern portion of the city, who thought that the new postmaster had not learned that the tax on postage was quite heavy enough, without their being compelled to submit to additional burdens in having to bring into requisition the penny post. On the other hand, it was said that the proposed removal would greatly accommodate the President and the heads of the departments; but the *Intelligencer* said the location of the post office was preferable to the proposed one by about the ratio of three hundred to thirty-five. Notwithstanding the protests of the citizens of the eastern part of the city, the post office was removed to the basement of Carusi's saloon, standing on Eleventh Street below Pennsylvania Avenue, and it was afterward removed to the corner of Louisiana Avenue and Four and a Half Street, opposite the City Hall. From this location it moved to Seventh Street, between E and F streets, and thence to F Street, opposite the Patent Office. In November, 1879, it was removed to the Seaton building, on Louisiana Avenue, where it remained until 1892' when it was finally removed to the new and elegant building erected especially for its use on Pennsylvania Avenue, between Eleventh and Twelfth streets.

The postmasters since Mr. Gunnell have been as follows: Charles K. Gardner, March 31, 1845, to June 28, 1849; William A. Bradley, June 28, 1849, to May 27, 1853; James G. Berrett, Dr. William Jones, Lewis Clephane, Sayles J. Bowen, Colonel C. M. Alexander, Judge James M. Edmunds, May, 1869, till his death in 1880; Colonel Daniel B. Ainger, 1880 to 1882; Thomas L. Tulloch, November 25, 1882, to June 23, 1883, when he died; Colonel D. S. Parker, one week, when he declined to serve; F. B. Conger, June 29, 1883, to January 30, 1888; John W. Ross, January 31, 1888, to September 30, 1890; and finally Henry Sherwood, appointed September 12, 1890.

At the main office, and at the sixteen branch offices, there were sold $500,000 worth of stamps in 1891; but as about seventy-five per cent. of the mail matter sent out from this office goes free, it is safe to say that, were none of it sent free, the income of the office would be $2,000,000. The regular delivery division, in 1891, handled 45,900,-000 letters, cards, etc., while the special delivery division handled 63,783 letters. This feature of the mail service was established in 1885, and for the year ending June 30, 1886, the special delivery letters numbered only 25,154. The number of registry pieces handled by the main office and its branches for the year 1891 was 2,394,806, the value of which was nearly $530,000,000. The weight of this matter was about 1,568 tons for the year. The weight of the mail handled by the mailing division amounts to nearly 30 tons per day.

The free delivery system was introduced in Washington July 1, 1863. This was the first day on which this system was used anywhere in the United States, and there were six other cities in which it was introduced on that day. The number of carriers now employed in the city is one hundred and forty-three.

CHAPTER VII.

GROWTH AND IMPROVEMENT OF THE CITY.

FROM the nature of things, it was to be expected that the growth of the Capital City would be slow. The establishment of a great city in the midst of what was a wilderness, in every respect, apparently, unfitted for the location of such a city, was a project entirely new, and without a precedent in the world's history. In addition to this, the plan of the proposed city was one of a magnitude without a parallel. The idea of the projectors of this grand city embraced within its scope the erection of a site for a Federal city that was to have at the outset buildings not only sufficient for the accommodation of the Government of the new Republic, but buildings that should be in keeping with the grandeur of the nation that was to be. Especially prominent among these buildings were the Capitol, for the accommodation of the legislative branch of the Government, and the house for the President. Other buildings for other purposes were also projected upon a scale simpler, it is true, than these, but yet sufficiently grand and commodious for the purposes that they were to subserve. All the ideas of the men who were principally concerned about this plan of the future Capital of the Nation were grand in every way, and looked to a future that was far beyond the conception of most of their contemporaries. These ideas, too, were far beyond what the accommodation of the Government at that time demanded, and were, indeed, in the opinion of many, far beyond what it was probable the Government ever would demand.

The very fact that these public buildings were placed, upon the plan of the Capital City, in positions so remote from each other, was calculated to retard the rapid growth of the Federal City. About this matter the notions of those who were placed in charge of the plan of the city vere very diverse, and it was not until almost the last moment that it was determined to locate the buildings destined as the meeting place of Congress and the residence of the President at so great a distance from each other. At one time it was thought best that the President's House should be in close proximity to the Capitol, and after the present location of the President's House was determined upon, there were several projects for using that building in connection with the legislative or the judiciary branch of the Government. However this may have been, and howsoever various the projects of those who were concerned in the erection of the public buildings, the fact remains that in this wilderness, selected to be the site of the Federal Capital, these buildings were erected so far apart as to make their connection by an inhabited city a matter of the slow development of many years.

It will be apparent to anyone who considers all the circumstances surrounding these beginnings of the city of Washington, that its early inhabitants must necessarily have been only those who were attracted by the operations of the Government, and, at the outset, particularly with reference to the erection of the public buildings. It is true, there may have been a few attracted to the city by the prospect it afforded for speculation in the purchase of lots in the new city. It may have been that a number of persons who were connected with the General Government were at that early day induced to select places for their future residences in part with a view to convenience and the further view of their possible speculative value. It may be that there were persons induced by the hope that the future Capital would offer a place for investments of various kinds, and that all of these classes sought to become inhabitants of the future city. But however all this may have been, we know from the history of the times that for years the population of the city was very sparse and limited in numbers, and confined almost exclusively to the persons and their families who were in one way or another employed by the General Government.

It is matter of fact, too, that several attempts made toward the improvement of the city by the erection of dwelling houses in any considerable number with the view of making profit of them by renting them to the citizens of the town, ended in failure. The history of the times plainly shows that the earliest improvements of any account were made at what was known as Greenleaf's Point, and that as early as 1800 those who write about the city of Washington speak of the houses erected in this locality as the handsomest and most commodious in the city. This seems remarkable at this day, because these buildings have been for many years mere ruins, and the places they occupied are so remote from the present residence portions of the city that it is surprising to us that such buildings should have been erected. Not very remote from this section of the city, too, were the buildings on what was known as "Twenty Building Hill," about which there is a legend that a row of houses was built which were never occupied, and soon fell into ruin. All these buildings of which we have spoken were erected in the direction at least of the Capitol building. Perhaps this was because, as in the early years of our history Congress had been by far the most important part of the Government, it was thought the Capitol would be the center of the Federal City, and for that reason the tendency of interest was in that direction. In this connection it may not be amiss to state that the President of the United States himself selected a site and erected a building in the neighborhood of the Capitol, which was afterward known for many years as the "Washington Property," and is pointed out to-day to strangers as the house built by General Washington. In this neighborhood, too, were several other old residences. The Chief Justice of the District of Columbia, William Cranch, the clerk of the local courts, and several other notables resided in this locality.

On New Jersey Avenue, south of the Capitol, a number of fine old residences existed in that early day. Among them was that of Dr. Frederick May, the leading physician of the city, and a building occupied by one of the local banks. For many years after the organization of the local courts of the District of Columbia they occupied buildings near the Capitol. But notwithstanding this apparent, or perhaps we ought to say real, tendency of improvement in the direction of the Capitol building, for some reason, of which mention need not be made here, the real progress of the city took another direction, and passing over the difficulties that existed in the road between the Capitol and the President's residence, the city soon began to make the most rapid progress in the location or vicinity of the presidential mansion. A row of houses known as the "Six Buildings" was among the first indications of this progress, and another row known as the "Seven Buildings" was erected. Then came O'Neil's hotel, known in later times as Gadsby's Row, and several others of minor importance erected in this neighborhood. Pennsylvania Avenue, the great thoroughfare between the Capitol and the President's House, seemed to offer the most advantageous location for the erection of houses of business, and before long this street, which L'Enfant had selected as the grand passageway between the legislative and executive departments, notwithstanding its line lay through what seemed to be an impenetrable morass and swamp, gave promise of being what he said it must be, a fine avenue. The effect of all this was that the business portion of the city soon began to be established on this avenue, and the city grew fast along this line which connected the two residence portions of the city, the one in the vicinity of the Capitol, the other in the vicinity of the presidential mansion, and the streets adjoining it, more particularly to the north. This then became the section of the city first built up by those seeking residences here, more particularly those connected with the Government.

At this early time, as may readily be conjectured, there were comparatively few residences of special note, size, or elegance; but there were some of such beauty of design as to merit particular mention. One of the earliest houses built in the city of Washington was the residence of Colonel John Tayloe, at the intersection of New York Avenue and Eighteenth Street. It was erected by Colonel Tayloe at the suggestion of President Washington, his personal friend, who subsequently watched the progress of the work when he visited the embryo city. This house was so erected as to face the Arlington House, on the opposite side of the river. It is in shape an octagon, and has always been known by that name. It still stands, but is now a ruin. Notwithstanding, however, its present dilapidation, it will pay anyone interested in such matters to examine the beauty and completeness of its interior arrangement.

Another house erected in those early days was the mansion of General Van Ness, on what was known as Mansion Square, near the river at the foot of Seventeenth Street. This house was, when it was first erected, pronounced the most elegant private mansion in the country. It was designed by Latrobe, and cost its owner a very large sum.

Mr. Benjamin O. Tayloe, son of Colonel John Tayloe, writing about the city of Washington in 1800, makes use of the following language, which may appropriately be introduced in this connection:

"I came to Washington in 1801, and remember it literally as *rus in urbe*, containing but a few thousand inhabitants scattered about in single houses apart from each other or in occasional groups, chiefly in the vicinity of the public buildings, from Georgetown to the Navy

Yard. There was scarcely any pavement, except in front of detached houses. The distinguished John Cotton Smith told me that when he was a Senator from Connecticut he attended President Adams's levee in Washington, in 1801, and that members of Congress living, like himself, on Capitol Hill, found it necessary to send to Baltimore for hackney coaches to convey them to the President's House; and to avoid the swamps of Pennsylvania Avenue, they had to travel along F Street and the high grounds adjoining. During Mr. Monroe's administration I have seen carriages mired in Pennsylvania Avenue, even then almost impassable, the city at that time not having less than ten thousand inhabitants. During my childhood, the Navy, War, and Post Office departments and the city post office were in one building on the site of the present War Department. That was sunk to the eves in a hollow prepared for it to make it on a level, as now, with the State and Treasury departments. Between the latter and the Capitol, its two wings only erected, there was but one building on Pennsylvania Avenue, then used as an apothecary shop, at the corner of Ninth Street, a small frame building built for public convenience by Dr. Bullus, of the navy, who was stationed at the Navy Yard."

In sketching the improvements of the early days of Washington it seems to be every way proper to make mention of those historical mansions within a short distance of the presidential residence which still give evidence of the taste displayed by our ancestors in the erection and arrangement of their homes. In describing these houses we shall be pardoned if we confine ourselves to the houses built around what is known as Lafayette Square, directly in front of and forming a part of the grounds of the President's Mansion.

The first private house erected on this square was known as the Decatur House. It was erected by Commodore Decatur. It is an elegant house to-day, and has been the residence, at different times, of some of the most distinguished men of the country. After the melancholy death of Commodore Decatur, it was occupied by the British minister, Mr. Stratford Canning, afterward Lord Stratford de Redcliffe. It was afterward occupied by the Russian minister, by Mr. Van Buren when he was Secretary of State, and by Sir Charles Vaughn, the British minister. After this, it became the property of Mr. John Gadsby, and after being his residence for some time, it was occupied by the brothers King, sons of Rufus King, and then by Vice-President George M. Dallas. It was subsequently occupied by Hon. Judah P. Benjamin, since then well known as one of the chiefs of the Southern Confederacy.

Almost directly opposite the Decatur House is the house which was for so long a time the residence of Mr. W. W. Corcoran, and where he ended his days. It was erected by Thomas Swann, formerly of Alexandria, one of whose sons was at one time governor of Maryland, and the other a distinguished physician at Philadelphia. It was for some time the residence of Baron Krudener, the Russian minister, and it was afterward the residence of Hon. Aaron Vail, Charge d'Affaires at London, England, during the negotiations which resulted in the securing of the Smithson bequest. Mr. Webster, when Secretary of State under General Harrison, occupied this house, and when he vacated it, it became the property of Mr. Corcoran. While in his possession, during his absence in Europe, it was occupied by the Marquis de Montholon, Minister of France to the United States.

Situated on this square and fronting its northeast corner is what has always been known as the Madison House, now owned and occupied by the Cosmos Club. It was the residence of Mrs. Madison, the relict of President Madison. It was built by the Hon. Richard Cutts, formerly member of Congress from the district of Maine. This house was the property for many years of Admiral Wilkes, who commanded the great exploring expedition sent out by our Government in 1838. He died in this house.

Near this mansion is the house of Colonel Benjamin Ogle Tayloe, now the residence of Senator Cameron, of Pennsylvania, and which has been for the greater part of half a century the scene of magnificent hospitality.

Next to this is the house built by Commodore Rogers, which was the residence of Roger B. Taney while he was Secretary of the Treasury, and of Mr. Paulding when Secretary of the Navy. During the War it was occupied by Secretary Seward, and it was in this house that the attack was made upon the Secretary and his son, Frederick W. Seward, at the time of the assassination of President Lincoln. It is at the present time owned and occupied as a residence by Hon. James G. Blaine, Secretary of State.

On the north side of the square stands the mansion built by Matthew St. Clair Clarke, at one time clerk of the House of Representatives, and which to-day is one of the handsomest residences in the city. This house was occupied at one time by Lord Ashburton, Special Ambassador from Great Britain, and at another time by Sir Henry Bulwer, the British minister. It was also the residence of Mr. George Riggs, and later of Mr. Meredith, when Secretary of the Treasury.

Not far from this mansion, on the same side of the square, is the house in which Thomas Ritchie, the great editor, had his home. Mr. John Slidell, Senator from Louisiana, afterward distinguished in Confederate annals, occupied this house, and Mr. Welles, while he was Secretary of the Navy, made it his residence.

Without dwelling further on the particular improvements of Washington in the early day, it may be sufficient to give here such statistics as are accessible concerning the improvements made for a period of years reaching up to about the year 1850.

According to John Sessford, a citizen of Washington who made the collection of such statistics a specialty, the number of houses and other buildings erected in the years from 1819, when he counted them himself, to 1853, both years inclusive, was as follows:

In 1819, there were 2,028 houses, and 129 other shops and other buildings; in 1820, there were erected 113 houses and 9 shops; in 1821, 90 houses; in 1822, 113 houses, 7 shops, and 6 additions; in 1823, 69 houses, 7 shops, and 9 additions; in 1824, 49 houses, 6 shops, and 8 additions; in 1825, 68 houses, 15 shops, and 10 additions; in 1826, 102 houses, 23 shops, and 15 additions; in 1827, 123 houses, 25 shops, and 23 additions; in 1828, 158 houses, 23 shops, and 24 additions; in 1829, 148 houses, 15 shops, and 17 additions. The total number of houses, etc., erected in Washington during the decade ending in 1829 was 1,033 houses, 130 shops, and 112 additions.

In 1830, the number of houses erected was 178, shops 24, and additions 14; in 1831, 148 houses and 38 shops; in 1832, 62 houses and 12 shops; in 1833, 72 houses, 12 shops, and 12 additions; in 1834, 63 houses, 11 shops, and 7 additions; in 1835, 42 houses, 10 shops, and 18 additions; in 1836, 41 houses, 15 shops, and 15 additions; in 1837, 63 houses, 18 shops, and 9 additions; in 1838, 85 houses, 21 shops, and 9 additions; in 1839, 141 houses, 12 shops, and 14 additions. Total number of houses, etc., erected in Washington during the ten years ending in 1839, was, houses, 895; shops, 173, and additions, 98.

In 1840, there were erected 178 houses, 13 shops, and 14 additions; in 1841, 216 houses, 23 shops, and 13 additions; in 1842, 295 houses, 14 shops, and 21 additions; in 1843, 322 houses, 10 shops, and 23 additions; in 1844, 357 houses, 18 shops, and 24 additions; in 1845, 338 houses, 28 shops, and 24 additions; in 1846, 208 houses, 16 shops, and 17 additions; in 1847, 128 houses, 6 shops, and 9 additions; in 1848, 141 houses, 11 shops, and 29 additions; in 1849, 184 houses, 9 shops, and 17 additions. Total number of houses, etc., erected during the ten years, 2,367 houses, 148 shops, and 191 additions.

In 1850, there were erected 292 houses, 25 shops, and 24 additions; in 1851, 453 houses, 28 shops, and 44 additions; in 1852, 632 houses, 19 shops, and 3 additions; in 1853, 556 houses, 22 shops, and 51 additions.

In 1850, according to Mr. Sessford, there was erected the first four-story building in Washington, and during the year there were erected 10 of these buildings. In 1851, there was erected 1 four-story building; in 1852, 25; and in 1853, 28.

By wards the number of houses erected was as follows: From 1819 to 1829, First Ward, 129; Second Ward, 251; Third Ward, 474; Fourth Ward, 68; Fifth Ward, 38; Sixth Ward, 73; total, 1,033.

From 1829 to 1839, First Ward, 141; Second Ward, 226; Third Ward, 296; Fourth Ward, 46; Fifth Ward, 175; Sixth Ward, 11; total, 895.

From 1839 to 1849, First Ward, 364; Second Ward, 472; Third Ward, 907; Fourth Ward, 217; Fifth Ward, 175; Sixth Ward, 123; Seventh Ward, 109; total, 2,367.

From 1849 to 1853, First Ward, 227; Second Ward, 342; Third Ward, 291; Fourth Ward, 390; Fifth Ward, 150; Sixth Ward, 104; Seventh, 429; total, 1,933.

In what we have said so far we have attempted to show the beginnings of this great enterprise of founding a capital city and its gradual progress through its early history to the date last mentioned. It will not be permissible to omit some notice of the fact that in the year 1814 this Capital City was invaded by the British troops and its public buildings destroyed by those ruthless invaders. The details of this attack upon the city of Washington will be related in another part of this work. Suffice it to say here, that not only were these buildings that had cost so much time and treasure in their erection destroyed so as to make them of little or no use for the purposes for which they had been constructed, but the question immediately arose as to whether they should be reconstructed at all or not. It is not material to our purpose in this history to recount here the various arguments that were used both for and against the permanency of the establishment of the Capital City. These debates were but a renewal of the controversy that existed at the time of the foundation of the city. A long struggle ensued, but it was finally determined to reconstruct the Federal buildings, and to continue the seat of government at the spot originally selected for its permanent residence. All this, of course, had the effect to retard seriously the progress, or in other words the growth and improvement, of the city of Washington. As far as we can ascertain from the records of those times, little or nothing was done toward the improvement of the streets and thoroughfares of the city, except by the Government authorities themselves in and about the public reservations and buildings. The streets were generally left in the condition of country roads or lanes, and were not at all in keeping with the dignity of the Federal City. The city, so far as its internal affairs were concerned, was in the hands of a local government consisting of a Mayor and two boards, one of aldermen and the other of councilmen, elected by the people, as has been related in another chapter of this history. Their powers and resources were altogether insufficient for purposes other than those pertaining to an inconsequential town.

In 1820, Congress granted a new charter to the city of Washington, by which it repealed all acts of incorporation theretofore granted, and enacted that the commissioners of the public buildings and other persons appointed to superintend disbursements in the city of Washington should reimburse to the city a proportion of the expenses incurred in improving any of the streets or avenues bordering upon or joining any of the public squares or buildings, and cause the sidewalks to be furnished with curbs and paved footways, whenever the corporation should direct such improvements to be made by the proprietors of the lots on the opposite side of the street or avenue, and directing also that such officer should defray such expense out of moneys arising from the sale of lots in the city of Washington belonging to the United States.

It will be seen from this that the provision made for the improvement of the streets, avenues, and sidewalks of the city of Washington at that early day was conditioned on the fact that the street to be improved bordered upon public reservations or other public property, and that the money used for such improvement was raised from the sale of lots reserved to the Government. The law in this respect remained in this condition for many years, and it is safe to say that there was no improvement to speak of in the city of Washington for many years after it was established.

In 1830, Congress took steps toward such an improvement of Pennsylvania Avenue as would make it a proper and convenient thoroughfare between the Capitol and the presidential mansion. A resolution to that effect was passed by the House of Representatives, and the Committee of the District of Columbia was instructed to inquire into the expediency of making provision for the repair and improvement of this avenue on the macadam or some other permanent plan. The committee to which this matter was referred made a report to the House of Representatives at the first session of the Twenty-first Congress, accompanied by a bill providing for the improvement of the avenue in question. It is significant in this connection that, in in this report, the committee used the following language:

"In reply to the suggestion which may perhaps be made, that the city of Washington ought to execute this work for its own accommodation, your committee beg leave to make a few remarks, in addition to the facts above stated, in relation to the importance of the work to the General Government. This city is already suffering under a burden of local taxation, more severe perhaps than any other portion of the country, and is therefore unable to incur so great an expense.

"At any rate, under their circumstances, their necessity for the proposed improvement does not justify the expenditure.

"Some of the causes of this oppressive state of things will be found in the fact that the Government has extensive domains in the city exempt from taxation, and in the embarrassment arising from the peculiar and unfortunate condition in which this entire district is placed. In connection with this it should not be forgotten how much the public lands here have been augmented in value by those extensive city improvements which have contributed largely to the existing burthens of the people. The extended scale upon which the Government originally laid out the city, and the number and width of its streets, have also greatly increased its expenses.

"Believing there has been some misapprehension in the public mind in regard to the amount of Government expenditures for the benefit of this District, compared with the amount of money received from the sale of land therein, beyond its cost, and the value of lands still unsold, your committee have thought proper to procure a statement of facts relating to this subject, which is hereto annexed.

"From this statement it appears that there has already been received, from the sale of public lands in this District, beyond the cost of all the lands purchased by the Government, the sum of $696,618.68; that the estimated cash value of lands still unsold amounts to $1,091,174.09, making in the whole $1,787,792.77.

"All the appropriations of money by Congress for the benefit of this District, independent of the public buildings for the General Government, amount to $186,860.48; of this sum there has been appropriated for a penitentiary, a courthouse, and jails, $144,295.79. There are many other considerations which might be presented to show that the General Government ought to exercise a liberal spirit toward this

District; but they will be reserved for a more important occasion, when its general concerns shall be exhibited in pursuance of another resolution of this House."

It is within the memory of many of the present inhabitants of this city that this project for the improvement of Pennsylvania Avenue was carried into effect, and that great thoroughfare was improved upon the plan of Macadam from the gates of the Capitol to the President's House. But it is worthy of remark that even in making this improvement Congress manifested how little the responsibility of the Government was realized in respect to its duty in the matter of improving the Capital City.

In 1835, a report was made by Senator Southard, of the Senate Committee on the District of Columbia, which is such a full exposition of the affairs of the District that an abstract of it is appropriate here. The report called the attention of the Senate to the fact that the city of Washington was then involved in pecuniary obligations from which it was utterly impossible that it could extricate itself by any means within its own control, or by any exertions which it might make, unaided by Congressional legislation. Its actual debts amounted then to $1,806,442.59, and according to the committee's view there was danger that the city might be driven to a surrender of its charter, and then be thrown entirely upon Congress for its support. A portion of the debt of the city had been incurred by its investment in the stock of the Chesapeake and Ohio Canal, and as the debt thus incurred must soon be discharged, and as the creditors were foreign bankers, they would in all probability become the owners of a large proportion of the property within the limits of the Capital.

Besides this, the people had done what they could to improve the streets; but owing to the unusual extent and magnitude of the plan of the city and the width of the streets and avenues, when compared with the entire number of the inhabitants, then numbering but little more than twenty thousand, little, comparatively, had been accomplished. The avenues varied in width from 160 feet down to 120 feet, and the streets, from 147 feet down to 80 feet; and the avenues and streets that had to be opened and repaired in order to fill up the plan of the city, extended to a distance of more than 60 miles. Upon the streets there had been expended since the year 1800 an average annual sum of $13,000, besides an equal amount assessed upon the citizens for gutters, pavements, etc. This expenditure made upon the streets was undoubtedly one of the principal causes of embarrassment to the city, and according to the committee making this

report, the inhabitants had had to bear much more than their proportionate share of the burden.

At the beginning of the occupation of this city as the seat of
government, that Government did not expect that the inhabitants
of the city should bear the burden that was then thrown upon them.
This was shown, first, by the consideration that the contract between
the Government and the owners of the lands gave to the Government
a large extent of the public lots, sufficient for all the edifices and
improvements which its convenience would require, and, in addition
to this, one-half of all the building lots within the limits of the city.
In the second place, the Government assumed exclusive control over
all the streets of the city, so that neither the corporate authorities
nor the people had any right to enlarge or diminish them, to open or
to close them. It could not, therefore, be held either reasonable or just
that the city itself should bear the expense of the improvement of the
streets, the property and control of which were absolutely in the Government.

There had been appropriated for the streets and paid out of the
public treasury $429,971, and in addition to this the inhabitants
had paid fully $200,000 for the improvement of the streets in vari-
ous directions. Previous to that year there had been made 106,371
feet of running pavement, besides curbstones and paved gutters,
which were paid for by a special tax upon the lots, and to which the
lots owned by the Government had contributed nothing, although
equally benefitted with the private lots. During all this time the
Government had expended upon its own streets only $208,905, all of
which, except $10,000, had been devoted to Pennsylvania Avenue
and the streets immediately in the vicinity of the Capitol and the
presidential mansion. The committee thought that Congress ought
to refund to the city one-half of the amount it had expended upon
the streets, namely, $214,985, to say nothing about the interest.

Another cause of embarrassment under which the city was then
laboring was the attempt to erect a City Hall, which so far as then completed had cost $50,000. To assist in the erection of this City Hall
a grant was made of the right to draw lotteries until the profits
should amount to $100,000. The drawing of these lotteries was
intrusted to men who failed in the discharge of their duties, and the
result was that the city was involved in a debt of $197,184.84, upon
which it had already paid $70,000 in interest. The number of build-
ing lots that were acquired by the Government was 10,136, a large
proportion of which had then been sold, and the account of the

13

Government with relation to these lots was as follows: It had received from the sale of building lots $741,024.45; it had given away to charitable institutions lots to the value of $70,000; it had remaining lots unsold valued at $109,221.84; it had received in grants from Maryland and Virginia, $192,000; making a total of $1,112,246.29, to which must be added the value of the public reservations, $1,500,000, making a grand total of $2,612,246.29.

The total appropriation for the benefit of the city made by the Government was $150,000, to enable it to complete the canal uniting the waters of the Potomac with those of the Eastern Branch.

In 1848, a committee, consisting of W. W. Seaton, Mayor of the city, John W. Maury, B. B. French, Ignatius Mudd, Lewis Johnson, Silas Hill, George E. Abbott, and G. H. Fulmer, was appointed to attend to the interests of the city of Washington before Congress. These gentlemen, who were the most prominent in the city at the time, and most thoroughly acquainted with its affairs, presented their views at length in the following statement:

When the present site was adopted by Congress for the Capital of the Nation, it consisted of a number of farms owned by eighteen or twenty different proprietors. These proprietors of the land conveyed the whole of it to the Government, for the purpose of establishing thereon a public city, according to such plan as the President might adopt. A plan was accordingly laid out, and adopted by President Washington, upon a magnificent scale, suited to the dignity of the Republic, and with a view to its resplendent future, with vast streets and avenues from 100 to 160 feet wide, and embracing an area of 7,134 acres. Of this great space, only 3,016 acres were appropriated in the plan to the building lots, the remainder (4,118 acres) being taken up with reservations for the Government edifices and other purposes, streets, avenues, and parks. Of the whole 7,134 acres, the Government paid the proprietors for but 512 acres, at the rate of £25, or $66.66, per acre, and returning to them one moiety of the building lots (1,508 acres), retaining as a free gift the entire residue of 5,114 acres, including one-half of the building lots. The proceeds of the sales of the building lots so retained by the Government, it was understood by the proprietors, were to be applied toward the improvement of the place, in grading and making streets, erecting bridges, and in providing such other conveniences as the residence of the Government might require. This promised improvement naturally devolved upon the Government, in whom was vested the right to the soil and the right of jurisdiction over the inhabitants. Yet for many years the Government failed in its performance, leaving everything to be done by private individuals. These improvements, so made by the city itself, and paid for by levying taxes upon the people, up to January 1, 1848, had cost the following sums: There had been made about 25 miles of streets, and there had been expended on streets, avenues, and parks, $625,000; there had been made 2,200,000 feet of paved footways, paid for by special tax upon the property, costing $110,000; there had been expended on the support of the poor and insane, $175,000; there had been expended in educating the children of the poor, $100,000; there had been expended on the police force, $32,000; and the city was burdened with a debt arising from various sources of $820,000, and it had paid in interest on this debt $850,000.

While the city of Washington had been doing all this, Congress or the Government had done comparatively nothing. Had the property of the Government been taxed as that of private citizens had been, it would have yielded about $60,000 per year; but the Government had paid nothing in the shape of taxes, nor anything out of the fund derived from the sale of lots granted to it by the proprietors. The most the Government had done for the corporation of Washington was to relieve it from the burden of the stock of the Chesapeake and Ohio Canal Company, from which, however, it had a debt on its hands of about $700,000 on account of interest and expenses connected therewith. The Government had received about $800,000 from the sale of its lots, $72,000 from Maryland, and $120,000 from Virginia, and the value of its property in the city at that time was about $7,625,000.

From the time of the close of the labors of John Sessford, in 1853, down to the organization of the permanent form of government, as explained in the Municipal chapter, there are no statistics accessible showing in detail the growth of the city as to the number of houses or other buildings erected from year to year, except those on the assessors' books, which are scattered through numerous volumes. To collect these statistics would involve very great labor with comparatively little result, and hence no attempt is made to make such a collection. Commencing, however, with the report of the inspectors of buildings for the year closing November 1, 1877, it is practicable to present in brief space this particular feature of the growth of the city from that time down to the present. From November, 1876, to November, 1877, there were erected, in the aggregate, buildings to the number of 1,508; to June 30, 1878, 1,001; to June 30, 1879, 1,981; to June 30, 1880, 1,921; to June 30, 1881, 1,792;

to June 30, 1882, 1,730; to June 30, 1883, 2,215; to June 30, 1884, 2,915; to June 30, 1885, 3,691; to June 30, 1886, 5,451; to June 30, 1887, 4,746; to June 30, 1888, 3,694; to June 30, 1889, 4,048; to June 30, 1890, 4,523.

In this connection the census of Washington, Georgetown, and the county outside, from 1850 to 1890, may here be introduced.

	1850.	1860.	1870.	1880.	1890.
Washington	40,001	61,121	109,199	147,293	188,932
Georgetown	8,366	8,733	11,384	12,578	14,046
County	3,320	5,226	11,117	17,753	27,414
Total	51,687	75,080	131,700	177,624	230,392

On January 4, 1885, the debt of the District of Columbia and of the then late corporation of Washington was, according to the published statement of Treasurer Wyman, *ex officio* commissioner of the sinking fund of the District, as follows:

BONDS OF THE DISTRICT OF COLUMBIA.	Registered.	Amount of Coupons.	Total Amount.
Permanent Improvement Bonds of 1871		$3,484,600	$3,484,600
Market Stock of 1871.		360,000	360,000
Market Stock of 1871–72	$100,000	46,450	146,450
Permanent Improvement, 1873		642,300	642,300
Water Stock, 1873		15,000	15,000
Fifty Year Funding, 1874–75	11,016,000	3,017,150	14,033,150
Twenty Year Funding, 1879–80	318,000	630,400	948,400
Washington Corporation—			
Three Year, 1870.		100	100
Twenty Year Funding, 1872		1,020,350	1,020,350
Thirty Year Funding, 1872		628,800	628,800
Total	11,434,000	$9,845,150	$21,279,150

The foregoing reports made to Congress and the statements of the citizens, of all of which we have given abstracts, serve to show not only that the city had made little or no progress down to the date to which we have last referred, but that all its attempts at progress had been obstructed by the want of interest taken in its affairs by the Congress of the United States, to which it had a right to look for at least a certain measure of support. The history of the years that succeeded is only a repetition of that of the years that had preceded. Little or nothing was done either by Congress or the people themselves toward putting the city into respectable condition or toward the development of its plan. The Government erected several elegant public buildings; the Capitol was extended, and the dome erected; the Patent Office, Treasury extension, Lafayette Square, and several other effective improvements were carried to completion. But in a general way matters remained in the unsatisfactory condition we have described, until the beginning of the War of the Rebellion, an account of which will be found in another part of this work. The effect of this war was to demonstrate more clearly than it had ever been shown before, the vast importance to the Nation of the preservation of the Capital City. Indeed this city was the great central point in the history of that war. The troops that were organized and sent to the field, to a great extent were first brought to this city, and their organization, their supplies, everything that conduced to their efficiency as troops, had origin and control within this city as a center of operations. The effect of all this was to bring to the city of Washington people from all parts of the country, and it is not too much to say that the sentiment of all American citizens with respect to the Capital City was one of disappointment at its condition, and surprise that so little progress had been made in its development in all the years that had succeeded its establishment. This feeling continued through years after the war. Some of the citizens fell back upon the old notion that the only remedy for this condition of things was the removal of the Capital from its present situation to a portion of the country where more respect would be shown for its progress and development.

This matter, though for some time publicly discussed in the newspapers, received little or no attention from Congress. But the feeling was so intense that it became manifest to the people of Washington that something must be done to make the city worthy of its name and its importance. There is no need to dwell upon this, an account of which would, of itself, fill a volume. Before leaving this subject,

however, it seems proper to refer to the fact that an effort was
made, under the old municipal form of government, to improve the
streets by paving them with wooden blocks, which was then a very
popular kind of pavement. The right to these pavements was the
property of several patentees. The general contract was given in
1870 to Lewis Clephane, as president of the Metropolitan Paving
Company, to pave Pennsylvania Avenue, and possibly other streets.
Work began on this avenue October 31, and was continued until the
paving of the avenue from the gates of the Capitol to Fifteenth Street
was completed, an event which was celebrated in an appropriate
manner.

But this was only a beginning. The wooden pavements, as might
have been expected, rotted away, became a dreadful nuisance, and had
to be removed. But they had the effect of presenting to the people
the advantages of smooth, durable surfaces on the public streets, and
of the benefits that would arise from the cleanliness derived from good
drainage, not only to the public health, but to the general appearance
of the city in every way. It is safe to say that from this time the
era of improvement that was so soon to transform the city takes
its beginning. A people that had once enjoyed the blessing of
smooth, clean thoroughfares were not willing to return to the mud
and discomfort of the olden times without an effort, at least, to save
themselves from that disaster. It was evident that the difficulty was
in the very nature of the affairs of the District, and that nothing
could be effected without first making a change in the methods of
government then existing. The result was that legislation was secured
that in the first place changed the nature of the government of the
city into a Territorial government for the entire District of Columbia,
which was under the control of a Governor and civil council; next, to a
temporary or experimental government by commissioners, appointed by
the President of the United States, and clothed with executive powers
over the affairs of the District; and lastly, into the present or permanent
form of government, consisting also of commissioners appointed by
the President and clothed with executive powers. In the debates
preceding the legislation out of which this form of government grew,
the question of its duty to the city as the Capital of the Nation was
presented to Congress. After considerable debate, in which projects
were offered and considered, it was finally determined that the
revenues of the District of Columbia collected from taxes imposed
upon its citizens should be paid into the treasury of the United States,
and disbursed under acts of appropriation passed by Congress, in every

respect as other public moneys of the United States are disbursed; and that it should be the duty of the Government of the United States, to the extent that the estimates made for the expenses of the Government should be appropriated by Congress, to appropriate the amount of fifty per centum thereof out of the public moneys of the United States. The act is as follows, on this point:

"To the extent to which Congress shall approve aforesaid estimates" (that is, the amount estimated for the support of the District Government), "Congress shall appropriate the amount of fifty per centum thereof, and the remaining fifty per centum of such approved estimates shall be levied and assessed upon the taxable property and privileges of said District Government."

This legislation, as a matter of course, changed the condition of things in the District of Columbia almost entirely. It may be well to mention what was done in the matter of this legislation more in detail, as an introduction to the history of the improvements which preceded and followed this final act of Congress.

The Territorial government, of which we have already spoken, went into operation June 1, 1871. On June 20, the board of public works, consisting of Henry D. Cooke, Governor, Alexander R. Shepherd, S. P. Brown, A. B. Mullett, and James A. Magruder, members, submitted to the Legislative Assembly of the District estimates for improvements amounting in the aggregate to $6,578,397, and recommended that the District should provide for the payment thereof by a loan of $4,000,000, and an assessment of $2,000,000. July 10, the Legislative Assembly passed a bill making an appropriation of $4,000,-000 for improvements in the District of Columbia, and authorizing an issue of twenty-year seven per cent. bonds in payment for the same. Application was made to the Equity Court for an injunction against the issue of the bonds, which being granted by Judge Wylie, the Legislative Assembly, on August 11, 1871, passed a supplemental appropriation bill of $500,000 for the purpose of avoiding the technical difficulties raised by the injunctionists, and work was immediately commenced. The injunction was subsequently dissolved, and by a later act the Legislative Assembly reduced the appropriations made by $500,000, thus putting the amount at $4,000,000, the original appropriation. The Legislative Assembly at the same time referred the $4,000,000 loan to the people at an election held November 21, 1871, and the proposition was almost unanimously sustained.

Thus sustained and fortified by the popular voice, the board of public works felt safe in inaugurating a system of improvements, particularly on the streets, which astonished the people of the District of Columbia by its magnitude and extent, and which caused much harsh and ungenerous criticism by people all over the country, and especially by those who were immediately concerned in the District itself, whose taxes were greatly increased, and whose convenience was seriously interfered with. Up to the time of the establishment of this board of public works, no system of grades had been established, and the inauguration of a system of sewers required numerous changes in the grades as they then existed, and some of these changes were of a very radical nature. This was the first great difficulty encountered by the board. The next difficulty was with the streets themselves, comprising, as they did and do, a greater percentage of the entire area of the city than those of any other city in the world.

The sewerage of the city had received almost no attention previous to the establishment of the board of public works. A large proportion of the drainage emptied into an open ditch, called the canal, and the current of water, depending as it did upon the ebb and flow of the tides, was wholly insufficient to carry off the deposits made at the outlets of the sewers emptying into it. The canal thus became an exceedingly offensive and disgusting object and a most prolific source of pestilence. How to abate this nuisance had been a great problem among scientific and practical men for twenty-five years, and it had not yet been solved. It soon became clear to this practical board of public works that an intersecting sewer at this point was a necessity, as all of the great sewers from the northern portion of the city had been let into the canal. At length it was determined to build an intersecting sewer from Seventh to Seventeenth Street, following a course parallel to the canal, and emptying into the river at the foot of Seventeenth Street; and another intersecting sewer from Sixth to Third Street, emptying into the Tiber arch on Third Street. These sewers vary in diameter from five to twelve feet. After their construction it was soon seen that the problem unsolved for a quarter of a century had found a solution.

The Tiber Creek sewer, which receives all the sewage of the city east of Sixth Street West, and which drains an extent of country northward of more than three thousand acres, is one of the largest in the world, varying in diameter from twenty-four to thirty feet, and is of abundant capacity for all future time. Other sewers were constructed in different parts of the city as needed, but it is not deemed necessary to particularize further on this subject.

Previous to November 1, 1872, there had been laid 116.36 miles

of street pavements of various kinds, including 34.26 miles of wood pavements, embracing those of Pennsylvania Avenue. and several other of the city streets. These wood pavements were of several kinds — the Ballard, Miller, Stowe, Moree, Keystone, Ingersoll, and De Golyer, Nos. 1 and 2. There were also 39.22 miles of gravel pavements, this kind of roads being made mostly in the country. Of asphalt pavements, the following kinds had been laid: The Scharf, the Evans, the Scrimshaw or Abbott, and the Parisian.

The improvement of the streets was by no means a small matter. It was necessary to equalize the grades; for while the city of Washington is situated on what is sometimes called a plain, yet it presents numerous and great inequalities. The White House grounds are but fifteen feet above mean low water; Capitol Hill is ninety feet above low water; Pennsylvania Avenue is, in some places, below high water mark; Observatory Hill is ninety-six feet above tide water; and in 1876 there were between Capitol Hill and Observatory Hill elevations of one hundred and three feet, which had to be cut down and the ravines and hollows filled up and made as nearly level as practicable when the necessary drainage was taken into account.

In addition to all the work done upon the streets, a great work was done by the parking commission, consisting of William H. Smith, William Saunders, and John Saul. Beginning in the spring of 1872 and continuing down to the present time, this commission has been steadily at work improving the streets and parks by the planting of trees, shrubs, and flowers, until the result is that all over the city the streets and parks are most beautifully shaded and the pleasantness and healthfulness thereof greatly enhanced, the city now being in this regard one of the most charming cities of the world. The transformation from an unhealthy, unsightly city to a city of fine, graded, graveled and paved, and shaded streets, well lighted at night, an extended system of sewerage, an efficient water supply, miles upon miles of shade, and acres upon acres of beautiful parks, including the Mall, the Smithsonian grounds, the Washington Monument grounds, the President's Square, Lafayette Square, and numerous others, was the most surprising and complete.

It is not improper in this connection to observe and to record for the benefit of future generations, that the presiding genius of this great transformation and improvement was Alexander R. Shepherd.[1]

---

[1] Alexander R. Shepherd was born in Washington City, January 31, 1835. At the age of ten he was apprenticed to a carpenter, and when seventeen, to the trade of a plumber; he became some years afterward a partner in the firm of John W. Thomp-

While the first Governor of the District of Columbia was Henry D. Cooke, a most estimable gentleman, Mr. Shepherd, in his position of vice-president of the board of public works, and afterwards when he became himself Governor, exercised superintendence over all the work that was done. Under Mr. Shepherd the rapidity and extent of the work performed was most extraordinary — so great, indeed, as far to exceed the authority of law under which he was working, and also so great as to call for the expenditure of money far in excess of the appropriations. The work was performed by Governor Shepherd with an honest purpose for the benefit of the city. His ambition was to make it the pride instead of the reproach of the Nation, and to render it, so far as anything could or can render it, the permanent Capital of the great American Government. As to the amount expended exceeding the appropriations, Governor Shepherd boldly told the committee of investigation appointed in February, 1874, to inquire into the proceedings of the board of public works, that inasmuch as the public buildings of the Government, which paid no taxes to the city, were greatly benefitted by the improvements made by the excess of expenditures complained of, the Government should in duty to itself assume that excess of liabilities; and there are now living those who believe that had Governor Shepherd retained his position and been permitted to complete the work begun by him, this result, so much to be desired, would have been accomplished. However this

son & Company, plumbers and gas fitters in the city of Washington, and finally succeeded to the business in his own name. When the Rebellion commenced he was one of the first to volunteer his services in the cause of the Union. In 1861, he was elected a member of the Common Council of the city of Washington and was chosen president of that body; he was a member of the Levy Court of the District of Columbia in 1867, and in 1869 was one of a committee of citizens selected to draft a bill for the better government of the District of Columbia, in which work he took a leading part. In 1870, he became president of the Citizens' Reform Association and was also elected an alderman of the city. In 1871, he was appointed a member of the Board of Public Works of the District of Columbia under the act of Congress of that year, abolishing the then existing government and creating a Territorial government for the District; he was elected vice-president of the board, the Governor under the law being *ex officio* president. He was, in 1873, appointed the second Governor of the District and remained in that office until June 20, 1874, when the form of the government of the District of Columbia was again changed by an act of Congress approved that day. Mr. Shepherd showed himself at all times, and in every position held by him, a man of distinguished ability, strong in his conviction of what was right, and always loyal to his convictions. He was ahead of his times in his opinion of what was best for the interests of the city of Washington, and to his boldness as a leader and his fearless adoption of the means in his hands is due, more than to all things else beside, the wonderful development of the beauties and advantages of the city of his birth. Mr. Shepherd has, for several years past, been a resident of Mexico, where he owns valuable mining interests, to which he is devoting his energies.

might have been, the results of his great work are everywhere visible; they are enjoyed by those who opposed and criticized him as well as by those who approved his work and stood by him. The great debt created has been advantageously funded, and will be paid by the future as well as by the present. At this time many of those who were his detractors have become his eulogists.

In closing this chapter it may be well to present in brief the number and extent of the public reservations and the length of the streets and avenues. The public grounds of the city of Washington consist of 331 reservations, containing 413.32 acres of land. Fifty-five of these are highly improved, and contain 231.28 acres; 47 of them are partially improved, containing 110.55 acres; and 229 remain unimproved, containing 71.49 acres. This statement does not include Rock Creek Park, lately condemned and converted into the largest park in the city, embracing within its limits nearly 2,000 acres, and costing nearly one million and a half of dollars.

Following is a summary of the length in miles and area in square yards of the various kinds of pavements at present upon the streets of Washington: Of sheet asphalt, 49.7 miles, 1,089,858 square yards; coal tar, 38.2 miles, 881,939 square yards; asphalt block, 10.1 miles, 242,736 square yards; granite blocks, 24.5 miles, 609,687 square yards; cobble and blue rock, 10.8 miles, 440,754 square yards; macadam, 10.4 miles, 293,218 square yards; gravel, 26.2 miles, 530,188 square yards. Total length of paved streets, 169.9 miles; total area, 4,088,380 square yards. The length of streets unimproved is 65.6, miles, making the total length of the streets 235.5 miles. The area of the unimproved streets is 1,167,672 square yards, making the total area of the streets 5,256,052 square yards.

The march of improvement in the city, begun in 1871, has been ceaselessly onward. Twenty years of constant, unremitting, intelligent attention to its progress has worked wonders in the appearance of the Capital. Pushing outward along the magnificent avenues, the grand plan of L'Enfant is being developed, as the city progresses, in a way that astonishes and delights its citizens. Already this progress has overleaped the old boundaries, and passing the confines intended by our forefathers, is peopling the hills that surround it like an amphitheater. The style of buildings is in keeping with the grandeur of the plan; while the beautiful parks, trees, flowers, and shrubs, the fountains, statues, and splendid public edifices, all combined, make it a city worthy of the name of Washington.

CHAPTER VIII.

MILITARY HISTORY.

THE War of 1812-15 had its remote origin in the fact that Great Britain claimed and exercised the right to impress seamen from American vessels into her own service, upon the principle that a subject of Great Britain could not expatriate himself. For several years before the commencement of actual hostilities, in fact as far back as the close of the Revolutionary War, the newspapers of the United States contained frequent advertisements in the form of lists of American citizens serving on board of American vessels, arbitrarily seized while engaged in the performance of their duty, and thus impressed into the service of that nation, together with appeals to their friends for proof that they were citizens of the United States, and for the adoption of measures that would lead to the recovery of their liberty. Then, too, deserters from the British navy sometimes enlisted in the service of the United States, to whom, when discovered, but little mercy was shown.

In the spring of 1807, three of the seamen of the British ship *Melampus* deserted her and enlisted as a portion of the crew of the American frigate *Chesapeake*, then being fitted out at the Navy Yard at Washington to join the Mediterranean squadron. Mr. Erskine, who was then British minister at Washington, made a formal demand upon the President of the United States for their surrender. The Government of the United States instituted an investigation into the case of these deserters, by means of which it was well established that all three of the men were American subjects previously to their enlistment on board the *Melampus*. Their names were William Ware, John Strachan, and Daniel Martin. Martin was a colored man and a citizen of Massachusetts; the other two being white men and citizens of Maryland. These facts being sufficiently authenticated, the Government of course refused to surrender them, and Mr. Erskine said no more upon the subject.

The failure to secure the surrender of these three men led Vice-Admiral Berkeley to an assumption of authority which caused a great deal of trouble between the two nations. Vice-Admiral Berkeley was on the Halifax Station, and a fleet under his command was at the time lying off Lynnhaven Bay, watching a French fleet that was on the coast, as well as American commercial movements. About the beginning of June, 1807, the *Chesapeake* sailed from Washington to Norfolk, where she reported as ready for sea to Commodore James Barron, the flag officer of the Mediterranean squadron, June 22. She sailed from Hampton Roads under the immediate command of Captain Gordon, armed with twenty-eight eighteen pounders on her gun deck and twelve carronades on her upper deck. Her crew numbered three hundred and seventy-five men. The British squadron in Lynnhaven Bay were watching her, as well as the French frigates, the *Leonard*, of the British squadron, being particularly on the lookout for the *Chesapeake*. The *Leonard*, mounting fifty-six guns, preceded the *Chesapeake* to sea several miles, until about three o'clock in the afternoon, when she bore down upon the *Chesapeake* and hailed her, informing Commodore Barron that she had a dispatch for him. The lieutenant of the British boat which came alongside, who was politely received by the Commodore in the cabin of the *Chesapeake*, informed the Commodore that he was in search of deserters, and, giving their names, demanded their release, in accordance with instructions issued June 1, 1807, by Vice-Admiral Berkeley, to all the captains in the British squadron. Commodore Barron replied that he knew of no deserters on board of his ship, and that his crew could not be mus-

tered except by their own officers. In the meantime, the officers of
the *Chesapeake*, suspicious of intended mischief, prepared the ship as
well as they could for action, and upon the retirement of the British
lieutenant, Commodore Barron, himself fearing hostile action in consequence of his refusal to surrender the deserters, called his men to
quarters. Soon afterward a shot was sent from the *Leonard* across the
bow of the *Chesapeake*, and in a few moments another, and then a
whole broadside was fired into the American ship. In several broad-
sides that followed, three of Commodore Barron's men were killed
and eighteen wounded. The *Chesapeake*, being really in a helpless
condition, could offer no resistance, and was compelled to surrender.
The three deserters above mentioned, and one other named John
Wilson, were found on board the *Chesapeake*, taken on board the
Leonard, and thence to Halifax, where Wilson, who was a British
subject, was tried and hanged. The other three were reprieved on
condition of reëntering the British service. One of the three Americans died in captivity, and the other two, in June, 1812, were restored
to the ship from which they had been taken.

This act of Vice-Admiral Berkeley, when brought to the attention of the British Government, was disavowed by Earl Canning, and
Berkeley was recalled from his command. The commander of the
Leonard was discharged from his command, and never again employed
by his Government. On the other hand, Commodore Barron was
greatly blamed by the American people for his misfortune. The
national pride was deeply wounded, and it was necessary that it
should be appeased. He was accused of neglect of duty, was tried
on this charge by a court martial, found guilty, and suspended for
five years without pay. Captain Gordon was also tried on the same
charge, as well as Captain Hall, but both were only privately repri-
manded, while the gunner was cashiered for not having sufficient
priming powder prepared. It is altogether likely, however, that the
blame rested with the Government more than with the officers of
the *Chesapeake*, though it is not deemed proper to pursue the investigation of this point in this volume.

The President, on July 2, issued a proclamation, in which he
complained bitterly of the habitual insolence of the British cruisers,
expressed his belief that the outrage on the *Chesapeake* was unauthorized, and ordered all British armed vessels to leave the waters of the
United States immediately. The schooner *Revenge* was sent to England
with instructions to the American ministers, Monroe and Pinckney,
who demanded reparation for insults and injuries in the case of the

Chesapeake, and insisted by way of security for the future, that the right of visitation of American vessels in search of British subjects should be totally relinquished. The British Government refused to treat on any subject except that of reparation. A disavowal of the act had already been made, and every disposition shown to be just and friendly. But no satisfactory understanding could be arrived at.

President Jefferson, in his message to Congress, December 18, 1807, on account of the attempted destruction by France under Napoleon, and by the British Government, of the commerce of the United States, by the operation of the Berlin decree of the former and the orders of the Council of the latter, suggested by way of retaliation the passage of an embargo act. And what is most remarkable, the Senate on the same day, after four hours' debate, passed such an act by a large majority. Three days later the House passed the same act, and on the 22d the President approved it. The object of this act was to preserve and develop the resources of the United States and to compel France and England to relinquish their hostility to the commerce of a neutral nation. But in both directions it was a failure, except that to a slight extent it tended to develop American manufactures. But how to develop commerce through its destruction is a problem that has not yet been solved. It turned out to be of assistance to France in her efforts to destroy the commerce of England, and the pride of England would not permit her to modify her action with reference thereto, she thinking she could endure the inconveniences of the American embargo as long as could the United States. In this position England was correct. The United States could not prosper without intercourse with the outside world, and the evils inflicted on her commerce by her own embargo were far greater than those inflicted on that of England or France. After considerable unfortunate experience, the policy of decree, orders, and embargo were alike abandoned.

On the occasion of the taking of the *Chesapeake*, the Tammany Society of Washington City sent an address to the "Grand Sachem of the Seventeen United Tribes of America," Thomas Jefferson, President of the United States, expressing regret that they had reason to believe that the calumet of peace was to be exchanged for the tomahawk of war, the Nation having been insulted and menaced by a foreign tribe. They beheld with horror the perfidious attack made upon our national canoe, the *Chesapeake*, on our own shore by the mercenary warriors of another tribe, beyond the wide waters, professing toward us amity and friendship.

About the time of these occurrences news came to Washington from all along the northern frontier that the English were exciting the Indians against the Americans, and making treaties with them to the end that they would certainly be on the side of the British in case of war. Even as far toward the north and west as Chicago it was firmly believed that war with Great Britain was inevitable. Then, too, to add to the gloom of the prospect, the embargo was bitterly denounced in many sections; though of course it was sustained by the friends of Mr. Jefferson and many others, who, though not especially his friends, yet were friends of their country without reference to his administration. The probable effect of the embargo was not understood by all, and many had so much confidence in Mr. Jefferson's wisdom that through this confidence they sustained the embargo, instead of through knowledge of its nature. "In 1794 an embargo did not produce a war, and we hope in 1807 it will avert one. If in this we should be disappointed it will at least yield the means of waging it with good effect."

In April, 1808, the names of seventy seamen claiming to be citizens of the United States were published by the War Department, with the request that their friends would supply the department with the proof necessary to establish their citizenship, and the promise was made that then measures would be taken to secure their liberty.

Thus matters continued until after Mr. Madison was elected President, and all through his first term,—the English persisting in their aggressions and the United States Government striving to avoid a war. At length, on July 24, 1811, President Madison, desirous of serving a second term, and hearing the ground trembling with dissatisfaction at his peaceful policy, convened Congress in extra session, to meet November 4, that year. This Congress, in January, 1812, passed a measure providing for the addition of 25,000 men to the military forces, which was the first war measure adopted. On February 21, 1812, appropriations were made for sustaining this additional force, and on the 24th nearly six hundred nominations of officers were sent into the Senate by the President, which nominations were confirmed March 12. During this month recruiting for the addition to the military was commenced, and by the 15th the mails were burdened with notifications of appointment to officers in all parts of the country.

April 4, 1812, another embargo was laid upon all ships and vessels in the ports of the United States, for ninety days from the passage of the act, with certain exceptions. April 13, a meeting was held at which was organized a company to manufacture solid shot, the factory established being named "Bruff's Pressed Shot Factory." By May 1, Thomas Ewell & Company had their gunpowder mills in operation, the capacity of which was two thousand pounds per day, both of these establishments being in the immediate vicinity of Washington.

War was declared by Congress, June 18, 1812. The enlistment of troops proceeded somewhat slowly until the surrender of Detroit by General Hull, August 16, 1812. This surrender filled the country with indignation, it being felt as an inglorious stain upon the country's honor. Then volunteers in great numbers flocked to arms, impelled by the noblest sentiments of patriotism. This sentiment now was well-nigh universal; for while previously there had been a difference of opinion as to the necessity or policy of war, yet, when actual hostilities commenced, and a stigma had been cast upon the American name, it became almost universally the opinion that no course but that of war was admissible. In Washington, the "Union Light Infantry Company" was organized, and commanded by Captain Davidson, and the "Washington Troop of Horse," by Captain Elias B. Caldwell. By September 29, a full company of one hundred and sixty men was ready for the field in Alexandria, having been organized on the 26th by the election of James McGuire captain, Robert Smith lieutenant, and Charles L. Nevitt ensign. Their services were tendered to and accepted by the President. The "First Legion of the District of Columbia" was officered as follows: William Smith, lieutenant-colonel, commanding; George Peter, adjutant; William Whann, quartermaster; Clement Smith, paymaster; Dr. Frederick May, surgeon; John Ott, surgeon's mate; E. Cummings, quartermaster's sergeant; John Simpson, fife major.

February 16, 1813, Adjutant George C. Washington, by order of Brigadier-General John P. Van Ness, required the commanding officers of the cavalry of the District to be ready to march at the sound of the trumpet, and on March 30 Brigadier-General Van Ness issued orders to the cavalry to hold themselves in readiness to march at a moment's notice. John Tayloe was lieutenant-colonel of cavalry. In connection with these orders was published a list of the officers of the several companies, together with the dates of their several commissions, as follows:

Columbian Dragoons — Captain, William Thornton, June 6, 1811; John Law, first lieutenant, June 6, 1811.

Georgetown Hussars — Captain, John Peter, June 6, 1811; first lieutenant, J. S. Williams, June 15, 1811; second lieutenant, William S. Ridgely, May 30, 1812.

14

Washington Light Horse—Captain, Elias B. Caldwell, May 30, 1812; first lieutenant, R. C. Weightman, May 30, 1812; second lieutenant, N. L. Queen, May 30, 1812.

Alexandria Dragoons—Captain, J. H. Mandeville, June 6, 1811; first lieutenant, William H. Maynadier, June 6, 1811; second lieutenant, John Dulany, May 8, 1811.

The regimental staff was as follows: Adjutant, George C. Washington; quartermaster, William Crawford; paymaster, Daniel Brent; surgeon, Dr. G. Clark; sergeant-major, Nicholas Worthington. Benjamin H. Latrobe was civil and military engineer at the Navy Yard.

May 8, 1813, there was a mass meeting of the citizens of Washington held to consider the propriety of adopting such measures as might further promote the defense of the city. Mayor Daniel Rapine was called to the chair, and Joseph Gales, Jr., made secretary. After some discussion it was determined to appoint a vigilance committee, whose duty it should be to consult with the citizens of the District and to communicate with the General Government on behalf of the city upon the subject of the probable security or danger of the city. The committee as appointed consisted of the Mayor and eight other citizens as follows: Thomas Munroe, John Davidson, Walter Jones, Jr., Peter Lenox, Buckner Thruston, Daniel Carroll of Duddington, Alexander McWilliams, and John Davis of Abel.

About this time the militia of the District was reorganized, with the following officers:

Major-general, John P. Van Ness; brigadier-generals, Robert Young and Walter Smith; adjutant-general, John Cox; assistant adjutant-general, George Peter; brigade-majors, Philip Triplett and John S. Williams; colonels, George Magruder, William Brent, and William Allen Dangerfield; lieutenant-colonels, James Thompson, Michael Nourse, and Adam Lynn; majors, Lawrence Hoof, Adam King, and Joel Brown.

Captains of infantry, Charles L. Nevitt, David Whann, Josiah M. Speake, Richard Johns, James Cassin, John Hollingshead, Elisha W. Williams, Craven T. Peyton, George Fitzgerald, and Alexander Hunter; captain of riflemen, Horace Field.

Captain of artillery, Benjamin Burch, with numerous lieutenants and ensigns, as follows: Lieutenants of infantry, Edward Edmonston, Abraham Wingart, John Fowler, Henry Beatty, Charles Warren, William Morton, Thomas L. McKenny, Bernard H. Tomlinson, Ambrose White, Thomas W. Peyton, Levin Moreland, Leonard Adams, Gustavus Harrison, Robert Smith, and Alexander L. Joncherez.

Lieutenant of riflemen, David Mankins; first lieutenant of artillery,

Alexander McCormick; second lieutenant of artillery, Shadrack Davis; lieutenant of grenadiers, John Goddard; ensign of grenadiers, George Ripple; ensign of riflemen, Francis Hucern; ensigns of infantry, Gustavus Alexander, Marsham Jameson, John Mitchell, James B. Holmead, William Williams, Francis Lowndes, Robert B. Kirby, and John Gilily.

May 11, 1813, Assistant Adjutant-General C. K. Gardner issued orders to Major-General John P. Van Ness that he should furnish from his division of militia the following detachment, to rendezvous at Washington on the 20th of the same month, under the law of February 28, 1795, and to report to Colonel Carberry, of the Thirty-sixth Regiment of United States Infantry:

Of infantry, 1 major, 4 captains, 4 lieutenants, 4 ensigns, and 400 rank and file; of artillery, 1 captain, 1 first lieutenant, 1 second lieutenant, 1 adjutant, 1 quartermaster, 1 surgeon's mate, and 100 rank and file.

The militia of the District had already, on the day before, been organized as follows, by Major-General Van Ness:

"The President of the United States having been pleased, under the authority vested in him by law, to adopt a new organization for the militia of the District of Columbia, better adapted to its present circumstances and more agreeable to the present army arrangements, whereby the militia of the District is formed into a division consisting of two brigades, each brigade to consist of two regiments," etc.

"In reminding the officers of the division of the late arrangements the Major-General thinks proper, in conformity therewith, to order that Colonels Magruder and Brent, and the regiments under their respective commands, compose the First Brigade, under the immediate command of Brigadier-General Smith; and that Colonel Dangerfield and Lieutenant-Colonel Commandant Tayloe, with the regiments under their respective commands, compose the Second Brigade, under the immediate command of Brigadier-General Young.

"Majors Robert Y. Brent and William S. Radcliff are selected as Major-General's aids-de-camp."

Brigade orders were issued, May 13, by Brigadier-General Walter Smith, to the effect that the militia of the District of Columbia, with the exception of the cavalry, should be formed into two distinct regiments, and constitute the First Columbian Brigade; the First Regiment to be commanded by Colonel George Magruder, assisted by Lieutenant-Colonel Thompson, and to consist of the following companies: Captains Ross's and Briscoe's infantry, and the infantry previously commanded by Captains Nourse, Keely, and Brown, who had been promoted; Captains Davidson's and Ruth's light infantry, Captain Stull's riflemen, and Captain Edmonston's grenadiers. The Second Regiment was to be commanded by Colonel William Brent, and to consist of Captains Morse's, McKee's, Parry's, B. King's, Bestor's, Blake's, Varnum's, and Hughes's infantry, Burch's artillery, and Cassin's, Lenox's, and Young's light infantry.

The "senior volunteers," who had enrolled themselves in the summer of 1812, were requested to meet May 20, in order to be reorganized into a company, and the citizens of the Third Ward who were above the age of forty-five were also requested to meet May 22 for the same purpose. Accompanying these requests, the hope went forth that no one was so old as to have no patriotism in his bosom. According to the *National Intelligencer*, there was a good deal of a military spirit manifest among the people at that time. There had then recently been formed several companies, as has been narrated in our late paragraphs, and particular mention was made of the artillery company under Captain Burch. Four hundred of the militia of the District, drafted in accordance with a requisition of the War Department, and under the command of Major King, had been placed in the command of Colonel Carberry, of the regular army, and were then encamped on the hill above Way's Glass Works, between Georgetown and the Potomac River. The Government was roused to the necessity of guarding against any possible danger, and it was believed that the steps taken were sufficient to defend the city against any invading force the enemy could bring against it.

On May 20, the corporation of the city of Washington made an appropriation of $5,000 to aid in the execution of such measures as the President might adopt for the safety and defense of the city. This sum of money was expended under the direction of Mayor Rapine, and John Davidson, Peter Lenox, Elias B. Caldwell, and Joseph Cassin.

May 29, 1813, a dinner was given at Davis's hotel in honor of the recent naval victories of the United States, which dinner was attended by a large number of citizens, without regard to party affiliations, from Washington, Georgetown, and Alexandria. Of this occasion it was said that it was the most numerous and respectable, and at the same time the most brilliant, assemblage of citizens that had ever been convened in the District. Among those present were the Vice-President of the United States, George Clinton; the Speaker of the House of Representatives, Henry Clay; and many members of Congress. General Robert Bowie, Governor of Maryland, acted as president of the day. Among the toasts drank were the following:

"The American People. Self-collected in prosperity, undaunted in adversity."

"The Genuine Republican. He that is ever ready to defend his country against her enemies."

"The Mission to Russia. As it is pledged to pacific intentions, so may it prove the precursor of an honorable peace."

"The Flag of Decatur. To the lightning of heaven it bows, to British thunder, never."

On Thursday, July 15, 1813, great excitement was produced in Washington by the report that the enemy's ships were approaching the city, his force in the Potomac consisting of fourteen sail. One-half of the regulars, drafted militia, and volunteers encamped at Warburton Heights, Thursday night, and the remainder within a few miles of them. The fort itself was in good order and well garrisoned, and the frigate *Adams* lay within a short distance. The Secretary of the Navy went down to Warburton on the same day that the report gained circulation, and arranged for the erection of a battery on the water's edge, which mounted nine heavy cannon. The Mayor of the city issued an order on the 15th requesting every man, whether or not subject to military duty, to enroll himself in some volunteer company for the defense of the city in case of an attack by the enemy. A meeting of the citizens was held in the afternoon of the same day in Capitol Square, at which it was resolved that the citizens who had not enrolled themselves should do so, and that a city commandant be appointed by a majority of the company officers, and that the Mayor be that officer. Regular patrols were organized among the citizens, which patrolled the city at night.

A strong detachment of United States artillery occupied Fort Warburton in Washington, and the ridge upon which the fort stood was held by a battalion of the Tenth and a company of the Twentieth United States Infantry, a battalion of drafted men, and a detachment from Captain Burch's men, all under the command of Colonel Nicholl, of the First Regiment of United States Artillery. On the road leading from Piscataway to Port Tobacco were the dragoons, supported by Captain Davidson's infantry, Captain Stull's riflemen, the Georgetown Grenadiers, and several companies of infantry. Near where the Warburton and Washington City roads meet, was the Thirty-sixth Regiment, under Colonel Carberry, with the remainder of Colonel Burch's artillery. This arrangement, besides guarding against the enemy's approach, admitted of a ready concentration of the American troops. At that time an invasion of the city seemed imminent. The various militia companies were under arms every morning at five o'clock, and through the day they were drilled and exercised, and fitted for the duties of the field. At Greenleaf's Point works were commenced upon which to erect a battery of heavy cannon, and furnaces were constructed with which to supply the cannon with red hot bolts. Below the Navy Yard, also, a similar fort was constructed. On Tuesday morning, July 22, 1813, the enemy's ships descended the river, and were then not in sight at Point Yates, about seventy miles away. A troop of cavalry under Captain Osburn, and two companies of infantry under Captains Lastly and Means, all from Loudon County, Virginia, arrived in Alexandria on Monday and Tuesday, July 19 and 20.

The British squadron was under the command of Admiral Warren. He having apparently abandoned his designs against Washington, an order was issued on Sunday, July 25, for the discharge of the volunteers, and they returned to their families and friends on the 26th, the regular troops and drafted militia remaining near Fort Warburton.

Matters were then quiet for several months. General Winder, who had been a prisoner of war in Canada, and who had been released on parole, arrived in Washington April 29, 1814. On July 17, 1814, quite alarming news was again received in Washington, that the enemy was at Patuxent, that he had burned the villages of Benedict and Lower Marlborough, and was in sight of Nottingham. Orders were immediately issued from the War Department to put on the march by 10:00 A. M., Saturday, June 18, detachments from the cavalry, artillery, and riflemen of this county to the number of about two hundred and fifty men. Contradictory advices being received in the afternoon of the same day, the above mentioned orders were countermanded. On Sunday, June 19, news was again received that the enemy was reëntering the Patuxent and had arrived opposite Benedict. Assistance was asked by the citizens of Nottingham, and the Secretary of War caused the necessary orders to be distributed by General Van Ness. By 10:00 A. M., the Georgetown Artillery and Riflemen, the Georgetown Dragoons, Captain Thornton's troop, of Alexandria, and Captain Caldwell's, of Washington, were ready to march, and all departed for the Patuxent under command of Major George Peter.

The *Intelligencer* said: "We learn that the enemy have pursued the same system of barbarous warfare that was commenced last summer under the notorious Cockburn. They have burned many dwellings and plundered many families on the shores of the Patuxent."

A new volunteer corps was organized about this time, known as the "Legion of Mounted Infantry," and composed of the *élite* of the entire District. The companies above mentioned reached Nottingham on Monday, June 20, and were immediately ordered to Benedict, where Colonel Wadsworth was in command of the troops previously collected. These troops included those under Major Peter, an artillery force with eight eighteen-pound cannon, and a battalion of the Thirty-eighth Regiment of United States Infantry from Baltimore. In connection with the notice of these movements of the soldiers, the *Intelligencer* said: "It is superfluous to notice the contemptible asseverations of facetious editors who rail at the National Government, without looking into the conduct of those whose willful neglect of duty has brought incalculable mischief upon a large portion of the citizens of Maryland."

On Tuesday, June 21, 1814, a slight battle was fought between the belligerent forces, in which one American named Francis Wise was killed. He was shot by a British soldier, "who most bravely fought until he was killed by repeated wounds, and who proved to be a sergeant of marines of proverbial courage and strength, and before he was disabled wounded another of the troops with his bayonet, and very nearly overpowered General Stewart, of the militia, who engaged him after Wise was killed." The British soldiers were, however, driven on board their ships, and the Americans withdrew out of reach of their guns. Six of the British were taken prisoners and brought to Washington on the 24th, and committed to the custody of the marshal. June 26, firing from the British vessels was kept up in St. Leonard's Creek all day, and fears were entertained for Commodore Barney, the British having been reënforced; but Barney extricated himself from his useless position in St. Leonard's Creek and went to Benedict on the Patuxent. Commodore Barney brought on this engagement, and in two hours the enemy "got under way and made sail down the river. They are now (10:00 A. M.) warping round Point Patience, and I am sailing up the Patuxent with my vessels. My loss is Acting Midshipman Asquith, killed, and ten others killed or wounded."[1]

In consequence of the retreat of the enemy down the Patuxent, the volunteers from Washington set out on their return on Wednesday, June 29, the cavalry arriving on the 30th, and the artillery and rifle companies on July 1. Commodore Barney arrived in the city on Thursday, June 30, his flotilla having moved up the river as far as Lower Marlborough.

The battle of St. Leonard's, at the mouth of St. Leonard's Creek,

[1] Commodore Barney's Report.

June 26, 1814, was the occasion of a great deal of controversy among
the officers of the American forces. Colonel Wadsworth, in his report
to the Secretary of War, reflected rather severely on the conduct of
Captain Miller, who commanded a portion of the artillery during the
day, and Captain Miller even more severely animadverted upon
the conduct of Colonel Wadsworth and his command. After moving
from his position on the hill down to the lower ground, in which
position he was disappointed, "finding that the barges which were
firing round shot were not only out of sight of this position, but completely out of range of any grape or canister that could be thrown
from my batteries," he therefore sought still another position, but
before he had reached one-half way to the spot he "discovered the
infantry retiring in good order along the low ground," and therefore
from this unfortunate movement of the infantry, himself "became one
of the number moving from the field," which he had held for
upward of two hours in constant firing upon the enemy's frigates,
employing his best exertions to annoy them, etc. He gave great
credit to Commodore Barney's flotilla, and the detachment from the
flotilla under Captain Cohagen.

July 14, 1814, the President of the United States made a requisition
upon the governors of the several States for militia from those States,
to be organized into regiments and held in readiness for immediate
action, to the number of ninety-three thousand and five hundred men.
He apportioned to Pennsylvania fourteen regiments, to Delaware one
regiment, to Maryland six regiments, and to Virginia thirteen regiments.

July 17, the enemy had a force of soldiers at Leonardtown, in
St. Mary's County, Maryland, about sixty-five miles from Washington.
The volunteers from this city and vicinity were then encamped near
the wood yard, about fifteen miles from Washington, from which
position they could in two hours reach either the Patuxent or the
Potomac. A battalion of volunteers, which had been enrolled for
the defense of Washington, was discharged July 23, 1814. They
were reviewed that day by General Winder, and by him highly com-
plimented on their soldierlike appearance. August 1, 1814, there was
a general review of the military of the District by General Winder,
of the Army of the United States, and commander of the military
department in which the District of Columbia was comprised. The
First Brigade, under Brigadier-General Young, was reviewed at Alexandria at 10:00 A. M., and the Second Brigade, which was under the
command of Brigadier-General Smith, was reviewed in front of the
President's Square, in Washington, at 2:00 P. M.

A volunteer corps of between sixty and seventy dragoons from Frederick and Washington counties, Virginia, passed through Washington, August 12, for the rendezvous at Bladensburg. A detachment of about three hundred men, under Colonel Gettings, from Montgomery County, Maryland, also reached Bladensburg about the same time.

August 9, the entire British fleet in the Potomac lay just below the mouth of the St. Mary's River—one 74-gun ship, the *Albion;* one razee, three frigates, two ships, two brigs, several sloops of war, one large schooner, and twelve smaller ones. The force in the Patuxent consisted of two ships and one brig, the ships being the *Severn* and *Prince William.* By the 19th of August, the British fleet was strengthened so as to consist of forty-six sail at or near Point Lookout, and besides there were five frigates off St. George's Island. On Thursday, August 18, the enemy's forces entered the Patuxent, and indicated an intention of ascending the river. Upon the receipt of this intelligence in the city, General Winder made requisition upon the governors of Maryland and Pennsylvania and upon various militia officers; and the militia of the District of Columbia was ordered out *en masse.* Colonel Monroe, with Captain Thornton's troop of horse, made a reconnoissance of the position of the enemy on Friday the 19th, and the militia of Washington and Georgetown were mustered on the same day. On the 20th, about 1:00 P. M., these, together with some other forces, commenced marching toward Benedict, and encamped for the night on the road to Upper Marlborough, about four miles from the Eastern Branch bridge. The British arrived at Benedict in force on the same day, with twenty-seven square-rigged vessels and other craft. Colonel Tiglhman and Captain Caldwell were ordered, with their cavalry, to remove and destroy forage and provisions in front of the enemy, and to impede his march as much as possible. Those who reconnoitered the position of the enemy estimated the strength of his forces at from four thousand to six thousand men, and he soon advanced upon Nottingham. Early on Monday, the 22d, a detachment of the Thirty-sixth and Thirty-eighth Regiments, and three companies from the brigade of General Smith, under the command of Major Peter, marched on the road to Nottingham, and the remainder of the army took up an elevated position. Commodore Joshua Barney had joined the army with the flotilla men, besides the marines under Captain Miller. The cavalry which met the British in their march retired before them, and this led the advanced corps to attempt to impede the march of the enemy, who took the road to Upper Marlborough, after coming within a few miles of General Winder's army, which was drawn up in line of battle to receive him. General Winder then fell back with his entire force to the Battalion Old Fields, about eight miles from Marlborough, and about the same distance from Washington. The British army arrived at Upper Marlborough about two o'clock, and remained there until next day, waiting for the return of the detachment sent against the flotilla under Commodore Barney, which was destroyed by the Commodore under orders from the Secretary of War. Late on the 22d, President Madison, together with the Secretaries of War and the Navy, and the Attorney-General, joined General Winder at Battalion Old Fields, and remained with him until the evening of the next day. On the morning of the 23d, the troops were reviewed by the President. At that time it was not known, and it could not be ascertained, what the purpose of the enemy was, whether it was to march upon Annapolis, upon Fort Washington, or upon the city of Washington. His forces were variously estimated, but it was generally believed that he had from five thousand to seven thousand men. General Winder's force was about three thousand, with five pieces of heavy artillery, two eighteen-pounders, and three twelve-pounders, and other smaller pieces, enough to bring the aggregate number of pieces of artillery up to seventeen. General Winder, induced to believe that the enemy intended to remain stationary through the day, ordered the troops under General Stansbury at Bladensburg, and one other corps, to move to Upper Marlborough, himself going to meet them, and leaving orders that the enemy should be annoyed in every possible way, either in his march or in his position; and that if he moved upon Bladensburg, General Smith should fall upon his flank, or be governed by circumstances as to his movements.

However, the enemy left Upper Marlborough and had a skirmish with Captain Stull's company, which was compelled to retreat after firing four or five rounds. The entire army was thereupon placed in a position favorable for defense, but upon General Winder's return, late in the afternoon, he decided to march upon the city of Washington. The object of this retreat was, as stated by General Winder, to unite his entire force, fearing a night attack by a superior enemy upon his undisciplined troops, as in a night attack his superiority in artillery would be of no avail. The march of the army to Washington was extremely rapid and precipitate, and the men were greatly exhausted before the camping ground was reached.

This precipitate march, or rather retreat, was of course after the battle of Bladensburg had been fought. It is difficult to give a correct account of that battle, because it was not very creditable to the American arms, and it was perfectly natural for all concerned in it to desire, after it was over, to prevent the precise facts from coming to light, especially where those facts reflected adversely upon their conduct. But the following account is as nearly accurate as the circumstances will permit. General Stansbury arrived at Bladensburg on the 22d of the month, and the Fifth Baltimore Regiment, together with the rifle corps and artillery, in the evening of the 23d. At twelve o'clock that night Colonel Monroe advised General Stansbury to fall upon the rear of the enemy forthwith, as it was understood that he was in motion for the city of Washington. General Stansbury, having been ordered to post himself at Bladensburg, did not consider himself at liberty to leave the place, and besides the fatigue of the troops under Colonel Sterret rendered it impracticable.

On the morning of the 24th, General Winder's headquarters were near the Eastern Branch bridge, arrangements for the destruction of which had been made. Detachments of horse were out in several directions as videttes and reconnoitering parties. Colonel George Minor arrived in Washington on the 22d, with his regiment of Virginia militia — six hundred infantry and one hundred cavalry, and reported to the President and Secretary of War for orders and United States arms. Next morning, after several delays in counting out the arms, it became rumored around that the enemy was marching upon the city by way of Bladensburg, and Colonel Monroe left the city with the view of joining General Stansbury, to aid him in forming a line of battle to meet the enemy. General Stansbury then occupied the ground west of Bladensburg, on the banks of the Eastern Branch. Here the front line of battle was formed. Over the Eastern Branch there was a bridge, from which a turnpike led to Washington. After the various forces at this point had been stationed, Colonels Beall and Hood, with the Maryland militia from Annapolis under Colonel Beall, crossed the bridge and took up a position on the right of the turnpike and upon the most commanding height, about three hundred yards to the right of the road, for the purpose of securing the right flank. About eleven o'clock in the morning, intelligence was received that the enemy was in full march toward Bladensburg. General Winder thereupon put his entire command in motion, with the exception of a few men and a piece of artillery at the Eastern Branch bridge, to destroy it. Upon the arrival of General Winder at Bladensburg in advance of his troops, he approved of the disposi-

tion made by General Stansbury and Colonel Munroe; but even if
he had not been able to do this, it would have been impracticable to
make any change, as the enemy at that moment, 12:00 м., appeared
on the opposite heights of Bladensburg, about a mile distant. General
Winder's troops were arranged in line of battle as they arrived. The
President, the Secretary of War, and the Attorney-General were all
upon the ground. As the enemy advanced into Bladensburg, the
second line of General Winder's troops was being formed. Commodore Barney's command came in at this time on the double-quick, and
were formed in line on the right of the main road. The heavy artillery
was placed in line under Captain Miller. Lieutenant-Colonel Kramer,
with a battalion of Maryland militia, was posted in a wood in advance
of Colonel Beall and Colonel Hood, and the other troops were properly
arranged. About half past twelve, while the second line was yet
forming, the enemy approached, and the battle commenced. The Baltimore artillery opened fire upon the enemy's light troops advancing
along the streets of the village, dispersing them, and they protected
themselves behind houses and trees as well as they could; but other
portions of their troops began throwing rockets, and his light troops
began to advance, concentrating near the bridge and pressing across
it, and also crossing above, where the river was fordable. The enemy's
column was thrown into some confusion while approaching the bridge,
but having gained it they rapidly crossed, and forming into line
moved steadily on, compelling General Winder's artillery and riflemen
to give way. Soon afterward the rockets from the enemy's force
assumed a more horizontal direction, and passing too near the heads
of Colonel Shutz's and Colonel Ragan's regiments, the right gave
way, and this, falling back, was followed in a few moments by a
general flight of the two regiments, in defiance of all the efforts and
exertions of General Winder and General Stansbury and the other
officers. Burch's artillery and the Fifth Regiment remained with firmness; but notwithstanding that the enemy's light troops were driven
back by the firmness of these two regiments, at length, the enemy
having gained the right flank of the Fifth, which exposed it, Burch's
artillery and Colonel Sterret, in command of the Fifth, were ordered
by General Winder to retreat, with a view of forming at a short
distance to the rear; but instead of retiring in order, the Fifth, like
the other two regiments, in a very few minutes was retreating in
disorder and confusion. Attempts were then made to rally the
troops, which were temporarily successful. They ultimately failed,
however, and the troops were badly routed. They retreated on the

road, which forked in three directions — one leading by Rock Creek to Tenley Town and Montgomery Courthouse, one leading to Georgetown, and the third to Washington.

After the retreat of the troops under Lieutenant-Colonel Kramer from his first position, the column of the enemy was exposed to a galling fire from Major Peter's artillery, which continued until they came in contact with Commodore Barney, and it was here that the enemy met with the greatest resistance and sustained the greatest loss. An eighteen-pounder was opened upon him by Commodore Barney, and this completely cleared the road for the time being, and several attempts were made to rally. He thereupon made a flank movement to the right, when Captain Miller opened upon him with three twelve-pounders with considerable effect; but they kept on with the flank movement and at length gained the rear of the right of the second line, and a retreat was ordered by Commodore Barney. After some further maneuvering and fighting, the troops, some of whom had remained firm in their positions, were ordered by General Winder to retreat, and after again forming were again ordered to retreat by the commanding general. And when General Smith's command came into the field and were in the act of forming in line, they were also ordered to retreat to Washington, expecting there to be united with the troops of the first line. Colonel Monroe covered the retreat. At the Capitol the troops were again halted while General Winder was in consultation with Colonel Monroe and General Armstrong.

However, the first line, which had been the first to break and retreat from Bladensburg, with the exception of Colonel Laval's, had most of them taken the road which led north of the District of Columbia, and others had dispersed and gone to their homes. Taking all these things into consideration the commanding general believed it would be impossible to defend the city against the invading forces of the enemy; nor did he think it would be proper to attempt to defend the Capitol building, as that would leave every other part of the city to the mercy of the enemy. On receiving the order to rally on the heights of Georgetown and abandon Washington to its fate, the troops, according to General Smith, evinced an anguish beyond the power of language to express. They were held at Tenley Town, and an attempt to collect them together was only partially successful. Some returned home, some went in pursuit of refreshments, and others gave themselves up to the feelings which fatigue, privation, and chagrin naturally produce. The forces collected were marched about five miles from the Potomac, and early in the morning of the 25th ordered to assemble at Montgomery Courthouse. This position seems to have been taken by General Winder with the view of interposing to protect Baltimore in case that city should prove to be in danger. On the 23d, General Winder had sent orders to the commanding officer at Fort Washington to place patrols in every road leading to the garrison, and in the event of his being taken in the rear to blow up the fort and retire across the river.

From Benedict to Washington *via* Bladensburg is about fifty miles. The battle of Bladensburg ended at 4:00 P. M., and the British forces reached Washington about eight o'clock in the evening. The British army was under the joint command of General Ross and Admiral Cockburn. As the former was riding toward the Capitol, his horse was shot under him by some one firing from a house in the vicinity, the design being apparently to kill the General. This so enraged the troops that, after setting fire to the house containing the sharpshooter, they marched quickly to the Capitol, and fired several volleys into its windows; then maching inside the building, they collected all kinds of combustible materials, piled the books and papers in the Congressional Library on the floors, and set the whole mass on fire. When the clouds of smoke issued from the roofs of the wings of the building, it seemed doomed to destruction, and doubtless more damage would have been done to it than was done, had it not been for the fact that in about half an hour after the fire was kindled a heavy shower set in and continued all the rest of the evening, and was the means of saving the walls, at least. While the fire was raging in the Capitol building, the British soldiers marched up Pennsylvania Avenue to set on fire the other public buildings. They did set on fire the Treasury, State, War, and Navy departments, and the President's House, destroying Mr. Sewall's house on Capitol Hill, a hotel belonging to Mr. Carroll, General Washington's house, and Mr. Frost's house. The public property destroyed was valued as follows: The Capitol building to its foundation was worth $787,163.28; the President's House, $334,334; the other public buildings, $93,613.82; total value, $1,215,111.10.

It may be proper to add to this detail a statement of the forces engaged on either side in the engagement at Bladensburg. The strength of the several corps on the part of General Winder's army was as follows: Dragoons of the United States, 140; Maryland militia, 260; dragoons of the District of Columbia, 40; dragoons of Virginia, 100; total dragoons, 540. The Thirty-sixth Regiment of Infantry, one battalion of the Thirty-eighth, and one company of the Twelfth, 500;

seamen and marines, 600; total, 1,100. Militia—Stansbury's brigade, 1,353; part of Stricker's, 956; Smith's brigade and Kramer's battalion, 1,800; Young's brigade, 450; Beall's regiment, 800; Minor's regiment, 600; sundry detachments of volunteers and militia, 450; total militia, 6,409. Total number, 8,049. There were in the battle twenty pieces of artillery of different caliber. The losses amounted to 10 killed and 30 wounded; total, 40.

The British forces numbered as follows: On Capitol Hill, 700; on Turnpike Hill, 2,000; wounded at Bladensburg, 300; attendants, 300; wounded and attendants at Washington, 60; killed at Bladensburg and Washington, 180; total, 3,540. The entire number in the British army was probably about 4,500.

On the evening of the 25th, after being in possession of the Capital of the Nation twenty-four hours, the British made the greatest exertions to leave the city. They had about forty horses, ten or twelve carts and wagons, and several gigs, which they sent to Bladensburg to move off the wounded; and these were preceded by a drove of sixty or seventy cattle. Arriving at Bladensburg, the surgeon was ordered to collect the wounded who could walk, and the forty horses were utilized to carry the wounded who could not walk, the carts and wagons being also used to carry the dead. About ninety of the wounded were left behind. At about midnight the British army passed through Bladensburg; parties continued to follow until morning, and stragglers until midday. The retreat was made in great haste, as if the enemy were conscious of the presence of the American army at Montgomery Courthouse, and were in dread of an attack by General Winder's forces.

The capture of the city of Washington by the British forces severely wounded the pride not only of the people of the District of Columbia, but also of the entire country. That the city should have been permitted to be captured, has ever since been looked upon as a disgrace to the country and a shame to those who were entrusted with its defense. Some writers, in their impartiality, have attempted to distribute the blame all round among the various officers of the Government, from President Madison down to the immediate commanding general; while others have sought to limit it to the commanding general. Those who have included the President in the list, do so mainly upon the ground that it was he who was responsible for the selection of such an incompetent general; but it is probable that one of the reasons for the ability of the British to march upon and capture the city with but little or no opposition, was

this; that most of the troops upon which General Winder had to
depend, were raw militia. Had they been disciplined veterans, as
were the British soldiers, or had they possessed confidence in themselves and in their general, the sting and stigma of the disgrace of
the capture would not have been experienced. At any rate the
prowess and valor of American soldiers have since been most amply
vindicated, on battlefields in Mexico, and on both sides in the war
of the late Rebellion; so that so far as that particular feature of the
case is concerned, there no longer remains any opportunity for criticism upon American soldiers, nor does there remain any reason to
doubt the ability of the United States to produce competent commanding generals.

In reviewing the events preceding the battle of Bladensburg, and
the battle itself, it may, in the first place, be well to introduce the
testimony of General Winder himself, with reference to the conduct
of the militia from the District of Columbia. In a letter published
October 8, 1814, he said: "I have no knowledge of any instance of
the conduct of the militia (from Washington and Georgetown) while
under my command which is not honorable to their zeal, spirit, and
subordination, and that they yielded a prompt and soldierly obedience
to all my orders. My situation on the field, in the battle of Bladensburg, with the front line, and subsequent efforts to form them on the
left of the Georgetown and other militias, prevented me from witness-
ing their conduct in the engagement. When I sent them orders to
retreat, the enemy were turning both their right and left flanks. From
the total flight of the front line and the troops posted on the right,
and when I came up to them shortly after their retreat commenced, I
found them retiring in order, and consequently inferred that they had
not left their position before receiving my orders to retire. They were
prepared and showed the utmost readiness to form again between the
Capitol and the turnpike gate to renew the contest, until I found
the total dispersion of the first line rendered it impossible to make
another stand with a number sufficiently great to afford any hope of
success. And they did, on my order, proceed through the city to
Georgetown and form on the heights of Tenley Town."

Then, too, the story of the battle is perhaps best told in General
Winder's own language:

"Our advanced riflemen, Pinkney's corps, now began to fire, and
continued it for half a dozen rounds, when I observed them to run
back to an orchard. They halted there, and seemed for a moment
about returning to their original position, but in a few moments

entirely broke, and retired to the left of Stansbury's line. The advance
artillery immediately followed the riflemen, and retired on the left of
the Fifth Baltimore Regiment, which had been pushed forward to
sustain them.

"The first three or four rockets fired by the enemy being much
above the heads of Stansbury's men, they stood them very man-
fully, but the rockets having taken a more horizontal direction, a
universal flight of the center and left of Stansbury's brigade was the
consequence. The Fifth Regiment and the artillery still remained, and
I hoped would prevent the enemy's approach, but the enemy approached singly, and their fire annoyed the Fifth considerably, when
I ordered it to retire, for the purpose of putting it out of reach of
the enemy: This order was, however, immediately countermanded,
from an aversion to retire before the enemy became stronger, and from
a hope that the enemy would issue in a body and enable us to act
upon him on terms of more equality.

"But his fire beginning to disturb this corps, and the Fifth Regiment still more by wounding some of them, and a strong column
passing up the road and deploying on its left, I ordered them to
retire. Their retreat became a flight of absolute and total disorder.
Beall's regiment was posted on a height to the right of the road, which
commanded the whole ground occupied by Stansbury's brigade. It
gave one or two ineffectual fires and fled." This retreat completes the
account of the fortunes and fate of the front line, which could not be
rallied, and which displayed all its activity in making its way home.

This, it will be seen, agrees with General Winder's letter given
above with respect to the conduct of the militia from the District of
Columbia, and hence it seems permissible to place the most of the
blame for the defeat at Bladensburg on the front line. The second line
was composed of Smith's militia brigade, the Thirty-sixth Regular
Regiment, one battalion of the Thirty-eighth Regiment, a detachment
of the Twelfth Regiment, and Commodore Barney's corps of seamen
and marines and the whole of the cavalry. General Winder did not
have this line under his immediate observation. It appears that Commodore Barney, in the pressure upon the front line, was entirely forgotten
at the Eastern Branch bridge, and would have remained there, much
against his inclination, had he not accidentally met the President and
Secretary of War, who advised him to hasten his march to Bladensburg
and join the army. The Commodore in his report said: "We came
up in a trot and took our position on the rising ground between
Smith's militia and Beall's, posted our marines and seamen, and waited

15

the approach of the enemy. During this period, the engagement continued, the enemy advanced, and our army retreating apparently in much disorder. At length the enemy made his appearance before us and halted. After a few minutes I ordered an eighteen-pounder to fire upon him, which completely cleared the road. A second and third attempt were made to come forward, but all were destroyed. They then crossed over into an open field and attempted to flank us. There he was met by three twelve-pounders, the marines and seamen acting as infantry, and was again badly cut up. By this time not a vestige of the American army remained, except a body of five or six hundred on a height on my right, and from which I expected great support. The enemy now pushed up their sharpshooters and began to outflank us on the right. Our guns were that way when we pushed up the hill toward the American corps, stationed as above described, which, to my great mortification, made no resistance, giving a fire or two and retiring. Finding the enemy now in my rear, and no means of defense, I ordered my officers and men to retire."

General Smith said: "The dispersion of the front line caused a dangerous opening on our left, of which the enemy was availing himself, when I ordered Colonel Brent, with the Second Regiment, to take a position still more to our left, and he was preparing to execute this order when orders came from General Winder for the whole of the troops to retreat."

Upon receipt of orders of this kind from the commanding general, of course fighting was out of the question. The orders that followed were but little else than a repetition of orders to form and counter orders to retreat. When what was left of the army reached Washington, the Secretary of War suggested the occupation of the Capitol building, believing that the Thirty-sixth and Thirty-eighth regiments, together with those portions of Commodore Barney's corps that could be collected, would be sufficient to sustain their position therein, provided General Winder could assure them of such exterior support as would be necessary to supply them with food, water, and ammunition. The General replied that he could not give the assurance, and that he proposed to retire behind the heights at Georgetown. The Secretary of War then assented to the measure which appeared to have been previously discussed and determined upon by the commanding general and the Secretary of State, and perceiving that no order was given to apprise the Navy Department of the determination to cross Rock Creek and to prevent the capture of the Navy Yard, he dispatched Major Bell to announce the retreat of the army. The garrison at Fort Washington was not more fortunate than their fellow-soldiers. The fort was destroyed and abandoned, though pressed by no enemy on either side.

It may not be improper to introduce testimony from the British side as to some of the features of this battle. An officer of the Eighty-fifth Royal Regiment, named Gleig, stated the facts in the following language: "This battle, by which the fate of the American Capital was decided, began about one o'clock in the afternoon, and lasted till about four o'clock. The loss on the part of the English was severe, since, out of two-thirds of the army which was engaged, upward of five hundred men were killed and wounded, and what rendered it doubly severe was that among these were numbered several officers of rank and distinction. Colonel Thornton, who commanded the Light Brigade, Lieutenant-Colonel Wood, commanding the Eighty-fifth Regiment, and Major Brown, who had led the advanced guard, were all severely wounded, and General Ross himself had a horse shot under him. On the side of the Americans the slaughter was not so great. Being in possession of a strong position, they were, of course, less exposed in defending than the others in storming it, and had they conducted themselves with coolness and resolution, it is not conceivable how the day could have been won. But the fact is, that with the exception of a part of the sailors from the gunboats, under the command of Commodore Barney, no troops could behave worse than they did. The skirmishers were driven in as soon as attacked. The first line gave way without offering the slightest resistance, and the left of the main body was broken within half an hour after it was seriously engaged. Of the sailors, however, it would be injustice not to speak in terms which their conduct merits. They were employed as gunners, and not only did they serve their guns with a quickness and precision which astonished their assailants, but they stood till some of them were actually bayoneted, with fuses in their hands; nor was it till their leader was wounded and taken, and they saw themselves deserted on all sides by the soldiers, that they quit the field."

General Ross, in his dispatch of August 30, said that his loss at the battle of Bladensburg was sixty-four killed and one hundred and eighty-five wounded and missing. The numbers given by Gleig comprised the entire loss of the British in killed, wounded, missing, and deserters, from the morning of the battle until their reëmbarkation, including the casualties at Washington.

"On the other hand, the citizen-militia escaped with their valuable lives, and, without forming again to impede the approach of the enemy

or to defend the Capitol and public buildings, disappeared entirely
from the District, leaving their wives and children to the mercy of
the victor."

The destruction of the Navy Yard followed almost immediately
after the defeat at Bladensburg. The Secretary of the Navy had given
orders to Commodore Tingey, that in case of defeat the shipping and
store at the Navy Yard should be destroyed, to prevent their falling
into the enemy's hands. At four o'clock the Secretary of War sent
a messenger to the Commodore informing him that no further protection could be given, and that officer forthwith proceeded to destroy
the buildings and vessels, notwithstanding earnest appeals were made
by the citizens to have the Navy Yard saved from destruction. At
twenty minutes past eight o'clock the match was applied, and the sloop
of war *Argus*, with ten guns mounted, five barges fully armed, two
gunboats, the frigate *Columbia* on the stocks, and a large quantity of
naval stores were consigned to the flames. The schooner and the
arsenal escaped destruction.

After leaving the Capitol the British army marched up Pennsylvania Avenue, and taking possession of Mrs. Suter's lodging house,
ordered supper. Meanwhile, they set fire to the Treasury building
and the President's House. The President himself had retired from
the city, with his cabinet, on horseback immediately after the close
of the battle of Bladensburg, crossing the Potomac at Little Falls and
recrossing it at the Great Falls. The table at the President's House
was found set for forty guests, in expectation of a welcome to the
victorious defenders of the city. The wine was cooling on the side-
board, the plates warming at the grate, and the meats were on the
spits in the kitchen. Ross and Cockburn, however, returned to
Mrs. Suter's house, and, after extinguishing the lights, ate their
repast by the light of the burning buildings. Later in the evening
General Ross rejoined the main army, then on Capitol Hill, and
Admiral Cockburn, with a few of his companions, passed the night
in a brothel. During the night, in a fit of rashness, the sentries were
attacked by a grandnephew of General Washington, a young sailor
named John Lewis, who was shot down in the street and was found
dead next morning where he fell. Had the militia at the battle of
Bladensburg showed the spirit manifested by this young nephew of
General Washington, the fortunes of the day would have been vastly
different. On the morning of the 25th, the two commanders renewed
the work of destruction by setting fire to the War and Navy departments. The Post Office and the Patent Office were spared by the

enemy on the appeal of Dr. Thornton to save private property stored in the building. General Washington's house, a dwelling owned by Robert Sewall, from behind which General Ross's horse was shot, that of Mr. Frost, and the hotel of Daniel Carroll were burned on Capitol Hill, when the British proceeded to the Navy Yard to complete the ruin commenced under the orders of the Secretary of War. There they burned the public works, the private ropewalks of Tench Ringgold, Heath & Company, and John Chalmers, and mutilated the monument erected by the officers of the navy to the valiant heroes who fell in the Tripolitan War.

After setting fire to the ropewalks they threw the torch into a dry well into which the Americans had previously cast a large quantity of gunpowder and other military stores. The immediate consequence was a tremendous explosion, which caused death and destruction to all around, nearly one hundred of the British soldiers being killed and wounded, and their mutilated remains scattered in all directions. In addition to the general consternation produced by this explosion, a frightful tornado swept over the city, throwing down buildings and dealing destruction to everything in its way. The inky blackness of the sky, the howling of the storm, the cataract of rain, the fierce gleaming of the lightning, the tremendous pealing of the thunder, and the crash of falling buildings, all conspired to render the scene terrific beyond description, and, as was natural, struck terror and dismay alike to the heart of friend and foe. Trees were torn up by the roots, roofs were hurled through the air like sheets of paper, and scores of the enemy, as well as of the inhabitants of the city, were buried beneath the ruins. The elements seemed to vie with the English in making the work of destruction as complete as possible. The British, taking a needless alarm, or pretending to be apprehensive of an attack from the brave militia that fought the battle of Bladensburg, stealthily withdrew from the city and took up their line of march for the point of embarkation.

President Madison, finally awaking to the seriousness of the situation, issued the following proclamation on September 1, 1814:

"WHEREAS, the enemy by a sudden incursion have succeeded in invading the Capital of the Nation, defended at the moment by troops less numerous than their own, and almost entirely of militia; during their possession of which, though for a single day only, they wantonly destroyed the public edifices having no relations in their structure to operations of war, nor used at the time for military annoyance; some of these edifices being also costly monuments of taste and of the arts, and others depositories of the public archives, not only precious to the Nation as the memorials of its origin and its early transactions, but interesting to all nations, as contributions to the general stock of historical instruction and political science; and

" WHEREAS, Advantage has been taken of the loss of the fort more immediately guarding the town of Alexandria, to place the town within the range of the naval force, too long and too much in the habit of abusing its superiority, wherever it can be applied, to require as the alternative of a general conflagration an undisturbed plunder of private property, which has been executed in a manner peculiarly distressing to the inhabitants, who had inconsiderately cast themselves upon the justice and generosity of the victor; and,

" W.HEREAS, It now appears, by a direct communication with the British commander on the American Station, to be his avowed purpose to employ the force under his direction in destroying and laying waste such towns and districts upon the coast as may be found assailable, adding to his declaration the insulting pretext that it is in retaliation for a wanton destruction committed by the army of the United States in Upper Canada, when it is notorious that no destruction has been committed which, notwithstanding the multiplied outrages previously committed by the enemy, was not unauthorized, and promptly shown to be so; and that the United States have been as constant in their endeavors to reclaim the enemy from such outrages, by the contrast of their example, as they have been ready to terminate on reasonable conditions the war itself; and,

" WHEREAS, These proceedings and declared purposes, which exhibit a deliberate disregard of the principles of humanity and the rules of civilized warfare, and which must give to the existing war a character of extended devastation and barbarism at the very moment of negotiations for peace invited by the enemy himself, leave no prospect of safety to anything within the reach of his predatory and incendiary operations but in manful and universal determination to chastise and expel the invader;

" Now, therefore, I, James Madison, President of the United States, do issue this, my proclamation, exhorting all the good people thereof to unite their hearts and hands, giving effect to the ample means possessed for that purpose. I enjoin it upon all officers, civil and military, to exert themselves in executing the duties with which they are respectively charged. And more especially I require the officers commanding the respective military departments to be vigilant and alert in providing for the defense thereof; for the more effectual accomplishment of which they are authorized to call to the defense of exposed and frontier places portions of the militia most convenient thereto, whether they be or be not parts of the quotas detached for the service of the United States under requisitions of the General Government.

"On an occasion which appeals so forcibly to the proud feelings and patriotic devotion of the American people, knowing what they owe to themselves, what they owe to their country and the high destinies which await it, what to the glory acquired by their fathers in establishing the independence which is now maintained by their sons with the augmented strength and resources with which time and heaven have blessed them.   JAMES MADISON."

Major-General Winfield Scott arrived in Washington, October 13, 1814. On that day the following officers captured at Bladensburg were released on their parole: Joshua Barney, commander of the United States flotilla; John Reagan, lieutenant of militia; Samuel Miller, captain of marine corps; Dominick Bader, captain of militia; G. Von Harter, lieutenant of militia; Robert M. Hamilton, master in United States navy; Thomas Duketant, acting master; Jesse Huffington, sailing master; Davidson Robertson, acting midshipman; John M. Howland, Fifth Regiment Baltimore Volunteers; J. B. Martin, surgeon, besides forty-one privates captured at Bladensburg and twenty-six captured at Baltimore.

But little of interest occurred in Washington after the battle of Bladensburg and the capture of the city, until the famous victory of General Jackson at New Orleans, January 8, 1815. The news of this victory reached Washington February 4, and in the evening of that day, which was Saturday, a general illumination of the city occurred in honor of the event. Rumors of peace were abroad in the city on February 13, and on the 14th the treaty of Ghent, signed on the 24th of December preceding, fifteen days before the victory at New Orleans, was delivered by Mr. Henry Carroll to the Secretary of State, and laid before the Senate of the United States on the 15th; and on Saturday night, February 18, 1815, there was a general illumination of the city and a grand celebration in honor of the peace secured by that treaty, which had been ratified by the Senate that day.

The next war in which Washington was engaged, in common with the rest of the country, was that with Mexico, brought on by politicians favoring the extension of slavery in order that the balance of power between the Slave States and the Free States might be maintained as nearly equal as possible. The details connected with the origin of this war have been so well presented in numerous histories that it is not deemed necessary to attempt to present them here. It may not be amiss, however, to call attention to the fact that two methods of annexation of the State of Texas to the Union attracted widespread attention, and were of universal interest to the American people in connection with this movement,—the one by treaty, the other by joint resolution of Congress. President Tyler negotiated a treaty with Texas for her annexation, which was rejected by the Senate by a vote of 35 to 16. According to Hon. Thomas H. Benton, who, with great power and vehemence, opposed the purposes and methods of the war, the rejection of this treaty postponed the war two years, and if the wisdom and patriotism of the Senate had had any influence with the executive department of the Government, there would have been no war with Mexico, and Texas would at the same time have been annexed.

Besides annexation by treaty there was but one other method by which that end could be peacefully accomplished, and that was by joint resolution. So far as Mexico was concerned, it would make but little or no difference as to the method by which her territory was procured, provided it were a peaceful one; but to the United States the question of method was all-important. To annex Texas by treaty would be to treat with that republic as an independent power or nation; and after annexation was accomplished she would seem to be always in a position of observing the treaty or not, as she might choose; and of pretending that the provisions of the treaty had been violated by the United States, whether such violation had or had not occurred; and by such pretense she would at any future time be able to influence her people to favor the abrogation of the treaty on their part; or, in other words, to secede from the Union. While on the other hand, if the whole matter were referred to the law-making power of the Government, instead of to the treaty-making power, as would be the case if Texas were invited to assume the position of a Territory of the Union, and then be admitted as a State, as had been all the other States, by the consent of Congress, she would become a member of an indissoluble Union, and would thereby become powerless to peacefully secede.

In accordance with this view a joint resolution, introduced into the House of Representatives by Mr. Douglas, December 23, 1844, for the annexation of Texas to the United States, "in conformity with the treaty of 1803 for the purchase of Louisiana," after a stormy debate, was passed, January 25, 1845, by a vote of 120 to 98. In the Senate the resolution was so amended on motion of Mr. Benton as to gain his support and that of one other Senator, and then passed by a vote of 27 yeas to 25 nays. The next day, February 28, as amended, it passed in the House of Representatives by a vote of 132 to 76. The Congress somewhat marred its work by adding to the joint resolution what was and is known as the "Walker Amendment," by which the President was authorized to set it aside and to proceed to "agree on the terms of admission and cession, either by treaty to be submitted to the Senate, or by articles to be submitted to the two Houses of Congress," which part of the amendment was perhaps, however, offset by the provision in the amendment itself, that the Republic of Texas "shall be admitted into the Union by virtue of this act *on an equal footing with the existing States*," etc. But the President, notwithstanding his predilection for the method by treaty, having on the 2d of March approved the legislation embodied in the joint resolution, chose to set aside the Walker Amendment, and on the next day, the last of his term of office, knowing that Congress did not intend to entrust him with the discretionary power, sent one of his relatives, a Mr. Waggaman, as an express to hasten to communicate to the Republic of Texas that he, as President of the United States, had made his election as to the alternative contained in the Walker Amendment looking to the admission of Texas into the Union, and that he had chosen the alternative by joint resolution. The proposition as thus submitted by President Tyler was accepted by Texas through her Congress and a convention, so that Texas was finally admitted into the Union under the authority of the joint resolution, and thus assumed a position as a part of the United States precisely similar to that maintained by each of the other States, and without any right to secede.

The assumption by President Tyler of the right to choose the alternative method of procedure effectually committed President Polk to the method thus chosen, especially as the Senate, on March 10, laid on the table by a vote of 23 to 20 a resolution introduced by Mr. Berrien, of Georgia, to the effect that the President would best conform to the provisions of the Constitution by resorting to the treaty-making power, for the purpose of accomplishing the objects of the joint resolution. But had President Polk attempted to secure the consent of Mexico to the annexation of Texas, and had he been satisfied with the proper boundaries of that republic, it is altogether probable that peaceful annexation would have been the result; but it appears perfectly clear to the student of the history of the entire movement that it was continuously the purpose of President Polk's administration to add very largely, if not as largely as possible, to the area of the United States. In pursuance of this policy President Polk, while carrying on a *quasi* negotiation with the President of Mexico for the settlement of the whole subject in dispute, gave orders on January 13, 1846, to General Taylor to proceed to the Rio Grande. General Taylor received these orders on February 4, left Corpus Christi on the 8th, and arrived at Matamoras on the 28th of that month. Inasmuch as at that time the Neuces, and not the Rio Grande, was the recognized boundary of Texas, the march of General Taylor's army to the Rio Grande was an invasion of Mexican territory, and was so considered by that country. As an act of invasion it was the real cause of the war, and drew from Mexico a declaration of war. On April 4, 1846, the Government of Mexico sent an order to General Arista to attack the forces of General Taylor with all the force at his command. The war thus having been brought on by the invasion of Mexican territory and by the consequent declaration of war by Mexico, the Congress of the United States, on May 12 following, declared that "by the act of the Republic of Mexico a state of war exists between that Government and the United States," and on the next day President Polk issued his proclamation to the American people, informing them of the fact of war, and of its declaration by Congress, and exhorting them, "as they love their country, as they feel the wrongs which have forced on them the last resort of injured nations, and as they consult as to the best means under Divine Providence of abridging its calamities, to exert themselves in observing order, in promoting concord, in maintaining the authority and the efficacy of the laws, and in supporting all the measures which might be adopted by the constituted authorities for obtaining a speedy, just, and honorable peace."

Thus, after the war had been in existence for more than two months by the action of the army under the orders of the President, without any necessity and without any justification, was the Congress brought to its sanction, and to the giving of a false reason for the part it took, by the declaration that war existed "by the act of the Republic of Mexico."

In pursuance of a call issued a few days before, a large and respectable meeting was held at the City Hall, May 15, 1846, which, on motion, was temporarily organized by the election as chairman of

Major Malay. Major Malay, after a speech explanatory of the object of the meeting, suggested the name of E. Brook for permanent chairman and Thomas M. Gleason as secretary, both of whom were unanimously elected. Mr. O'Brien then moved that a committee of five be appointed to wait upon Ex-President Houston, of Texas, and Senator Jarnagin, of Tennessee, to request their attendance at an adjourned meeting to be held at the same place Saturday evening, May 16. William O'Brien, E. Brook, Thomas M. Gleason, John W. Mount, and Major Malay were appointed. This adjourned meeting was organized by the election of Dr. Bronaugh, of Missouri, as chairman. Lieutenant W. D. Porter delivered an address, alluding to the many depredations committed on the people of the United States by Mexico, and trusting that the young men of the city of Washington would come boldly to the rescue. Hon. Barclay Martin, of the Sixth Congressional District of Tennessee, followed in a very eloquent speech, telling the young men the necessity of buckling on their armor and going to the war. Colonel R. M. Johnson then spoke "in his usual style of oratory," saying he was not in favor of stopping at the Rio Grande, but would march into the interior of Mexico, and cut their departments right and left. He spoke of cutting off California from Mexico and annexing that country to the United States. Hon. F. G. McConnell then entertained the meeting, as did also Hon. F. P. Stanton and Mr. St. John, of New York. The latter urged the young men to enroll themselves for the war, and at the close of his speech forty-five of them presented themselves as volunteers.

On May 18, a meeting was held at the Franklin Engine House, of which J. Cooper was made chairman. J. E. Norris addressed the meeting, and a company of volunteers, called "Washington Volunteers, No. 1," was organized by the election of John Waters captain, William Parham first lieutenant, and Eugene Boyle second lieutenant. No men were to be taken in this company who were under eighteen years of age.

At a meeting at the City Hall, addresses were delivered by Robert Ratcliffe, Robert Bronaugh, and Hon. John Wentworth of Chicago. Thirty-five young men enrolled themselves, which ran the number in this company up to eighty-six. The name adopted for this company was the "Washington City Riflemen," and its officers elected as follows: Robert Bronaugh, captain; Phineas B. Bell, first lieutenant; William O'Brien, second lieutenant, and four sergeants and four corporals. Dr. W. L. Frazier was chosen surgeon. The sergeants were as follows: John W. Mount, Josephus Dawes, Lewis F. Beeler, and William A. Woodward; the corporals, Andrew Kemp, John Kelly, Jacob C. Hemmrick, and John P. White. These companies went into the United States barracks to drill, preparatory to going to the front. Three companies from Baltimore, namely, the first and second companies of the Baltimore Volunteers, and the Chesapeake Riflemen, were also in the barracks at the same time. These several companies were removed to Fort Washington June 10, 1846, under the command of Lieutenant-Colonel Watson, to await embarkation for the southern army, the steamship *Massachusetts* having been chartered by the Government of the United States to take the entire battalion to the Rio Grande. A company of volunteers was formed in Alexandria June 12, which elected officers as follows: Captain, M. D. Corse; first lieutenant, C. S. Price; second lieutenant, T. W. Ashly, and first sergeant, Benjamin Waters, Jr. The Secretary of War was, however, obliged to decline their services at that time, as the battalion from this city and Baltimore was already filled. June 16, the battalion from Baltimore and Washington sailed from Alexandria in the ship *Massachusetts* for the Rio Grande. The officers of this battalion were as follows: Lieutenant-colonel, William H. Watson; adjutant, F. B. Shaffer; surgeon, G. M. Dove. Company A — Captain, J. E. Stewart; first lieutenant, B. F. Owen; second lieutenant, Samuel Wilt. Company B — Captain, James Piper; first lieutenant, M. K. Taylor; second lieutenant, I. Dolan. Company C — Captain, Robert Bronaugh, etc., as already given. Company D — Captain, John Waters, etc., as given above. Company E — Captain, J. R. Kenly; first lieutenant, F. B. Shaffer; second lieutenant, Odon Bowie. Company of light infantry — Captain, James Boyd; first lieutenant, Joseph H. Rudduch; second lieutenant, R. E. Hustel.

The battle of Monterey was fought September 21, 1846, the battalion from Baltimore and Washington being engaged in the storming of the place, and Lieutenant-Colonel Watson was killed. James E. Stewart, who succeeded to the command, wrote from the camp, near Monterey, September 26, as follows:

"The battalion of Maryland and the District of Columbia volunteers, under the command of Lieutenant-Colonel Watson, connected with the First Regiment of Infantry, the whole under the command of Lieutenant-Colonel Wilson, were ordered to march at about eight o'clock in the morning of the 21st inst., for an attack on Monterey. The battalion were out in their full strength, save Company C, Captain Bronaugh, which was ordered to remain on guard duty at the camp, and Lieutenant Owen, of Company A, with a detachment of twelve men, were ordered on picket duty by General Twiggs. The battalion marched toward the city, and charged in a most gallant manner on a battery, under a galling fire, in which it sustained some loss. The point of attack was then changed by order of Colonel Garland, and we entered the city exposed to a destructive fire from several batteries, supported by a large number of infantry, which raked the streets. We remained in the city for nearly half an hour, when we were ordered to retire. In doing so the battalion became separated. Colonel Watson fell by a musket shot whilst gallantly leading on to a second assault on the city. A portion of the battalion was then formed under Captain Kenly, and remained on the field of battle until it was ordered back to camp by General Twiggs, having been under a heavy fire for nearly nine hours, losing in the action six killed and eighteen wounded. I take pleasure in noticing the gallant conduct of the battalion throughout."

On Sunday, November 22, 1846, Captain Samuel H. Walker arrived in Washington from the battlefields in Mexico, and was given a most hearty reception in Odd Fellows' Hall. Speeches appropriate to the occasion were made by Messrs. Ratcliffe, C. S. Wallach, E. H. Harriman, Joseph H. Bradley, D. Wallach, Lewis F. Thomas, and Mayor W. W. Seaton. Captain Walker responded, expressing his gratification at receiving such a flattering testimonial of respect, and the entire number present—about one thousand—took him by the hand. Captain Walker, in January, 1847, raised a company of mounted riflemen for the regiment to which he belonged, in Washington and its vicinity, and on February 6 his company left Washington for Baltimore in a special train *en route* for the seat of war. Twenty of the young men in this company were from Prince George's County, Maryland.

A meeting was held at the city Council chamber Friday evening, January 22, 1847, for the purpose of raising a company of soldiers for the Mexican War, the Mayor of the city making the address. The company was organized by the election of officers as follows: Captain, John M. Thornton; first lieutenant, Edmund Barry; second lieutenant, Hume Young; orderly sergeant, David Westerfield, Jr. The name adopted for this company was "Washington's Own." About April 25, 1847, the Secretary of War called upon the major-general of the District to furnish three companies of volunteers, to form, with two companies from Maryland, a battalion for immediate active service, to be under the command of Lieutenant-Colonel Charles Lee Jones. This was the last recruiting done in Washington for the war.

On February 21, 1848, a treaty of peace signed by Mr. N. P. Trist on the part of the United States, and by the Mexican authorities, was received in Washington, and on March 10, after two weeks' debate on the part of the Senate, was ratified by that body by a vote of 38 to 14. On May 25, it was ratified by the Mexican Senate by a vote of 33 to 4. July 4, President Polk issued a proclamation declaring peace established, and on the 6th of the same month sent a message to Congress announcing the end of the war.

Article V. of this treaty was as follows: "The boundary line between the two republics shall commence in the Gulf of Mexico three leagues from land, opposite the mouth of the Rio Grande, otherwise called Rio Bravo del Norte, opposite the mouth of its deepest branch, if it should have more than one branch emptying directly into the sea; thence up the middle of that river, following the deepest channel, where it has more than one, to the point where it strikes the southern boundary of New Mexico; thence westwardly along the whole southern boundary of New Mexico [which runs north of the town called Paso] to its western termination; thence northward along the western line of New Mexico until it intersects the first branch of the river Gila, or if it should not intersect any branch of that river, then to the point on said line nearest to such branch, and thence in a direct line to the same; thence down the middle of the said branch and of the said river until it empties into the Rio Colorado; thence across the Rio Colorado, following the division line between Upper and Lower California, to the Pacific Ocean."

By Article XII. of this treaty, the United States agreed to pay to Mexico for the territory acquired from her, Texas and Upper California, fifteen millions of dollars,—three millions immediately on the ratification of the treaty by the Mexican authorities, and thereafter three millions per year until the whole should be paid, and also interest on what remained unpaid at the rate of six per cent. per annum.

Hon. A. H. Sevier, United States Senator from Arkansas, and the Attorney-General, Nathan Clifford, were appointed commissioners to exchange ratifications, and the latter was ordered to remain in Mexico as the resident minister from the United States.

The War of the Rebellion really began many years before actual hostilities commenced in 1861. That the existence of slavery was the cause thereof, no one can now seriously doubt who is tolerably well informed. Slavery came near preventing the formation of the Union in the first place, and was, so long as it existed, a constant menace to the existence of the Union. At the beginning of the Revolutionary War, the entire country was a slaveholding country; but while that war was going on, the New England and some of the Middle States, perceiving the inconsistency of striving for their own liberty and at the same time striving to perpetuate the subjection of another race, passed acts of immediate or gradual emancipation of the slaves within their boundaries. Massachusetts passed an act of immediate emancipation in 1780, and Pennsylvania in the same year passed an act of gradual emancipation. Indeed, there were many individuals in the South as well as in the North who were deeply impressed with the inconsistency of fighting to establish freedom for themselves while they were denying freedom to others, who, under the laws of nature, had the same right to it as they. Rhode Island and Connecticut gradually emancipated their slaves. In 1799, New York passed a gradual emancipation act, and in 1817 another act declaring all slaves free July 4, 1827. New Jersey passed a gradual emancipation act in 1804, and thus slavery was abolished in all of the New England and Middle States long prior to the breaking out of the Rebellion.

But the States south of Pennsylvania adhered to the institution, and indeed some of them, notably South Carolina and Georgia, made its perpetuation by constitutional provision a condition of the ratification by them of the Constitution itself. This condition is thus expressed: "Representatives and direct taxes shall be apportioned among the several States which may be included within this Union, according to their respective numbers, which shall be determined by adding to the whole number of free persons, including those bound to service for a term of years, and excluding Indians not taxed, three-fifths of all other persons." Thus was the Constitution of the country made the bulwark of the institution, and the country divided into two hostile sections, which continually became more hostile to each other as time rolled on. The joy and gratitude felt by the people of both sections for the success of their arms in the struggle with Great Britain, and for the successful establishment of a national government of their own, were such that for years but little attention was given to the institution of slavery. It was known to all that under the Constitution the importation of slaves must cease in 1808, and also that in the States Congress by that Constitution had been rendered powerless to interfere with the institution. Little could therefore be done in a practical way, except to abolish slavery in the District of Columbia, for which consummation petition after petition was presented to Congress, causing more and more acrimonious debate as the years rolled by. The Missouri Compromise came, and then its repeal. Afterward came the Nebraska Bill, designed to give

two more States to the Union, but which in reality gave two more
Free States, Kansas and Nebraska, to the Union, and this effect proving
to be the practical working of the Squatter Sovereignty doctrine,
demonstrated to the South that the ultimate result of the struggle, of
the irrepressible conflict, that was not only irrepressible but certain
to continue until either freedom or slavery should win a final victory
if the South should remain in the Union, determined for her her
course with reference to the Union.

It is not proper to attempt to relate in this volume with any
degree of minuteness the steps in either section of the country which
led to the secession of the Southern States, for in the first place, that
is not the object for which the work is written, and in the second
place, that work has been done by others much better than it could
be done herein; yet, while this is the case, it is proper to refer
briefly to a few of the facts and incidents which preceded and produced
that secession. While, during many years previous to 1850, there had
been heard here and there in both the East and the South a few
voices demanding the dissolution of the Union, yet no great alarm
was felt for the safety of the Union previous to that year. But the
question had been raised in the First Congress by the introduction
of a memorial to the House of Representatives from the "Annual
Meeting of Friends," of New York and Philadelphia, in October,
1789, in obedience to a sense of duty they felt incumbent upon
them as religious bodies, etc. It was not long after this that a
memorial was presented from "The Pennsylvania Society for the
Abolition of Slavery," signed by Benjamin Franklin, president,
praying for the abolition of slavery. In this way, as has been said,
by the presentation of petitions to Congress upon the subject, a
subject upon which Congress was powerless under the Constitution
as it then stood, was the question persistently kept under discussion,
with but little fear of danger until the debate upon the admission of
California into the Union as a Free State, in the session of 1849–50,
when the subject assumed alarming proportions to all those, both
North and South, who desired that the Union should be preserved, and
even to those who desired its preservation merely as secondary to the
preservation of the institution of slavery. For a long time the specter
of the Nashville Convention, which convened in Nashville in 1850, was
a dreaded thing to lovers of the Union in both sections; but when it
was discovered that the Southern States were slow to elect delegates
thereto, and when it had been held and had resulted in failure, there
not being then sufficient disunion sentiment to give it sustenance, that

specter melted away, leaving scarcely a wreck behind. What it might have accomplished, however, was shown on May 28, 1851, by Hon. H. S. Foote, United States Senator from Mississippi, in a speech in Attala County, that State, in which he said: "The idea of demanding amendments to the Constitution, and in case of failing to obtain them, resorting to secession, was first broached by Mr. Calhoun after our October convention in 1849"; that Mr. Calhoun told him that he had no expectation of obtaining these amendments; but Mr. Calhoun thought that if they should be refused, then the South would unite in favor of a Southern convention, and that Mr. Calhoun had prepared a constitution for the new republic which was to have been formed out of one of the fragments of the Union as it then existed. All of this revelation by Hon. Mr. Foote as to Mr. Calhoun's plans and purposes was in perfect accord with Mr. Calhoun's prediction, made in 1846, that within a generation there would be formed a Southern Confederacy, and that Atlanta, Georgia, would be its capital.

The insurrection at Harper's Ferry occurred October 16, 1859. The particulars of this insurrection are so well known that it is not necessary to more than refer to them in this connection, and no attempt is made in this work to do more than to narrate the events transpiring in Washington immediately connected with that foolhardy affair, which in itself was equally unnecessary and unjustifiable with the later and much greater insurrection which had for its object the breaking up of the Government of the United States, except that the motive actuating the insurrectionists at Harper's Ferry was the liberation of the slave. The outbreak came without premonition, and was caused by no special provocation. Of course great excitement was caused in this city, as elsewhere, and during the day following the announcement of the outbreak there was manifested the greatest eagerness to learn of its progress and success. At three o'clock of the morning of October 18, Governor Wise, of Virginia, arrived in Washington, accompanied by the Greys of Richmond, about sixty in number, and the Alexandria Rifles. Governor Wise found Mayor James G. Berrett at the City Hall, surrounded by the police, and remained there most of the time until six o'clock, when he took the train for Harper's Ferry. At three o'clock in the afternoon the mail boat from Acquia Creek, and other boats on the Potomac River, brought up five companies of the Virginia troops, numbering about three hundred men, two or three of which companies marched immediately to the railroad depot, but receiving there a dispatch from Governor Wise, they returned, the Young Guard of Richmond taking

16

the opportunity to parade along Pennsylvania Avenue. The order and quiet in Washington for the next succeeding two or three days were painful in the extreme, no one knowing what to expect, and hence fearing the worst. On Sunday, November 20, 1859, Governor Wise, with a regiment of Virginia volunteers from Richmond, four hundred and four strong in rank and file, arrived in Washington, leaving for Harper's Ferry at 10:00 A. M. that day. In the afternoon three companies from Petersburg arrived, and as they could not get out of town they remained until next morning.

November 27, 1859, a company of troops arrived in Washington for Charlestown, Virginia, and on the 28th three other companies arrived for the same destination, notwithstanding there were then stationed at that point six hundred and fifty men, and in the entire county there were under arms not less than one thousand men; thus showing the supposed necessity for a strong force to prevent the spreading of the John Brown heresy into Virginia. The execution of John Brown followed in a few days afterward, on December 2, with a promptness and certainty which were commendable.

The excitement caused by this episode in American history did not subside before other causes of excitement arose. The Republican Association of Washington, on May 28, 1860, held a meeting to ratify the nomination of Abraham Lincoln and Hannibal Hamlin to the positions of Presidency and Vice-Presidency, respectively. B. B. French, president of the association, addressed the assemblage, which was in front of the southwest portico of the City Hall, and read a series of resolutions expressive of the sentiments of the Republican Party. Hon. J. R. Doolittle, Senator from Wisconsin, presented very briefly the positions of the two great parties. Hon. Israel Washburn, of Maine, said that while he had favored Mr. Seward, yet he would do all he could to secure the election of Mr. Lincoln. Hon. B. F. Wade, Hon. G. A. Grow, Hon. Henry Wilson, Hon. Ely Spaulding, Hon. John A. Bingham, and Mr. McKean of New York, each made short addresses.

On July 3, 1860, another ratification meeting was held at the same place, to ratify the nomination of Stephen A. Douglas and Herschel V. Johnson to the same offices. A large banner was thrown to the breeze, bearing the inscription, "No Secession," in large letters. The meeting was addressed by George W. Brent of Alexandria, Ellis B. Schnabel of Philadelphia, and Dr. Culver of Washington.

On July 9, a similar meeting was held by those favoring the election of Hon. John C. Breckinridge and Hon. Joseph Lane. Their motto was, "The Constitution, and the Equality of the States." Mayor Berrett, of Washington, presided, and James M. Carlisle, A. B. Meek of Alabama, Isaac I. Stevens of Washington Territory, A. G. Brown of Mississippi, and Jefferson Davis made addresses.

Still another ratification meeting, and the largest of all, was held in front of the City Hall August 8, 1860, to ratify the nomination of Hon. John Bell and Hon. Edward Everett to the same positions. The central portion of the City Hall was used on this occasion, and a large platform erected between the two wings. Mr. B. O. Tayloe called upon Philip R. Fendall to preside, who claimed that Mr. Bell, like Themistocles, on a former occasion, was the second choice of all the parties that had candidates in the field, and argued hence that he was at least fit to be the first choice of all. Robert E. Scott of Fauquier County, Virginia, Hon. J. Morrison Harris of Baltimore, Robert J. Bowie of Maryland, B. L. Hodge of Louisiana, Hon. Alexander R. Boteler of Virginia, and Joseph H. Bradley of Washington, addressed the meeting.

Mr. Lincoln was elected November 6, 1860, and on the next day occurred what may perhaps be called the first battle of the subsequent civil war. Late at night on the day of election, it became known what the result was, and toward midnight it was proposed and agreed to, at the Breckinridge headquarters, on Pennsylvania Avenue between Four and a Half and Sixth streets, that the fifty or sixty members of the National Volunteers should repair in a body to the Republican headquarters at the corner of Indiana Avenue and Second Street, and "wreck the shanty." There was then a large party of Breckinridge men at Brown's Hotel, which united with the National Volunteers, making the combined strength of the two parties about three hundred men. Proceeding to the Republican building, they began, when in front of it, to fire pistols and throw stones at the windows, soon demolishing all in the second story of the building. Going around to the Second Street side, they broke open the door, which was locked, went up stairs, and began the destruction of the paraphernalia and furniture of the rooms. They also entered the room above the wigwam and destroyed the stands of type, and scattered type all around the room. Some half dozen scared Republicans retreated to the roof of the building. Soon several policemen, headed by Lieutenant McHenry, entered and took possession of the rooms, and made arrests of those in the building, including three Republicans and five of the Volunteers. An investigation was had at the office of Justice Donn, but no very severe punishment was inflicted.

That it was the full determination of the Southern leaders to take their States out of the Union, in case of the election of Mr. Lincoln, —toward which they lent their powerful and essential assistance by breaking up the Democratic Party at Charleston, South Carolina, in the summer of 1860,—though then not so widely known as now, was yet well known to those who had opportunities of finding out the truth. Notwithstanding the well-known fact that many patriotic citizens were preparing to meet in convention in Washington, at the call of the State of Virginia, to agree upon measures which they intended to propose to the people of the United States as a basis of compromise for all serious difference between the sections, yet on the 5th of January, 1861, there was held a caucus in this city by Southern secession Senators from Florida, Georgia, Alabama, Mississippi, Louisiana, Arkansas, and Texas, at which these gentlemen in effect resolved to assume to themselves the political and military power of the South, to control all political and military movements for the immediate future, and telegraphed to their followers in the South to complete the plan by seizing forts, arsenals, customhouses, and other property belonging to the United States; and advised the conventions then in session and soon to be in session, to pass ordinances of secession; but themselves, in order to thwart any operations of the General Government, were to retain their places in the Senate. These Senators at this caucus also advised, ordered, or directed the assembling of a convention of delegates from the seceding States to be held at Montgomery, Alabama, about February 13, 1861, which could be done only by the seceding conventions usurping the powers of the people and sending delegates over whom they would lose control in the establishment of a provisional government, which was the plan of the caucus members. This same caucus also resolved to take the most efficient measures to influence the legislatures of the States of Tennessee, Kentucky, Missouri, Arkansas, Texas, and Virginia, into following in the wake of the seceding cotton States; nor was Maryland to be forgotten or overlooked.

This was a most remarkable and startling exposition: Senators of the United States, representing sovereign States and sworn to support the Constitution of the United States, looked to by at least a portion of their constituents to effect some method of adjustment by which civil war might be avoided, deliberately considering and concocting a conspiracy by means of which the Government might be the more easily, and thus the more surely, overthrown—that Government which they were at the time under the most solemn of oaths to maintain and support, the contemplated overthrow to be accomplished through such military organizations as the Knights of the Golden Circle, Committees of Safety, Southern Leagues, and other similar agencies, all at their command, thus dividing the South from the North, and then dividing the South among themselves.

Only a day or two afterward, the Washington correspondent of the Baltimore *Sun* corroborated the statement, as given in substance above, by saying that the leaders of the Southern movement were consulting together as to the best method of consolidating their interests into a Southern Confederacy, under a provisional government, etc.

Not only in corroboration of, but in full demonstration of, the accuracy of this remarkable exposition, was the letter of Hon. D. L. Yulee, United States Senator from the State of Florida, which is here introduced.

"WASHINGTON, D. C., January 7, 1861.

"MY DEAR SIR: On the other side is a copy of resolutions adopted at a consultation of the Senators from the seceding States in which Georgia, Alabama, Louisiana, Arkansas, Texas, Mississippi, and Florida were present.

"The idea of the meeting was that the States should go out at once, and provide for the organization of a Confederate Government not later than the 15th of February. This time is allowed to enable Louisiana and Texas to participate.

"It seemed to be the opinion that if we left here, force, loan, and volunteer bills might be passed, which would put Mr. Lincoln in immediate condition for hostilities; whereas, by remaining in our places until the 4th of March, it is thought we can keep the hands of Mr. Buchanan tied, and disable the Republicans from effecting any legislation which will strengthen the hands of the incoming administration.

[Another paragraph followed, which is of no historic interest in this connection.] "D. L. YULEE.

"To Joseph Finegan, Esq.,
    "Sovereignty Convention,
        "Tallahassee, Florida.'

The resolutions referred to in this letter as having been adopted at the caucus of January 5, were as follows:

"1. That in our opinion each of the Southern States should, as soon as may be, secede from the Union.

"2. That provision should be made for a convention to organize a confederacy of the seceding States, the convention to meet not later than the 15th of February, at the city of Montgomery, in the State of Alabama.

"3. That in view of the hostile legislation that is threatened against the seceding States, and which may be consummated by the 4th of March, we ask instructions whether the delegates are to remain in Congress until that date for the defeating of such legislation.

"4. That a committee be and are hereby appointed, consisting of Messrs. Davis, Slidell, and Mallory, to carry out the objects of this meeting."

Soon afterward, upon the solicitation of the State of Virginia, speaking through her legislature, a peace convention, above referred to, assembled in Washington, meeting in Willard's Hall, on F Street, between Fourteenth and Fifteenth streets. This convention was organized February 4, 1861, with Ex-President John Tyler as its chairman, and S. C. Wright as secretary. Much was hoped from this convention by the Northern and border Slave States, but nothing by the more southern Slave States, because, as has been intimated before, they were determined to secede irrespective of what might be done by any portion of the people, or by the Government itself. On the same day that this Peace Convention met in Washington, the delegates to the Confederate Congress met in Montgomery, the States of South Carolina, Georgia, Alabama, Mississippi, Louisiana, and Florida being represented. President Tyler addressed the convention, saying that the members thereof had as grand a task before them as had been performed by their "godlike fathers" in the founding of the glorious Constitution and Government which was then imperiled by the secession movement. On the 23d of February, the convention, having completed its labors by formulating an amendment to the Constitution, closely resembling the Crittenden compromise, which it proposed to the country for adoption, and by passing a resolution advising the Government of the United States not to make war on the seceded and seceding States, adjourned.

About the middle of January, there were rumors afloat of combinations being formed to interfere with the inauguration of Mr. Lincoln. Of course the city of Washington was interested in knowing the truth or falsity of these rumors, and in order to learn something definite, if possible, as to their truth, Mayor James G. Berrett wrote to Marshal George P. Kane, of Baltimore, receiving a reply dated January 16, to the effect that so far as Baltimore was concerned, nothing could be further from the truth. Such rumors, however, continued to circulate. One form these rumors took was that the President-elect had contemplated coming to Washington over the Baltimore and Ohio Railroad, but that on account of apprehended dangers had changed his purpose. Mayor Berrett therefore, on February 1, wrote to John W. Garrett, president of that company, asking information as to the truth of alleged threats against Mr. Lincoln's safety. February 4, Mr. Garrett replied that there was not, nor had there been, the slightest foundation for any of the rumors to which the Mayor referred. On the same day that Mr. Garrett wrote this letter to Mayor Berrett, Major-General R. C. Weightman, in command of the militia of the District of Columbia, requested of the Mayor of Washington the names and residences of the police for both day and night service, because, as he said, if the assistance of the police should be required it would be of importance to have the means of reaching them as early as practicable. To this request the Mayor replied that he was not ignorant of the fact that secret organizations were alleged to have been set on foot in Washington and in the adjoining States of Virginia and Maryland for the purpose of seizing upon the District of Columbia by force of arms with the view of effecting a revolution in the Federal Government by preventing the inauguration of the President-elect; nor was he ignorant of the fact that in order to oppose and thwart the supposed conspiracy in the execution of its unhallowed designs, orders had been issued, and were in process of execution, for enrolling, arming, and disciplining the militia of the District, while for the same purpose unusual numbers of Federal troops were concentrating at this point. And more than that, not-withstanding he had used every possible effort to ferret out the conspiracy, yet he had been unable to find one tittle of evidence that any such conspiracy existed. The Mayor closed by declining to furnish the desired information.

It was generally expected that Mr. Lincoln would arrive in Washington on Saturday, February 23, 1861, and thousands of the citizens of both sexes determined to witness his entrance into the city. This determination was, however, defeated by the arrival of Mr. Lincoln some time during the preceding night, having come directly through from Harrisburg, Pennsylvania, instead of stopping at Baltimore on Saturday and reaching Washington in the afternoon or evening of Saturday, according to the original arrangement. This was not merely surprising, it was actually amazing, to the people of the entire country, as it was flashed over the wires on the morning of the 23d. Several theories were immediately in circulation to account for this sudden and secret change of plan on Mr. Lincoln's part. One explanation was, that he had been telegraphed to be present during the meeting of the Peace Convention. Another was, that he had been advised to come direct to Washington, to prevent possible disturbances that might grow out of conflicting purposes of political clubs in Baltimore — of the Republican clubs to honor him, and of Democratic clubs to prevent any such demonstration. Of course there was great disappointment in Baltimore. On the 26th of February, it was given out, on the authority of Marshal Kane, of that city, that Mr. Lincoln had passed quietly through Baltimore, to avoid any demonstration that might be made by his political friends; for, while there was no doubt that Mr. Lincoln would be treated with all the respect due to him person- ally, yet there was no assurance that his political friends, in giving him a welcome, would be treated in the same manner. The Baltimore *American* said that Mr. Lincoln's incognito entrance into Washington was in accordance with his wish to escape from his pretended friends, and thus to prevent a breach of the peace, which would be disgraceful to the city and derogatory to the American character.

Upon arriving in the city, Mr. Lincoln went to Willard's Hotel, where he was met by Mr. Seward, and they together called upon President Buchanan. On the following Wednesday, the Mayor and Council of Washington waited upon him and tendered him a welcome. The next evening he was serenaded by the Republican Association, accompanied by the Marine Band. At his inauguration there was a greater display of military force than had ever been seen on a similar occasion. Nearly twenty of the well-drilled companies of the militia of the District of Columbia were out, comprising a force of more than two thousand men. In addition, Georgetown contributed companies of cavalry, infantry, and artillery of fine accomplishments. Collected at two or three points, as at the City Hall and at Willard's Hotel, they were centers of attraction for the citizens. After attending at the Capitol in the morning, President Buchanan, accompanied by the Senate committee, left the Executive Mansion, went to Willard's Hotel to receive the President-elect, and the party thus composed, attended by distinguished citizens in carriages, on horseback, and on foot, proceeded along Pennsylvania Avenue, with military in front and rear, and at a quarter past one in the afternoon the President and President-elect entered the Senate chamber, and soon afterward pro- ceeded to the east front of the Capitol, where Mr. Lincoln read his inaugural address, listened to by at least ten thousand of his fellow-citizens, at the close of which the oath of office was administered to him by the venerable Chief Justice of the United States. The military preparations were so thorough and complete that it would have been practically impossible for anyone to have successfully attempted violence to the President on this occasion; but when all was over, apprehensions were allayed and all breathed with their accustomed freedom, so far as the question of the safe inauguration of the President was concerned.

On April 10, there was a hurried gathering of all the members of the various military companies in the city, the order having been issued late on Tuesday night, the 9th inst. Inspections took place at different places; of four companies at Temperance Hall by Colonel Stone, and in front of the War Department all the companies were inspected by A. A. G. McDowell in the presence of Adjutant-General Thomas and several other officers of the army. Ten companies in all were inspected, eight from Washington and two from Georgetown. The object of the inspection was to muster them into the service of the United States. Several of the men, however, refused to take the oath, though this refusal it was said was based upon the supposition that the Government wanted to send them outside of the District. The names of the companies, together with the numbers composing them, were as follows: Washington Light Infantry Battalion, Colonel Davis, 125 men; Company A, Captain E. C. Carrington, 100 men; Companies A, B, C of the National Guard, each company about 100 men; the Washington Rifles, Captain Balbach, 50 men; Company B of the Union Regiment, Captain Kelly, 60 men; the National Rifles, Captain Smead, 27 men; the Carrington Home Guard, Captain Goddard, 60 men; Potomac Light Infantry, of Georgetown, Captain McKenny, 61 men.

The demand for the surrender of Fort Sumter was made April 11, and the batteries on Sullivan's Island and at other points opened upon the fort at four o'clock the next morning. Then came the call for troops from all over the South. Fort Sumter was surrendered April 13, and on Monday, the 15th, came the proclamation from the President calling for seventy-five thousand men to suppress combinations of men too powerful for the ordinary means of the Government, and to cause the laws to be duly executed, and also convening Congress in extra session on July 4, 1861. The law under which the militia was thus called out by President Lincoln was the act of 1795, enacted by Congress for the purpose of providing means to suppress the Whisky Insurrection in Pennsylvania, when several thousands of insurgents were in arms against the Federal Government.

On the Saturday previous to the issuance of the proclamation, about 40 men were mustered into Captain Carrington's company, and 20 into Captain Kelly's. The Anderson Rifles, from Georgetown, to the number of 52, all were mustered in, which made the tenth company mustered. On the 15th, the enlistment of men into the United States service went forward as rapidly as practicable, the greater part of the day being thus occupied. Captain Gerhardt, of the Turner Rifles, added 30 men to his company, making 120 in all; the Metropolitan Rifles, Captain Nalley, added 17 men, making the number up to 100; Captain Thistleton, of the Putnam Rifles, added 30 men to his company; the howitzer corps at the Navy Yard numbered 100 men; the Henderson Guards, consisting almost exclusively of residents of the First Ward, under Captain Foxwell, numbered 80 men; Captain Kelly's company added 22 men; Captain Patrick H. King, Company A, National Guard Battalion, had 70 men; and the National Rifles, to the number of 42, came forward and were mustered in. On April 16, the Henderson Guards increased their number to 100; the Carrington Home Guard, of Georgetown, was increased to the number of 52; the President's Mounted Guard, Captain S. W. Owen, numbering about 80 men, tendered their services, which were not accepted, as cavalry was not then needed. The troops were placed at different points in the vicinity of the city, the artillery on the heights and roads leading out of the city, and twenty-five cart loads of cartridges, grape shot, and other missives taken up the avenue to be placed near the cannoneers and other soldiers. On this same day, Colonel E. E. Ellsworth left Washington for New York for the purpose of raising a regiment of Zouaves for the war. A call was made on the 18th of the month upon the members of the Association of the Soldiers of the War of 1812 of the District of Columbia to meet at the City Hall on the next Monday for the purpose of adopting a military organization and of offering their services to the Government for the defense of the city. On this same day, about five hundred men, consisting of infantry, artillery, and cavalry, were stationed at the Long Bridge, to repel any attempt of the rebels to cross the Potomac at that point. On the evening of the 18th, seventeen car loads of soldiers arrived in Washington from Harrisburg, Pennsylvania, and were quartered in rooms in the Capitol building, having passed through Baltimore about five o'clock the same day without molestation. These troops were the Washington Artillery Company and the National

Light Infantry of Pottsville, the Ringgold Light Artillery of Reading, the Logan Guards of Lewiston, and the Allen Light Infantry of Allentown, in all five hundred and thirty men. During the entire day of the 18th, all avenues to the city were closely watched, cannon were placed on commanding heights so as to sweep the entire range of river front, and the cannon were supported by infantry. Mayor Berrett on this day issued a proclamation exhorting all good citizens and sojourners to be careful to so conduct themselves as neither by word nor deed to give occasion for any breach of the peace.

On April 9, a military department had been created consisting of Maryland and the District of Columbia, as originally bounded, called the Department of Washington, and placed under the command of Brevet-Colonel C. F. Smith. On the 19th, this department was increased so as to include Delaware and Pennsylvania, and placed in command of Major-General Patterson, and Major-General Scott placed volunteer soldiers along the railroad from Wilmington, Delaware, to Washington, to guard the railroad and telegraph between the two points. April 22, a proposition was made by several citizens of Washington to form a light artillery company, the services of which were to be tendered to the Government. The office of this proposed organization was at 355 Pennsylvania Avenue, where books were open for signatures. Notice of the proposed movement was signed by L. Oppenheimer, Henry Meling, Johann Walter, Joseph A. Schell, Louis Landrock, August Bruehl, H. Diebeitsch, E. C. Randolph, William Geriske, Charles Werner, and Alexander McRee. This was afterward changed into a rifle company. By April 24, this company had over forty members, and was organized with the following officers: Captain, Thomas J. Williams; first lieutenant, E. C. Randolph; second lieutenant, W. H. Standiford; third lieutenant, E. Hunt; orderly sergeant, Henry Kaluzowski; quartermaster sergeant, Charles Werner. The name chosen was "The Turner Rifles." On April 20, a meeting was held on Capitol Hill for the purpose of organizing a company of men who, from their age, were exempt from military duty. They were to aid in the defense of the National Capital. Martin King was chairman of the meeting, and Stephen G. Dodge secretary. The name selected was "The Silver Greys." By vote of those present Robert Brown was chosen captain. On the 22d, a number of French and Italian citizens held a meeting at the European Hotel, and resolved to form a company to be called "The Garibaldi Guards," and twenty-two members immediately enrolled. On the same day, a meeting of the old soldiers of 1812 was

held, Colonel John S. Williams taking the chair, and Richard Burgess
acting as secretary. A committee was appointed to prepare a program
and report the next day at 4:00 P. M., consisting of Dr. William
Jones, William A. Bradley, and Richard Burgess. At the adjourned
meeting the hope was expressed that the time was not remote when
the country would be again united; but in the meantime they held
themselves in readiness to perform any duty to which they might be
assigned by the Government of the United States for the protection
of the city of Washington. They invited all persons exempt by law
from military service to unite with them in offering their services to
the Government. The next day they tendered their services to the
Secretary of War, which were accepted, and a written response promised in a few days. On the 25th, another meeting was held and an
organization was effected as follows: Captain, John S. Williams; first
lieutenant, Edward Semmes; second lieutenant, A. W. Worthington;
third lieutenant, F. R. Dorsett; surgeon, Dr. William Jones; orderly
sergeant, A. Baldwin.

One of the incidents of the times was the arrest on the 25th of
April of five young men, who were captured in the act of carrying
arms away from the city. The arrest was made by two members of
the Metropolitan Rifles, named Bigley and Frazier. These two young
men had watched the five enter the tavern of Christopher Boyle,
and were suspicious that all was not right. At length the suspected
characters rode away, in a wagon driven by a negro, toward Bladensburg. The two young men followed them, and though they were
armed with nothing more effective than brickbats, challenged them,
took them prisoners, and brought back to the city the entire outfit. By
order of the Mayor they were taken to the guardhouse, and upon
examination a bundle in the wagon was found to contain effective
firearms. The names of the five men thus arrested were William
Stanton, William Harding, Augustus Hand, William Eugerman, and
Thomas Davis. Three of the five were quite heavily armed.

Enlistments still went on, and by the 25th of April there were
about ten thousand troops in the city. The wounded of the Massachusetts Sixth, which had reached Washington on the evening of the
19th, who were being taken care of at the infirmary, passed resolutions
of thanks to the officers thereof, to the surgeons, and the Sisters of
Mercy for their kindness and sympathy. On this day, the Seventh New
York Regiment came into Washington and marched up Pennsylvania
Avenue, making a magnificent appearance. They were received with
the wildest demonstrations of delight by the citizens. On the 26th,

a large body of troops arrived from Annapolis, consisting of one-half of the Rhode Island regiment, commanded by Governor Sprague, and the Butler Brigade of Massachusetts, numbering one thousand and four hundred men, and commanded by Colonel Benjamin F. Butler. Troops now daily arrived, and at this time there were fully seventeen thousand soldiers in the city.

On April 27, the Seventy-first New York and the Fifth Pennsylvania regiments reached Washington. April 29, the Eighth Massachusetts came in, and in the afternoon of the same day the steamers *Anacostia, Baltic,* and *Pocahontas* arrived. The *Baltic* brought about six hundred Pennsylvania and Ohio troops. About this time treachery in the Navy Yard was discovered, a large quantity of bombshells being found filled with sawdust and sand. On April 30, the Twelfth New York Regiment came in, and the other half of the Rhode Island regiment arrived in the steamer *Bienville* from New York, bringing with them an unusual quantity of supplies, and on their march through the streets displaying the infrequent features of four *vivandiéres* appropriately uniformed. It was said of this regiment, "For completeness of appointment in all respects, nothing can excel the Rhode Island regiment."

The Twenty-fifth New York came in on the 30th of April, and the Sixty-ninth New York, the afterward famous Irish regiment, under Colonel Michael Corcoran. A notable event took place on the 2d of May, in the raising of a flag over the United States Patent Office in the presence of a large concourse of citizens. The Rhode Island regiment, which was quartered in that building and in command of Governor Sprague, formed in line on Seventh Street. The Metropolitan Rifles, Captain Nalley, were on the roof of the portico, formed in line just behind the entablature, facing to the front. At the appointed time President Lincoln appeared on the roof, and hoisted the flag to the top of the staff, a stout hickory pole fifty feet high. On this day the Rhode Island artillery arrived in the city, having a battery of six pieces, and the Seventh New York took up its quarters at Camp Cameron on Meridian Hill. The Sixty-ninth New York were quartered near the Georgetown college buildings. At this time the Government had six steamships running up and down the Potomac to protect merchant vessels plying upon it. On May 5, Sunday, the Twelfth New York Regiment was on parade on Pennsylvania Avenue, and afterward was drawn up in the form of a hollow square in front of the City Hall. In this position they listened to their chaplain read a chapter from St. Paul's Epistle to the Romans, after which the whole regiment joined in the singing of "Old Hundred," accompanied by the band. The Twenty-eighth New York arrived on the 6th, and the First and a portion of the Second New Jersey. May 8, James A. Tait, Charles Everett, and Lemuel Towers were mustered into the United States service as lieutenant-colonels; P. H. King, A. Balbach, and J. McH. Hollingsworth, as majors. Colonel Ellsworth's Zouaves were sworn into service on the 7th, one thousand strong. The Fourth Pennsylvania, Colonel John F. Hartranft, arrived on the 9th.

The officers of the militia of the District of Columbia, commissioned by the President about this time, were as follows: Of the Cameron Guards — James Elder, captain; Thomas Mushaw, Oliver Birkhead, and John W. Glover, lieutenants. Company D, Union Regiment,— J. M. McClelland, captain; Alexander Tait, J. H. Dubant, and J. H. Posey, lieutenants. Potomac Light Guards — Robert Boyd, captain; C. A. Offut, W. H. Burch, and B. McGraw, lieutenants. Company E, National Guard Battalion,— William McCormey, third lieutenant. Arthur W. Fletcher, brigade quartermaster. John R. Dale, captain of the District of Columbia Rifles. National Guard, Company F — W. P. Ferguson, captain; J. T. Carroll, first lieutenant; W. Nottingham, second lieutenant, and J. B. Davis, third lieutenant. Union Volunteers, Company F — James Fletcher, captain; Henry P. Duncan, first lieutenant; Isaac E. Owen, second lieutenant, and J. Clement Reynolds, third lieutenant. Washington Light Infantry — Colonel, Thomas A. Scott: Company A — Lemuel D. Williams, captain; C. H. Uttermehle, first lieutenant; Marvin P. Fisher, second lieutenant, and James Coleman, third lieutenant. Sherman's celebrated light artillery arrived May 9, commanded by Major T. W. Sherman. The District brigade of volunteers, numbering about three thousand and five hundred, were out on parade May 13, under command of Colonel Stone. This brigade was composed of eight battalions, commanded as follows: First Battalion, Major J. McH. Hollingsworth; Second Battalion, Lieutenant-Colonel Everett; Third Battalion, Major J. R. Smead; Fourth Battalion, Lieutenant-Colonel Towers; Fifth Battalion, Lieutenant-Colonel Tait; Sixth Battalion, Major J. Grey Jewell; Seventh Battalion, Major P. H. King; Eighth Battalion, Captain Gerhardt. At their head in the parade was the President's Mounted Guard, Captain Owen.

May 17, the volunteers of the District were mustered with the militia of the District, and field officers appointed to each. The complete organization was as follows:

First Battalion, from Georgetown,—Major J. McH. Hollingsworth; Company A, Anderson Rifles, Captain Rodier; Home Guards, Captain Goddard; Potomac Light Guard, Captain Boyd; Andrew Johnson Guards, Captain McBlair.

Second Battalion—Major J. Gray Jewell; Henderson Guards, Captain Foxwell; Company A, Union Regiment, Captain Carrington; Company B, Captain Kelly; Company D, Captain McClelland; Company E, Captain Callan.

Third Battalion—Major J. R. Smead; National Rifles, Lieutenant Davis; Company F, Union Regiment, Captain Fletcher; Slemmer Guards, Captain Knight; Cameron Guards, Captain Elder.

Fourth Battalion—Lieutenant-Colonel Lemuel Towers; Company A, Washington Light Infantry, Captain Williams; Company E, Zouaves, Captain Powell; Washington Light Guard, Captain Marks; District Union Rifles, Captain Dale.

Fifth Battalion—Lieutenant-Colonel Everett; Constitutional Guards, Captain Degges; Company A, Putnam Rifles, Captain Thistleton; Metropolitan Rifles, Captain Nalley; Jackson Guards, Captain McDermott; Company B, Putnam Rifles, Captain Grinnell.

Sixth Battalion—Lieutenant-Colonel Tait; Company A, National Guard, Captain Lloyd; Company C, Captain McKim; Company E, Captain Morgan; Company F, Captain ———.

Seventh Battalion—Major P. H. King; City Guards, Captain Clarke; Mechanics Union Rifles, Captain Rutherford; Company D, Washington Light Infantry, Captain Cross; Company C, Union Regiment, Captain Miller.

Eighth Battalion—Major A. Balbach; Washington Rifles, Captain Loeffler; Company A, Turner Rifles, Captain Gerhardt; Company B, Captain Kryzanowski.

The Washington Zouaves, on Wednesday, May 15, displayed a handsome flag at their headquarters, in Thorn's building. They had then been on duty several weeks at the arsenal, at Long Bridge, and about the several departments.

About that time, an incident occurred which attracted considerable attention in connection with the First New Jersey Regiment, encamped near Meridian Hill. A party of its soldiers called upon a Mrs. Baker, a widow, who kept a market garden near their camp, and asked her for some onions and other vegetables for one of their number who was sick. She freely complied with the request, and would take no pay. Next day the party returned, and made Mrs. Baker a present of a handsome Bible, which she accepted as of more value than money, thus bringing to memory the measure of meal of the widow of Zarephath, which, in consequence of her kindness to the wayfaring prophet, was never again allowed to be empty.

General Benjamin F. Butler arrived in Washington May 16, and was waited upon at the National Hotel by numerous friends, and at night was serenaded by Withers's Band. The Eighth New York was encamped at Camp Mansfield, on Kalorama Heights. A flag was raised over the General Post Office May 22, in presence of a large assemblage of citizens. General St. John B. L. Skinner was chairman of the committee of arrangements, and made an address, stating that the flag about to be raised was the contribution of the clerks of the Post Office Department. President Lincoln then, upon request, raised the flag. The Hartford Cornet Band played the "Star Spangled Banner," and addresses were made by Postmaster-General Blair, Secretary Seward, and Secretary Smith.

The night of May 23 was a beautiful one on the Potomac. The moon shone brightly and peacefully down, and perfect quiet prevailed all over the valleys and hills in the neighborhood of Washington. But a most important movement was begun that night. The troops in the city were ordered to occupy the heights in Virginia opposite Washington. At eleven o'clock on the night of the 23d the Washington Light Infantry, Company A, was posted some distance up Maryland Avenue from the Long Bridge. A squad of infantry was posted near the Washington Monument, to keep an eye on boats going out of the canal. Near the Long Bridge and on it were the infantry, a company of Rhode Island soldiers, a company of United States cavalry, a company of United States artillery, the Putnam Rifles, the Turner Rifles, Metropolitan Rifles, Company F Union Volunteers, Company E Washington Light Infantry, and the Constitutional Guards, occupying the Virginia end of the bridge. A short time after midnight Captain Powell's Zouaves and Captain Smead's company of National Rifles advanced across the bridge to the vicinity of Roach's Spring, and soon the Virginia pickets set spurs to their horses and made off for Alexandria. The Constitutional Guards, to the number of about eighty, were on duty on the bridge. Upon being asked by Colonel Stone, of the District Volunteers, if they would go beyond the District of Columbia, they replied that they would go anywhere in defense of the Union. They were therefore sent forward as far as Four Mile Run. The Virginia picket guard, stationed near Roach's Spring, ran away, and about an hour later the alarm bells were rung in Alexandria.

On Friday morning, the 24th, a large body of troops crossed the Potomac into Virginia. Ellsworth's Zouaves in two steamers left their camp on the Eastern Branch, making directly for Alexandria. The Michigan regiment, accompanied by a detachment of United States troops and two pieces of Sherman's battery, proceeded by the Long Bridge to Alexandria. The Seventh New York was held under orders at Hughes's Tavern. The Second New Jersey was at Roach's Spring, one-half mile from the bridge. The New York Twenty-fifth, the Twelfth New York, and the Third and Fourth New Jersey proceeded to occupy Arlington Heights, joined by other troops which crossed over the Georgetown aqueduct.

At 4:00 A. M., Ellsworth's Zouaves landed at Alexandria, and, though fired upon in landing by the few Virginia sentries posted in the town, which fire was returned by the Zouaves on the decks of the steamers, immediately on landing marched directly into the center of the town, meeting with no resistance. Reaching the city flagstaff they hoisted an American flag, and then perceiving a rebel flag floating from the Marshall House, Colonel Ellsworth proceeded there with a squad of men and requested the proprietor, James Jackson, to take it down. This request not being complied with, Colonel Ellsworth went to the top of the house and hauled it down, and wrapping it round his body started down the stairs. As he was descending, the proprietor, who had concealed himself in a dark passage, discharged the contents of one barrel of a double-barreled gun into his body, killing him instantly. Private Francis E. Brownell, of Colonel Ellsworth's Zouaves, instantly discharged the contents of his own musket into Jackson's brain and pierced his body with his bayonet as he fell, the other barrel of Jackson's gun going off as he fell. The news of the assassination of Colonel Ellsworth reached the city at an early hour in the morning, and when it was confirmed all the flags in the city were displayed at half-mast. The remains of the patriotic and brave Colonel were escorted to the Navy Yard by the steamer *Mount Vernon*, and the funeral occurred from the Executive Mansion at eleven o'clock the same morning, whence the body was taken to the railroad depot for conveyance to New York.

Intrenching tools were conveyed over the river, and on Saturday, the 25th, the work of fortifying the city began in earnest on the Virginia side. One of the New Jersey regiments threw up fortifications at the Junction of the Washington, Alexandria, and Columbia Turnpike, and another work of the same kind was commenced by another New Jersey regiment on the next height above, on the road

17

toward Alexandria. The Sixty-ninth Regiment was engaged in destroying communications between Alexandria and Leesburg, by the destruction of bridges, etc., on the Loudoun and Hampshire Railroad. The fortifications thus commenced on the 25th of May, 1861, subsequently became of immense extent, and together with those on other sides of Washington, consisted of forty-eight works, mounting three hundred guns. The entire circumscribing perimeter of these fortifications was about thirty-five miles in length.[1]

To the National Rifles of Captain J. R. Smead is due the honor of first entering upon the sacred soil of the Old Dominion, crossing the Long Bridge at an early hour on the night of May 23, driving in the advance pickets of the rebels, and with other District troops holding the roads to Alexandria. Captain Powell's Zouaves were among the first, as were also the Metropolitan Rifles, under command, at the time, of Lieutenant Chauncey, and all were prompt and meritorious in the discharge of their duty.

At Fort Washington, on the Potomac, a few miles below Alexandria, on the Maryland side of the river, Major Haskins was in command. The Ninth New York Regiment, which was the first regiment to offer its services to the Government for three years, arrived in Washington May 28. J. W. Stiles was the colonel of this regiment. The Fifth Regiment, District of Columbia Militia, was mustered into the service May 29, Colonel W. H. Philip commanding. The several companies were commanded by Captains S. B. Elliott, W. B. Webb, Hilton, Clark, French, Emory, Jillard, Burchell, and Robinson. The regiment was four hundred strong, and was made up of citizens residing between Seventh and Seventeenth streets and H and Boundary streets.

May 30, the Sixty-ninth New York Regiment raised their flag at

---

[1] These forts and batteries thus erected for the defense of the Capital of the Nation were as follows, commencing at the south of Alexandria, then along the Virginia shore, crossing the Potomac above Georgetown, and extending north of the city and along the ridge east of the Anacostia down to the river opposite Alexandria: Forts Willard, O'Rourke, Weed, Farnsworth, and Lyon; Battery Rodgers; Forts Ellsworth, Williams, Worth. Ward, Reynolds, Garesche, Barnard, Berry, Richardson, Craig, Scott, Albany, Runyon, Jackson, Tillinghast, Cass, Whipple, Woodbury, Morton, Strong, Corcoran, Bennett, C. F. Smith, Ethan Allen, and Marcy; two batteries near the distributing reservoir; Batteries Cameron, Parrott, Kemble, Martin, Scott, Bailey, Vermont, Alexander, and Benson; Forts Sumner, Kerby, Cross, Davis, Mansfield, Simmons, Bayard, and Reno; Battery Rossell; Fort Kearney; Batteries Terrill and Smeade; Fort De Russey; Batteries Kingsbury and Sill; Forts Stevens, Slocum, Totten, Slemmer, Bunker Hill, Saratoga, Thayer, Lincoln, Mahan, Shaplin, Meigs, Dupont, Davis, Baker, Wagner, Ricketts, Stanton, Snyder, Carroll, Greble, and Foote.

Fort Corcoran, their new camp at Arlington Heights. Colonel Hunter, of the Third United States Cavalry, who was assigned as commander of the Aqueduct Brigade, composed of the Fifth, Twenty-eighth, and Sixty-ninth New York regiments, made a speech on this occasion, as also did Captain Thomas F. Meagher. Mr. Savage's new national song was then sung by the author, the entire body of troops present joining in the chorus. The New Jersey troops threw up intrenchments at the Columbia Springs early in June, placing some thirty-two-pound cannon in position, as well as other artillery. The volunteer battalion near the chain bridge, two miles above Georgetown, was well fortified, and had guns so mounted as to sweep the bridge and the Virginia shore in case of necessity.

On the 9th of June, an important movement was made up the Potomac from Washington. The Rhode Island battery, under Colonel Burnside, was sent to join General Patterson at Chambersburg, and on the 10th Colonel Stone's command, consisting of the National Rifles under Major Smead, the Slemmer Guards under Captain Knight, the Cameron Guards under Captain ———, Captain Magruder's battery of United States artillery, the First Pennsylvania, and the Ninth New York, and the First New Hampshire, moved up the Rockville road toward Edward's Ferry, about midway between Washington and Harper's Ferry. It was the only crossing for teams between the District of Columbia and the Point of Rocks, and was at that time a general thoroughfare for the transit of secessionists and military stores from Maryland into Virginia. The quota of the District in this movement was one thousand, and was promptly furnished to the Government by Washington and Georgetown.

June 18, 1861, Professor T. S. C. Lowe made a number of ascensions in his balloon, taking along a telegraph instrument connected by a wire with the White House. When the balloon was at its greatest elevation, about one-half mile, the following telegram was sent down:

"Balloon Enterprise, Washington, D. C., June 18, 1861.

"*To the President of the United States:*

"This point of elevation commands an area of near fifty miles in diameter. The city, with its encampments, presents a superb scene. I have pleasure in sending you this first dispatch from an aërial station, and in acknowledging indebtedness to your encouragement for the opportunity of demonstrating the availability of the science of aëronautics to the military service of the country.

"T. S. C. Lowe."

June 24, the Councils of Washington passed a bill appropriating $5,000 for the support of the families of the District of Columbia volunteers, payable out of the general fund. The first grand review of the Army of the Potomac occurred July 4, 1861. Major Jewell's battalion of District volunteers, after an arduous campaign of some weeks on the line of the Potomac, returned to Washington on the morning of July 4. The same day, the Third Battalion of District Volunteers returned to Washington from Edward's Ferry, having rendered effective service to the Government. Regiments of troops continued to arrive in Washington in such numbers that any attempt to enumerate them would not be of interest. After the 4th of July, they passed over into Virginia in considerable numbers. On the morning of the 9th, two soldiers who had been killed in a skirmish at Great Falls, named Riggs and Uhl, were buried from the armory in the new German cemetery near Glenwood. This appears to have been the first burial of soldiers of the District of Columbia killed in defense of the Union. The term of service of the District volunteers having expired, several of the companies were mustered out, July 10, the companies thus mustered out being Company A, Union Regiment, Captain E. C. Carrington; Campany A, Washington Light Infantry; the Washington Zouaves; Company E, Washington Light Infantry; the Anderson Rifles, the Potomac Light Guard, the National Rifles, the Home Guards, and the Andrew Johnson Guards.

July 16, 1861, Edward Thompson, a private soldier in the Watson Guards, died at the age of sixty-four years. The Watson Guards were, at the time, under command of Captain Callan. In 1814, he was at the battle of Bladensburg; in 1836-37, he was in the Florida war; in 1846-47, he served with the District of Columbia volunteers under Colonel Watson in the war with Mexico; and in April, 1861, he volunteered to defend the National Capital against the rebels, in the Watson Guards.

Several regiments went over into Virginia, July 20, 1861. The battle of Manassas Junction, or the first battle of Bull Run, was fought on Sunday, July 21, commencing about 10:30 A. M., and lasting until 4:00 P. M. The history of this battle is sufficiently well known not to need recital in this work, though it may not be out of place to note that for several days after it was fought, it was continuously asserted to have been the fault of non-combatants that there was a rout and a stampede of the Union forces. General McDowell's official report, however, set the matter before the public in its true light. After the rout, many of the soldiers made their way to Washington as fast as possible, and were picked up and made comfortable by members of the National Rifles, of the District volunteers, in their fine armory in Temperance Hall. There were others that wandered about the streets, seeking shelter from the driving rain which fell on the day after the battle, which fact — that is, the fact of the shower of rain — was seized upon by certain meteorologists to direct attention to their theory that rain always follows heavy cannonading.

July 27, there was a fearful explosion at the Navy Yard, in the rocket house, which killed two men and wounded two others. The killed were Francis C. Brown and John P. Ferguson, and the wounded William Martin and Nicholas Ray.

A. Porter, colonel of the Sixteenth United States Infantry, was appointed provost-marshal of the District of Columbia, August 1, 1861. His General Order No. 1 was issued August 2, ordering all officers and enlisted men to remain in camp unless absent by permission; and all officers and soldiers were forbidden to be in the streets, at hotels, or at other places, after 9:00 P. M.

Following are names of Washingtonians killed at the battles of Stone Bridge and Bull Run, July 18 and 21, in the First Regiment Virginia Volunteers: Captain C. K. Sherman and Isidore Morris.

August 6, the first company of Colonel Everett's new regiment of District of Columbia volunteers was mustered into the service, with Captain Knight in command. Captain Geary's company of cavalry was mustered in for three years, as were also the Everett's Guards about the same time, with Maurice Tucker captain, James R. Harrover first lieutenant, Jeremiah O'Leary second lieutenant, and George Augerton orderly sergeant.

One of the important institutions of Washington pertaining to the war was the army bakery, located in the Capitol, in the exterior vaults. It was in control of Lieutenant Thomas J. Cate, of the Twelfth United States Artillery, who, upon the necessity for such an institution arising, offered his services to build the ovens. This work being performed he employed one hundred and seventy hands, dividing them into day and night squads. By this bakery the soldiers were supplied with fresh and wholesome bread. In the employ of the bakery were twelve wagons, which were kept constantly going, loaded with bread, carrying out nearly sixty thousand loaves per day. Each loaf weighed twenty two ounces. In October, 1861, this bakery was consuming one hundred and fifty barrels of flour per day. A yeast room was attached to the bakery, employing eight men. The ovens were large and well built, and each was capable of baking about four thousand three hundred loaves in twenty-four hours.

November 5, 1861, the mansions of Senator Douglas, Senator Rice, and Mr. Corbin, known as Minnesota Row, were engaged for a military hospital, at an annual rental of $7,000.

The Navy Yard was kept busy all the time during the war. December 1, 1861, Captain Dahlgren, in charge, had at work under him eighteen hundred men. A number of very large anchors, weighing from eight thousand pounds downward, were made there, as also many chain cables.

The Second District Volunteer Regiment was mustered into the service of the United States for three years in February, 1862, and by the 20th of this month all of its companies but three were full. The regimental officers were as follows: Colonel, Isaac K. Peck; major, Charles Alexander; adjutant, C. M. Lienbeck; quartermaster, James P. Sanderson; surgeon, Dr. J. B. Keasby; assistant surgeon, Dr. L. C. Hoole, and chaplain, Rev. Mr. Lockwood. The captains of the several companies were as follows: Company A, Captain Garrett; Company B, Captain Dubant; Company C, Captain Drew; Company D, Captain Ditmarris; Company E, Captain Callan; Company F, Captain Steele; Company G, Captain Stockbridge; Company H, Captain Blything; Company I, Captain Duncan; Company K, Captain Krouse. On May 21, this regiment was presented with a handsome flag, having in gold letters the following inscription: "President's Guard, Second Regiment District of Columbia Volunteers." The flag was mounted on a staff bearing this inscription: "Presented to the President's Guard by the Ladies of Washington, May 21, 1862." The presentation speech was made by Major B. B. French, and the response by Colonel Peck.

At the beginning of the year 1862, there were the following numbers of soldiers in and around Washington, including the various armies as noted: At Fortress Monroe, under General Wool, 15,000 men; south of Washington and partly on the Maryland side of the Potomac, General Hooker's division, including General Sickles's brigade, about 10,000; southwest of the city was the mass of General McClellan's army, consisting of eight divisions, nearly 160,000 men, and other troops on the line of the Baltimore and Ohio Railroad toward Baltimore, making the grand aggregate nearly 200,000 men.

The force designed for the special defense of Washington, while General McClellan was engaged on the Peninsula in front of Richmond, was described as follows, the forces being placed in command of Brigadier-General James Wadsworth, according to General McClellan's orders, dated April 1, 1862: "The garrisons in the forts around Washington amount to 10,000 men, other disposable troops now with

General Wadsworth being 11,400 men. The troops employed in guarding the various railroads in Maryland amounted to some 3,350 men. These it was designed to relieve, they being old regiments, with dismounted cavalry, and send them forward to Manassas. General Abercrombie occupied Warrenton with a force which, including General Geary's at White Plains and the cavalry to be at their disposal, amounted to 7,780 men, with twelve pieces of artillery. Besides these General McClellan requested that troops be sent to Manassas so as to make the command of General Abercrombie equal to 18,000 men. Thus, to summarize, the troops designed for the defense of Washington were as follows: At Warrenton, 7,780 men; at Manassas, 10,860 men; in the Shenandoah, 35,470 men; on the Lower Potomac, 1,350; in all, 55,460 men. In front of Washington there were to be left 18,000 men, exclusive of the batteries of artillery, which were as follows: Battery C, First New York Artillery, 2 guns; Battery K, First New York Artillery, 6 guns; Battery L, Second New York Artillery, 6 guns; Ninth New York Independent Battery, 6 guns; Sixteenth New York Independent Battery, 6 guns; Battery A, Second Battalion, New York Artillery, 6 guns; Battery B, Second New York Artillery, 6 guns; total number of guns, 32.

On August 6, a great war meeting was held in front of the Capitol building. At 5:00 P. M., a salute of thirty-four guns was fired and the bells of the city were rung. The Marine Band played at this place instead of its accustomed place. The President and his cabinet were in attendance. The Mayor of Washington presided, and Samuel E. Douglass was secretary of the committee of arrangements. The speakers were the Hon. George S. Boutwell, Commissioner of Internal Revenue; Hon. Leonard Swett of Chicago, Hon. R. W. Thompson of Indiana, L. E. Chittenden, Register of the Treasury; President Lincoln, General Shepley, Military Governor of Louisiana; Senator Harlan of Iowa, and General E. C. Carrington, United States District Attorney for the District of Columbia. The meeting lasted until 10:15 P. M. A series of resolutions was adopted, expressive of the sentiments of the meeting, regarding the dismemberment of the Union as an event not to be contemplated in any possible contingency; that the hesitation then manifested by loyal citizens was owing solely to their misgivings as to the prosecution of the war; urging the President to adopt effectual means of assuring the people that he was resolved to prosecute the war on a scale limited only by the resources of the country; that the measures adopted should be such as would bear with the most crushing weight upon those in rebellion, whether in arms or not; that the leaders of the Rebellion should be regarded as irreclaimable traitors, and either deprived of life or expelled from the country; that the National Capital was eminently the place where treason should be instantly denounced and punished, and that the most stringent measures should be adopted by the proper authorities without delay to arrest the disloyal men and women within the District of Columbia; approving the act of Congress subjecting to confiscation the property of rebels, and declaring free such of their slaves as should take refuge within our lines; that the Federal Government should be sustained, no matter what administration was in power, and pledging to the President and his cabinet the most earnest, cordial, and determined support; and lastly, pledging themselves to make ample pecuniary provision for the support of the families of such of the citizens of the District of Columbia as were in the military service of their country.

The speech of the President was a noteworthy one, being uttered at a time when much criticism was being indulged in by friends of himself and those of General McClellan, for opposite reasons, and when there was dissatisfaction with the results of the campaign on the Peninsula. Omitting the mere introductory portion of the speech, the President said:

"There has been a very widespread attempt to have a quarrel between General McClellan and the Secretary of War. Now, I occupy a position that enables me to believe, at least, that these two gentlemen are not nearly so deep in the quarrel as some presuming to be their friends. General McClellan's attitude is such that in the very selfishness of nature he cannot but wish to succeed, and I hope he will be successful. The Secretary of War is precisely in the same situation. If the military commander in the field cannot be successful, not only the Secretary of War, but myself, for the time being the master of them both, cannot but be failures. Sometimes we hear a dispute about how many men McClellan has had. Those who would disparage him say that he has had a very large number, and those who would disparage the Secretary of War insist that General McClellan has had but a very small number. The basis for this is that there is always a wide difference between the grand total on McClellan's rolls and the men actually fit for duty; those who would disparage him talk of the grand total on paper, and those who would disparage the Secretary of War talk of those present and fit for duty.

"General McClellan has sometimes asked for things that the Secretary of War could not give him. General McClellan is not to blame for asking for what he wanted and needed, and the Secretary of War is not to blame for not giving what he had not to give. And I say here, that so far as I know, the Secretary of War has withheld nothing from McClellan without my approval, and I have withheld nothing at any time in my power to give. I have no accusation against him. I believe he is a brave and able man, and I stand here, as justice requires me to do, to take upon myself what has been charged upon the Secretary of War as withheld from him."

The second battle of Bull Run was fought on the 29th, 30th, and 31st of August, 1862, resulting, as is well known, in the serious defeat of the Union forces under General Pope. In consequence of the great losses to the Union army in wounded, there was great demand for surgeons and nurses to care for them, and a corresponding activity in the departments and among the people at Washington in response to the demand. Fully one thousand persons, employees of the Government and others, assembled at the corner of Maryland Avenue and Eighth Street South at four o'clock in the afternoon of Saturday, the 30th, expecting speedy transportation to the battlefield; but owing to the failure to notify the engineer of the train that civilians were to go on it, there was a delay of four hours in getting started. At length, however, at eight o'clock, the train got under way with its load of humanitarians, to carry succor to the sick and wounded. After a ride of ten hours, they reached Fairfax Station, and then could proceed no further, except on foot, and on their own responsibility, the bridge over Bull Run having been destroyed by the rebels the night before; and then there was a march of fifteen miles before them. if they went on. The few that did make the attempt to reach the battlefield were peremptorily ordered back; so all gave up and returned to Washington. The next day, the medical director of the District, John Campbell, published a request that all who were willing to receive into their houses convalescent soldiers, in order to make room for wounded soldiers, would send their names to him, together with the number they could accommodate. The movement thus begun at Washington, to send surgeons and other assistance to the battlefields, instantly spread to all the larger cities of the Northern States, and packages of all kinds of clothing, etc., were forwarded therefrom in great abundance.

On September 1, a consultation was held by the President, General Halleck, and General McClellan, as to the defenses of the city, and a number of gunboats came up the Potomac, anchoring at different points off the city, so as to be ready in case of an attack upon the city, which was then with good reason apprehended. Quite a number of clerks from the departments went down to the boat-landing at Sixth Street, to assist in transferring the wounded, about fifteen hundred of whom reached the city that day. Carriages, wagons, omnibuses, and ambulances were all pressed into the service. The influx of wounded after this battle made it necessary to convert every place capable of use in this way into hospitals for the sick and wounded, the upper story of the Patent Office, the Capitol, and numerous other buildings being converted into hospitals.

On September 2, General McClellan was placed in command of the fortifications of Washington and of all of the troops for its defense, and the patrolmen were all busy closing all retail liquor establishments. September 3, the remains of Colonel Fletcher Webster, son of Hon. Daniel Webster, having been embalmed at Alexandria, were brought to Washington, as were also those of General Kearney. The entire army of General Pope, which commenced falling back from Centerville on Monday morning, September 1, reached its position in front of the fortifications on the south side of the Potomac on Tuesday night, General McClellan assuming command of this army, as also of General Burnside's. In consequence of the threatened danger to the city, the clerks in the several departments of the Government were organized into military companies for the defense of the Capital. In the Interior Department a company was formed containing 120 men, under Captain J. M. Edmonds. The Census clerks formed a company of 85 men; the Patent Office, one of 100 men. The Post Office employees made a company containing 87 active men, and 30 reserves, with captain, R. K. Scott; first lieutenant, C. F. McDonald; second lieutenant, William H. Frazer. The Treasury Department also organized a company, but the War Department was too busy with its regular duties to give any attention to local military organizations. The employees of the Government Printing Office organized a company containing about 170 men. The total number of employees of the Government thus organized into companies for the defense of the city was about 1,800 men. The National Rifles, about 80 strong, tendered their services. Including this latter company there were, by September 4, 18 companies organized, the Interior Department furnishing 8, the Treasury Department 5, the Printing Office 2, the Coast Survey 1, the Post Office Department 1, and the National Rifles. On the same day, the One Hundred and Thirty-ninth Pennsylvania Regiment arrived in the city, and the One Hundred and Twenty-second New York and the Twentieth Michigan. The German Relief Association, organized to relieve and comfort the sick and wounded soldiers, performed unusually acceptable service at this time. The clerks of the Third, Fourth, and Fifth Auditors' divisions were organized on Wednesday evening, September 3, with captain, D. H. Lusk, first lieutenant, A. J. Bentley, second lieutenant, J. Hackett. The stonecutters and laborers at work on the Capitol on the same day organized two companies, one company being officered as follows: Captain, Richard Morgan, first lieutenant, H. Ellis, and second lieutenant, P. Fritz; the other as follows: Captain, A. Johnson, first lieutenant, A. Carroll, and second lieutenant, Joseph Sullivan. Other employees at work on the building organized another company, with captain, C. F. Thomas, first lieutenant, C. Magruder, and second lieutenant, G. Miller.

In consequence of the invasion of Maryland by the successful rebels, and the capture of Fredericksburg, a force of troops left Washington on Sunday, September 7, General McClellan following at 6:40 P. M., General Banks being left in charge of the defense of Washington. On Saturday night, the troops had been placed under marching orders, and the new levies made the night air resound with their shouting and their cheers, while the old troops, having had considerable severe experience in actual warfare, were much more quiet. The great battle of August 17, at South Mountain, was one of the severest of the war, resulting in a victory for the Army of the Potomac. During the 18th, the firing was not renewed, General McClellan having agreed to an armistice, proposed by the enemy, to bury the dead. After this great battle, the Sanitary Commission was very active in sending supplies to the army. At this time there were the following hospitals in Washington for the care of the sick and wounded soldiers:

Ascension Hospital, at the corner of H and Ninth streets; Armory Hospital, on Seventh Street, south of the canal; Baptist Hospital, Dr. Samson's, on Thirteenth Street, near G; Baptist Hospital, Rev. Mr. Kennard's, on E Street, near Sixth; Caspion's House, near the Capitol; Carver's House, near Boundary, between Seventh and Fourteenth; Capitol Hospital; Columbian Hospital, Columbian College, on Fourteenth Street; Cliffburne Hospital, near Columbian College; Douglas Hospital, at the corner of I and First streets; Ebenezer Hospital, on Fourth Street, near G; Eckington Hospital, near the Gales mansion; Emory Hospital, at the Sixth Cavalry Barracks, east of the Capitol; Epiphany Hospital, on G Street, between Thirteenth and Fourteenth streets; Finley Hospital, near the Eckington Hospital; Harewood Hospital, Corcoran's Place, near the tollgate; Judiciary Square Hospital; Kalorama Hospital, Twenty-first Street and Kalorama Heights; Methodist Hospital (Southern), Eighth and I streets; Mount Pleasant Hospital, Fourteenth Street, near Columbian College; Ninth Street Hospital, between G and H streets; Odd Fellows Hospital, Eighth Street East, near the Navy Yard; Patent Office Hospital; Ryland Chapel Hospital, Tenth and D streets; Seminary Hospital, Gay and Washington streets, Georgetown; St. Elizabeth Hospital, Government Insane Asylum; Stone's Hospital, Fourteenth Street, east of the college; Trinity Church Hospital, Third and C streets; Union Chapel Hospital, Twentieth Street, near H; Union Hotel Hospital, Georgetown; Unitarian or Cranch Hospital, Sixth and D streets; St. Aloysius Hospital, near St. Aloysius Catholic Church. Besides these there were ten hospitals in Alexandria.

It would be impossible to do more than justice to those who attended the sick, wounded, and dying soldiers in these hospitals. Ladies of every class in society, including the most refined, and members of families of foreign diplomats, all moved by a sympathy for suffering humanity common to all hearts, and as honorable as common, were constantly at work at the bedsides of those needing aid. The amount of good done in this way is inestimable.

After the issuance of the Proclamation of September 22, 1862, a serenade was given the President on Wednesday evening, the 24th. In response, the President said: "I have not been distinctly informed why it is that on this occasion you appear to do me this honor. I suppose—["It is because of the proclamation!"]—I was about to say I suppose I understand it. What I did I did after very full delibera- tion, and under a very heavy and solemn sense of responsibility. I can only trust in God that I made no mistake." Secretary Chase, Cassius M. Clay, and Attorney-General Bates were also visited and serenaded, and all made speeches approving of the proclamation.

The First Regiment, District of Columbia Volunteers, in October, 1862, were sent to Alexandria to act as provost guard, Colonel Tait relieving General Slough as military governor of the city of Alex- andria. This regiment had been in the severe campaigns of Banks and Pope, but notwithstanding this fact had at this time nearly five hundred men in ranks fit for duty, and only twenty-five absent without leave. The Second District of Columbia Regiment was for some time previous to October 31 engaged in duty on the Upper Potomac, but was relieved about this time, and came to the city.

Island Hall Hospital was established at the corner of Sixth Street and Virginia Avenue about November 1, and was under the care of

Surgeons Hayes and Schenck. Up to January 1, 1863, bounties were given to such persons as should enlist in the District of Columbia regiments, but at that time this practice was abandoned, because very few of the inhabitants availed themselves of the bounty, and because most of the enlistments were by parties from abroad, who in some instances were deserters from other regiments. At the close of the year 1862, there were about fourteen thousand sick and wounded soldiers in the hospitals in Washington, Georgetown, and Alexandria. But notwithstanding there were so many, there was sufficient room for all in the regular hospitals, and the Fourth Presbyterian Church, the Church of the Ascension, and the Methodist Episcopal Church South were vacated, when all the churches were vacated which had been in use by the Government for this purpose. On February 18, 1863, Lieutenant-Colonel W. E. Doster was relieved at his own request as provost-marshal of the District of Columbia, and Captain Henry B. Todd, of the First New York Cavalry, appointed in his stead.

March 31, 1863, a great war meeting was held in both halls of Congress, under the auspices of the two boards of the city Council. Mayor Richard Wallach presided in the hall of the House of Representatives, and Lewis Clephane and Alexander R. Shepherd in the hall of the Senate, the former during the first part of the meeting, and the latter during the latter part. In the House of Representatives, Ex-Governor Bebb, of Ohio, submitted a series of resolutions strongly in favor of fighting the war to a successful termination, and quoting John Bright, as to the destiny of the Republic, as follows:

"We cannot believe that civilization, in its journey with the sun, will sink into endless night, to gratify the ambition of the leaders of this revolt, who seek to 'wade through slaughter to a throne,' and 'shut the gates of mercy on mankind.' We have another and far brighter vision before our eyes. Through the thick gloom of the present we see the brightness of the future as the sun in the heavens. We see one vast confederation, stretching from the frozen North in one unbroken line to the glowing South, and from the wild billows of the stormy Atlantic to the calmer waters of the Pacific main; and we see one people, one law, one language, and one religion, and over all this wide continent the home of freedom and a refuge for the oppressed of every race."

Alderman Sargent then offered a resolution to the effect that there were two classes of people in this city, the loyal and the disloyal; and "that we owe it to ourselves to ferret out the disloyal and send them to their friends in Richmond." All the resolutions were unanimously adopted. Hon. Green Adams then addressed the meeting, as did also Admiral Foote, Chief Justice D. K. Cartter, Hon. Horace Maynard, Hon. Andrew Johnson, and General E. C. Carrington. In the Senate chamber Ex-Governor Bebb offered the same series of resolutions offered in the House of Representatives, and speeches were made by General Martindale, then Military Governor of the District of Columbia, Admiral Foote, Rev. Mr. Phillips of New York, L. E. Chittenden, Register of the Treasury, L. A. Whitely of Maryland, Horace Maynard, Governor Bashford of Wisconsin, and Dr. Daily of Indiana.

In June, 1863, in consequence of reduction in the size of its companies, the First District Regiment was consolidated into a battalion of four companies. Upon this consolidation the officers mustered out were: Colonel James A. Tait; Captains H. M. Knight, James Coleman, James Fisher, P. E. Rodier, and Joseph Mundell; First Lieutenants C. P. Wroe, R. W. Barnaclo, C. T. Barrett, and Joseph Venable; Second Lieutenants Jerome Callahan, P. McChesney, W. E. Morgan, and Edward Carroll. Those retained were: Lieutenant-Colonel Lemuel Towers, and staff officers; Captains E. S. Allen, Robert Boyd, Robert Clark, and M. P. Fisher; First Lieutenants John Donn, B. F. McGrew, C. W. Sherwood, and W. W. Winship; Second Lieutenants William Young, Walter Dobson, J. W. Atwell, and D. F. Stiles.

Toward the latter part of this month, when it was learned that the rebel General Lee was marching northward into Pennsylvania, orders were issued by Provost-Marshal-General James B. Fry to Major-General George C. Thomas, then in command of the District of Columbia militia, that eight regiments of the militia infantry of the District be called into immediate service for sixty days, and providing that if the volunteer cavalry and infantry of the District should tender their services they would be accepted. Major-General Thomas thereupon issued the orders necessary for calling out and enrolling the eight regiments. On the morning of July 6, the various regiments composing the District militia assembled on their parade grounds, and were informed that as General Lee had been defeated at the great battle of Gettysburg, and was compelled to retreat back into Virginia, their services would not be needed. On Tuesday, July 7, there was great rejoicing in Washington over the victories of General Meade in Pennsylvania, of General Grant at Vicksburg, and of General Rosecrans in Tennessee. A large number of citizens of Washington, headed by the band of the Thirty-fourth Massachusetts

Regiment, marched to the Executive Mansion and serenaded the President, who made to them a speech, paying glowing tribute to the brave men in the armies, but declining to mention any soldier by name, for fear of omitting some who were equally meritorious with those whom he might name, should he name any of them. Secretary Stanton and General Halleck, and also Senators Wilson, Wilkinson, and Lane, and Hons. E. B. Washburn, Isaac Arnold, and General Martindale, made speeches.

Under the President's call for 500,000 men, July 18, 1864, there was a draft in the District of Columbia for her quota. The District was divided into twelve districts, of which each of the seven wards of the city of Washington was one; that part of Georgetown east of High Street was the eighth; that part west of High Street the ninth; that part of the county west of Rock Creek the tenth; that part between Rock Creek and the Eastern Branch the eleventh, and that part south and east of the Eastern Branch the twelfth. Captain Sheetz, who was provost-marshal under the Conscription Act, made a return of the names enrolled for the first class toward the latter part of July, as follows: First Ward of Washington, 4,000; Second Ward, 2,500; Third Ward, 2,000; Fourth Ward, 3,000; Fifth Ward, 1,700; Sixth Ward, 1,200; Seventh Ward, 2,400; eighth district, 800; ninth district, 700; tenth district, 400; eleventh district, 500; twelfth district, 300; total, nearly 20,000; or, to be exact, 19,327; of which number there were 14,242 whites, and 5,085 blacks. The apportionment of the District was 3,865, to which was added fifty per cent. to allow a margin for exemptions; or, in all, 5,798. The draft commenced on Monday, August 3, with the First Ward. The number to be drawn from each subdistrict was as follows: First Ward, 1,180; Second Ward, 741; Third Ward, 607; Fourth Ward, 896; Fifth Ward, 513; Sixth Ward, 337; Seventh Ward, 719; eighth district, 239; ninth district, 216; tenth district, 116; eleventh district, 155, and twelfth district, 79; total, 5,798. The drawing commenced at 9:00 A. M., a blind man named Thomas C. Burns drawing the names from the box. The drawing for the First Ward closed at 2:00 P. M. Of the persons drawn, 874 were white and 306 black. The drawing for the Second Ward was completed the same day, and of the number drawn 494 were white and 247 black. The drawing for the Third Ward came off on the 4th, resulting in 502 whites being drawn, and 105 blacks. There were drawn in the Fourth Ward 736 whites and 160 blacks; in the Fifth Ward, 344 whites and 169 blacks; in the Sixth Ward, 286 whites and 51 blacks; in the Seventh Ward, 684 whites and 235 blacks;

in the eighth and ninth districts, 390 whites and 65 blacks, and in the rest of the county 350 persons in all. The board of enrollment met on August 10, to hear applications for exemptions.

The result of the draft in the District of Columbia was reached September 30, the work of the board of enrollment closing on that evening. This result was as follows: Total number drawn, 5,784; quota, 3,863; number of drafted men who reported, 4,115; number failing to report, 1,679; number accepted, 285; number of substitutes, 675; number paying commutation, 212; number exempted, 2,943. Of the number of soldiers obtained by means of the draft (960), there were 336 negroes.

In October, the President called for another 300,000 men. Under this call the District of Columbia, with the rest of the country, was called on for its quota. On November 6, there was a meeting at the City Hall, preliminary to a large mass meeting which was held August 6, for the purpose of aiding enlistments, so that if possible there might be no necessity for another draft. The quota of the District under this call was 2,730—from Washington and the county, 2,516, and from Georgetown, 214. At this meeting a committee was appointed to solicit funds with which to assist the families of soldiers of the District serving in any of the armies of the Union. The committee consisted of B. B. French, Henry Addison, Richard Wallach, Samuel E. Douglass, George H. Plant, Hudson Taylor, Frank Taylor, John M. Brodhead, George R. Wilson, John H. Semmes, E. J. Middleton, William B. Todd, William J. Murtagh, Joseph F. Brown, Judson Mitchell, William H. Tenney, John Marbury, Jr., George W. Beall, and Henry D. Cooke. The subscriptions very quickly amounted to $20,745, $18,726 of which was distributed among the families of the soldiers, the rest, $2,019, being retained to commence operations for the winter.

On July 24, 1863, Judge Wylie, of the Supreme Court of the District of Columbia, made a decision under the Confiscation Act with reference to the property of Dr. A. Y. P. Garnett, which was before the Court for condemnation, and which was the first case argued before the Court. The Judge, in making his decision, said that it was a most important case. The confiscation did not, as was generally supposed, treat the inhabitants of the so-called Confederate States as traitors, but as alien enemies, and in that point of view their property of every description was liable to absolute forfeiture and alienation to the use of the Government. There was no distinction between real estate and personal property. Nor did the

Constitution forbid this absolute forfeiture of real estate. But the joint resolution of Congress, passed on the same day as the Confiscation Act, under the provisions of which the property in question was sought to be confiscated, was a declaration by them that, in a spirit of kindness, they would confiscate the real estate of rebel owners only during their lifetime. The Judge was, he said, bound by the joint resolution, and therefore he condemned the real estate only during the lifetime of the owner, and the personal estate absolutely. Judge Wylie referred to a number of authorities, among them the legislatures of Maryland and Pennsylvania, confiscating absolutely the property of Americans who remained loyal to England during the Revolutionary War.

The decree of condemnation was then ordered against the property of Thomas D. Allen, Francis Hanna, E. A. Pollard, Charles S. Wallach, Cornelius Boyle, French Forrest, J. N. Maffit, C. W. C. Dunnington, Martin L. Smith, Daniel and Mary F. Radcliffe, E. M. Clark, Samuel Lee, Henry B. Tyler, William F. Phillips, C. W. Havenner, Lavinia Boyle, and Samuel L. Lewis.

In August, 1863, the marshal of the District of Columbia, by direction of the attorney for the District, made seizure of the following property:

Two two-story frame houses of Craven Ashford, formerly a justice of the peace in Washington, but then in the South; lots 1 to 12, inclusive, of George S. Houston, formerly a member of Congress from Alabama, and of Governor Letcher, of Virginia, on Capitol Hill; lot improved by a four-story dwelling, on E Street, between Second and Third streets, northwest, in the name of W. H. Thomas, then in the Confederate Army; lot at the corner of Vermont Avenue and K Street, improved by a two-story house, in the name of H. H. Lewis, of Virginia; lot near the corner of the canal and South Capitol Street, in the name of Oscar R. Hough, formerly of the National Rifles, but then connected with the provost-marshal's office at Richmond; subdivision of lots near the Baltimore and Ohio Depot, and several lots on South Capitol Street, near N Street, used as a brick yard, in the name of David A. Windsor. While there was considerable other property confiscated, yet it is probable that enough detail has been here given.

The Ladies' Relief Association, for the relief of the soldiers of the District of Columbia, held a meeting December 21, 1863, at the residence of Hon. Sayles J. Bowen, to elect officers. Major B. B. French was chosen president, Henry D. Cooke vice-president, Selah

18

Squires secretary, and Mrs. L. E. Chittenden treasurer. A committee of arrangements for a fair, which was then in contemplation, was appointed, consisting of four gentlemen and seven ladies; also, an executive committee, a finance committee, a committee for each ward, as well as a committee for Georgetown, a committee at large, and a committee for each of the twenty-three of the loyal States. The great hall of the north front of the Patent Office was offered by Hon. J. P. Usher, and accepted by the association, for the purposes of the fair. The ladies of the association made application to the proprietor of Canterbury Hall for assistance in this work, and in response to this appeal Mr. William E. Sinn offered either $25 in money or a benefit at his establishment, the ladies choosing the latter, to be given January 8, 1864. Jay Cooke & Company, bankers in Washington, donated $1,000 toward the objects of the fair. January 18, a committee, on behalf of the association, requested Mr. Leonard Grover, proprietor of the New National Theater, to give a benefit, with which request Mr. Grover complied, fixing upon January 23 as the date for the benefit, which netted to the association $437.15. On the 22d of the same month, a benefit performance was given at the Variety Theater, on Pennsylvania Avenue and Ninth Street, of which Messrs. Hamblin & Company were the proprietors. The fair opened in the Patent Office building February 22, 1864, upward of one thousand tickets being disposed of at the door that evening, a large number having been sold throughout the District during the preceding three weeks. Contributions to the fair came from many of the loyal States, as well as from the District of Columbia. This fair yielded a net sum of $12,721.35, and from individual subscriptions and from other sources there was received the sum of $2,588.69, making $15,310.04. To this sum there was added the $2,027.25 mentioned above as being left over from other subscriptions, making a fund of $17,337.29, available for the relief of the families of soldiers of the District.

There was another fund, of which John H. Semmes was the treasurer, named the Volunteer Fund. By December 31, 1863, this fund amounted to $3,597.50, and Mr. Semmes had paid out for bounties the sum of $4,800; for premiums, $480; for recruiting expenses, $130.72; in all, $5,410.72, and was creditor to the fund to the amount of $1,813.22. By February 17, 1864, Mr. Semmes reported that there had been obtained 404 recruits, exclusive of the 300 obtained by Captain Sheetz. All that was needed, he said, to enable the District to avoid the draft, was money. On March 7, Mr. Semmes reported that the amount of money received into this fund was $53,938; the amount expended — $47,000 for bounties; for premiums, $5,865; for printing, $516; total amount expended, $53,381. The whole number of recruits up to March 5 was 598, costing on the average $89.16 each. By the 16th of that month 99 more recruits had been obtained, and at the same time about 150 soldiers of the First District Regiment had reënlisted, and about 600 of the Second District Regiment. The quota of the District under the call that was then being complied with was 820, and by May 1, 1864, Mr. Semmes reported that 893 had been obtained, 73 more than enough.

In July, 1864, when General Grant was besieging Petersburg, a diversion was made by General Lee, in the hope of directing Grant's attention to the safety of the city of Washington, by sending General Early on a raid into Maryland with about twenty thousand men, and menacing Washington from the north. On July 7, there was a battle at Frederick, Maryland, and on the 10th there was a great battle at the Monocacy, lasting from nine o'clock in the morning until 5:00 P. M. In the evening of this same day, a body of rebels made a dash through Rockville, and on Monday morning there was a skirmish between them and Colonel Lowell's cavalry force in the vicinity of Rabbitt's Creek Post Office, between Rock Creek and Tennallytown. About noon on Monday, the rebels were in the vicinity of the Claggett farm, on the Seventh Street turnpike, and the residence of Francis P. Blair. In consequence of what appeared to be, on the part of the rebels, a determination to make an attack upon Washington, the District militia was called out on the 11th for sixty days by Major-General George C. Thomas, the details of their organization being placed in the hands of Brigadier-General Peter F. Bacon. On the 12th, the rebels destroyed communication by both rail and telegraph between Washington and Baltimore. In the vicinity of Fort Stevens, formerly Fort Massachusetts, out on Seventh Street, there was a skirmish between the rebel and Union forces, and some houses which the former had used for protection in firing upon the fort were destroyed by the latter. The houses thus burnt belonged to Richard Butts, W. Bell, J. H. McChesney, Abner Shoemaker, and W. M. Morrison. On Tuesday, the 12th, there was some skirmishing between Fort Stevens and Fort De Russy, in the Widow Carberry's woods, but on the 13th the Michigan infantry threw a few shells into the woods, when the rebels worked around to the right, making an attempt to get in between Fort Stevens and Fort Slocum. The Confederate forces in front were those of General Rhoad, General Ramser, and General Gordon, all under the command of General John C. Breckinridge.

Laurel Bridge was destroyed by the rebels. On account of the near approach to Washington of the rebel forces, and its apparent danger, the Union Leagues of the city tendered their services to General Halleck for its defense, and these were accepted, Major-General Doubleday being assigned to the command. The National Rifles also offered their services. On Tuesday evening, General McCook determined to dislodge the rebel sharpshooters at the Carberry place, and especially from the house of Mr. Lay, on Rock Creek, to the left of Fort Stevens. A shell was sent out from the fort which exploded in the house, throwing the brick and woodwork in all directions, and setting fire to the house, causing the rebels to retreat. A charge was then made by the Sixth Corps, and the rebels retired a mile or more, the Union line advancing beyond the house of Francis P. Blair. The loss of the Union forces in this charge was about three hundred in killed and wounded, and the rebels left one hundred wounded at the house of Mr. Blair.

While the volunteers and militia of the District in considerable numbers were mustered into the service on Wednesday, the 13th, yet there were not enough of them to warrant the Government in accepting their services; but the clerks in the various departments appeared in such strength that they were taken into the service, and the National Rifles were mustered in as an independent company. The Union Leagues were represented by several well-filled companies, and were mustered in. The Navy Yard employees formed a regiment about eight hundred strong. But notwithstanding the readiness of these forces to defend the city, they were all mustered out on Wednesday evening, after serving one day, the enemy having retired from the vicinity of the city. On their way out, however, they burned the country seat of Postmaster-General Blair and rifled that of his father, Francis P. Blair. After the danger had passed and there was time to reflect upon the conduct of the citizens and of the volunteers and militia of the District, Major-General George C. Thomas published a card, thanking Colonel W. W. Daniels, of Louisiana, and James C. Welling, S. A. Peugh, J. H. Leavenworth, C. S. Noyes, Tyler Southall, Charles H. Armes, Captain John B. Tanner, Charles W. Morris, H. A. Goldsborough, Colonel Lemuel Towers, Lieutenant S. S. Bach, Charles W. Boteler, Jr., B. B. French, Jr., Selden Hetzel, Alpheus N. Brown, and several officers of the Seventy-first New York Volunteers.

Under the call of the President, of July 18, 1864, for 500,000 men, the quota of the District of Columbia was 2,910. For the purpose of raising the quota Mayor Wallach appointed as recruiting agents, Arthur Shepherd for Eastern Virginia, George T. Finnegan for North Carolina, William Finley for Mississippi, C. E. Green for Georgia and Alabama, and George H. Mitchell for South Carolina and Florida. Applicants for substitutes were required to leave their names and $300 at the Bank of Washington. The provost-marshal at the time was Captain J. C. Putnam. From advance enlistments the quota of 2,910 was reduced to 2,225, and this latter number was divided among the several districts as follows:

	Enrollment.	Whites.	Blacks.	Quota.
First Ward.........	3,890	2,950	940	415
Second Ward.........	2,890	1,920	970	232
Third Ward.........	2,100	1,760	340	200
Fourth Ward.........	4,060	3,180	880	355
Fifth Ward.........	1,880	1,290	590	170
Sixth Ward.........	1,420	1,160	260	135
Seventh Ward.........	2,700	1,800	900	246
Georgetown, Eighth and Ninth Districts.....	1,631	1,068	562	142
Giesboro, Tenth District.........	275	166	109	25
Eleventh District......... ....:.....	1,260	620	640	136
Twelfth District......... ....:.........	1,500	990	510	169
Total.........	23,606	16,904	6,702	2,225

At the time the draft commenced, to fill this quota, the District had received a credit of one thousand seven hundred and eighty-four, leaving a deficiency of one thousand one hundred and twenty-six to be made good by the draft, which began on September 19. On the 26th of the month, the Councils of the city passed an act authorizing the Mayor to anticipate the revenue of the corporation to an amount not exceeding $50,000, to enable the corporation to pay bounties to volunteers, and to purchase substitutes for those who had been or might be drafted, the money to be paid out only to such *bona fide* residents of Washington as were registered as voters on the 31st of December, 1863. The draft was closed in Washington September 30, and in Georgetown, October 1, 1864; but as many of the men drafted did not report, the number required was not forthcoming. An effort was then made by many of the prominent citizens to have the quota reduced because of the alleged fact that a large number of persons in the employ of the General Government had been enrolled as citizens of the District who were but temporarily resident therein, and that by this means the enrollment of the District was greatly increased beyond what it should be. Provost-Marshal-General Fry, however, declined to make the desired reduction.

Under the call of the President for 300,000 men, December 19, 1864, the quota of the District was 3,019, apportioned among the several districts as follows: First Ward, 575; Second Ward, 348; Third Ward, 111; Fourth Ward, 490; Fifth Ward, 213; Sixth Ward, 224; Seventh Ward, 355; eighth district, 71; ninth district, 105; tenth district, 24; eleventh district, 219; twelfth district, 284. While there was a general conviction that this quota was excessive, strengthened when taking into account the fact that under the former call for 500,000 the quota was only 2,910, yet there was manifested on the part of the people a determination to see that the quota was filled, while at the same time there was a determination to secure, if possible, a correction of the list. Meetings were held in all the districts for both purposes, and at length a reduction was secured in the quota, so that the number required was only 2,222. Lieutenant Knox was, at that time, commissioner of the board of enrollment, but on February 13 he was succeeded by the appointment of H. A. Jones, in order that there might be a permanent officer in this position. The draft for the filling of the quota of the District under the call for 300,000 began February 21, 1865. But this draft was not completed, as, before sufficient time had elapsed for this, it became so clearly evident that the Rebellion could not last, that efforts were relaxed.

On Monday, April 3, 1865, the joyful news reached the Capital that both Petersburg and Richmond had been evacuated by General Lee, who was in full retreat. It would be impossible to adequately describe the feelings of the people of this city when this news flashed over the telegraphic wires. No such attempt will therefore be made. All were fully conscious that the war which had devastated the country for four years was at last near its close. The religiously inclined gave "Thanks to God, who giveth us the victory," and that victory which had been long hoped for and impatiently waited for was to emancipate not only those to whom the Proclamation of Emancipation applied, but also all the rest of the black race, and

many loyal and Union loving people of the Southern States, from a
military despotism such as the world had never seen, as well as from
the despotism of political errors as powerful and cruel in its influence
on the public mind as the military despotism had been on the persons
of the Southern people, many of whom, if not the majority, never
wanted war. In the streets of Washington all men, young and old,
greeted each other most ardently; ladies flung to the winds their
miniature flags, and the judges of the courts deserted the hall of
justice, satisfied that for a time at least the blind goddess would not
note their absence. The public schools dismissed their scholars, business was deserted on all hands, and all repaired to the vicinity of the
public buildings to acquire a fuller knowledge of the incidents of
the three days' terrible fighting which immediately preceded the fall
of the two cities, the fate of which had so long been linked together.
A scene of wild excitement was presented at the Patent Office when
the news of the fall of Petersburg was received, and a few hours
later, when the news of the fall of Richmond came, it was evident
everywhere that a great weight of anxiety had been lifted from the
public mind. Patriotic exercises were immediately extemporized in
the open air in front of the Patent Office building. A gentleman
named Thompson began to sing "Rally Round the Flag," the crowd
joining in the chorus. Mr. Holloway, Commissioner of Patents, then
addressed the assemblage, and was followed by Hon. J. P. Usher, who
alluded to the evacuation, when some one in the crowd suggested that
the Interior Department be evacuated, and at once the entire crowd
took up its line of march for the Department of State, where they
were felicitously addressed by the Secretary of State, who still predicted, as he had continued to do from the beginning, that the war
would end in ninety days. The Hon. Preston King, Hon. J. W. Nye,
and others spoke after the Secretary, and at length came the turn
of the Hon. Edwin M. Stanton, whose remarks were characterized
by a deep feeling of patriotism and religion. At the close of his
remarks he presented to the assemblage the boy Willie Kettles, fourteen years old, an operator in the military telegraph office, who
had received the dispatch announcing the fall of Richmond at 8:15
A. M. that morning, April 3. From the residence of Francis P. Blair,
Vice-President Andrew Johnson made an eloquent speech, and from
the balconies of all the hotels poured forth a chorus of patriotic
music and oratory. Hon. Richard Yates spoke from the steps of the
National Hotel and Major-General Butler from in front of Willard's.
General Butler said that the God of Justice works by means, and

perhaps there could be found in history no more striking and suggestive instance of retribution than that of the corps of colored troops
under General Weitzel being the first to enter Richmond after its
fall, and the planting of the flag of freedom by them over the rebel
capital.   Four regiments of the Veteran Reserve Corps and two
squadrons of cavalry, accompanied by a fine band of music, paraded
the principal streets of the city. The northern portico of the War
Department building was tastefully decorated with flags, and the
Veteran Regiment band played patriotic airs at the Circle. A salute
of eight hundred guns was fired near Franklin Square — five hundred
for Richmond and three hundred for Petersburg, and the city in all
directions was decorated with the Union banner. None rejoiced more
sincerely than the sick and wounded soldiers in the hospitals. Work
was generally suspended in the departments, the clerks rushing into
the streets to unite with their fellow-citizens in the general rejoicing.
At the Navy Yard and the Arsenal the suspension of work was also
universal, and the vessels all around the city were gaily decked with
bunting. The colored population had perhaps a double reason for the
demonstration of their joy, for not only had peace dawned upon
the land, but the day of their deliverance had also dawned at the
same time.

But the illumination of the city and the display of fireworks on
the evening of April 4 surpassed in magnificence anything that had
ever been seen in the Capital of the Nation. The Capitol building
shone resplendent, the whole massive dome being most brilliantly
illuminated with innumerable lights, possessing a most beautiful and
imposing appearance. The National Conservatory exhibited one of
the most beautiful features of the display. All the public buildings,
the National Bank, the residences of the heads of departments, the
Executive Mansion, the offices of all the subordinate officers of the
Government, and most of the business houses and private residences
in all parts of the city were illuminated, in expression of the general
rejoicing. In Georgetown the illumination was equally universal; the
customhouse, the post office, the Bank of Commerce, the police station,
the Seminary Hospital, the Vigilant Engine House, the Union Hotel, the
Ellis Hotel, and business houses and private residences generally exhibited the joyful emotions of the people at the prospective close of
the war.

On Friday, April 7, it was rumored that General Lee and his
entire army had surrendered. A salute of one hundred guns was
fired, and a general jubilee prevailed. On the 10th of the month,

however, official news of the surrender of Lee was received, and a salute of two hundred guns was ordered to be fired at the headquarters of every department, and at every post and arsenal of the United States, in commemoration of the surrender. On this day the rejoicing and excitement in Washington were renewed with all the intensity of the former day. The President was visited, but declined to make more than a few remarks, in the course of which he said that the tune of "Dixie" was one of the best he had ever heard, and that he had insisted, the day before, that with the fall of Richmond the tune of "Dixie" likewise fell into our hands; that he had submitted the question to the Attorney-General, who had decided that the tune of "Dixie" was a lawful prize. At his request the tune of "Dixie" was then played by the band, as was also that of "Yankee Doodle," both of which tunes, therefore, should henceforth be considered national airs. Other demonstrations were made, and continued through the day and evening. But the formal celebration occurred on the evening of the 11th, on which occasion the President made a prepared speech, dealing with the question of reconstruction as it was then exhibited in the State of Louisiana. This address is invaluable to any and all who would be pleased to speculate upon what would have been, or at least what might have been, the President's plan of reconstructing the rebellious States, had he been permitted to live and attempt to reinstate those States in their proper relations to the Government of the United States. In accordance with resolutions adopted by both the city Councils, the city was brilliantly illuminated on the evening of April 13, the Capitol being illuminated even more fully and brilliantly than on the evening of the 4th. Probably no building in the world ever presented so gorgeous and beautiful a spectacle as did the Capitol on the evening of April 13. The entire city on the same occasion was "literally ablaze," which terms cover the ground better, perhaps, than any detailed description could.

But in the midst of this rejoicing came the terrible announcement of the brutal, cowardly, and extremely foolish assassination of President Lincoln, as he sat in a box of Ford's Theater in the evening of April 14. During the third act of the play, when there was a temporary pause, a sharp report of a pistol shot was heard, but which at first was supposed to be a part of the play. Immediately afterward, however, the assassin jumped upon the stage with a long dagger in his hand, and crying, "*Sic semper tyrannis!*" made his escape. The details of the assassination have so often been published that no more is done in this work than merely to refer to it, in passing, as to its effect upon the public mind at the time. . The principal emotion in connection with it was that a great and good man had fallen, one who had the power and the disposition to a greater degree than any other man living, to heal the wounds of the war, to bring order out of chaos, and to reëstablish the Union in the affections of the entire people, North and South. Considerations like these illustrate better, perhaps, than anything else, the enormity of the crime by which the President's life was brought to an untimely end.

The depression of spirits caused by this national calamity was, at least, equal to the elevation caused a few days before by the great victories of the armies in the field. The day after the death of the President was Sunday, and upon that day in all the churches the crime of the 14th gave tone to all the sermons, in which appropriate allusions were made to the distinguished and honored dead, and these allusions found ready appreciation, and were heartily responded to by the hearts of the people in the various congregations. The services in the churches were made none the less impressive by the fact that they were held on Easter Sunday.

The city Councils adopted a resolution appropriating $20,000 as a reward for the arrest of the assassin; the various corporation offices were closed until after the funeral, as well as the public schools. Ward H. Lamon, United States Marshal of the District of Columbia, had charge of the funeral arrangements and ceremonies, which were held on Wednesday, April 19, and were the most imposing pageant that had ever been witnessed in the Capital of the Nation. The remains of the President lay in state in the east room of the Executive Mansion, eight hours being allowed for visitors to pass and view the familiar features, but even then thousands were disappointed. The funeral address was delivered by Rev. Dr. Gurley, and a song was sung, composed for the occasion by Rev. T. N. Haskell, of Boston, Massachusetts. The citizens of every State, resident at the Capital, held meetings at which suitable resolutions were adopted.

On May 5, a notice was published to the citizens of the District of Columbia, signed by a large number of persons, one hundred and three of whose names were published with the notice, calling a mass meeting at the City Hall for the 9th of the month, for the purpose of consultation as to the best means of preventing such of those who, having been at the outbreak of the Rebellion citizens of the District, had entered the military service of the Confederate States, from returning to their former homes and enjoying the privileges enjoyed by loyal citizens. At this meeting, held in accordance with the call, there were but few present, not more than enough to cover the central portico and steps of the City Hall. Hon. John Wilson was elected president of the meeting, and there were chosen twenty-three vice-presidents and six clerks. After a brief address by President Wilson, a committee on resolutions was appointed, consisting of W. A. Cook, J. W. Deeble, Z. D. Gilman, R. B. Clark, Lewis Clephane, Asbury Lloyd, D. S. M. McKim, W. H. Terry, J. R. Elvans, and Z. Richards. Mr. Joseph F. Brown, one of the vice-presidents, made an address, in which he said that those who had sought to make their homes among rebels and traitors should be made to understand, at least, that their room was better than their company. The committee on resolutions then made a report of a series of resolutions, stating that those who organized the Rebellion had sought to accomplish their designs not only by the ordinary means of warfare, but also by the commission of every crime that distinguished the ferocity and degradation of barbarism, and that, approving of its purpose, a considerable number of the citizens of the District of Columbia, at its inception and during its progress, voluntarily abandoned their homes and entered the military service of the Confederacy, and that some of these same persons had already returned to the District, and others proposed to return, and therefore it was resolved that it was the duty of citizens to protect themselves from physical and moral evil; that the citizens of the District earnestly resisted the settlement here of those who during the past four years had been directly connected with the Rebellion, and especially those who had formerly been residents of the District should not be allowed to return; that they approved of the opinion of the Attorney-General that the rebel officers included under the surrender to General Grant had no homes within the loyal States, and had no right to come to homes which were theirs before going into the Rebellion; that the same rule should apply to those who had entered the civil service of the Rebellion, and recalled to mind the fact that the President of the United States had not been murdered by the open and avowed enemies of the Government, but by secret and resident miscreants. The president of the meeting was requested to appoint a committee, composed of two members from each ward in Washington and Georgetown, to present the proceedings of the meeting to the proper authorities, and the resolutions quoted the words of President Johnson, that "mercy without justice was a crime." W. H. Terry, of Georgetown, then made a speech very strongly against permitting rebels and traitors to return to the District of Columbia. He said: "After loafing around this District last summer,

ready to come in and point out the homes of loyal men and have
their dwellings burned and the owners hung—that you should be
permitted to come here now and be received with honor, we say it
shall not be." The city Councils expressed similar sentiments in the
form of resolutions adopted in regular meeting, and called upon
President Johnson to issue an order which would carry into effect the
opinion of Attorney-General Speed.

May 23 and 24 were days ever to be remembered in the history
of Washington. On those days occurred the grand review of the
Union armies, the Army of the Potomac on the 23d, the armies of
Georgia and Tennessee on the 24th. Thousands of interested and
glad spectators crowded the streets, sidewalks, and roofs of houses
on both days to witness the grandest spectacle that every occurred in
the United States. The different corps, brigades, and other organizations of the Army of the Potomac crossed the Potomac River during
the early morning of the 23d, and arranged themselves on the various
streets and avenues, ready to fall into line at the appointed time.
These streets and avenues had been thoroughly sprinkled during the
preceding night by the fire department, and barrels of water were
placed along the sides thereof for the soldiers to drink as they passed
along in the procession. The cavalry formed north of the Capitol, the
line extending far beyond the city limits. The children of the public
schools were tastefully arrayed, and arranged on the high ground
north of the Capitol. Thousands of banners bore thousands of
mottoes, expressive of joy and welcome to the victorious veterans
of the army, one of which in particular may be repeated here: "The
Only Debt We Can Never Pay is the Debt We Owe to the Victorious
Union Soldiers." At the head of the victorious Army of the Potomac
rode Major-General George G. Meade, accompanied by his staff. Then
came the cavalry, immediately after the headquarters escort, in command of Major-General Merritt. The Third Cavalry Division was in
command of Major-General George A. Custer, and the entire cavalry
force followed in brigades and divisions. Then came the Ninth Army
Corps, in command of Major-General John G. Parke; the Fifth Corps,
in command of Major-General Charles Griffin; and the Second Corps,
in command of Major-General A. A. Humphreys. The procession
began to move at 9:00 A. M., and the passage of troops continued
until three o'clock in the afternoon.

On the 24th, the grand Army of Georgia and that of Tennessee
were reviewed, the crowd upon the sidewalks, the streets, and the
housetops being greater even than the day before. General Sherman

and his command were received with unbounded enthusiasm all along the route. The head of the column formed on A Street Northwest, and at the firing of the signal gun at nine o'clock the column began to move. General O. O. Howard rode with Sherman, and they were followed by Major-General W. B. Hazen at the head of the Army of the Tennessee, of which Major-General John A. Logan was in command. The Seventh Army Corps came next, commanded by Major-General Francis P. Blair, and then, leading the Army of Georgia, came Major-General H. W. Slocum. This army was composed of the Twentieth and Fourteenth corps, the former commanded by Major-General J. A. Mower, the latter by Major-General Jeff. C. Davis. The review of the 24th was in every way as grand a spectacle and as great a success as was that of the day before. From this time the thousands of veterans dispersed to their homes to enter again the peaceful pursuits from which duty had called them four years before, and the War of the Rebellion was at an end.

The principal results accruing to the District of Columbia from the final and complete suppression of the Rebellion were, first, the abolition of slavery therein; and second, the improvement of the cities of Washington and Georgetown. The latter subject has already been discussed; while the former is briefly presented here, as it is more immediately connected with the war than either of the others. The act for the emancipation of the slaves in the District of Columbia was passed by Congress April 16, 1862, and provided that all persons loyal to the United States having claims to the service or labor of persons discharged therefrom by the act itself, might within ninety days from its passage, but not afterward, present to the commissioners to be appointed petitions for compensation not to exceed $300 for each slave; but no person who had borne arms against the Government should receive any pay for any slave. One million dollars was the maximum amount appropriated under the act for the purpose of paying for the slaves.

The commissioners appointed were Daniel R. Goodloe, Horatio King, and John M. Broadhead. These commissioners met at the City Hall, April 28, 1862, and chose William R. Woodward secretary, and by January 15, 1863, had reported favorably upon 999 entire petitions, and upon 21 petitions in part. They had rejected 36 petitions entirely. The whole number of slaves for whom compensation had been allowed was 2,989, and the whole number for whom compensation had been withheld was 111, making a total of 3,100 included in 1,056 petitions. As regards loyalty there were but few instances in which the evidence was of such a nature as to warrant the commissioners in withholding compensation. Afterward, because of the impossibility of submitting proof of their loyalty by some of the residents of the District in time to claim compensation under this law, the time was extended, and 28 more slaves were paid for, making the total number paid for 3,017.

After the close of the war and the consequent disbandment of the armies, there were still kept up, or organized, in the District of Columbia military organizations of various kinds; but to trace minutely the history of each would only add to the length and tediousness of this chapter. However, the present military establishment it is proper to give. A law was passed by Congress March 1, 1889, providing for the enrollment of the militia of the District of Columbia, every able-bodied male citizen resident in the District, between the ages of eighteen and forty-five, being required to be enrolled. Under the law the President of the United States is commander-in-chief of the militia, and was required to appoint a commander of this militia, which consists of the National Guard of the District of Columbia, in part. This National Guard is composed of a brigade of two regiments, each having three four-company battalions, and one independent battalion of infantry, one battery of light artillery, one troop of cavalry, one engineer corps, and one ambulance corps, armed, uniformed, and equipped in conformity with the regulations of the United States army. Brigadier-General Albert Ordway was appointed commander of this militia, and under his assiduous and skillful training has attained a high state of discipline.

CHAPTER IX.

TRANSPORTATION.

IN this chapter on "Transportation," an attempt will be made to describe, somewhat in detail, the means and methods of transportation, and the developments in these means and methods which have been employed and made from time to time, since the first historic exploration of the Potomac River, with the view of improving its navigability, by the great founder of the city of Washington, the District of Columbia, and, indeed, of the Nation itself. This exploration was of the river above tide water, as but little, if anything, was necessary to be done below the location of the District of Columbia, which, indeed, had not been decided upon at the time; but it is well known that the future President of the United States had, in his own mind, selected the present location even long before the exploration under consideration was made. It is also stated by numerous writers, doubtless on sufficient authority, that the present situation of the Capital of the United States was chosen, in part, because it is on a tidal river, the tide water of which penetrates farther into the heart of the country than any other, so that when communication should be necessary between the Atlantic seaboard and the interior of the country, it would, from this point, be the most easy and inexpensive. Of course, this means of communication was to be by the improved navigation of the Potomac River, or by means of a lateral canal, as railroads had not then been considered. Indeed, for many years after the practicability of this latter means of travel had been demonstrated,

many of the people could not be convinced that anything was superior
to a canal.

But at the risk of repeating what has been stated so many times,
we must introduce at the outset in this chapter a brief account of
the famous exploration referred to above. It took place in 1783, and
in a canoe, or pirogue, hollowed out of a large poplar tree, and was
undertaken for the purpose of determining whether the Potomac
River could be navigated above tide water at Georgetown. General
Washington was the principal character engaged in this work, for
which he was eminently qualified by his early education and practice
as a surveyor. There were several other gentlemen in the exploration
party with him in the pirogue, among whom was Governor Johnson,
of Maryland, who had been a gallant soldier in the Revolutionary
War. The humble bark, when ready for the water, was hauled to
the banks of the Monocacy on a wagon, launched into the stream,
and received its distinguished burden. It immediately started on its
interesting and important reconnoisance. As night came on, the party
would land and seek accommodations of the planters or farmers along
the banks of the river, who were then, as now, far-famed for their
genial hospitality. The work of the exploration was accomplished,
and was followed, as a result, by the organization of a company for
the improvement of the river. This company expended, in the attempt
to render the river navigable, nearly a million of dollars, in a series of
years, and at length gave way to a more extensive company working
on a different and more feasible plan.

The company first referred to was called the Potomac Company.
This company was incorporated by the legislatures of Maryland and
Virginia in 1784. Its affairs were managed by a president and four
directors, who were elected at a general meeting of the stockholders
on the first Monday in August each year. The purpose for which
the company was incorporated was to extend the navigation of the
Potomac River from tide water to the highest practicable point on
the North Branch. While a great deal of money was expended, yet
the object was but imperfectly accomplished on account of the natural
obstacles in the way, and for want of experience in such matters in
this country at that time. The fall in the river between Cumberland
and tide water was as much as 578 feet, and the distance was one
hundred and eighty-five miles; hence the difficulty of rendering the
Potomac River navigable. The company did, however, execute great
and beneficial works, as the locks at Little Falls, overcoming a fall
of 37 feet; the canal and locks at Great Falls, overcoming a fall of

77 feet; the long canal at Harper's Ferry, and several other small canals around falls in other parts of the river.

The locks at Great Falls were opened in 1800, and from that time to August, 1826, there were brought down 1,308,911 barrels of flour, 48,909 barrels of whisky, and other articles, the aggregate in value being $10,534,000.

At the Great Falls the canal was 1 mile long, 25 feet wide, and 6 feet deep; and the descent of 77 feet was made through 5 locks, each 100 feet long and 12 feet wide. The canal at Little Falls was of the same capacity, and 2½ miles in length, furnished with 3 locks. These locks were constructed of wood, and were each 100 feet long and 18 feet in width. Of the five locks at Great Falls, two were cut in the solid rock, and the other three were made of wood and stone.

Besides these canals with locks, there were constructed 3 canals without locks. The first was below Harper's Ferry, at Shenandoah Falls, where the Potomac breaks through the Blue Ridge, and was 1 mile in length. The second, along the Seneca Falls, was ¾ of a mile in length, and the third, at House's Falls, five miles above that at Shenandoah Falls, was 50 yards in length.

On the Shenandoah River there were 5 locks, each 100 feet long and 12 feet wide; and 6 canals, each 20 feet wide, 4½ feet deep, and extending 2,400 yards. But navigation, in 1830, of the main or North Branch of the Potomac River, extended to Western Port, near its source, a distance of 219 miles above tide water.

The South Branch of the Potomac was navigable for 100 miles above its junction with the main branch, and the north fork about 60 miles.

The boats used for the navigation of the Potomac and the Shenandoah were 75 feet long, 5 feet wide, and drew 18 inches of water. They carried 20 tons.

The original capital stock of the company consisted of 701 shares, which, at $444⅔, amounted to $311,560. Of these shares, 220 belonged to Maryland, and 70 to Virginia.

In 1821, the affairs of the Potomac Company became the subject of investigation. Commissioners appointed by Maryland and Virginia assembled at Georgetown June 2, 1822, and afterward reported that the company had expended not only the whole of their stock, but in addition had incurred heavy debts, which their resources could never enable them to pay; that not only the whole of their original stock, but also all their tolls had been expended in an attempt to improve the river; and that the failure to accomplish the objects of their incorporation was attributable to lack of information on the subject

19

at the time they were incorporated. Accordingly, a low water survey of the condition and depth of water was made at the suggestion of the commissioners, which was taken minutely from day to day in 1822, as the river was descended; from which it was ascertained that the Potomac, from its confluence with the South Branch to Goose Creek, below the mouth of the Monocacy, is one hundred and fifty-seven miles long; that there was no section of ten miles at all navigable in low water by loaded boats of any kind or description, and that for more than eighty miles obstructions from shallows sufficient to stop a skiff were to be met with. A full text of this low water survey is to be found in Jonathan Elliott's "Ten Miles Square."

But from the survey it was evident that the floods and freshets gave the only navigation then used; that these floods and freshets occurred from September 1 to June 20, and much of this time there was ice in the river; and there were times between the floods and freshets when navigation lasted not more than about ten days for full loaded boats late in the year, and about thirty-five days in the spring. These periods were, however, longer below the Great Falls and less above them. Besides the shortness of the navigable seasons, there was considerable danger from rocks and the windings in the torrent, which it was hoped would be overcome by the construction and completion of the contemplated Chesapeake and Ohio Canal.

The Chesapeake and Ohio Canal Company was incorporated by the Legislature of Virginia in December, 1823. This action of the State of Virginia was confirmed by the State of Maryland and also by the Congress of the United States. On May 16, 1825, the Potomac Company assented to the provisions of this legislation, surrendering all their rights to the newly incorporated company, and conveying in due form of law to the said company all the property, franchises, rights, and privileges it possessed. The deed of surrender was signed by John Mason, president of the company, Jonah Thompson, John Laird, and C. Smith, in the presence of William Cranch. Robert Barnard was secretary of the company at the time.

The following statement shows the condition of the finances of the Potomac Company at the close of its career:

	Number.	Amount.
Capital stock		$311,111 11
Shares held by Virginia	120	53,333 33
Shares held by Maryland	220	97,777 77
Shares held by individuals	360	160,000 00
		$311,111 11

The total amount of the expenditures of the company from the commencement, in 1784, to August 1, 1822, including original improvements, repairs, interest, and expenses of collecting toll, was $729,387.29.

The debts due by the company, August 1, 1822, including interest, were as follows:

To subscribers to the Monocacy loan, 1803	$3,876 49
To subscribers to the Shenandoah loan, 1812	4,608 77
To subscribers to the Antietam loan, 1812	17,026 33
To subscribers to the Cumberland loan, 1813	7,642 12
To the State of Maryland, 1814	39,950 00
To banks of the District of Columbia	101,192 88
To sundry individuals	1,500 00
Total	$175,796 59

During the period of twenty-three years, from August 1, 1799, to August 1, 1822, the aggregate of the tonnage of articles and goods of all kinds brought by this company was as follows:

Barrels of flour shipped, 1,135,761; whisky, 38,382; hogsheads of tobacco, 426½; tons of iron, 5,476; estimated value of other articles, $215,151.75; value of goods retransported, $180,597.29; tonnage, 162,798.

Work on the Chesapeake and Ohio Canal was commenced immediately after the incorporation of the company, but the surrender of the Potomac Company to that company, referred to above, was not finally made until August 15, 1828. The work on the Chesapeake and Ohio Canal for the first year was principally for the purpose of ascertaining whether the undertaking was practicable. During the following year the survey of the route was made, and the data secured necessary to form a general plan of the work, and to make an estimate of the probable expense of construction. The Chesapeake and Ohio Canal was to extend from Georgetown to Pittsburgh, in the State of Pennsylvania, a total distance of 341 miles, 1,450 yards; nearly 342 miles. It was divided into sections, as follows: Eastern section, from Georgetown to Cumberland, 186 miles; middle section, from Cumberland to the mouth of Casselman's River, 70 miles, 1,010 yards; western section, from the mouth of Casselman's River to Pittsburgh, 85 miles, 440 yards.

The descent in feet from Cumberland to Georgetown was 578 feet; in the middle section, 1,961 feet; and in the western section, 619 feet, making the entire ascent and descent 3,158 feet. The estimated number of locks in the eastern section was 74; in middle section, 246, and in the western, 78; total number 398. According to estimates made by General Barnard, the cost of constructing the eastern section would be $8,177,081.05; of the middle section, $10,028,122.86, and of the western section, $4,170,223.78; making the cost of the entire canal from Georgetown to Pittsburgh $22,375,427.69. An estimate of the cost of the canal was made at the same time by Geddes & Roberts, who made it $12,528,019, a difference of $9,847,408.69. The sequel will show how wide of the mark both of these estimates were.

Congress passed three acts relative to this canal — first, the one mentioned above, confirming the incorporation of the company, approved May 5, 1828; second, an act authorizing subscriptions to the stock of the company, approved May 24, 1828; third, an act to enlarge the powers of the several corporations of the District of Columbia, etc., approved May 24, 1828.

Act No. 2 authorized the United States to subscribe for 10,000 shares of the stock of the company, and No. 3 authorized the corporations of Washington, Georgetown, and Alexandria to subscribe for stock in the company. Under the authority thus granted the United States subscribed through commissioners for 10,000 shares of the stock; the city of Washington for 10,000 shares; Georgetown for 2,500 shares, and Alexandria for 2,500 shares. Each share was $100. By May, 1829, the entire number of shares taken was 36,089, or $3,608,-900, and these, together with the Holland loan, placed the company in possession of funds sufficient to complete the eastern section of the canal.

The first officers of the company were as follows: Hon. Charles Fenton Mercer, president; Directors, Phineas Janney of Alexandria, Joseph Kent of Maryland, Peter Lenox and Dr. Frederick May of Washington, Walter Smith of Georgetown, and Andrew Stuart of Pennsylvania. The treasurer was Clement Smith, of Georgetown, and the clerk, John P. Ingle, of Washington. Robert Barnard was assistant clerk. The corps of engineers was composed of Benjamin Wright, of New York, engineer-in-chief; Nathan S. Roberts and John Martineau, of New York; Robert Leckie, of Scotland, inspector of masonry, and Philibert Rodier, of France, draughtsman.

Having thus briefly glanced at the organization of the Chesapeake and Ohio Canal Company, it may not be uninteresting or devoid of value to briefly present the measures taken by the people themselves of Maryland and Virginia which led up to this organization. Among the first of the meetings held by the people, looking toward the accomplishment of this great object, was one held at Fredericksburg, Maryland, August 12, 1823, at which the project of constructing this canal was discussed. It was held to hear read a report of a committee previously appointed to correspond on the subject of a canal with those who, it was supposed, were in favor of it, and who might be able to carry it forward.. Delegates were present from Baltimore, Washington, Georgetown, Alexandria, Leesburg, and Rockville. The meeting viewed with great gratification the efforts of the Legislature of Maryland, and the noble-minded participation of the Legislature of Virginia, to effect the contemplated water communication by canal from Cumberland down the Potomac to tide water, and it also felt increased pleasure at the contemplated connection of the Potomac with the Ohio, "thereby affording our fellow-citizens of the western parts of Pennsylvania and Ohio, 'whom we cannot consider in any other point of view than as members of our great political family,' the same facilities and advantages which we shall ourselves enjoy."

A meeting was held in Frederick County, Virginia, October 6, 1823, to take into consideration the subject of a convention to be held at the city of Washington, November 6, 1823, to deliberate upon the best means of improving the navigation of the Potomac. A similar meeting was also held in Prince William's County, Virginia, on the same day for the same purpose. Committees were appointed in each case, and a preliminary meeting was held in Washington, October 18, for the same purpose. Delegates were appointed also in Alexandria, in Prince George's County, and in Washington County, Maryland, and many other places. The convention itself was a grand assemblage of citizens from the District of Columbia, Virginia, Maryland, Pennsylvania, and Ohio. The *National Intelligencer* said of it: "A volunteer assemblage of citizens so numerous, so respectable, had never been seen before in any part of the Union," and it looked upon the connection of the waters of the Ohio and the Potomac and the Atlantic Ocean as truly a national object. Albert Gallatin was present from Pennsylvania; Bushrod C. Washington from Virginia; Robert W. Bowie from Maryland; and G. W. P. Custis from the District of Columbia.

The convention assembled in the hall of the Supreme Court. Joseph Kent, from Maryland, was made chairman, and General Walter Jones, of Washington, secretary. General Mercer, from Virginia, presented a series of resolutions reciting what had been done to effect the object contemplated, and then made a very learned speech, manifesting an extensive and accurate knowledge of canals, both in this country and in Europe, which was of great service in directing the deliberations of the convention. Up to this time the name used in connection with the projected improvement was "The Union Canal," but at this meeting the name, "The Chesapeake and Ohio Canal," was substituted. The convention lasted three days, the 6th, 7th, and 8th of October, and the following preamble and resolutions were adopted:

"WHEREAS, A connection of the Atlantic and Western waters by a canal leading from the seat of the General Government to the river Ohio, regarded as a local object, is one of the highest importance to the States immediately interested therein, and considered in a national point of view, is of inestimable consequence to the future union, security, and happiness of the United States:

"*Resolved, unanimously,* That it is expedient to substitute for the present defective navigation of the Potomac River above tide water, a navigable canal by Cumberland to the mouth of Savage Creek, at the eastern pass of the Allegheny Mountains, and to extend the canal as soon thereafter as practicable to the highest constant steamboat navigation of the Monongahela and Ohio rivers.

"That the most eligible mode of attaining this object will be by the incorporation of a joint stock company, empowered to cut the said canal through the territory of the United States in the District of Columbia, and in the States of Virginia, Maryland, and Pennsylvania, and therefore that committees be appointed, each consisting of five delegates, to prepare and present in behalf of this assembly, and in coöperation with the central committee hereinafter provided for, suitable memorials to the Congress of the United States and the legislatures of the several States before named, requesting their concurrence in the incorporation of such a company and their coöperation, if necessary, in the subscription of funds for the completion of said canal," etc.

The other resolutions were very long, but covered the following points: Accepting the act of the State of Virginia of February 22, 1823, as a basis for the incorporation of any new stock company, and accepting it as a charter for the proposed company, with certain modifications; changing the name to the Chesapeake and Ohio Canal . Company; that the canal should be not less than 40 feet wide at the top, 28 feet wide at the bottom, and not less than 4 feet in depth; permitting the States of Maryland and Virginia to construct lateral canals, and using the waters of the Potomac River. The convention also proposed that in case of necessity there be a subscription to the stock to the amount of $2,750,000, to be divided as follows: Maryland, $\frac{2}{11}$; Virginia, $\frac{3}{11}$; the United States, $\frac{4}{11}$; and the three cities of the District of Columbia, $\frac{2}{11}$, to be divided among them as they might determine. It was also proposed that a committee be appointed of five delegates to prepare a memorial to the State of Ohio, inviting her coöperation in the work of completing the Chesapeake and Ohio Canal, and its ultimate connection with Lake Erie, etc.

By August, 1824, the board of engineers, having finished their first general reconnoissance, of the eastern and middle sections of this great national design, and having no doubt of its practicability, made out instructions for the different brigades of engineers ordered upon the work. They then went to examine the Monongahela River to Pittsburgh, and also that portion of the proposed canal which was to unite the Ohio River with Lake Erie by the Beaver and Grand rivers.

During the succeeding winter the legislatures of Maryland and Virginia incorporated the Chesapeake and Ohio Canal Company, and on May 16, 1825, the stockholders of the old Potomac Company assembled, four hundred and sixty shares being represented, and came to a unanimous determination to assent to the charter granted to the new company in the terms of the act of Virginia. On the 17th of May, the central committee of the Canal Convention met at Brown's Hotel in Washington, those present being Charles Fenton Mercer, John McLean, Frisby Tilghman, John Lee, A. B. Powell, John Mason, and H. L. Opie. Commissioners were appointed by the 1st of July, to open subscription books to the stock of the Chesapeake and Ohio Canal Company, as follows: For the District of Columbia, Samuel H. Smith, Anthony C. Cazenove, and Clement Smith; for Maryland, Governor Sprigg, Colonel Frisby Tilghman, and Philip E. Thomas; for Virginia, General John C. Hunter, Colonel William Ellzey, and Richard H. Henderson.

Their appointment completed the legal requirements to the establishment of the Chesapeake and Ohio Canal Company. But the consent of Pennsylvania had not yet been obtained for the extension of the canal beyond the line of Maryland to Pittsburgh; in fact, that consent had, in the winter of 1824-25, been refused, with the peculiar wisdom that is so often found in legislatures. But on August 29, 1825, a large meeting of citizens was held at Uniontown, Pennsylvania, which passed resolutions forcibly approving of the canal project, and viewing "with apprehension and alarm the extraordinary and unaccountable vote of the last legislature." Subscriptions to the stock also remained to be secured, but there was every reason, and even stimulus, to cause these subscriptions to be made, both on the part of individuals and the States, as well as the District of Columbia. The price of lands beyond the Allegheny had already been augmented, as a result of the movement, as had also the thousands of unimproved lots in the city of Washington.

The central committee of the Chesapeake and Ohio Canal Company met at Brown's Hotel, in Washington, August 30, 1826, and adopted an address to the members of the convention, and to the inhabitants of the counties, and corporations of the West, and Pennsylvania, Maryland, and Virginia, who felt an interest in the object to be accomplished, and giving such information as it could regarding the progress of the work. They said it could scarcely be questioned that the markets of Philadelphia and Baltimore might be brought, by the connection of the Potomac and the Susquehanna above the Blue Ridge and by the Patapsco below it, into fair competition with those of the District of Columbia.

On July 8, 1827, a meeting of the citizens of the District of Columbia east of Rock Creek urged the commencement of active operations on the canal, and the appointment by the Mayor of Washington, R. C. Weightman, of nine citizens to act as a committee, together with the Mayor and two citizens east of Rock Creek, to take into consideration the future of the canal company. Hon. Charles Fenton Mercer was present at the meeting, and was publicly thanked for his services in behalf of the project. ;The committee appointed by the Mayor was as follows: Daniel Carroll of Duddington, John P. Van Ness, Thomas Law, Thomas Munroe, Walter Jones, C. McLean, Joseph Gales, Jr., William A. Bradley, John Davis, for Washington; and Samuel H. Smith and Joseph Pearson, for the county. This committee reported to a meeting held July 17, 1827. In their report they said that it was greatly to the interest of this city that the canal be completed as soon as practicable. It would save to the city in fuel alone, by the substitution of coal for wood, more than $100,000 per year, small as the city was at that time; and there would be a diminution in the prices of grain, flour, lumber, butter, whisky, meat, marble, iron, and the various other commodities that were brought in from a distance, which would be paid for with the fish and manufactures of the city, etc. The corporation of the city of Washington was therefore advised to subscribe to the stock of the company $1,000,000, on the condition that Congress was to be applied to to grant authority to do whatever was necessary to enable the city legally to assist the canal, etc. This was the first decisive step taken by the city, although the inhabitants had all along approved of the project and wished it to go forward; but they had done nothing but to invoke the aid of Congress, and of the States of Maryland

and Virginia. As some at the time expressed it, "they had been upon their knees invoking .Hercules, but Hercules would not alone put his shoulder to the wheel; the citizens must themselves put their shoulder to the wheel, and then it might be, if they needed assistance, that Hercules would condescend."

Subscription books were opened at the Branch Bank October 1, 1827. The amount of each share was $100 in current money, and $1 must be paid on each share subscribed for at the time of subscribing, the rest to be paid upon the call of the president and directors of the company, but not more than one-third was payable each year. On the first day the books were opened there was subscribed in Washington, including the city itself, $1,066,300, and in Georgetown, including the subscriptions of that city, $425,000; total in the two places, $1,491,300. The work was to begin when $1,500,000 was subscribed; so the first day's subscriptions rendered its beginning a certainty.

But, notwithstanding this auspicious beginning, by November 6 those interested in the project living in the District of Columbia became considerably alarmed at the prospect, because of the proposed construction of the Baltimore and Ohio Railroad from Baltimore to the Ohio River. This railroad project deprived the canal company of much of the money it had expected from many of the citizens of Baltimore, and from the towns and country through which the railroad was to be constructed. It therefore devolved upon the District of Columbia to take that step which would immediately be decisive of the fate of the canal, which would not only embark in it a liberal contribution, but which would be a most efficient means in securing the powerful and decisive aid of Congress. A strong and earnest appeal was therefore made to every man 'to do all in his power in furthering the canal. Committees were appointed for each of the wards of the city to procure further subscriptions as follows:

First Ward, ———— and Charles Vinson; Second Ward, James McLeary and James Larned; Third Ward, Andrew Way and Andrew Coyle; Fourth Ward, J. P. Ingle and James Young; Fifth Ward, Griffith Coombe and E. S. Lewis; Sixth Ward, Adam Lindsay and William Easley.

The Congress of the United States, in response to the petitions of the citizens, passed the Chesapeake and Ohio Canal bill in May, 1828, by a large majority in both Houses, and the papers then burst forth with congratulations somewhat as follows:

"We may congratulate ourselves on the passage of a bill which contemplates, and which will, no doubt, secure, the execution of a work so beneficial to this District, to the States through which it will pass, and to the country at large.   Georgetown and Alexandria, in whose streets the grass now grows green, will become once more the scenes of commerce and wealth.   Washington, which is now poverty-stricken and humbly dependent on the regular or casual expenditures of individuals attached to the Government, will be able to hold up her head among the cities of the country, and to participate with them in some of the benefits resulting from population, capital, and productive industry. The intentions and anticipations of the Father of his country, as to the city which bears his name, may now be fulfilled and realized. The city of Washington may be made worthy of its founder, and worthy of remaining forever the metropolis of the Union,' etc.   "The author of this great enterprise is Charles Fenton Mercer, of Virginia. He will be called the 'Clinton of the South,' a title more honoring than the proudest which heraldry can boast."

In honor of the success of the preliminary steps taken in this enterprise, the citizens of Georgetown gave a public dinner to Hon. C. F. Mercer, on the 26th of June, 1828.

A meeting of the stockholders of the canal company was held June 20, 1828, at the City Hall, to receive the report of the board of commissioners on the part of the United States, and the States of Maryland and Virginia, and to organize the company by the election of a president and six directors.   On motion of General John C. Hunter, Hon. Richard Rush, Secretary of the Treasury, was invited to preside; but on account of the possibility of his having to attend to official business before the meeting should close, he proposed the Mayor of Washington, Joseph Gales, Jr., for chairman, and Mr. Gales was selected accordingly.   Clement Smith acted as secretary.   The report of the commissioners was read by Samuel H. Smith, and in this report it was shown that the subscriptions to the stock of the company then amounted to $3,090,100 in money, and $10,149.77 in the stock of the old Potomac Company.   The salaries of the officers of the company about to be organized were then settled, and the company organized as stated in former pages.   Notice was then given that subscriptions, which should be first offered in whole shares up to $6,000,000, would be received at the Bank of the United States in Washington, and that these subscriptions should take precedence over others later received.

June 28, 1828, it was resolved that the municipal authorities of the three cities within the District, the president and directors of the canal company, and guests specially invited, should proceed by water on July 4, to the point where the ground was to be broken on that day, for the beginning of the canal. This spot was just within the limits of the District, near the powder magazine and above the Little Falls bridge. The ceremonies of the day were intended to be, and were, very imposing in their nature. At an early hour, the invited guests assembled at Tilley's Hotel, the President of the United States arriving at 7:30 A. M. There were also present the Secretaries of the War, Navy, and Treasury departments of the Government; the Postmaster-General, Senators, and Representatives, and many of the ministers of foreign countries. At eight o'clock, the procession formed and moved to High Street wharf, whence the steamer *Surprise*, two other steamers, and a line of barges moved up the Potomac to a spot just above the lower termination of the canal. On leaving the "River of Swans," the procession marched a few hundred yards to the canal boats prepared to receive them, at the upper bridge across the canal, from the banks of which "there shot up along its entire course a large variety of the most beautiful native trees, whose branches, interwoven above, would have excluded the rays of the most piercing sun. . . . Noiseless, but in crowds, the people moved forward on the bank of the canal, keeping even pace with the long line of boats, whilst airs, now animated, now plaintive, from the Marine Band, placed in the forward boat, lightened the toil of the work."

Upon reaching the ground selected for the beginning of operations, one or two hundred yards east of the Washington Canal, the procession formed a hollow square, in the center of which was the spot marked by Judge Wright, the engineer of the company, for the commencement of the work. At that precise moment, the sun burst forth from behind a cloud, and the Mayor of Georgetown handed the spade to Hon. Mr. Mercer, president of the company, who stepped forward from the column and addressed the assembled multitude as follows:

"FELLOW-CITIZENS: There are moments in the progress of time which are counters of whole ages. There are events the monuments of which, surviving every other memorial of human existence, eternize the nation to whose history they belong, after all other vestiges of its glory have disappeared from the globe. At such a moment we have now arrived; such a monument we are now to found."

Then turning to the President of the United States, Hon. John Quincy Adams, who stood near, Mr. Mercer addressed him in a short speech, and then presented to him the spade with which he was to perform the ceremony of breaking ground. The President himself made an address of considerable length, at the conclusion of which a national salute was fired, when the chairman of the committee of arrangements delivered an address, and was followed by Mr. Stuart. At the conclusion of Mr. Stuart's speech, sods of earth were dug in succession by the President of the United States, the president of the canal company, the mayors of Washington, Georgetown, and Alexandria, the Secretaries of the War, Navy, and Treasury departments of the Government, the Postmaster-General, the Commander of the Army, the Revolutionary officers present, and the directors of the canal company, followed by a great many other persons. The procession then returned to the canal, thence to tide water, and thence down to Davidson's wharf, where they all landed. "Thus ended the most delightful commemoration of this eventful day that we have ever witnessed, and thus auspiciously was begun the work upon the Chesapeake and Ohio Canal."

The company established its offices in the City Hall, in the second story, on the west side. John P. Ingle was the clerk, and served for many years.

July 8, 1828, the Board of Aldermen and Common Council of the city of Washington requested the Mayor to ask the officers of the canal company to locate and mark with as little delay as possible the route of so much of the said canal as passed through the city of Washington to the Eastern Branch; and that he be further requested to communicate the result of such application to the board as soon as practicable.

In response to this resolution the board of directors of the canal replied, that it would be inexpedient to expend any part of the capital stock in an extension of the canal below the entrance to the canal then in existence, at the head of the Little Falls of the Potomac, before the line of the canal leading thence to the mouth of the Shenandoah had been put under contract; that the president and directors of the Chesapeake and Ohio Canal Company were not under any obligation to prescribe the eastern termination of the canal in the District of Columbia; and further, that if it were the desire of the corporation of the city of Washington, notwithstanding, that the eastern termination of the canal should be then fixed by a vote of the company, the president and directors would, upon the request of the corporation, or of the directors residing within the limits of the city, call a general meeting of the stockholders for the purpose of submitting that question to their judgment. The request was accordingly made, and a meeting of the stockholders was held in the City Hall, September

10, 1828. With reference to the local question — as to the eastern termination of the canal — to decide which the meeting had been called, Mr. Mercer said that his belief was, that the point of termination was not fixed by the charter; that its most advisable termination was at the basin above Georgetown; but that he had never doubted that it would ultimately pass through the city of Washington, under distinct legislation of Congress, and concluded with submitting as the result of the deliberations of the board of directors a series of resolutions, to the effect that if the Attorney-General of the United States should be of the opinion that the charter of the company conferred authority therefor, and the corporations of Washington, Georgetown, and Alexandria should respectively assent thereto, the canal should extend to the mouth of Rock Creek, on the plan of the engineers, Benjamin Wright and John Martineau.

September 17, an adjourned meeting was held and the above proposition was approved; that is, that the canal should terminate at a basin to be erected by the corporation of Washington at the mouth of the Tiber, and it was also agreed that it might be continued to Alexandria, and a branch be extended to the Navy Yard in Washington. Payments on subscriptions were made as follows: October 3, $2; November 3, $2; December 3, $2; and so on monthly, $2 per month, at any of the banks in the District of Columbia, the Hagerstown Bank, Maryland, or the branch of the Valley Bank at Charlestown, Virginia.

Preparations were made to lay the corner stone of the first lock of this canal on July 4, 1829, but the ceremony had to be postponed until a later day on account of the inclemency of the weather. On March 30, 1830, the water was let into the canal from the powder house down to the old locks, and navigation, which had been for some time obstructed by operations on this part of the canal, was then resumed, several boats having come down to Georgetown from the river above. This piece of the canal, which was about two miles in length, was described as a beautiful sheet of water, and as answering all the expectations of its projectors and managers. Its beauty was of course enhanced by its prospective commercial value. One boat had traversed the entire two miles in fifteen minutes. The canal was permanently opened for navigation the same day, that is, March 30, 1830. It was from eighty to one hundred feet wide, and its minimum depth was six feet. In addition to the two miles of the new canal, one-twentieth of a mile of the old Potomac Canal was used, connecting it with the river at the head of Little Falls. The prism of the Chesapeake and Ohio Canal was more than double that of the Erie Canal, thus giving much greater facility of draught. The line up to Seneca was under contract, and it was expected to be completed that far by June 1, 1830.

The same officers were elected in June, 1830, that had previously served the company. The canal was completed, including the construction of the locks from Georgetown to Seneca, a distance of 22 miles, by July 4, 1830. In this distance there were 24 locks of hewn stone, a large basin common to Washington and Georgetown, covering eight acres, and embracing 1½ miles of wharf; 5 or 6 stone bridges in Georgetown; 8 large culverts and several small ones; 2 dams built on an entirely new plan, of solid masonry, and several walls, varying from 40 to 50 feet in height. The canal was nearly completed to the "Point of Rocks," and but for the legal controversy with the Baltimore and Ohio Railroad Company, it was believed the canal would have been completed that year to Harper's Ferry. In the distance from Georgetown to Seneca, there was about 190 feet of lockage, a little more than one-third of the entire lockage from tide water to Cumberland, so that the canal had passed through the most difficult part of the distance.

About April 1, 1831, the Legislature of Pennsylvania passed a resolution requesting their Senators and Representatives in Congress to endeavor to procure the passage of a law authorizing the United States to subscribe $1,000,000 toward the completion of the western end of the canal. The canal was to be completed to the Point of Rocks that year, but the twenty-seven miles between Seneca and the Point of Rocks would be useless unless it was constructed beyond the Point of Rocks to the feeder. This point was involved in litigation between the canal company and the Baltimore and Ohio Railroad Company. The canal was in operation from Seneca to Georgetown, and its usefulness was demonstrated by the fact that one boat could bring down in one day as much produce as could be brought down by four horses and a wagon in a month. It formerly cost fifty cents per barrel to get flour from Seneca to Georgetown, but by the canal it could be brought down for seven cents per barrel. The canal was opened for the season of 1831, on March 21, and by the end of the month there was received $8,400 in tolls. The amount of produce which passed down to Georgetown by May 14, that year, was as follows: Flour, 83,106 barrels; whisky, 752 barrels; wheat, 7,401 bushels; bacon, butter, and lard, 84,540 pounds; corn, 202 bushels; hemp, 4,000 pounds; iron, 85 tons; bran, etc., 1,190 bushels; besides a large quantity of stone, firewood, etc. The tolls amounted in that time to $17,049. The packet boat, *Charles Fenton Mercer*, left the bridge at Frederick Street, Georgetown, for Seneca, at seven o'clock every morning; fare to Crommelin, 37½ cents; to Seneca, 50 cents; breakfast, 31¼ cents; dinner, 50 cents; supper, 25 cents; wine at from 50 cents to $1.50 per bottle.

The first 48 miles of the canal were laid out and marked on the ground by Dr. John Martineau, a civil engineer, under the supervision of Benjamin Wright. They were divided into about 90 sections, and comprehended in that distance 2 aqueducts — one of three and the other of seven arches, of 54 feet span each; 74 culverts; a dam across the Potomac at the head of Little Falls, 1,750 feet long, and another at the head of Seneca Falls 2,500 feet long; 27 lift locks, besides a tight lock and a guard lock; 17 houses for the lock keepers, two of which were built large enough to serve as places of rest for passengers; 3 feeders from the river and one from an intermediate stream; several basins, one of which was designed as a capacious harbor for boats, and was sustained by a mole across Rock Creek, erected in 20 feet of water, and was 1,000 feet long and 160 feet wide, through which a lock connected the navigation of the canal with the tide water of the Potomac.

The progress of the canal was arrested by the injunction of the Chancellor of Maryland, granted almost immediately after the organization of the company, and brought at the suit of the Baltimore and Ohio Railroad Company. This injunction was continued until reversed by the Court of Appeals of Maryland, January 5, 1831, during all of which time the canal from Seneca Falls to the Point of Rocks was awaiting a supply of water from Harper's Ferry; and after the dissolution of the injunction the canal had to be extended through the fourteen miles of disputed territory and up to Harper's Ferry Falls, where there was a dam already erected by the United States Government. This portion of the canal was speedily let to experienced contractors, as well as that portion between Rock Creek basin and the mouth of Tiber Creek, the eastern terminus of the Chesapeake and Ohio Canal. Thirty-six miles above the head of Harper's Ferry Falls were also contracted for, in order to complete one hundred miles of the canal in five years, as required by the charter. Sixty-four miles of the canal were completed and capable of navigation by October, 1833.

Up to December 1, 1833, there had been received into the treasury of the company the following sums of money: Subscriptions to the

capital stock, $3,589,252.64; on account of the compromise, $177,-
333.35; tolls, $94,538.27; old houses and materials sold, $514.80; sums
paid agents, refunded, $752.31; profit on the sale of Maryland
stock, $4,703.03; interest received from delinquent subscribers, $989.79;
costs of suit recovered, $3,847.62; on debts of the Potomac Com-
pany, $784.82; loans at the several banks, $55,000; total amount,
$3,927,716.63. The entire expenditures had been up to the same
time, $3,707,262.43.

In explanation of the above amount received on account of
compromise, it should be stated that some months previously the
two litigant companies, the Chesapeake and Ohio Canal Company
and the Baltimore and Ohio Railroad Company, had compromised
their difficulties by the acceptance on the part of each of an act of
the Legislature of Maryland passed for the purpose of securing the
construction of the Baltimore and Ohio Railroad to Harper's Ferry.
By this compromise the railroad company bound themselves to pay
·to the canal company, in consideration of the damage that might be
done to the canal, and of the interruption or hazard to which its
navigation would be unavoidably exposed in the construction of the
railroad along the margin thereof, for grading the four and one-tenth
miles of the road between Harper's Ferry and the Point of Rocks,
described below, the sum of $266,000. The said four and one-tenth
miles consisted of a space to be laid off between the entrance of the
bridge at Harper's Ferry and a point two miles therefrom, according
to the location of said road, which was to be below Millar's Narrows;
of one mile and one-twentieth extending from a point opposite to the
door of the chief public house at the Point of Rocks up the valley
of the Potomac, comprehending the lower Point of Rocks; and one
mile and one-twentieth extending above and below the upper Point
of Rocks so as to comprehend the same; making all that part of
the canal at those places in which an interference exists, between the
location of the canal and the railroad.

Shortly after this compromise was effected, an election of president
and directors of the canal company was held in June, 1833, at the
City Hall in Washington. It resulted as follows: John H. Eaton
received 5,054 votes to C. F. Mercer's 3,430. The directors elected
were William Price, J. J. Abert, W. Gunton, W. Smith, Phineas
Janney, and R. H. Henderson. To the friends of Mr. Mercer his
defeat was a sore disappointment, as they looked upon him as the
great promoter of the canal. They could, however, console themselves
only with the reflection that it was the shares of stock that elected

Mr. Eaton, while the individual stockholders were very largely in favor of Mr. Mercer, the vote on this basis standing 2,362 for Mr. Mercer, to 1,030 for Mr. Eaton.

In order to assist the company in completing the canal, the Legislature of Maryland, in March, 1835, offered to loan the company $2,000,000 on certain conditions. At a general meeting of the stockholders, held at Washington, April 22 following, after full discussion of the proposition, it was resolved by the company to accept the loan with the terms. At that time the navigation of the canal was continuous for a distance of 110 miles from Washington, exclusive of 9 miles of slack water navigation above dam No. 5.

In February, 1836, a report was made by the company to the Legislature of Maryland, showing that 109 miles of the canal were in operation. These 109 miles had cost $4,838,271, and it was estimated that to extend the canal from the 109th mile to the Great Cacapon, a further distance of 27 miles, would cost $1,022,534; to the line near the South Branch, 31 miles, $1,793,048, and to Cumberland, a distance of 19½ miles, $745,037; making a total of $8,398,890. George C. Washington was then president of the company, and he was reëlected June 22, 1836, and again in 1837.

At this point it may not be improper to digress sufficiently to narrate the construction of the Alexandria Canal, and the aqueduct across the Potomac at Georgetown by which it was supplied with water. The first spadeful of earth was thrown up in the construction of this canal, July 4, 1831. The aqueduct itself was begun in 1833. At first the engineer was overruled, and several contractors failed in their attempts to build circular cofferdams in which to sink the piers. The board of directors then placed Major William Turnbull, of the corps of topographical engineers, in charge of the work, and he held the position until it was completed. The aqueduct was built across the Potomac at Georgetown, and conveyed the water from the Chesapeake and Ohio Canal to the Alexandria Canal. It consisted of two abutments and eight massive stone piers one hundred feet apart, supporting a wooden trunk, which was originally designed to be of stone. The foundation of these piers rested on the rocky bottom of the river, reached through twenty feet of water and twenty feet of mud. When completed, it was said of it, "As a hydraulic work it ranks number one, and may be boldly pointed to in comparison with anything of the kind at home or abroad." After several attempts and considerable difficulty, the canal was at length opened to Alexandria on December 2, 1843. The canal was seven

20

miles long from the aqueduct to Alexandria, with no lock or other interruption to navigation. The president of the canal company, the Mayor of Alexandria, and a large number of citizens went up to the aqueduct in the morning, and there, with the engineers and other officers of the company, embarked in the canal boat *Pioneer*, and after a passage of a little more than an hour reached the termination of the canal at the junction of Washington and Montgomery streets. In the afternoon of the same day, a canal boat came down from Washington County, Maryland, loaded with flour. The officers of the canal company at that time were William Fowle, president; Hugh Smith, Phineas Janney, Robert H. Miller, Thomas E. Baird, Robert Jamieson, and G. H. Smoot, directors.

During the years 1838 and 1839, the company experienced great difficulty in completing the upper end of the canal, because of the actual expense so far outrunning the estimates; and it began to be feared by the friends of the canal that the Legislature of Maryland, which State was the great stockholder and supporter of the enterprise, would decline to render further assistance, unless the canal were turned over to her as security for money advanced, and to be advanced. Up to March, 1839, the various sums invested in the canal were as follows: First, her commuted stock in the old Potomac Company; second, $500,000 subscribed to the original capital; third, $125,000 to save the dams; fourth, $2,000,000 on loan to the company on pledge of the revenue of the canal; fifth, $3,000,000 subscribed on a guaranty of six per cent. per year on the amount, after the expiration of three years. Thus she was guaranteed the entire revenue of the canal. The Government of the United States had $2,500,000 of stock, and she, together with the State of Virginia and the individual stockholders, who, in 1839, had been for ten years and more lying out of their money and out of any dividends upon it, could receive no dividend until Maryland had received her six per cent. upon her advances. There was then needed, to complete the canal to Cumberland, $2,320,871 more than had been estimated, and it was this unexpected state of affairs which caused the contemplation of a policy which, had it been pursued, would have been suicidal in the extreme.

In April, 1839, water was let into 27 miles of the canal at the upper end, making 137 miles of this great work completed, and leaving only 50 miles to finish to Cumberland. In the meantime, the State of Maryland had decided to subscribe to the stock of the company $1,375,000 more, to which the company at a general meeting of the stockholders agreed, May 11, 1839. They also, at the same time, agreed to the proposal of the State to exchange $3,200,000 of five per cent. sterling stock of the State for the $3,000,000 six per cent. stock already subscribed by the State.

On June 3, 1839, Francis Thomas was elected president of the company. The chief engineer of the company at that time was Charles B. Fisk. His estimate of the entire cost of the 50 miles above mentioned as necessary to complete the canal to Cumberland, was $4,440,657, upon which, however, there had then been expended about $950,000. In March, 1840, according to the report of the same engineer, there had been expended on the six-sevenths of the canal that were completed a little over $10,000,000, and there was needed to complete the remaining one-seventh $2,300,000. He said that the canal could not prove profitable to the stockholders until this remaining one-seventh should be finished. At a meeting of the company at Washington, held in the City Hall, July 20, 21, and 22, 1840, it was decided to remove the offices of the company from Washington, where they had been ever since the organization of the company in 1828, to Frederick, Maryland, and it was unanimously resolved that the thanks of the company be extended to the corporate authorities of Washington for the gratuitous use of the apartments of the City Hall during that length of time.

Early in 1841, George C. Washington was compelled to retire from the presidency of this company. He said it was under party proscription of his own State, and that of the United States, the Secretary of the Treasury being the agent voting the stock of the United States. The indebtedness of the company at that time was somewhat more than $3,000,000, and the assets were $4,936,937. At a meeting of the stockholders, held April 1, 1841, Michael C. Sprigg was elected president, to succeed President Washington.

An act was passed by the Legislature of Maryland, at its session of 1841, to secure the completion of this canal. Section 1 of this act provided that whenever the Chesapeake and Ohio Canal Company should agree to all the provisions of the act, it should then be the duty of the commissioner of loans of the State to issue, from time to time, to the company in sums of not less than $100 certificates of stock of the State, to an amount not exceeding $2,000,000, irredeemable for thirty years, and redeemable afterward at the pleasure of the State, bearing six per cent. interest, payable semi-annually.

Section 4 provided that for the purpose of providing for the payment of the debt thus authorized the annual sum of $25,000 should be paid from the tolls of the canal.

"SECTION 10. AND WHEREAS, It is to be apprehended that the canal will reach Cumberland before any effective effort will be made to open and complete the several railroads which are to connect the canal with the coal mines, in which case there is danger that the State may be compelled to make these railroads at the public expense;

"*Therefore be it enacted,* That before any contract shall be made for the completion of the said canal to Cumberland, or bond or certificate issued under the provisions of this act, the treasurer of the Western Shore shall certify, under his hand and seal of office, to the president and directors of said Chesapeake and Ohio Canal Company, that the companies hereinafter named, incorporated by the Legislature of this State, to wit: 'The Baltimore and New York Coal Company,' 'The Maryland and New York Iron and Coal Company,' 'The Maryland Mining Company,' and 'The Clifton Coal Company,' have severally given satisfactory bonds to the State of Maryland, conditioned for the construction and completion of a railroad adequate to convey to the canal the products of their prospective mines, the same to be completed, ready for use, simultaneously with the completion of the Chesapeake and Ohio Canal to Cumberland."

"SECTION 12. That no part of this bill shall be operative until one or more of the incorporated companies, coal or iron, in Allegheny County, shall have entered into bonds, with security, to the State of Maryland, to be approved by the treasurer of the Western Shore, to pay $200,000 per annum for five years, for the transportation of their own coal, iron, or other materials or goods, at the expiration of each and every year from and after six months after the completion of the said canal to Cumberland"; and they were not to be released from the payment of this amount on the whole amount of articles transported by them until the same, at the rate of tolls charged by the canal company, exceeded in cost the sum of $200,000.

For the year 1841, according to the report of Charles B. Fisk, chief engineer of the company, there had been done on the fifty miles of unfinished canal, $231,107 worth of work, and the amount needed on January 1, 1842, to complete the canal was $1,591,136. During that year the canal had been navigable for about 300 days. The canal was 6 feet deep, and the locks 15 feet wide and 100 feet long. A boat load was 80 tons, and the toll on the canal for coal was $1 per ton, from Cumberland to Georgetown.

On June 2, 1842, a joint resolution was introduced into the Senate of the United States, recommending that the stock of the United States and a portion of that of the cities of the District of Columbia be transferred to the State of Maryland, in order to enable her to complete the canal. This resolution was introduced on the strength‛ of a report made by the Committee on Roads and Canals, which summarized the history of the subscription to the stock of the company, showing that, up to January, 1842, there had been subscribed the following amounts: By the United States, $1,000,000; by Maryland, $5,000,000; by Virginia, $250,000; by Washington, $1,000,000; by Georgetown, $250,000; by Alexandria, $250,000; and by sundry individuals, $457,518.36. Of these various sums all had been paid, except $151,881.36, which was due from some of the individual subscribers. The State of Maryland was also credited with $43,280 on account of a debt due that State from the old Potomac Company, which surrendered its charter to the Chesapeake and Ohio Canal Company, and also with the sum of $120,444.44 on account of 220 shares of stock transferred from the Potomac Company to that State, making $163,724.44. The canal company also owed the State $2,000,000, loaned under authority of an act of 1834. The report in which these facts were submitted was very long, and recommended that Congress deal liberally with the State of Maryland, as she would be the greatest sufferer if the canal were not completed, because she was the greatest stockholder, and suggested that the $1,000,000 of stock of the United States, and $750,000 of the $1,500,000 of stock deposited with the Secretary of the Treasury of the United States by the cities of Washington, Georgetown, and Alexandria, be returned to the cities of the District. The favor thus suggested to the three cities was because they had suffered severely by the losses sustained by them in the payment of interest and expenses on the Holland loan, the city of Washington having paid on her portion of the debt $449,650, Georgetown $116,795, and Alexandria $111,715, an aggregate amount of $678,160. The committee proposed, therefore, by way of indemnity to the cities, the redelivery of the remaining $750,000, deposited with the Secretary of the Treasury under the act of Congress of May 20, 1836,— to the city of Washington, $500,000; and to the other two cities, each $125,000. The question of consent to the joint resolution was submitted to the Boards of Aldermen and Common Council of Washington July 1, 1842, and received their assent. The outcome of this movement will appear later in these pages.

On December 3, 1842, the Hon. M. C. Sprigg, who had been reëlected to the presidency of the company in the preceding June, resigned his position, and was succeeded by Major-General William Gibbs McNeill. With reference to the resignation of Colonel Sprigg, the Baltimore *Patriot* said, that the canal could have been completed under him if his political opponents had extended to him the confidence and assistance to which his elevated character entitled him; but these were withheld, it believed, merely from party purposes. And it was hoped that the distinguished engineer that succeeded him would not encounter similar opposition.

On January 2, 1843, the Common Council of Washington took up the question of the surrender of its stock, and discussed it more fully than before. Mr. Haliday introduced the following resolution:

"WHEREAS, The Governor of the State of Maryland, in a letter to the President of the United States, which was communicated to Congress January 1, 1840, requesting a surrender to the State of Maryland of the stock of the Chesapeake and Ohio Canal Company belonging to the United States, and to the cities of Washington, Georgetown, and Alexandria; and

"WHEREAS, This corporation, by its committee, on the 11th of March, 1840, presented to both Houses of Congress, a remonstrance against the surrender, so far as related to the stock owned by this corporation; which remonstrance, among the many facts and arguments it contains to show that Maryland is not entitled to any bonus or gratuity, especially at the expense of the people of this city, proves that whatever loss has arisen from delay in the completion of the canal is attributable solely to the legislation of that State. On this subject the remonstrance says: 'The State of Maryland originally embarked in this enterprise, as the corporation did, under the impression that a canal suited to its purposes could be constructed at an expense entirely within the means then estimated. But this was no favorite project with her legislators or with her people. They looked to another avenue and another great outlet for her exhaustless mineral wealth, which should lead directly to her city, Baltimore; and as it early ascertained that no route for a canal to that city could be found except through the District of Columbia, all her energies were directed to the railroad. Her legislation and the political power of the State were equally devoted to this object. She granted a most favorable charter to the railroad company, and the first serious obstacle to the progress of the canal is to be clearly traced to that legislation. The work of the canal was obstructed in most vexatious, tedious, and most expensive litigation, producing a train of evils from which the canal company never recovered. But the greatest injury was in the progress of the work itself, and the discouragements produced by the delay. The history of her subsequent legislation shows how regardless she was of these injuries, and how pertinaciously she adhered to her original design of diverting all the trade of the Potomac, and all the vast products of the region watered by its tributaries, from its natural channel, and to force it to Baltimore. Year after year, while this corporation was exhausting its means and oppressing its citizens to carry on the canal, Maryland was taxing the ingenuity of her ablest men to defeat the canal, demanding the right to cut a canal through this city, and in every way seeking to secure to herself every advantage from the investment of this corporation, and never relaxing these efforts until she was well assured that this was the only practicable means of bringing into use the great wealth of her mountains.'

"AND WHEREAS, Congress, satisfied with the justice of the position assumed by the corporation of Washington in the defense of its rights and those of its citizens, and of the injustice of the State of Maryland in asking for a surrender of their property; and

" WHEREAS, A joint resolution having been presented in the Senate of the United States in December, 1841, soliciting the surrender to the State of Maryland of the canal stock owned by this city, as previously required by the Governor of the State, a remonstrance on the part of this corporation was again laid before the Senate by the Mayor of this city, which remonstrance is in the following words:

"'The original subscriptions to the stock of the Chesapeake and Ohio Canal Company, made in 1827 and 1828, were as follows: [These have been previously presented.]

"'In the year 1834, the State of Maryland made a further subscription of $125,000 to the stock of the company, payable in five per cent. bonds, which yielded the company only $120,000, a loss of $5,000. In 1835, the State made a loan to the company in six per cent. bonds of $2,000,000 on the condition that the State should have the privilege of converting this loan into stock of the company at any time within a year after the canal should be completed; that until that time the books of the company should be closed, and no other subscriptions received; that for the payment of the principal and interest of this loan the whole property of the company should be mortgaged to the State, and that the bonds should be sold at a premium of fifteen per cent., to be paid to the State. The bonds actually sold for more than fifteen per cent., which went into the State treasury, and the six per cent. interest has been paid to her up to the year 1840. In 1836, the State authorized a further subscription to the company of $3,000,000 in six per cent. bonds, on the conditions that the Baltimore and Ohio Railroad Company should be allowed to construct its works where the law had denied it the right to do so; that the bonds should produce twenty per cent. premium to the State, and that the property of the company should be mortgaged to insure and pay her six per cent. interest on the subscription, thus making herself a preferred stockholder, in positive violation of the charter, which provides that all the stockholders should share equally in all profits, according to their respective shares. These bonds, it is to be further observed, could not be made available to the company for three years, and then only yielded $2,464,000, the company losing half a million on them.

"'In 1839, the State made a further subscription of $1,375,000, payable in five per cent. sterling bonds at pár, the State taking a further mortgage to secure a dividend of six per cent. on this subscription, in violation of the charter, as in the other case, while the sale of the bonds yielded to the company only seventy-seven per cent. on the nominal value, a further loss of $317,000.

"'This subscription, as well as the preceding one, of $3,000,000, was resisted by the corporation of Washington, but it was forced on the company, with its onerous conditions, by the almost solid vote of the State of Maryland herself, which then had a majority of the stock.

"'Coupled with the act authorizing the last subscription was a direction to the Governor to ask of Congress a surrender to the State of the $2,500,000 of stock originally subscribed by the United States, and the corporations of Washington, Georgetown, and Alexandria, and if granted, the State pledged herself to buy out all individual stockholders at fifty per cent. On the 23d of February, 1841, fifteen days after the Senate of the United States had passed a resolution giving her the said $2,500,000 of stock and had sent it to the House of Representatives for concurrence, and when it was expected that the House also would pass the bill, a bill was introduced into the Senate of Maryland and instantly passed both branches of the legislature, quietly revoking this obligation to which she had pledged herself to Congress, to pay the private individuals fifty per cent. This repealing bill was in the following brief and unostentatious form:

"'"A Supplement to the Act Passed at the Session of December, 1838, Chapter 396, Entitled, 'An Act Relating to the Chesapeake and Ohio Canal Company':

"'"Be it enacted, That the second and third sections of said act be, and the same are hereby, repealed."

"'Fortunately, the surrender of our stock did not pass the House of Representatives, and this act of the Legislature of Maryland releasing the State from her obligation was of no avail. We make no comment on this proceeding.

"'The proposition for this surrender has, however, been renewed, and is now again before the Senate; but if that honorable body will look into the relative exertions, sufferings, and claims of the several classes of partners in the canal company, it is believed that the State of Maryland will be found to possess less title to this great boon than others, and to grant which, while it would be signally unjust to her suffering copartners, would, in fact, not afford her the least aid in completing the canal. The .impulse given by the subscriptions, corporate and private, of the District of Columbia, was mainly instrumental in starting the work, and while the corporation of Washington and its citizens subscribed $1,500,000, the State of Maryland took but half a million. The United States, it is true, assumed the principal of the corporation subscriptions, but from borrowing money to pay the annual interest on the subscription before the transfer, a debt of nearly half a million was incurred, and is now established on the city, and while Maryland has been exacting of the company an .illegal payment of six per cent. profit on the greater portion of her subscription to the work running through her own State, and for her own peculiar benefit, the poor citizens of Washington have been sinking the interest on their subscriptions for fourteen years, and can never receive one farthing on their stock until the State of Maryland shall have first received six per cent. on her immense investment. Under these circumstances Maryland asks Congress to strip the corporation of Washington of $1,000,000 of stock which it subscribed, leaving the city encumbered with an enormous debt of half a million of dollars as its only reward for giving the first effective impulse to a work of which Maryland herself is ever to reap the chief benefit.

"'In addition to all this, when Maryland was pressing her petition on Congress to grant to her the above $2,500,000 of stock, her legislature passed an act (to wit: at the session of 1840–41) ordering a foreclosure of the mortgage, imposed by her own vote on the company, to secure her preferred dividend of six per cent. on her subscription.

"'In behalf of the Committee of the Corporation of Washington,
"'W. W. SEATON, Chairman.'

"AND WHEREAS, No information has been submitted to this board since January, 1842, tending to show the justice or propriety of making at this time the transfer of the city to the State of Maryland, and thereby leaving a debt of half a million of dollars, with an annual interest of $30,000, to be borne by the people of the city, with no provision for the payment of the principal or interest but by taxes upon their property; and,

"WHEREAS, On the 1st of July, 1842, the Board of Aldermen passed a resolution and sent it to this board, seeking a concurrence, which resolution is now pending in this board, giving the assent of this corporation to the passage by Congress of a joint resolution before Congress whereby it is proposed to transfer as a gratuity to the State of Maryland $500,000 of the $1,000,000 of the stock subscribed and paid for by the corporation and now held by the United States on certain conditions, and upon which this corporation has paid, besides the $1,000,000, in interest, etc., nearly $700,000; and,

"WHEREAS, on the 2d of June, 1842, a joint committee was appointed by the two boards to attend the meetings of the Chesapeake and Ohio Canal Company and vote on the above-mentioned stock, which committee, since their appointment, have attended several meetings of the company, at the last of which it is understood measures were adopted of great interest to the stockholders in general — measures which the committee appointed on the part of this board declared, in a debate in this chamber on the 12th of December last, would render it unnecessary to sacrifice the rights and interests of a part of the stockholders to complete the canal to Cumberland; and

"WHEREAS, It is indispensably necessary to the members of this board, before they can with due regard to the interests of their constituents proceed to act on a subject of so great importance as to give away to the State of Maryland without an equivalent the stock of this corporation, on the pretense that it is necessary in order to induce her to complete the canal, to have a full knowledge of all the proceedings referred to; and

"WHEREAS, The Board of Aldermen rejected the joint resolution calling upon the committee for a report of the proceedings of the meetings of the stockholders which they attended as representatives of this corporation; therefore,

"*Resolved*, That the committee appointed on the part of this board, who attended said meetings, be requested and is hereby directed to communicate to this board at the earliest convenient moment a statement in full of the proceedings of said meetings, embracing the means adopted by the company to complete the canal, and which, in his opinion, will render it unnecessary to sacrifice the interests of a portion of the stockholders to complete the object."

This resolution was then laid on the table by a vote of 12 to 4. In reply, however, to the resolution, Lewis Johnson, who attended the meetings of the canal company on the part of the Board of Common Council, published a statement in which he said that he had not asserted that measures were adopted that would render it unnecessary to sacrifice the interests of a portion of the stockholders in order to complete the canal; but that he had expressed the sanguine hope, which he entertained, that the course adopted by the convention would prove to be the foundation of measures which would lead to the completion of the canal to Cumberland.

Notwithstanding the strong reasons furnished by the above report, which, as has been said, was laid upon the table, the two boards of the city's government assembled at the call of the Mayor for the purpose of taking decided steps in reference to the proposed transfer of stock, and adopted the following ordinance:

"*Resolved*, By the Aldermen and Common Council of the City of Washington, that the assent of this corporation be, and the same is hereby, given to the transfer of the stock originally subscribed by this city to the Chesapeake and Ohio Canal Company, as proposed by and upon the terms, conditions, and restrictions contained in the joint resolution introduced in the Senate of the United States from the committee on roads and canals, on the 2d day of June, 1842, entitled 'A Joint Resolution Directing the Transfer of the Stock Held by the United States in the Chesapeake and Ohio Canal Company to the State of Maryland, and the Cities of Washington, Georgetown, and Alexandria': *Provided*, It shall be further conditioned, that the State of Maryland shall cancel and abandon all mortgages or liens which the Chesapeake and Ohio Canal Company may have executed to said State, and all claims to priority under said mortgages executed by said company to the said State in the year 1835, for a loan of $2,000,000, and shall agree not at any time to foreclose the last-mentioned mortgage, or any other mortgage or mortgages which may be executed to the State of Maryland by the Chesapeake and Ohio Canal Company, so as to divest the State of Virginia, the said cities, corporations, or individuals, of their respective proportions of stock now held by them, or hereinafter to be held in the manner and under the circumstances mentioned in the said joint resolution."

This ordinance was adopted January 14, 1843, and was signed by all the proper officials. The Senators and Representatives in Congress from Maryland agreed to support a joint resolution embodying the above conditions.

In July, 1843, the president of the canal company, General William Gibbs McNeill, made a contract for the completion of the canal between dam No. 6 and Cumberland, with Thomas W. Letson and John Rutter, which contract having been made on his own sole authority, and not by the directors, or a majority of them, as required by the charter of the company, the contract was disapproved by the directors, and General McNeill resigned his position as president, July 19, 1843, and was succeeded by Colonel James M. Coale. About this time an arrangement was made with the Baltimore and Ohio Railroad Company to carry coal from Cumberland to dam No. 6, whence it was carried to the District of Columbia by the canal. This afforded an excellent opportunity for the introduction of Allegheny coal into this market. Colonel Coale was reëlected president of the company, June 4, 1844.

The delay in the work of completing the canal was to some inexplicable, while it was understood by others. William Price, in writing on this subject, quoted from the reports of the Baltimore and Ohio Railroad Company as follows:

"The canal has progressed too far and combines too many interests to warrant the belief that it will not, at an early day, be completed to Cumberland; and if the railroad be permitted to linger for any great length of time at that point, all must see that for the transportation of merchandise and produce to and from the west, the canal must become a formidable rival.

"Reaching Cumberland in wagons across the mountains, a choice must then be made between the canal and the railroad, and in either event commissions for handling and forwarding must be paid. A selection of the cheapest route for the port of exportation may be expected, and therefore, unless the railroad consents to reduce its charges below the point of profit, Baltimore may be deprived of the trade."

The enormous cost of the work thus far was $13,915,469, while according to the estimate of General Barnard it should have cost only $9,195,457. But of this excess $2,616,744 was easily accounted for, and ought to be deducted from the $4,720,012 which had been expended over and above the estimate of General Barnard. The smaller sum mentioned here as easily accounted for, was accounted in the following manner: Almost at the outset, the work was stopped by the injunction of the railroad company at the Point of Rocks for more than three years, and then again, when it reached dam No. 5, it stood still for nearly two years more. Afterwards it was interrupted, checked, and partially stopped, the mere appearance of a force being sustained upon the line. Then it was carried on under great difficulty for about three years, and again totally suspended in 1841, remaining in that condition until August, 1844. Then, after the State had subscribed its $3,000,000 and its $1,375,000, the prices of labor unexpectedly rose fully forty per cent., so that common laborers were paid $1.25 per day. Again, when the laborers could not be paid in full, they formed combinations against the contractors, who were in consequence compelled to abandon their sections. Then the payments of the company, even in its best days, were often made in scrip, which added to the cost. All these and other circumstances were surely sufficient to account for at least a portion of the excess over the estimate of General Barnard.

An act was passed by the Legislature of Maryland, March 11, 1845, for the completion of this canal, which required a guaranty for the annual transportation upon the canal from Cumberland to Georgetown, after its completion, of one hundred and ninety-five thousand tons per year. An ordinance was passed by the corporation of Washington, April 15, 1845, agreeing to indemnify any citizen or citizens of Washington who should become guaranty for the transportation of twenty-five thousand tons. The company was also authorized to issue bonds to complete the canal, and in consequence of giving this authority, the two boards of the corporation of Washington, on August 4, 1845, passed a resolution requesting the Mayor to appoint a committee of two citizens from each ward to invite individuals to make investments in the company's bonds. The next day the Mayor appointed the following gentlemen as the committee: First Ward, S. H. Smith and William Easby; Second Ward, Lewis Johnson and John Sessford; Third Ward, G. C. Grammer and J. W. Maury; Fourth Ward, B. B. French and J. P. Ingle; Fifth Ward, J. C. Fitzpatrick and Thomas Blagden; Sixth Ward, A. H. Lawrence and James Tucker.

In consequence of the above-recited action of the Legislature of Maryland and of the popular movements incited thereby, the company was enabled in September, 1845, to make a contract with Walter Gwynn and others, to complete the canal to Cumberland, the work to be done within two years. The work was to be begun within thirty days from September 25. At the time this contract was made there were eighteen and three-tenths miles of the canal to be completed, the contract price for which was $1,625,000.

April 14, 1847, the corporation of Washington passed an act to aid the company to complete the canal to Cumberland, by which the proposition was to exchange $50,000 in the stock of the corporation, bearing six per cent. interest, redeemable at the pleasure of the corporation, for $50,000 of the stock of the canal company bearing six per cent. interest, provided that the contractors should show to the satisfaction of the committee appointed to transact the business, that with the aid of this $50,000 sufficient funds had been secured to complete the canal, and that the interest on the bonds would be punctually paid.

On October 10, 1850, after many delays, the canal was opened to Cumberland, and water communication was thus opened from that point to the three cities in the District of Columbia. The ceremonies at Cumberland were of a very interesting nature. William Price delivered the address. The first boat from Cumberland, loaded with coal, reached Georgetown November 1, 1850, "and yet we hail its advent with no rejoicings, and welcome the event with no show of joy," etc. The basin at Georgetown was dry, and everything at the lower end of the canal was out of order. The Chesapeake and Ohio Company not being able to put it in order, the corporation of Washington appropriated $1,500 toward that end on December 5, 1850.

February 28, 1851, at a meeting at Gadsby's Hotel, Samuel Sprigg, of Maryland, was elected president of the company, to succeed General Coale, resigned. March 14, 1851, the appropriation of December 5, 1850, was increased to $3,000, and the president and directors of the company were tendered the use of rooms in the basement of the City Hall, in case they should remove the offices of the company to Washington.

By November 12, 1851, the canal was completed from end to end, and from forty to fifty boats had arrived with coal from Cumberland, some of them carrying as much as one hundred and twenty-five tons. Wheat at that time coming in on the canal sold at eighty-five cents per bushel. There were then two passenger boats running, and one other ready to be added, and there was plenty of custom for them all. One of the features of interest connected with the canal was the steam tug *Virginia*, owned by R. S. Demy & Company, of Worcester, Massachusetts, put upon the canal for the purpose of towing boats, and on November 17 it was said that up to that time the experiment had worked well. The *Virginia* could easily tow six boats at a time. Her paddle wheels were so constructed that the recoil was reduced to a minimum, and, in fact, was almost annihilated.

The steam canal boat *President* arrived August 19, 1852, at Georgetown from Cumberland. This boat belonged to Ward's line, and had two propellers, worked by a twelve horse-power steam engine. She traveled six miles per hour without injury to the banks of the canal. She was eighty-eight feet long by twelve feet beam, and commenced running regular trips from Georgetown to Harper's Ferry and Cumberland August 23, 1852. For the year 1852, the tonnage of the canal was as follows: Ascending, 16,226 tons; descending, 151,369 tons; total, 167,595 tons. The tolls amounted to $92,248.90.

Other efforts to use steamboats on this canal were subsequently made, but none of them were entirely satisfactory, no matter how promising they at first appeared. The canal steamer *James L. Cathcart* made a trial trip June 30, 1857, from Georgetown to Alexandria, her speed being five miles per hour. October 26, 1858, this propeller made a trip from Cumberland to Georgetown in sixty-four and a half hours, the quickest trip made up to that time.

To close this account of the construction of the Chesapeake and Ohio Canal, the following statement is interesting. It shows the stock and debts of the company and the actual cost of the canal, exclusive of interest on $3,718,000: Preferred debt, $3,837,651; stock not belonging to the State, $3,718,000; State stock, bonds, and interest, $9,049,000; State loss by interest paid on bonds for its stock, $5,000,000; total, $21,604,651.

A brief account of the Washington Canal is here inserted. It was a project early contemplated, as on September 1, 1792, proposals for cutting it were received. The proposals were to cut it from tide water in the Tiber to tide water in James Creek, a length of about one and one-eighth miles;' its breadth at the bottom to be 12 feet, and at the top 15 feet. The depth was not to be uniform, but the greatest depth was not to exceed 12 feet, and the bottom was designed to be two feet below ordinary low water. Mr. Herbaugh calculated the cut to contain 21,760 solid yards, but not relying implicitly on Mr. Herbaugh's calculations, the commissioners proposed to pay by the cubic yard. This was the beginning of the enterprise. Not to dwell too long on the details of the history of this canal, as it was never of much commercial value to the city, but was a great expense, and toward the last, at least, when the city had become one of considerable size, a great nuisance, it is deemed sufficient to summarize its history, and give a general description of it as it was when completed. It commenced at the lock of the Georgetown Canal near the foot of Seventeenth Street, forming a large triangular basin called "The Mouth of the Tiber." Between that street and West Fifteenth Street it ran from the eastern extremity of the basin along North B Street to a point between West Seventh Street and Sixth Street, a distance of about 5,200 feet. Here it took a southern course for about 775 feet. Again turning to the east and after running 1,570 feet it came to West Third Street. It then turned south and ran to Maryland Avenue, a distance of 623 feet, and there shunting off toward the southeast for a distance of 2,365 feet it reached South Capitol Street, along which it ran 705 feet to a point below Virginia Avenue. It then ran 1,988 feet to Second Street East, where it took a southern course down to the Eastern Branch, a distance of 2,100 feet, making the entire length of the canal 15,326 feet.

The breadth of the canal at its eastern extremity was 150 feet; from the first bend down to Maryland Avenue it was 70 feet wide; from this point down to South N Street it was 40 feet wide; below the bridge across New Jersey Avenue it was 19 feet wide; and south of South N Street it formed a basin 100 feet wide. The sole of the canal was originally four feet below low water, and either level or very nearly so.

A great deal of money was expended from time to time on this canal, but it was never made of much use for the original purposes for which it was constructed, viz., that of affording means of transporting goods into the center of the city; and at length, when the era of improvement came upon the city, in 1871, the canal, as has been said in another chapter, was cleaned out and arched over, and converted into a sewer, one of the largest in the world, so that now it is serving a most useful purpose.

The history of the Baltimore and Ohio Railroad commences, like that of the Chesapeake and Ohio Canal, in the old Potomac Company; hence this connection between the two is here briefly related. The commissioners who were appointed, in 1822, to examine the state of navigation of the Potomac River, pointed out the advantages of a continuous canal from Cumberland to tide water, to be connected with Baltimore by a lateral canal from the Monocacy or Seneca, or by an extension through the District of Columbia. In 1825, Maryland assented to the act incorporating the Chesapeake and Ohio Canal Company, with a reservation of the right to construct any lateral canal whatever within her own territory, and upon the expressed condition that Congress should provide some safe or practicable mode whereby the right should be secured to her of constructing a canal to Baltimore, from that part of the main canal which should be in the District of Columbia. In 1826, Maryland authorized a subscription of

$500,000 to the capital stock of the main canal, and the same amount to the stock of the company for making or extending the canal to the city of Baltimore, upon the condition that Congress should subscribe $1,000,000 to the eastern section, and by law expressly secure to her the right to take and continue the canal aforesaid; and provided further, that the practicability of constructing the canal to Baltimore should be demonstrated.

In 1827, Congress not having subscribed, and General Barnard, with the corps of United States engineers, after making the survey of the route for the canal with scientific precision, having estimated the entire cost to be $22,375,427.69, and that of the first section alone from Cumberland to tide water, in the District of Columbia, at $8,177,081.05; and it being also ascertained by the survey of Dr. Howard that it was impracticable to make a lateral canal to Baltimore by any of the routes through Montgomery County, as proposed by the commissioners in 1822, and that the extension of the main canal through the District of Columbia would cost $3,000,000, all hope began to abate of accomplishing the object by means of a canal; and it was then that Maryland gave her countenance to the aid of a railroad, coming before her, as it did, with the experience of Europe to prove the practicability of such a road. In consequence of the use of steamboats and other improved facilities opened by New York and Pennsylvania for the purpose of securing the trade and commerce of the great and growing West, the trade of Baltimore was at that time notably diminishing. Baltimore, therefore and thereupon, took hold of the building of the Baltimore and Ohio Railroad, from that city to the Point of Rocks, and ultimately to some point on the Ohio River. Philip E. Thomas, who was then commissioner on the part of the State of Maryland in the Chesapeake and Ohio Canal Company, resigned that position, and in connection with George Brown, devoted himself thenceforth to the formation of the Baltimore and Ohio Railroad Company. George Brown was a brother of William Brown, afterward a member of the English Parliament, and was frequently in receipt from this English brother of documents containing much valuable information on the progress of the Manchester and Liverpool Railroad. Mr. Thomas also had a brother, Evan Thomas, of Baltimore, who was then in England, and who there collected many facts relative to the successful operation of the many short railroads then in existence in England, which facts he sent to his brother in this country. These facts and documents, upon being compared by Philip E. Thomas and George Brown, led them to the

21

conclusion that a railroad could be built and made practicable between Baltimore and the Western waters, and that on the early consummation of this enterprise depended the future commercial prosperity of Baltimore.

A meeting was therefore called, to be held at the residence of Mr. Brown on February 12, 1827, "to take into consideration the best means of restoring to the city of Baltimore that portion of the western trade which has lately been diverted from it by the introduction of steam navigation, and by other causes." The facts and documents above referred to, illustrating the efficiency of railroads for conveying articles of heavy carriage at small expense, were presented to the meeting, which became convinced that this mode of transportation was far superior to either common turnpike roads or canals, and a committee was appointed to collate and report upon the facts so presented, and to recommend the best course to be pursued to accomplish the object proposed. This committee was composed of Philip E. Thomas, George Brown, Benjamin C. Howard, Talbot Jones, Joseph W. Patterson, Evan Thomas, and John V. L. McMahon. Their report, a very able document, was presented to an adjourned meeting, held February 19, 1827. In this report they stated that even then 2,000 miles of railroad were "completed or in a rapid progress in that country, and that they had fully answered the most sanguine expectations of their projectors"; and they recommended "a double railroad" from Baltimore to the Ohio River. Maryland, in view of the activity of her citizens, incorporated the Baltimore and Ohio Railroad Company, in February, 1827, and at the same time repealed the condition of her subscription to the canal, that Congress should subscribe to the eastern section thereof. March 8, 1827, the charter of the company was enacted by Virginia, and on the 24th of April, the stock of the company having been subscribed, the company itself was organized, with the following directors: Charles Carroll of Carrollton, William Patterson, Robert Oliver, Alexander Brown, Isaac McKim, William Lorman, George Hoffman, Philip E. Thomas, Thomas Ellicott, John B. Morris, Talbot Jones, William Steuart. Philip E. Thomas was elected president of the company, and George Brown treasurer.

Upon application to the General Government a corps of engineers was deputed to survey a route for the railroad, consisting of Captain William Gibbs McNeill, Lieutenants Joshua Barney, Isaac Trimble, Richard E. Hazzard, William Cook, Walter Gwynn, and John L. Dillahunty, of the United States artillery, and William Har-

rison, Jr., assistant engineer. The company's engineers were Colonel
Stephen H. Long and Jonathan Knight.

On June 20, following, these engineers commenced their reconnoisance preparatory to selecting the route and site for the road. February
28, 1828, Pennsylvania chartered the railroad company in that State,
and on March 3 Maryland, mainly through the efforts of John V. L.
McMahon, authorized the subscription of half a million of dollars, on the
condition that the company locate the road so that it should go to or
strike the Potomac River at some point between the mouth of the Monocacy River and the town of Cumberland, in Allegheny County, and that
it go into Frederick, Washington, and Allegheny counties. The United
States engineers, on April 5, recommended that the route of the railroad from Baltimore should be along the valley of the Patapsco, and
then to the Point of Rocks, and afterward the company's engineers confirmed this opinion, saying that the route by the valley of the Potomac
possessed many advantages in respect to economy of construction, cost
of motive power, and prospective commercial advantages. Agents were
therefore sent out to secure the title to the lands along the proposed
route, along which, however, there was but little choice to be had.

The subscription books of the Baltimore and Ohio Railroad Company were closed March 31, 1827, on which day there were taken
13,387 shares, making in all 41,788 shares taken, of which 5,000 shares
had been taken by the city of Baltimore. The amount of money
subscribed in Baltimore alone was $4,178,800, divided among 22,000
persons or names.

The Baltimoreans were really in earnest, it began to be discovered,
about this railroad business, for by April 30, 1828, they were devising
a railroad from Baltimore to Washington. They applied to Congress
to allow them to make that part of it falling within the limits of the
District of Columbia on terms similar to those granted them in
the State of Maryland, the charge on the transportation of goods to
be not more than one cent per ton per mile for toll, and three cents
per ton per mile for transportation, and for passengers it was not to
exceed three cents per mile.

On the 4th of July, 1828, the corner stone of the Baltimore and
Ohio Railroad was laid by the venerable Charles Carroll, in the
presence of many thousands of people.

In January, 1829, four of "Winan's wagons" were put to work
on the Baltimore and Ohio Railroad, on a part of the road where
there was a curve of about five or six hundred feet radius; and, while
the rails made only a temporary road, and were not true, either

horizontally or on the curve, yet upon this road a horse drew these four wagons, loaded with gravel and sand which, together with the wagons, weighed fifteen tons, backward and forward upon the road with ease; and it would therefore appear that upon a road properly graded and graduated, one horse could perform the work of thirty horses on a common turnpike road.

For some time after work on this railroad commenced, the question of the use of locomotives remained unsolved. In March, 1829, their engineers were in England, observing the success of railroads in that country. Their attention was given particularly to locomotives, and they found that they could be used where the ascent was as much as 72 feet per mile. On a part of the Killingsworth Railroad, where the inclination was 50 feet per mile, a locomotive descended with 20 loaded cars and ascended with the same number of empty ones. On the Stockton and Darlington Railroad they saw a locomotive of ten horse-power descend a slope of 10 feet per mile with a train of 12 loaded cars at 15 miles per hour, and return with the same wagons loaded at the rate of 10 miles per hour. The weight of each wagon was 25 hundred-weight, and the load of coal weighed 53 hundred-weight, or in other words, the load was in the aggregate 45 tons. From observations such as these, it became evident that the power on railroads would soon be furnished by steam.

In January, 1831, application was made to Congress, by the Baltimore and Ohio Railroad Company, for permission to extend their road to the District of Columbia; but in this connection it was readily seen that if this company should be granted that privilege, the Washington Turnpike Company would be ruined. This company, some fifteen years previous to the time of asking for the privilege of extending the railroad, that is, in about 1815, when it was dangerous to attempt to travel over the wretched road then connecting Baltimore and Washington, and when at the best the journey took the better part of two days, had at great expense constructed their turnpike, and had accommodated the public in many ways. The turnpike had been largely advantageous to the two cities, and, in fact, to the entire country between them adjacent to the turnpike, and to everybody but to the stockholders themselves, who, a writer in the *National Intelligencer* said, did not for the first twelve years after constructing the road receive a cent in dividends; but that for the few years previous to 1830, the road had yielded something in the way of dividends; and then the Baltimore and Ohio Railroad Company "very modestly" came forward and proposed to make a railroad parallel to the turnpike, thus monopolizing a rich harvest and at the same time ruining the turnpike company. Such a course, though abstractly legal, was thought by some to be eminently unjust, inequitable, and impolitic; and hence it was argued that if Congress should give the Baltimore and Ohio Railroad Company the privilege of constructing its railroad from Baltimore to Washington, it was necessary, in order to be just, to compensate the turnpike company in some way for the losses that they would inevitably suffer.

As has been stated, the "corner stone" of this road was laid July 4, 1828, and with great ceremony. During the fall of 1829, the laying of the rails was commenced within the city of Baltimore, the first rails being laid on wooden sleepers, at the eastern end of the Mount Clare premises, under the direction of Major George W. Whistler and John Ready. The first division of the road was opened for passengers May 22, 1830, and during the first few months afterward the people of Baltimore continued to throng the depot to try the new mode of travel; and although but one track was completed and the number of cars limited, and these cars drawn by horses, yet the receipts up to the 1st of October amounted to $20,012.36. During the first year, there being no settled means of propulsion, Evan Thomas constructed a sailing car, which he named "The Eolus," which attracted wide attention. throughout the United States, and even in foreign countries. December 1, 1831, the opening of the branch road to Frederick was celebrated, and on April 1, 1832, the whole line was opened to the Point of Rocks, making seventy-three miles of the road then finished and in operation.

January 4, 1831, the company offered liberal inducements to the inventive genius and mechanical skill of the country for the production of locomotive steam engines. "The Baltimore and Ohio Railroad Company, being desirous of obtaining a supply of locomotive engines of American manufacture, adapted to their road, the president and directors hereby give public notice that they will pay the sum of $4,000 for the most approved engine, which must be delivered for trial upon the road on or before the 1st of June, 1831, and they will also pay $3,500 for the engine which. shall be adjudged the next best and be delivered as aforesaid," subject to nine separate conditions, one of the most notable of these conditions being that the engine "must not exceed three and a half tons in weight, and must on a level road be capable of drawing day by day fifteen tons, inclusive of the weight of the wagons, fifteen miles per hour." The company agreed to furnish Winan's wagons for the test.

The result of this call upon American mechanics was that three locomotives were produced, only one of which, however, answered the purposes of the company. This was made by Davis & Gartner, of York, Pennsylvania, and was named the "York." This locomotive traveled between Baltimore and Ellicott's Mills, a distance of about 12 miles, at the rate of from 15 miles per hour on curved portions of the road, to 30 miles per hour on straight portions of the line, though it did not displace horses for some time; indeed, the demands upon the road for transportation of freight and passengers were so great that it was not for some time after this that it had locomotives enough to allow of the doing away with horses. About October 1, 1831, the editor of the *National Intelligencer* had a ride on a railroad car for the first time, and as his paper had consistently favored the canal in preference to the railroad, it is interesting to note the impressions made on his mind by this novel mode of travel. He said: "We traveled in a large car, drawn by one horse, carrying eight or ten persons, capable, we suppose, of carrying thirty or forty. In the distance between Baltimore and Ellicott's Mills the horse was changed but once going and coming, and in returning, the whole distance, thirteen miles, was traveled in fifty-nine minutes. The locomotive steam machine, by which cars loaded with persons are occasionally drawn, is propelled at about the same rate, and might be propelled much more rapidly if it were desirable, but for our part we have no desire to be carried by any mode of conveyance more than thirteen miles per hour. . . . And we do not think we should feel safe on a railroad in traveling by night at anything like that speed. . . . We owe it to the general reader to say that nothing occurred in the short examination we were able to give to the matter to change the opinion we have heretofore advanced of the relative value of railroads and canals as great highways of commerce."

In January, 1832, the *Intelligencer* was still of the opinion that canals were much superior to railroads for all the purposes of commerce. This was, however, before the locomotive had become a success on railroads, and this fact ought to be taken into consideration when reflecting upon the pertinacity with which many people adhered to the same opinion. Canals were, of course, fully developed then, while railroading was in its infancy, though this fact, so clear now, was not capable of recognition then.

Both the Baltimore and Ohio Railroad and the Chesapeake and Ohio Canal were delayed in their construction two or three years by litigation brought on by the latter company obtaining an injunction from the county court of Washington County, restraining further proceedings of the railroad company in obtaining titles to lands over which their railroad must pass, and over which it had already been located. This was followed by the railroad company obtaining an injunction restraining the canal company from taking any further steps in the construction or location of the canal which might render unavailable a decision in favor of the railroad company on the first injunction. And as the owner of the fee simple to the title of the pass of the Potomac on the Catoctin Mountain at the Point of Rocks, the railroad company still continued to prosecute the construction of its road at that place. Then followed a second injunction by the canal company, restraining the railroad company from constructing the road at all in Frederick County, although the greater part of the railroad through that county could never come in collision with the canal. This last injunction was, however, afterward withdrawn by the canal company, so far as it related to land east of the Point of Rocks.

In January, 1832, the Court of Appeals decided the injunction cases by the Chesapeake and Ohio Canal Company against the railroad company, the decision preventing the railroad company from appropriating or using land for the railroad until the canal company should have located its canal between the Point of Rocks and Harper's Ferry, and the progress of the railroad was thus for a time arrested again. The available space in the district to be preoccupied by the canal was either too narrow to admit the parallel passage of both the canal and railroad, or would at least be used by the canal company at its usual extreme breadth, and this would effectually exclude the railroad. There were, therefore, but four alternative modes of procedure:

1. To procure the permission of the canal company for the construction of the two works side by side from the Point of Rocks to Harper's Ferry.

2. To construct the railroad alongside of the canal upon such site as might remain after the canal company had exercised its right of choice.

3. To cross the Potomac at the Point of Rocks and ascend the valley on the Virginia side.

4. To tunnel through the mountain spurs.

After a great deal of trouble and delay and perverseness on the part of both companies, an adjustment was at length made by the passage of a law by the State of Maryland, March 22, 1833, by which the railroad company was to pay the canal company $266,000 for all claims under the law, which was called the compromise act, this adjustment being brought about mainly through the influence and efforts of Charles F. Mayer, effectively assisted by B. S. Pigman, of Allegheny County. May 9, 1833, therefore, the canal company commenced the joint construction of the canal and railroad, from the Point of Rocks to Harper's Ferry, and on December 1, 1834, the road was opened for travel and freight transportation to Harper's Ferry.

In the meantime, the corps of engineers, under the direction of Benjamin H. Latrobe, were rapidly bringing to a close the surveys of a branch of the road to Washington, and on March 9, 1833, an act was passed under which this branch was constructed, and by which the Washington and Baltimore Turnpike Company, the destruction of whose interests were so much feared by some, was permitted to subscribe for a certain amount of the stock of the railroad company. The bridge over the Patapsco River was immediately put under contract. When completed, this bridge was a magnificent granite viaduct, consisting of eight elliptical arches, each of fifty-eight feet span, with the roadway sixty-six feet above the surface of the water. It was designed by Benjamin H. Latrobe, and was at that time the largest structure of the kind in the United States. In the case of this viaduct, as well as that of the branch road to Washington, the expense of construction was actually within the estimate.

This lateral branch of the railroad from Baltimore to Washington was in an advanced stage of progress in April, 1835. The contractor for that portion of it that lay within the limits of the District of Columbia was Mr. Ennis, who broke ground upon his portion of the road April 21. Mr. Belt had the contract from the limits of the District to Bladensburg, and had then considerable of his work completed. On July 1, the president and directors, together with the principal officers of the railroad, accompanied by several citizens of Baltimore, made a trip of inspection over this road, coming down to Bladensburg, at which place they were met by the Mayor of Washington and others. The rails laid- down on this branch were of improved construction, and greatly superior to any previously in use. The locomotive which brought the party down from Baltimore was " of great power," and each car comfortably accommodated sixty passengers. The road would have been completed to Washington by that time, but for the delay in the arrival of a cargo of iron, which did not sail from England until May 16, but which should have sailed a month earlier. On Wednesday, July 8, 1835, the company began running passenger trains between Baltimore and Bladensburg, passengers being taken from Washington to Bladensburg by stage coaches.

"By applying our modern mode of computing distances,—by hours, instead of days and miles,—the distance between the two cities of Baltimore and Washington is henceforth to be two hours; that from Washington to New York, twenty-six hours; and from Washington to Boston, forty hours! Are we in a dream?"

On Monday, July 20, 1835, trains commenced running down to the District line, twice each day, occasionally making twenty miles per hour. The first locomotive run on the Baltimore and Washington Railroad was named the "General Washington," and others succeeding this one were named after the Presidents of the United States. William Gwynn was the engineer of the "General Washington," which locomotive was a kind of marvel of the times, running thirty successive days, conveying a train of passenger cars more than seventy miles per day, without requiring to be repaired!

On August 25, 1835, occurred the opening of the Baltimore and Washington Railroad to Washington. "Two cars will leave the ticket office at the intersection of Second Street West and Pennsylvania Avenue this day [Sunday] at 4:00 P. M., to convey the invited guests to Baltimore, to join the train from Baltimore on Tuesday. A car will leave Washington on Tuesday morning at ten o'clock to convey the members of the corporations of Washington, Alexandria, and Georgetown to Bladensburg to meet the trains from Baltimore." August 25, 1835, was a great day in Washington. "It was a glorious sight to see four trains of cars, each with its engine, extending altogether several hundred yards in length, making their entry by this new route, to the delight of thousands, to a spectator on elevated grounds north of the Capitol." The number of persons brought in on the trains from Baltimore was about one thousand, accompanied by two brass bands. They marched to Gadsby's and Brown's hotels, at both of which bounteous and sumptuous entertainments had been provided. The trains arrived in Washington about one o'clock, and started on the return trip about four o'clock.

On September 15, 1835, the trains began to run on schedule time, leaving Washington at 9:00 A. M., and 4:30 P. M., and leaving Baltimore at 8:15 A. M., and 4:00 P. M. "As there is no standard time in Washington, it is recommended to passengers to be at the depot before the hours named for the departure of the cars."

The receipts of this road for the following four months in 1836 were as follows: April, $19,230.33; May, $22,189.45; June, $18,613.91; July, $17,648.07; total, $77,681.76.

In July, 1842, an arrangement was made with Messrs. Baring Brothers, of London, England, by which they agreed to furnish the iron requisite to finish the Baltimore and Ohio Railroad to Cumberland, on a credit of seven years, $50,000 to be paid each year, thus, it was thought, placing the construction of the road to Cumberland to that point, early the ensuing fall, beyond doubt. In 1849, the road was extended west of Cumberland twelve miles. When it was determined to extend the road from Cumberland to Wheeling, T. W. Ward, attorney for the Barings, of London, under date of December 31, 1849, telegraphed to Thomas Swann, president of the Baltimore and Ohio Railroad Company, "The contract is made at five pounds ten." Twenty-three thousand tons was the amount purchased at this price.

This company, in 1851, erected some valuable improvements in this city: First, an engine house; second, a car house; third, the main building, which was 119 feet on New Jersey Avenue, was two stories high, and had a tower 100 feet high. J. H. McMachen, of Baltimore, superintended the work, and M. G. Emery, of Washington, executed the granite work.

A most interesting experiment was made on the Baltimore and Ohio Railroad on the last Tuesday in April, 1851, by Professor Charles G. Page, with his electro-magnetic locomotive, running it from Washington to Bladensburg and back. It was made, however, with only half the power the engines and batteries were capable of yielding. Each engine was estimated by Professor Page at twelve horse-power, which would make the locomotive twenty-four horse-power. The locomotive, with batteries full charged, weighed ten and a half tons. With the seven passengers taken on the trip it weighed eleven tons. Under the most favorable arrangements, eight pounds were required to start a ton on a perfectly level rail, and seven pounds would barely keep a ton in motion. The magnetic locomotive, the first of its kind ever made, being imperfect and full of stiffness in all its parts, ran very hard. A horse-power, on the usual estimates, is one hundred and fifty pounds running two and a half miles per hour, or three hundred and seventy-five pounds running one mile per hour. The speed of the magnetic locomotive was fifteen miles per hour on a level road, and its traction was two hundred pounds. It was therefore estimated that this locomotive developed eight horse-power, when in motion. But it had a greater power at a lower speed. After the engine was on the road it was found necessary to throw out of action five of the helices, and these at the most important part of the stroke. This difficulty could not be overcome without taking out both of the engines, which could not be done at the time. Another difficulty encountered on this experimental trip was the breaking of the porous cells in the battery, causing a mixture of the two acids and the interception of a large portion of the power. In all, seven of the porous cells broke, which took away one-half of the power. Going to Bladensburg the locomotive was stopped five times, or the run would have been made in thirty minutes. One very important and interesting feature of this magnetic locomotive was that its reversing power was greater than its propelling power, nearly twice as great, in fact, which Professor Page had demonstrated several years before.

In October, 1851, Professor Page presented his locomotive to the Smithsonian Institution, which, with its accompanying electro-magnet, forms one of the most prominent and interesting features in the philosophical department. This is the same engine that worked the Morse telegraph in 1844. It was constructed with reference to the maximum quantity of electricity to be obtained by magneto-electric excitement, to ascertain whether the electricity so obtained would be sufficient to operate an electro-magnetic engine, which in its turn should furnish sufficient magnetic power to keep the magneto-electric machine in motion, but it was never tested for this purpose.

The Baltimore and Ohio Railroad was so far completed in December, 1852, that the first train passed over it from Baltimore to Wheeling on the 31st of that month, in fifteen hours and fifteen minutes.

On March 3, 1853, Congress passed an act providing that whenever Maryland should incorporate a company to lay out and construct a railroad from any point in connection with the Baltimore and Ohio Railroad, at or near the Point of Rocks, to Georgetown, in the District of Columbia, the right of way should be granted to such company, provided, that before any such road, or its depots, or its fixtures should be located in Georgetown, the consent of the citizens of that place should be obtained. May 5, 1853, the Maryland Legislature incorporated the Metropolitan Railroad Company, naming John W. Maury, W. W. Corcoran, W. W. Seaton, David English, Francis Dodge, and Frederick W. Risque, of the District of Columbia; Charles E. Trail, Jacob M. Kenkel, and Meredith Davis, of Frederick County; Robert T. Dade, William Lingan Gaither, and Frances C. Clopper, of Montgomery County; David Weisel, James Wason, and Elias Davis, of Washington, as commissioners to receive subscriptions to the capital stock of the company, requiring them to keep the subscription books open, the first time they were open, for at least ten days; and then, if sufficient subscriptions were not received, they might keep them open from time to time for twelve months, or until a sufficient amount of stock were subscribed to warrant the organization of a company. The capital stock was fixed at $2,000,000, in shares of $50 each, and as soon as ten thousand shares should be subscribed the company was declared incorporated, by the name of the Metropolitan Railroad Company.

The commissioners held the first meeting at the Union Hotel in Georgetown, and it was there determined to open books for subscriptions June 6, and to keep them open until the close of the 16th of the month. The banks at Washington, Georgetown, Frederick, Maryland, Boonesborough, and at Hagerstown were to act as agents to receive subscriptions. The result of the subscriptions for the first ten days was that at Washington there were subscribed 1,806 shares; at Georgetown, 6,723; at Rockville, 220; at Hagerstown, 216; and at Frederickstown, 115; total, 9,080. Thus there was a deficiency of 920 shares, and a necessity for a second opening of the books. These books closed the second time on July 2, 1853, at which time the subscriptions stood as follows: Georgetown, 7,057; Washington, 2,200; Montgomery County, 388; Frederick County, 140; Washington County, 224; total, 10,009; though in order to make up this number the commissioners from Georgetown and two of those from Washington, themselves, on July 5, took about 400 shares. The counties through which the road was to pass took very little interest in the road, as may be seen from their subscriptions. The number of shares having been subscribed, a meeting was held at Union Hotel July 28, for the purpose of electing twelve directors, who were elected, as follows: John W. Maury, W. W. Corcoran, George Parker, and Joseph Bryan, of Washington; David English, A. H. Dodge, William M. Boyce, A. H. Pickrell, and H. C. Matthews, of Georgetown; F. C. Clopper, of Montgomery County; Meredith Davis, of Frederick County; and Daniel Weisel, of Washington County.

June 28, 1854, at a meeting of the directors, the report of the engineer on the subject of the location of the route was received, the following route having been selected: Leaving Georgetown on Prospect Street, passing around south of the college, up the Fountain Branch and on toward Drover's Rest; thence to the easterly part of

Rockville; thence passing on near Gaithersburg, about one mile east of Barnesville; then passing the west side of Sugar-Loaf Mountain and running to the Baltimore and Ohio Railroad, about five miles west of Monocacy Viaduct; thence direct to Frederick; from Frederick to Hagerstown by way of Getzenstanner's Gap, on the Catoctin Mountain, and Turner's Gap, on the South Mountain, passing east of Boonesborough to Hagerstown.

The route having been selected, the great question still remained, which could only be determined by the public, and that was: Should the work of construction be commenced. It could not commence without substantial aid from the upper counties through which it was to pass, and they had shown how much interest they took in the project by the number of shares of stock for which they had subscribed. Francis Dodge was president of the company at that time.

In January, 1863, President Lincoln sent a message to each branch of Congress on this subject. Its great benefits to Washington were fully and graphically set forth in the public prints, and an estimate was made of what it would have saved the Government had it been completed before the war. So far, of course, all efforts to construct this road had resulted in failure.

July 1, 1864, an act of Congress to incorporate the Metropolitan Railroad Company was approved, and amended by an act approved March 3, 1865, three years being given in which the company might complete the road. In March, 1865, an act was passed by the Maryland Legislature naming as commissioners to receive subscriptions to the stock of the company, G. W. Riggs, Richard Wallach, and Henry Willard, of Washington; Henry Addison, Henry D. Cooke, and John T. Mitchell, of Georgetown; Francis C. Clopper, Walter M. Talbott, Allen B. Davis, Thomas Lausdale, and Nicholas D. Offut, of Montgomery County; and Charles E. Trail, Jacob M. Kemkel, and Robert H. McGill, of Frederick County, Maryland. The capital stock of the company was as before fixed at $2,000,000, in shares of $50 each, and when ten thousand shares were subscribed the commissioners were to call a general meeting of the subscribers for the purpose of selecting directors to manage the affairs of the company.

The Metropolitan Railroad afterward became a part of the Baltimore and Ohio Railroad system, and is now operated as such. It was completed May 28, 1873, and is forty-two and three-quarters miles long.

The Baltimore and Potomac Railroad Company was organized under a charter granted by Congress, May 6, 1853. December 18, 1858, at a meeting held at Upper Marlborough, seven directors were elected, as follows: Edward Robinson, of Virginia; J. S Sellman, of Anne Arundel County; Edmund J. Plowden, of St. Mary's; John W. Jenkins and Walter Mitchell, of Charles County; W. D. Bowie and W. W. Bowie, of Prince George's County. The contemplated road was to extend from Baltimore to a point on the Potomac River opposite Acquia Creek, and to have a branch running into Washington. But little was accomplished on this work for a number of years. About March 1, 1867, the first five miles were graded, extending from the crossing of the Annapolis bridge to the Patuxent River. It was then taken hold of by Northern capitalists and pushed forward with considerable energy, and the road was so far completed that it was opened for travel July 2, 1872, the first train leaving Baltimore at 9:15 A. M., and reaching Washington at 1:00 P. M. Trains from Alexandria and Fredericksburg also began arriving at the Sixth and B Street depot on the same day. The road was completed to Pope's Creek January 1, 1873. The main line, extending from Baltimore to Pope's Creek, is 73.13 miles long, and the branch running from Bowie Station to Washington is 18.93 miles in length. This railroad is a continuation of the Pennsylvania system, and connects with the Southern railroads through the National Capital and over the Long Bridge.

The Washington and Alexandria Railroad Company was incorporated by an act of the Legislature of Virginia, passed February 27, 1854, the commissioners to receive subscriptions, named in the act, being James S. French, John W. Maury, A. J. Marshall, Cornelius Boyle, George French, Edgar Snowden, and R. W. Latham. The capital stock of the company was limited to $300,000, in shares of $100 each. The purpose of the company was to construct a railroad on the plan of J. S. French, "as set forth to the House of Delegates in document No. 65, session of 1850-51," and whenever two thousand shares should be subscribed the company was to be considered incorporated, under the name of the Alexandria and Washington Railroad Company. Mr. French claimed for his plan greater security for passengers, and the ability to use lighter machinery.

This road was completed so that the first train passed over it November 1, 1856. The first train consisted of four cars drawn by the locomotive "John T. Towers." Cars commenced running on regular time November 25, 1856. The road was eight miles in length. It was sold April 10, 1862, to Alexander Hay, of Philadelphia, for $12,500, subject to a judgment of $250,000. May 3, 1862, the company was reorganized under the name of the Washington and

Georgetown Railroad, with a board of five directors — Alexander Hay, Joseph Thornton, Horace M. Day, Silas Seymour, and Joseph B. Stewart. Mr. Hay was elected president, Mr. Stewart secretary, Mr. Thornton treasurer, and Mr. Seymour general superintendent.

The gentlemen thus placed in charge of the interests of the company endeavored to secure from Congress a new charter for the company, for the erection of a branch across the Potomac River and the right of way through certain streets of the city of Washington.

This was in time accomplished, and the road received the name of the Washington City and Point Lookout Railroad Company, under the charter granted in 1871. The company was required to build a railroad from Washington to Point Lookout, a distance of eighty miles. The work of grading this road was commenced in 1872, and that portion of the road extending from the Baltimore and Ohio Railroad at Hyattsville to the Potomac River, opposite Alexandria, completed in 1875. It was leased to the Baltimore and Ohio Railroad Company for $36,000 per annum, payable in gold, one-tenth part of which was annually appropriated to extinguishing the issue of bonds maturing June 1, 1913. Default of interest was made July 1, 1882, and under a decree of foreclosure granted September 1, 1885, the road was sold for $75,000 January 13, 1886, and the bondholders formed a new railroad company in April, 1886, under the name of the Washington and Potomac Railroad Company.

The Washington and Chesapeake Beach Railway Company was chartered in 1882, with an authorized capital of $100,000. It has very recently secured power to establish a seaside resort at Chesapeake Beach, in Calvert County, Maryland, and will construct a railroad twenty-eight miles long, connecting with the Baltimore and Potomac Railroad at Upper Marlborough, and with the Baltimore and Ohio Railroad near the east line of the District of Columbia. It is expected that the road will be completed about August 1, 1892.

The first bridge across Rock Creek was built in 1792 or 1793, by the commissioners of the District of Columbia. It was on K Street, and consisted of a single arch, the arch being composed of stones representing the several States of the Union, as they were then. The keystone had upon it the shield of Pennsylvania, and it is believed that it was from this fact that Pennsylvania has always been known as the "Keystone State." The theory of making K Street as wide as Pennsylvania Avenue was, that a great deal of wagoning would cross the creek and go on out toward Bladensburg.

In the winter of 1807–08, an act was passed by Congress authorizing the construction of a bridge across the Potomac River within the District of Columbia. Subscription books were opened at Stelle's Hotel, April 1, 1808. Subscriptions were authorized up to two thousand shares, $10 of each share to be paid at the time of subscribing, and the residue to be paid in installments of $10 each when called for by the commissioners. The commissioners appointed under this act were Robert Brent, Daniel Carroll of Duddington, Thomas Munroe, James D. Barry, Frederick May, Samuel H. Smith, Jonah Thompson, Jonathan Swift, Thomas Vowell, Cuthbert Powell, Elisha Janney, and Charles Alexander. These commissioners were authorized to open subscription books for raising a capital stock not to exceed $200,000, in shares of $100 each, for the purpose of erecting a bridge over the Potomac between the city of Washington and Alexander's Island. Whenever nineteen hundred shares of stock should be subscribed for, in accordance with the provisions of the act of Congress, they were to be considered a corporation under the name and style of the Washington Bridge Company; and as soon thereafter as practicable the commissioners were required to call a meeting of the stockholders for the purpose of electing five directors, a clerk, and a treasurer, and such other officers as might be deemed necessary. A meeting was therefore held on Monday, May 2, 1808, at Stelle's Hotel, for the election of the above-named officers, the directors being Daniel Carroll, George Blagden, Frederick May, William Harper, and Robert Young. Daniel Carroll was elected president. On May 4, the company advertised for timbers of various kinds with which to build the bridge, and also for the iron work, carpenters, and laborers. Thomas Vowell was elected treasurer, and Samuel Elliott, Jr., clerk. The bridge was so far completed as to be opened for travel May 20, 1809, but as it was not quite finished, passage to and fro was free for a few days.

Up the Potomac River, about three miles above Georgetown, a bridge was built across the river by Mr. Palmer. It was of wood, and in about seven years fell to pieces from the natural processes of decay. The second bridge erected at this place was by Mr. Burr, architect of the celebrated Trenton bridge, and on the same principles, and was also of wood. This bridge lasted about six months, having cost about $80,000; but the abutments were not destroyed when the bridge itself gave out. The third bridge was erected upon the principles of that built a few years before by Judge Findley near Uniontown, Pennsylvania, over Jacob's Creek. It was a suspension bridge, supported solely by iron chains thrown over piers erected upon the abutments about twenty feet high. These chains were four in number, and the pendents were hung upon the chains alternately about five feet apart, so that each chain received a pendent in every ten feet. This manner of construction was, however, in violation of the instructions of the inventor, Judge Findley, who said that one chain on each side would have been sufficient, and one-half the pendents, so that the bridge as constructed had more than twice the strength that it would ever need, and of course cost a great deal more than was necessary. The four chains, hanging as they did, were able, according to Judge Findley, to sustain from 225 to 280 tons, and from the manner in which the pendents were strung on the chains it was next to impossible that any one of the pendents would ever have to bear one-fortieth of what it was able to bear. The span of this bridge was 128½ feet, the width 16 feet, and the weight 22 tons. The cost was less than $4,000. The wood part of this bridge could easily be repaired, and it was confidently expected that the iron portion would last a century. Judge Findley's plan of bridge building was considered the most valuable then discovered, combining great strength and durability, and also extreme cheapness.

On February 13, 1840, this chain bridge was entirely carried away by a freshet, and its timbers floated down the river.

The Washington Bridge, mentioned above, was opened for traffic May 31, 1809. It had cost $100,000. It had a broad carriage way in the center and a footway on each side, set off by a double rail for the protection of pedestrians. It was a wooden structure, and nearly a mile long. The toll was twenty-five cents for a man and horse, and $1 for a four-wheeled horse-carriage and a pair of horses. But this toll never paid a reasonable profit to the company. Notwithstanding that this toll was enormous, it superseded the use of any adjacent ferry for twenty years, and furnished continuous communication between the two sides of the Potomac. Neither was there any serious accident to it until February 22, 1831, when a freshet swept away a considerable portion of it. For some time afterward its use was suspended.

The company asked Congress for assistance to rebuild the bridge, but during the discussion of the question a bill was introduced, and finally became a law, appropriating $20,000 to purchase the rights of the bridge company, and $60,000 to reconstruct the bridge, the plan to be approved by the President. The plan approved by the President was a most elaborate one, reported by George C. Gratiot and Colonel James Kearney. These engineers reported the plan of an iron bridge,

22

which would cost probably about $1,293,250, while a wooden bridge would not cost more than about $706,110. President Jackson, in ‑a message to Congress, stated that he had adopted the wooden bridge in preference to the iron one. Congress soon afterward appropriated $200,000 toward the construction of any bridge that the President might approve, and on April 11, 1833, proposals were published by order of the President, through the Secretary of the Treasury, for the construction of a bridge with stone abutments and with piers and arches of stone, and by May 1 it was currently reported in the District of Columbia that a contract had been entered into for the construction of a bridge, and that the bridge so contracted for would cost nearly $2,500,000. But a misunderstanding arising between the contractors and the Secretary of the Treasury, no contract was in reality completed, and consequently the commencement of the work was delayed. Soon afterward O. H. Dibble, who had been for some years a contractor on the Chesapeake and Ohio Canal, offered to construct the proposed bridge, substituting solid masonry for stone piers and abutments resting on piers, and to do all the work for $1,350,000. The proposition of Mr. Dibble was accepted December 6, 1833. Congress was then in session, but the question was not submitted to that body as to whether it approved the substitution of a bridge costing $1,350,000 for one for which it had appropriated $200,000.

Charles Fenton Mercer was a member of Congress, at that time, from Virginia. On the 20th of December, Mr. Mercer offered a resolution in the House of Representatives couched in the following language: "That the President of the United States be requested to lay before this House a copy of any contract which may have been made for the construction of a bridge across the Potomac River at Washington, together with the authority under which the contract may have been made; the names of the contractors and their securities, if any; and the plan and estimate of the cost of such bridge."

An answer was received to this resolution, January 7, 1834, and referred to the Committee on Roads and Canals. This committee promptly decided that it was incompetent to proceed with the construction of the stone bridge across the Potomac, which would cost, according to the estimates of the best engineers, anywhere from $2,000,000 to $5,000,000; and the chairman of the committee, Mr. Mercer, on the 10th of February, reported a bill to repeal all acts theretofore passed on the subject of the Washington Bridge, except so much of the first act — that of July 14, 1832, — as authorized the contract with the Washington Bridge Company and the reconstruction of the bridge at a cost not exceeding $130,000, on the site and plan of the old bridge, provided that upon the shoals between the main channels a solid embankment might be made, not exceeding one thousand, six hundred and sixty feet in length, which was one-third of the space between the abutments of the old bridge.

According to surveys made in the winter of 1832–33, the width of the river at the point where the bridge was constructed was 4,984 feet, as follows: Middle channel, 575 feet; flats, 943 feet; swash channel, 437 feet; flats, 1,716 feet; Virginia channel, 942 feet; to the shore, 371 feet. Of all this breadth there was not more than 450 feet of firm bottom, and in some places this firm bottom could not be reached at a less depth than 26 feet. It was thought that 42 feet in height would be sufficient to permit the passage of steamboats, without taking into account the height of chimneys, as they could be lowered. According to Lieutenant-Colonel Kearney, the bridge would be somewhat as follows, if built in conformity to the act of Congress:

Proceeding from the Maryland abutment, for 3 arches and 3 piers, 292 feet; for the Washington draw and pier, 88 feet; for 33 arches and piers, to the opening of the Georgetown pier, 3,734 feet; for the Georgetown draw and pier, 88 feet; for 4 arches and 6 piers, 452 feet; for 3 arches and 2 piers descending, 270 feet; total, 4,924 feet.

The plan decided on by the President for a bridge across the Potomac is interesting, as showing what he would have done had he not been prevented by the economical spirit of Congress. He had decided upon it previous to April 11, 1833, as he was required to do by Congress. That plan was as follows: The bridge was to have had 41 arches and 2 draws; 42 piers and 2 abutments with their half-piers. The arches were to have been of 96 feet span, and 25 feet rise above the springing line, and were to be curves of several centers, all semi-elliptical. The piers and abutments were to have risen 7 feet above low water. The draws were to have been 66 feet wide, one to be placed at the Maryland channel, the other at the Virginia channel. The bridge was to have been 36 feet wide between the parapets, and the piers, arches, and abutments were to have been of granite. A full and particular description of this proposed bridge of. President Jackson, which the engineers estimated to cost from $2,000,000 to $5,000,000, was published by Hon. Louis McLane, Secretary of the Treasury, commencing with April 12, 1833.

The bridge that was built in the place of this proposed one was opened for traffic October 29, 1835. George W. Hughes was the engineer of construction. According to his report the bridge cost $113,126, nearly $17,000 less than the sum appropriated for it by Congress. The engineer said that he considered the bridge very uncertain as to its existence. Under favorable circumstances it might last thirty years, and it might be destroyed within a year. But no one was to blame for the building of such a bridge but Congress, which should not have permitted the erection of anything but a substantial bridge.

The doleful predictions of the engineer as to the existence of this bridge began to be realized in May, 1836, in which month a freshet did considerable damage to it. On June 7, Congress passed a joint resolution authorizing the Secretary of the Treasury "to have all repairs made to the bridge across the Potomac River which have become necessary from the late flood; and that the expense of said repairs be paid out of the money heretofore appropriated for the erection of said bridge, and which is now in the treasury unexpended." December 7, 1836, Hon. Levi Woodbury, Secretary of the Treasury, submitted a statement to Congress showing that in the aggregate there had been expended on the repairs to the bridge, to the causeway, to the draws, to the abutments, etc., $11,992.65, and that there was still left of the original appropriation $4,194.18, which was applicable to the grading, graveling, and planting of Maryland Avenue.

On March 3, 1839, the jurisdiction of the corporation of Washington was extended over this bridge. In February, 1840, a freshet occurred, which carried away the chain bridge above the Little Falls and did great damage to the Long Bridge. This disaster caused inquiry into the propriety of the location of Long Bridge, and some were of the opinion that a better one could be found where the Alexandria Canal Company's aqueduct crossed the river. These people reasoned that the Alexandria and Falmouth Railroad Company would soon be seeking a passage across the Potomac, and it was thought that the railroad should cross the river in connection with the aqueduct. Others thought there was no insuperable obstacle to making Long Bridge a permanent structure, nothing being required to this end but stone piers at each of the draws, and ice-blockers above, strong enough to resist and check the mass of floating ice. What was necessary was to cause the ice to float, for then it would not dam up the stream and cause an immense pressure of water against the bridge. The difficulty in the way of getting a good bridge built was that committees of Congress were not in the habit of consulting with men who understood the work that was to be done.

"Ignorance, even when opportunity has existed to remove it, assumes a humble degree of respectability when it candidly shows itself; when it seeks to disguise itself in the habit of knowledge it becomes ridiculous; but, unfortunately, the consequences of the deceit are sometimes too mischievous to be contemptible."

In the winter of 1856-57, an attempt was made on the part of certain persons to secure the discontinuance of the Long Bridge. Of course this movement was opposed by others. A meeting of the citizens of Alexandria was held February 20, 1857, for the purpose of expressing hostility to the proposed removal of the bridge. They considered that the aqueduct as a point of transit from one side of the river to the other would make their northern connection by ordinary means exceedingly inconvenient, and earnestly urged their Representatives and Senators in Congress to use their best efforts to avert the calamity. There was also a movement started in Alexandria to prevent the piers of the aqueduct over the Potomac from being used for the support of a railroad bridge. A committee of citizens waited on the committee of the House of Representatives, February 25, 1857, addressing them on the immediate reconstruction of the bridge, making the offer of the Washington and Alexandria Railroad Company to repair the bridge and keep it in repair if Congress would permit the construction of a railroad track over it. Georgetown was not asleep on this subject. Mayor Addison called a meeting of the citizens to formulate an expression of their sentiments, the meeting to be held on the 26th of the month. Citizens of Washington also assembled in mass meeting in the evening of the 26th, in the City Hall, for the same purpose. At this meeting the Mayor presided, and J. Carroll Brent acted as secretary. A series of resolutions was presented and adopted, expressing hearty sympathy with the people of Alexandria in their desire for the continuance of the Long Bridge, the site upon which it stood being best adapted for communication between the north and south sides of the river. A committee was appointed consisting of twenty persons, afterward enlarged to twenty-six, to lay the whole subject before Congress; this committee consisting in part of the Mayor, W. B Magruder, and Ex-Mayors W. W. Seaton, Peter Force, Walter Lenox, and John T. Towers.

Without pursuing this subject into detail, it is sufficient to say that the movement of the citizens in the way above described, prevented the entire destruction of Long Bridge by Congressional authority, and in due time measures were taken to again repair the bridge, the Councils of the city of Washington appropriating $5,000 toward that object. This was on May 25, 1857. By November 1, 1858, the bridge was again repaired so as to be put in use.

In February, 1867, the Long Bridge was carried away by floating ice, rendering communication between the two sides of the river impossible, except by way of the chain bridge, involving an ordinary day's journey. In the emergency thus created, the lessees of the canal offered the Government the use of the piers of the aqueduct for the erection of a permanent bridge over the Potomac. This offer, however, was not accepted, and Long Bridge has been kept up until the present day.

The first movement looking toward the construction of a street railroad in Washington was made in 1854, a memorial of the citizens of Washington and Georgetown being presented to Congress about February 1, that year, praying that authority might be granted to George W. Yerby and others to construct a horse-power railroad through Pennsylvania Avenue and other public thoroughfares of the city of Washington. This memorial was signed by a great number of citizens. This project aroused considerable opposition, those opposed saying that such a railroad was uncalled for by either public or private necessity; that it would be hurtful to the true interests of the city, most injurious to the convenience and beauty of the principal thoroughfares of the city; that it would make the avenue totally unsuitable for the purposes for which it was originally designed.

But little, if anything, appears to have been accomplished in the direction of the construction of this road until May 25, 1858, on which day the House of Representatives passed a bill, authorizing Gilbert Vanderwerken, Bayard Clarke, Asa P. Robinson, and their assigns, to construct and lay down a double-track railroad on Pennsylvania Avenue and Fifteenth Street, from the west gate of the Capitol grounds to the city line of Georgetown, the cars to be drawn by horse power, and the rate of fare not to exceed five cents. The charter of the road was for twenty-five years.

That the corporation was not opposed to this enterprise is shown by the action taken by the Councils, December 30, 1858, on which day they adopted the following resolutions:

"That the joint committee of the Councils to attend to the interests of the corporation before Congress be, and they are hereby, instructed to request and urge upon Congress to pass such law or laws as will give to this corporation full power and authority to authorize the construction of railroads in the streets of the city of Washington, and to control, regulate, and tax the same.

"That the Mayor be, and he is hereby, requested to have a copy of these resolutions transmitted to the President of the Senate and the Speaker of the House of Representatives, and to every member of the Senate and House of Representatives of the United States."

A meeting was held November 10, 1859, to further the effort to construct a railroad from the Navy Yard in Washington to some point in Georgetown. Mr. George Mattingly submitted a report, accompanied by articles of agreement, and a bill to be submitted to Congress at its next session for enactment. The principal feature of the articles of compact was that not more than ten shares of stock should be taken by any one person, until after the public had had three days' opportunity to subscribe. The act also provided that there should be a president and nine directors to superintend the construction of the road, which should not be of less than four feet gauge, which must be commenced within six months from the passage of the act, and be completed within two years.

A third meeting of the citizens was held Tuesday, November 15, at which time a petition for a charter received forty-eight signatures, and $33,000 of stock was subscribed. A committee of five was appointed to· solicit additional signatures, and a second committee of five to appoint a committee of thirty to secure the charter from Congress. At another meeting, held on the 25th, a little over $100,000 was subscribed, and by the 26th the subscription had reached $190,000. By December 1, the entire $200,000 was secured, taken by four hundred and fourteen subscribers.

In 1862, it began to be hoped that the city would enjoy the privileges of a street railroad. The war was concentrating in and around Washington a population of nearly 200,000, including the encampments. Officers and men complained of the inconveniences of moving about from one part of the city to another. There were but few hacks, and they could not be obtained except at a rate of $2 per hour, or for a visit to the camps, even within the city limits, without making a $10 job of it. An act incorporating this company was approved May 17, 1862, and books for the subscription of stock were opened May 23. The name of the company thus incorporated was the Washington and Georgetown Railroad Company. By this charter the capital stock was required to be not less than $300,000 nor more than $500,000, and the Bank of Washington was selected as the depository of its funds. E. Kingman was chosen president, and J. J Coombs secretary. Of the 6,000 shares of stock issued, 1,327 were taken in Washington, 42 in Georgetown, and the rest mainly in New

York and Philadelphia. But in the apportionment of directors, four were given to the District of Columbia, two to Philadelphia, and one to New York. Work on the road was immediately commenced, and by August 13 it was completed to Georgetown, with the exception of a small piece across the aqueduct bridge over Rock Creek, and there were fifteen cars running as far as the Circle, in connection with omnibuses to Georgetown, at five cents from one end of the line to the other. October 2, 1862, the cars commenced running to the Navy Yard, and then the whole line was in operation from the Navy Yard to Georgetown. The line down Seventh Street to the river was completed November 14, 1862.

In July, 1865, the statistics of this road were as follows: Number of cars per day, 60; number of trips, 941; average number of trips for each car, 16; whole number of trips during the year, 343,465; number of passengers carried during the year, 8,651,223; gross earnings of the road during the year, $450,000.

The officers of the Washington and Georgetown Railroad Company since its organization have been as follows: Presidents — H. D. Cooke, 1862–63; George S. Gideon, 1863–67; William Duning, a few months in 1867 and 1868; S. S. Riker, 1868–74; Samuel L. Phillips, six months in 1874; Henry Hurt, 1874 to the present time. Secretaries and Treasurers — H. C. Fahnestock for the first few months; William C. Greenleaf, 1862–67; A. W. Nichols, 1867–70; Henry Hurt, 1870–74; C. M. Koones, 1874 to the present time.

The Seventh Street road was changed to a cable road May 1, 1890. The plant by which the cable is propelled is situated on Square No. 504, between Water and Four and a Half streets, and fronting on the Arsenal. In this power house are two engines, each of two hundred and fifty horse-power, but capable of developing five hundred horse-power each. The legislation under which this cable road was built was permissive only, but in 1890 Congress passed a supplemental act requiring the entire system of the Washington and Georgetown Railroad to be operated by cable or electricity, and the change to be completed in two years from the passage of the act. Under this legislation, which was really unnecessary, as the company intended to change from horse power to the cable system, the change to the cable system is now in progress, and will be completed within the time required by law, which expires August 6, 1892. The power house in which the machinery will be located is being erected on Square No. 255, between Thirteen and a Half and Fourteenth streets, and D and E streets Northwest. The estimated cost of the machinery to be erected in this building is $150,000. There will be two seven hundred and fifty horse-power engines, and eight one hundred and eighty-four horse-power boilers. The total length of the cable road belonging to this company will, when completed, be eleven miles of double track, and the entire cost of the change is estimated at $3,500,000.

The Metropolitan Railroad Company was organized under an act of Congress approved July 1, 1864, with the following-named incorporators: A. R. Shepherd, Richard Wallach, Lewis Clephane, S. P. Brown, Nathaniel Wilson, Franklin Tenney, M. G. Emery, Samuel Fowler, John Little, J. C. McKelden, S. J. Bowen, J. H. Semmes, D. C. Forney, W. W. Rapley, W. G. Moore, Thomas Lewis, J. B. Keasby, and Charles H. Nichols. This company has about ten miles of double track. Its east and west line runs from Thirty-fifth and O streets to Twenty-fifth Street, to P Street, to Connecticut Avenue, to Seventeenth and H streets, to Fourteenth Street, to F Street, to Fifth Street, to Louisiana Avenue, to East Capitol Street, to Lincoln Park.

Its north and south line begins on Brightwood Avenue, above Florida Avenue, and runs south on Ninth Street to the Market House, to Missouri Avenue, to Four and a Half Street, to O Street, to the steamboat wharves; also, a line on Brightwood Avenue, past the Soldiers' Home to Brightwood.

The first president was S. P. Brown, M. G. Emery being treasurer, both of whom served until March, 1865. From March, 1865, to July, 1884, J. W. Thompson was president. George W. Pearson has been president since July, 1884. William W. Moore was secretary and treasurer from January, 1865, to January, 1887, and since then William J. Wilson has been secretary and treasurer.

The present board of directors is composed of George W. Pearson, A. A. Wilson, A. A. Thomas, Dr. Daniel B. Clarke, Robert Bell, John Cammack, and Robert Weaver. The company is about to change its motive power from horses to electricity, and expects to complete the change during the summer of 1892.

The Columbia Street Railroad Company was organized under a charter granted May 24, 1871, with the following board of directors and officers: J. G. McKelden, president; William H. Clagett, secretary; George H. B. White, cashier of the National Metropolitan Bank, treasurer, and Alexander R. Shepherd, Hon. A. M. Clapp, N. B. Fugitt, Colonel S. S. Smoot, and M. M. Rohrer. The route of this company commences at Fifteenth Street and New York Avenue; thence along this avenue to K Street; then past the old Northern

Liberties Market on the south side; then down Massachusetts Avenue to II Street, and then on H Street to the tollgate, a distance of nearly three miles. Originally a single track was laid, with turn-outs, but in October, 1871, it was decided to construct a double track, which was completed in March, 1872. The cost of the road, as a double-track road, together with nine cars, forty horses, land, and stables, was $99,971.19. The present equipment of the road consists of one hundred and forty-four horses, sixteen two-horse summer cars, and sixteen two-horse winter cars. It is designed to change to an exclusively mechanical equipment as soon as practicable.

The officers of the company have been as follows: Presidents — J. C. McKelden, 1871 to 1874; H. A. Willard, 1874 to 1889; W. H. Clagett, May, 1889, to March, 1890; W. J. Stephenson, March, 1890, to the present time. Vice-Presidents — So far as the records show, Henry Dickson, to 1885; E. G. Davis, 1885 to the present time. Secretaries and Treasurers — William H. Clagett, 1871 to May 30, 1889; R. F. Baker, 1889 to the present time.

The Anacostia and Potomac Railroad Company was incorporated March 9, 1872, the original incorporators being L. W. Guinand, John Hitz, Thomas R. Riley, Alfred Richards, Thomas A. Richards, Zadok Williams, John Grinder, John A. Ruff, George B. Smith, and Madison Davis. Nothing was done until 1875, when a new charter was granted, under which a reorganization was effected, the board of directors being Dr. Noble Young, Edward Temple, R. B. Clarke, L. W. Guinand, H. A. Griswold, John Webster, Alfred Richards, Zadok Williams, and George A. Rohrer. The first officers were L. W. Guinand, president; Madison Davis, secretary; Thomas A. Richards, treasurer. By this second charter Congress prescribed the route of this road, as follows: From the Treasury by way of Fourteenth Street to Water Street; then along M Street to Eleventh Street; then across the Navy Yard bridge and along the Good Hope road to the District line, an entire distance of about seven miles. In 1876, the charter was so amended as to require the road to be built by way of Ohio Avenue to the Center Market. In 1888, the right was given to build the road from Eleventh and M streets Southeast, along Eleventh, G, E, Canal, and Third streets, Missouri Avenue, and B Street, to the Center Market; and also along G, Seventeenth, and E streets to the Congressional Cemetery. This portion of the road was constructed in 1889 and 1890, and was completed in January, 1891. Additional franchises were granted, allowing the construction of the road, by way of Second and M streets, to connect with the main or G Street line at Canal Street, which road was constructed in 1891, making the entire length of the line operated by this company thirteen and one-half miles. Should the bill now before Congress become a law, providing for the building of the road from Center Market by Ninth Street to G, then to Eleventh and E streets, and back by Ninth Street, the entire length of the line will be about sixteen miles.

All the old tracks of this road have been relaid with standard girder construction, with a view to the adoption of an improved electric or other motor power. The equipment of the road at the present time consists of one hundred and fifty horses, sixteen summer cars, and twenty-eight winter cars, all two-horse.

The officers of the company have been as follows: L. W. Guinand, president; H. A. Griswold, secretary and superintendent, and Thomas A.. Richards, treasurer; Mr. Guinand serving until his death in October, 1880; then H. A. Griswold, president and superintendent, until the present time; Thomas E. Smithson, secretary, until July, 1886, then J. Beacham Pitcher, until the present time. Mr. Pitcher subsequently succeeded Mr. Richards as treasurer, and is now serving in that capacity also.

The Capitol, North O Street, and South Washington Street Railroad Company was incorporated by a special act of Congress, approved March 3, 1875, the following gentlemen being named as the incorporators: Joseph Williams, William J. Murtagh, Hallet Kilbourn, Benjamin F. Fuller, William J. Cowing, Samuel R. Bond, William Saunders, George W. Goodall, George A. McIlhenny, L. A. Bartlett, and L. H. Chandler. The route along which this company was authorized to lay down their road, which might be either a single or double track, was as follows: Commencing on First Street West, in front of the Capitol grounds, and running thence due north along First Street to G Street North; thence west to Fourth Street; thence on Fourth Street to O Street; thence to Eleventh Street; thence to E Street; thence to Fourteenth Street; thence to Ohio Avenue; thence to the intersection with Twelfth Street; thence to Virginia Avenue; thence to Maryland Avenue; and thence to First Street, the place of beginning.

This act was amended, May 23, 1876, so as to authorize the extension of the line on Fourth and Eleventh streets West, from O Street to P Street, and to lay a single track and run its cars one way upon P Street, between Fourth and Eleventh streets. The charter was again amended, March 3, 1881, so as to authorize the company to remove its track from Ohio Avenue and Twelfth Street Southwest, and to lay a single or double track from the intersection of Ohio Avenue and

Fourteenth Street to C Street Southwest, eastwardly along C Street to Virginia Avenue, to connect with its line at the junction of this avenue and street; and also to lay a single or double track from its line on P Street and Eleventh Street Northwest, north on Eleventh Street to Boundary Street; and to lay a single or double track from the intersection of C and Eleventh streets Southwest, along Eleventh Street to Water Street, and then to M Street South, this to be the southern terminus of the road. The charter was again amended, March 1, 1883, authorizing the company to extend its line, by laying a single or double track, commencing at the intersection of Eleventh and E streets Northwest, along E to Ninth Street, along Ninth to Louisiana Avenue, then to Ohio Avenue, and then to the junction of Ohio Avenue and Twelfth Street Northwest. Then, in May, 1888, an amendment was made to the charter so as to authorize the construction of the road beginning at Fourteenth and B streets Southwest and extending along B Street to Twelfth Street Southwest, to connect with the company's line on the latter street. The entire length of line of travel is now about eight and one-half miles; and its present equipment consists of two hundred and thirty horses and fifty-two cars. The rails are for the most part eighty-pound grooved rails, and the ties are of white oak, hewed, and placed three feet, six inches apart. The board of directors are very active in securing for the road the best equipment that is practical, and within the law of Congress on the subject of street railways in the District. They have purchased Square No. 330, at the head of Eleventh Street Northwest, where they intend to erect a power house adapted to the necessities of that form of mechanical equipment which shall ultimately be adopted, and when this power house shall be erected they will abandon their present plants at Third and B streets Southwest, and at Twelfth and V streets Northwest. The capital of this company, at first $200,000, has been increased to $500,000.

The first meeting of the incorporators of this company was held December 30, 1874, and the company was organized March 8, 1875, by the election of Joseph Williams president, W. J. Cowing secretary, B. F. Fuller treasurer, and S. R. Bond attorney. The office of attorney was abolished February 23, 1875. May 3, George A. McIlhenny was elected president, and upon his resignation William Saunders was elected, October 14, 1875. S. R. Bond was elected December, 1875; Edward Temple served from 1876 to 1879; Charles White, May 12, 1879, to 1889; W. J. Cowing, November 29, 1889, to 1890; George White, May 12, 1890, to the present time. Vice-Presidents — A. M.

Clapp, December 26, 1889; W. J. Cowing, May, 1890; Charles Flint, 1891 to the present time. Secretaries and Treasurers — W. J. Cowing, until May 8, 1876; R. S. Cowing, 1876 to 1878; R. S. Chew, November 23, 1878, to 1881; W. E. Boughton, May 23, 1882, to 1889; H. A. Haralson, December 30, 1889, to 1890; H. K. Gray, March 3, 1890, to the present time. Superintendents —John La Rue, until May, 1877; Mr. Armstrong, for a short time; John W. Belt, May 22, 1878, to September 1, 1878; S. S. Daish, September 1, 1878, to July 1, 1881; E. L. Barnes, July 1, 1881, to May 26, 1884; Andrew Glass, May 26, 1884, to the present time.

The Rock Creek Railroad Company was organized under a charter granted by Congress, June 22, 1888, the incorporators being Gardner G. Hubbard, George Truesdell, Samuel W. Woodward, Otis F. Presbrey, John F. Waggaman, B. K. Plain, John Ridout, A. F. Stevens, Leroy Tuttle, Lawrence Sands, Edward C. Dean, James B. Wimer, Samuel S. Shedd, Leroy Tuttle, Jr., Robert J. Fisher, Jr., and Pitman Mann. Active work did not commence, however, until the amended charter was secured, May 28, 1890, by which the route of the road was changed so as to extend to the line of the District of Columbia on the line of Connecticut Avenue extended. The road now begins at the junction of Connecticut and Florida avenues and runs on Florida Avenue to Eighteenth Street, on Eighteenth Street to the Columbia road, thence to Rock Creek, and then on the line of Connecticut Avenue extended to the District of Columbia line. From this point the road has been graded and built into Maryland. The company has done a great deal of grading on Connecticut Avenue extended, and has built two very expensive bridges on its line. The entire main line was completed and put in operation about May 15, 1892. It is a double-track road, equipped with the Thomson-Houston system of overhead electric wires. It began operation with eighteen cars. The length of the road, including its branch road from Eighteenth Street and Florida Avenue along U Street and Florida Avenue to North Capitol Street, is about eight miles. The power house is located at the end of the line in Maryland, and is equipped with two engines, each of a nominal horse-power of two hundred and fifty, and four dynamos, of eighty kilowatts each. The officers of the company at the present time are Francis G. Newlands, president; Edward J. Stellwagen, vice-president; Thomas M. Gale, treasurer; Howard S. Nyman, secretary; and other directors, Henry E. Davis, John J. Malone, and Albert W. Sioussa. General A. J. Warner is superintendent of construction, and W. Kesley Schoepf, engineer.

The Eckington and Soldiers' Home Railway Company was chartered June 19, 1888, the incorporators being Edward F. Beale, Edward C. Dean, A. L. Barber, George Truesdell, James L. Barbour, George E. Moore, C. C. Duncanson, Michael Connor, and Joseph Paul. The company was organized August 2, 1888, with the following officers: George Truesdell, president; C. C. Duncanson, vice-president; Joseph Paul, secretary, and E. Kurtz Johnson, treasurer. These officers still retain their respective positions. G. S. Patterson has been superintendent since 1890.

By its charter, this company was authorized to build a road from the intersection of Seventh Street and New York Avenue, along New York Avenue to Boundary, along the boundary to Eckington Place; then north along Eckington Place to R Street, along R Street to Third, along Third to T Street, and along T Street to the car house. This road was built and the cars commenced running thereon October 17, 1888, the cars being propelled by means of the Thomson-Houston electric system, and was thus one of the first electric street railroads in use in the United States. The company, by its charter, was also authorized to extend its line along New York Avenue to Ivy City. In the spring of 1889, it began operating cars on Fourth Street, and added four vestibule motor cars and seven double-decked tow cars. In the fall of the same year, it added three vestibule motor cars and three double-decked tow cars. In the summer of 1889, the road was extended along Lincoln Avenue and B Street nearly to Glenwood Cemetery. The charter was amended April 30, 1890, authorizing the extension of the track from New York Avenue to Fifth Street, then to G Street, and along G Street to Fifteenth; and also, beginning at the terminus of the cemetery branch, along Lincoln Avenue to a point opposite the entrance to Glenwood Cemetery; also, beginning at the intersection of New York Avenue and North Capitol Street, along the latter to the south boundary of the Soldiers' Home. The road was built along G and Fifth streets in the spring of 1891. Two storage-battery cars were run temporarily, as an experiment, from the spring of 1891 to August 16, 1891, on which day the insulation of six new cars was completed, and these commenced running November 1, 1891, and are still running.

In the early part of 1891, the company commenced constructing the North Capitol Street tracks, and completed the road as far as T Street. Cars are not yet running on this road. The cemetery extension was completed May 29, 1891, and cars commenced running thereon May 30, Decoration Day.

The power house is located on Fifth Street, above T Street, Northeast, at Eckington. The power house contains four Thomson-Houston eighty horse-power generators and four one hundred horse-power engines, three one hundred and ten horse-power boilers and two forty horse-power Electric-Dynamic Company's generators, and one one hundred horse-power engine, the latter being used in charging the batteries of the storage cars, the other engines being used in propelling the trolley cars. In 1889, the number of passengers carried was 538,870; in 1890, 750,833; and in 1891, 1,076,744.

At the last annual election, held on the second Wednesday in January, 1892, the following gentlemen were elected directors: C. C. Duncanson, E. Kurtz Johnson, Joseph Paul, M. M. Parker, J. H. Lane, L. M. Saunders, Thomas Somerville, George Truesdell, and B. H. Warner.

The Georgetown and Tennallytown Railroad was organized in 1888, and their railroad, which is an electric one, equipped with the Thomson-Houston system, extends from Water and Thirty-second streets, Georgetown, out on Thirty-second Street to the District line, a distance of four and a half miles. The power house of this line is situated about one mile from Water Street, and is equipped with one two hundred and fifty horse-power Corliss engine, and one one hundred and twenty-five horse-power Corliss engine, propelling four dynamos, each of eighty horse-power. The first officers of this company were General R. C. Drum, president; R. H. Goldsborough, vice-president; John E. Beall, secretary; and George H. B. White, treasurer. General Drum resigned the presidency in a few months, and was succeeded by Mr. Goldsborough, and W. A. Gordon was chosen vice-president. At the last annual election, held January 13, 1892, Spencer Watkins was elected president, R. D. Weaver vice-president, John E. Beall secretary, and George D. Ashton treasurer.

At the District line this road connects with two other electric roads, the one owned by the Glen Echo Railroad Company, and extending to Glen Echo, a distance of about three miles, the other owned by the Tennallytown and Rockville Railroad Company, and extending now to Bethesda Park, a distance of about three and a half miles. It is expected that this line will ultimately be extended to Rockville, Maryland.

The Norfolk and Washington, District of Columbia, Steamboat Company was chartered by the Legislature of Virginia in February, 1890, with a capital of $100,000, which was increased in 1891 to $300,000. The company was organized the following month with

William E. Clark, president; Levi Woodbury, vice-president; C. C. Duncanson, treasurer; John Keyworth, secretary, and John Callahan, superintendent. Subsequently, Mr. Duncanson resigned and Mr. R. F. Baker was elected treasurer in his stead. Contracts were made in May, 1890, with the Harlan & Hollingsworth Company, of Wilmington, Delaware, for the construction of two steamers, the *Washington* and the *Norfolk*, which were completed and commenced running, the former on March 28, 1891, and the *Norfolk* on April 3, 1891. These two steamboats are each of iron, and two hundred and sixty feet in length, and each cost $235,000. Some time afterward, the company purchased of the Potomac Company their wharf and steamer, *George Leary*, which boat they have had entirely repaired and refitted, at an expense of about $20,000. The two new steamers are first-class in every respect, and are capable of running from nineteen to twenty miles per hour. Their time between Washington and Norfolk is usually twelve and a half hours, a distance of two hundred miles.

The Mount Vernon and Marshall Hall Steamboat Company has been in existence for several years. Its boats, the principal ones of which are the *Charles Macalester* and the *River Queen*, the latter an elegant new steamer, ply between Washington and Alexandria, Mount Vernon, Marshall Hall, and other points on the Potomac River, running to Mount Vernon in connection with the Ladies' Mount Vernon Association, and charging $1 for the round trip to the latter, which includes admission to the grounds. The officers of this company are Joseph C. McKibben, president; L. L. Blake, vice-president; Thomas Adams, secretary and treasurer; Samuel C. Ramage, general manager.

The Washington Steamboat Company, Limited, is the successor to the Potomac Ferry Company, which originated in 1864; the Washington Steamboat Company being organized in 1881. It has five steamboats plying on the Potomac between Washington and points below. These boats are named the *Wakefield, T. V. Arrowsmith, Columbia, City of Alexandria,* and *City of Washington*. The officers of this company are C. W. Ridley, general manager; J. B. Padgett, general agent, and Jonathan P. Crowley, treasurer.

Other steamboat lines are those of the People's Washington and Norfolk Steamboat Company, the successor to the Inland and Seaboard Coasting Company, which latter company was the successor of the Washington, Georgetown, Alexandria, and New York Steamship company, organized as early as 1867; the Independent Steamboat and Barge Company, organized in 1889; and of E. S. Randall, and George L. Sheriff.

CHAPTER X.

HISTORY OF BANKING.

The Bank of Columbia — The Bank of the United States — Office of Discount and Deposit in Washington — "The Produce Bank of the Potomac" — The Bank of the Metropolis — The National Metropolitan Bank — The Bank of Washington — The National Bank of Washington — The Union Bank of Georgetown — The Central Bank of Georgetown and Washington — The Farmers and Mechanics' Bank — The Patriotic Bank — Confusion of the Finances — The Second National Bank — John C. Calhoun on the National Bank — Directors of the Branch Bank in Washington — President Jackson's Animosity to the National Bank — Suspension of Specie Payments — Extension of Charters of the District Banks — Troubles with the Currency — President Tyler's Vetoes — The Banks of the District Practically Extinguished — The Freedman's Saving and Trust Company — Riggs & Company — First National Bank — Merchants' National Bank — National Bank of the Republic — National Savings Bank — National Safe Deposit Company — National Capital Bank of Washington — Second National Bank — Citizens' National Bank — Washington Safe Deposit Company — Columbia National Bank — Washington Loan and Trust Company — American Security and Trust Company — Lincoln National Bank — West End National Bank — Traders' National Bank — Ohio National Bank — Private Banking Institutions.

THE Bank of Columbia was established at Georgetown in 1793, and was the first institution within what afterward became the District of Columbia. It was established by Samuel Blodgett, assisted by Mr. Stoddert and Governor Johnson, of Fredericktown. Samuel Hannon was cashier from its establishment up to 1801, when, notwithstanding his earnest protest, he was superseded by William Whann. When the Bank of Potomac was established in 1804, there were immediately made severe criticisms on banks as institutions, and Mr. Blodgett, in September of that year, made an elaborate defense of them, and of his own course in connection with them. "I trust it is now universally known that the invariable and only effects of the American banking system, as it has been hitherto practiced with astonishing success, have been almost immediately to extend the commercial and mechanical operations of every eligible place where these institutions have been formed, and finally, on account of the great profits attained to the stock and realized in semi-annual dividends, to draw foreign capital for the purposes thereof, and often at an advanced premium — a clear gain to the community." He also said:

"An ignorance of the effects, at the time, occasioned the exclusive monopolizing clause in the constitution of the Bank of the United States. Congress seeing how that foreigners, by holding almost the whole of this bank, are benefited, against the principles of equality which we cherish in our commercial regulations for the general benefit of our fellow-citizens, they will therefore repeal the injurious clause in any application for a renewal of the charter now nearly expired. They will then grant the same privileges, not only to the Bank of Potomac, but to several others I hope to see instituted in the Territory of Columbia in due time. We have now about $39,000,000 of banking capital in the United States. England alone has about $600,000,000 of banking capital, and to equal her beneficial experience we might, for six millions of people, if more compactly situated, carry our banking capital to at least seven times its present sum, and to the same advantages," etc.

On March 20, 1809, directors of this bank were elected, as follows: John Mason, C. Worthington, William Marbury, John Cox, John Threlkeld, Walter Smith, Henry Foxall, Marshall Waring, James Dunlop, Philip B. Key, Jeremiah Wins, and Thomas Peter. John Mason was elected president, and was continued in this office until 1816. N. Frye, Jr., succeeded General Mason, and was himself succeeded, in 1828, by Richard T. Lowndes, who continued to serve until 1837. William Whann served as cashier up to within a few months of his death, on February 5, 1822, in Cecil County, Maryland, whither he had gone in hope of recovering his health, but in vain.[1] Mr. Whann was succeeded as cashier by D. Kurtz, who served until 1828, when he was succeeded by Richard Smith.

---

[1] A friend of Mr. Whann, immediately after his death, wrote of him as follows:

"Perfection is not given to mortals, but if there ever was a truly good man the deceased was one. He was indeed the good citizen, the kind parent, the true friend, the sincere Christian. Hoping to find restoration of health in the quiet of a country life, and a calm for his wounded feelings, caused by a succession of afflictions and misfortunes which had recently come to him, he resigned a position which he had held for more than twenty years, and went to his immediate relatives; but it was all in vain, and he died on the day above given.

> "Then, reader, forgive this friendly zeal to save
> Virtues like his from an oblivious grave.
> I seek not his pure monument to raise
> On the weak basis of a mortal's praise;
> Nor yet to give, with still a vainer aim,
> His modest merit to the voice of fame:
> No—let his virtues in our bosoms rest,
> To life's last hour indelibly impressed."

Who was president after Mr. Lowndes, if anyone, or cashier after Richard Smith, could not be ascertained, nor the precise date of the failure of the bank, notwithstanding more time was spent in the attempt to ascertain these facts than was warranted by their intrinsic value. The last legislation by Congress relating to this bank was approved February 25, 1836, by which its charter was extended to March 4, 1839. It also provided that no discounts should be made except such as might be deemed proper to renew such notes as had already been discounted, and that no more promissory notes should be put in circulation. This legislation also provided that instead of a president and nine directors, as then required by law, a board should be elected on the first Thursday in March, 1836, and each year thereafter, so long as the law itself remained in force, who should elect one of themselves president; and the stockholders were authorized to choose trustees to wind up the affairs. It is therefore altogether probable that this bank ceased to exist about 1839.

On February 4, 1806, at a meeting of the president and directors of the Bank of the United States, the following gentlemen, from Washington, Georgetown, and Alexandria, were elected directors of the office of discount and deposit for the District of Columbia for one year: Joseph Carleton, Thomas Tingey, William Brent, James D. Barry, John P. Van Ness, Caleb Swan, Thomas Munroe, Joseph Nourse, David Peter, William Stewart, Lewis Leblois, Benjamin Shreve, Jr., and Phineas Janney. On the 3d of March, John P. Van Ness was elected president of the board. February 3, 1807, the same gentlemen were again elected directors, and Mr. Van Ness president. February 2, 1808, the same board was again elected, with the exception that John Tayloe was chosen in the place of Joseph Carleton. February 7, 1809, the following gentlemen were elected members of this board: John P. Van Ness, William Stewart, Thomas Tingey, Caleb Swan, Joseph Nourse, James D. Barry, Thomas Munroe, Lewis Deblois, Elias B. Caldwell, Walter Hellen, William Brent, David Peter, and John Tayloe. February 6, 1810, the same gentlemen were again elected, except that James Sanderson was chosen in place of Caleb Swan.

This appears to have been the last election of officers for the branch of the Bank of the United States in the District of Columbia; and the bank itself soon became extinct through the failure of Congress to renew its charter. The main reason for this refusal was the fact that the directors and a majority of the stockholders were Federalists, and hence the institution itself was looked upon as a Federal institution. But notwithstanding this feeling of prejudice, which should not have actuated any member qualified to be a member of Congress, the bill providing for its recharter passed the House of Representatives, and in the Senate received seventeen votes to the same number against it, its fate being decided by the vote against it of Vice-President Clinton, who had been opposed to the formation of the Federal Constitution, and to any institution more national than those authorized by the old Confederation, and at the time of voting against the recharter of this bank still cherished the same tendencies, slightly modified. At the present day, this fact would seem to have been a sufficient reason for electing some other person, one in favor of the National Constitution and of national institutions, to the Vice-Presidency.

After the expiration of the charter of this bank, in 1811, the business of the office of discount and deposit in Washington was conducted for a time by a temporary board of agents, of which John P. Van Ness was chairman. Still later, a committee was appointed, consisting of Messrs. Tayloe, Munroe, Hellen, Peter, Sanderson, and Rowles, to manage the business, with a view of winding up its affairs. This having been accomplished, it was soon found necessary to make an attempt to establish another bank in Washington, there being then but one little bank, on Capitol Hill, which had not funds sufficient for the canal, road stock, and for the business houses in the vicinity of its own property. The extension of the Bank of Columbia in the Treasury Department had been felt only as a nuisance, stimulating hope with the certainty of ending in disappointment, and even this feeling of hope had been felt only by a few, as no reasonable man could calculate upon an accommodation in Georgetown, except upon the usual principles of accommodating to secure greater wants. In short, the people were distressed for want of bank accommodations, the commerce of the Potomac being nearly at a standstill in consequence of limited bank facilities. The building of the then late office of discount and deposit was soon upon the market, and available for the use of any new institution of the kind that might be established, and the citizens of Washington were invited to attend a meeting at Davis's Hotel on Wednesday, March 25, 1812, to appoint commissioners to open subscriptions to the stock of a new bank. Among the principles to be determined at this meeting were these, according to the gentleman calling it: First, as to the exclusive accommodation of dealers in the produce of the Potomac—hence the suggestion that the bank should be named "The

·Produce Bank of the Potomac"; second, the extent of the capital of the new bank, which the same gentleman suggested should be $1,500,000; third, the commissioners to open the subscriptions. The following names were suggested as those of proper persons: Colonel John Tayloe, John P. Van Ness, Commodore Tingey, Charles Carroll of Bellevue, Lewis Deblois, Elias B. Caldwell, Thomas Munroe, Walter Hellen, Tench Ringgold, Buller Cocke, James Davidson, Silas Butler, C. W. Goldsborough, William Simmons, John Graham, and D. Sheldon.

At the meeting held in pursuance of the above suggestion, Charles Carroll, of Bellevue, was elected chairman, and Edmund Law secretary. It was then resolved, unanimously, that there be appointed seventeen commissioners to draw up articles of association and to open subscription books for the proposed new bank. Of the above-named gentlemen all were appointed, except Lewis Deblois, Tench Ringgold, William Simmons, John Graham, and D. Sheldon; and in addition, there were appointed Washington Boyd, Roger C. Weightman, Andrew Way, James D. Barry, Phineas Bradley, and James H. Blake. These commissioners were authorized to fix upon a "scite" for the bank, the capital stock, and the president's house. At a subsequent meeting the commissioners submitted articles of association for an institution to be named "The President and Directors of the American Bank." The association was to continue twenty-one years. The capital stock was to be $1,000,000, divided into shares of $40 each, and the copartnership was to transact its business in the city of Washington. After several attempts to hold meetings and to secure subscriptions, the commissioners gave up the attempt to establish the bank; and at length, on January 20, 1813, the citizens of Washington who were desirous of having a second bank opened in the city were requested to meet at McLeod's Tavern on the 25th of that month for the purpose of choosing commissioners to carry out the project. General John P. Van Ness was called to the chair, and Alexander Kerr made secretary. But little was accomplished at this meeting, and a second meeting was held, February 1, 1813, at which it was resolved that, as it was not known that there was any application before Congress for a new bank when they commenced operations, they would await the result of that application before proceeding any further.

This application does not appear to have resulted in the establishment of any banking institution, and in November, 1813, the movement postponed, as above related, was again taken up, and at a meeting held at Davis's Hotel, on the 25th of that month, thirteen commis-

sioners were appointed to act under articles of association adopted at
that meeting. The next meeting, held at Davis's Hotel, January 3,
1814, was of the stockholders of the new bank, which was named "The
Bank of the Metropolis." John P. Van Ness was chosen president of
the new bank, and Alexander Kerr cashier. The location of this bank
was at the corner of F and Fifteenth streets, east of the Treasury
building. John P. Van Ness was continued as president of this bank
until 1842. Alexander Kerr was cashier until his death, in 1832, when
he was succeeded by George Thomas, who was succeeded in 1846 by
Richard Smith. In 1829, the capital of this bank was $500,000, and
its total assets $645,815.15. Toward the close of the War of 1812-15,
when General Jackson made an appeal for funds with which to pay
the American soldiers, this bank loaned largely to the Government.
After General Jackson became President of the United States, he kept
his private accounts with this bank, and after the removal of the
deposits from the United States Bank this bank was made a public
depository. After the retirement of General Van Ness from the presidency of this bank, John W. Maury served in that capacity, and
Richard Smith continued as cashier for many years. At length, it
was organized under the National Banking law as the National Metropolitan Bank, with John B. Blake president, and Moses Kelly cashier.
Mr. Blake remained president until 1874, when he was succeeded by
John W. Thompson,[1] who is still the president. Moses Kelly was
succeeded as cashier, in 1874, by George H. B. White, who is cashier
at the present time. When Mr. Thompson became president, the
surplus amounted to about thirty per cent. of the capital of the bank,

---

[1] John W. Thompson, one of the leading bankers, business men, and financiers
of Washington, came to this city from New York City in 1849. Upon his arrival here
he at once entered into an active business life. During the War of the Rebellion, he
was identified with the Government of the United States. He was afterward connected
with the Board of Aldermen, and was appointed by President Grant to the upper
house of the Legislature of the District of Columbia. He was president of the New
York, Alexandria, Washington, and Georgetown Steamship Company, established for
the purpose of trading between New York City and the District of Columbia. He
was one of the principal movers in the building of the Metropolitan Street Railroad,
and was for several years president of the company. He has been connected with
numerous businesses, and has been and is to-day one of the most successful business
men in Washington. This success has led to his selection to fill important positions,
both in business and civic circles. He was chairman of the Garfield inauguration
committee, and under his management the committee was able to return all the money
subscribed as a guaranty fund, for the first time in the history of the country. He
has been president of the National Metropolitan Bank since 1874, and his high
standing in business and social circles and in the church is the best evidence of the
estimation in which he is held by his fellow-men.

which was then, and is now $300,000, while at the present time the surplus and undivided profits, on the first of March, 1892, amounted to $329,286.68.

The Bank of Washington was chartered in 1809, and was the first bank established in Washington. The capital stock was $100,000. Daniel Carroll, of Duddington, was its first president, and Samuel Eliot, Jr., its first cashier. The capital, after the first payment, was paid in in installments, Mr. Eliot, the cashier, on February 10, 1810, notifying the subscribers that the fourth installment of $2 on each share would be due on March 3, following, at the temporary banking house of the institution, which was located on Capitol Hill, near New Jersey Avenue. A committee was appointed to erect a banking house, and to receive proposals up to July 25, 1810, of which committee Frederick May was chairman. Just where this banking house was erected has not been ascertained. The last installment on the capital stock was due on September 4, 1810, and had to be paid in order to avoid forfeiture of what had already been paid in. Sometime between 1820 and 1830, the business was removed from the building erected by the committee mentioned above to the National Hotel, and on September 27, 1831, a resolution was adopted that the brick building owned by John Stetinus, and occupied by Mauro & Son, auctioneers, standing where now stands the fine marble building of the National Bank of Washington, at the junction of Louisiana Avenue and C Street Northwest, be purchased, and into this building the bank moved in 1832. Daniel Carroll, of Duddington, served as president of the bank until September, 1819, when he was succeeded by Samuel H. Smith, who served in this capacity until February, 1828; George Culvert was then president until September, 1830; Thomas Munroe, until January, 1835; William Gunton, until December, 1880; Edward Temple, until January, 1888; and Charles A. James, until the present time.

Samuel Eliot, Jr., served as cashier until June, 1819, when he was succeeded by William A. Bradley, who served until July, 1826, when he resigned, and was succeeded by Roger Chew Weightman. Mr. Weightman served until October, 1834; John H. Reilly, until November, 1836; James Adams, from November, 1836, until July, 1870; Charles A. James, from July, 1870, until January, 1888; and C. E. White, from January, 1888, until the present time.

In January, 1886, this institution was organized as the "National Bank of Washington," with officers as noted above. According to its last published statement, its capital is $250,000, and its surplus and undivided profits amounted at the same time, March 1, 1892, to $100,644.48.

The Union Bank of Georgetown, District of Columbia, was chartered by Congress, March 11, 1811. The capital stock of the bank was $500,000, in $50 shares. For most of the time during the existence of this bank, Robert Beverly was its president, and David English appears to have been cashier during its entire existence. In 1840, it went into liquidation, but its charter was extended from time to time until 1849, to allow its affairs to be fully settled.

The Central Bank of Georgetown and Washington was chartered March 3, 1817, and when organized John Tayloe was president, and A. R. Levering cashier. Mr. Tayloe resigned the presidency in May, 1818, and was succeeded by Francis Dodge, who remained president during the bank's short existence. March 2, 1821, Congress passed an act authorizing this bank to pay off its debts and close its affairs, there being then too many banks in the District of Columbia.

The Farmers and Mechanics' Bank of Georgetown was started in 1814, at a meeting held February 15, at Crawford's Hotel. The gentlemen present were William Marbury, Thomas Turner, John Lee, J. Melvin, R. Riggs, L. H. Johns, George C. Washington, T. B. Beall, T. Robertson, and Charles W. Goldsborough. William Marbury was elected president, and Thomas Van Swearingen, of Shepherdstown, was chosen director in his place. A committee was appointed to memorialize Congress for a charter, consisting of William Marbury, T. B. Beall, and John Lee. The salary of the president was fixed at $500 per year, and that of the cashier at $1,600 per year. Clement Smith was then elected cashier. A committee was then appointed, consisting of the president, cashier, and L. H. Johns, T. Robertson, and T. Turner, to receive proposals for a banking-house site. March 1, 1814, Mr. John Peters offered to sell the house at the corner of Bridge (now M) and Congress (now Thirty-first) streets for $14,000, and this offer was accepted by the new bank, payable in eight months from the 15th of March, 1814. On March 21, 1814, the cashier was allowed the privilege either of living in the banking house, or of accepting in lieu of this privilege $400 additional per year as salary. On April 4, John I. Stull was appointed teller, Horatio Jones bookkeeper, and Robert Reed discount clerk. On May 17, 1814, the following resolution was adopted: "That the cashier be authorized and required to take to the amount of $50,000 of the last loan of the United States for the use and benefit of the bank, provided it can be obtained as original subscribers, with all the benefit and advantages that have or may accrue to them."

July 8, 1817, Clement Smith was elected president of the bank, but soon afterward Thomas B. Beall was elected, and served until 1820, Clement Smith continuing to serve as cashier until 1820. The original capital of the bank was $500,000, and in January it was resolved that the capital should not be reduced to less than $450,000. Clement Smith became president of the bank in 1820, and John I. Stull cashier. December 18, 1823, Thomas Wilson resigned as a member of the board of directors, and Raphael Semmes was chosen in his place. On January 1, 1829, the capital of this bank was $485,900, and its entire assets $793,191.97. April 12, 1834, its board of directors resolved to suspend specie payments, saying, in explanation of their course: "They foresee that the present prostration of business confidence, and consequent derangement of the currency, must eventually reduce them to this course, and they prefer to anticipate the event by yielding at once to the pressure, rather than to avert it by holding out during the short practical period of delay, at the expense of sacrificing the permanent interests of the bank. This measure is of temporary duration. The board see no necessity, in the condition of the bank, for extending it beyond the present singular crisis in the banking history of the country, and confidently anticipate the resumption of active business on a specie basis as soon as this crisis shall pass away."

John Kurtz succeeded Mr. Smith as president in 1841; Robert Reed became president in 1850; George Shoemaker, in 1862, and Henry M. Sweeney, in 1865. John I. Stull served as cashier until 1841; Alexander Suter, until 1848; William Lang, until 1851, and William Laird became cashier in that year.

The original charter of this bank was dated March, 3, 1817, and it was renewed by Congress from time to time, and the stock of the bank, which, on account of the varying fortunes of the banking interests of the country, fluctuated considerably during the "singular crisis," precipitated by the opposition to these interests manifested by one of the great political parties, gradually rose from fifty cents on the dollar in 1838 to above par in 1870.

On January 15, 1872, this bank was organized as a national bank under the name it now bears, "The Farmers and Mechanics' National Bank of Georgetown." At the time of this organization, the following nine directors were elected: Henry M. Sweeney, Philip T. Berry, William C. Magee, Evan Pickrell, William King, Francis Wheatly, John Davidson, Charles M. Matthews, and Evan Lyons.

Henry M. Sweeney was continued as president of the bank, and is still its president, having served in that capacity during a period of thirty-six years. William Laird was continued as cashier, and served in the same capacity for forty years.

The Patriotic Bank was established in May, 1815, and on June 5, following, the following directors were elected: Robert Brent, Thomas Law, James D. Barry, Daniel Porter, Timothy Winn, Phineas Bradley, George Way, Thomas Munroe, William Prout, Stephen Pleasanton, George Beall, David Ott, and Nicholas Young. On June 7, Robert Brent was chosen president, and Overton Carr cashier. Joseph Pearson was elected president in 1824, and also in 1825. On June 28, 1825, this bank opened its business in its new banking house, at the intersection of Seventh and D streets Northwest, opposite the office of the *National Intelligencer.* On June 1, 1829, the capital stock was $250,000, and its total assets $503,133.87. In 1832, G. E. Dyson was cashier, he having sometime before succeeded R. T. Weightman. On April 14, 1834, at a special meeting, it was resolved that, in the opinion of the board of directors, the interests of the bank and of its creditors required that the payment of specie for its obligations ought to be suspended; that the bank was able to pay 110 per cent. to the stockholders, and that the creditors of the bank be requested not to sacrifice their claims. "In making known this determination, the board need hardly say that nothing but the extraordinary juncture of affairs could have brought them to the painful necessity of this annunciation"—signed by W. A. Bradley, president, and G. E. Dyson, cashier. This bank resumed specie payment July 10, 1836, by unanimous resolution, but on May 12, 1837, it was again compelled to suspend, in common with the other banks throughout the country. This was done at the request of the shareholders of the bank. At that time, a brief statement of the condition of the bank was made public, as follows: Debts due by the bank, $326,560.48; debts due to the bank, including real estate, $528,256.67; capital stock outstanding, $171,040; entire surplus, $30,656.19. P. Thompson was cashier in 1839, and C. Bestor in 1846, Mr. Bradley remaining president. In 1846, this bank opened a savings department, receiving sums of $5 and upward, upon which it paid interest until the money was withdrawn. This was the first savings bank in Washington.

During the War of 1812–15, with Great Britain, the finances of the country fell into inextricable confusion; the Government was obliged to borrow money at a ruinous rate of interest, giving $100 for $88, and taking the proceeds in the notes of banks which could not pay specie, the notes being worth from sixty to ninety ·cents on the dollar. Under such disastrous and distressing circumstances as these the evils inflicted on the country by Vice-President Clinton's vote against the renewal of the charter of the old National Bank, already referred to, were plainly visible to those who understood financial matters, and the necessity of such an institution was painfully experienced. In this state of things, at the session of Congress of 1813-14, Hon. Felix Grundy, of Tennessee, introduced a measure into the House of Representatives looking to the establishment of a national bank, which was referred to the proper committee. Action upon the question was not taken at that session "for want of time," although Mr. Grundy was of the opinion that there was plenty of time; but in November, 1814, the question again came up, and in connection with the discussion the *National Intelligencer* said: "Those in Congress who doubt the constitutional power of Congress to establish a national bank are not few; and if we add to the number those who are opposed to the measure for sustaining the public credit, inasmuch as nothing would delight them more than to see the wheels of government stopped by national bankruptcy, we shall find a formidable phalanx in Congress arrayed against a national bank, however organized."

These remarks were designed for the Federalists, many of whom believed the war with Great Britain wholly unnecessary. The bill, as presented in the House of Representatives, November 14, 1814, named only Boston, New York, Philadelphia, Baltimore, Richmond, Charleston, and Pittsburgh, as places where subscriptions to the capital stock were to be received, thus confining the opportunities to subscribe almost exclusively to the Atlantic cities. This was far from satisfactory to many Western members of Congress, and upon motion of Mr. Sharp, of Kentucky, Lexington was added; on motion of Mr. Robertson, New Orleans; on motion of Mr. Harris, Nashville, Tennessee; on motion of Mr. Lewis, Washington, District of Columbia, Raleigh, North Carolina, Savannah, Georgia, and New Brunswick, New Jersey, were also added, and Pittsburgh stricken out.

For Washington, District of Columbia, Robert Brent, Walter Smith, and Thomas Swann were made the commissioners to receive subscriptions. Mr. Lewis then made a motion contemplating the location of the principal bank in Washington, but this was opposed by Mr. Fisk, of New York, the Ways and Means Committee having selected Philadelphia for that honor. Of this committee Hon. John C. Calhoun, of South Carolina, who had entered Congress about the beginning of the war, was chairman, and in this responsible position he introduced the bill, ably advocated it, and really carried it through the House. This, however, was on its final passage. Previously to its reaching this point, its history is of considerable interest. On January 2, 1815, the bill, coming up for final action in the House of Representatives, was apparently carried by 81 affirmative to 80 negative votes. But the Speaker, Hon. Langdon Cheves, from South Carolina, called attention to the rule of the House which permitted the Speaker to vote in two cases, of which this was one, and, declaring his conviction that the bill was a dangerous measure, cast his vote against it, and thus made the vote in the House a tie, and then decided that the bill was lost. On January 8, however, in an amended form, the bill passed the House by a vote of 120 to 38, and it passed the Senate by a good majority. But on January 30, President Madison returned it, without his approval, to the Senate.

On April 5, 1816, however, the bill, having passed the House of Representatives by a vote of 80 yeas to 71 nays, passed the Senate by a vote of 22 yeas to 12 nays, and on the 10th of the same month it was signed by the President, and thus became a law. Of those who voted for the bill more than two-thirds were "Republicans," or "Democrats," as they were indifferently called, in contradistinction to the "Federalists," who numbered about three-fourths of those who voted against the bill. But all of those who thus voted were not opposed to a national bank, being opposed only to certain features of the bill, and voted against it in the hope of throwing it back again into the committee, and of thus having an opportunity to eliminate the features which were objectionable to them.

This was a great triumph for the friends of a sound currency, and for those who were in favor of a vigorous prosecution of the war. The bank went into immediate operation, but for some years the sanguine anticipations entertained of public advantage from its operations were not realized. The difficulties were, that the country, at the close of the Revolutionary War, was flooded with $200,000,000 worth of foreign fabrics, which were sold at any price that could be obtained, with the view of breaking down the manufacturing industries of the young Republic, and the entire country was overwhelmed with both public and private debt; and in addition to these things, the currency was in a most deplorable condition, as a consequence of the failure to renew the charter of the old National Bank. For these reasons it was an impossibility for the bank to restore everything to a prosperous condition in a short period of time, even by affording every facility in its power. After a time, however, aided by a more efficient tariff and an improved management of the affairs of the bank itself, the country began to emerge from its embarrassments, and from 1819 to 1834 the bank prospered, and gave to the country the best currency that the world had ever seen.

When everything was in this prosperous condition, when the National Bank was recognized as a most useful institution, Hon. John C. Calhoun, to whom credit has already been given for the success of the efforts in Congress to charter this bank, said, in 1832: "I may say with truth, that the bank owes as much to me as to any other individual in the country; and I might even add, that had it not been for my efforts it would not have been chartered. · I might content myself with saying that, having been on the political stage without interruption from that day to this, having been an attentive observer of the question of the currency throughout the whole period, the bank has been an indispensable agent in the restoration of specie payments; that without it such restoration could not have been effected short of the utter prostration of all monied institutions in the country, and an entire depreciation of bank paper; and that it has not only restored specie payments, but has given a currency far more uniform, between the extremes of the country, than was anticipated or even dreamed of at the time of its creation."

Under this act the president of the bank appointed as commissioners to superintend the taking of subscriptions in Washington, General John Mason of Georgetown, Thomas Swann of Alexandria, and General John P. Van Ness of Washington. Subscription books were opened on Monday, July 1, 1816, and closed on the 23d of the same month. The amount subscribed here up to that time was $1,293,000, an amount far exceeding what had been anticipated. By the same time the subscriptions in Richmond amounted to $1,702,000; in Baltimore, to $4,014,100; in Wilmington, Delaware, to $465,600; in Trenton, New Jersey, to $130,000; in New York City, to $2,500,000; etc. By August 29, the total amount subscribed amounted to $25,000,000. The deficiency of $3,000,000 was subscribed by Stephen Girard, "a wealthy citizen of Philadelphia."

On January 27, 1817, the following gentlemen were appointed directors of the Branch Bank of the United States in Washington: Richard Cutts, Thomas Munroe, B. Thruston, R. C. Weightman, G. Bomford, G. Graham, and William Brent, of Washington; Thomas Tudor Tucker, J. Deane, and Thomas Swann, of Alexandria, and W. Smith, W. S. Chandler, and R. Parrott, of Georgetown. Richard Smith was chosen cashier, and the office began business on Saturday,

February 8, 1817. General John P. Van Ness was elected president of this branch. This branch bank continued in successful operation until the main bank was slaughtered, when, from the necessities of the case, it wound up its affairs.

During the Presidential campaign of 1828, at the close of which Andrew Jackson was elected to the Presidency, his elevation was urged on every imaginable ground except that of the overthrow of the United States Bank. Although some of his zealous partisans adduced even the failure of the crops in certain localities as evidence that nothing could flourish under the rule of such an administration as that of John Quincy Adams, yet no man complained of the currency, or demanded any radical change in the American banking system, thus showing most conclusively that that system was universally popular. But soon after General Jackson's inauguration, he managed to involve himself needlessly in a controversy with the management of the United States Bank. His Secretary of the Treasury demanded the removal of Jeremiah Mason, president of the branch of this bank at Portsmouth, New Hampshire, because President Mason was not a stanch friend of the Jackson administration. But as this demand was not accompanied by any evidence of, or even any allegation of, misconduct or incompetency in President Mason, compliance therewith was necessarily declined. Nicholas Biddle was then president of the United States Bank, and during this controversy had of course stood by President Mason, and this was sufficient reason for President Jackson to make war on the institution of which Mr. Biddle was president.

In his annual message to Congress soon afterward, he took occasion to observe that the time would soon arrive when the question of granting a recharter to the Bank of the United States would come before that body, and stated that "both the constitutionality and expediency of such an institution had been well questioned." The portion of the message containing this assertion was referred by the House to its Committee of Ways and Means, of which the Hon. George McDuffie, of South Carolina, was chairman. The entire committee, including its chairman, were supporters of General Jackson, and hence their report on this extraordinary statement is of special value. This committee gave grave consideration to the whole subject, and made a lengthy report, strongly in favor both of the constitutionality and expediency of a national bank. On the point of constitutionality, they said, in part,—for only brief extracts can be given in this work, and that more for the purpose of indicating the direction of their thought than of presenting the argument in full:

"If the concurrence of all the departments of the Government, at different periods of our history, under every administration, and during the ascendency of both political parties into which the country has been divided, soon after the adoption of the present Constitution, shall be regarded as having the authority of such sanctions by the common consent of all well-regulated communities, the constitutional power of Congress to incorporate a bank may be assumed as a postulate no longer open to controversy. In little more than two years after the Government went into operation, and at a period when most of the distinguished members of the Federal Constitutional Convention were either in the executive or legislative councils, the act incorporating the first Bank of the United States passed both branches of Congress by large majorities, and received the deliberate sanction of President Washington, who had then recently presided over the deliberations of the convention. The constitutional power of Congress to pass this act of incorporation was thoroughly investigated, both in the Executive Cabinet and in Congress, under circumstances in all respects propitious to a dispassionate discussion. . . . No person can be more competent to give a just construction of the Constitution than those who had a principal agency in forming it; and no administration can claim a more perfect exemption from all those influences which sometimes pervert the judgment even of the most wise and patriotic, than that of the Father of his Country during the first term of his service."

On the point of expediency, the committee said: "Indeed, bank credit and bank paper are so extensively interwoven with the commercial operations of society, that, even if Congress had the constitutional power, it would be utterly an impossibility, to produce so entire a change in the monetary system of the country as to abolish the agency of banks of discount, without involving the community in all the distressing embarrassments usually attendant on great political revolutions, subverting the titles of private property."

The committee also said, and this proved to be in the nature of a prediction, if not of a prophecy: "If the Bank of the United States were destroyed, and local institutions left without its restraining influence, the currency would almost certainly lapse into a state of unsoundness. The pressure which the present bank would cause in winding up its concerns would compel them either to curtail their discounts, when most needed, or to suspend specie payments. It is not difficult to predict which of these alternatives they would adopt under the circumstances in which they would be placed. . . . It has this decided advantage over the army and navy; while they are of scarcely any advantage except in the time of war, the bank is not less so in peace. It has another advantage still greater. If, like the army and navy, it should cost the nation millions annually to sustain it, the expediency of the expenditure might be doubtful; but when it actually saves to the Government and to the country more millions annually than are expended in supporting both the army and navy, it would seem that, if there was one measure of national policy upon which all political parties of the country should be brought to unite by the impressive lessons of experience, it is that of maintaining a national bank." The report which this committee made was concurred in by Congress, and the subject dropped for a time.

But neither reason nor the lessons of experience had any effect upon President Jackson's mind, especially where his friendship or enmity was strongly enlisted, as the latter was in this case against the president of the United States Bank; and he therefore continued to press the matter upon the attention of Congress. At length, in 1832, a bill was reported by a committee of his political friends in the Senate and passed through both Houses of Congress, which were strongly in his favor, rechartering the United States Bank. As was to be expected, President Jackson vetoed this bill, but explicitly stated that, had he been applied to, he would have furnished a plan of a charter which would have been constitutional. An attempt to pass the bill over the veto failed for want of the two-thirds majority required by the Constitution. Had it not been, therefore, for this constitutional requirement, that in order to pass a bill over a veto two-thirds of each branch of Congress must sanction it, the United States Bank would have been rechartered, and the widespread derangement of the currency that followed, and the long-continued distress in all departments of business and of life, would not have occurred. The experience of the country with the veto power in this instance, and in numerous other instances in the subsequent history of the country, would seem to indicate the necessity, or at least the wisdom, of so amending the Constitution that a majority of both Houses of Congress should be as potent in passing a measure over a veto as in passing it in the first place. The wisdom of the President would thus be equally available as under the present system, and his power for evil would be reduced to a minimum.

Returning now to the narration of local events connected with the banks of the District of Columbia, it should be stated that in 1819 there was considerable excitement throughout the country in reference to the suspension of specie payments. But one old merchant and banker of Georgetown, named Romulus Riggs, publicly announced that the banks of the District were paying specie for their notes, and also stated that he held himself responsible for the announcement to that effect. The banks that were then in existence in the District were as follows: The Bank of Columbia, the Farmers and Mechanics' Bank, the Union Bank, all of Georgetown; the Central Bank of Washington and Georgetown; the Bank of the Metropolis, the Patriotic Bank, the Bank of Washington, all of Washington; the Bank of Alexandria, the Union Bank of Alexandria, and the Bank of Potomac, all of Alexandria; and besides these, the Branch Bank of the United States at Washington. So that Mr. Riggs apparently assumed a good deal of responsibility, but it does not appear that he was ever called upon to make good any of the paper of any of these banks.

A peculiar feature of the monetary history of the District was this: that in 1820 the practice prevailed of cutting paper dollars in such a way as to make change. In the latter part of May of this year, the banks adopted a resolution which was calculated to banish from circulation "such an inconvenient and unsightly sort of currency, and to bring silver into use in its place. Those who have cut notes on hand would do well to exchange them for silver before to-morrow evening." This advice was published May 31, so that it appears that June 1 was the last day on which these cut notes were received at the banks.

In 1834, three of the banks in the District of Columbia only, suspended specie payments, the others keeping therefrom by the presidents and directors of each, with the exception of the Bank of the Metropolis, each pledging his individual property as security for the debts of their respective banks. The Bank of the Metropolis had other means of accomplishing the same results. Later, at the near approach of suspension of specie payments by the several banks of the District, together with the winding up of the affairs of the Branch Bank of the United States, it was suggested that it would be a most laudable act if the presidents and directors of all future banks established in the District, and the stockholders as well, should be required by the several charters to pledge their individual fortunes for the debts of the banks in which they were interested. The good effects, it was thought, which would follow such a requirement would

24

be, first, extended confidence in each of the banks; second, the impossibility of loss to the community, even if such a bank should suddenly close its doors; third, increased devotion to the interests of the bank by the officers, and a more lively interest in the management of the bank by the stockholders.

In 1835, when it was thought the completion of the Chesapeake and Ohio Canal was near at hand, and the commerce of the cities of the District was about to be increased a hundred fold, it was plain that the means of carrying on such commerce was at the same time to be rudely taken away. The National Bank, it was conceded, must fall, and of course its branch in Washington, which had furnished from $1,000,000 to $1,500,000 of the circulating medium, must necessarily close its doors. Besides this, the charters of the several banks in the District would expire in March, 1836, and it was at least problematical what disposition Congress would manifest toward them; and then, too, even if these charters should be renewed it was thought they could not supply capital sufficient for the necessities of trade, as they were small institutions, and the competition among them had caused a limited circulation of their notes. In order, therefore, to prevent the difficulties as thus portrayed to the minds of the public, it was thought necessary to establish a new bank to be called the Bank of the District of Columbia.

In December, 1835, Congress took up the question of the recharter of the banks of the District of Columbia, but not before it was necessary for them to do so, as the charters of all of them expired March 3, 1836. The debate was upon the resolution offered by Mr. Thomas, of Maryland, which was as follows:

"*Resolved*, That a select committee be appointed to inquire into the condition of the currency of the District of Columbia, to whom shall be referred all other memorials which may be presented to the present Congress, praying for an extension of the charters of the existing banks in said District of Columbia, or for the establishment of any other bank or banks in their stead, and to inquire into the condition of the currency in said District, to inspect the books and to examine into the proceedings of said banks, to ascertain whether their charters have been violated or not, and whether any abuses or malfeasances have existed in their management — to send for persons and papers, to examine witnesses on oath, and to appoint a clerk to report their proceedings."

This resolution, after warm debate, in which the Hon. John Quincy Adams bore a most conspicuous part, and after it was amended by striking out the words, "to whom shall be referred all other memorials which may be presented to the present Congress," was adopted, and the following select committee appointed: Mr. Thomas of Maryland, Mr. Pierce of New Hampshire, Mr. Reed of Massachusetts, Mr. May of Illinois, Mr. Beaumont of Pennsylvania, Mr. Huntsman of Tennessee, Mr. Pinckney of South Carolina, Mr. Garland of Louisiana, and Mr. Claiborne of Mississippi.

On January 5, 1836, Mr. Benton, in the Senate, introduced a resolution for the appointment of a select committee of five members to act with those appointed by the House, which was laid on the table. In consequence of there having been made charges of mismanagement on the part of the banks of the District of Columbia, a certain citizen of Washington published in the *National Intelligencer* of January 16, 1836, a statement showing that the banks of the District were prepared to meet their liabilities immediately, if necessary, in the following ratio: The Bank of Washington, 49.84 per cent.; Patriotic Bank of Washington, 71.81 per cent.; Bank of the Metropolis, 46.88 per cent.; Union Bank of Georgetown, 78.30; Farmers and Mechanics' Bank of Georgetown, 54.52 per cent.; Farmers' Bank of Alexandria, 43.21; Bank of Potomac, 51.85 per cent.

For each dollar of liabilities, except capital stock, each bank had assets as follows: Bank of Washington, $3.30; Patriotic Bank, $1.64; Bank of the Metropolis, $1.39; Union Bank of Georgetown, $2.46; Farmers and Mechanics' Bank of Georgetown, $3.05; Farmers' Bank of Alexandria, $1.57; Bank of Potomac, $2.32.

The entire circulation of the seven banks of the District at that time was $964,799.90. The specie possessed by them was $643,585.52. The aggregate liabilities of the seven banks, exclusive of their capital stock, was $2,813,925.26, and their cash funds amounted to $1,492,814.56. To meet these balances the banks had discount notes amounting to $3,141,559.95; real estate, $318,688.25, and stocks, $228,301.93; total, $3,688,550.13, a surplus of $2,367,439.43.

The bill rechartering the banks of the District was at length passed by Congress in June, 1836, their several charters being extended to July 4, 1838. In August, 1836, the Branch Bank of the United States, in Washington, Richard Smith cashier, advertised its property for sale. In Washington this property consisted of somewhat more than forty lots, some of them vacant, and some of them having houses upon them. In Georgetown there were several lots with houses upon them; and besides all these, there was a tract of land in Virginia and another in Maryland.

On May 13, 1836, a notice was published in the press by the Bank of Washington, and by the Bank of the Metropolis in almost identical language, to the effect that notwithstanding information had reached Washington of the suspension of specie payments by the banks in New York, as well as by some of those in Philadelphia and Baltimore, they had determined to continue to pay specie; and, satisfied of the strength of their respective banks, "the president, directors, and cashier have determined to pledge their private fortunes for all just claims against the institution." This was a part of the notice in the case of each bank. Of the Washington Bank, W. Gunston was president, and J. Adams cashier; of the Bank of the Metropolis, General John P. Van Ness was president, and George Thomas cashier. The Farmers and Mechanics' Bank of Georgetown also refused to suspend.

The determination to suspend specie payments had been arrived at in New York on May 11, and was the result of the peculiar and great stringency of the times. This great stringency was itself the result of President Jackson's "Experiment," and was brought to a crisis by his famous "Treasury circular," issued a short time previously, exacting specie in payment for all public lands, under the operations of which circular the receipts for public lands was reduced from $24,800,000 in 1836, to $6,700,000 in 1837. This circular, however, permitted duties on imports into the Atlantic cities to be paid in bank notes. It is a singular circumstance that the Government itself, by one of its deposit banks, was the first to refuse the payment of specie. This occurred about May 1, 1836, at Natchez, Mississippi, Treasury drafts for a large sum of money being refused payment by the Planters' Bank of Mississippi, and protested. "All this comes of the ignorance and folly which enforced the Treasury circular. The Administration, however, in thus warring against the prosperity of the country, by undertaking to regulate the deposits, and the currency, for party purposes, has dug its own grave, and would bury the country also in it, rather than retract its wicked measures or acknowledge its errors. We anticipate that you must also suspend specie payments in the North, and look with deep anxiety for news by every mail." [1]

It was explained in the interest of the New York banks, that their suspension was rendered necessary by a continual drain upon their specie resources in response to demands from Philadelphia and

---

[1] Letter written from Natchez, May 3, 1836, to a correspondent in Philadelphia.

Baltimore; and the benefit of the measure was realized by the united action of the banks of New York. Then, when New York refused to pay specie in her dealings with Philadelphia and Baltimore, and other cities, it of course became necessary for those other cities to refuse to pay specie in their dealings with New York. The suspension thus became general throughout the country, the Bank of the United States acting in concert with the other banks, and including also the Treasury banks; for, when the Treasury banks refused to pay specie, why should other banks pay specie to the Treasury banks? The Bank of the United States pursued this course, believing the measure to be a temporary and precautionary one, and with the desire to preserve its strength unbroken, so as to be able to lead the way to resumption as soon as the Government should become able to pay its creditors in specie.

But this universal suspension of specie payments by the banks of the country was a most striking object lesson; it was a most unequivocal confession of the complete impotence of the banking system then in vogue. It also most clearly exposed the quackery of the politico-financial invention known as the Safety Fund, which, by being to a great extent relied upon, produced a delusion of safety, and, like a safety-valve which gets out of order for want of attention, became one of the most efficient causes of the suspension which ensued. It taught the banks to rely upon the supervision of a common authority, and to the chances of a common security, instead of upon that precaution and sagacious foresight which regulate individual enterprise.

But one of the most interesting and instructive features of the times was that already alluded to, with reference to the Government itself suspending specie payments. In Philadelphia, on May 12, some of that city's merchants called at the customhouse to make payment of bonds, in order to avoid suit for non-payment, as threatened by the Secretary of the Treasury in an order issued May 8. These merchants offered notes on the Government deposit bank in payment of the bonds, which were refused, the Government requiring payment in gold or silver. On the same day, the customhouse in Philadelphia, having certain liabilities to meet, refused to pay specie. On May 13, a merchant in Philadelphia, having to pay a certain sum to the Government, tendered payment to the Government deposit bank in its own notes, and they were refused, the merchant being told that the Government would receive nothing but gold or silver.

This refusal was in accordance with the following order, issued May 12:

"*To Collectors of Customs:*

"If the bank where you deposit should suspend specie payments, you will yourself collect, and keep in your own hands, the public money for all duties at your port until further directions are given to you by this department how to deposit, transfer, or pay it. You must, of course, continue to adhere to the existing laws of Congress, and to the former instructions of the Treasury, in respect to the kind of money receivable for customs, and by which it is understood to be your duty to require payments to be made in specie and in the notes of specie banks that are at par.

"LEVI WOODBURY,

"Secretary of the Treasury."

A New York merchant, on May 12, 1837, wrote: "Had the President but intimated that specie would come back in time, or that drafts of New York for specie would be avoided, or that the circular would be revoked in the summer, it would have given confidence; and that is all that was wanted. But nothing — no, nothing was done, and the greatest disgrace any Administration has suffered to rest upon its head has fallen upon the present.

"To the dominant authority, then, I would say: You have failed; you have failed in establishing a 'better currency'; you have failed in the 'experiment'; you have failed in regulating exchanges; you have failed in a specie currency; you have failed in your safety-fund plan; you have failed in putting the deposits in safe keeping; you have failed in relation to the currency; you have failed in every thing but but one — you have succeeding in destroying the National Bank."

Throughout the country a national bank was the great desideratum. This was the constant and continuous refrain: "Give us a national bank." But that had been destroyed, because, as has been said before, of President Jackson's hostility to the president of that institution, not because of his understanding anything connected with the principles of banking or political economy, for of these he understood but little. The result was wide-spread distress. Bank notes in one part of the country were at a great discount, in another part of the country entirely worthless, and the people in the various cities were busy in fabricating paper representatives of every part of a dollar. In New York, merchants had recourse to checks upon restaurants in the payment of small sums. In Washington, all kinds of paper were in circulation, the extreme limit being reached in the issue of notes by a certain barber, whose name might be given, who, upon the presentation of his notes for redemption, said: "What do I want of those things? I don't want anything to do with them; go and buy something with them!"

May 16, 1837, the Bank of the Metropolis of Washington issued printed notices announcing its suspension of specie payments, and then the Bank of Washington, which had sustained for three days a heavy run upon it for specie, finding itself standing alone in the city, resolved to close its vaults. It was, however, then prepared to redeem its circulating notes to the last dollar; but it was thought that such a course would only tend to embarrass the mercantile classes, without relieving the public. This bank, therefore, also suspended on the 16th, and was thought to be the last bank to suspend in the Union.

The fundamental vice of President Jackson was in introducing and carrying out his "experiment"; not so much in his antipathy to the Bank of the United States. His animosity could not so easily have destroyed that institution and caused the great evils that succeeded, had that animosity been confined within constitutional limits. But he permitted his animosity to lead him to the destruction of the bank, which the will of the people clearly indicated they wished to stand; and afterward, when the representatives of the people expressed their opinion by a vote of one hundred and nine to forty-six that the Bank of the United States was a safe place to keep the public deposits, and notwithstanding that the law had given to the Secretary of the Treasury unqualified and exclusive power over them, when the Secretary of the Treasury refused to remove them, then President Jackson removed the Secretary of the Treasury and placed another Secretary in his place who had no scruples as to their removal.

Next came one of President Jackson's greatest official mistakes. This was in permitting the law which passed the House March 1, 1837, designed to counteract the evil effects of the specie circular,— by providing that, under certain conditions, and in accordance with certain regulations, no duties, taxes, or sums of money payable for lands should be collected or received otherwise than in the legal currency of the United States, or in notes of banks which were payable and paid on demand in said legal currency of the United States,—to fail, by retaining it in his possession until after Congress had adjourned. This act was passed by the Senate by a vote of 41 to 5, and by the House by a vote of 143 to 59.

The nature of the financial distress may be inferred from the fact that on Saturday evening, May 20, 1837, a public meeting was

held to consider the propriety of an issue of corporation notes to
serve the purpose of change during the suspension of specie payments
by the banks. Thomas Munroe was called to the chair, and Edward
Hanley and Henry Bradley made secretaries. Two series of resolutions were introduced, opposed to each other, one favoring the issue
of corporation notes, the other opposing such issue. Speeches were
made by several gentlemen on either side of the question. Mr. Cunningham and Mr. Hoban spoke against the proposition, and Mr. G.
Sweeney and Mr. D. Clagett in favor of it. But when the corporation
came to act on the suggestion of the meeting, they found that a law
of Congress, which had been approved June 30, 1834, forbade the
corporations of Washington, Georgetown, and Alexandria to issue any
new promissory notes or bills of a less sum than $10; hence the entire
subject was indefinitely postponed.

The banks of Washington which had suspended specie payments
were requested by resolution to resume, so far as the $5 notes were
concerned. To these resolutions each bank replied separately. These
banks were the Bank of the Metropolis, of which John P. Van Ness
was president; the Patriotic Bank, of which W. A. Bradley was
president, and the Bank of Washington, of which Richard C. Washington was president; the first on the 29th of May, and the other
two on the 30th. The substance of each reply was, that while the
bank was anxious to comply with the request, yet it could not be
done with safety or with benefit to the public by any one bank or
by the banks of any one city. The Chesapeake and Ohio Canal
Company, unable to obtain corporation notes of $1 and $2, determined
to issue notes of its own in sums of $2, $1, and fifty cents, in order
to carry on its business. These notes, while serving the purposes of
the company, found their way among the people generally, and
"enabled them to transact their little everyday business."

An act was passed by Congress May 25, 1838, which was in part
as follows:

"*Be it enacted,* That the charters of the Farmers and Mechanics'
Bank of Georgetown, the Bank of the Metropolis, the Patriotic Bank
of Washington, the Bank of Washington, and the Farmers' Bank of
Alexandria, and the Bank of Potomac, in the town of Alexandria, be,
and the same are hereby, extended to the 4th of July, 1840, provided
that said banks, each for itself, shall conform to the following conditions:

"1. To cease receiving and paying out all paper currency of a
less denomination than $5, on or before the promulgation of this act.

"2. To redeem all their notes of the denomination of $5, in gold or silver, from and after the first day of August of the present year.

"3. To resume specie payments in full on or before the first day of January, 1839, or sooner if the principal banks of Baltimore and Richmond shall sooner resume payments in full."

These conditions were justly considered very harsh by the banks. With respect to the first, it was clearly seen that to prohibit the use of notes less than $5 could only cause great inconvenience to persons who had to pay out small sums; and the prohibition to circulate their own $5 notes, or, in other words, the requisition that they should pay them in full in specie on and after the 1st of August (which meant the same thing, for so large a part of the District circulation was in $5 notes), made it necessary for the banks to considerably reduce their discounts. It was freely declared that the conditions imposed upon the banks of the District were such as the several Congressmen would not have imposed on the banks of their respective States.

Specie payments were generally resumed early in 1839, and in this connection, when Nicholas Biddle resigned the presidency of the United States Bank, March 29, 1839, it was said of him by a friend of General Jackson, who was at the same time an opponent of the bank, that Mr. Biddle's course with reference to cotton, the great staple of the country, during the eighteen months previous to his resignation, had saved the country $25,000,000, and had enabled the banks to resume specie payments. This resumption was not, however, of long duration. Distress began to be felt in the succeeding summer, and finally, on October 10, the banks in Philadelphia suspended, giving as the reason therefor that the failure of the harvests in England, in 1838, caused a demand on the Bank of England for more than £6,000,000 for export to the Continent in payment for grain. The withdrawal of so large an amount of specie produced at once a depression of the value of cotton and other American produce, and lessened our means in England of paying for the large amount of importations of foreign merchandise. There had been for this reason a continual drain upon the banks for specie to ship to Europe to supply this deficiency. The banks, therefore, thought it best to suspend, and thus to keep the gold and silver at home. On the 11th of October, the banks of Baltimore followed the lead of the Philadelphia banks, and on the same day the banks of the District of Columbia, at a meeting of the representatives of several of them, passed the following resolutions:

" WHEREAS, Information is received that the banks of Philadelphia and Baltimore have suspended specie payments for the present, and it being the opinion of the several banks in the cities of Washington here represented that the safety of the banks and the interests of the community will not be promoted by an attempt to sustain specie payments while the suspension of Northern banks shall continue; and

" WHEREAS, The banks here have abundant means to meet all their liabilities, yet as a considerable part of these means has become unavailable for the present, as specie funds, by the suspension of the banks of Philadelphia and Baltimore; be it therefore

" *Resolved*, That it be, and is hereby, recommended to the several banks here represented, to suspend specie payments for the present, with the pledge of said banks to resume as soon as the banks of Philadelphia and Baltimore shall do so."

The Patriotic Bank was not represented at this meeting and did not suspend, as it had some time before reduced its circulation considerably. At this time, there were six banks in the District—two in Alexandria, one in Georgetown, and three in Washington. In order to show that they were worthy of public confidence, the following statement of their condition on the 1st of February, 1840, was published:

Amount of capital, $1,762,880; notes in circulation, $651,640.65; post notes, $12,000; individual deposits, $749,304.44; public deposits, $248,377.90; due to other banks, $250,209.60; unclaimed dividends, $14,900.24; profit and loss, $270,873; total liabilities, $3,960,185.83. Resources—Amount of bills and notes discounted, $2,447,600.65; specie, $323,689.89; specie funds, $154,753.75; due from banks, $256,-801.41; notes of other banks, $197,373.38; real estate, $218,152.99; sundry stocks, $286,142.28; legal expenses, $25,077.81; suspense accounts, $50,593.67; total, $3,960,185.83. Surplus, profit and loss above, $270,873; from which, after deducting suspense accounts, errors, etc., equal to $94,220.50, there remained a net surplus of $176,652.50.

On July 1, 1840, the question came up in Congress as to whether the charters of the banks of the District should be continued, on that part of a motion by Mr. Cooper, of Pennsylvania, which was an amendment to Mr. Petrikin's, which prohibited, after a certain day, the issue of notes of a denomination less than $20. It was decided in the negative by a vote of 83 to 98, so that this part of Mr. Cooper's amendment was rejected. The question then recurred on so much of Mr. Cooper's amendment as prohibited after the 1st of January, 1841, the issue of notes of a less denomination than

$50, and it was decided in the negative by a vote of 60 to 106. The question then came up on agreeing to the following amendment: "*Provided, also,* that the president and directors of each of the banks shall jointly and severally, in their individual capacity, be liable for all notes issued or debts contracted by said banks respectively, from and after the day this act goes into effect, to be recovered as other debts of like amount are recovered." This was decided in the affirmative by a vote of 92 to 90.

The question then came up on the following amendment: "*Provided,* that said banks shall not make any dividends during the time the said banks shall refuse to pay all their liabilities on demand," which was decided in the affirmative by a vote of 145 to 25. The question then came on this further amendment: "And the president and directors of any of the said banks, who shall make any such division of profits, or declare any such dividend, or consent to or vote for the same, shall be liable to pay double the amount of the sum so. divided or declared, to be recovered of them, in their individual capacity, by any person suing for the same, as debts of like amount are recoverable, one-half of said forfeiture to go to the person suing, and the other half to the corporation where said bank is located." Justices of the peace within the District of Columbia were given jurisdiction in all actions for debt against the banks whose charters were extended, for sums not exceeding $100, and no appeal was allowed unless the president or one or more of the directors of the bank should make affidavit that such appeal was not taken for the purpose of delay. This amendment passed by a vote of 94 to 78.

An amendment was then passed, by a vote of 96 to 76, that the said banks should not 'issue notes of a less sum than $10. Then followed an amendment that their notes should be redeemable at all times in specie, or, on failure to redeem as required, the charter of any bank so failing should be forfeited. This amendment passed by a vote of 101 to 77. Then came the following amendment: "That in case said banks, or any of them, shall refuse or fail to pay their notes in specie, any person shall and may have remedy by judgment and execution at law, at a notice of ten days, before any justice of the peace of the said District." This was passed by a vote of 87 to 71.

The question then came up on ordering the above amendments to be engrossed and the bill to be read a third time, when it was decided in the negative by a vote of 69 to 90. A motion to reconsider the question was lost by a vote of 94 to 86, not two-thirds in the affirmative.

Mr. Halleman then introduced a bill to continue the charters of the banks in the District of Columbia for certain purposes: "That the provisions, restrictions, and enactments of the Act of Congress of May 25, 1838, entitled 'An Act to Extend the Charter of the Union Bank of Georgetown, in the District of Columbia,' be, and the same are hereby, extended to the Farmers and Mechanics' Bank, of Georgetown; the Bank of the Metropolis; the Bank of Washington; the Patriotic Bank, of Washington; the Bank of Potomac, and the Farmers' Bank, of Alexandria. *Provided*, that whenever in the original act the 4th of July, 1838, occurs, it shall be construed to mean the 4th of July, 1840, and whenever the 4th of July, 1842, occurs, it shall be construed to mean the 4th of July, 1844."

On Friday, July 3, 1840, Mr. Underwood moved to amend the bill by adding:

"That if the said banks, or any or either of them, shall, within ninety days from and after the passage of this act, resume specie payments, then the said banks, or such of them as shall so resume, shall be entitled to all the rights and privileges conferred by their present charters until the 4th of July, 1842, unless Congress shall at any time otherwise direct; but if such banks so resuming shall at any time after such resumption again suspend specie payments, or refuse to pay any of their notes or other obligations in specie, then such suspension or refusal shall operate as a forfeiture of their respective charters, except for the purpose of winding up their affairs under the provisions and restrictions contained in this act; *and provided, further,* in all cases where the said banks, or either of them, thereafter refuse payment of any of their notes or obligations, there shall be a summary remedy therefor before any justice or judge having jurisdiction of the case by giving five days' notice, wherein there shall be no *supersedeas,* stay, execution, or injunction, or *certiorari* allowed, nor any appeal, except upon an affidavit of merits by the president, cashier, or directors.

"SECTION 2. That if the president and directors of either of said banks shall violate the provisions aforesaid, they, and each of them, shall be fined in a sum not less than $100 nor more than $1,000 for every offense, to be recovered by presentment or indictment in any court of record having jurisdiction thereof."

This amendment was sustained by a vote of 98 to 70. The bill as thus amended was ordered to be engrossed for a third reading by a vote of 108 yeas to 69 nays. It was then read a third time, and passed by a vote of 115 to 75, and sent to the Senate. In this body it was reported without Mr. Underwood's amendment; was returned to the House, and there passed by a vote of 124 to 19; again sent to the Senate, and then to the President, for his signature.

Upon this action of Congress, the *National Intelligencer* said: "As things now stand, the people of the District of Columbia are made an exception to the privileges enjoyed by all the rest of the American people, by being deprived of the use of those facilities indispensable, under the existing circumstances of the country, to the prosecution of almost any branch of trade or manufactures. The extension of the charters of these banks was resisted by a large proportion of the friends of the Administration with a dogged preseverance which cannot fail to fix the attention and excite the surprise of every distant reader, as it has excited the surprise of everybody, in and out of Congress, who was not privy to the design to abolish the banks entirely."

While the bill above referred to was under discussion, Mr. Dawson, of Georgia, made a very able speech in opposition to the attempt to compel the banks to resume specie payments. He said: "I am against destroying the relation of creditor and debtor. I will not vote to depreciate the value of property, to raise the value of money, and thereby to empower the creditor to bring all the property of the debtor under the hammer. That will be the operation of the bill. All you, by voting for this bill, appreciate money one hundred per cent., and depreciate all property fifty per cent. At one blow, you cut off the five heads of these District banks, and throw them bleeding into these ten miles square; and you tell them, 'Now die, and close up your respective concerns — for you may live no longer.' For the sake of your political experiment in bringing a 'hard money currency' into this devoted District, you stand by with stony hearts and look upon the ruin of these defenseless people as if it were a spectacle exhibited at a theater, all to carry out your beautiful scheme of reform and a 'hard money currency.' Well, sir, let the example be carried out; let those who are for compelling these defenseless people of the District to use nothing but hard money go into their own States and get the State legislatures to collect the taxes in hard coin, and to pay for all their works of improvement in the same hard money. Try it there, and how long do you think your Government will exist? I call upon you to come out from the bushes and show your faces. Do to the people of this District as you are willing to do to the people of your own States," etc.

When Congress adjourned, July 21, 1840, after having failed to take action looking to a continuance of the corporate existence of the banks, bank privileges were suspended in the District, on July 4. After that day no bank could reissue its notes, make any discounts or loans, or incur or receive any new obligation. The result was that bank notes of any kind could scarcely be found in quantities sufficient to transact the daily business of the community. By many it was believed there was no hope for the District except in a change in the administration. During several years the people of the District had been for the most part intensely Whig in their political sentiments, and this was sufficient for many in Congress to do what they could in any way to punish them. This fact is more clearly set forth in the chapter on municipal affairs, and hence is only referred to in this connection in order to point out briefly the reasons for the non-action of Congress in regard to a matter of grave import to the commercial interests of the people of the District.

As every one knows, the change in the administration so long hoped for by these people at length came, in the election of William Henry Harrison to the Presidency, and of John Tyler to the Vice-Presidency. Not long after the result of this election became known, a memorial to Congress was circulated for the signatures of merchants, tradesmen, mechanics, and other citizens of Washington, setting forth that "the condition of your memorialists resulting from the present state of the incorporate banks in the city of Washington is such as, in their opinion, calls for some effectual and speedy remedy to be applied by your honorable body," and closing with the following: "Your memorialists therefore humbly pray that the act passed by your honorable body, at your last session, entitled, 'An Act to Continue the Corporate Existence of Certain Banks in the District of Columbia for Certain Purposes,' may be speedily repealed, and that the banks of the city of Washington may again be chartered for a reasonable time, with such provisions for the security of the public interests as may seem just and proper, and not inconsistent with a due degree of usefulness to your memorialists and their fellow-citizens."

The next day after the adjournment of Congress, Hon. William Cost Johnson, member from the Fifth District of Maryland, and one of the ablest men in the House, issued an address to the people of the District of Columbia, in which he made use of the following language:

"It was known that the voice of the District, if not their votes, was against the continuance of the present Executive head, and that fact was at once the reason and the cause why the House of Representatives would not, in an eight-months' session, grant a single request of the committee [the District Committee of the House, of which Mr. Johnson was chairman], or even give a single request or measure emanating from the committee a decent hearing or respectful consideration.

"A Congress professing to be Democratic, and the Constitution, which they have sworn to support, making it the Legislature for the District, and with the fullest knowledge of the sentiment of the people of the District in relation to various measures — this Congress, thus constituted and thus advised, whilst they were vociferous and declamatory about their Republican principles, set all the obligations of the Constitution in this respect at defiance. Not only did they disregard every principle of Republicanism in refusing to obey the will of the people of this District in relation to their own measures and business, but to punish the people who have the temerity to refuse allegiance to Mr. Van Buren, they went counter in their vindictive feelings to their own pretended principles, refused to recharter one of the banks of the District which had not suspended specie payments, and again refused to recharter the banks generally with a condition that they should immediately resume specie payments. With a malignant pleasure, they seemed to revel in their work of ruin and destruction, in serving the President and maintaining their principles; principles as disreputable to the head as they were perverting to the heart."

In the meantime, two of the banks of the District, the Bank of the Metropolis, and the Farmers and Mechanics' Bank of Georgetown, resolved to pay all their notes and other obligations in specie, this action being taken on July 6, 1840. The published notice of the former bank was signed by John P. Van Ness, president, and Richard Smith, cashier; and that by the latter by J. I. Stull, cashier.

It is well known that one of the principal reasons for the over-throw of the Democratic Party in 1840, by the election of William Henry Harrison, was that there might be a reform of the currency, which had been thrown into almost inextricable confusion by President Jackson, and continued in that condition through the administration of President Van Buren. In order to effect this reform as soon as possible, President Harrison called Congress together in extra session, and at this extra session Congress passed a bill providing for a "Fiscal Bank," which was only another name for a national bank, to be located in the city of Washington. Henry Clay was one of the principal supporters of the proposed bank, remaining in Congress mainly for the purpose of assisting to perfect this and other necessary legislation. But, unfortunately for the country, President Harrison died before the opportunity came for him to assist this necessary work by his signature, and the Vice-President, John Tyler, became the President. President Tyler, when the bill establishing the Fiscal Bank was presented to him for his signature, returned it to Congress with his objections, two in number — first, that he was conscientiously opposed to a national bank, because in his view such an institution was clearly unconstitutional, and he had taken an oath to support and defend that sacred instrument. This was a great surprise and a great disappointment to the party that had elevated him to power, but he said that the Whigs, when they nominated him for the Vice-Presidency, knew what his views had always been, and so in fact had no one to blame but themselves for finding themselves in the condition that they were. President Tyler's other reason for vetoing the Bank bill was that there was a possibility of some one or more of the States having a Branch Bank of the United States established within her or their borders against the will of the people, as under the bill as it was presented to him such branch could be established in any State, provided that State should not decide against it at the first meeting of its legislature after the passage of the bill by Congress. So that all the States that desired precisely such an institution were deprived of the great benefits that would have followed the establishment of such an institution within their limits because of the fear in the President's mind that some one State might have a branch bank established, and thus have its benefits forced upon her against her consent. This latter reason of the President was in all probability as flimsy an argument as has ever appeared in a state paper; and then, with reference to the first reason, — his conscientious opposition because it was in his view unconstitutional, — it may be said that such conscientious convictions with reference to the organic law were hardly sustained by his subsequent career in the Presidential office. After the veto of the Fiscal Bank bill, Congress attempted to frame one which, as they understood it, was in accordance with the President's views as to what a national bank should be, giving to it the name of a "Fiscal Corporation," to be located within the District of Columbia, with a capital of $21,000,000. The bill providing for this Fiscal Corporation was likewise vetoed by the President, because he was unable to see the difference between a "Fiscal Bank" and a "Fiscal Corporation." If one was unconstitutional, so was the other.

Here again were strikingly illustrated the evils of which the veto power is capable. Had Congress been able to pass a measure over the veto by a majority vote, instead of a two-thirds vote, the country would have been enabled to possess all the advantages of a sound currency, and prosperity would have again smiled upon the labors of all classes of people. But instead of this great blessing, the currency kept on going from bad to worse. In Washington, "if our sufferings are not intolerable, they are too grievous to be borne, the best of our currency being the outstanding certificates of deposit thrown into circulation by the banks. Congress has indeed reinstated the charters of the banks, but with the conditions that, so long as the banks of States on either side of us do not pay specie, our banks can keep out no circulation, and, of course, can do no business." The bankable paper of the District at that time consisted of the notes of the banks of the District, certificates of deposit of those banks, and notes of the banks of Baltimore and of banks in cities north of Maryland. By far the greatest part of the bank circulation, however, was of the Virginia banks, which, for some reason that was not then clear, could not then be made bankable, except at a loss of $3 per hundred to the possessor. Besides this, there was a flood of the notes of the Baltimore and Ohio Railroad Company, of denominations less than $5, which, up to near the latter part of 1841, circulated at par, and then becoming depreciated in Baltimore, they also, of course, settled in Washington to about ten per cent. below par. So great was the loss and confusion that was occasioned, that the merchants of Baltimore agreed not to receive them in payment for anything except at their actual value.

The following figures relate to the condition of the banks on December 31, 1841: Bank of the Metropolis — Capital, $500,000; deposits, $223,040.02; circulation, $21,620.26; specie on hand, $81,680.61. Richard Smith was cashier at that time. Bank of Washington — Capital, $359,840; deposits, $170,372.21; circulation, $7,180; specie funds and Treasury notes, $71,269.68. James Adams was then cashier. Patriotic Bank, of Washington,— Capital, $250,000; circulation, $25,686. Farmers and Mechanics' Bank, of Georgetown,— Net capital, $317,265.

In January, 1842, the rates of discount in Washington were as follows: Baltimore and Ohio Railroad notes, 20 to 25 per cent. discount; Virginia notes, from 4 to 5 per cent. discount; specie was from 3 to 3½ per cent. above Baltimore bank notes, while the notes of the banks of the District were equal to specie, and the certificates of deposit of the Patriotic Bank were equal to Baltimore bank notes.

Congress, during its extra session of 1841, labored hard and faithfully to remedy the evils inflicted upon the country by the derangement of the currency, but all their efforts were unavailing because of what, at length, in the language of the times, came to be

known as President Tyler's "conscientious" scruples as to the constitutionality of the measures by it adopted. From the termination
of the extra session to the opening of the next regular session,
and during the regular session, the condition of the currency was
persistently growing worse. In three-fourths of the States there
was, in fact, nothing that could be called currency, except by courtesy.
In Philadelphia, there was no bank paper which any man would hold
a moment longer than was necessary to rid himself of it. In Washington, the notes of the banks of several of the States, which were
in tolerably fair credit at home, could not be converted into funds at
less than from five to twenty per cent. discount, while the notes of
banks of other States could not be converted into funds upon any
terms. A remarkable illustration of the condition of the currency in
1842, the result of fourteen years experiment by incompetent hands,
was furnished by the following notice, published in the Mobile *Prices
Current*, June 29, that year: "A sight check on New York for
$5,000 was yesterday sold at forty-two per cent. premium." Another
instance was cited in the public prints — that of a gentleman in
Philadelphia, who had just received a remittance from St. Louis in
Virginia money, for which the St. Louis agent had paid ten per
cent. premium, and which, on its arrival in Philadelphia, was found
to be at a discount of about ten per cent., causing a loss of twenty
per cent. on the transaction. Such facts as these demonstrated to all
business men, and all other rational men, that the great necessity of
the country was a national currency, of equal value in all parts of the
Union. Such a currency could not be furnished by State banking
institutions. President Jackson's "better currency" was little else
than an aggravation everywhere, because it was practically a fraud
and a delusion. The specie standard was established at various
points, as at Cincinnati, Louisville, St. Louis, New Orleans, etc., and
yet the traveler at the West or South, starting from any of these
points, often found it necessary to change his funds, and at every
change he was compelled to lose from three to ten per cent. At
Louisville, specie-paying New Orleans funds were from five to ten
per cent. discount, and in Indiana three per cent. At St. Louis,
Kentucky paper was at a discount of from four to five per cent. There
was no money then in the country that would pass for its face
everywhere but American gold, and that could not be had for less
than three per cent. premium in silver.

One of the strongest statements made, or possible to be made,
with reference to the condition into which the currency had been

brought by the administrations of President Andrew Jackson and President Martin Van Buren, was contained in a letter to the Hon. John C. Calhoun by General James Hamilton, then an ex-member of Congress from South Carolina, and a stanch friend of General Jackson at the time of his elevation to the Presidency, and for several years thereafter. The letter was written in London, England, September 29, 1842, after several months' observation as to the credit of the several States, and of the United States, in Europe. He said that the great necessity of the country was a uniform circulation, which should be of the same value in New Orleans and in Boston. "This circulation, in the recesses of financial wisdom which is past finding out, was destroyed by our friend, General Jackson, when he slew the Bank of the United States, with the arm of Samson, and almost 'with the selfsame weapon,' too, when we recollect all the twaddle of the old gentleman on the subject. He, as Burke said, was certainly 'a consummate architect of ruin' in his time and tide, and had the happy faculty of impersonating, in his mind's eye, a corporation for the purpose of hating it as cordially as he once did you and Mr. Poindexter. When, thereafter, Mr. Biddle entered into a contest with this hero of two wars, he forgot the wisdom of a Spanish proverb, 'that he who sits down to dine with the Devil should eat with a long spoon.' What has been the result of this feast of broken meat and empty plates you well know. It has left our country hungry of flesh, indeed, and poor in spirit. I doubt, since the creation of the world, whether such an example can be exhibited as we have presented for the last sixteen years, of folly and misgovernment. No Southern planter would permit his plantation for an hour to be governed with such a lack of all sense and providence. The Caffres and Hottentots, in reference to their condition, I doubt not, have been governed with a policy far more vigilant and enlightened. A country of immense resources, in a period of profound peace, on the verge of bankruptcy! No man who has ever read Hume's essay on 'Public Credit,' and on 'Money,' can be at any loss to trace our present condition to its true cause. . . . This result has been, first, in the constant action of the Federal Government, or their supposed meditated action, on the banks of the States, which created a universal panic; and next, the General Government permitted to remain in criminal abeyance their several functions to supply a currency equal to the wants of the country, and to regulate its value. . . . But, my good sir, the day of reckoning must come. The account will be adjusted now, or by posterity. One of its first sums will be to settle what the victory at New Orleans has cost us. Napoleon's victories, in cost, were no more to be compared to the victory at New Orleans than a penny whistle is to Baron Munchausen's celebrated clarion under an April thaw. I calculate that the victory of the 8th of January cost us $500,000,000, besides the small expense of entailing upon the country a set of drivelers, whose folly has taken away all dignity from distress, and made even calamity ridiculous. You will say: 'Hold! You and I were greatly responsible for this hero's getting into power.' Yes, it is true! Willingly would I expiate this sin, sir, with my blood, if I could recall the fatal past, but this is impossible," etc.

But the "Whig Congress" adjourned, March 4, 1843, without granting a recharter to the District banks, and as showing the feeling of the opposition party toward these banks, the following from the Ohio *Statesman*, of March 7, is extremely expressive:

"There was one bright and glorious spot in the close of this Congress besides its eternal dissolution; namely, the District banks failed to get a recharter. The rotten things are now defunct, and their putrid carcasses are left to dry up in the summer's sun, for a more corrupt and rascally set of Whig shaving shops did not exist in the Union."

But notwithstanding this outburst of malice, the fact was that these banks were honestly conducted, they paying specie even when other banks did not, and always when other banks did. They were at that time paying specie, and were quite as able to meet their engagements as any banks in the States on either side of the District. But the triumph of the enemies of the District banks was not destined to be permanent. In March, 1844, a bill to extend their charters was reported to the House of Representatives, which became a law June 17, 1844. This law, however, did not specifically extend the charters of any of the banks in the District of Columbia. It only provided that each of them might be party to a suit at law, by which debts due by or to any of them might be collected. Afterward, there was no legislation upon banking in the District, except such as provided for the temporary extension of the charter of the Union Bank of Georgetown for the specific purpose of winding up its affairs, until after the beginning of the War of the Rebellion, and the District banks existed merely as financial institutions, without special banking privileges.

The Freedman's Savings and Trust Company was incorporated by an act of Congress approved March 3, 1865, with fifty incorporators — thirty-one of whom were from New York, seven from Massachusetts, two from Rhode Island, six from Pennsylvania, and four from Ohio. These incorporators were also made by this act the first trustees of the institution, and were required to elect from their own number a president and two vice-presidents. Other officers were also provided for. The object of the incorporation was to receive on deposit such sums of money as might be, from time to time, offered by or on behalf of persons previously held in slavery, or their descendants, and to invest them in the stocks, bonds, Treasury notes, or other securities of the United States. The books of the company were to be open to inspection to such persons as Congress should appoint.

The business of the company was at first, and for some time, conducted in New York City, with the following officers: President, William A. Booth; first vice-president, Mahlon T. Hewitt; second vice-president, Walter S. Griffith; secretary, J. W. Alvord. When the headquarters of the company were removed to Washington, J. W. Alvord became president, D. W. Anderson vice-president, and W. J. Wilson cashier. The business of the bank was prosperous and well conducted until the original charter was so amended, May 6, 1870, as to authorize the trustees and officers of the company to make loans to the extent of one-half of the deposits on unincumbered real estate situated in the vicinity of the several branches of the company, to the extent of one-half the value of such real estate. By this amendment to the original charter, and by Section 6 of the act of incorporation creating an available fund, Congress opened the door to trouble, which eventually wrecked the institution. And this event was not long delayed. Some of the funds of the bank were recklessly invested, and not always, or perhaps often, with a view to the benefit of the depositors. The business was very extensive. There were thirty-four branches of the company, in all parts of the country. The growth of the business was extremely rapid, the deposits for the year ending March 1, 1866, amounting to $305,167, while for the year ending March 1, 1871, they were $19,952,647.36. When it was discovered that the affairs of the company were in an unsatisfactory condition, a board of commissioners was appointed to take charge. These commissioners were John A. J. Creswell, Robert Purvis, and Robert H. T. Leipold. The deposits then in the aggregate had amounted to about $56,000,000, and about $53,000,000 had been paid back to the depositors, leaving about $3,000,000 still due to nearly seventy thousand depositors. To settle up the accounts with this immense number of depositors was the task assumed by these commissioners. By March 7, 1881, they had paid out $1,450,000, and at the present time sixty-two per cent. of the total amount due the thousands of depositors has been paid to all who have called for their dividends. However, the original commissioners have not been continued in charge of the work during all the years it has been going on, they having been relieved of the labor at their own request, March 7, 1881, under the provisions of an act of Congress approved February 21, 1881. Since then, the work has been in charge of the Comptroller of the Currency. Up to December 5, 1891, there had been paid to the depositors the sum of $1,722,340.58, from the assets of the company, a showing quite creditable to the commissioners and the Comptroller of the Currency, and one equal to, if not better, than that made by most of the financial institutions which failed in consequence of the panic of 1873.

Mr. W. W. Corcoran commenced the brokerage business in Washington in 1837, in a small store, ten by sixteen feet in size, on Pennsylvania Avenue, near Fifteenth Street. His business here was eminently successful, and in 1839 he moved to the old Bank of the Metropolis building, on the corner of Fifteenth and F streets. In 1840, he received into partnership George W. Riggs, son of Elisha Riggs, of New York, broker, the firm name being Corcoran & Riggs. In 1845, Corcoran & Riggs purchased the old United States Bank building, at the corner of Fifteenth Street and New York Avenue, together with all its property and effects uncollected. The business of this firm having been successful, Mr. Corcoran settled with all his old creditors of 1823, the aggregate amount required to settle all these old accounts being about $46,000. This act of Mr. Corcoran's was a great surprise to his old creditors, none of whom had any legal claim upon him. Mr. T. C. Rockhill, of Philadelphia, who had received on such an account $1,415.50, in acknowledging its receipt, said: "This extraordinary act has been done by you without solicitation on my part, and I will take this occasion to say that, having been engaged in mercantile pursuits for thirty years, and during that period having sold upward of $23,000,000 to various persons in different States of the Union, and having compromised claims for very large amounts, yours is the only instance in which a man ever came forward (after recovering his fortune), in the honorable manner you have done, and paid me in full."

About this time, the house of Corcoran & Riggs took on its own account nearly all the loans made by the Government of the United States. July 1, 1848, Mr. George W. Riggs retired from the firm, and Elisha Riggs, also a son of Elisha Riggs, of New York, by another

Chas C Glover

wife, was taken in as a junior partner. He remained in the firm until 1854. On the 1st of April of this year, Mr. Corcoran withdrew from the firm, and the business was continued by Mr. George W. Riggs, under the firm name of Riggs & Company, until his death, August 24, 1881, since which time the same name has been retained, and the business conducted under it by E. Francis Riggs, Thomas Hyde, Charles C. Glover,[1] and James M. Johnston.

The First National Bank of Washington was organized in September, 1863, under the National Banking law of Congress, and opened its doors for business on the 22d of that month, at the corner of Fifteenth and G streets. H. D. Cooke was president, and William S. Huntington cashier. The capital of the bank was $500,000, and its business was very prosperous until the panic of 1873, when it failed, and was placed in the hands of E. L. Stanton, son of the Secretary of War, Edwin M. Stanton, who wound up its affairs.

The Merchants' National Bank was organized in September, 1864, with William Bayne as president, and L. Huyck cashier. In October, 1865, Mr. Bayne resigned as president, and was succeeded by Mr. Huyck in that position, Charles A. Sherman being elected cashier. Charles W. Boteler, Jr., was elected vice-president of the bank January 1, 1866. In March, 1866, this bank became involved with a Baltimore firm which failed, the result of which was that the bank itself failed, and the president, being accused of placing large sums in the hands of the Baltimore firm without authority, was arrested and thrown into jail. Without entering into the details of the

---

[1] Charles Carroll Glover, one of the ablest and one of the youngest financiers of Washington, was born in Macon County, North Carolina, November 24, 1846. His grandfather, Charles Carroll Glover, in the early years of the century was a large property holder and a prominent and respected citizen of Washington. His father, Richard L. Glover, was a native of Washington, and married in 1845 Miss Caroline Percy, in about 1845, moved to a farm and coffee house a few miles from Asheville, North Carolina, and were living there when he was born. When he was eight years old, his parents moved to Washington, and here he attended Rittenhouse Academy, taught by Otis S. Wight, one of the prominent teachers of the city. At the age of sixteen, he entered Frank Taylor's bookstore, remaining three years. On June 30, 1866, he entered the Washington office of Jay Cooke & Company. He soon rose to be the teller in the bank. On January 1, 1874, upon the invitation of Mr. Riggs, he became a member of the firm, and so remains to the present time, and it is since that time that most of his important work has been performed. In 1878, he joined the management of the Washington and Georgetown Railroad Company, which afterward became a prosperous corporation. In 1881, he entered the directory, and became vice-president of the company a few years later, resigning in 1891 both the vice-presidency and the directorship, and leaving the corporation one of the finest in the country. He

Chas C Glover

wife, was taken in as a junior partner. He remained in the firm until 1854. On the 1st of April of this year, Mr. Corcoran withdrew from the firm, and the business was continued by Mr. George W. Riggs, under the firm name of Riggs & Company, until his death, August 24, 1881, since which time the same name has been retained, and the business conducted under it by E. Francis Riggs, Thomas Hyde, Charles C. Glover,[1] and James M. Johnston.

The First National Bank of Washington was organized in September, 1863, under the National Banking law of Congress, and opened its doors for business on the 22d of that month, at the corner of Fifteenth and G streets. H. D. Cooke was president, and William S. Huntington cashier. The capital of the bank was $500,000, and its business was very prosperous until the panic of 1873, when it failed, and was placed in the hands of E. L. Stanton, son of the Secretary of War, Edwin M. Stanton, who wound up its affairs.

The Merchants' National Bank was organized in September, 1864, with William Bayne as president, and L. Huyck cashier. In October, 1865, Mr. Bayne resigned as president, and was succeeded by Mr. Huyck in that position, Charles A. Sherman being elected cashier. Charles W. Boteler, Jr., was elected vice-president of the bank January 1, 1866. In March, 1866, this bank became involved with a Baltimore firm which failed, the result of which was that the bank itself failed, and the president, being accused of placing large sums in the hands of the Baltimore firm without authority, was arrested and thrown into jail. Without entering into the details of the

---

[1] Charles Carroll Glover, one of the ablest and one of the youngest financiers of Washington, was born in Macon County, North Carolina, November 24, 1846. His grandfather, Charles Carroll Glover, in the early years of this century, was a large property holder and a prominent and esteemed citizen of Washington. His father, Richard L. Glover, was a native of Washington, and with his wife, formerly Miss Caroline Percy, in about 1845, moved to a farm on Valley River, about twenty miles from Asheville, North Carolina, and were living there when Mr. Glover was born. When he was eight years old, his parents moved to Washington, and here he attended Rittenhouse Academy, taught by Otis C. Wight, one of the prominent teachers of the city. At the age of sixteen, he entered Frank Taylor's bookstore, remaining there three years. On June 30, 1866, he entered the banking house of Riggs & Company, and in time rose to be the teller in the bank. On January 1, 1874, upon the invitation of Mr. Riggs, he became a member of the firm, and so remains to the present time, and it is since that time that most of his important work has been performed. In 1876, he joined the management of the Washington and Georgetown Railroad Company, which afterward became a prosperous corporation. In 1881, he entered the directory, and became vice-president of the company a few years later, resigning in 1891 both the vice-presidency and the directorship, and leaving the corporation one of the finest in the country. He

difficulty, it may be sufficient to say that the Merchants' National Bank did not survive the shock, and was at length closed entirely.

The National Bank of the Metropolis was organized in 1865, was located at No. 452 Fifteenth Street, opposite the Treasury, and went into liquidation the latter part of the year 1868.

The National Bank of the Republic, of Washington, was organized in 1865. It purchased the property of the old Patriotic Bank, of Washington, located at the southwest corner of Seventh and D streets. At this time, the officers of the old bank were John Purdy, president; M. Chauncey Bestor, teller; Charles Bradley, bookkeeper, and J. M. Duncanson, clerk. The new bank building was built by William H. Baldwin, afterward one of its directors. The first board of directors of the new bank were as follows: Fitzhugh Coyle, Matthew G. Emery, Samuel Norment, J. M. Brodhead, William A. Bradley, Leonidas Coyle, John H. Semmes, Daniel B. Clarke, and L. D. Gilman, gentlemen all well known and highly esteemed. Mr. Fitzhugh Coyle was unanimously elected president of the board, and continued in that position until his death, in 1877. Matthew G. Emery afterward became president of the Second National Bank; Samuel Norment, of the Central National Bank, and J. M. Brodhead, First Comptroller of the Treasury. Charles Bradley was elected cashier of this new bank, March 8, 1865, and J. M. Duncanson teller. The bank became a Government depository in May, 1865, and invested its capital in Government bonds. William A. Bradley died August 28, 1867, and on September 18, following, William H. Baldwin was

became a director in the National Safe Deposit, Savings, and Trust Company before it assumed its present name, and is now vice-president of the institution. He was one of the originators of the Columbia Fire Insurance Company, and is now its vice-president. In 1881, he began the effort which resulted in the reclamation of the Potomac Flats, which gave to the city another beautiful park containing about four hundred acres of land, adding much to its beauty as well as to its healthfulness; and he was also largely influential in securing the extension of the waterworks, by which extension they are equally efficient with any system in the country. He is one of the trustees of the Corcoran Art Gallery, and was the last to enter the board previous to Mr. Corcoran's death. In 1891, he succeeded in inducing the trustees to purchase a large tract of land on Seventeenth Street and New York Avenue with the view of erecting thereon a new gallery, which will be done as soon as practicable. He has been for a long time connected with the Church of the Epiphany, and has been vestryman for a number of years. The crowning event of his life, however, is doubtless the success attending his labors in securing the condemnation of about two thousand acres in Rock Creek Valley for a national park, called Rock Creek Park. This work was commenced in 1888, and continued until the bill passed Congress in September, 1890, assuring the success of the project. From the facts of Mr. Glover's comparative youth

appointed to the vacancy. Leonidas Coyle died in August, 1868, and in October, following, W. H. Morrison was appointed to the place. C. S. Bradley became bookkeeper in November, 1865, and assistant cashier in January, 1874. Edwin L. Stanton, son of the great Secretary of War, G. M. Wight, W. R. Riley, and W. J. Sibley became directors in January, 1874. L. D. Gilman died March 15, 1876. Major J. C. Cash became director in 1876, and died February 8, 1877. Mr. E. L. Stanton died in September, 1877. Mr. Fitzhugh Coyle died September 30, 1877, and Dr. Daniel B. Clarke[1] was elected to the presidency October 3, 1877. R. K. Elliott and T. E. Waggaman were elected directors in January, 1878. G. M. Wight resigned in December, 1878, and E. K. Goldsborough was appointed to fill the vacancy in 1879.

The dividends declared were ten per cent. up to July, 1879, when they were reduced to eight per cent., at which they have since continued. Up to July 1, 1880, the total dividends declared amounted to $352,000, or $152,000 more than the capital stock. During the years from 1867 to 1872, inclusive, the tax on each semi-annual dividend was also paid by the bank. The directors in January, 1881, were Daniel B. Clarke, W. H. Morrison, W. R. Riley, W. J. Sibley, James M. Farr, R. K. Elliott, T. E. Waggaman, E. K. Goldsborough, and C. C. Duncanson. Mr. Charles Bradley, cashier, died August 26, 1881, and C. S. Bradley was elected to the vacant position, September 7, following. A. A. Wilson was elected director January 10, 1882. B. F. Bigelow's defalcation was discovered June

and his great success in the past, it may perhaps be safely predicted that he will be one of the wealthiest citizens of Washington, as he is now one of the most public-spirited.

[1] Daniel Boone Clarke, capitalist and banker, was born in Washington, District of Columbia, March 3, 1825. He is a descendant in the seventh generation of the Hon. Robert Clarke, who came from England in 1636, who represented the Jesuit fathers in the colonial assemblies, who was surveyor-general of Maryland, privy councilor under Lord Baltimore, and who voted in the assembly of 1649 for the celebrated Maryland Federation Act. The Clarkes of Maryland had their large landed estates confiscated in the Revolution of 1689. William Clarke, born March 16, 1750, great-great-grandson of Hon. Robert Clarke, was a second lieutenant in one of the eight companies constituting the Seventh Regiment, Maryland Line of Regulars, of General William Smallwood's brigade, in the Revolutionary War. His son, Walter Clarke, born in June, 1777, and married to Rachel Boone September 20, 1814, was the father of Dr. Daniel Boone Clarke. Young Clarke was educated in the private schools of Washington, and in 1841 entered a pharmaceutical establishment in this city. When twenty-one years old, he went into business on his own account in South Washington, and in 1857 graduated from Georgetown University with the degree of M. D. In 1859, he

22, 1882, being in amount $40,000. The bank had him arrested and tried, and sent to the penitentiary for a term of years. He was afterward pardoned out by the President of the United States.

Up to June 30, 1891, the total dividends paid since the organization of the bank amounted to $560,055.20, and the amount placed to the surplus fund to $200,000. The total of other profits was $13,318.32, making the total amount of the profits of the business of this bank up to that time $773,373.52.

Mr. George E. Lemon was elected director in January, 1890, and A. A. Wilson vice-president in June of the same year. In addition to the officers supplied by this bank to other banks, mentioned above, there may be noted John E. Herrell, president of the National Capital Bank; William R. Riley, president of the West End National Bank, and two cashiers, Brent L. Baldwin, of the Traders' National Bank, and William B. Baldwin, of the National Capital Bank. The surplus and undivided profits of this bank on March 1, 1892, amounted to $226,777.76.

The National Savings Bank was chartered May 24, 1870, and opened for business on November 1, that year. Henry A. Willard was the first president of the bank, William Stickney vice-president, Lewis Clephane secretary, and B. P. Snyder treasurer. According to the report of Mr. Willard, president, the first year's business was as follows: Receipts, $499,756.83; payments, $228,059.95, and the expenses, $3,417.39. The location of the bank was at the corner of New York Avenue and Fifteenth Street. At the time of the second annual statement, there were 2,114 depositors, no one of whom was

purchased the establishment in which he had learned and practiced pharmacy, and made a gratifying success of his business. Subsequently, he erected on Pennsylvania Avenue a large building, into which he moved, and about a year afterward retired from business. When James G. Berrett was Mayor of Washington, Dr. Clarke was elected a member of the city Council, and he has been for many years a member of the Washington National Monument Association. Since the death of J. B. H. Smith, he has been its treasurer. He is a director in the Franklin Insurance Company, of the Metropolitan Railroad Company, of the United States Electric Light Company, is president of the Franklin Insurance Company, and since 1877 he has been president of the National Bank of the Republic. This institution, under Dr. Clarke's management, is one of the solid and most prosperous financial institutions in Washington. Dr. Clarke is a brother of Richard H. Clarke, LL. D., the celebrated lawyer and Catholic historian, and president of the Society of American Authors, and of the late Rev. Father William Francis Clarke, S. J., at one time president of Gonzaga College.

Dr. Clarke was married to Anna M. Cripps, only daughter of William McLean Cripps, January 14, 1847, by whom he had three children. The eldest married Thomas E. Waggaman, and, dying in 1889, left three children; the second daughter died at the age of sixteen; the third is the wife of Alexander Porter Morse.

permitted to deposit more than $1,000. The presidents of this bank have been H. A. Willard, one year; William Stickney, 1872 to 1881; B. P. Snyder, 1881 to 1891. The vice-presidents have been William Stickney, one year; Lewis Clephane, 1872 to 1891. The secretaries have been Lewis Clephane, M. G. Emery, J. H. Lathrop, A. L. Sturtevant; and the treasurers, B. P. Snyder and A. L. Sturtevant. In 1891, this bank went out of business so far as to cease receiving deposits, which at that time amounted to more than $1,300,000. The accounts have, since that time, been steadily reduced with the view of entirely closing them.

The National Safe Deposit Company, of Washington, was chartered by special act of Congress, approved January 22, 1867, and commenced business July 27, 1867, at the corner of New York Avenue and Fifteenth Street. The first directors of this company were George H. Plant, H. D. Cooke, S. P. Brown, George O. Evans, William S. Huntington, Nathaniel Wilson, and B. P. Snyder. The first officers were S. P. Brown, president; George O. Evans, vice-president; William S. Huntington, treasurer, and B. P. Snyder, secretary. Since that time, the presidents have been George H. Plant, 1869 to 1877; William Stickney, 1877 to 1881; B. P. Snyder, 1881 to the present time. The vice-presidents have been George W. Riggs, 1869 to 1881; C. C. Glover, 1881 to the present time. Secretary, A. L. Sturtevant, 1881 to the present time. Treasurers, A. L. Sturtevant, 1872 to 1882; John Cassels, 1882 to 1885; T. L. Riggs, 1885 to 1889; E. Francis Riggs, 1889 to the present time.

The fine new building in which this company is now located was completed in August, 1889, at a cost of $250,000. It is of brick and cement, and rests on a concrete foundation. This company now has over $1,000,000 in deposits, consisting largely in transfers from the National Savings Bank. The departments of the business conducted by this company consist of receiving money on deposit from ten cents upward, upon which interest is allowed, and of loaning money on standard collaterals and real estate; of deposits of securities and valuables; a trust department; collection of income; registration and transfers of loans and stocks of corporations.

The National Capital Bank, of Washington, was organized in September, 1889, with a capital of $200,000. It commenced business at the corner of Pennsylvania Avenue and Third Street Southeast, in a leased building, while erecting its own fine building at 314 and 316 Pennsylvania Avenue Southeast, moving into it in March, 1891. The capital remains as at first, and the surplus and undivided profits on March 1, 1892, were $39,608.15. The deposits at the same time amounted to a little more than $600,000. The officers of this bank have been, since its organization, John S. Herrell, president; Thomas W. Smith, vice-president, and W. B. Baldwin, cashier.

The Second National Bank was established about July 1, 1872, with a capital of $200,000. On the above date, at a meeting of the stockholders, the following directors were elected: John C. McKelden, George W. Balloch, D. L. Eaton, Thomas L. Tulloch, F. H. Gassaway, John O. Evans, George F. Gulick, W. W. Burdette, J. L. Barbour, Lewis Clephane, and F. H. Smith. John C. McKelden was elected president, John O. Evans vice-president, D. L. Eaton cashier, and F. H. Gassaway assistant cashier. Business was commenced at No. 631 F Street, the bank remaining here but a short time, however, when it removed to No. 509 Seventh Street, its present location.

Mr. McKelden served as president until 1877, when he was succeeded by Matthew G. Emery,[1] who has been president ever since. D. L. Eaton was cashier for about one year, when H. W. Griffith took the place temporarily, and then, in 1874, Mr. H. C. Swein became cashier, and has been in that position up to the present time. John C.

---

[1] Hon. Matthew Gault Emery was born in Pembroke, New Hampshire, in 1818. Himself and five brothers spent their youth on the farm which had been their grandfather's, upon which their father was born and spent his life, and where he died in 1868, at the age of ninety-two. Joseph Emery, the grandfather of M. G. Emery, served six years in the War of the Revolution, first as a lieutenant, then as a captain, in the Thirteenth Regiment, New Hampshire Militia. Matthew Gault, the maternal grandfather of Mr. Emery, served four years in the patriot army, having enlisted July 11, 1775, at the age of nineteen. His regiment of "Rangers," raised by the colony of New Hampshire, served first with General Montgomery's northern division of the Continental Army. Matthew Gault afterward became a member of Captain Samuel McConnell's company, with which he marched to Bennington and Stillwater.

The pioneers of the Emery family in this country were two brothers, John and Anthony, who emigrated with their families from Romsey, Hants, England, landing in Boston April 3, 1635, and settling in "Ould Newberrie," of the Massachusetts colony.

Matthew Gault Emery attended the best schools and academies in his native town, and in 1837 he went to Baltimore, where an elder brother was living, and here determined upon his future vocation, that of builder and architect. He patiently served the time required to make himself a skilled stonecutter, and in 1840 went with a force of men to the quarry and directed the cutting of the stone for the Post Office Department building in Washington. In 1842, he established his permanent residence in Washington, thus debarring himself from participation in general elections; but voted, however, in 1840, for William Henry Harrison for President, the only Presidential candidate for whom he has ever voted.

Mr. Emery has had contracts for the construction of many important buildings in Washington, both public and private. He did much of the stone work of the Capitol, and cut and laid the corner stone for its extension in 1851, Daniel Webster delivering the oration. He also cut and squared, free of expense, and on July 4, 1848, himself

Yours Truly

M. G. Emery

Eckloff is assistant cashier. In 1884, Mr. M. W. Beveridge succeeded John O. Evans as vice-president, and still remains in that position.

The capital of this bank, as stated above, was originally $200,000. In 1873, it was increased to $300,000, and in 1880 decreased to $225,000. At the present time, it is $225,000, and the bank has a surplus on hand of $75,000. The present board of directors consists of M. G. Emery, M. W. Beveridge, William F. Mattingly, Lewis Clephane, George W. Pearson, W. W. Burdette, Samuel Fowler, Seymour W. Tulloch, John L. Vogt, and A. A. Thomas.

The Citizens' National Bank was organized in 1874, and occupied the building formerly occupied by the First National Bank. The capital of the bank at first was $200,000, and it was raised in 1875 to $300,000. The first president was Jacob Tome, who served in this office until 1875, when J. A. J. Creswell was elected, and served until 1888, when the present president, E. Kurtz Johnson, was elected. The first vice-president was A. R. Appleman, who served until 1878, after which John Van Riswick was elected, and served until 1885, when he was succeeded by E. Kurtz Johnson, who served in that

laid, the corner stone of the Washington Monument, for which service he received the thanks of the board of directors in a series of resolutions, signed, among others, by John Quincy Adams, Henry Clay, and Robert C. Winthrop.

Before the breaking out of the War, Mr. Emery organized a militia company, of which he was made captain. His commission, signed by President Lincoln and Secretary of War Simon Cameron, is dated May 16, 1861. His company was several times called out for the protection of the Government buildings, and to perform patrol duty, until the arrival of the Sixth Massachusetts Regiment. During the War, Mr. Emery was treasurer of the New Hampshire Soldiers' Aid Association in Washington, and assisted in the care of the sick and disabled soldiers from his native State, in the discharge of these duties visiting Gettysburg and other battlefields. A piece of his country property, adjoining Fort Stevens, was injured during the War to the extent of several thousand dollars, but no claim was ever presented for damages. Early in the War, he gave up his Brightwood home for the use of the officers of the Union army. Being the highest point of land in that vicinity, it was made a signal station, and many were the messages transmitted between it and the dome of the Capitol. Evidences of the occupation of "Brightwood" by the soldiers, in the shape of raised plateaus for the flooring of tents, etc., are still visible, and are looked upon by the family with patriotic pride.

Mr. Emery was for many years a member of the Board of Aldermen, his services proving of great value to the city. In 1870, after a memorable struggle, he was elected Mayor of Washington, as the "Citizens' Candidate," by a majority of 3,194, being the last Mayor of Washington, as shown in another chapter.

In 1872, at the end of thirty years' labor in the business of builder, contractor, and architect, in accordance with a resolution formed at the time of entering upon that business, he disposed of his interests therein to his brother, Samuel Emery, and he has since devoted himself to his other business interests.

capacity until elected president of the bank; and since that time the vice-president has been Thomas Somerville. The first cashier was W. E. Weygant, who served one year, and was succeeded by W. N. Roach, who was cashier until 1878, when followed by the present cashier, Thomas C. Pearsall. The surplus and undivided profits, according to the statement published March 1, 1892, amount to $93,764.49.

The Central National Bank succeeded the Metropolis Savings Bank, and was organized as a national bank April 11, 1878. For several years, it occupied the old Bank of Washington building, but

Mr. Emery was one of the seven persons who organized the Metropolitan Methodist Episcopal Church, was chairman of the building committee, and has for twenty years been president of its board of trustees. He has been a regent of the Smithsonian Institution, and was for a long period a trustee of Dickinson College. For ten years or more, he has been a regent, and he is now vice-chancellor, of the National University, organized in Washington. He is also one of the incorporators of the recently established American University; he is one of its regents and is also its treasurer. He has been president of, and is now a director in, the Night Lodging Association, and has been for many years a director and treasurer of the Associated Charities of the city.

In 1854, he was a charter member of the Mutual Fire Insurance Company, and is still one of its directors; he was for some time president of the Franklin Insurance Company and of the National Capital Life Insurance Company, a director of the Metropolitan Insurance Company, and was first treasurer of the Metropolitan Street Railway Company. He was one of the organizers of the Washington Market House Company, was its president for eighteen years, and is still a director. He was for many years a director in the United States Electric Light Company of Washington, and has been its vice-president. At an early day, he was a director of the Patriotic Bank, and afterward, in connection with Mr. Fitzhugh Coyle, he established the National Bank of the Republic, of which he was a director for eight years, and one year the acting president. In 1877, he was elected president of the Second National Bank, and has held the position ever since. He was one of the organizers, and for twenty years a director, of the National Savings Bank, and is a director of its successor, the National Savings and Trust Company. He is also a director of the American Trust Company, and is president of the American Printing Press Company.

The home of Mr. Emery, in Washington, is one of a row of three spacious houses built in 1860, by Stephen A. Douglas, John C. Breckinridge, and H. S. Rice, all of which were used for hospital purposes during the War. After the War, they were completed, and the Breckinridge mansion soon purchased and presented to General Grant by his friends. When General Grant was elected President of the United States, the house was purchased and presented to General Sherman by his friends. When General Sherman removed to St. Louis, in 1873, the house was purchased by Mr. Emery, and has since been his home.

During a residence of half a century in Washington, Mr. Emery has been constantly identified with all the most important movements for the improvement of the city, has been unceasingly active in the cause of education, unremitting in his efforts to advance the best interests of the people, without regard to race or religion, and above reproach in fulfilling the many positions of trust and honor to which his fellow-citizens have so frequently called him.

Eng. by E.G.Williams & Bro. NY

later it purchased and moved into its present spacious and handsome quarters at the junction of Pennsylvania Avenue and C Street at Seventh Street, April 1, 1888. The capital of the bank is $100,000. Its career has always been a successful one. It has paid out in dividends more than $82,000, and has on hand more than $10,000 in undivided profits. Mr. Samuel Norment[1] was the president of the bank from the date of its organization up to the time of his death, March 23, 1891, when he was succeeded by Mr. William E. Clark.[2] Mr. J. A. Ruff was cashier from the organization of the bank

[1] Samuel Norment, one of the most prominent business men and bankers of Washington, was born in Virginia. He came to Washington City about 1846, and at first found employment in the Treasury Department. His business capabilities enabled him soon to take a front rank, and when the War came on he held the highest position in his division, which position he then resigned. He soon became engaged in the lumber business, and after a successful career of seventeen years he determined to enter upon the business of banking. Upon the organization of the Central National Bank, April 11, 1878, he became its president, and retained the position until his death, March 23, 1891. For several years, he was a regent of Dickinson College. He was also a director of the National Bank of the Republic, and one of the commissioners of the police. He was a large stockholder in the Washington Gas Light Company, in the Washington and Georgetown Railroad Company, in the United States Electric Light Company, in the Kingsley Company, in the Mutual Fire-Insurance Company, and in the Inland and Seaboard Coasting Company.

Mr. Norment was a strong believer in the education of the young, and was thus led to make numerous munificent gifts to institutions of learning. He was also exceedingly liberal in his donations to charitable institutions, an instance of this liberality being the endowment of the free bed in Garfield Hospital for the benefit of sick and disabled policemen. He was originally a member of Wesley Chapel, but later became one of the original trustees of the Metropolitan Methodist Episcopal Church.

Mr. Norment was married twice; first to a daughter of Rev. Ulysses Ward, by whom he had three children, all of whom are living. His second wife was a daughter of George W. Utermehle, by whom he had two children, both of whom are living. Mr. Norment was buried March 25, 1891, in Rock Creek Cemetery. Mr. Norment was a most successful business man, a true friend of education, and a zealous supporter of charitable and religious enterprises. In his death the community suffered a severe if not irreparable loss.

[2] William E. Clark, president of the Central National Bank, was born in Washington County, Pennsylvania, March 16, 1835. His father, Abner Clark, was a farmer, and William E. Clark was brought up on his father's farm. He was educated at Jefferson College, leaving there in 1855. He then removed to Baltimore and engaged in the live-stock business, remaining there for several years. In April, 1861, he came to Washington, and again in 1862 became engaged in the live-stock business, and has been interested in that business ever since. Upon the death of Samuel Norment, he became president of the Central National Bank. He is also president of the Washington Abattoir Company, vice-president of the United States Electric Light Company and of the National Mutual Life Insurance Company, and is president of the Norfolk and Washington Steamboat Company. Mr. Clark, in the year 1871, was married to Miss Fannie W. Wilhelm.

until 1890, when he was succeeded by his son, A. B. Ruff. The present board of directors are as follows: Albert Gleason, William B. Webb, H. Browning, B. Charlton, William E. Clark, O. T. Thompson, J. L. Edwards, Levi Woodbury, W. K. Mendenhall, and C. F. Norment. On March 1, 1892, the surplus and undivided profits amounted to $147,340.98.

The Washington Safe Deposit Company was incorporated April 25, 1883, and organized with the following officers: W. G. Metzerott, president; John T. Lenman, vice-president, and Samuel Cross, secretary and treasurer. Mr. Metzerott remained president one year, when John T. Lenman became president, and James L. Barbour vice-president. Mr. Lenman remained president until his death, March 17, 1892, when he was succeeded, April 4, by W. A. Gordon. Mr. Barbour was succeeded as vice-president in 1886, by W. A. Gordon, who was followed, April 4, 1892, by William H. Hoeke. Mr. Cross has been secretary and treasurer since the organization of the company. This company's business is conducted at No. 916 Pennsylvania Avenue.

The Columbia National Bank was organized in February, 1887, with a capital of $250,000. Its first officers were B. H. Warner, president; A. T. Britton, vice-president, and E. S. Parker, cashier. This bank is located at 911 F Street Northwest, in a building erected especially for its use, at a cost of $70,000. It conducts a general banking business, receives money on deposit, makes loans in large or small amounts, and discounts good paper. This bank makes a specialty of collections. The officers at the present time are E. S. Parker, president; A. F. Fox, vice-president, and Pliny M. Hough, cashier. The other directors are as follows: Charles B. Bailey, W. E. Barker, C. C. Duncanson, John Joy Edson, John B. Larner, Benjamin F. Leighton, Frank B. Noyes, M. M. Parker, O. G. Staples, George Truesdell, B. H. Warner, H. K. Willard, and S. W. Woodward. The capital of this bank remains at $250,000, and its surplus at the present time is $85,000. Previously to becoming connected with this bank, its president, Mr. E. S. Parker, had had twenty-three years' experience in the banking business in Mifflintown, Juniata County, Pennsylvania.

The Washington Loan and Trust Company was organized August 15, 1889, with a capital of $600,000, which, during the first year of its existence, was increased to $1,000,000. The original purpose of its organization was that of "buying, selling, loaning upon and negotiating bonds, stocks, promissory notes, and other property, and of guaranteeing, certifying, registering, endorsing, and supervising the issuance of bonds, stock, and other securities," etc. The officers of the company

W E Clark

at first were B. H. Warner, president; J. J. Edson, vice-president; C. P. Williams, secretary; William B. Gurley, treasurer; John B. Larner, general counsel; J. J. Darlington and A. S. Worthington, advisory counsel, and Albert F. Fox, George Truesdell, A. A. Wilson, and O. C. Green, executive committee. The number of directors was twenty-five. This organization was made under the laws of West Virginia. Business was commenced by the company October 1, 1889, with the office located at the northwest corner of Tenth and F streets, where it worked under the West Virginia charter until December 13, 1890, at which time it reorganized under the act of Congress providing for the incorporation of trust companies in the District of Columbia, approved October 1, 1890. The act is entitled, "An Act to Provide for the Incorporation of Trust, Loan, Mortgage, and Certain Other Corporations within the District of Columbia." This act authorized the transaction of three classes of business, the first of which, and the class conducted by this company, is therein styled, "A safe deposit, trust, loan, and mortgage business."

Upon the reorganization of the company under this act, the following officers were elected: B. H. Warner, president; J. J. Edson, vice-president; William B. Robison, secretary; W. B. Gurley, treasurer; John B. Larner, general counsel; J. J. Darlington and A. S. Worthington, advisory counsel. The board of directors consists now of thirty members.

The building into which the company moved October 19, 1891, was erected during that and the preceding year. It is a ten-story building, located at the southwest corner of Ninth and F streets. The building committee was composed of J. J. Edson, chairman; S. W. Woodward, A. A. Wilson, George Truesdell, A. F. Fox, John A. Hamilton, and B. H. Warner. The architect was James G. Hill, late supervising architect of the Treasury building. W. C. Morrison was the builder. The principles governing the building committee in the erection of this fine structure were beauty, safety, and convenience. It is constructed of rock-faced granite, of a light color, giving it a massive effect. The frontage on F and Ninth streets is divided architecturally into three divisions by prominent string courses. The frontage on F Street is 52 feet, while that on Ninth Street is 116 feet. An L on the west side continues the south front to a distance of 112 feet. In this magnificent building there are 190 rooms occupied exclusively as offices. The building is fire-proof, and cost $500,000.

As stated before, this company commenced business October 1, 1889, the paid-up capital being then $68,000. It began to issue certificates of deposit December 26, 1889, and on January 2, 1891, began to receive accounts subject to check. The growth of the business since this latter date has been really marvelous among even the sound and prosperous financial institutions of Washington, the records showing total deposits March 1, 1891, .$91,542.25, and on March 1, 1892, $1,095,940.07, making a gain during the year of $1,004,-397.82, this amount being represented by 1885 new accounts. One peculiarly attractive feature of this company's method of doing business, is the paying of interest on accounts subject to check, a feature seldom met with in banking.

The officers of this company at the present time are as follows: Brainard H. Warner, president; John Joy Edson, vice-president; John A. Swope, second vice-president; John R. Carmody, treasurer; William B. Robison, secretary, and Andrew Parker, assistant secretary.

The American Security and Trust Company was incorporated October 12, 1889, under the general incorporation laws of the State of Virginia. It was incorporated and reorganized November 11, 1890, under the act of Congress approved October 1, 1890. Its business was conducted, temporarily, at 1419 G Street Northwest, but in the latter part of the year 1891 it removed to a fine new building erected for its own use at No. 1405 G Street. It executes all kinds of trusts, and acts as executor, administrator, guardian, assignee, receiver, and trustee, and accepts the management of estates and property generally. Money received on deposit is subject to check on demand, and interest is paid on such accounts at a rate agreed upon. It loans money on real estate and approved personal security. It issues its own debenture bonds upon deeds of trust or mortgages of real estate, in series and in sums of $100, $500, or $1,000, payable in a stated period, with quarterly or semi-annual interest, as may be agreed upon. Its safe deposit feature is noteworthy, the vaults being constructed with every precaution against fire and burglars. Its storage warehouse department is also a valuable feature, the warehouse being situated at 1140 Fifteenth Street. It is especially planned for storage purposes, and is constructed exclusively of stone, brick, iron, and cement. This company also acts as financial agents in the matter of countersigning and registering certificates of stocks, bonds, or other obligations of any corporation, association, State, or public authority, and manages sinking funds on such terms as are agreed upon; and it also acts as agent or attorney for the collection of interest, dividends, and all forms of income, and as attorney in fact for the interest of non-residents and others who may desire to be relieved of the care and attention of property.

A. T. Britton

A. T. Britton[1] is president of the company; C. G. Bell, first vice-president; A. A. Thomas, second vice-president; Percy B. Metzger, treasurer and trust officer, and George E. Emmons, secretary. The directors are A. T. Britton, C. S. Noyes, Robert Dornan, James E. Fitch, M. M. Parker, James G. Payne, W. S. Thompson, C. C. Duncanson, Henry A. Willard, S. S. Sharp, C. G. Bell, M. W. Beveridge, M. G. Emery, John E. Herrell, Martin F. Morris, Harry F. West, Henry F. Blont, Nathaniel E. Janney, John S. Jenks, Daniel Donovan, A. A. Thomas, Charles Porter, Caleb J. Milne, Alan H. Reed, H. S. Louchbeim, John R. McLean, W. M. Coates, William Venner, John N. Hutchinson, and Benjamin H. Warder.

The Lincoln National Bank, of Washington, District of Columbia, was organized February 27, 1890, with a capital of $200,000, and

[1] Alexander T. Britton, lawyer and financier, was born in New York City, December 29, 1835. His father and uncles were among the last captains of the old "Liners" plying between London, Liverpool, and New York. He is a charter member of the Sons of the American Revolution of the District of Columbia, being a great-grandson of Major Isaac Coren, aid-de-camp to General Braddock, and afterward major of artillery in the Continental Army under General Knox. His grandfather, Captain John Towers, first utilized the water power of the Schuylkill River at a mill at Manayonk, Pennsylvania.

A. T. Britton graduated at Brown University in 1857, and was admitted to the bar through the Supreme Court of Rhode Island in March, 1858. He practiced his profession in that State until 1860, and then at Madison, Florida, until the War of the Rebellion compelled his return North. In March, 1861, he was appointed a clerk in the General Land Office, and entered the service of the United States on April 15, 1861, as a member of the National Rifles, to protect the Capital during the early days of the War. Since that time, with an interval in 1864, when practicing law in California, Washington has been his home. In 1864, he organized the firm of Britton & Gray, and has since then by his ability made his name a leading one among the lawyers of the city. In 1877, he was appointed by President Hayes a commissioner to codify the public land laws, the result of his labors being a codification in three volumes, which have several times been published by authority of Congress.

He has served Washington in many high and responsible positions. He was the last president of the board of police commissioners in the early seventies. He is now director in the Emergency Hospital, Columbia Fire Insurance Company, and Foundling Asylum, and was one of the promoters and directors in the Georgetown and Tennallytown Railroad Company, the Eckington and Soldiers' Home Railroad Company, and the Columbia National Bank. He is a trustee in the Tunlaw Syndicate, which has added so much to the beauty of Georgetown Heights. He built the Pacific Building in 1885, and is president of the Atlantic Building. He was chairman of the inaugural committee having charge of President Harrison's inauguration, and is one of the World's Fair Commissioners from the District. In 1890, he organized, and was made president of, the American Security and Trust Company, and in many other ways has aided in making Washington the handsome Capital it now is. Mr. Britton is, and has been for many years, one of the progressive citizens, in favor of all measures calculated to add to the city's progress and growth.

opened its doors for business on March 25. At its organization, its board of directors were selected from the most enterprising and successful business men of the city. This board of directors consisted of the following individuals: William E. Abbott, H. Bradley Davidson, Edward W. Donn, Augustus Burgdorff, William O. Denison, Peter Latterner, Job Barnard, Jesse C. Ergood, Frederick W. Pratt, James F. Oyster, Willie S. Hoge, Frederick A. Schiffely, Augustus B. Coppes, and Richard A. Walker. The board was organized by the selection of John A. Prescott, president; J. Harrison Johnson, vice-president, and Frederick A. Stier, cashier. The success attending the business operations of this bank during its first year was unprecedented in the banking business of the city. At the end of this year, at the reorganization of the board, Mr. Prescott and Mr. Johnson resigned their positions as president and vice-president, and were succeeded respectively by Mr. Jesse B. Wilson[1] as president, and by Mr. H. Bradley Davidson as vice-president. Mr. Stier retained his position as cashier.

[1] Jesse B. Wilson, president of the Lincoln National Bank, was born in Prince George's County, Maryland, in 1830. His father was Nathaniel Wilson, who belonged to one of the old and hospitable Maryland families; but both father and mother died before young Jesse was seven years old. He was then apprenticed by his uncle to a coach maker, in Anne Arundel County, near Ellicott's Mills, and by the terms of the apprenticeship, which lasted about seven years, was to have one year's schooling during that time. However, when the time was within six months of coming to an end, the stipulation with regard to education not having been complied with, his uncle took him to his home in Howard County, and gave him two years' education in the public schools.

Early in 1842, learning that a brother of Mr. Washington Adams intended to retire from the grocery business, young Wilson set out on foot for Washington and made application for the vacancy. He was taken into the employ of Mr. Adams, and, developing an unusual aptitude for business, he was afterward induced to enter the establishment of Messrs. George & Thomas Parker, which occupied two buildings on Market Space, fronting on Pennsylvania Avenue, between Seventh and Eighth streets. Soon after this promotion, he became the junior partner in the grocery firm of Morsell & Wilson, and in the fall of 1851 he bought the interest of Mr. Morsell in the business. This business he conducted himself on the south side of Pennsylvania Avenue, between Sixth and Seventh streets, for nearly twenty years, increasing it year by year, until 1872, when on account of failing health he retired from business for a time; but upon regaining health he became engaged to a greater or less extent in the real-estate business, making this, too, a success. He then became president of the Mutual Fire Insurance Company, serving in this capacity until December, 1890, when he was elected president of the Lincoln National Bank. For several years, he has been president of the Northern Market Company, and he has been a member of the Board of Trade since its organization. Mr. Wilson married Miss Scrivener, of Washington, in 1849. Since 1870, he has been a member of the Mt. Vernon Place Methodist Episcopal Church. His election to the presidency of the Lincoln National Bank is a sufficient indication of the estimation in which he is held by his fellow-men.

The bank has continued to merit and receive the patronage of the public to a large degree by its careful, conservative method of doing business, and in all probability has a long and honorable career in the future. The surplus and undivided profits of this bank on the second anniversary of its establishment, March 25, 1892, were $20,-353.59.

The West End National Bank was organized in 1890, with a capital of $200,000. It was originally located at the corner of Nineteenth Street and Pennsylvania Avenue, in the west end of the city, and for this reason was named the West End National Bank; but after a year's experience, it was moved to its present location, No. 1415 G Street Northwest. On the opening day of its business, the deposits amounted to $40,000, and at the time of the removal the deposits amounted to $130,000. The deposits at the present time amount to $330,000, and the business is steadily increasing.

William R. Riley has been president of this bank since its organization. The vice-president, at the time of organization, was George A. McIlhenny, who was succeeded by Dr. A. P. Fardon, the present incumbent of this office. Charles P. Williams has been cashier since the organization of the bank. The directors are John F. Vogt, Horace S. Cummings, Conrad Becker, Edward S. Westcott, R. H. Goldsborough, W. R. Wilcox, Le Roy Tuttle, Jr., John H. Moore, F. C. Stevens, John H. Magruder, George A. McIlhenny, Henry C. Winship, and George E. Emmons.

The Traders' National Bank was organized March 3, 1890, with a capital of $200,000, and with the following officers, who still retain their positions: George C. Henning, president; William A. Gordon, vice-president; Brent L. Baldwin, cashier. The present site was bought in June, 1890, and the fine banking building erected and completed in time for occupation on June 1, 1891. The directors, in addition to the president and vice-president, are as follows: E. F. Droop, O. C. Green, Isadore Saks, Emil G. Schafer, Samuel S. Shedd, George A. Shehan, Emmons S. Smith, and John T. Varnell. The capital remains as at first, and on March 1, 1892, the surplus and undivided profits amounted to $50,763.25.

The Ohio National Bank is the youngest national bank in the city, having begun business February 24, 1891, at the corner of G and Twelfth streets Northwest, in a rented building. Most of those concerned in the movement were Ohio men, and hence, in part at least, the name of the bank. Its capital was, and is, $200,000, and at the end of the first year's business the surplus was about $3,000. The officers and directors of the bank at its organization were, Hon. Joseph D. Taylor, member of Congress from the Eighteenth Ohio District, president; John O. Johnson, of Pennsylvania, vice-president; Charles H. Davidge, formerly of Indiana, cashier; C. A. Baker, assistant cashier; directors — Hon. J. D. Taylor, John O. Johnson, A. P. Lacey, Hon. William Lawrence, Hon. C. S. Baker, F. J. Dieudonne, L. M. Saunders, J. B. Wimer, William C. Morrison, C. F. Scott, George H. LaFetra, J. F. Batchelder, William Mayse, John Lynch, T. A. Harding, and Bushrod Robinson. This banking company is at the present writing erecting a fine building on the northwest corner of Twelfth and G streets Northwest, at a cost, including the land upon which it stands, of nearly $125,000. It is of granite, Indiana limestone, and New Jersey buff brick. It is six stories high above the basement, and is an elegant and commodious structure.

The private banking firm of Lewis Johnson & Company commenced business February 1, 1858, at the corner of Pennsylvania Avenue and Tenth Street. It was then composed of Lewis Johnson, David Walker, and Lewis J. Davis. June 1, 1891, it removed to its present location, No. 1315 F Street Northwest. At the present time, the firm consists of Lewis J. Davis, David Walker, and Charles N. Wake. A general banking business is conducted by this firm.

Many other private banks have existed for a longer or shorter time in Washington. Without attempting to exhaust the list, the following may be mentioned as in existence at the present time, and as enjoying the confidence of the community in a high degree: William Mayse & Company, 516 Ninth Street Northwest; Bell & Company, 1406 G Street Northwest; Corson & McCartney, 1419 F Street Northwest; Crane, Paris, & Company, 1344 F Street Northwest; and Lewis G. Tewksbury & Company, 1335 F Street Northwest.

The firm of Woods & Company is composed of Thomas E. Woods and H. T. Woods, and others. It was organized for general banking business in July, 1890, and commenced business in a building owned by W. B. Moses, but in November, 1890, selected a site at No. 1222 F Street Northwest, where they erected a new banking house especially for their own use, and in April, 1891, transferred their business to this location. While this firm transacts a general banking business, and deals in foreign exchange, it also receives money on account and on deposit, the lowest sum received being five dollars. On certificates of deposit, interest is paid monthly, quarterly, or annually, at the option of the depositor. Money is also loaned to any amount on approved security.

The Capital City Savings Bank was organized in October, 1888, with a capital of $50,000. It is located at No. 804 F Street Northwest. It is the only bank in Washington owned and conducted exclusively by colored men. Its officers are Hon. John R. Lynch, president; J. W. Cole, vice-president; Henry E. Baker, secretary; L. C. Bailey, treasurer; and Douglass B. McCary, cashier. In its business transactions race lines entirely disappear, all classes of citizens dealing with it with equal freedom.

The Union Savings Bank was established June 10, 1891, in the basement of the Second National Bank building, No. 509 Seventh Street Northwest. It has a guaranty fund of $100,000. Its officers are F. H. Smith, president; I. G. Kimball, first vice-president; A. M. Lothrop, second vice-president; John Tweedale, secretary; T. A. Lambert, treasurer, and T. T. Stewart, assistant treasurer. Ordinary deposits are received, and are entitled to four per cent. semi-annual dividends. Installment deposits, payable at any stated period for a term of five years, share in the earnings of the bank, the dividends being compounded semi-annually. This plan, though in use in other cities for years, is new in Washington, and is worthy of attention. This bank also uses the savings bank stamp system. Agencies have been established in over fifty stores in all parts of the city and suburbs for the sale of five-cent and twenty-five-cent stamps, and when a page of a book, supplied by the agent for the purpose, is filled with one dollar's worth of stamps, they may be deposited as so much money, and an account with the bank.

The financial institutions of Washington are well managed and sound. Their business is large and steadily increasing. On March 1, 1891, the national banks, and the three great loan and trust companies, the Washington, the National Safe Deposit, and the American Security and Trust Company, had an aggregate capital of $5,866,300, and a surplus of $1,682,783; their loans and discounts amounted to $11,828,923, and their total deposits to $13,980,261.

CHAPTER XI.

MERCANTILE HISTORY.

THE city of Washington has never been a great commercial center; primarily, it is believed, because it was, up to the War of the Rebellion, surrounded by Slave States, the institution of slavery being inimical to commerce as well as to manufactures, and nearly all forms of industry. The necessities of the inhabitants of the city had, however, to be supplied, and there were consequently the usual number of retail establishments of different kinds, that number increasing, of course, as the city itself increased in population. As this volume is devoted to local history, there will be given the names of such business men as were prominent in their several lines, especially of those in the earlier days.

In 1800, the Washington Bookstore was kept by Rapine, Conrad, & Company, at the corner of South B Street and New Jersey Avenue. In November, this firm advertised the recent receipt of "Letters from Alexander Hamilton, Concerning the Public Conduct of John Adams, Esq., President of the United States," and also a choice assortment of books on History, Law, Medicine, Divinity, the Arts and Sciences, Classics, School Books, Novels, Romances, Biography, etc., as well as all kinds of stationery, the best Dutch quills, black lead pencils, blank books, etc.

In the same month, John Barnes, of Philadelphia, opened for sale a large assortment of articles; fresh teas, spices, liquors, coffee, stationery, ink powder, and English and American playing cards.

Henry Ingle, about the same time, opened a hardware store on New Jersey Avenue, Capitol Hill, keeping a general assortment of ironmongery, cutlery, saddlery, glassware, and building material, among which he specified the following articles: Iron pots, frying pans, chafing dishes, iron and japanned candlesticks, patent metal teapots and saucepans, japanned tea trays, waiters and bread baskets, sadirons, mathematical instruments, mahogany knife cases filled with ivory-handled knives and forks, cruet stands, ladies' dressing cases, mill-pit and crosscut saws, fifty-six-, twenty-eight-, and fourteen-pound iron weights, also scale beams to weigh from five to ten hundredweight,—"just imported in the ship *Missouri* from Philadelphia."

Jonathan Jackson appears to have been one of the first real-estate dealers in the city, as he commenced advertising November 12, 1800, offering for sale both improved and unimproved property. John Kearney, in the same kind of business, commenced advertising November 17, 1800. A conveyancer's office was opened about December 1, 1800, by Thomas Herty, on New Jersey Avenue, opposite the Little Hotel.

Kid, Eliot, & Company commenced advertising as hardware dealers December 18, 1800, also keeping a large quantity of brandy, spirits, sugar, tea, and coffee, at the brick store opposite Blodgett's Hotel.

Adlington & Powers in February, 1801, opened a grocery and dry-goods store on New Jersey Avenue, near the Sugar House.

In this connection it is interesting to note the advertised prices of "all kinds of hammered and cut nails" in Washington in February, 1801. Samuel McIntire was selling hammered nails and brads as follows: Twentypenny nails by the hundredweight or half hundredweight, at $12\frac{1}{2}d.$ per pound; twelvepenny nails, $13d.$ per pound; tenpenny nails, $13\frac{3}{4}d.$; eightpenny nails, $15d.$ per pound. By retail, under 56 pounds, twentypenny nails were $13\frac{1}{2}d.$ per pound; twelvepenny nails, $13\frac{3}{4}d.$ per pound; tenpenny nails, $14\frac{1}{2}d.$ per pound; eightpenny nails, $15\frac{1}{2}d.$ per pound. Cut nails and brads were sold at the following prices: Twentypenny nails, from $9\frac{1}{2}d.$ to $10\frac{1}{2}d.$ per pound; tenpenny nails, from $10d.$ to $11d.$ per pound; eightpenny nails, from $11d.$ to $12d.$ per pound; sixpenny nails, from $12d.$ to $13d.$ per pound; fourpenny nails, from $13\frac{1}{2}d.$ to $14d.$ per pound; threepenny nails, from $14\frac{1}{2}d.$ to $15d.$ per pound.

John Ott opened a drug store in April, 1801. Richard Dinmore removed his grocery from Georgetown to Washington in April, establishing himself on Square 119, opposite the Seven Buildings, on Pennsylvania Avenue. In June, 1801, Brohawn & Bogs opened a lumber yard, "conveniently situated to the Capitol and President's Square." "The schooner *Dolphin and Kitty* will continue to take freight from this point to Annapolis and Baltimore every three weeks."

Sharpless & Smith opened a new store, in which they kept hardware and dry goods, in November, 1801. Robert Cherry carried on the grocery and liquor business on New Jersey Avenue, near the Sugar House. The *Mail Pilot*, at this time, plied between Washington and Baltimore, Philadelphia and New York, leaving Washington about 6:00 A. M. and arriving at Baltimore at 3:00 P. M., leaving Baltimore next morning and reaching Philadelphia in about twenty-four hours, carrying baggage "at the risk of the owner."

In June, 1802, Duane's Bookstore advertised for sale a few copies of the suppressed book, "The History of John Adams's Administration," which was suppressed by Mr. Burr; also, a number of books of European importation, cheaper than before the peace in Europe.

Among the receipts in merchandise noted in 1803, was a cargo of "Plaister of Paris," certified to be genuine and of the first quality. It was for sale by Stewart & Beall.

A new market was opened in Washington in December, 1801. The people were advised, through the public prints, to sustain the market, and farmers in the vicinity were advised to take their produce there for sale.

In the latter part of 1803 and the beginning of 1804, a movement was inaugurated looking to the development of the commercial interests of the city. This movement consisted in the establishment of a commercial company. At the outset, however, it was seen that the great difficulty to be overcome in this movement was the fact that there were but few engaged in the Government employ, and these few were in the city but part of the time. They had for the most part residences of their own, and would cause but little extra business to spring up. The city, however, was situated on a great and noble river, which came down through a rich country, and there was a harbor here capable of accommodating a large quantity of shipping, where vessels of the largest tonnage could load and unload with facility. And though there were perhaps but few willing to "risque" their property for the general good, yet there were some desirous of forming, by subscription, a capital to be applied to commercial purposes, and it was presumed there would not be lacking either industry or enterprise to make that capital productive. It was thought that if this city could become a market for the sale of domestic and foreign manufactures, even on a small scale, it would not be long before the doors of commerce would be open to individual enterprise, etc.

By the census of 1803, it was found that the professions, occupations, and trades of the inhabitants were as follows: Architects,

4; merchant tailors, 2; notaries public, 1; clerks, 10; merchants, 21; stonecutters, 16; lumber merchants, 2; carters, 18; tailors, 17; gentlemen, 15; nailers, 2; peddlers, 8; painters, 4; painters and glaziers, 2; carpenters, 63; joiners, 12; physicians, 6; cabinet makers, 7; printers, 10; laborers, 82; bricklayers, 18; turners, 1; sailmakers, 2; coopers, 1; nail cutters, 1; house carpenters, 13; limners, 2; shoemakers, 23; pump makers, 3; millwrights, 1; tavern keepers, 9; "plaisterers," 13; bakers, 6; carvers and gilders, 1; brickmakers, 1; stone masons, 7; booksellers, 2; grocers, 2; officers of the Government, 24; brewers, 1; lawyers, 4; blacksmiths, 8; masons, 2; ministers of the Gospel, 3; schoolmasters, 5; shop keepers, 33; chair makers, 2; coach makers, 2, etc.

In 1804, preparations were made for the holding of a fair in Washington. Great good, it was thought, would result, both to the city and to the farmers of the vicinity. The first fair commenced May 1, 1805, and continued three days. James Hoban, Joseph Hodgson, and Henry Ingle were appointed the first directors of the fairs held in the city.

October 18, 1805, the sloop *Mary Ann*, from Guilford, Connecticut, arrived at the Navy Yard, and had for sale on board potatoes, onions, cheese, hay, clover seed, table fish, etc. About the same time, the schooner *Ann* arrived at Lear's wharf with eighteen hundred bushels of "coals," from Nicholson & Heath's black pits, Richmond, the "coals" being reputed the best in Virginia. They were offered for sale on board the schooner.

An act of the Council of Washington, adopted April 17, 1806, with reference to the baking of bread, is of considerable interest. The act regulated the weight and quality of bread. It provided that after the 1st of June, 1806, bread made or offered for sale in the city of Washington should be made from inspected flour, either superfine, fine, or middling, without any intermixture of the same, or the addition of any Indian meal or flour from any other grain. All bread offered for sale was required to be stamped with the initials of the maker. Any bread offered for sale not thus stamped was to be forfeited to the would-be purchaser, or to the trustees of the poor of the city of Washington. Single and double loaves of bread, of all qualities, were to be of the weights as given below: From fine flour worth from $4 to $4.50 per barrel, a single loaf was to weigh 31 ounces, double loaf, 62 ounces; from flour worth from $4.50 to $5 per barrel, a single loaf was to weigh 30 ounces, a double loaf, 60 ounces; from flour worth from $5 to $5.50 per barrel, a single loaf was to weigh 27 ounces, and a double loaf, 54 ounces; from flour worth from $6 to $6.50 per barrel, a single loaf, 22 ounces, and double one, 44 ounces; from flour worth from $6.50 to $7, a single loaf was to weigh 20 ounces, and a double one, 40 ounces; from flour worth from $7 to $7.50, a single loaf was to weigh 19 ounces, and a double one, 38 ounces; from flour worth from $9.50 to $10, a single loaf was to weigh 13 ounces, and a double one, 26 ounces, and so on as flour increased in price. The price of flour was to be ascertained the last week of every month by the Mayor, or by the register in the absence of the Mayor, from respectable merchants living in the county of Washington, and published in the city newspaper for the benefit of those concerned; and this price was to govern the size of the loaves of bread for the next month; except that in case of any sudden rise in the cash price of flour, the Mayor was authorized to establish the standard price of flour each week.

William S. Nicholls, in 1806, was one of the leading dry-goods merchants in the city, keeping a great variety of goods in a store then lately occupied by a Mr. Melvin.

In February, 1807, P. Mauro notified the public that he had just imported direct from London, England, four English pianofortes, with additional keys, Astor, maker, together with other musical instruments. "The above instruments have been examined by the subscriber, who (flattering himself to be a judge) will, when sold, warrant them to be of superior quality and without any defect."

Tunis Chaven, dry-goods merchant, in February, 1808, removed to his new store near the Navy Yard gate. About this time, F. A. Wagler offered for sale two "fortepianos," made by Broadwood, and they were probably superior to any in the place; also, all kinds of dry and wet goods, "among the latter being brandy six years old."

The Washington Commercial Company was organized at a meeting held March 16, 1808, at Stelle's Hotel. Twelve directors were chosen, as follows: Thomas Tingey, Peter Miller, John McGowan, C. W. Goldsborough, Joseph Forrest, James D. Barry, Alexander Kerr, Adam Lindsay, John P. Van Ness, William Prout, Samuel N. Smallwood, and James Cassin. Joseph Forrest was chosen president of this company, which carried on a general wholesale business. In August, 1808, they received from New York a large shipment of various kinds of goods, liquors, sugars, teas, coffees, spices, and groceries. This company continued to do business many years.

The city continued to grow slowly until after the War of 1812–15. At the close of this war, the number of stores in Washington was so limited that the inhabitants were compelled to go to Georgetown or

Alexandria to procure necessary articles of dry goods, hardware, groceries, china, glassware, etc., but by 1816 there had been such an increase in the growth of business houses in the central part of the city that every article of necessity, convenience, and even of luxury, could be had without difficulty at home. At this time, the number of stores on Pennsylvania Avenue, between the Capitol and the President's Mansion, was as follows: Dry goods, 16; groceries, 7; hardware, 2; china, glassware, etc., 2; drug stores, 2; millinery stores, 3; confectioneries, 3; hats, shoes, etc., 2; books and stationery, 2; leather stores, 1; cabinet stores, 3; chair factories, 1; "merchant taylors," 3; plate, jewelry, etc., 3; and at the same time there were plenty of mechanics in the different branches, two extensive hotels, and a reading room well supplied with books, papers, etc.

In February, 1819, there was prepared and published a tabular statement with reference to the commerce of the District of Columbia. It commenced with 1801, as there were no statistics for 1800. The entire value of exports in 1801 was $894,467; in 1802, $774,063. In 1803, the value of foreign and domestic produce was as follows: foreign, $32,938; domestic, $1,112,056; in 1804, foreign, $294,803; domestic, $1,157,195. From this time on, the value of foreign produce generally diminished until 1812, when it was $12,096; but in 1818 it had increased to $138,717. With reference to the value of domestic produce, it was, as has been said, in 1804 $1,157,195, and with fluctuations from year to year, it was in 1818 $1,264,751. In 1804, the first year in which the tonnage of the District was recorded, it was 9,915 registered tons; enrolled, 3,514; licensed, 868. And in 1816, it was, registered, 7,743; enrolled, 8,976; licensed, 1,938.

Among the bookstores in the city in 1819, were those of Davis & Force, and Henry Guegan. Pishey Thompson came later, but not many years after 1820. On January 12, 1829, Mr. Thompson advertised, for the first time in Washington, Webster's Dictionary, in two large quarto volumes; price to subscribers, $20 in boards, and $25 in cloth. Mr. Thompson was the author of a history of Boston, England, highly commended.

In 1833, Richard Wright advertised Schuylkill coal for sale at $9 per ton on the wharf, and Seth Sturdevant had Lackawanna coal for sale at the "reduced price of $9 per ton."

In September, 1854, the price of coal in Washington was so high as to cause great dissatisfaction. Public complaints were numerous and forcible against the dealers, who were called upon for some explanation. Coal was then selling for from $8 to $9 per ton, an advance upon the price of the previous year of from $1 to $2 per ton. This increase in the price was in defiance of the fact that the output of coal for that portion of the year then passed that for the corresponding portion of the year 1853. Up to August 5, 1854, about 103,000 tons more coal had reached tide water from the Cumberland mines than in the previous year; over the Reading Railroad the increase had been 306,000 tons; by the Schuylkill Canal the increase had been 52,000 tons, making from three principal sources of supply an increase of 460,000 tons, or about 25 per cent. more than was forwarded the year before. The price of coal in London, England, was then from $3 to $4 per ton the year round, and the cost of transportation from the mines was quite as great there as in this country.

The amount of coal shipped to market from the Cumberland mines for the year ending August 26, 1854, was 403,143.12 tons, of which 103,894.17 tons passed through the Chesapeake and Ohio Canal, the rest passing over the Baltimore and Ohio Railroad. The amount shipped to the same time in 1853 was 289,555 tons.

In answer to the objections to the high price of coal then ruling, a "Retail Dealer" said that the price was about thirty per cent. higher than it was the year before; and to justify this increase in the price, said that it was on account of the increased cost of labor at the mines, the advance of tolls on railroads, the increased cost of labor in shipping, the advance of freights over the year before of about thirty per cent., and the increased expenses of retail dealers. But above all of these items, there was the greatly increased consumption of coal, which would almost of itself justify the increase complained of in the price of coal. This increase in consumption of coal had been occasioned in part by the substitution of coal for wood on steamboats and locomotives, and in manufacturing establishments, which latter had greatly increased in number during the few years previous.

But there was another reason for the increase in the price in coal, which was quite as potent as any given by the "Retail Dealer." This was that the operators of the anthracite mines in Pennsylvania combined for the purpose of restricting the shipments of coal from the mines. This combination was seriously condemned by the public generally as a conspiracy against their rights, and was unfavorably compared with the conduct of the Dutch, some years before, owners of the spice islands, who, in order to keep up the prices of spices, allowed only a certain amount to be sent to the market, burning all the rest. The conduct of the coal operators was considered worse than that of the Dutch in this, that the Dutch interfered only with the price of a luxury, while the Pennsylvania coal barons combined to keep up the price of an article which was a necessity to the poor as well as to the rich. Purchasers were seriously advised to limit their consumption of coal in order to bring the coal operators to terms. Such movements as these of the coal operators and the Dutch producers of spice, are far from being exceptional in the history of the world. The Knights of Labor in the United States have frequently combined to limit the amount of labor in the market, with the view of controlling its price, and in the year 1891 the Farmers' Alliance combined, to a considerable extent, to limit the amount of wheat offered for sale, in order to force up the price to an unnatural height. All such movements are conspiracies against the public interests, and alike subject to condemnation.

Some time previous to 1856, the precise date not ascertained, there was an attempt to organize a Merchants' Exchange. An annual meeting of this society was held December 5, 1856, with Mr. James B. Dodson, vice-president, in the chair. Numerous topics of interest were discussed, and the following resolution was adopted:

"That Messrs. G. W. Riggs, William B. Todd, Hudson Taylor, M. W. Galt, Philip Otterback, and John H. Semmes, being one from each ward of the city, be, and they are hereby, appointed a committee to urge upon the city authorities the absolute necessity of erecting a new market house in the central portion of the city."

The officers of the association then were as follows: Samuel Bacon, president; James B. Dodson, vice-president; John F. Ellis, secretary; William Wall, treasurer; Walter Harper, S. P. Franklin, T. J. Fisher, J. B. Clagett, A. E. Perry, T. Parker, William F. Bayly, George Burns, B. F. Morsell, William B. Todd, Benjamin Beall, and Hudson Taylor, board of directors. This society, however, was not permanent, probably because it was premature. In February, 1862, several of the merchants again attempted to revive the subject of a Merchants' Exchange, inasmuch as the city was then assuming rank as a commercial center; but it was not until 1865 that such an organization became prominent. This organization, known as the Board of Trade, will be treated of in succeeding pages. General commercial interests will for the present claim attention.

In 1856, the coal trade was but little more satisfactory to the general public than in 1853. This was because of the breaking of two of the principal dams of the Chesapeake and Ohio Canal, by means of which canal Cumberland coal reached the city. Some of the dealers, however, had unlimited confidence in the final success of the trade. Mr. Alexander Ray, in this year, expended $30,000 in putting up docks and sheds, and in 1857 he expended other large sums and flanked his dock with two railroads, connecting with the Chesapeake and Ohio Canal.

Another enterprise which at that time promised to be of great importance was the shipping of timber direct to foreign countries. Benjamin Thornton, of Fairfax, though formerly of England, dispatched the brig *Wabash* from Alexandria to Liverpool, England, with three hundred tons of timber on board, and had, besides, three thousand tons ready for shipment from the Washington City wharves. As there was then abundance of timber on the river, both above and below the District of Columbia, it was confidently anticipated that the shipping of timber would become an extensive portion of the business of the District.

In 1859, there was considerable commerce being carried on at the deep water wharves above Easby's Point. Within the week ending August 27, eight seagoing vessels arrived at these docks, their cargoes consisting of coal, plaster, lumber, ice, etc. A vessel was dispatched with agricultural fertilizers for lands on the Patuxent. At the ship-yard and marine railway of the Easbys, the repair of vessels was constantly going on. The machinery at these works was capable of hauling out of the water vessels of from four hundred to five hundred tons.

About this time, an event of considerable importance transpired with reference to the commerce of the District. This event was the opening of the "New York and Washington Screw Steamship Line." The first steamship of this line to arrive at the West Washington wharves was the *Mount Vernon*, a screw steamer, Captain F. C. Smith, September 6. The line of steamers of which the *Mount Vernon* was the pioneer, was owned by H. B. Cromwell & Company, of New York, and was designed to run between New York and the District of Columbia. The *Mount Vernon* was of seven hundred tons, and had an engine of five hundred horse-power. She drew twelve feet of water, and her speed was fifteen knots an hour. The vessel was fitted up for both freight and passengers, with accommodations for about thirty of the latter. The fare to New York was $7.50; round trip, $13. The event of the opening of this line was fittingly celebrated on Tuesday evening, September 6, at the house of Thomas T. Everett, on M Street, in the northern liberties. At this banquet George D. Fowle, of Alexandria, made an address, in which he called attention to the advantages this enterprise furnished to the people of the District, and those of Virginia and Maryland in the vicinity,—certain, safe, regular, and cheap means of communication and commerce between the Capital of the Nation and the metropolis of the Nation. This steamship continued to make regular trips between the two cities until the breaking out of the War, when she entered the service of the Government. The chief obstacle to her progress she found during this time was a sand bar in the Potomac River, which was, however, removed by dredging in the year 1860, the work being completed by August 1. The length of the area dredged was 1,500 yards, and the breadth 100 yards. 900 yards in length was dredged 6 feet deep, and the remainder from 4 to 5 feet, making the sand excavated about 275,000 cubic yards. The channel at the shallowest point then had a depth of 14 feet. Early in April, 1861, Hirman Barney, collector of the port of New York, informed the proprietors of this line that he could not grant clearances to any ports of the United States where the functions of the Federal officers had been usurped by State authorities, and soon afterward the steamers of this company were engaged in the service of the United States.

The prices of the various commodities in the markets of Washington in February, 1865, were as follows: Flour, superfine, $11.50 per barrel; extra, $11.75 and $12; Welch's family, $13.75 in fifty-barrel lots, and $14 per dray load; Royal York, $12.75; corn—yellow, $1.95; white, $1.95 to $2.05 per bushel; corn meal, $2.05 per bushel; potatoes, $6 per barrel; butter, 53 to 58 cents per pound; cheese, 22 to 24 cents per pound; dried beef, 20 cents per pound, and other things in proportion.

Early this year, the enterprising merchants and business men of the city, in order to insure safety, speed, and regularity in the transportation of goods between New York and the District of Columbia, established a new line of steamships. They started with three regular steamers, namely, the *E. C. Knight*, Captain J. J. Mason; the *Ann Eliza;* and the *John Gibson*, Captain W. C. Geoghegan. The steamers were built by Cramp & Son, of Philadelphia. The agents for the new line in Washington were William R. Snow & Company, and Messrs. Flowers & Barnes, of Alexandria, in that city. The steamer *E. C. Knight* arrived in Georgetown March 26, the time of sailing from New York to her dock in Georgetown being forty-one hours and twenty-five minutes. The name of the company operating this line of steamers was "The Atlantic Steamship Company." Another company similarly engaged was the New York and Washington Steamship Company, having three steamers, named the *Baltimore*, the

27

Rebecca Clyde, and the *Empire*. C. P. Houghton was their agent at Georgetown, and M. Eldridge & Company at Alexandria.

One of the large firms to establish themselves in business early after the War was Thomas Davis & William Marbury, in the wholesale salt business. Mr. Davis had long been in the salt business, and, more largely than any other man, had dealt in salt between Washington and New York. His largest warehouse was at No. 23 Water Street, Georgetown, which was full of salt; and in addition to this, he had warehouses in different parts of the city, filled with various kinds of salt — as Ashton, refined Liverpool, etc. He had also one warehouse filled with ground alum.

On October 17, 1865, there was a meeting held at the City Hall for the purpose of organizing a Merchants'. Exchange. S. Norment was called to the chair, and John R. Elvans appointed secretary. Speeches were made by Mr. Elvans, G. Perkins, of Chicago, A. R. Shepherd, R. M. Hall, and others. The merchants of Georgetown were invited to unite in the movement. The firms represented at this meeting were King & Burchell, C. W. Boteler, Jr., H. Senken, W. R. Snow & Company, W. G. Metzerott, R. M. Hall, J. T. Walker & Company, Phillip & Solomons, A. R. Shepherd, Samuel Bacon & Company, W. H. Clagett, Barbour, Semmes, & Company, S. Norment, Lansburg & Brother, J. B. Bryan & Brother, Blanchard & Mohun, C. B. Bayley & Company, John R. Elvans & Company, J. P. Bartholow, and R. Cohen. On motion of Mr. Shepherd, a committee was appointed to prepare a plan of organization, consisting of Mr. Shepherd, Mr. Perkins, Samuel Bacon, C. W. Boteler, Jr., R. M. Hall, John R. Elvans, and J. P. Bartholow.

At a meeting held October 24, 1865, the following names were announced for membership: Kidwell & Son, Mohun & Son, Henry R. Searle, J. D. Edward & Company, Kellau, Moore, & King, John F. Bridget, C. S. Noyes, John F. Ellis, Ulysses Ward, William P. Mohun, T. Edward Clark, Hall & Hume, J. H. Semmes & Company, Thomas Thompson, M. McNeal, C. S. O'Hare, H. O. Hood, Hays & Cropley, John G. Adams, G. F. Clark, Harper & Mitchell, James T. Close & Company, James Y. Davis, Z. D. Gilman, C. H. Utermehle, McKnew & Bell, H. S. Johnson, Wall, Stephens, & Company, Elijah Edmonston, John B. Turton, James Moore, F. L. Harvey, B. F. Morsell, C. B. Baker, Hudson Taylor, R. B. Clarke, Thomas A. Tolson, W. H. & O. H. Morrison, Daniel B. Clarke, Webb & Beveridge, Nagle & Company, W. S. Teel, H. Burns & Company, J. E. Hoover, J. W. Clampitt, J. R. D. Morrison, G. M. Wight, and A. J. Dietrich.

Mr. A. R. Shepherd submitted a report of the committee on the constitution, under which the merchants present organized themselves into a Board of Trade of the District of Columbia. Under this constitution the annual contribution of each member was $10, a sum which some considered too small to accomplish the purposes which the new organization had in contemplation. One of these purposes was to compete with the great monopoly, the Baltimore and Ohio Railroad. Mr. Shepherd, the week before, had said that if the merchants of Washington would organize, and make the city what it should be — a commercial city, and not a mere appendage of Baltimore, as it then was, they could build up the city, and make it independent. He was in favor of including all citizens in the benefits to be derived from the organization of a board of trade, and was opposed to following the example of the corporation of Washington, which, in the magnitude of its wisdom, had ordained that none but citizens should engage in corporation work. The Southern trade was what was wanted, and Mr. Shepherd said that if each merchant would subscribe $300 or $400, the monopoly above referred to could successfully be opposed.

At a special meeting of the Board of Trade held December 6, 1865, the question discussed was as to the adoption of a resolution offered by Mr. Shepherd, inviting an expression of opinion as to the propriety of urging Congress to consolidate the cities of Washington and Georgetown, and the county of Washington, under one municipality. In his remarks in favor of the resolution, he called attention to the fact that in the District of Columbia there were five distinct governments: the corporations of Washington and Georgetown, the Levy Court, the Metropolitan Police Commissioners, and the Commissioner of Public Buildings. The corporation of Washington had but little control, as Congress could at any time enact obnoxious laws, and it would therefore be better if Congress had complete control. Mr. Mitchell, of the Common Council of Georgetown, said that he had already introduced into that body a resolution favoring the uniting of the two corporations.

The Board of Trade of the city of Washington continued in existence several years, but it seems not to have impressed the city very strongly with its importance, and it was permitted by the business community to lapse. Georgetown also had an organization known as a board of trade, established in 1866. On March 22, 1869, the third annual meeting of this board was held, and the chairman thereof then stated that during the previous year there had been received seven hundred and four thousand bushels of wheat, all of which had been manufactured into flour, and the corn received amounted to about five hundred thousand bushels. He also hoped for increased interest in the Board of Trade. This hoped for increased interest did not make itself felt, for this exchange, like the old Washington Board of Trade, soon ceased to exist.

In recent years, an organization has been effected under the name of the Washington Board of Trade, which is, however, something more than its name implies. ·It was organized December 2, 1889, with the following officers: Myron M. Parker, president; S. W. Woodward, first vice-president; S. E. Wheatley, second vice-president; A. T. Britton, general counsel; B. H. Warner, treasurer; Alexander D. Anderson, secretary. The directory consisted of thirty-one members. There have been, since this organization was effected, numerous committees to carry on its affairs, and it is sufficient to present the names of these committees in order to show the wide range of the work of this Board of Trade, which might perhaps as well be called a board of promotion, as its objects, as stated in its by-laws, are "the consideration of, and action upon, matters concerning the commerce, prosperity, and advancement of the material interests of the National Capital, and the dissemination of information relating thereto." These committees are the executive, with E. Kurtz Johnson, chairman; finance, Beriah Wilkins; taxation and assessments, Henry Wise Garnett; railroads, B. H. Warner; transportation, William A. Wimsatt; arbitration, A. T. Britton; commerce, Isidor Saks; public buildings, Thomas Somerville; membership, Thomas W. Smith; parks and reservations, C. J. Bell; streets and avenues, George Truesdell; charities, John H. Magruder; public health, F. L. Moore; trade organizations, Samuel Ross; water supply, Charles Baum; improvement of the Potomac River, S. E. Wheatley; harbor improvements, C. B. Church; Mount Vernon Avenue, Frank Hume; universities, Alexander D. Anderson; bridges, Theodore W. Noyes; insurance, Simon Wolf; Rock Creek Tunnel, S. E. Wheatley. The membership of this board at the present time is about two hundred.

In addition to the work ordinarily performed by boards of this kind in the various cities of the country, the committee on universities, of which Mr. Alexander D. Anderson is chairman, is performing great and valuable public service in aiding to build up and foster the great universities established, or proposed, for the city of Washington. The purpose is to make Washington the great educational center of the United States.

Washington has had market houses, one or more, ever since its earliest days. But the old market houses were destroyed in 1870-72, when the era of improvement commenced. There are now eight public markets in the District, six in Washington and two in Georgetown. The largest, and one of the finest in the country, is the Center Market, between Seventh and Ninth streets, and Pennsylvania Avenue and B Street. This market house took the place of one that had for years been an eyesore to the residents of the city. It was erected by a private company, chartered by Congress for the purpose. The entire stock of this company was taken in October, 1870, 10,000 shares at $50 each. Mayor Emery subscribed for 1,000 shares; Fitzhugh Coyle, 500 shares; A. R. Shepherd, 1,000 shares, and later for 500 shares more; Moses Kelly, 500 shares; H. D. Cooke, 500 shares; E. M. Tinker subscribed for 1 share each for five persons, one of the five being Hiram Sibley, and 10 for himself; Mr. Chandler subscribed for 1 share each for several different persons, and 1,245 for himself, and afterward he subscribed for 1,250 more shares for himself; Mr. Hildreth subscribed for 5 shares for F. B. Whiting, and 1,245 for himself; Mr. Ordway subscribed for 1 share each for five individuals, and 1,245 for himself; several shares were taken by parties whose names were not ascertained; then, it being found that there were only 220 shares left, Mr. Chandler took them. November 5, 1870, the incorporators were organized by the election of directors in the persons of H. D. Cooke, A. R. Shepherd, H. S. Dawes, S. S. Smoot, C. Cushing, H. Van Aerman, N. M. Ordway, John Roche, M. G. Emery, E. M. Tinker, T. C. Connolly, W. E. Chandler, and T. A. Hildreth. H. D. Cooke was chosen president; Moses Kelly, treasurer; and a building committee of six was chosen as follows: Shepherd, Ordway, Davis, Tinker, Hildreth, and Smoot. Adolph Cluss was selected as the architect, who drew up plans for the building; which, as it stands at the present time, is as follows: Whole length of market houses on Seventh, Ninth, and B streets, 740 feet; average width, 82 feet; length of wholesale store building, 274 feet; width, 37 feet. In the central portion of the building is the armory, and in the second story of the Ninth Street portion is the drill room. The buildings were completed in 1872, and are of the most substantial character. The retail building is a one-story brick, and covers 60,172 square feet of ground. The retail market has 666 stalls, and cost $350,-000. The average monthly rental of the stalls is $8.35. As has been intimated in the above, this market is owned by a private corporation; all the other markets, brief mention of which follows, are public.

North Liberty Market is on the corner of Fifth and K streets

Northwest. It is a one-story building, covering 41,600 square feet of ground. It contains 284 stalls, and cost $152,000. The average rental of the stalls is $5.90.

Riggs Market is on P Street, between Fourteenth and Fifteenth streets. It a one-story frame structure, 130 x 70 feet, contains 60 stalls, and cost $5,000. The average rental is $4.33⅓.

Corcoran Market is a low frame building on O Street, near Seventh Street, Northwest. It contains 187 stalls, the average rental being $3.56.

Western Market is on the southeast corner of Twenty-first and K streets Northwest. It contains 105 stalls, which rent for $3.63 each per month.

Butchers' Market, on High Street, between First and Second streets, in Georgetown, is a one-story brick structure, 80 x 60 feet, and cost $5,000. It contains 48 stalls, each of which rents for $3.80 per month.

Georgetown Market, on Bridge Street, fronting on Market Street, is a one-story brick building, 36 x 240 feet. It contains 75 stalls, and cost $60,000. Each stall rents for $1.92 per month.

Eastern Market is on Seventh and C streets Northeast. It is a one-story brick building, 205 x 47 feet, cost $90,000, and contains 85 stalls, each of which rents for $3.75 per month.

While not a part of the commercial history of Washington, yet it is believed that no more fitting place in this volume can be found than this for a brief outline of the movement resulting in the Columbian Exposition to be held in Chicago in 1893. It is due to Washington, and it is also due to the truth, that such a statement should somewhere herein be made. It is a matter of fact and of record that this coming Exposition at Chicago is the outgrowth of the proposed Three Americas' and World's Exposition at Washington. The author and projector of this proposed Exposition was Mr. Alexander D. Anderson, of Washington, who, backed by the citizens of Washington and of Baltimore, spent four years' time and $33,000 in money in promoting the movement. The project was first foreshadowed by him in an interview in the New York *Herald*, November 19, 1884. He submitted it in writing to the president of the Baltimore and Ohio Railroad Company, January 1, 1885, and presented it in detail to the citizens of Washington at a public meeting February 26, 1886, at which meeting committees were appointed, headquarters opened, and a vigorous campaign commenced. The memorial of the committee was presented to the Senate of the United States in

April, 1886, by Arthur P. Gorman, of Maryland, and this memorial was published in full in the *Congressional Record.*

The local board was then converted into a national board of promotion, and, in response to notices of appointment sent out, Mr. Anderson received formal letters of acceptance from the governors of forty States and Territories, the mayors of fifty-five of the leading cities, one hundred and seventy-six presidents and secretaries of boards of trade, and the officers of thirty State and Territorial granges, approving of the movement, and pledging coöperation.

June 16, 1888, Hon. Perry Belmont, of New York, submitted a report to the House of Representatives in favor of the project, and naming Washington as the place for holding the Exposition. But before the report of the committee could be acted upon by the House, New York, in the summer of 1889, attempted to appropriate the work of Washington, and to secure the great Fair for herself. Against this attempt Chicago made a vigorous protest, and it was only when the latter city saw that New York was determined to have the Fair, and that there was danger of her securing it away from Washington, that she herself determined to secure it away from New York. The result of the contest between Chicago and New York is well known to everybody.

Mr. Anderson thereupon publicly stated that it had become the duty of every American citizen to aid the Exposition to the best of his ability, and to make it a success worthy of the Nation. He projected an amendment to the Exposition bill, providing for a grand review of the navies of the world in the New York harbor and Hampton Roads, preceding the opening of the Fair at Chicago, which amendment Senator Daniel, of Virginia, introduced into the Senate, and which is now Section 8 of the Exposition act. This grand review is to take place in April, 1893, immediately preceding the opening of the Exposition itself at Chicago.

CHAPTER XII.

MANUFACTURING.

Early Establishments — A Nail Factory — A Hat Factory — The Steam Engine — Thresh-
ing Machine — The Columbia Manufacturing Company — Foxall's Foundry — Manu-
factory of Fire Engines — The Columbia Rolling Mills — .Paper Mills — Pope's
Threshing Machine — Bomford's Flouring Mill — George Page, Shipbuilder — Steam
Marble and Brown Stone Works — George Hill, Jr.'s Paper Mill — William Stick-
ney's Envelope Manufactory — The Washington Gas Light Company — The United
States Electric Lighting Company — Summary of Manufacturing Establishments in
Existence at the Present Time.

WITH reference to manufacturing establishments, the same remarks
may be made as have been already made with regard to commerce. Washington has had, from year to year, a considerable number
of such establishments of different kinds, and yet not enough to
render the city a distinctively manufacturing center. In December, 1800,
Wilson & Handy commenced the manufacture of furniture on New
Jersey Avenue, between the Episcopal church and the Sugar House.
They expressed their confidence that they should be able to give
general satisfaction, from the experience they had had in the principal
shops in Europe and America. The articles made by this firm were
secretary desks, portable writing desks, chests, card tables, etc.

A nail factory was established about February 1, 1801, on F
Street, where all kinds of cut nails were made. John Minchen
moved his shoe factory from Philadelphia to Washington about this
time, locating near the Eastern Branch, and afterward on New
Jersey Avenue, near the Capitol.

In April, 1802, Benjamin Henchey gave notice that he would
exhibit his new mode of obtaining light in a variety of thermo lamp,
commencing the next Friday evening after the 14th of the month, and
continuing until May 18, at Mr. Thompson's new brick house on
Pennsylvania Avenue. Tickets were $1, which would admit one gen-
tleman twice or a gentleman and lady twice.

Joel Brown, in 1803, established himself in Washington as a man-
ufacturer of hats, and in February, 1804, removed to Georgetown. In
February, 1806, Evan Evans advertised for sale an improved straw-

cutter, at his house between the Six Buildings and the Potomac. "He forms the steel of this machine aslant so as to cause the knife to cut off the straw at an angle of twenty-two and one-half degrees, which makes it cut much easier than at right angles." Oliver Evans, of Philadelphia, was the maker.

February 19, 1806, John James Dufour made a remark about the steam engine worthy of note, to the effect that many people attributed the great prosperity of England to it, and that its introduction into the United States would certainly produce the same result; but the great question of iron, which it required for its construction, and the complicated mechanism necessary to produce a rotary motion from its natural motion, would operate for some time to prevent its adoption. He therefore advertised an invention of his own, whereby the rotary motion could be easily effected, and urged capitalists to take an interest in his invention.

Tunstall's patent threshing machine was one of the noted machines of the day. Cast-iron wheels for this valuable machine could be bought at H. Foxall's Georgetown foundry, and also of T. Hogan, on F Street, Washington. This machine was capable of threshing, with two horses or oxen, three hundred bushels per day, and it sold for about $150. A quantity of straw, supposed to contain about two hundred bushels of wheat, had been threshed with this machine, and then rethreshed with flails, and this second threshing produced only a pint and a half of grain.

June 15, 1808, the Mayor of Washington, Robert Brent, called a meeting of citizens of Washington at Stelle's Hotel for the 21st of the month, for the purpose of taking into consideration the expediency of organizing a plan for the encouragement of domestic manufactures. Of this meeting Mr. Brent was elected chairman, and John Law secretary. Samuel H. Smith offered a series of resolutions, which were in substance as follows: That at a time when our rights are trampled upon with unprecedented audacity and injustice by the belligerent nations of Europe, it became the duty of the people either to make sacrifices for their country or to unfold their energies; and that whether peace or war should come, it was the duty of the people to make themselves independent of the workshops of Europe; that it was the duty of all sections of the Union to encourage the establishment and extension of domestic manufactures; that the city of Washington, for various reasons, was eminently fitted for attaining manufacturing importance, and that a plan should be reported to a subsequent meeting. A committee was appointed, and authorized to call another meeting when they were ready to report. This committee was composed of Samuel H. Smith, William Cranch, Gabriel Duval, Cornelius Cunningham, A. Cutting, George Blagden, Buller Cocke, and Robert Brent.

The adjourned meeting was held in accordance with the call of the committee, which reported articles of association for the Columbia Manufacturing Company. There were nine articles adopted. The first declared that the object of the association was to carry on the manufacture of cotton, wool, hemp, and flax, and to promote such other domestic manufactures as should be thought advisable. The second article provided that the capital stock of the company should be $50,000, to be raised by subscription, shares to be worth $25 each, and the books to be opened on August 1, that year. As soon as five hundred shares should be subscribed, a meeting was to be called for the purpose of devising a plan for conducting the business. If five hundred shares should not be subscribed within six months from the time of opening the books, then the money which had been subscribed should be returned. Application was to be made to Congress for the incorporation of the company. The chairman of the meeting, Robert Brent, was authorized to appoint nine commissioners to receive subscriptions, three from Washington, three from Alexandria, and three from Georgetown. The commissioners from Washington were William Cranch, William Brent, and George Blagden, and the books were opened August 1, 1808, at the office of the clerk of the Circuit Court.

On the 14th of February, 1809, John Gardiner congratulated the commissioners on having made a successful start, and offered his services as secretary of the company without compensation, and also offered to devote his leisure time to the superintendency of the factory, only asking that at the end of the year, if he then had served the interests of the company well, he receive some honorary testimonial to that effect.

But upon the organization of the company, on the 22d of February, 1809, the following directors and officers were chosen: Directors — Robert Brent, Nicholas King, Michael Nourse, William Cranch, Charles Jones, Samuel H. Smith, John P. Van Ness, Thomas Munroe, and Joseph Huddleston. Robert Brent was elected president, Samuel H. Smith and Michael Nourse vice-presidents, and Thomas Carpenter secretary.

In November, 1809, the question was whether the company could succeed in getting a start, and a series of resolutions was adopted at a meeting of the directors, in which the opinion was expressed that the success of the institution depended upon the prompt payment of the installments due upon the stock subscription, and requesting the president of the company to have prepared and published a statement of the financial condition of the company. Accordingly, the secretary and treasurer, Thomas Carpenter, under date of November 20, presented a statement of the condition of the company, in which it was shown that there had been four hundred shares subscribed, and that the amount of money paid in was $1,414.33, of which $1,320.10 had been paid out. Of this latter sum $500 had been paid for a carding machine, and $222 for a billy of forty-four spindles and a jenny of sixty-six spindles. One bale of cotton had been purchased for $51.64. In order to compel the payment of the installments due, it was determined to put in operation a rule of the company by which delinquent subscribers forfeited their rights and interests in the company, so that all of those who, by the 22d of February, 1810, had not paid in nine installments should lose their interests in the company. An election was held the same day for nine directors and a secretary. The factory was located on Greenleaf's Point. The company continued in operation for several years, and in 1812 John Gardiner was the secretary.

One of the historic institutions of the early day in Washington was the Foxall Foundry, established in 1800, by Henry Foxall. At this foundry most of the heavy guns were cast that were used in the War of 1812-15. Previously to coming to Washington, Mr. Foxall had operated in Philadelphia, in partnership with Robert Morris, the great financier of the Revolution, a similar institution, called the "Eagle Foundry." The guns made at the Foxall Foundry were the first bored guns made in this country, and many of them were dragged across the country by oxen to the lakes. It is said that they were used by Commodore Perry in his battle on Lake Erie.

After Mr. Foxall's death, the foundry passed into the hands of General John Mason, and for some time afterward was known as the Columbian Foundry. In 1843, an addition was erected at its eastern end, and in this eastern addition were cast most of the heavy guns used in the Mexican War. After the close of this war, the building was used as a distillery for some time, and early in the fifties it was converted into a flouring mill, and is still used for the purpose of manufacturing flour.

In the early part of the century, there was situated on Rock Creek what was known as the Federal Mills, within one-fourth of a mile of Georgetown. These mills had four pairs of stones, capable of manufac-

turing into flour fifty thousand bushels of wheat in a season.   They
were the property of John F. Rowles up to the time of his death, in
1812.   What became of the property afterward was not ascertained.

In December, 1810, Philip Pyfer, Jr., commenced the manufacture
of hides, on Pennsylvania Avenue, opposite the Central Market, where
anyone, by calling, could be accommodated with hides of any kind
"on the lowest terms imaginable."   John Helmer was also a manu-
facturer of hides at that early day, and was located opposite Dr.
Thornton's residence.   About the same time, a blanket manufactory
was established in Georgetown by Elkanah Cobb and Daniel Bussard
& Company.

John Achmann, who had "been regularly brought up in Europe
to the making of engines," carried on the manufacture of fire engines
in Washington for several years, commencing in 1812.   He had a fire
engine in Fredericktown, Maryland, of the following description: The
box of copper, the pumps of brass, and the rest of the engine, except
the carriage, of iron.   It conveyed the water through a tube three-
fourths of an inch in diameter one hundred feet, through a hose one
hundred and four feet in length, then, with a tube one-half inch in
diameter, it was conveyed seventy feet.   He took out letters patent
for his "new invented fire engine," and offered rights for sale.

The Washington Brewery was established in 1811, and was located
at the foot of New Jersey Avenue,—J. W. Colbert & Company, proprietors.   In December of that year, this company advertised malt
liquors of a superior quality.   Table ale was $3 per barrel, strong ale
$4 per barrel, and ale $5 per barrel.

In May, 1813, R. Parrott & I. W. Westerman, of England, were
established in the city as manufacturers of machinery for spinning
and carding wool and cotton.   They were then setting up machinery
of their own manufacture at R. Parrott's mill, at the foot of his
ropewalk.   R. Parrott & Company had also a "grocery warehouse"
on the wharf.

The Columbia Rolling Mills were situated near Georgetown, and
were the property of George French.   They turned out rolled iron of
all descriptions.

In May, 1817, the Washington Knit Stocking Factory went into
operation, at which were manufactured cotton and woolen pantaloons,
cotton and woolen stockings, cotton and woolen waistcoats without
sleeves, cotton and woolen drawers, Berlin lace or tulle, etc.   Isaac
Keller was the proprietor of this establishment.   The Columbia Mills
went into operation about the same time.   Of these mills George

Johnson was the proprietor, and at them woolen goods were manufactured.

The Window Glass Factory of A. & G. Way was established in Washington in 1810 or 1811, on the bank of the Potomac, near the mouth of the Tiber. At this factory there were produced an average of three thousand boxes of glass per year, each box containing one hundred square feet of glass.

A paper mill on Rock Creek was offered for sale in December, 1821. This mill was one hundred and twenty feet long, three stories high, the first story built of stone. It was a two-vat mill. A flour mill belonging to the same property, situated at the Little Falls bridge, three miles above Washington, was also offered for sale at the same time. It was a three-buhr mill. A woolen factory adjoining the flour mill was also offered at the same time. This was a two-story stone building one hundred and ten feet long, with carding machines, billies and jennies, twelve broad looms and a number of narrow ones, and, including the flour mill, cost $40,000.

In February, 1824, Pope's patent threshing machine, adapted either to hand or horse power, was on exhibition at Mr. Steuart's coach maker's shop, on Pennsylvania Avenue, at the foot of Capitol Hill. This machine, with the ordinary power of one horse, and with one man to feed it and one man to take away the straw, was guaranteed to thresh with ease eight bushels of wheat per hour. It was invented by Joseph Pope, of Massachusetts, greatly celebrated both in Europe and the United States for his philosophical researches and attainments. The orrery then in the philosophical and astronomical department of Harvard College was of his invention. The threshing machine combined all that had long been wanting in such a machine — strength and simplicity of construction, and in its operation economy of labor, with the most powerful effects.

George C. Bomford had a large flouring mill in Georgetown, which was burned down in 1844. Upon the ruins Mr. Bomford erected a cotton factory, with a water wheel thirty feet high. The building was four stories in height, and had three thousand spindles and one hundred looms. It furnished employment to about one hundred laborers, male and female. In order to encourage the industry, the corporate authorities of Georgetown exempted the machinery from taxation. At this same time, a Mr. Davis had a flouring mill in Georgetown, grinding from three to four hundred barrels of flour per day.

About the first of the year 1851, George Page began the building of ships in Washington, on the river at the foot of Seventh Street. He had in June, of that year, just completed a steamboat called the *Champion*, which was one hundred and fifty feet long, twenty-four foot beam, and eight feet in depth of hold. Her engine was of one hundred horse-power, and her wheels twenty-four feet in diameter. Her captain was H. J. Strandberg, of Baltimore. He also had on the stocks a steamboat one hundred and seventy-five feet long, twenty-four foot beam, and nine feet depth of hold, the timbers for which were cut from the logs by machinery invented by Mr. Page. He was also then constructing a wharf at Seventh Street, four hundred feet long, from which vessels were to run to Mount Vernon. This one hundred and seventy-five foot steamer was named *William Selden*. He also built, about the same time, a boat which was owned largely by the workmen, named the *Jenny Lind*, one hundred and twenty feet long and of a proportionate width. Then came a ferryboat designed to ply between Washington and Alexandria, two hundred and fifty feet long and thirty-four feet broad.

The *William Selden* was a very fast boat for those times. Upon one occasion, in September, 1851, a New York built steamer, named the *George Washington*, made a fast run from New York to Washington, and Mr. Page, in order to try the speed of the *William Selden* in comparison with that of the *George Washington*, went down to Piney Point, and as the *George Washington* passed, began a race with her to Washington. When the *William Selden* started from Piney Point, the *George Washington* was about six miles ahead. The *William Selden*, however, after some time overtook and passed the *George Washington*, and came to her wharf at the foot of Seventh Street in five hours and fifty-six minutes, the entire distance being about one hundred miles, and gaining about ten miles on the *George Washington*.

In 1852, there were several important manufacturing establishments in full operation in Washington, furnishing employment to a large number of workmen, concentrating considerable capital, and building up a home market for country and other produce.

In November, 1856, Messrs. Coltman & Duncanson, who were well known and highly esteemed by the citizens of Washington, erected what they named Metropolitan Mills, near the Twelfth Street Bridge. Their building was large and commodious, and their engine was a fine piece of machinery from the manufactory of Messrs. Ellis.

In 1860, Mr. Alexander Rutherford had an establishment called the Pioneer Steam Marble and Brown Stone Works, on the south side of Pennsylvania Avenue, between Thirteenth and Fourteenth streets, which, as its name implies, was the first of its kind in Washington, though Mr. Rutherford had himself been a long time in the business in the city.

During the War, there was, of course, but little, if anything, done in the way of establishing new manufactures in the District of Columbia. The War overshadowed everything. But in January, 1865, George Hill, Jr., began the manufacture of paper at the foot of Potomac Street, Georgetown, on an extensive scale. His building was at the northwest corner of Water and P streets, and it contained machinery worth about $20,000. The factory was a three-story brick structure, forty by ninety-five feet in size. Mr. Hill had previously been engaged in the manufacture of paper, having had mills at the Chain Bridge, at Paper Mill Bridge, and at Cabin John Branch.

In August, 1865, William Stickney began the manufacture of envelopes at 375 D Street, near Seventh Street. The machine selected by Mr. Stickney was that patented by Mr. Negbaum, of New York, August 25, 1863, which was then used in the largest envelope manufactories in the United States. The process of making envelopes is extremely simple. Everything was done in Mr. Stickney's establishment by machinery, except gumming the flap. He had in his factory four folding machines, making four different sizes of envelopes on each machine, so that he manufactured sixteen different-sized envelopes in all. In September, 1865, he was employing twelve hands, seven females and five males. At this time, it was thought that Mr. Negbaum's machine was the best made. By its use Mr. Stickney was enabled to sell good envelopes at $2 per thousand, and official envelopes at $3.75 per thousand. However, the most wonderful machine for the manufacture of envelopes then known was that invented by James P. Heron, of Ohio, which cut, gummed, folded, counted, and packed entirely, without the aid of hands, and made three hundred thousand per day.

It is a remarkable fact in the history of civilization, that up to about the beginning of the present century there was no good artificial light,—none better than candle light. Artificial light is obtained either as a result of combustion, or as the effect of chemical action, or of heat without chemical action. Those substances which give out flame are rich either in carbon or hydrogen, as wax, gas, and oils, which are consumed in the burning either of candles or lamps.

The phenomenon of the burning of natural gas is familiar to the citizens of most parts of this country, but it is altogether probable that few are familiar with the history of the origin of the use of artificial gas for lighting purposes. By common consent the merit of the discovery and application of artificial gas for lighting purposes belongs to Great Britain. Sir James Lowther and Dr. James Clayton are believed to have been the first persons to collect and burn coal gas, the experiments of the latter being made in 1739. In 1767, the subject was pursued by Dr. Richard Watson, afterward Bishop of Landarff; by Robert Murdoch, of Scotland, in 1792, at Birmingham and Manchester, England; and by Mr. Winsor, in London, in 1803 and 1804. Mr. Murdoch did not succeed, however, in lighting up the workshop of Boulton & Watt, at Birmingham, until 1798. Dr. Henry, of Manchester, also assisted in the development of the infant art of gas lighting, as did also Mr. Clegg, who succeeded Mr. Murdoch at the works of Boulton & Watt.

Recurring to the dates given above, it may be said that the nineteenth century, in most respects the brightest and best in all history, was ushered in by the light of coal gas, the most pleasant, convenient, and safe, with the possible exception of the incandescent electric light, of all artificial lights yet discovered or invented.

Gas is obtained from petroleum, from oil, from resin, from wood, and from peat. Oil gas was manufactured in New York from 1824 to 1828, and sold at $10 per one thousand cubic feet; resin gas was supplied in New York from 1828 to 1848, at $7 per one thousand cubic feet most of the time. Oil gas, under the name of "solar gas," was introduced into Washington in the latter part of 1846; and in January, 1847, Mr. Crutchett, the inventor of what was called here and in Dayton, Ohio, a little later, "Crutchett's Solar Gas," lighted with this gas Capitol Hill and North Capitol Avenue, having nine "solar gas lamps" burning between the Capitol gate and his residence, at the corner of First and C streets. The light emitted by this gas was said at the time, by a newspaper, to be so strong and brilliant that a person could read fine print by it in the streets without the least difficulty. Mr. Crutchett kept on experimenting as well as he could with his gas for a year or two. The east room of the President's House was lighted for the first time with this gas on December 29, 1848, to the satisfaction of the President and others. Mr. Crutchett was then engaged in erecting his gas works in Washington. During this year, the Washington Gas Light Company was organized for the purpose of supplying the citizens of Washington with "solar gas," it appearing that this gas could be successfully manufactured from oil. On January 14, 1850, this company published an address to the public, in which they said that they were able to furnish light equal to that from seventy-five thousand cubic feet of coal gas per day, and that in a short time they should increase their capacity by thirty thousand feet per day. They claimed they could manufacture gas from oil cheaper than it could be manufactured from coal anywhere in the United States, and that they sold it cheaper than coal was sold for anywhere in the country, except in Pittsburgh and Philadelphia. One foot of solar gas, they said, was equal to two and a half feet of coal gas, and while they were selling solar gas for $8 per one thousand cubic feet, coal gas was being sold for $3.50 per one thousand cubic feet. Thus coal gas light equal in quality to $8 worth of solar gas light would cost $8.75.

From further experience, however, it was found that the manufacture of solar gas could not be made a success, and the company erected coal gas works east of Four and a Half Street, between Maryland Avenue and the City Canal, on Square C. The main buildings were eight in number. The smoke stack or tower was 70 feet high, and the excavation for the gasometer was 90 feet in diameter and 20 feet deep. The walls were $3\frac{1}{2}$ feet thick, and required 400,000 brick. The mast in the center of the gasometer was 50 feet long, and projected into the air 20 feet. The old gas works were south of Tenth Street, and cost $100,000, and the new works cost $150,000, making the cost of the new establishment $250,000. In December, 1851, the new establishment commenced furnishing to the inhabitants of Washington gas from coal. Pipes were laid from the works on Square C up Four and a Half Street to Pennsylvania Avenue, and then both ways on Pennsylvania Avenue toward the Capitol and the President's House.

In a circular published by the company March 14, 1856, over the signature of Mr. Silas H. Hill, then president, he says:

"On account of the widely scattered population of Washington, and the apparent impracticability of uniting governmental and individual effort in the establishment and maintenance of a company for the supply of gas light, even in the more important parts of the city, several years passed away before any organized effort was made to accomplish this desirable object. It was not regarded by our citizens as a business promising a fair remuneration, and consequently this city, with all its apparent advantages, and with a fixed population of forty thousand inhabitants, was among the last in the Union to enjoy this almost indispensable means of illumination."

The capital is stated as "$424,000, every dollar of which has been judiciously and economically expended."

28

A retort house containing 28 benches of 3 retorts each, in all 84 retorts, had been erected; this was capable of producing 280,000 cubic feet of gas every twenty-four hours. Also, two gas holders, respectively 120,000 feet and 280,000 feet. The number of consumers had reached 1,681.

"A line of six-inch pipe, over a mile in length, was laid from the vicinity of the Capitol to the Navy Yard, with only one widely scattered row of street lamps, passing many squares with scarcely a dwelling house on each, and double lines of pipe are in that part of Pennsylvania Avenue near Georgetown, with quite as uninviting a prospect of private consumption."

The amount paid to their numerous employees exceeded an average of $2,000 per month, and their city taxes amounted to over $1,000 per annum.

"For four out of the eight years of the company's existence, nothing was realized but actual expenses, and since that period the board have been enabled to declare dividends semi-annually of profits of three, three and a half, and, latterly, five per cent. on the capital stock; not at any time more than the last-mentioned rate."

"Since the completion of the new works, in 1851, the board have constantly acted on the design of supplying all the habitable parts of the city with gas, having laid in this period nearly twenty miles of street mains."

"The average annual consumption of gas is less here, in proportion to the length of street mains, than in any other city. This company have thirty miles of street mains, and an annual average consumption of 944,000 cubic feet of gas per mile. In Baltimore the average is 1,648,000 cubic feet per each mile of pipe; in Philadelphia it is 2,083,000; in New York, 1,765,000; in Boston, 2,700,000; in Albany, 2,000,000; in Brooklyn, 1,330,000; in St. Louis, 1,318,000; and in Charleston, 1,546,000. In most of these cities, also, the average number of consumers of gas on every hundred feet of street mains is five, while in Washington the number is not quite one."

"The gas is manufactured, condensed, and purified in the most approved manner, and the intention always has been to produce the very best quality. Superior bituminous coals suitable for this purpose, and at high prices, have been procured with this view, and the board are confident that, with rare exceptions, the gas here has been equal to that used in any city throughout the entire Union. Careful examination and measurement with the photometer have placed this matter beyond cavil. It is true that sometimes coals from the same mines

are found, on trial, to be of unequal strength, though perfectly uniform in appearance, and the purifying process may be deficient from a similar invisible cause, but these defects are immediately corrected as soon as discovered. Extraordinary severity of weather, prolonged for months, as during this season, may interrupt the flow of gas, and thus incommode so many consumers at the same time as to render prompt relief impossible. These are contingencies against which no foresight can effectually guard, and, during the past winter, they have operated as seriously against other gas companies, and thereby caused as much annoyance to the public, as they have done in Washington."

"With a capital of $424,000, actually and economically expended in the business, and unincumbered by debt, with works of acknowledged excellence, and capable of producing a supply of superior gas equal to any demand; with thirty miles of street mains, covering, as with a network, almost all the populous parts of the city, and so laid as to admit of any future extension; with one thousand six hundred and eighty-one consumers, and this number daily augmenting, our business systematized and now generally understood, the company have every motive for not only accommodating the public to their utmost requirement, but also for reducing the price of gas, from time to time, as the adoption of every valuable improvement and the increased consumption may justify."

At the present time, the company has two hundred and forty miles of street mains, nearly twenty-three thousand consumers, and an annual sale of gas of about eight hundred million cubic feet. It supplies gas to nearly five thousand public lamps, and pays forty thousand dollars for taxes and license per annum.

The officers of this company have been as follows: Presidents — John H. Callan, July 14, 1848, to April 14, 1849; Ulysses Ward, April 14, 1849, to January 2, 1851; Silas H. Hill, January 2, 1851, to June 1, 1856; George W. Riggs, June 1, 1856, to November 11, 1864; Barnabas H. Bartol, November 11, 1864, to November 15, 1883; George A. McIlhenny,[1] November 15, 1883, to the present time. Secretaries

[1] George Alexander McIlhenny was born in the north of Ireland in 1835. At the age of eight, he came to the United States. He was educated at the public schools of Philadelphia, and learned the engineer's and machinist's profession in the same city. After quitting the public schools, he paid particular attention to gas engineering, and at the age of twenty-two he took charge of the gas works at Macon, Georgia. He came to Washington and took charge of the Washington Gas Company's works on the 7th of March, 1865, and has had charge of them every since. He was one of the organizers and the first president of the Belt Line Railroad Company, and is the author

—Jacob Bigelow, July 14, 1848, to April 16, 1849; E. Lindsley, April 16, 1849, to January 8, 1851; Joseph F. Brown, January 8, 1851, to January 24, 1866; Charles B. Bailey, January 24, 1866, to the present time. Treasurers—Until the accession of Joseph F. Brown, the duties of treasurer were performed by the president; then Whitman C. Bestor, January 24, 1866, to November 13, 1873; Charles B. Bailey, *pro tempore*, November 13, 1873, to January 3, 1874; Charles C. Glover, January 3, 1874, to October 26, 1881; John C. Poor, October 26, 1881, to the present time. Assistant Secretaries—James D. Clay, February 26, 1884, to March 12, 1885; William B. Orme, March 12, 1885, to the present time. Engineers—The office of engineer was created March 20, 1865, and has been continuously filled by Mr. George A. McIlhenny, the present president and engineer.

The United States Electric Lighting Company had its origin in a novel manner. In the fall of 1881, the survivors of the Army of the Cumberland gathered together in Washington to dedicate their statue of General Thomas, in the Thomas Circle. The people of Washington contributed to the success of that occasion, and committees were appointed to carry out various plans for the entertainment of the visitors. One of the new ideas proposed was to illuminate Pennsylvania Avenue from the Peace Monument to the Treasury Department with the electric light, at that time beginning to be used in a few cities, but entirely unknown in Washington. Guys were stretched at intervals from housetop to housetop, and arc lamps suspended therefrom over the middle of the street. A dynamo was connected with the engine of a sawmill on Thirteenth Street, and at the appointed time thousands of citizens and visitors thronged the avenues to witness the novel display and to behold night transformed into day.

Strange to relate, however, the attempt to light the avenue in this way was a melancholy failure; but the interest awakened in the subject was not permitted to die out. Messrs. Stilson Hutchins, D. B. Ainger, William Dickson, Moses Kelly, and George A. Kelly organized a company, named the Heisler Electric Light Company. A

of the ticket system in the street railroad service. He is at present a director and vice-president of the West End National Bank; a director in the Washington and Georgetown Railroad Company; he is one of the executive committee having in charge the construction of the cable railroad; is a director in the Corcoran Insurance Company, and is president and engineer of the Washington Gas Light Company. He is president of the board of trustees of the West End Presbyterian Church. He is an inventor of several gas appliances, and a writer on subjects connected with the use of gas. He has had several patents issued to him, and his articles have been published in the proceedings of the American Gas Light Association.

small experimental 'plant was established in the Washington *Post* building, with a circuit of a few lights in the vicinity of Tenth Street and Pennsylvania Avenue. These ran most of the time during the winter, and in the meantime a small station was commenced in the rear of the *Post* building, under the supervision of George A. Kelly. Mr. Kelly resigned in the spring of 1882, and Mr. Seymour W. Tulloch was requested to act in his stead.

The company experienced considerable difficulty in maintaining its service, and in November transferred all its property to the United States Electric Lighting Company, a company organized under the laws of West Virginia, October 14, 1882, with a capital of $300,000, by Stilson Hutchins, William Dickson, Robert Boyd, James L. Barbour, and A. W. Fletcher. This company was organized November 9, 1882, by the election of the following officers: James L. Barbour, president; Robert Boyd, vice-president; Martin Maloney, treasurer; William Dickson, secretary, and N. W. Ellis, superintendent. An entire new set of dynamos and lamps was ordered from the United States Electric Light Company, of New York, and the first large contract made to supply light was with the Baltimore and Ohio Railroad Company, for eleven lights about their station. February 14, 1883, the present efficient general manager and superintendent, A. M. Renshaw, was elected, and the entire business placed in his charge. May 1, 1883, the first dynamo for incandescent lighting was ordered, with a capacity of one hundred lights. At the first annual meeting, held November 9, 1883, there were reported ninety-one arc lights and one hundred incandescent lights in operation.

On January 8, 1884, the company resolved to apply for a permit to lay an underground conduit along Pennsylvania Avenue and other streets where circuits extended. This conduit was laid at great expense, under the supervision of an expert from Europe. From this time on, in deference to the wishes of the citizens, and in harmony with the legislation of Congress, the company took front rank in underground construction, and through its experiments succeeded in perfecting its present system, which is considered the best all-round system in existence, and has to-day over thirty-five miles of conduits through the principal streets of the city.

The company lighted Pennsylvania Avenue without any return for two years or more, but during the fall of 1884, at the request and by the subscriptions of property holders and merchants along F Street, preparations were made to light the same by means of underground conduits, and this bit of enterprise was the beginning of a movement which resulted in F Street becoming the business street of the city, and in the greatly enhanced value of its real estate.

The discussion of the question of an enlarged plant was brought to a speedy determination on the night of July 16, 1885, the entire station being that night consumed by fire. While the fire was blazing, arrangements were made to lease the original Baltimore and Ohio Railroad Depot, then lately occupied by the Brush Electric Light Company, and on the 18th of the month a new equipment was ordered from the United States Electric Light Company, of New York. Within two weeks, the principal lights were again in operation from a Brush dynamo. On the 20th of August, the Thomson-Houston system was adopted as the standard arc light of the company. During September, the stockholders of the Brush Electric Light Company became identified with this company, and on December 1, 1885, there were two hundred and thirteen arc, and two hundred and sixty incandescent, lamps in operation.

At the annual meeting held November 9, 1886, the stockholders voted to purchase the lot, one hundred by one hundred and twenty feet, at the corner of Thirteen and a Half and B streets, on which a portion of the present station is located, and the officers were authorized to build and equip a permanent station. The Edison system of central station lighting was adopted by the company, and at the annual meeting held November 8, 1887, the president reported the station nearly completed. To meet the cost of the station and its partial equipment, and the construction of the incandescent circuits, the capital stock was increased, September 4, 1888, from $300,000 to $500,000, and an issue of convertible debenture certificates authorized, the first of their kind in the city. At the annual meeting in November, 334 arc and 4,236 incandescent lights were in operation. April 19, 1890, the property of Mr. George Bogus, adjoining the station, and containing 22,000 square feet, was purchased, and on April 14, 1891, the charter of the company was amended, authorizing an ultimate capitalization of $2,000,-000; and steps were taken to extend the station to an ultimate capacity of 1,000 arc and 40,000 incandescent lamps, of which at the present time 542 arc and 16,829 incandescent lamps are in operation.

The officers and directors of the company are as follows: A. A. Thomas,[1] president; William E. Clark, first vice-president; Robert

---

[1] Ammi Amery Thomas was born in Genesee County, New York, in 1847. He received a common-school and academic education in Wisconsin, in which State he enlisted as a soldier at the breaking out of the War of the Rebellion in 1861. He was taken prisoner by the Confederates, and detained in the prisons at Cahawba, Alabama,

A. A. Thomas

Boyd, second vice-president; Seymour W. Tullock, secretary and treasurer; A. M. Renshaw, general manager; George W. Pearson, C. C. Duncanson, Daniel B. Clarke, John Paul Jones, Emmons S. Smith, and Peter H. Hill.

Having thus presented brief references to some of the institutions devoted to manufactures, the following summary, as given in the late Census Bulletin No. 158, it is believed will fittingly close this chapter, showing as it does, as nearly as may be, the condition of these industries in the District of Columbia at the present time. It is also believed that the purposes of this work will be subserved as well by combining in one summary the statistics for 1880 and 1890, as they would be by presenting the two summaries separately, and, besides this, the comparison between the two can be most readily made if they are together. The general statistical table is as follows:

General Subjects.	1880.	1890.
Number of establishments reported............................	970	2,300
Capital invested.................	$5,527,526	$28,876,258
Number of hands employed.............................:.......	7,146	23,477
Amount of wages paid..	$3,924,612	$14,638,790
Cost of material used...	5,365,400	17,187,752
Miscellaneous expenses...	....	1,603,548
Value of manufactured goods...............................	11,882,316	39,296,259

It is necessary to explain, however, that while the census report of 1890 is as full and complete as it was possible to make it, that for 1880 omitted several classes of industries included in that for 1890, and hence the increase as shown by the above table is apparently

and Columbia, South Carolina, for upward of six months, during which period he experienced more than the usual amount of privation, suffering, and humiliation, together with no small amount of romance. After an honorable discharge from the army, he entered upon the study of law at Milwaukee, was admitted to practice, and in 1870 was appointed United States Deputy Marshal for the State for the purpose of taking the census. He afterward removed to Kansas, where he received the appointment of register of the United States Land Office at Kirwia, holding that position there and at Cawka City more than four years. At the expiration of this service, he removed to the city of Washington to engage in the practice of law, naturally drifting into the prosecution of claims before the several departments. In 1881, he commenced publishing a periodical named *The Reporter*, with the determination of securing reforms in

greater than it really was. The industries included in the table for 1890 that were not in the report for 1880 were, china and pottery; decorating; women's clothing; druggists' preparations, except prescriptions; the manufacture of heating and illuminating gas; and slaughtering and meat packing, except retail butchering.

It is also nécessary further to explain that in these details is included the manufacturing carried on by the Government of the United States for its own purposes, as the lock and mail-bag repair shops of the Post Office Department; the public printing office and binding, the Bureau of Engraving and Printing, the Navy Yard ordnance and ordnance stores, and the carpenter shops operated by the War, Navy, and Treasury departments. The statistics of the above Government operations are as follows: Capital employed, $7,-477,290; miscellaneous expenses, $27,815; amount of wages paid, $3,-821,176; cost of materials, $1,782,645; value of product, $5,960,931; number of hands employed, 4,592.

Deducting these various sums from the corresponding amounts in the preceding table, the remainders are the amounts to be credited to the private manufacturing enterprises of the District of Columbia, and the general result is that $22,093,131 in value, in one shape or another, has been added to the wealth of the District during the ten years preceding June 30, 1890.

The total number of the different kinds of industries in the District of Columbia, as reported by the census bulletin, is 120, and the total number of separate establishments, 2,300. Forty of these industries employ less than 10 men each, and there are four of them employing more than 1,000 hands each. These last are, carpentering, 2,428 hands; brick and tile, 1,204; printing and publishing, 3,597; and paper hanging and painting, 1,134. Each of five of these industries employs a capital of more than $1,000,000; namely, carpentering, $1,-212,239; engraving on steel, including plate printing, and also including

some of the methods in the departments, which had become generally obnoxious, and in this determination he was thoroughly successful. Prompted by a desire to become more actively engaged in business pursuits, he became a director in the Second National Bank, in the United States Electric Lighting Company, in the American Security and Trust Company, in the Metropolitan Railroad Company, and in various other business enterprises. He is now president of the United States Electric Lighting Company, vice-president of the American Security and Trust Company, and in all of these companies he takes a leading part in their advancement. His career throughout has been one of great activity and abundant success. Captain Thomas is yet a young man, and is conspicuous among that class of young men who have contributed so much toward making the Capital City one of the finest cities on the globe.

the United States Bureau of Engraving and Printing, $1,546,425; malt liquor, $1,174,191; painting and paper hanging, $1,108,050; and printing and publishing, including the United States Printing Office, but not including the value of the lands of the latter, $1,731,504. The classes of business each of which has over 100 establishments, are the following: Boots and shoes, 232; carpentering, 171; men's clothing, 116; women's clothing, 143; painting and paper hanging, 156.

The classes of business each of which annually use more than $1,000,000 are the following: Carpentering, $2,928,490; flouring and grist-mill products, $1,358,238; printing and publishing, $1,254,130.

The twenty-five principal industries are the following: Bottling, employing 208 hands and paying in the aggregate $118,957 in wages. Brick and tile — hands, 1,204; wages, $442,929. Carpentering — hands, 2,428; wages, $1,754,367. Carriages and wagons — hands, 290; wages, $160,170. Confectionery — hands, 349; wages, $165,907. Engraving on steel — hands, 997; wages, $849,332. Flour and grist mills — hands, 149; wages, $85,718. Foundry and machine shops — hands, 311; wages, $172,297. Furniture — hands, 161; wages, $94,048. Iron work — hands, 309; wages, $186,412. Malt liquors — hands, 120; wages, $82,422. Lithographing and engraving — hands, 127; wages, $79,568. Planed lumber, sash, doors, and blinds — hands, 440; wages, $258,438. Marble and stone work — hands, 391; wages, $305,631. Masonry — hands, 661; wages, $537,180. Painting and paper hanging — hands, 1,134; wages, $748,728. Paving and paving materials — hands, 878; wages, $404,523. Plastering and stucco works — hands, 237; wages, $148,093. Plumbing and gas fitting — hands, 646; wages, $432,567. Printing and publishing — hands, 3,099; wages, $2,494,406. Printing and publishing newspapers — hands, 498; wages, $389,731. Saddlery and harness — hands, 106; wages, $58,636. Tinware, etc. — hands, 424; wages, $259,120. Tobacco, cigars, and cigarettes — hands, 159; wages, $83,279. Watch, clock, and jewelry — hands, 126; wages, $83,224. From these figures the average annual wages paid in the different industries may be easily deduced.

CHAPTER XIII.

HISTORY OF THE PRESS.

THE Washington *Gazette* was first published June 15, 1796, by Benjamin More, a bookseller. It was a semi-weekly paper, issued on Wednesdays and Saturdays, at $4 per annum, from the office then lately owned "by Thomas Wilson, deceased, but subsequently, for a few weeks, in possession of Mr. John Crocker." The *Gazette* was a good paper for the times in which it was printed; well made up, neatly printed, and ornamented with an engraving of a shield, centered with an eye darting rays in all directions, and with the encircling motto, *Nunquam dormio.* Mr. More continued to publish his paper for more than a year, and then, in his number of July 26, 1797, he published the following notice: "The Washington *Gazette* will not be published again until the publication is attended by some profit to the publisher"; and he also stated that "nothing but want of money stops the paper." How its publication was ever to be attended with profit unless it were published, is somewhat difficult for an Anglo-Saxon intellect to perceive. However, Mr. More found encouragement of some kind soon afterward, for on September 16, 1797, the Washington *Gazette* again appeared, but this time as a weekly paper, containing the following announcement: "The Washington *Gazette* again makes its appearance, and its editor hopes to receive that encouragement from the public which will enable him to continue the publication uninterrupted, until he shall be able, from experience, to sing of mercy as well as of judgment." Precisely what was meant by this last allusion must be left to conjecture. After a further struggle of about thirty-five weeks, Mr. More, in his number of March 24, 1798, announced as follows: "I shall not be able to continue the publication of the Washington *Gazette* unless some friend should lend a helping hand. Hope has led me into a thicket of difficulties, and appears to be departing from me." At that time, there was not a large constituency for any paper, and besides this it has been suggested that Mr. More was somewhat caustic in his criticisms of the commissioners then engaged in laying out the Federal District, and was at the same time a Federalist. So far as is known, the Washington *Gazette*, under Mr. More's management, did not appear again.

The *National Intelligencer* was established in Washington in October, 1800, about the time of the removal of the Federal Government from Philadelphia to Washington. The first number of this paper appeared October 31, and it was published in a row of brick buildings on New Jersey Avenue erected by Thomas Law. The editor and proprietor was Samuel Harrison Smith, a biographical sketch of whom appears in another chapter. His residence, while he lived in Washington, was one of the conspicuous objects in the vicinity, being situated on a commanding site about three hundred feet above tide water. The paper was published three times each week, and was thus what is generally called a tri-weekly publication. Mr. Smith in his prospectus said: "The appearance of the *National Intelligencer* has been protracted to this day [October 31, 1800] by the inevitable though unanticipated embarrassments attending the removal of the printing office. The vessel which contained the greater part of the material sailed from Philadelphia on the 20th of September, but did not arrive in this city until the 25th inst., owing to her having been driven on shore by the violence of the late storm. . . . The editor, at the commencement of his duties, considers it as not improper to state the nature of the plan which he intends to pursue, and concisely to notice the principles by which he proposes to regulate his own conduct as well as those by which it is expected that correspondents will regulate theirs," etc. After showing the necessity of the freedom of the press, he said: "But while the editor classes with our dearest rights the liberty of the press, he is decidedly inimical to its licentiousness. As, on the one hand, the conduct of public men and the tendency of public measures will be freely examined, so, on the other hand, private character will remain inviolable, nor shall indelicate expressions be admitted, however disguised by satire or enlivened by wit."

Whatever may be said of this paper, as to its "interminable diatribes," or as to its general character as a "National Smoothing Plane," or as to its first editor as "Silky, Milky Smith," the high tone indicated in the above extract from its first prospectus was steadily maintained by all its managers from 1800 down to 1870, when it ceased to exist.

The terms of publication were at first announced as follows: First, the paper shall be published three times a week, on good demy paper, and with new type; second, the annual subscription shall be $5, paid constantly in advance, by all subscribers not residing in the city of Washington, and $6 by those residing in the city, in which case the payment shall be half-yearly; third, all letters shall be postpaid.

Politically, the *Intelligencer* supported Mr. Jefferson for the Presidency, to succeed President John Adams. On Monday, November 3, 1800, it said that on the Saturday before, November 1, President Adams arrived in Washington, and took up his residence in the house appropriated to him by the commissioners, the house, however, not being then finished.

Mr. Smith is entitled to great credit for the struggle he made for the right to publish the debates in Congress as they occurred. In his paper of January 19, 1801, he details his interview with the Speaker of the House of Representatives in reference thereto, explaining that he could only secure the Speaker's consent to his having such papers as the clerk of the House should permit him to copy, and that he might publish an account of anything upon which the House had come to a decision. The position of the Speaker, in full, was as follows: "I have no objection to your obtaining copies of those papers that are proper to be published; but you must know it would be manifestly wrong to publish papers that relate to papers in an unfinished state. For instance, a member may make a motion that refers to a particular subject; it may be made inadvertently — its meaning may be equivocal. To publish it in this immature state, before the House has decided upon it, might be to produce misconceptions, and might essentially injure the respect of the people for the Government. Such papers ought not to be published. But in cases in which the House has come to a conclusion, you may publish what has been decided upon."

Theodore Sedgwick, of Massachusetts, was then Speaker of the House of Representatives, and John Holt Oswald, of Pennsylvania, clerk. The progress made by the press in securing the right to publish the proceedings of Congress may be readily measured by comparing the present condition of things with that indicated by the above-outlined position of Speaker Sedgwick; and as to whether the respect of the people for the Government has been diminished, that also may be estimated by a similar comparison.

Mr. Smith continued to edit and publish the *Intelligencer* alone until 1809, when Joseph Gales, Jr., of Raleigh, North Carolina, entered his employ as stenographic reporter of proceedings in Congress. This fact of itself is a suggestive indication of the progress already made in the direction referred to. Young Mr. Gales's services proved so acceptable to Mr. Smith that he was soon taken into partnership, and in September, 1810, he bought out the entire establishment. The paper continued to be anti-Federal, supporting Madison and Monroe. To the war with Great Britain, which was declared in the fourth year of Mr. Madison's first term, it gave a hearty support. In October, 1812, Mr. Gales was joined by his brother-in-law, William Winston Seaton, a native of King William County, Virginia, a printer by trade, who had served his apprenticeship in the office of the *Virginia Patriot*, at Richmond.

The *Daily National Intelligencer* was established January 1, 1813, because of the necessity of the more prompt publication of the news of the war. The price was $10 per annum, payable in advance. When the British entered Washington in 1814, they partially tore out the *Intelligencer* office, and as a consequence it did not appear from August 24 to October 1, though it did not suffer so much as might have been expected. The paper continued to support the administration in power until President Jackson's time, when it became a strong Whig paper, teaching that Whig principles were the principles of the Presidents in power from Jefferson to Jackson. It was strongly in favor of what would in this day be called "civil service reform," and hence could not tolerate President Jackson's appointment to office of personal friends as a political reward, a policy at once discovered to be laden with manifold evils, and from which it has not yet been found possible to extricate that service. From day to day, during 1829, the first year of President Jackson's incumbency, it published reports of the progress made in the "reform" going on in the various departments. The editors were very friendly to the Chesapeake and Ohio Canal, and extremely doubtful as to whether railroads could ever be made a success in this country.

The weekly edition of the *Intelligencer* was established June 5,

1841, at $2 per annum, payable invariably in advance. The *Intelligencer*, after the death of President Harrison, was extremely reluctant to part company with President Tyler, but was at length compelled to do so, because of President Tyler's abandonment of the principles upon which he had been elected. With all its ability and conscientiousness it fought the annexation of Texas, and as an evidence of its influence it published the following letter:

"DEPARTMENT OF STATE, WASHINGTON, May 8, 1844.

"To the Publishers of the National Intelligencer:

"GENTLEMEN: I am directed and required to discontinue the copies of your semi-weekly and daily papers sent to this department for the legations abroad.

"I am, Gentlemen,

"Your obedient servant,

"EDWARD STUBBS, Agent."

Upon the receipt of this letter, the editor remarked: "Were it not for the narrow spirit which it evinces on the part of the Secretary of State,[1] in regard to the freedom of the press, we should feel proud of this letter as a testimonial to the proprietors of this paper of their having discharged their duty to their countrymen, even at the hazard of the displeasure of these official personages."

The paper continued to be published by Gales & Seaton until the death of Mr. Gales, which occurred at Eckington, his country seat, July 21, 1860, in the seventy-fifth year of his age. August 30, Mr. Seaton announced that Mr. James C. Welling would be associated with him in the editorial conduct of the paper in the future. Mr. Welling had then been connected with the paper about ten years. On Saturday, December 31, 1864, Mr. Seaton retired from the proprietorship of the paper, and its editorial management. James C. Welling also retired on the same day, and the new proprietors, Snow, Coyle, & Company, took possession. April 1, 1865, the paper was enlarged to a seven-column sheet. Afterward, the *Express* was consolidated with it, and the name changed to the *Intelligencer and Express*. Snow, Coyle, & Company continued the publication of the paper until November 30, 1869, when they sold out to Alexander Delmar, then late Chief of the Bureau of Statistics of the Treasury Department, who announced his intention of placing it in the front rank of journalism. But on January 10, 1870, he was compelled to discontinue its publication.

[1] Hon. John C. Calhoun.

It has been said of the *Intelligencer* that it was "Jeffersonian till Jackson's time, and then Whig till Lincoln's time, when it became rebel Democratic, and went into the lobby under Johnny Coyle."[1] This is partly true and partly false. It never became "rebel Democratic." Its motto always was "The Union and the Constitution." It was always true to the Union, and, in its own way, it was always true to the Constitution. In 1860, its devotion to slavery, that institution being protected by the Constitution in the States at least, led it to support Hon. John Bell for the Presidency as against Abraham Lincoln, Mr. Lincoln being the anti-slavery candidate. In 1864, it supported General McClellan for the Presidency, because it could not even then see that slavery had forfeited its right to exist by attempting to overthrow the Constitution by which it had been protected. President Lincoln and his emancipation policy were both too intricate and mysterious for the understanding of the *Intelligencer*, and hence it had to sustain what it could understand — the restoration of "The Union as it Was," that is, with slavery still unimpaired. Through the stormy reconstruction period, the *Intelligencer* was a strong supporter of Andrew Johnson and his plan of reconstruction, and it continued on this line of political thought until it gave up the ghost in 1870.

It may not be generally known that Joseph Gales, when driven from England for the freedom which he exercised in the publication of his paper at Sheffield, learned stenography on his way across the Atlantic. This art he found extremely useful in the service of Claypoole in Philadelphia. His son, Joseph Gales, Jr., as one of the editors of the *National Intelligencer*, found the same art also extremely useful, as did likewise his partner, W. W. Seaton; one reporting the Senate, the other the House. Had it not been for the presence of Gales in the Senate, the great speeches of Hayne and Webster in 1830 would have been entirely lost to the world, and very few of the debates of earlier Congresses would have been preserved but for the efforts of Gales and Seaton, editors of the *National Intelligencer*. The action of Congress authorizing them to write up and publish their reports of the early proceedings was one of great wisdom, as through this action we have preserved to us the debates of Congress in the early days. Posterity is indebted to them for these, as it is to James Madison for the debates of the Constitutional Convention which framed the Constitution of the United States.

The Washington *Daily Gazette* was started in Washington October

---

[1] "Washington Outside and Inside," by G. A. Townsend.

1, 1800, at $5 per annum, payable half yearly in advance. The projector, in his advertisement, said: "It shall be conducted on a fair, impartial plan, open to political discussions; but no personal pieces or irritating animadversions on parties or individuals shall be admitted." This was signed by Charles Cist. How long this paper was published is not known.

The Washington *Federalist* was published for several years in the early part of the century, as a contemporary of the *National Intelligencer*, but advocating opposite views. It is believed to have existed about four years, but no authentic data with reference to this point could be obtained.

The *Weekly Register of Political News* was first published in November, 1807, by J. B. Colvin. How long it was published is not known.

The Washington City *Gazette* was established in 1812 or 1813, by William Elliott. It was edited by George Watterston. William Elliott was a native of England, and died December 30, 1838, at the age of sixty-four years. He was a man of considerable scientific attainments, and was one of the earliest and most zealous members of the Columbian Institute.

The Washington City *Weekly Gazette* was started in 1815, by Jonathan Elliott, who was also an Englishman. He continued the publication of this paper as a weekly until 1817, when he changed it to a daily.

The Washington *Republican* was first issued in 1822, by James C. Dunn & Company, as a semi-weekly paper. It was published in the interest of John C. Calhoun. It afterward passed into the hands of Haughton & Company, and was the ostensible forerunner of Force's semi-weekly *National Journal*, begun in November, 1823, and of the *Daily National Journal*, begun in 1824.

The *Weekly Messenger* was started in 1807, by John B. Colvin, who, in 1808, changed the name to the Washington *Monitor*. This paper was soon succeeded by the Washington *Expositor*, conducted by Dinmore & Cooper.

The *Weekly Messenger* was first published in 1817, by Mrs. John B. Colvin, the talented widow of John B. Colvin.

The *National Register* was first issued in 1816, by J. K. Meade, and edited by George Watterston.

The Washington City *Chronicle* was started in 1828, by A. Rothwell and T. W. Ustick, and edited by George Watterston. It was a literary paper, published weekly. It was transferred in November, 1830, to James C. Dunn, and in 1832 it was the property of B. Homans.

The Washington *Mirror* was commenced October 18, 1834, by William Thompson, an Englishman. The name was afterward changed to the *Metropolitan*, and edited by Rufus Dawes. Mr. Dawes made his paper popular and successful for some time, but this popularity was not of great duration. In 1836, the paper was merged into the *United States Telegraph*. Mr. Thompson assumed the position of city editor on the *National Intelligencer*, and on July 17, 1846, he started the *Saturday Evening News*, which he continued until 1858, when, on account of an affection of the eyes, he abandoned its publication.

The *African Repository* was first published in 1835, by Ralph R. Gurley, secretary of the American Colonization Society, who continued its publication for several years.

The *United States Telegraph* was established in 1826, by Duff Green. Upon the inauguration of Andrew Jackson as President of the United States, the *Telegraph* became the organ of the Administration; though, if the Hon. Thomas H. Benton is good authority, it was more the organ of John C. Calhoun than of President Jackson. Some time afterward, a very strong article against nullification appeared in the Frankfort *Argus*, published in Kentucky, to which was called the attention of the President, who, upon being informed that it was written by Franklin P. Blair, invited him to Washington, and the *Globe* was the result. At any rate, it can be stated that the *Globe* was established because of differences betweeen President Jackson and Mr. Van Buren.

The *Globe*, upon its establishment in December, 1830, became at once a power in the Government. While it was not in the Cabinet, it had a cabinet of its own, widely known as the "Kitchen Cabinet." Soon after its establishment, John C. Rives became a partner with Mr. Blair, and Amos Kendall became a regular contributor to the paper. Amos Kendall wrote the broadside editorials of the *Globe*, at the dictation of the President, but, of course, greatly improving the President's English; for, while he could not write elegantly, yet he was a vigorous thinker. The *Globe* had the public printing and advertising for eleven years, or until General Harrison was inaugurated, ceasing to be the Government organ on March 3, 1841; but it did not cease then to be the chief organ of the Democratic Party. The *National Intelligencer* then resumed its old position. The death of President Harrison, however, brought confusion to the Whigs, and the vetoes of President Tyler against the Bank bills disrupted the relations of the *Intelligencer* with the Government, the *Intelligencer* adhering to the fortunes of Henry Clay and the Whig Party.

20

A new paper, called the *Madisonian*, which had been started August 1, 1837, then became the organ of the President. At its establishment, it announced that it would be devoted to the elucidation of the principles of the Democracy, as delineated by Mr. Madison. In its prospectus, it said that the commercial interests of the country were overwhelmed with embarrassment, and every ramification of society was invaded by distress. The social edifice seemed threatened with disorganization, and the General Government was boldly assailed by a large and respectable portion of the people as the direct cause of their difficulties. Open resistance to the laws was publicly encouraged, and a spirit of insubordination was fostered as a necessary defense to the pretending usurpations of the party in power. Some, of whom better things were hoped, were making confusion worse confounded by a headlong pursuit of extreme notions and indefinite phantoms totally incompatible with the wholesome state of the country. The paper was at first edited by Thomas Allen, and then by John Jones. However, on account of the uncertainty regarding the *Intelligencer*, with Daniel Webster in the Cabinet, a new paper was begun in December, 1841, edited by Edward N. Johnson, Joseph Segar, and John H. Pleasants. About the 1st of April, 1845, this paper passed into the hands of Theophilus Fisk and Jesse E. Dow, who changed it to a daily, semi-weekly, and weekly Democratic paper, under the name of the *Constellation*.

When Amos Kendall severed his editorial connection with the *Globe*, he began to publish, in 1841, a paper which he called *Kendall's Expositor*, as a semi-weekly periodical, and continued its publication until April, 1844.

The *True Whig*, a weekly paper, was first issued in 1841, by Calvin Colton. In 1842, he converted it into a daily, and soon afterward ceased its publication.

After the establishment of the *Globe*, the *United States Telegraph* was continued under the management of Duff Green, still as the organ of John C. Calhoun. In 1835, it was merged with the Washington *Mirror*.

The *Globe*, after giving up its official position, became the publisher of the Congressional debates, Blair and Rives being awarded the contract for their publication in 1846. In 1849, Blair sold out his interest to Rives, who continued to publish them until his death, after which the *Globe* was published by his sons.

The *Washingtonian* was started in 1836, by A. F. Cunningham, as a temperance paper. It was a quarto in form, and its publication was continued for a year.

The *Metropolitan Churchman* was first issued in November, 1838, under the editorship of Rev. Philip Slaughter, of Virginia. It was an Episcopal periodical, and in after years it became the *Southern Churchman*. For a long series of years it was a power in the Church.

In 1843, John T. Towers established the *Whig Standard* in the interest of Henry Clay, and continued its publication until the election of James K. Polk.

In the same year, the *Daily Capitol* was started by an association of printers. It was a penny paper, and had considerable popularity. Its ostensible publishers were Coale, Dickinson, & Devaughn. In 1844, it was transferred to Smith, Murphy, & Company, the name being then changed to the *Democratic Capitol*, and it was made a Democratic campaign paper. Its publication ceased with Mr. Polk's election to the Presidency.

The *Daily Bee* was first published August 19, 1845, by Gobright, Melvin, & Smith. Its publication continued for twenty-four days, when it suspended.

The *Columbian Fountain* first appeared January 4, 1846, under the superintendence of Rev. Ulysses Ward. It was at first a temperance paper, but in 1847 it became a pronounced Whig paper. Its chief editor was supposed to be Worthington S. Snethen.

The *Weekly Democratic Expositor* was started about the same time as the *Fountain*, by Rev. Theophilus Fisk and Jesse E. Dow. The former had a most varied experience, and the latter was editor of the *Expositor* from January, 1846, until it ceased to exist. Mr. Dow had for a long time contributed articles to the *Globe* under the pseudonym of "Old Ironsides."

The *Native American* was established in 1837, by the Native American Association, which was organized a few months previously. Its objects were to secure the repeal of the naturalization laws, and the establishment of a national character and the perpetuity of the institutions of the country through the means of the natives of the United States. The subscription price of the paper was $2.50 per year. T. D. Jones was secretary of the association in 1839.

The *Columbian Star* was a weekly paper published in Washington by a committee of the General Convention of the Baptist denomination of the United States. Its publication was commenced, probably, in 1823. It was a useful and instructive publication, being faulty only in one particular, namely, that of its bigotry. "The editors of the *Star* seem to think it rank heresy to confide in the representations of a Catholic." This paper was published in Washington until about

June 1, 1827, when it was removed to Philadelphia, where it was committed to the care of Rev. William T. Brantly, pastor of the First Baptist Church of that city. While it was in Washington it was edited by Rev. Baron Stow.

We, the People, was the name of a weekly paper started in Washington March 8, 1828, to oppose the pretensions of Andrew Jackson to the Presidency. It was friendly to the administration of John Quincy Adams. It was published every Saturday, at $3 per annum, Jonathan Elliott being both editor and publisher.

The *Christian Statesman* was a weekly paper, commenced in Washington in January, 1838, by R. R. Gurley. This paper advocated the cause of African colonization of the negro as meriting the earnest and liberal support of the Nation. The price was $3 per annum payable in advance.

The *Columbian Gazette* was started in Georgetown July, 1, 1829, by Benjamin Homans, who had lost his office on the accession of Andrew Jackson to the Presidency. The *Gazette* was a handsome tri-weekly paper. In 1835, the *Metropolitan* appeared in Georgetown, at the instance, as it was understood, of Joel R. Poinsett, an anti-Calhoun South Carolinian, and was edited by Samuel D. Langtree, having as an associate John L. O'Sullivan. After about two years, the paper was removed to Washington, and the *Potomac Advocate* became the town paper of Georgetown. This paper was owned by Thomas Turner, but Mr. Turner soon tired, and sold it to Fulton & Smith, who, after a time, dropped the word "Potomac" from the name, and called their paper simply the *Advocate,* and still later, the *Georgetown Advocate.* Mr. Smith at length retired from the paper, and John T. Crow became either part or sole owner, and conducted it until about 1844, when he went to Baltimore and became employed on the Baltimore *Sun.* Afterward, the *Advocate* was conducted by Joseph Crow, a brother of John T. Crow, until its sale soon afterward to Ezekiel Hughes, of Fredericktown, Maryland. Mr. Hughes continued the paper for about fifteen years, when he abandoned it because he could not make it pay.

Several other papers were published in Georgetown before the War, but as they were all short-lived, it is not deemed worth while to trace their brief careers.

The Washington *Union* was started immediately after the election of James K. Polk to the Presidency. The Nashville *Union* had been the home paper of the Polk wing of the Democratic Party, just as the *Globe,* in Washington, was published in the interest of the Van Buren wing. The Richmond *Enquirer* had been instrumental in defeating Van Buren in the convention. From the Nashville *Union* and the Richmond *Enquirer* there were brought to Washington two men, Thomas Ritchie and John P. Heiss, who purchased the *Globe* of Blair & Rives, and established the Washington *Union*, the first number of which appeared May 1, 1845. The *Union* continued to be the organ of the Government until 1849, when the Whig Party came again into power. At this time, the *Republic* was established as the organ of the Government. The *Union* continued to be edited and published by Thomas Ritchie until 1859, when he sold it to A. J. Donelson, who had been private secretary to President Jackson, *Chargé d'Affaires* to Texas, Minister to Prussia, and also to the Germanic Confederation. The sale was made by Mr. Ritchie because of the immense amount of printing thrown upon him by Congress, and because of an unfortunate contract made by him, which involved him heavily in debt. Mr. Donelson said in his salutatory that he "threw himself upon the indulgence of the Republican-Democratic Party for the support which may be due to one who can promise so little to justify in advance the confidence which has been given to me in advance."

During the same year, George W. Bowman purchased the *Union*, and changed the name to the *Constitution*, announcing his purpose to be to make the *Constitution* a thoroughly Democratic paper, advocating the principles which the Democratic Party all over the country claimed as common property. William M. Browne became the owner of this paper early in 1860, and continued it until January 31, 1861, when he said he was making arrangements for its reissue elsewhere under more favorable auspices.

The *Republic* was started, as has been stated, immediately after the inauguration of President Taylor, who did not recognize the *National Intelligencer* because it was devoted to Daniel Webster, and Daniel Webster had said that the nomination of Taylor was one "not fit to be made." Alexander Bullitt, of the New Orleans *Picayune*, and John O. Sargent, of the New York *Courier and Enquirer*, were the first editors of the *Republic*, but for certain reasons they could not succeed in Washington. Upon the death of President Taylor, and the succession of Vice-President Fillmore, with Daniel Webster in the Cabinet, the *National Intelligencer* once more resumed its old place as Government organ. But it was the last of its line — that is, of the Whig organs to the Government. With President Pierce in the Executive Mansion, the *Union* was again the Government organ, and continued to sustain this relation to the Government through both the administrations of Presidents Pierce and Buchanan. It then became somewhat confused in its political relations, as did the Democratic Party itself, and, as has been already stated, ceased to exist about the close of the control of the Government by the Democratic Party.

The *Spectator* was published in Washington under the influence of Senator Rhett, of South Carolina. It had succeeded the *Telegraph* as the organ of the South Carolina section of the Democratic Party. It was published by Martin & Heart, with Virgil Maxcey as one of its editors. After Martin went to Paris, William A. Harris became the partner of Heart, and they changed the name of the paper to the *Constitution*. Subsequently, Harris went to Buenos Ayres as *chargé d'affaires*, and Heart joined the Charleston, South Carolina, *Mercury*, when the *Constitution* closed its career. Harris, on his return from Buenos Ayres, became connected with the *Union*.

The *National Era* was established in 1847, the first number appearing January 7 of that year. A fund of $20,000 was raised by the friends of freedom, with which it was established. Lewis Tappan was at the head of these gentlemen. Dr. Gamaliel Bailey, of Cincinnati, Ohio, was selected as the editor, and Lewis Clephane was their clerk. The publishers of the paper were Martin Buel and William Blanchard. Dr. Bailey was at the time well known throughout the country, having, though a young man, had an eventful career. In 1834, he cordially espoused the cause of freedom and did not look back. In 1836, he became connected with James G. Birney (who afterward, by accepting the nomination of the Abolition Party for the Presidency, defeated Henry Clay for that high office) in the editorship of the *Philanthropist*, of Cincinnati, which paper was devoted to the cause of the slave. About August 1, 1836, the office of the *Philanthropist* was attacked by a mob, the type scattered about the streets, and the press thrown into the Ohio River, causing a suspension of the paper for a few weeks; but late in September it again appeared, printed in a neighboring village, but published in Cincinnati. Dr. Bailey soon became sole proprietor and editor, and conducted the paper without incident worthy of special note for five years, or until September, 1841, when on account of the commission of some improprieties by negroes, not in any way connected with the paper, a mob assailed the office with a violence which defied the municipal authorities for four days, during which time the type was scattered all over the streets and the press broken in pieces and thrown into the river. This second destruction of the office, however, caused a delay in the publication of the *Phil-*

anthropist for only a few days, when it resumed publication and went on as before.

Dr. Bailey, in the fall of 1846, as intimated above, was invited to Washington to take editorial control of the new anti-slavery paper to be established here in the then near future, where ¦no pretense of State rights could be urged as a motive or offered as an apology for the suppression of, or interference with, the freedom of the press. From the first, the elevated tone of its able editorials and correspondence commanded the respect of all intelligent men. The regular corresponding editor was John G. Whittier. Dr. James Houston, an accomplished Irishman, wrote a series of graphic sketches of men and things about Washington, and H. B. Stanton, author of "Modern Reformers," was also an able contributor. Theodore Parker, Alice and Phœbe Cary, Dr. Pierpont, and William D. Gallagher were occasional contributors. Later in the history of the paper, such characters as Edward Everett Hale, S. P. Chase, Charles Sumner, Wendell Phillips, Harriet Beecher Stowe, Gail Hamilton, and Mrs. Dr. Bailey contributed to its columns. Mrs. Stowe's "Uncle Tom's Cabin" first appeared, in 1851, as a serial story in the columns of the *National Era.*

The most interesting event connected with the history of the *National Era,* in Washington, was the attack upon its office by a mob, on Tuesday night, April, 1848, the attack being occasioned by the supposed interest taken by the paper in the attempted escape of seventy-seven slaves from their masters in this city. Of these seventy-seven slaves, thirty-eight were men and boys, twenty-six were women and girls, and thirteen were children. The attempted escape was made in a sloop, named the *Pearl,* which sailed down the Potomac with a fair wind on Sunday, April 16, and came to anchor in Cornfield Harbor, on the Maryland side of the river, near Point Lookout. A party of volunteers in the steamer *Salem* started in pursuit, overtook the *Pearl,* and brought her and her cargo of fugitives back to Washington, where H. C. Williams, a magistrate of the city, summoned the parties engaged in the kidnapping of the slaves before him, and committed the slaves as runaways, and Edward Sayres, the captain of the *Pearl,* and Caleb Aaronson, for further examination. These two individuals were afterward tried and appropriately punished according to the laws of those days.

On the 20th of the month, the *Era* gave an account of the attack, highly commending Captain Goddard and others who had vigorously sustained him in the preservation of order, for saving the press and the honor of the city. The press of the entire country condemned the mob—even that of the Southern States, which, while it condemned the principles advocated by the *Era*, yet spoke in the highest terms of Dr. Bailey. The office of the *Era* was at this time on Seventh Street, between F and G streets. It was afterward removed to the corner of Indiana Avenue and Second Street, into what is now the Trémont House, and here, upon the election of Mr. Lincoln to the Presidency, it was subjected to another attack by a mob, in common with the Republican headquarters, which were in the same building. Only slight damage was, however, done on this occasion.

While it is perhaps within limits of safety to say that, at the time of the beginning of the war with Great Britain in 1812, Federalism was confined mainly to the New England States, yet there were many Federalists in other parts of the country. This was particularly the case in Maryland. A number of these Maryland Federalists in Frederick, Montgomery, and Prince George's counties, desiring to extend their views among their fellow-citizens as much as possible, united their means and established a newspaper in Baltimore for this purpose. This paper thus established was named the *Federal Republican*, and it had for its editor Alexander Contee Hamilton, who was assisted by a Mr. Wagner. On Saturday, June 20, 1812, two days after the declaration of war with Great Britain, the *Federal Republican* contained an article unusually bitter in its denunciation of the Administration. It had, therefore, in the minds of the friends and supporters of the Administration, fully identified itself with the enemy of the country. The population of Baltimore became very much excited over this publication, and a mob of them turned out on the following Monday night, pulled down the office, scattered the type, and broke the presses to pieces. The Federalists throughout the country were very much excited, and did not hesitate to intimate that the Government at Washington was implicated in the riot. The friends of the *Federal Republican* resolved that if possible the liberty of the press should be vindicated in the republication of their paper, and on the following Monday, July 27, 1812, it reappeared from a rented building on Charles Street, though it had been set up and worked off in Georgetown, District of Columbia. This issue of the paper was extremely severe in its condemnation of the people, mayor, and courts of the city of Baltimore. Anticipating the result of the course they were pursuing, they had taken the precaution to station throughout the building a considerable number of their adherents, and when, in consequence of their animadversions upon the people of Baltimore, an attacking party appeared in front of the building, throwing stones at and breaking some of the windows thereof, those inside, for the purpose of repelling any attack that might be made, fired a volley at them, killing a Dr. Gale, an electrician of Baltimore; and wounding several others. The next morning, about seven o'clock, the garrison of the rented building, about twenty-three in number, were marched to the city jail by the military under General Stricker. Everything was quiet throughout the day, and at nightfall it was unfortunately deemed by the authorities safe to permit the military to repair to their homes. Taking advantage of the unguarded condition of the jail, a terrible mob assembled in front of the jail, broke it open, and with clubs and other weapons made a furious assault upon the unarmed and unprotected inmates, killing General Lingan outright, and so fearfully maltreating General Harry Lee, of Virginia, "Light Horse Harry," the father of the rebel chieftain, General Robert E. Lee, that his eyesight was ever afterward permanently impaired. Eleven of the others were fearfully beaten, eight of them being thrown out in front of the jail for dead, and two escaped. One of these eight was Dr. Peregrine Warfield, afterward a distinguished member of the medical profession of Georgetown. The *Federal Republican* did not appear in Baltimore. It was removed to Georgetown, and was largely patronized by the Federalists throughout the country.

The *American Telegraph* was started as an afternoon paper, March 25, 1851, by Connolly, Wimer, & Magill. This paper is remarkable for being the first in Washington in which the word *telegram* was used as a heading for telegraphic dispatches. The date was the 27th of April, 1852. The editor at that time was Thomas C. Connolly. He thus introduced the word *telegram:* "*Telegraph* means to write from a distance; *telegram*, the writing itself. *Monogram, logogram*, etc., are words formed upon the same analogy and in good acceptation, hence *telegram* is the appropriate heading of a telegraphic dispatch. Well, we'll go it; look to our heading." Mr. Connolly was, however, following the example set by the Albany *Evening Journal*, which, on April 6, 1852, first used the word in this way.

This heading was continued for some time, but, as it found no favor with the press of the country generally, it was dropped on May 18, 1852, and the old heading, "News by Electric Telegraph," resumed.

The Washington *Sentinel* was established by Beverly Tucker, in September, 1853. He said in his announcement that he should support the principles of the great Democratic-Republican Party of the United States; but would permit his paper to be the organ of no department.

The paper would uphold the Union upon the basis of the rights of the States under the Constitution. The paper was, however, of little ability, and of short life. August 20, 1856, Mr. Tucker published a card in the *National Intelligencer*, informing his friends of his intention to abandon the publication of the *Sentinel*, and it was thereupon abandoned.

The *Constitutional Union* was established in 1863, by Thomas B. Florence, who had for some years been a Democratic member of the House of Representatives from Pennsylvania. It was a conservative daily paper, and struggled on for three or four years with varying but not with satisfactory success. Mr. Florence afterward published the *Sunday Gazette* in Washington. Mr. Florence had previously published the *National Democratic Quarterly Review* in this city, commencing it in 1859.

The *American Organ* was established in Washington as a daily and weekly paper by an association of native Americans. In their prospectus, they said: "We have reached an important crisis in our political history. The two leading parties of our country, hitherto separated by broad lines, either of principle or of policy, differ now scarcely in anything but in name. A national bank, formerly an essential point of difference between the rival parties, has now no advocates. A protective tariff for the sake of protection, which once divided parties and distracted our national councils, has become obsolete as a question of party policy, simply because a revenue tariff affords incidental protection to American manufacturers. The distribution of the proceeds of the public lands, the improvement of the rivers and harbors by Congressional aid, and other such questions have become obsolete; and a new era has arrived which has to be distinguished by being the 'Era of Patriotism,'" etc. The daily, every afternoon except Sunday, was $5 per year, and the weekly, every Monday, $2 per year. Francis S. Evans was the agent of the association. The first number of this paper appeared November 13, 1854. It was under the editorial control of Vespasian Ellis, with R. M. Heath as associate. Mr. Ellis found it necessary to deny that he belonged to the Whig Party, having, as he said, mostly supported Democrats for office. This paper was not published many years, and this notice of it is introduced to exhibit a phase of thought that passed over the country a few years before the War.

The *Sunday Morning Chronicle* was established in Washington early in 1861, as the property of John W. Forney, of the Philadelphia *Press*. It was published by James B. Sheridan & Company, from the building at the northeast corner of Pennsylvania Avenue and Seventh

Street. It was announced as entirely independent of party politics, although strongly devoted to the Union of the States. Joseph A. Ware was editor of the paper from the beginning, but in August, 1863, he resigned, and accepted a position as private secretary to Adjutant-General Thomas. John W. Forney soon became clerk of the House of Representatives, and later, of the Senate, and the *Sunday Morning Chronicle* was overshadowed by the *Daily Morning Chronicle.* This paper moved into new quarters on August 1, 1863, on Ninth Street, between E and F streets,—a brick structure one hundred and seventy by twenty-two feet in size and three stories high, of which Thomas U. Walter was the architect. The *Chronicle* was sold in 1870 to John M. Morris, ex-clerk of the United States Senate, who was also the proprietor of the South Carolina *Republican,* and John W. Forney went back to the Philadelphia *Press.* This paper has always been Republican in politics, and has been published since 1882 by J. Q. Thompson & Company, Mr. Thompson being the editor.

The *National Republican* was established in 1860, the first number appearing on Monday, November 26, that year. While this paper disclaimed all design of becoming an organ, yet it proposed to support, so far as possible, the then incoming administration of Mr. Lincoln. Lewis Clephane was the principal member of the company which established this paper. The paper remained true to the Government throughout the War, but toward the latter part of the sixties relaxed somewhat its political tone and thereby gained somewhat in circulation. In 1867, or 1868, the original proprietors sold it to William J. Murtagh and S. P. Hanscom, the latter becoming its editor. Afterward, Mr. Harris, formerly of the *Patriot,* became editor, then Mr. Connery, and then John P. Foley. The paper continued to be published for several years.

The *Daily Patriot* was the result of an effort made by several wealthy gentlemen in the Atlantic cities to collect a fund of $100,000 with which to found a conservative Democratic paper at Washington. The office began operations November 14, 1870. It was at that time the only Democratic paper in the city. Its chief editor was James E. Harvey, with Oscar K. Harris as chief of the news department, the business manager being James G. Berrett, formerly Mayor of Washington. By 1872, all of these gentlemen had retired from their positions, and the general direction of the paper was then in the hands of Colonel W. H. Philip, J. C. McGuire, and R. T. Merrick. A. G. Allen was the editor-in-chief, and Louis Bagger local editor. This paper is not now published.

The *Evening Star* was first issued as a specimen paper, December 12, 1852, the regular daily issue beginning December 16. Its original size was but little larger than a good-sized letter sheet, and its edition was but little more than eight hundred. The printing was done on a hand press. It was first issued by Captain J. B. Tate at the corner of Eighth and D streets, but the next year it was removed to the corner of Sixth Street and Pennsylvania Avenue. In May, 1854, it was removed to the second story of a blacksmith shop on D Street, near Twelfth Street, Northwest, on the site of the present Franklin Engine House. Soon after this removal, Mr. Tate sold the paper to W. D. Wallach and W. H. Hope, Mr. Wallach becoming sole proprietor a short time afterward. Toward the latter part of 1854, the office was removed to the corner of Eleventh Street and Pennsylvania Avenue, the corner recently occupied by Dowling, the auctioneer, but now included in the city post-office site. In 1855, C. S. Noyes, the present editor-in-chief, became connected with the paper. Mr. Wallach retained his ownership until 1867, at which time he sold it to C. S. Noyes, S. H. Kauffmann, Alexander R. Shepherd, Clarence Baker, and George W. Adams, for $110,000. In 1868, these gentlemen were incorporated into the Evening Star Newspaper Company, by a special act of Congress. Some time afterward, Messrs. Baker and Shepherd sold their interests. In about 1863, a Hoe rotary press was introduced into the establishment.

In 1881, the rapid growth of the paper demanding for it more commodious quarters, the *Evening Star* moved to its present location, at the northwest corner of Pennsylvania Avenue and Eleventh Street, and at the same time added to its facilities by the introduction of a modern perfecting press and folding machine. But even this press, with its wonderful speed, was unable to keep pace with the growth of the paper's circulation, and the following year another press of similar character was added, and since then still another press has been put in, so that now three of the fastest presses which invention has produced, having a combined capacity of twelve hundred papers a minute, are required to print the *Star* every evening in time for early distribution to its subscribers. The *Star*, when it moved to its present location, purchased the property fronting on the avenue, and also the adjoining building fronting on Eleventh Street. These two buildings, however, were not sufficient to meet the growing demands of the paper; so, in 1890, the company erected an additional four-story building on Eleventh Street, having a front of fifty-five feet and a depth of one hundred feet, making the entire frontage of the *Star* buildings

Crosby S. Noyes

on Eleventh Street one hundred and eighty feet. Recently, the company purchased the building on Pennsylvania Avenue, adjoining the corner, and now occupies a portion of that also. One great characteristic of the paper is its devotion to local interests, and the care and fullness with which it covers Washington news; but its enterprise does not stop here, for it gives every evening, with a completeness and fullness never exceeded by any evening paper, the news of the day from all the world. Special wires bring into the office the latest intelligence from all over the globe up to the moment of going to press; private telephone wires, with improved long-distance telephones, connect the office with the Capitol and the District Government buildings, and other long-distance telephones give ready communication not only with every point in the District, but with distant cities as well. The *Evening Star*, though so preëminently a local paper, has a reputation as the representative paper of the Capital, and its writers furnish much of the reading in the way of Washington news that the people of the country get, for the Washington correspondence of newspapers in different parts of the country is largely borrowed from the columns of the *Star*, that which appears in the *Star* in the evening being telegraphed away, and appearing the next morning in the dailies throughout the country. The circulation of the *Evening Star* averaged, for 1891, thirty-three thousand, seven hundred and seventy-five copies daily.

Shortly before nine o'clock, April 13, 1892, a fire broke out in the *Star* building, which caused a loss of $22,000, in the aggregate, $14,000 of which was covered by insurance. This was on the building and printing materials. The paper was, however, issued as usual on the same day, and on Saturday, April 16, it was printed on the same presses as before the fire, and with the usual-sized page.

The editorial staff of the *Evening Star* is composed of Crosby S. Noyes,[1] editor-in-chief; Theodore W. Noyes, associate editor; Ru-

---

[1] Crosby S. Noyes was born in Maine in 1825. He is a journalist, thoroughly trained in every branch of his profession. In his youth, while employed in a cotton mill, in Maine, he wrote a dialect sketch, relating with rich humor the unhappy experiences of "A Yankee in a Cotton Factory," which was printed in the *Yankee Blade*, of Boston, and widely copied. Other sketches in a similar vein were equally successful, and his youthful productions made their way into such books as "The Harp of a Thousand Strings," which collected the best work of the recognized humorists of the day. Ill health drove him from Maine to a milder climate. He entered Washington on foot in 1847, and became a Washington correspondent of some Lewistown, Boston, and Philadelphia papers. His letters were keen, witty, and picturesque. Some of them gave admirable descriptions of exciting scenes in Congress, and of the pecu-

dolph Kauffmann, managing editor; H. P. Godwin, city editor; Franklin T. Howe and Alexander T. Cowell, news editors; Philander C. Johnson and Cicero W. Harris, editorial writers. Besides, there is a large staff of reporters, special writers, and suburban correspondents. The reportorial staff includes John P. Miller, George H. Harries, W. B. Bryan, Victor Kauffmann, Thomas C. Noyes, T. H. Brooks, James Croggon, J. E. Jones, Helena McCarthy, Rene Bache, N. O. Messenger, and R. W. Dutton.

The business management of the paper is in charge of Mr. S. H. Kauffmann, president of the Evening Star Company; Mr. Frank B. Noyes, treasurer and assistant business manager, and Mr. J. Whit Herron, cashier. Mr. Richard A. McLean is foreman of the composing room.

The Washington *Post* was established December 6, 1877, by Mr. Stilson Hutchins. It was a well-printed four-page paper, and at once attracted attention by the force and originality of its editorial management and its comprehensive news service. Politically, the *Post* was Democratic. It was not then so well understood as it is now that the interests of neither of the great political parties required representative organs at the seat of government, where politics has no organized foothold.

The *Post* at once became the leading morning newspaper at the National Capital, and its establishment became an assured success. January 1, 1889, Messrs. Frank Hatton and Hon. Beriah Wilkins became the sole proprietors of the *Post*. Mr. Hatton had had many years' experience in the newspaper business as editor and manager,

---

liarities of the great men that figured in them. In 1855, he enlarged his information and broadened his views by a foot-tramp in Europe, after the Bayard Taylor fashion, and described his experiences in an interesting series of letters to the Portland *Transcript*. At the close of the same year, he became a reporter on the *Evening Star*, his connection with which paper still continues. After a successful career as an enterprising news-gatherer, he was made assistant editor, and in 1867 he became editor-in-chief and part proprietor of the *Star*, from which time his public history and that of the *Star* have been the same. As assistant editor and editor, he gave to it the precise character which fitted the situation and tended to make it the paper of the people. At the start, when it had a place to win for itself, it was made audacious and aggressive, but since his paper gained its present circulation and influence, he has been more conservative, as befitted the paper's larger responsibilities. Through his paper, Mr. Noyes has been a potent factor in the development of the modern Washington. With Alexander R. Shepherd, he chafed at the spectacle of the Capital held up to the world's contempt because of local old-fogyism and national neglect, and in the columns of his paper fought steadily and effectively to assist Shepherd to put into practical operation in the National Capital those noble projects about which

and later was Postmaster-General in President Arthur's Cabinet. Mr. Wilkins had been a Democratic member of Congress for several terms from Ohio, before which he had been a successful banker. Under this ownership, the *Post* became an independent newspaper, and entered upon a broader and more successful career than it had ever before enjoyed.

The *Post* is an eight-page, eight-column paper, with from sixteen to twenty-four pages on Sunday, and is at this time the only morning newspaper in Washington. It has the exclusive news service of the Associated Press and of the United Press for a morning paper, and together with its special service, its news facilities are unsurpassed. Its circulation throughout the South and West is larger than that ever before attained by any paper at the National Capital.

Der Volks-Tribun was established in 1875, by E. Waldecker and Carl Roeser, as a German Republican weekly. It has been continued by them in the same relations to the present time. Mr. Roeser had previously been connected with some of the largest German papers in the United States.

The Washington *Critic* was established in 1868, as an independent daily, and in the early part of its career it enjoyed considerable prosperity. It was an evening paper, published every evening in the week except Sunday. In 1881, it was published by Ringwalt, Hack, & Miller. Subsequently, it passed into the hands of Hallett Kilbourn, and still later into those of Richard Weightman and his associates. On May 14, 1891, it passed into the hands of a receiver, and in a few days thereafter its outfit, United Press franchise, type, etc., were purchased by the Evening Star Newspaper Company.

they had dreamed and planned while fellow-members in the local Common Councils in 1863. Afterward, he was among the foremost in the movement which led to the assumption by the National Government of one-half of the debt and expenses of the District of Columbia, and the reclamation of the Potomac Flats. And in every great work for Washington, from that time down to and including the establishment of Rock Creek Park, he has played an influential and important, though unostentatious, part. Commencing in 1863, he served one term as a member of the city Council, and then two successive terms as alderman, from the old Seventh Ward, now South Washington, since which time he has steadily declined public service. In his later years, he has traveled much, and has contributed to his paper many articles containing vivid pictures of scenes and events in foreign lands. Under a mild, quiet, unassuming exterior he conceals a strong will, a steady, unflinching purpose, and the capacity for a vast amount of brain work of the highest order. There could be no higher tribute to his journalistic abilities than the fact that in Washington, noted, as it is, as the graveyard of newspaper enterprises, he has made a conspicuously successful newspaper, one which everybody reads, from the President of the United States down to the casual visitor to the city of Washington.

The *Capital* was started in 1870, and was published by the Capital Publishing Company. The paper was edited for a number of years by Don Piatt, who made for it a national reputation. In 1880, A. C. Buell became the editor, and its publication was continued until 1889, when it was discontinued.

The *Government Official* was established by John E. Peterson, who, after a time, took into partnership a Mr. Smith, of Hobert, Indiana, and a Mr. White, of Fort Wayne, Indiana. In 1891, they retired, and Mr. Peterson sold one-half interest to Gilbert E. Overton, and later in the same year he sold the other half to Mr. Overton, so that Mr. Overton became sole proprietor. About the same time, the name of the paper was changed to the *Public Service*, and it is now published by the Public Service Company, which is incorporated with a capital of $50,000. James R. Young, formerly executive clerk of the United States Senate, is the president of the company. There are three vice-presidents, and Mr. Overton is secretary and treasurer. This paper, while admitting that the civil service of the Government has its faults, yet advocates the elimination of these faults in preference to the abolition of the system.

The *Home Magazine* is a monthly periodical of twenty-four pages, published by the Brodix Publishing Company, at 614 Eleventh Street Northwest. It is now in its fourth year, the April number of 1892 being No. 6 of the fourth volume. It is a magazine for the home, and is filled with fresh material important to the home and social circle. It is edited by Mrs. John A. Logan.

The *Sunday Herald* was established in 1866, by Captain I. N. Burritt, and when the *National Intelligencer* was discontinued in January, 1870, Captain Burritt, having acquired title to the property, added to the title of his paper "*and National Intelligencer*," which title it has retained to the present time. In a more limited field, the *Sunday Herald* has been a worthy successor of the *National Intelligencer*. Its aim has always been to be a high-class social and literary paper, devoted to the interests of Washington and her people. In 1889, upon the death of Captain Burritt, the paper passed into the hands of its present proprietors, Messrs. Soule & Hensey, who have extended its field of usefulness, enlarged its size, and improved it in many ways, and it has a large local circulation.

The *Republic*, a straight-out Republican paper, issued early every Sunday morning, was established in 1875, by John Brisben Walker, now editor and proprietor of the *Cosmopolitan*, with offices at the northwest corner of Pennsylvania Avenue and Eleventh Street, Northwest. Mr. Walker sold it to the late H. J. Ramsdell in 1876, who, in 1883, sold it to M. V. S. Wilson, of whom its present proprietor, Rufus H. Darby, purchased it in 1884. Up to about six years ago, it was in pamphlet form with a green cover. It was changed to its newspaper form by its present proprietor. Its weekly edition averages about five thousand in circulation. Its present location is at No. 1308 Pennsylvania Avenue Northwest.

The Washington *Sentinel* was established July 1, 1873, by its present proprietor, Mr. Louis Schade. The *Sentinel* is devoted to general liberty, personal and religious, and it assigns that reason for leaning toward the Democratic Party. It is not, however, strictly a party paper, as it reserves the right to oppose the Democratic Party. When that party is not pursuing the right, the *Sentinel* opposes it, as was the case in 1878, when Hon. Thomas Ewing was candidate for Governor of Ohio, and again in 1891, when Hon. James E. Campbell was the Democratic candidate.

The *National Tribune* was established in 1877, by Captain George Lemon, the present owner, in an office at 1405 G Street Northwest. Here it remained until more room was needed for its growing business, when it removed to its present location in the Lemon building, at 1729 New York Avenue Northwest, an elegant five-story brick structure. The *Tribune* has developed into a great national paper, its average circulation during 1891 being one hundred and fifty-six thousand. Its subscribers live in every State and Territory of the Union. Its specialty is the interests of the old soldiers of the Union Army, and the history of the War of the Rebellion. John McElroy is editor, and Charles Flint business manager, of the *Tribune*.

The National Tribune Company purchased, in February, 1892, the *American Farmer*, which was established in April, 1819, and which claims to be the oldest agricultural paper in the United States.

The *National View* was established in May, 1878, as an independent Greenback-Labor journal of education, by Mr. Lee Crandall, editor and proprietor, both of which relations he still sustains to the paper. It continued in the same line of thought until the Silver Convention assembled in St. Louis in 1889, at which time it began the advocacy of the free and unlimited coinage of silver. While it is not an organ, it represents to the best of its ability the interests of the People's Party, which was called into existence at Cincinnati in 1891, of the national committee of which Mr. Crandall is a member. He is secretary of the National Silver Committee and of the National

30

Executive Silver Committee. The offices of the *View* are at No. 1202 Pennsylvania Avenue.

The *American Anthropologist* is the principal journal in the United States devoted to the science of anthropology. The initial number was issued by the Anthropological Society in January, 1888. It is an octavo quarterly, of ninety-six pages, and is published on the first of January, April, July, and October, the subscription price to non-members being $3 per annum. Its pages contain many contributions from various parts of the country by writers not connected with the society.

Owing to the rapid growth of the society, and the accumulation of numerous valuable papers presented at its meetings, the publication of the *Anthropologist* became a necessity, that there might be some means of disseminating their contents. The first editor of the periodical was Mr. Thomas Hampton, whose death was announced April 25, 1888. His successor, Mr. Henry W. Henshaw, the curator of the society, has performed the duties of editor-in-chief from that date to the present time.

The *Vedette* is a monthly journal devoted especially to the interests of the surviving veterans of the Mexican War. Alexander M. Kenaday is the editor and proprietor. It was established in 1878, for the purpose of advocating the claims of those veterans to be placed upon the pension rolls upon the same footing as those of the War of 1812, and through its advocacy of their cause, in part at least, the movement was at length a success, Congress on the 29th of January, 1887, passing an act placing about twenty-eight thousand survivors and widows on the rolls at $8 per month. In 1889, the publication of the paper was temporarily discontinued. But in 1890, Congress having passed a Pension bill allowing dependent soldiers of the Union Army in the War of the Rebellion from $6 to $12 per month, Mr. Kenaday decided to reissue the *Vedette* for the purpose of advocating an equalization of pensions, so that his comrades of the Mexican War should have pensions of at least $12 per month during their natural lives. The headquarters of the National Association of Veterans of the Mexican War is at No. 507 F Street, from which office the *Vedette* is published. The local association of survivors numbers about three hundred members, survivors and widows.

Kate Field's *Washington* was established January 1, 1890, by Miss Kate Field as editor and proprietor. Caroline Graysingle is managing editor, and Ella S. Leonard publisher. This paper is a national independent review, devoted principally to literature, society news, poetry, and stories.

The *Congressional Record* is a Government publication, devoted to the measures introduced into Congress, together with the speeches thereon, and to the proceedings of Congress generally. It was established to take the place of the *Globe*, after the *Globe* ceased to be published.

Public Opinion was established in 1887, by F. S. Presbrey, at No. 306 Ninth Street. This periodical is unique in its field of work, being devoted to the collection and publication of the opinions of the press and of leading thinkers on all leading and current questions. It is similar in its plan to *Littell's Living Age*, but it is much wider in its scope. It has recently moved into elegant quarters in the Washington Loan and Trust Company's building.

There are numerous other newspapers published in Washington, devoted severally to a great variety of purposes, among them the following: The *Sun*, established in 1877, and still published by W. D. Hughes; the Washington *Law Reporter*, established in 1874, by Hugh T. Taggart, since then published by different parties, and at the present time by the Law Reporter Company; the *Western Land Owner*, established in 1874, now named *Copp's Land Owner*, published by Henry M. Copp; *American Annals of the Deaf*, by Edward A. Fay, Ph. D., and published at the National Deaf Mute College, Kendall Green; and several others.

In this chapter on the "Press," it may not be out of place to present a brief history of the first successful electric telegraph established in this country, though, perhaps, not the first electric telegraph in the history of the world. On this point, too, it may be well to state that, according to the decision of Levi Woodbury when a Justice of the Supreme Court of the United States, messages were sent by means of electricity so long ago as in 1827 or 1828, the inventor of this telegraph being Harrison Gray Dyar. He was proved by a Mr. Cornwell to have constructed a telegraph on Long Island, at the race course, with wires on poles, using glass insulation. Dr. Bell fortified this statement, having seen some of the wires, and understood its operation to be by a spark sent from one end of the wire to the other, which made a mark on paper prepared by some chemical salts.

In 1831, Professor Joseph Henry, of Princeton College, described a method of forming magnets of intensity and quantity produced from correspondent batteries, by the use of which, with relay magnets prepared by him, magnetic effects could be produced at a distance of from one thousand to two thousand miles.

Professor S. F. Morse, in 1835, produced a rude working model of a telegraphic instrument, thus anticipating Steinheil in the matter of a recording telegraph. In October, 1837, Professor Morse entered his first *caveat* for an American electro-magnetic telegraph, claiming that his first thought upon the subject of a magnetic telegraph was on his passage across the Atlantic in 1832.

On September 7, 1837, "A New American Invention" was referred to in the public prints, and at the same time a certain writer claimed that this invention by Professor Morse was only a repetition of a French invention. To this Professor Morse replied, that if it were true that his method of communicating intelligence by means of the electro-magnetism had been previously invented, and if he could be assured of that fact, he would be the last to attempt to detract from the honor of the real inventor, or of his country.

Professor Morse's claims to the invention of the electro-magnetic recording telegraph were, of course, recognized and sustained, and after several years' delay, Congress on February 23, 1843, passed an act making an appropriation for the construction of a telegraph line from Washington to Baltimore. This line was completed on May 24, 1844, and on the next day, Saturday, the batteries were charged and the telegraph put in operation, conveying intelligence between the Capitol and the Pratt Street Depot in Baltimore. The first message, according to many writers, was sent from the Capitol to Baltimore by a young lady named Miss Annie Ellsworth, to whom Professor Morse was at the time ardently devoted, a granddaughter of the famous Governor Ellsworth, of Massachusetts, and whose father at the time was Commissioner of Patents. This first message was in these words: "What hath God wrought?" At 11:30 A. M., the question was asked from Baltimore: "What is the news in Washington?" and almost instantaneously the answer was flashed back: "Van Buren stock is rising." Sixteen persons witnessed the experiment in the Capitol. This was May 25. On the 27th, the working of this wonderful instrument won universal admiration from all who were fortunate enough to be spectators. Messages passed between Baltimore and Washington at intervals during each hour throughout the day. At 1:40 P. M., information was received in the Capitol building of the nomination of James Carroll for Governor of Maryland; a few moments later came the news of the nomination by acclamation, by the Tyler Convention, of John Tyler for President of the United States, and also of a speech of more than two hours in length by Benjamin F. Butler, in favor of the majority rule in the convention. On Wednesday, the 29th, the telegraphic news from Baltimore caused

great excitement at the north end of the Capitol building, in that it
announced on that day .the nomination of James K. Polk, "a subal-
tern," for the Presidency, by the Democratic Convention. This announcement was of so surprising a nature, and the telegraph was
of so recent introduction, that neither the announcement nor the
telegraph was believed; and in order to ascertain the truth, two
special messengers were dispatched by railroad to Baltimore, but of
course the result of their mission was only to confirm the telegraphic
announcement.

Among the many reasons given by different persons for the
continuance of the seat of government at the city of Washington,
was that of the invention of the Morse telegraph. In locating the
seat of government, one of the requisites was centrality, and Mr.
Madison remarked that "if there could be any means of instantaneously
promulgating the laws throughout the country, the center would be
of less consequence." This means was supplied by the electric telegraph, and hence it was inferred by some that the seat of government
would never be removed.

On Monday, April 5, 1847, connection was made between Baltimore and Alexandria by means of the telegraph passing through
Washington.

In the summer of 1846, the first attempt was made to determine
longitude by means of the telegraph. A line of wire was extended
from the General Post Office in Washington to the Naval Observatory,
and another was carried from the High School observatory in
Philadelphia to the main Baltimore line. Still another wire was
carried from the Jersey City telegraph office to the Presbyterian
church. The observations at Washington were made under the
direction of Mr. Sears C. Walker; those at Philadelphia, under Professor Kendall, and those at Jersey City, under Professor Loomis. Each
observer had at his command a good clock and a transit instrument
for regulating it with precision. The signal used in determining
the difference of longitude of these three places was the click of a
magnet. Signals were exchanged between Washington and Philadelphia, October 10, 1846, but none were obtained for Jersey City. On
August 3, 1847, the experiments were resumed upon the following
plan: Commencing at Jersey City at 10:00 P. M., the operator strikes
a key, and simultaneously a click is heard at each of the three places.
The observer at each place recorded the time of the click, each by
his own clock. Ten seconds afterward, the same sign is repeated, and
so on for twenty signals. The series of signals was then repeated for

Washington and Philadelphia, and from these sixty signals, averaged up, the difference of time was obtained with almost perfect accuracy. The difference of time thus obtained between Jersey City and Philadelphia was four minutes and thirty seconds.

On February 9, 1848, a paragraph in the London correspondence of some American paper noticed the fact that the electric telegraph had begun its work in England, the price charged for sending one hundred words from London to Liverpool, a distance of two hundred and twenty miles, being £5, while at the same time, in this country, the rate charged for sending a telegram of one hundred words from Washington to New York, a distance of two hundred and twenty-five miles, was only $5.

The Associated Press and the United Press both have offices in Washington, as well as all of the leading newspapers in the country, many of which have private telegraph wires.

CHAPTER XIV.

PREVIOUS to the establishment of the public-school system in the city of Washington, there were here, as in all other towns and cities of the United States, numerous private schools, and these were as various in their characters as were the teachers who established them. It is manifestly impracticable to present a detailed history of every one of these private schools, and it is altogether probable that such a detailed history would be far from acceptable if practicable; hence, the history of private education in the city of Washington, as given in this volume, will be found to be more illustrative than exhaustive.

The Columbian Academy, of Georgetown, was one of the first of these private schools. It was in existence as early as 1803, and was then under the care of Rev. David Wiley, and had been for some years. In 1803, there were seventy-five pupils in attendance, but the building was capable of accommodating one hundred. The studies pursued were the common branches and the learned languages.

A Young Ladies' Academy was opened, July 16, 1806, by Mrs. Reagan, in a commodious house on F Street, between Captain James Hoban's and Josiah W. King's. The branches taught were tambouring, embroidery, open work, marking, all kinds of plain sewing, filigree, painting, waxwork, French, music, dancing, reading, and writing. Young ladies could also be accommodated with board.

Hugh Maguire, then late a professor in St. John's College, Maryland, where he had been employed for eleven years, and a teacher of twenty-three years' experience, opened an academy near the Seven

Buildings, in August, 1807. In this academy, he taught Latin, Greek, mathematics, geography, bookkeeping, etc., for $40 per annum; English grammar, reading, writing, and arithmetic, for $24 per annum. At first, he had as an assistant Samuel Cantwell. After teaching this school a short time, he was selected principal of the public academy, and in a year established a school at Bladensburg, which failed of support. He therefore returned to Georgetown, and opened a school near the Union Tavern, on the 6th of January, 1812. In this school he taught Latin, Greek, and the common English branches. Some time afterward, he removed his school to commodious apartments in the rear of Congress Hall, and again associated with himself, in the teaching of the common English branches, Mr. Simon Cantwell, who had taught with him before, and who was highly approved of in the neighboring county of Prince George, for capacity and industry in his scholastic duties for the then past thirty years.

A school was opened in 1802, by the Rev. A. T. McCormick, on Capitol Hill, in which he taught the common branches and the higher mathematics. Rev. Mr. McCormick kept on with this school until 1819, in February of which year he was succeeded by P. Edwards, under whom the instruction was almost completely changed.

Francis Donnelly opened a school on Monday, May 30, 1803, in a building then lately occupied as an auction store, near the West Market. Mr. Donnelly taught spelling, reading, writing, arithmetic, English grammar, bookkeeping, history, and geography.

About the same time, a new school was opened by J. Sewell, on North F Street, in a room then lately occupied by Mr. Coates, opposite the Little Hotel. For teaching English grammar, writing, etc., he charged $4 per quarter; for common arithmetic, $5 per quarter; for merchants' accounts, geography, algebra, mensuration, surveying, plain navigation, astronomy, and the other branches of mathematics, and the principles of mechanics, $8 per quarter.

Madam du Cherray, a French lady, then lately arrived from Moscow, Russia, where for several years she had been at the head of one of the most reputable academies in that city, under the immediate protection of his Majesty, Alexander the First, Emperor of all the Russias, opened an establishment similar to the one she had taught in Moscow, in the year 1808, in which she received both boarders and day pupils. In her academy, she taught English, French, history, geography, mythology, writing, arithmetic, embroidery, all sorts of needlework, drawing, music, and dancing. She also taught miniature portrait painting.

One of the most prominent and peculiar of the earlier teachers in Washington was John McLeod. He commenced teaching here in 1808, near the Navy Yard, with four pupils. Soon afterward he employed an assistant teacher, and in four or five years erected an academy building which cost him $6,000. After the destruction of the Navy Yard in the War of 1812–15, he removed from that locality and erected the Central Academy in 1816, for this purpose borrowing a large sum of money. During both summer and winter, both himself and his assistant teachers were at the schoolhouse by daylight, and they spent daily from nine to ten hours in the schoolroom, instructing the youth committed to their care. This plan, Mr. McLeod said, had an excellent effect upon the minds and constitutions of the pupils. They enjoyed fair health, and in their early and regular attendance at school they acquired good conduct and made great improvement in their studies. They were not excelled, nor, perhaps, equaled, by any pupils of their age in this country or any other; and in rewarding their noble conduct, he had been more liberal than his circumstances would warrant. "At thirty-four public examinations in Washington, I gave away upward of $2,000 in premiums. My last examination cost me $200. To aid me in this expense, I never received a cent from any person, except $15 from Major-General Brown. This generous and unexpected present merits my warmest thanks. Perhaps there is not a private institution more costly than mine, of great or of no title. Unconnected with any faction, I look for no indulgence; I know my situation well. Should I succeed in this arduous and important undertaking, I expect no praise; should I fail, no sympathy. My system of education, rules, and regulations are fruits of my long experience. Having everything at stake, and dependent entirely on my own exertions, I must attend at my post, perform my duties, and my teachers must be able and willing to do the same.

"I have spent $16,000 in erecting literary institutions and in rewarding my pupils since my commencement in this metropolis. All those of my profession have not laid out one-fourth of that sum in the same manner since the first foundation was laid in it. There were thirty here when I commenced, and all of them have deserted the employment long ago. Thus have I stated my history since I came to Washington, and my present situation, which I hope will be sufficient apology for changing my system.

"It is now the beginning of a new year, and I must settle my accounts the best way I can, and be more exact in the future. I have

$6,000 or $7,000 due, the third of which I never expect to see. This is my own fault. I have almost ruined myself by indulging people. My expenses are very great, and without a change the Central Academy cannot stand. I therefore respectfully request those whose bills are due six months, or longer, to settle before the first of next month, or withdraw their children. Tuition bills must be actually paid at the end of every quarter. I assure my beneficiaries and the public that imperious necessity compels me to adopt these measures."

In 1814, when the British army approached Washington, Mr. McLeod dismissed one hundred and seventy-two students from the Eastern Academy, which was, as has been said, near the Navy Yard. At that time, it was the only decent schoolroom in Washington. In 1827, although it had been occupied since its abandonment by Mr. McLeod by twelve or fourteen different teachers, it was in a very bad condition, and the Bank of Washington was compelled to take it to prevent it from becoming a nuisance to the neighborhood, as the Western Academy building was at that time. "O angels and ministers of grace, protect the Central Academy from a similar fate; at least, until its visionary and enthusiastic founder shall have paid the last farthing of his debts in this world and in the next! Should this prayer be granted, perhaps it may serve the last generation."

Mr. McLeod erected the Columbian Academy in 1835, making the third academy building erected by him. In July, 1839, in his advertisement he was very severe upon the practice of giving vacations. His school bell was rung by the dawn of day at all seasons of the year. His establishment was in complete order, and his teachers were at their posts at that early hour to receive their pupils, and both teachers and pupils were on duty from nine and a half to ten hours each day in the summer time, and about eight hours in the winter. Notwithstanding this fact, Mr. McLeod said that there was not a more active set of pupils in the entire Union than the pupils of Columbian Academy. "The subscriber intends finishing his days in the instruction of youth, and is resolved never to give more than four days holiday in succession. For some days before vacation, it is impossible to make pupils study. The girls must get new dresses to visit in, and often where they are not welcome. Boys spend their time in idleness and wickedness, disturbing the public peace, destroying their health and character, by committing all manner of vice they are capable of," etc. Mr. McLeod complained of, or perhaps rather pointed out, the fact that "since the commencement of the Western Free Academy, about thirty years before, the pupils attending it had not been more than one-half the time in school that they should have been, and, of course, the able and virtuous teacher [Henry Ould], as the trustees call him, has received during that time about $10,000, without teaching one lesson for this immense sum. The citizens of Washington and myself are of the opinion that the youth of this school are going exactly as they are taught and encouraged to go!'"

In 1841, Mr. McLeod was still teaching. He then said that in addition to the $20,000 he had expended in buildings, he had paid out in premiums, at forty-two public examinations, more than $6,000. His motto, he said, when he commenced, was, "Order is Heaven's First Law," and in his advertisement this year he said that in support of this motto he had sacrificed much, and "could, if necessary, sacrifice life itself." He was glad to be able to boast that he had had under his direction, during the thirty-three years of his professional life in Washington, more pupils than any other teacher in the Union.

Mr. O. C. Wight represents him as having been a stern disciplinarian, with whom the rod was a potent factor in government. He hesitated not to use it, both freely and frequently.

January 2, 1811, Charles Bowman, late professor in Georgetown College, opened a school on F Street, near St. Patrick's Church, in the house then lately occupied by Major Bowling. For reading, English grammar, writing, and arithmetic, he charged $5 per quarter, and for Latin and Greek, either or both, he charged $8 per quarter.

The first Lancasterian school in the United States was established in Georgetown. The corner stone of the building was laid on Monday, June 24, 1811, by the Mayor of Georgetown, after appropriate ceremonies and a prayer by the Rev. Mr. Sneethen, of the Methodist church. The Mayor was *ex officio* member of the Lancasterian Society. After the conclusion of the ceremonies, there was an oration by Mr. Henry Beatty. The plan of the building and the directions for its construction were sent over from England by Mr. Joseph Lancaster, the reputed author of the system. The system, however, originated with Andrew Bell, D. D., an ordinary of the Church of England, who, in 1795, while engaged in the management of the orphan children of the European military at Madras, British India, on account of his arduous duties in this position, resorted to the expedient of conducting the school by the aid of the pupils themselves. In 1797, after Dr. Bell's arrival in England, he prepared a pamphlet suggesting a system by which a school might teach itself, under the superintendence of the master, which pamphlet, coming under the notice of Joseph

Lancaster, suggested to him the method of organizing schools in such a way that the necessary teaching force could be thus most economically provided. And it was through the efforts of Mr. Lancaster that this method of conducting schools became so widely known and so popular throughout Germany, England, and the United States, and it was because of his success in securing .for the system such a large measure of public recognition that it was called the Lancasterian System. It was otherwise called the Monitorial System, each pupil who had the management of a class of his fellow-pupils being called a monitor. The number of pupils that could be taught on this system depended almost altogether on the number of monitors that could be found in the school, and might be, for one head master, as many as three or four hundred.

The building erected in Georgetown, according to the directions sent over by Mr. Lancaster, was 32 x 70 feet in size, and calculated to accommodate 350 pupils. The teacher, Mr. Robert Ould, who was selected the first principal of this school, was recommended by Mr. Lancaster. From the second annual report made to the trustees, December 7, 1813, the following facts were taken: The opening of the school occurred November 18, 1811. During the first two years, 410 pupils were admitted; 242 had left it for various employments; 168 remained on the rolls, and 18 teachers had been sent out to different parts of the country to instruct on the Lancasterian plan, and there were left 3 in Georgetown. This school was continued for several years, and was very popular on account of its novelty and economy. Its subsequent history is referred to in subsequent pages in this chapter.

Miss Charlotte Ann Taylor opened a female boarding school near the house of General Van Ness, February 15, 1813. She taught the common English branches, French, Italian, music, drawing, and needlework. She was late from London, England. In Washington she was a successful teacher, and in 1813 moved her school to G Street, near Dr. Elzy's house. For the common English branches, together with plain sewing, marking, etc., she charged $10 per quarter; for French and Italian, $2.50 per quarter extra; and for music, painting, dancing, and drawing there was an extra charge.

Ezekiel Hildreth, then late of Harvard College, on January 13, 1815, opened a school for both sexes in the house contiguous to Washington Boyd's, on F Street. For the classics he charged $7 per quarter, and for other branches, $5 per quarter.

Mrs. Howard, "having at the solicitation of several families of distinction" removed her seminary to Washington, opened it on June 5, 1815, teaching therein the common and higher English branches, and all kinds of plain and fancy needlework, as well as French, music, and dancing.

Mrs. Stone opened an academy in her house November, 1816, for young ladies. In her school she taught geography, English grammar, reading, spelling, history, composition, and needlework. Mr. Stone taught French, writing, arithmetic, drawing, landscape painting in oil and water colors, etc.

On January 4, 1819, D. McCurdy opened a school at his residence near the Navy Yard, where he taught the common branches of an English education. He also published a book called the "Columbian Tutor's Assistant," a work on arithmetic.

Mr. and Mrs. Webber opened a classical, mathematical, and commercial school for young men, and a seminary for young ladies, January 4, 1819, at the corner of Bridge and Green streets, Georgetown. Their plan of education consisted of an "interrogatory and an explanatory system by which the pupils are enabled to understand their lessons with pleasure to themselves, and satisfaction to their teachers."

The Washington Eastern Academy was opened in 1818, by Edward Ferris, A. M. He said that in his academy his pupils were taught to learn, because he had witnessed in more than one university in Europe the bad effects of employing masters to do the duty and execute the tasks of the pupils.

Dr. Horwitz came to Washington in the fall of 1819, and for some time taught the Hebrew language to private students. In noticing the work of Dr. Horwitz, the *National Intelligencer* said that the Hebrew was "perhaps the most regular, rich, and philosophical of all the tongues spoken in the world." Dr. Horwitz was considered not only a perfect master of the Hebrew, but also a thorough classical scholar, and deeply versed in Oriental learning.

Mrs. Fales started a boarding school for young ladies November 1, 1820, at the house then lately occupied by Mr. Petre, the French consul, on Thirteenth Street, between the Avenue and F Street. In her academy she taught the common branches, drawing, and ornamental painting on wood and velvet, embroidery, etc., besides music and dancing. She had been a teacher in Marietta and Philadelphia.

William Elliott commenced a course of lectures on mathematics November 13, 1820, in the "Long Room," on C Street. His course consisted of five lectures on numerical calculations, including logarithms; fifteen lectures on algebra, twenty on geometry, and ten on conic sections.

The Union Academy of Georgetown and Washington was opened for students in February, 1821, under the superintendence of James D. Cobb. In it were taught the common branches, Latin, Greek, geography, history, chronology, and the various branches of mathematics. Both sexes were admitted.

D. Hewett commenced teaching stenography in Washington in October, 1823, charging $5 for a course of twelve or fifteen lessons, which he said was sufficient to acquire the theory, yet anyone could attend without additional charge until the art should be effectually acquired. Mrs. Hewett taught the lady pupils.

Franklin Academy was located on F Street, north of the General Post Office. The principal of this institution was James Caden. The course of instruction embraced all the branches of an English education, bookkeeping, Latin, Greek, French, and Spanish; and for young men desirous of qualifying themselves for the countinghouse, a course of lectures was given on domestic, factory, and commercial accounts. Neither holidays nor vacations were given, nor were any deductions made for loss of time. The terms ranged from $5 to $12.50 per quarter.

The Washington Academy was located at the corner of H and Ninth streets Northwest, directly east of General Van Ness's family mausoleum. It opened in a new building erected especially for its use, on Monday, July 2, 1827, for the reception of boys. The common branches of an English education, history, mathematics, Latin, Greek, French, and Spanish were taught. "Long convinced of the beneficial effects resulting from very early and regular attendance, the academy will be open through the year for scholars at sunrise." Z. D. Brashears and R. Kirkwood were the principals.

Mrs. McClenchan opened a school for young ladies, in 1827, on Ninth Street, which she maintained for several years. Robert II. McClenchan opened a school for young gentlemen, which he named the English and Mathematical School, on Eleventh Street West, over the city library. He taught the English branches and a full course of mathematics.

Miss Heaney's Academy opened for students April 4, 1831, in the house then lately occupied by Madam Bonfils, on the corner of F and Twelfth streets. Miss Heaney was from Boston, Massachusetts, and had been for some years principal of the Derby Academy, at Hughens. She taught the elementary English branches, and also those of a liberal education.

The Washington Female Seminary was established in 1824, by Mrs. E. M. Haven, assisted by Miss Laura A. Haven and Miss Jane A. Hoskins, in a large and commodious building on G Street, two doors west of Eighteenth Street. In this academy four courses of study were pursued. The terms for board, tuition in English, French, and pencil drawing, were $150 for five months; for lessons and use of piano, $25; oil painting and *papier-maché* work, $10; floral, leather, and pastel drawing, $5; Latin and phonography, $5.

Masonic Hall Academy was established in 1827, by John Devlin. In the latter part of this year, he advertised that he would continue to enforce the same rigid observance of scholastic discipline, to pursue the same efficient system in the communication of instruction, and to use the same untiring industry in the discharge of his professional duties, which had previously invariably distinguished him. In his school were taught the common English branches, and a thorough course of mathematics. Mr. Devlin concluded his advertisement as follows:

"At a time like the present, when every pretender to literature and science lauds in turgid language his own institution and everything connected with it, the principal of the Masonic Hall School, conscious of the extent and solidity of his researches in the branches of the sciences above enumerated, has the confidence to assert that he will instruct the youth in them, not superficially, but according to principles susceptible of conclusive proof in the rigid language of irrefragable demonstration."

Mr. Delvin taught in Washington about six years, and then opened the Prince Street Academy, in Alexandria. Still later, in 1833, he associated with himself Philip·Smith, and opened a school on F Street in Washington, in which were taught the common English branches, the mathematics, and the classics.

Miss English's Academy, in Georgetown, was opened February 27, 1826, in a small two-story brick building on the corner of Washington and Gay streets. The building gradually grew in size, by additions, until it was a large building, and it was known for many years as "Miss English's Seminary." It was six and three stories high, and contained about twenty rooms. Miss English died in 1865, at the age of sixty-six. She was the daughter of Mr. David English, a gentleman well known for many years as the cashier of the Union Bank. When she retired from her profession as teacher, she was succeeded by Rev. Mr. Clarke, and he was succeeded, in 1857, by Miss Harrover.

Difficulties in the way of educating colored youths were, in the early days, quite numerous. Prejudice, stronger a third of a century after the founding of the city than at its inception, compelled all efforts to partake largely of a personal character. The race, however, began to establish schools within two years after the whites organized their work. Many of their schools were taught by colored, but most of them by white, teachers.

The first schoolhouse erected especially for the education of the colored youth was built about 1807, by George Bell, Nicholas Franklin, and Moses Liverpool, all of whom had been reared as slaves, in Maryland and Virginia. It was a fair one-story frame building, and stood on the site of the present Providence Hospital. As soon as it was finished, a full school was opened under the management of Mr. Lowe, a white teacher. It continued for several years, when the building was used for a dwelling.

At that time, the total colored population of Washington was one thousand, four hundred and ninety-eight, of which number the aggregate free colored, from which class only such a school could be recruited, was four hundred and ninety-four.

Of these colored pioneers in school work, Franklin and Liverpool were calkers at the Navy Yard, to which place they had come from the lower parts of Virginia. They were freemen, but it is not known how they secured their liberty. They were unable to read and write, but were desirous that their children and the children of their neighbors should be more fortunate. In this educational enterprise, the leading spirit, however, was George Bell. He lived beyond the Eastern Branch, and had been the slave of Anthony Addison. His wife, Sophia Browning, saved from the sale of market products $400, with which she purchased her husband's freedom. He, in turn, subsequently bought hers for five pounds, Maryland currency. In process of time, they purchased the freedom of their children.

Bell and his family were, for a time, the recognized leaders of the colored people in all matters educational and religious, and fully impressed their personality upon the future of their race in the city.

In 1818, the Bell Schoolhouse, which had for a number of years been used for a dwelling, was again taken for educational purposes. The school was known as the "Resolute Beneficial Society," of which William Costin was president, James Harris secretary, and George Bell treasurer. An evening school was organized in October, to continue through the season. Children were instructed in reading, writing, arithmetic, English grammar, or other branches. The school continued several years, with an average attendance of sixty pupils.

The first teacher was a Mr. Pierpont, of Massachusetts, and the second was John Adams, the first colored teacher in the District.

The third school was established by Henry Potter, an Englishman, about 1809, in a brick building which stood on the southeast corner of F and Seventh streets. He had a large attendance; but after several years, removed to Clark's Row, on Thirteenth Street, between G and H streets.

About this time, Mrs. Anne Maria Hall began a school on Capitol Hill, on First Street East. She changed about quite frequently, and continued in the work, with great success, for some twenty-five years.

Of the early teachers of colored children in Washington, none are mentioned with greater reverence than Mrs. Mary Billings, the projector of the first colored school in Georgetown. She was an Englishwoman. Her husband, a cabinet maker, came from England to Washington in 1800, and dying in 1807, left his wife to maintain and educate three children. At first she taught both white and colored pupils, but prejudice arising, she concluded to devote her energies wholly to colored youth. Accordingly, she established a school, about 1810, in a brick house on Dunbarton Street, between Congress and High streets, and continued it until the winter of 1820–21, when she came to Washington and opened a school on H Street, near the Foundry Church. She conducted a night school, and had pupils from Bladensburg and the surrounding country. She died in 1826.

Mrs. Billings's successor at Georgetown was Henry Potter; and following him, Mr. Shay, an Englishman, who subsequently came to Washington, and for many years conducted a large colored school in a brick building known as the "Round Tops," in the western part of the city, near the Circle. Later, he removed to the Western Academy, corner of I and Seventeenth streets. He continued until about 1830, when, for assisting a slave to freedom, he was convicted, and sent to the penitentiary.

About 1823, Henry Smothers, a pupil of Mrs. Billings, built what was known as the Smothers Schoolhouse, in the rear of his own dwelling on the corner of Fourteenth and H streets. He had taught in Georgetown, on Washington Street, opposite the Union Hotel, and removing to Washington, opened his work in the old corporation schoolhouse built in 1806, but subsequently known as the Western Academy. His own house being completed, he removed to it in 1823, and for two years conducted a flourishing school, the attendance reaching one hundred to one hundred and fifty pupils.

In 1825, John W. Prout, a man of rare ability, succeeded to the

31

management of the school. It was placed under a board of trustees, and known as the "Columbian Institute." Tuition for a time was nominally free, a charge of twelve and one-half cents per month being made. The attendance averaged one hundred and fifty, necessitating the employment of Mrs. Anne Maria Hall as assistant.

In August, 1834, Prout was succeeded in the school by John F. Cook, brother-in-law of George Bell, of whom mention has been made. He had been a slave, whose liberty was purchased eight years previous by his aunt, Alatheia Tanner. He had been for some time assistant messenger in the Land Office. His school numbered a hundred pupils in the winter, and a hundred and fifty in the summer. His prosperity, however, was interrupted. What was known as the Nat Turner Insurrection in Virginia, in August, 1831, and the Snow Riot, or "Snow Storm," in Washington, in September, 1835, created a panicky feeling among both colored and white people. The feeling in Washington was extremely intense. Colored citizens, private houses, churches, and schoolhouses were assaulted, and in some cases destroyed. To avoid violence, Cook fled from the city and went to Columbia, Pennsylvania, where he taught school for a time. Returning in August, 1836, he resumed his labors in the school which had, for several years, been known as Union Seminary. The course of study embraced three years, and the line of work was quite thorough, attracting much attention.

Shortly after, Mr. Cook began to study for the ministry, and was finally ordained, and served in that capacity for some twelve years. Teaching and preaching constituted his occupation until the time of his death, March 21, 1855. His son, John F. Cook, continued the work until May, 1857, when it passed into the hands of a younger son, George F. T. Cook, who changed it from the old Smothers house to the basement of the Presbyterian church, in the spring of 1858, and maintained it until July, 1859. An interregnum existed from this date until 1862, owing to the outbreak of the War. In 1862, however, John F. Cook, Jr., having erected a new schoolhouse on Sixteenth Street, reorganized the work, and continued it until the founding of schools throughout the city in 1867 rendered his work no longer necessary, and he retired to other fields.

Louisa Parke Costin's school was established, as a contemporary of the Smothers school, in 1823, on Capitol Hill. The Costins came to Washington from Mount Vernon shortly after the death of Martha Washington, in 1802. The father, William Costin, whose death occurred in 1842, had been a messenger for twenty-four years in the

Bank of Washington. Louisa Parke Costin opened her school at the age of nineteen, in her father's house, and continued it with success until her sudden death in 1831. After her death, her younger sister, Martha, who had been educated in a colored convent in Baltimore, took the school and continued it some eight years.

James Enoch Ambush, a colored man, began, April, 1833, a large school in the basement of Israel Bethel Church, on Capitol Hill, and continued it in various places for ten years, until 1843, when he built a schoolhouse on E Street South, in which was established the Wesleyan Seminary. It maintained a successful existence until August, 1865. Mr. Ambush studied medicine, and became a Botanic physician.

The first seminary for colored girls in the District was established in 1827, in Georgetown, by Father Vanloman, a Catholic priest. Maria Becraft, a talented young colored woman, was the teacher in charge. She became so popular and successful in her work that she was finally transferred to a convent in Baltimore, where she was a principal teacher until she died.

The Myrtilla Miner Seminary for colored girls originated in Washington. The projector, Myrtilla Miner, was born in Madison County, New York, in 1815. Burning with a zeal to accomplish something beyond the mere drudgery of domestic life, she sought every opportunity to qualify herself for philanthropic work. She finally prosecuted her studies in a seminary at Rochester. Subsequently, she went to Mississippi to superintend the education of planters' daughters. While there, she saw so much of the despotism of slavery that she returned to the North, determined to do what she could for the amelioration of the colored race. She chose Washington as the field of her labors. In the autumn of 1857, she commenced her work in a small room, fourteen feet square, on Eleventh Street, near New York Avenue. After many changes and discouragements, she was instrumental in securing, from various prominent sources, means with which to purchase a school site of three acres bounded by Nineteenth and Twentieth, and N and O streets, Northwest. The price paid was $4,000. The building, a small frame dwelling of two stories, and three small cabins, constituted the outfit for this institution. Miss Miner was encouraged by W. H. Seward and his wife, and prominent members of Congress; and yet the feeling of opposition and persecution was bitter against her. She was threatened with conflagration. Even the Mayor of the city, Walter Lenox, decried against her through the public press. This bitter feeling culminated in the spring of 1860 in the firing of her house while she was asleep. She was aroused, however, in time to save herself and the building from the flames. The War coming, and her health constantly failing, she relinquished her post to regain her health and collect funds for the erection of suitable buildings on her chosen site. In this work she continued until her death, December, 1866.

After her death, the trustees sought means by which to build a structure and continue the enterprise. General O. O. Howard offered $30,000 for erecting a suitable building. The scheme did not materialize; and not till within the last three years has the school reappeared; then in a building on the corner of Four and a Half Street and Maryland Avenue Southwest. It is a primary institution, under the management of trustees.

Charles H. Middleton began his career about the time when Johnson was retiring. He was encouraged to engage in his work by Jesse E. Dow, a member of the Common Council. It was really the first movement for a free colored public school, and occurred in 1848-49.

With the opening of the War of the Rebellion, a new condition of things began. Schools were disorganized. The city was filled with troops and refugees, necessitating the organization of work by societies. One of these, the Colored Orphans' Home, was the outgrowth of the efforts of some philanthropic women. It was incorporated as "An Asylum for Aged and Destitute Colored Refugees and Colored Orphans," February 16, 1863. It first took possession of a property on Georgetown Heights, owned by Richard S. Cox, a major in the Confederate service; but he having been pardoned by President Johnson, the society had to relinquish its claim, and buy another site north of the city for $2,000. The Freedmen's Bureau erected a temporary home. Its work, however beneficent, was cramped for the lack of adequate means.

Other agencies occupied this period of chaos and strife. Among these were St. Aloysius' school for girls, the Colfax Industrial Mission, Miss Walker's Industrial School, the Wayland Theological Seminary, and Howard University.

Slavery in the District of Columbia was abolished on the 16th of April, 1862. On the 21st of May, following, Congress passed an act requiring "ten per centum of taxes collected from persons of color in Washington and Georgetown to be set apart for the purpose of initiating a system of primary schools for the education of colored children." This provision of the law was a failure, the receipts in Washington in 1862 being $256.25; in 1863, $410.89; in Georgetown, in the latter year, $69.72; total, $736.86.

Hence, another act was passed June 25, 1864, giving the colored people a due proportion of the funds available to the District. On the 23d of July, 1866, an additional act was passed, still further equalizing the revenues arising for school purposes. It accomplished its aim, the funds enabling the trustees to inaugurate a system of public colored schools in the two cities.

The first public colored school in the District was opened March 1, 1864, in the Ebenezer Church of-the city. Miss Emma V. Brown, of Georgetown, an educated colored girl, was employed as teacher at $400. Her associate was Miss Frances W. Perkins, from New Haven, Connecticut. The attendance began with forty, but soon increased to more than one hundred.

Miss Perkins was instrumental in securing the first public school-house for colored children. From a lady in New Haven she obtained $1,000, to aid in the enterprise. The trustees, securing some additional means, purchased a lot, forty-two by one hundred and twenty feet, on Capitol Hill, on C Street, between Second and Third streets, and erected, in the winter of 1864-65, a two-story frame building, forty-two feet square, two rooms on each floor. The school was moved into it, and dedicatory services were held May 1, 1865.

The question of the establishment of public schools attracted early attention in Washington. In June, 1804, a committee, appointed by the chambers of the city Council, reported a bill which they advised be made into a law, and which contained the following provisions:

1. That the superintendence of the public schools in the city of Washington be placed under the supervision of thirteen trustees, seven of whom should be chosen by the joint ballots of the Councils, and six to hold their appointments for life by contributing to the promotion of the schools as provided in the bill. In case of a vacancy in the number of the life members; the board itself was empowered to fill the vacancy, the newly chosen member to be a life member; and in case of a vacancy occurring among the members elected by the Councils, the Councils were authorized to supply the vacancy, the person chosen to serve until the next succeeding annual election. This board was to make ample provision for the education of the children residing within the city, whose parents were unable to send them to school.

2. The tax already laid, or to be laid, on slaves and dogs, on licenses on carriages and on hacks, for ordinaries and taverns, for the retailing of wines and spirituous liquors, for billiard rooms, for theatrical and other public entertainments, for hawkers and peddlers,

should be appropriated to the support of such schools as should be established under the act.

3. The two chambers of the Council, within three weeks after the passage of the act, were to appoint three of their own number to take all necessary preliminary steps for carrying the act into effect, and they were themselves, or through agents, to solicit subscriptions at a distance; and at a time to be fixed upon, all persons who should have contributed $10 or more were to meet in person, or by proxy, and elect the six life members.

The bill was passed by the first chamber, unanimously, July 3, 1804, the members being Cunningham, Smallwood, Herford, Smith, Alexander, Carpenter, Rapine, Blagden, and Bromley. In the second chamber, the vote for the bill was Nicholas King, Mr. Hodgson, and J. C. King; and against it, Andrews, Sinclair, McCormick, and Jones.

"Thus has a measure destined to be of incalculable benefit to the city, by enlightening the minds and impressing the morals of the rising generation, by rescuing the metropolis from its darkest regret, and by rendering it worthy of the esteem of the rising Nation, failed for the want of a single vote," etc. Twelve members of the two Councils voted for the bill, and four against it, thus causing its defeat, and showing how thoroughly were the rights of the minority protected in a republican form of government.

Afterward, however, the movement for the establishment of public schools on this plan was made a success, and a meeting of the board of trustees was held August 5, at the Capitol. Thomas Jefferson, President of the United States, was chosen president of the board, but, as he was absent, Robert Brent was chosen chairman of the meeting, and Nicholas King secretary. It was found from the returns that the following gentlemen composed the board: Thomas Jefferson, Robert Brent, John Taylor, Nicholas King, Gabriel Duval, John Dempsie, Thomas Tingey, Thomas Munroe, William Brent, William Cranch, George Blagden, James Barry, and Samuel H. Smith.

Mr. Smith moved the appointment of a committee to report to the board the proper steps to be taken for carrying into operation the act of the Council establishing the "Permanent Institution for the Education of Youth in the City of Washington." In accordance with this motion, Messrs. Smith, Tingey, Cranch, Blagden, and Duval were appointed.

On September 19, the board published their by-laws for the establishment of the Academy, these by-laws providing that this academy should consist of as many schools as circumstances would permit, but that at first it should consist of but two, one of which should be situated within half a mile of the Capitol, and the other within half a mile of the President's House, subject to removal. Poor children were to be taught reading, writing, grammar, and arithmetic free of expense, while the price of tuition to others was fixed at $5 per quarter. The board was authorized to appoint a principal for each school, who should receive for his services $500 per year, and in addition to this the tuition money of pupils until they amounted to fifty, and beyond, as determined by the board. But out of his income he was to pay schoolhouse rent, for his fuel, and for such other incidentals as might be necessary, and also for such assistants as he might need. There was provided a committee of three for each school, who were styled the superintending committee, whose duties were to see to the admission of poor children, etc. Robert Brent was vice-president of the board, and Washington Boyd secretary.

The Washington Academy opened for the reception of pupils January 20, 1806, under the direction of Mr. White, principal teacher at the schoolhouse on Pennsylvania Avenue, west of the President's House, and near Major Sevan's. For the admission of pay pupils, application was made to Mr. White; and for the admission of those whose parents could not afford to pay, application was made to the superintending committee, which at that time consisted of Samuel H. Smith, Nicholas King, and Thomas Munroe.

The school in the eastern part of the city was opened, May 19, 1806, in a commodious brick building owned by Daniel Carroll, north of Stelle's Hotel. The first principal in this school was Rev. Robert Elliott, A. M. Pay pupils applied for admission to Mr. Elliott, while others applied to William. Cranch, William Brent, or John Dempsie, superintending committee.

July 14, 1806, the following gentlemen were elected trustees of the Washington Academy, by the city Council: Thomas Jefferson, William Cranch, Nicholas King, Abraham Bradley, William Brent, Frederick May, and Samuel Hanson. On July 21, the contributors elected the following trustees: Gabriel Duval, Robert Brent, James Davidson, Elias B. Caldwell, James Laurie, and Samuel H. Smith.

In November, 1806, the trustees of the public schools determined to erect two schoolhouses, one in the eastern and one in the western part of the city, and appropriated $2,400 for the purpose. Mr. Elliott taught his school the second year, and engaged an assistant teacher. On October 16, 1807, Hugh Maguire, who is mentioned elsewhere as having just previously established a private school, was engaged as principal of the west side school, in place of Mr. White, who had resigned. Mr. Maguire remained in this position until 1810, at which time the compensation was $400 per year from the children of the poor, and $20 per pupil from each one that paid.

In July, 1810, the trustees of this institution elected by the corporation were Thomas H. Gilliss, Daniel Rapine, E. B. Caldwell, Tunis Craven, Moses Young, John P. Van Ness, and Alexander Kerr. Those elected by the contributors were Samuel H. Smith, James Laurie, Gabriel Duval, Robert Brent, William Cranch, and Joseph Mechlin.

On July 15, 1811, the following trustees were elected: By the contributors, Samuel H. Smith, Gabriel Duval, James Laurie, Thomas H. Gilliss, Joseph Mechlin; and by the corporation, William Cranch, John P. Van Ness, Elias B. Caldwell, Daniel Rapine, Buller Cocke, Moses Young, and Buckner Thruston.

On July 19, 1813, the contributors elected as trustees Gabriel Duval, James Laurie, Elias B. Caldwell, George Blagden, James Davidson, and Joseph Mechlin. On July 28, the Boards of Aldermen and Council having failed to elect trustees, the Mayor appointed the following persons: Samuel N. Smallwood, Alexander McWilliams, Franklin Wharton, Andrew Hunter, William Matthews, Moses Young, and John Haw.

In November, 1813, it was determined to build and endow two public schools in Washington, and to build a penitentiary. To this end a lottery was established, or provided for, by the corporation, and three citizens from each ward appointed managers of the lottery — from the First Ward, John Davidson, Thomas Munroe, and John Hewitt; Second Ward, Washington Boyd, Andrew Way, Jr., and Joseph Gilliss, Jr.; Third Ward, William Brent, John Law, and S. N. Smallwood; Fourth Ward, Buller Cocke, William Brent, and John Dobbyn.

At a meeting of the board of trustees held August 14, 1814, the following officers were elected: President, Rev. James Laurie; vice-president, Thomas H. Gilliss; secretary, John D. Barclay; superintending committee for the Eastern School, George Blagden, Samuel H. Smith, and William Dougherty; and for the Lancasterian School, Rev. William Matthews, Andrew Way, and Moses Young.

August 1, 1815, the Mayor appointed Josiah Meigs, Dr. William Matthews, Benjamin Homans, Moses Young, S. N. Smallwood, George Blagden, and William Prout trustees of the public schools. On the 7th, the board organized as follows: President, Rev. James Laurie;

vice-president, Josiah Meigs; secretary, John D. Barclay; treasurer, Moses Young. The superintending committee of the Western Academy were Benjamin Homans, Rev. James Laurie, and Joseph Mechlin; of the Eastern Academy, William Brent, George Blagden, and William Dougherty; and of the Lancasterian School, Rev. William Matthews, Moses Young, and Andrew Way.

On June 28, 1816, the city was divided into two school districts, the First and Second wards constituting the first district, and the Third and Fourth wards the second. Each district had a separate board of trustees, that of the first consisting of nine members, six of whom were chosen by the joint ballot of the two parts of the city Council, of which number three were taken from the First Ward and three from the Second, and the three remaining members were to be chosen annually by the contributors who had contributed $10 or more toward the support of the schools. The board of trustees of the second district was chosen annually by both parts of the city Council, and consisted of seven members. The contributors elected as trustees Joseph Anderson, James Davidson, and Andrew Way, Jr. The trustees elected by the corporation were Rev. James Laurie, Rev. William Matthews, Josiah Meigs, Benjamin Homans, Joseph Mechlin, and Moses Young.

The Lancasterian School was carried on successfully for four years, when a gale of wind so injured the building that it was considered unsafe. This was in the spring of 1816. The house was then advertised for sale, and then, in consequence of the rapid increase of population in the Second Ward, the superintending committee could find no building at all. The lottery authorized by law, by means of which it was hoped to raise the money necessary to build the Lancasterian schoolhouse, failed to raise the amount, and on this account Mr. Robert Ould was retained at a reduced salary until the schoolhouse should be built; but, in December, 1816, having no hope from the lottery, and not knowing when the corporation would build a schoolhouse, the trustees rented a room on F Street, between Ninth and Tenth, and in that room opened the school on December 17, 1816.

The officials of the public schools elected August 3, 1817, were as follows: President, Rev. James Laurie; vice-president,————————; secretary and treasurer, John D. Barclay. The superintending committee for the Washington Academy were Joseph Anderson, Rev. James Laurie, and Rev. William Hawley; and for the Lancasterian School, Josiah Meigs, Rev. William Matthews, and Thomas H. Gilliss.

A most interesting occasion was that of the visit to this country of Mr. Joseph Lancaster, who delivered a lecture in Congress Hall January 26, 1819.

July 3, 1820, the trustees elected were, for the first district, Josiah Meigs, William Williamson, James Hoban, William Matthews, James H. Handy, John P. Van Ness, and Andrew Coyle; for the second district, Andrew Hunter, Daniel Carroll of Duddington, Charles B. Hamilton, John Crabb, George Watterston, Daniel Rapine, and James Carberry. The board for 1822 was as follows: First district, Thomas Munroe, James H. Handy, William Williamson, C. W. Goldsborough, James Hoban, William Matthews, and George Sweeney; for the second district, Edmund S. Lewis, George Watterston, A. T. McCormick, S. N. Smallwood, M. Wright, Daniel Rapine, and Samuel Miller.

In June, 1826, the following trustees were appointed: First district, Rev. William Matthews, Rev. Robert Little, Rev. David Baker, C. W. Goldsborough, Christ Andrews, John Wells, and George Sweeney; second district, Rev. A. T. McCormick, Rev. Ethan Allen, George Watterston, George Blagden, Daniel Rapine, Edmund S. Lewis, and Timothy Winn.

Robert Ould was still principal of the Lancasterian School, established in 1811, into which there had been received 1,101 pupils; 879 had left, and 222 remained.

June 29, 1827, the trustees elected for the first district were Rev. William Matthews, Daniel Baker, Robert Little, C. W. Goldsborough, John N. Moulder, James Larned, and George Sweeney; for the second district, Rev. A. T. McCormick, Ethan Allen, George Watterston, John Coyle, Jr., William A. Smallwood, Charles B. Hamilton, and G. W. Peter.

June 27, 1828, the trustees of the public schools elected were: For the first district, Rev. William Matthews, Rev. William Hawley, James Larned, George W. Dashiell, John N. Moulder, William G. Elliott, and George Sweeney; for the second district, Rev. A. T. McCormick, George Watterston, G. W. Peter, Charles B. Hamilton, John Coyle, Jr., C. T. Coote, and Edward W. Clarke.

For the public schools, trustees were annually elected until 1837, up to which time the only system of public education recognized in the District of Columbia was that supported in part by the corporation and in part by individual subscriptions. The free schools, of which there were two, were started by the corporation with money derived from lotteries; but so far, the free schools were totally inadequate to the necessities of the youth of the city. There were then about 3,000 white children from five to fifteen years of age, and of these about 1,200 were being educated at private academies, and about 350 only at the public schools. Thus about 1,400 of the children of the ages mentioned were entirely destitute of educational facilities, and if the same ratio were applied to the entire District, it appeared that there were upward of 2,300 children growing up in ignorance within the Ten Miles Square. At the same time, there were many among the poorer classes who would not send their children to the free schools for fear of incurring the stigma of having them educated by public charity. This unreasonable, but natural, feeling could only be removed by some such admirable system as that of the public schools of New England, where the children of the poor men enjoyed the same privileges as the children of the rich, and where there was made no discrimination in the public mind as to the different classes of children attending the public schools. In such a system of education no stigma applied to one that did not apply to all, and hence there was no stigma at all applied to any.

Congress had not appropriated any money for schools in the District of Columbia. This was not attributed, however, to the parsimony of Congress, but to the neglect of the city authorities of Washington, who had never presented the claims of the children of the District to that body of legislators. In fact, the corporate authorities of the city, instead of placing the subject of education among those of first importance, had always treated it as of but minor consequence. They had spent their time upon canals, railroads, banks, and other public institutions, and permitted public education to suffer and almost perish from neglect.

But in the early part of 1837, the trustees of the corporation free schools, by the direction of the Council, appointed a committee to bring the necessities of the District of Columbia to the attention of Congress, and to ask of that body such assistance as would lay the foundation of a general system of education to embrace the entire population of the District of Columbia from five to fifteen years of age. The memorial prepared by this committee was presented to the appropriate committee of the Senate during its session of 1836-37, but, as that session drew to a close with but little prospect of action, it was suggested to the citizens of Georgetown and Alexandria that they appoint committees to make similar demands upon Congress at the beginning of its session of 1837-38, so that measures might be adopted which should apply to the children of the entire District of Columbia, and under which the children of the poorest should enjoy the same educational privileges and advantages as the children of the rich.

On July 3, 1837, trustees of the public schools were elected as follows: First district, Rev. William Matthews, Rev. William Hawley, Lewis H. Machem, James Larned, John D. Barclay, John W. Maury, and William B. Magruder; second district, Rev. A. T. McCormick, John Coyle, Thomas Blagden, Richard Barry, William Speiden, James Marshall, Marmaduke Dove, and James Carberry.

In the first district, for the year 1836-37, J. Laurens Henshaw was the teacher. According to his report, made to the trustees, for the year ending June 28, 1837, there had been admitted to the school, which was still conducted under the act of October, 1808, from its commencement, in February, 1812, 1,488 boys and 675 girls, an aggregate of 2,163 pupils; and at the time of making the report, there were in attendance 207 pupils—186 boys and 21 girls.

In 1839, the question again arose as to why it was that the corporate authorities paid so little attention to the education of girls. In the Western Free Schools they were not admitted at all, in consequence, it was thought, of the immoral tendency of mingling together so great a number of the two sexes, both in and out of school. While this exclusion, for this reason, was considered proper, yet it was not thought proper that no provision should be made for the education of the girls.

July 1, 1841, J. Laurens Henshaw made his report of the condition of the schools in the first district, consisting of the First and Second wards. There had been in attendance two hundred and sixty-nine pupils in school during the year.

The condition of education in Washington in February, 1842, is shown by the following statistics: The number of public schools was 2, and of private schools 19. The number of white persons under twenty years of age was 9,000; the number between five and fifteen years of age, 4,488; and it was estimated that the number between four and sixteen years of age was 4,900. The estimated number under four and above sixteen, of school age, was 500; so that the total school population of the city was 5,400. From official sources it was learned that the number in actual attendance at school was 989, leaving the large number of 4,411 that did not attend school at all. The cost of educating the 989 that did attend was estimated to be as high as $35,000, and some thought it was considerably higher; and it was believed that by means of a thorough system of public schools all the children in the city might be educated for a less sum.

Such considerations as the above led the committee on public schools to submit to the Boards of Aldermen and Common Council, a report in relation to the establishment and support of common and high schools in the city of Washington. This report was submitted November 7, 1842. The annual message of the Mayor had discussed the subject of education, and the committee said: "Provision should be made for the education of the entire youth of the community at the public expense and at the earliest possible period. At present, no systematic or efficient plan exists," etc. The cost of educating the one thousand two hundred children, or thereabouts, that attended school, including the cost of books, stationery, etc., fell but little, if any, short of $40,000 per year. One-half of that amount judiciously expended, so it was thought, would give equal if not better instruction to the school population of the city. The committee therefore suggested the establishment of a number of schools sufficient to meet the wants of the people, by the imposition of a tax upon the assessable property of the city.

The committee, at that time, had in contemplation the establishment of a high school in connection with the proposed system of common schools, admitting to the high school those who proved most proficient in scholarship in the common schools. Their proposition was to erect seven schoolhouses, and to appropriate $15,000 with which to pay the teachers and to purchase the necessary books, stationery, etc. Their report was quite long, and very able and comprehensive. The committee consisted of James F. Haliday, C. A. Davis, John T. Towers, John A. Lynch, John E. Neale, and E. W. Clarke.

But in Washington, as in all other parts of this country, when it was proposed to establish schools in which the children of the poor should be educated at the expense of the rich, there were those who could not be convinced of the justice of the system by even the most forcible and logical reasoning. And here, as elsewhere, the objection was raised, that under this plan the poor would be taxed to educate the children of the rich! This was, of course, a great perversion of reasoning faculties, and a great misapprehension of the purposes and plans of the committee.

On January 16, 1843, the Board of Aldermen convened to listen to a report from the committee appointed to take into consideration the advantages to be derived from the establishment of common and high schools in the city. The report was not long, but it is not deemed necessary to present it in full in this connection; it is therefore summarized, as follows: The corporate authorities of the city of Washington have the necessary power to establish such a system of schools, granted to them in the charter in the following words:

"The corporation shall have full power and authority to lay and collect taxes upon the real and personal property within the said city, provided that no tax shall be laid upon real property at a higher rate than three-fourths of one per centum on the assessed value thereof, except for the special purpose hereafter provided"; and "the said corporation shall also have power and authority to provide for the establishment and superintendence of public schools, and to endow the same; and to lay and collect taxes for the expense thereof."

But, notwithstanding the fact, as the committee reported it, that the corporation had sufficient authority to establish such schools, it yet thought that it would be inexpedient to exercise the power at that time, for the reason that when the rate of taxation was increased to pay the interest on the Holland loan, the result was to check and almost to prevent the making of improvements in the city. "The noise of the busy workman, so cheering to the friends of the city, was rarely heard." "When, however, through the kind liberality of Congress, the load of debt under which we were struggling was partly removed and the taxes restored to the original rate, the city, rousing from its lethargy, has increased and prospered at a ratio which, under all circumstances, has rarely been exceeded by any city east of the mountains. Shall we again, by an increased imposition of taxes upon real and personal property, the very means by which our city is extended and improved, check those improvements, and again have to lament the stagnation of mechanical and other business, and the cessation of our present prosperity? We are sure that the voice of the people will answer, No!" etc. The committee was therefore opposed to imposing a tax upon real and personal property at that time. They were also opposed to taxing certificates of stock and also to asking aid from Congress. They then recommended the indefinite postponement of the petition. Their report was adopted by a vote of yeas, 9, to nays, 2.

On July 24, 1843, the Mayor, W. W. Seaton, submitted to the Boards of Aldermen and Common Council some statistics with reference to the schools. The teacher of the Western Free Schools reported the attendance, during the year then closing, of 336 pupils, an increase of 134 over the previous year. The teacher of the Eastern Free School reported 174 scholars in attendance. The two female charity schools, to which the corporation had for some years contributed pecuniary aid, continued to flourish, and to do honor to the benevolent ladies by whom they were instituted. The report of the managers of the Central Schools showed that the number of pupils registered was 80, and the attendance 60. The Capitol Hill school had 85 registered pupils.

Mr. Seaton then said that he regretted the postponement of the adoption of the public-school system. "Anxious as I was to see introduced the wise and admirable system of the North, by which education is amply placed within the reach of the poor and rich alike, the diversity of views which the scheme has encountered, and the doubts which are found to exist in regard either to the power of imposing taxes for its support, or the expediency of imposing them, must, I fear, forbid for the present the hope for its adoption."

Notwithstanding the adverse action of the Council, the Mayor recommended the establishment of an additional public school. The income from the school fund was then $3,000, and the two schools then in operation cost the city but $1,800 per year, leaving a surplus of $1,200, which might be devoted to the support of a third school. Yet the Councils did not take immediate action on the Mayor's recommendation.

There were members in the Council quite as anxious as was the Mayor for a system of public education. On October 2, 1844, Ignatius Mudd introduced a bill into the Common Council entitled, "An Act to Increase the Number of Public Schools," which was read twice, and referred to the committee on public schools by a vote of 13 to 5. At length, on December 6, 1844, an ordinance was adopted by the corporate authorities to increase the number of public schools in the city of Washington and for other purposes. By this act the city was divided into four public-school districts, as follows: The first district was composed of the First Ward and that part of the Second Ward north of the canal; the second district consisted of all that part of the Third Ward north of the canal; the third district consisted of the Fourth and Sixth wards and that part of the Fifth Ward east of the canal, and the fourth district, the rest of the city.

This act provided for the election by the Boards of Aldermen and Common Council of a board of school trustees of three persons from each school district, who, together with the Mayor of the city, should have the management of the schools of the city. The Mayor was authorized to have erected a good and substantial schoolhouse on that portion of Judiciary Square granted by the President of the United States for that purpose, for the second district; and he was required to secure ground and have erected thereon a good schoolhouse for the fourth district. The cost of the schoolhouse in the second district was not to exceed $2,000, and that of the house in the fourth district was not to exceed $1,800. There was appointed one male teacher for each of the schools, who was the principal thereof, and who had charge of the school. All white children between the ages of six and sixteen years were admitted to the schools under this act, at a tuition not to exceed fifty cents per month, to be paid in advance.

On December 16, 1844, the trustees elected under this act were as follows: First district, Robert Farnham, George J. Abbott, and John F. Hartley; for the second district, Peter Force, Thomas Donoho, and John C. McKelden; third district, John P. Ingle, Noble Young, and William M. Ellis; fourth district, Isaac S. Miller, Ignatius Mudd, and Thomas Blagden.

February 28, 1845, an act was passed by the corporation, appropriating $475 to procure a lot and to cause to be erected thereon a good and substantial schoolhouse for the fourth district, sufficient to accommodate not less than one hundred and fifty pupils. On April 7, Dr. T. Watkins was elected teacher in the second district, and Henry Hardy in the fourth.

In the summer of 1848, the pay feature of the public-school system was abolished, and it was hoped that all the dissatisfaction which had existed under the old system would disappear, and that in a short time all classes would be united in the support of the public schools.

November 22, 1850, the corporation established four male primary schools, to which females were not, under any circumstances, admitted, either as pupils or teachers. For the support of these four schools the following appropriations were made: For compensation to teachers, $1,637.50; for books, maps, and stationery, $100; for fuel, $60; for furniture and desks, $280; for rent of schoolrooms, $180; for contingent expenses, $45; total, $2,302 50.

By 1851 the public schools of the city were placed in a flourishing condition, and great interest was taken in their success by the people. Prizes and diplomas were given to meritorious pupils. August 16, 1851, Dr. Tobias Watkins, who had been principal of the Second District School ever since the establishment of the system, declined a renomination for the position, and was succeeded by T. M. Wilson. The expenses of the public schools for 1850 were $11,519.14, and for 1851 $12,935.92. Under the law of November 22, 1850, mentioned above, four new primary schools were established at the beginning of the following year, making the total number in active operation 23 — 19 primary and 4 district schools. There were 33 teachers — 23 males and 10 females. The number of pupils admitted through the year was 3,317, and the average attendance for the year ending June 30, 1851, was 1,755. In 1854, there were 36 teachers, at an aggregate annual salary of $12,400. The highest salary paid at that time was $800 per annum. The lowest was $200. All white children between the ages of six and sixteen were admitted to the schools. The act under which the schools were then operated imposed a tax of $1 upon all white male citizens of twenty-one years of age and upward. In September, 1854, there were still four school districts in the city. In the first district there were 10 teachers; in the second, 10; in the third, 11, and in the fourth, 6. The principals in the districts were as follows: First district, S. Kelly; second district, Thomas M. Wilson; third district, John Fell; fourth district, J. E. Thompson. There was as yet no superintendent of the public schools, nor any high school. The total expenses of the schools for the year were $17,633.88. The number of pupils on the roll was, in the first district, 552; second, 504; third, 631, and fourth, 378; total in the four districts, 2,065.

From 1854 to 1861, much improved school furniture was introduced, the municipal authorities coöperating with school trustees in extending facilities for instruction.

An attempt was made in 1857 to establish the office of superintendent of public instruction, but the measure was vetoed by the Mayor. The total appropriations for this period were $257,721.74.

The period from 1862 to 1866 begins to mark the development of the school system. Thirty schools of different grades were authorized. The Wallach schoolhouse, the pioneer of the present excellent public-school buildings, was erected at an expense of some $30,000. It was pointed at by many at the time as "Wallach's folly"; but time has vindicated the wisdom of its erection. Steps were taken also for the erection of the Franklin building. The aggregate expenditures for this period were $390,727.10. The gross appropriations for school purposes within the District from 1805 to 1866, a period of sixty-one years, were $918,090.89.

September 1, 1862, an act was passed by the city Councils grading the public schools and fixing the salaries of the teachers. This act provided that the schools should be known as primary, secondary, intermediate, and grammar schools. There were then four school districts, each of which was divided into male and female grammar schools, male and female intermediate schools; and there were as many secondary and primary schools as were necessary. The preceptors of the male grammar schools received under this act $1,200 per annum; of the female grammar schools, $550 per annum; the

32

teachers of the male intermediate schools, $500 per annum; and of the female intermediate schools, $450 per annum. Other teachers received smaller salaries.

When the schools opened in the fall of 1864, there were 8 grammar schools, 8 intermediate schools, 27 secondary schools, and 20 primary schools; total number of schools, 63; capacity of the buildings, 3,780.

A new public-school building was erected in 1869 on Four and a Half Street in South Washington, between M and N streets. It was two stories high, thirty-two by seventy-two feet in size, and cost $6,500. It contained four schoolrooms, each thirty feet square in the clear.

In 1870, the statistics for the public schools were as follows: There were 131 schools authorized by law, and there were established 117. The four districts had the following numbers of scholars: District No. 1, 1,271; No. 2, 1,430; No. 3, 1,554; and the fourth, 1,156; total, 5,411. Of the teachers then employed, J. E. Thompson was first appointed in December, 1847; Mrs. M. E. Rodier, in 1849, as was also Miss Moss; Miss Emily Billings, in 1850; and Mrs. Emily Myers, in 1852. In the four districts the lots upon which the public schoolhouses stood were valued at $94,864, and the buildings at $319,000. The furniture, apparatus, etc., in the four districts were valued at $40,115; total value of school property, $453,979.

The period from 1867 to 1876 was marked by some new departures in school administration. The office of public superintendent was created in September, 1869. In 1873 a normal school was established, and Miss Lucilla E. Smith was chosen the first principal.

In 1871, the municipal government was changed and placed under the control of a Territorial governor and legislative assembly. It continued until 1874, when the present triumvirate commission was established. The aggregate expenditures on schools during this period (1867 to 1876) were $2,404,000.

The superintendency of the city schools has been confined to but few men. The first was Zalmon Richards. He was succeeded, after many years' service, by Professor J. Ormond Wilson, who held this position for some fourteen years, to be followed by the present incumbent, Professor W. B. Powell, from Illinois.

The colored schools have likewise a superintendent, Professor G. T. Cook, who is equally responsible with Superintendent Powell for the management of the schools of his race.

The following table, showing list of public-school buildings owned and occupied, has not only statistical but historical interest:

PUBLIC SCHOOL BUILDINGS OF THE CITY OF WASHINGTON.

HISTORICAL TABLE.

Name.	Location.	Description of Building.	Heated.	Erected.	No. of Rooms.	Value of Site.	Value of Building.	Total.
High School	O St., bet. 6th and 7th	Brick, 198x75, 3 stories and basement	Steam	1883	38	$75,000	$118,078	$193,078
Abbott School	Cor. New York Ave. and 6th St	Brick, 103x42, 3 stories and basement	Furnace	1876	9	5,158	20,000	25,158
Amidon	Cor. 6th and F sts., S. W	Brick, 81x69, 2 stories and basement	Furnace	1882	8	5,949	18,232	24,181
Anacostia	9th St. and Virginia Ave., S. E.	Brick, 38x24, 2 stories	Stoves	1840	2		2,000	2,000
Grant	G St., bet. 21st and 22d sts., N. W	Brick, 92x88, 3 stories and basement	Steam	1882	12	8,000	40,428	48,428
Bowen	Cor. 9th and E sts., S. W	Brick, 88x45, 2 stories	Stoves	1867	8	1,672	5,000	6,672
Banneker	3d St., bet. K and L sts., N. W	Brick, 81x69, 2 stories and basement	Furnace	1882	8	3,500	20,000	23,500
Brent	Cor. 3d and D sts., S. E	Brick, 81x69, 2 stories and basement	Furnace	1883	8	2,135	22,065	24,200
Chamberlin	East St., Georgetown	Frame, 88x40	Stoves		12	169	1,000	1,169
Cranch	Cor. 12th and G sts., S. E	Brick, 79x36, 3 stories and basement	Steam	1872	6	622	16,000	16,622
Curtis	2d St., bet. High and Newmarket sts., Georgetown	Brick, 97x79, 3 stories and basement	Steam	1875	8	1,908	60,000	61,908
Force	Massachusetts Ave., bet. 17th and 18th sts., N. W	Brick, 90x73, 3 stories and basement	Steam	1879	12		36,215	36,215
Franklin	Cor. 13th and K sts., N. W	Brick, 148x79, 3 stories and basement	Steam	1869	16	17,564	188,000	205,564
Gales	Cor. 1st St. and Massachusetts Ave., N. W	Brick, 90x66, 3 stories and basement	Steam	1881	12	10,000	40,116	50,116
Garnott	Cor. 10th and M sts., N. W	Brick, 90x73, 3 stories and basement	Steam	1880	12	7,120	35,000	42,120
Greenleaf	4½ st., bet. M and N sts., S. W	Brick, 72x32, 2 stories	Stoves	1869	4	1,500	8,000	9,500
Henry	P St., bet. 6th and 7th sts., N. W	Brick, 89x73, 3 stories and basement	Steam	1880	12	25,000	45,000	70,000
Jefferson	Cor. 6th and D sts., N. W	Brick, 172x88, 3 stories and basement	Steam	1872	20	18,896	50,000	68,896
John F. Cook	O St., bet. 4th and 5th sts., N. W	Brick, 96x58, 3 stories	Furnace	1868	11	2,160	18,000	20,160

HISTORICAL TABLE—CONTINUED.

Name	Location	Description of Building.	Heated.	Erected.	No. of Rooms.	Value of Site.	Value of Buildings.	Total.
Lincoln	Cor. 2d and C sts., S. E.	Brick, 75x68, 3 stories and basement	Steam	1871	10	3,460	20,000	23,460
Lovejoy	Cor. 12th and D sts., N. E.	Brick, 60x35, 2 stories and basement	Stoves	1872	6		10,000	10,000
McCormick	3d St., bet. M and N sts., S. E.	Brick, 55x45, 2 stories and basement	Furnace	1870	4	407	7,000	7,407
Morse	R St., bet. New Jersey Ave. and 5th St.	Brick, 81x60, 2 stories and basement	Furnace	1883	8	4,578	23,670	28,248
Peabody	Cor. 5th and C sts., N. E.	Brick, 90x90, 3 stories and basement	Steam	1879	12	2,500	38,150	40,650
Potomac	12th St., bet. Maryland Ave. and E St.	Brick, 72x32, 2 stories	Stoves	1870	4	584	4,500	5,084
Randall	Cor. 1st and I sts., S. W.	Brick, 90x72, 3 stories	Furnace	1876	10	727	40,000	40,727
Seaton	I St., bet. 2d and 3d sts., N. W.	Brick, 94x67, 3 stories and basement	Steam	1871	11	11,325	35,000	46,325
Stevens	21st St., bet. K and L sts., N. W.	Brick, 88x48, 3 stories and basement	Steam	1868	10	4,944	15,000	19,944
Summer	Cor. 17th and M sts	Brick, 94x69, 3 stories and basement	Steam	1871	11	18,875	70,000	88,875
Thompson	12th St., bet. K and L sts., N. W.	Brick, 91x28, 3 stories and basement	Furnace	1877	6	2,906	8,000	10,906
Twining	3d St., bet. N and O sts., N. W.	Brick, 81x69, 2 stories and basement	Furnace	1883	10	4,681	24,070	28,751
Wallach	Pennsylvania Ave., bet. 7th and 8th sts., S. E.	Brick, 99x76, 3 stories and basement	Steam	1864	12	14,517	40,000	54,517
Webster	Cor. 10th and H sts., N. W.	Brick, 107x164, 3 stories and basement	Steam	1881	12	15,000	41,053	56,053
Odd Fellows' Hall	Cor. 7th and G sts., S. E.	Brick, 40x22, 2 stories	Stoves	1840	2	433	1,200	1,633
Odd Fellows' Hall	Cor. High and Market sts., Georgetown	Frame, 58x30, 2 stories and basement	Stoves		2	584	3,000	3,584
Threlkeld	Cor. Prospect and Lingan aves	Brick, 75x29, 2 stories and basement	Stoves		4	670	5,000	5,670
Dennison	S St., bet. 13th and 14th sts	Brick, 92x89, 3 stories and basement	Steam	1884	12	11,627	45,181	56,808
Blair	I St., bet. 6th and 7th sts., N. B.	Brick, 70x84, 2 stories and basement	Furnace	1884	8	3,500	22,071	25,571
Wormley	Prospect Ave., bet. 33d and 34th sts	Brick, 70x84, 2 stories and basement	Furnace	1884	8	3,750	23,495	27,245
Addison	P St., bet. 32d and 33d sts., N. W.	Brick, 54x98, 2 stories and basement	Furnace	1885	8		29,313	29,313
Maury	B St., bet. 12th and 13th sts	Brick, 70x84, 2 stories and basement	Furnace	1886	8	3,382	25,598	29,180
Weightman	Cor. 23d and M sts., N. W.	Brick, 76x83, 2 stories and basement	Furnace	1886	8	13,574	29,234	42,808

Name	Location	Construction	Heating	Year	Rooms			
Towers	Cor. 8th and C sts., S. E.	Brick, 56x104, 2 stories and basement	Furnace	1887	8		24,999	24,999
Magruder	M St., bet. 16th and 17th sts.	Brick, 56x104, 2 stories and basement	Furnace	1887	8		25,973	25,973
Carberry	5th St., bet. D and E sts., S. E.	Brick, 70x84, 2 stories and basement	Furnace	1887	8	6,456	29,980	36,436
Phelps	Vermont Ave., bet. T and U sts.	Brick, 70x84, 2 stories and basement	Furnace	1887	8	10,466	24,521	34,987
Giddings	G St., bet. 3d and 4th sts.	Brick, 70x84, 2 stories and basement	Furnace	1887	8	7,188	24,952	32,140
Blake	North Capitol, bet. K and L sts.	Brick, 70x84, 2 stories and basement	Furnace	1887	8	9,985	24,973	34,958
Bradley	13½ St., bet. C and D sts.	Brick, 70x84, 2 stories and basement	Furnace	1857	8	5,000	24,992	29,992
Smallwood	I St., bet. 3d and 4½ sts., S. W.	Brick, 70x83	Furnace	1888	8	8,519	26,652	35,171
Adams	R St., bet. 17th St. and New Hampshire Ave., N. W.	Brick, 70x83	Furnace		8	16,322	26,652	42,974
Jones	Cor. 1st and L sts., N. W.	Brick, 67x83	Furnace		8	10,500	25,396	35,896
Arthur	Arthur Place, N. W.	Brick, 67x83	Furnace		8	10,605	27,652	38,257
Corcoran	28th St., near M St., N. W.	Brick, 68x82	Furnace		8	7,100	25,952	33,052
Briggs	Cor. 22d and E sts., N. W.	Brick, 67x83	Furnace		8	8,500	24,619	33,119
Lenox	5th St., bet. G St. and Virginia Ave., S. E.	Brick, 70x83	Furnace		8	4,000	25,135	29,135
Berret	Cor. 14th and Q sts., N. W.	Brick, 50x100, 3 stories and basement	Furnace		9	15,000	25,049	40,049
Bell	1st St., bet. B and C sts., S. W.	Brick, 67x83, 2 stories and basement	Furnace		8	9,536	25,609	35,145
Madison	Cor. 10th and G sts., N. E.	Brick, 70x84, 2 stories and basement	Furnace	1889	8	6,468	25,644	32,112
Jackson	Road St., bet. 30th and 31st sts.	Brick, 70x84, 2 stories and basement	Furnace	1889	8	10,000	28,031	38,031
Ganison	12th St., bet. R and S sts., N. W.	Brick, 70x84, 2 stories and basement	Furnace	1889	8	8,250	24,540	32,790
Ambush	L St., bet 6th and 7th sts., S. W.	Brick, 70x84, 2 stories and basement	Furnace	1889	8	11,750	23,885	35,635
Harrison	13th St., near V St., N. W.	Brick, 75x101, 2 stories and basement	Furnace	1890	8	17,644	27,796	45,440
Tyler	11th St., near G St., S. E.	Brick, 70x84, 2 stories and basement	Furnace	1890	8	8,691	25,972	34,663
Phillips	N St., near 28th St., N. W.	Brick, 70x84, 2 stories and basement	Furnace	1890	8	11,400	26,066	37,466
Slater	P St., near North Capitol, N. W.	Brick, 70x84, 2 stories and basement	Furnace	1890	8	11,000	26,067	37,067
High School (Colored)	M St., bet. New Jersey Ave. and 1st St., N. W.	Brick, 80x147, 3 stories and basement	Steam	1890	24	24,592	82,317	106,909
Wilson	Meridian Hill (Mount Pleasant)	Brick, 70x84, 3 stories and basement	Furnace	1891	8	9,000	25,537	34,557
Taylor	Cor. 7th and G sts., N. E.	Brick, 70x84	Furnace	1891	8			
Logan	Cor. 3d and G sts., N. E.	Brick, 55x101, 2 stories and basement	Furnace	1891	8	8,436	26,514	35,000
Eastern High School	7th St., bet. C St. and Pennsylvania Ave., S. E.	Brick, 80x147, 3 stories and basement	Steam	1891	20			75,000

The report of the city schools for the school year ending June 30, 1891, contains some statistics which show progress in the development of popular education. They are significant, when compared with the facts given in the preceding portion of this chapter.

The first table shows the enrollment of pupils, with the per cent. of increase, from 1880 to 1891, inclusive.

Year.	Enrolled.	Per Ct.	Year.	Enrolled.	Per Ct.	Year.	Enrolled.	Per Ct.
1880	21,600	....	1884	23,867	1.11	1888	28,553	2.95
1881	22,061	2.13	1885	25,157	5.40	1889	29,565	3.54
1882	22,826	3.46	1886	26,911	6.97	1890	30,366	2.70
1883	23,594	3.36	1887	27,733	3.05	1891	31,301	3.07

During the school year closing June 30, 1891, the following exhibit was made:

SCHOOL.	TOTAL ENROLLMENT.			TEACHERS EMPLOYED.		
	WHITE.	COLORED.	TOTAL.	WHITE.	COLORED.	TOTAL.
Normal..	45	26	71	....	....	....
High..........	1,659	376	2,035	....	....	....
Grammar & Primary	22,525	13,745	36,270	....	....	....
Total..............	24,229	14,147	38,376	530	265	795

The aggregate expenses for all causes during the year were: For day schools, $683,120.33; night schools, $6,468.85; total, $689,589.18. Compared with the expenditures prior to the War, these figures are quite startling, and show that the schools are firmly planted in public confidence.

Georgetown was incorporated as a city in November, 1789. No trace of legislation touching public schools is found prior to December, 1842, when the system was established. Prior to 1810, educational opportunities were confined to private schools. About the close of the year 1810, the "Lancasterian School Society" was organized. Under its protection a school was opened, November 18, 1811, by Robert Ould, a pupil of Joseph Lancaster, the founder of the system.

This school was maintained by private aid until 1815, when the Georgetown corporation appropriated $1,000 for its support, and continued that appropriation annually until 1842, when the school was suspended. Subsequent to this time, the primary education of the place was taken charge of by the board of guardians, and schools became practically *free to all.*

In August, 1844, the city authorities authorized the guardians to receive donations for the support of the schools. Four years later, the guardians were directed to charge, not exceeding $1 per month, all pupils whose parents were considered able to pay tuition.

In August, 1849, the board of guardians were authorized to purchase a church edifice, on Montgomery Street, for school purposes, and to issue bonds in the sum of $1,200 for its payment. The sum of $800 was also appropriated to refit the property. Appropriations ranging from $1,500 to $2,500 were made annually to support the schools, and this arrangement continued until 1857, when the Washington plan of assessing $1 upon each free white male resident twenty-one years of age and upwards was adopted. In 1859, the city made the requisite appropriation to build a commodious house on High Street, at an expense of $4,500. In April of the next year, application was again made to Congress for an appropriation for educational purposes, but in vain.

Georgetown College, located on the Potomac, within the District of Columbia, is the oldest Catholic and one of the first American institutions of learning. The germ of the college may be traced to a promise, made about 1640, almost contemporaneous with the founding of Harvard University, by the English provincial of the Jesuits to Father Ferdinand Poulton, who was sent from England, in 1638, as superior of the Maryland missions. One of Poulton's darling schemes, on coming to America, was the establishment of a seat of learning in Maryland; and it is asserted by those versed in the origin of the institution, that his purpose was to locate it at or near the present site of the city of Washington. Accordingly, he wrote to the English provincial to obtain sanction, and received, in reply, this assurance: "The hope of establishing the college which you hold forth, I embrace with pleasure, and shall not delay my sanction to the plan when it shall have reached maturity."

This plan, in its gradual unfolding, included work done by migratory academies near Calverton Manor, on the Wicomico River; at Newton Manor, and at other places. In these peripatetic institutions, driven hither and thither by frenzied persecution, were developed both the men and the principles which should ultimately guide the cherished enterprise to success. One of these men, John Carroll, was specially trained for his work. He became the first Archbishop of Baltimore. The cherished "maturity" had finally arrived. Accordingly, with a zeal nursed in the thorough appreciation of the necessity for scholastic training, Father Carroll began to move toward the establishment of a place of higher education.

At a meeting of the clergy, held at Whitemarsh, November 13, 1786, Dr. Carroll laid before that body a plan for the establishment of an academy, and recommended the site finally selected.

The following year, a committee, of which Dr. Carroll seems to have had large control, agreed with William Deakins, Jr., and John Threlkeld for a tract enclosing about an acre and a half, the price being seventy-five pounds.

Much difficulty was experienced in securing a building. It was a three-story brick structure, fifty by sixty-three feet, capable of accommodating all the students likely to enter its walls. In a letter to his friend Plowden, under date of February 24, 1790, Dr. Carroll said: "I am greatly obliged to you for your anxiety about our proposed academy, as well as for your generous intentions respecting it. I think we shall get enough of it completed this summer to make a beginning of teaching; but our great difficulty will be to get a proper president—a superintendent. The fate of the school will depend much on the first impression made upon the public, and a president of known ability and reputation would contribute greatly to render that impression a very favorable one."

As a result of his earnest desire, Bishop Carroll finally succeeded in securing Rev. Robert Plunkett, a man of great piety, learning, and experience, to preside over the new institution. It opened its doors for students in September, 1791. The first pupil to matriculate was William Gaston, of North Carolina. He was a young man of great brilliance, and became an orator of remarkable power. He was a compeer, in Congress, of such men as Webster, Calhoun, and Clay, the latter of whom, it is alleged, he once vanquished in debate. Rev. Plunkett remained in charge of the institution but two years, 1791-93, and then resigned, to enter the missionary work of the Church. His labors, however, were sufficient to impart an educational impulse to the academy, and established it in the confidence of the people.

Rev. Plunkett was succeeded in the presidency by Rev. Robert Molyneux, June 14, 1793. Shortly after his installation, preparations began to be made for the enlargement of facilities. A rectangular lot north of the other tract, and containing about two· acres, was purchased of John Threlkeld for £97 5s. In 1795, a new building, with a frontage of one hundred and fifty-four feet and an elevation of three stories on one side and four on the other, was erected, adding to the facilities and patronage of the school.

It will not be within the scope of this work to follow this institution through all the changes and trials which have characterized its development. That has been faithfully done in a large memorial volume, giving a history of its first century's growth, to which the reader is referred. It is proper, however, to note that on the 27th of January, 1815, William Gaston, a former student, but then an active member of Congress, introduced into the House a resolution which greatly increased its scope, by empowering it to confer the usual college degrees. The bill was approved by President Madison, March 1.

Prior to this date, the college was under the charge of the incorporated clergy of the State of Maryland. Gentlemen under twelve years of age paid $200 per year, and those over twelve paid $220 per year, except in cases where the student in theology, having extraordinary expenses, had indulgences allowed him, and paid $250 per year. The students were taught English, Latin, Greek, all the branches of a classical education, sacred and profane history, geography, the use of globes, arithmetic, algebra, and geometry, and all other portions of mathematics. The greatest care was taken to teach the students the duties of religion and morals, and they were constantly under the eye of some of the professors. While the institution was a Catholic one, yet students of any faith, or of no faith, were admitted; and about this time (1815), the course of study was enlarged to include German, French, and Spanish, rhetoric, *belles-lettres*, the fine arts, and divinity.

In 1831 was begun, under the administration of Rev. Thomas F. Mulledy, S. J., the erection of a large building for chapel, refectory, study hall, and rooms for students. Mrs. Decatur, widow of a distinguished naval officer, aided by the loan of $7,000 for that purpose.

In 1851, initial steps were taken to enlarge the sphere of the institution by adding a medical department. Dr. Joshua A. Ritchie, a graduate of the class of 1835, was the moving spirit. The organization began with a full faculty, on the 1st of May, 1851. Improvised rooms had to be secured for this new department; finally, in 1882, a new building was erected on H Street, between Ninth and Tenth streets, the old quarters on the corner of Tenth and E streets proving insufficient.

The law department was established in 1870, its regular courses beginning in October of that year. Its organization consisted of Rev. John Early, president; Judge Charles P. James, vice-president; Charles W. Hoffman, secretary and treasurer, and a full corps of professors. The new structure erected in 1891 is a fine one, on E Street between Fifth and Sixth streets.

On the 12th of December, 1877, the first stone of a new college structure was laid, and by the next December the roof was placed on the completed north pavilion. During the next two years, other important additions were made to the structure.

During the first century of its active existence, Georgetown College has been presided over by some of the ablest men within the ranks of the Church of which it has been the pioneer institution of learning. The following is the list:

Rev. Robert Plunkett, 1791-93; Rev. Robert Molyneux, 1793-96; Rev. William L. Du Bourg, 1796-99; Rt. Rev. Leonard Neale, D. D., 1799-1806; Rev. Robert Molyneux, S. J., 1806-08; V. Rev. William Matthews, 1808-10; Rev. Francis Neale, S, J., 1810-12; Rev. John Grassi, S. J., 1812-17; Rev. Benedict J. Fenwick, S. J., 1817-18; Rev. Anthony Kohlmann, S. J., 1818-20; Rev. Enoch Fenwick, S. J., 1820-22; Rev. Benedict J. Fenwick, S. J., 1822-25; Rev. Stephen L Dubisson, S. J., 1825-26; Rev. William Feiner, S. J., 1826-29; Rev. William Beschter, S. J., 1829; Rev. Thomas F. Mulledy, S. J., 1829-37; Rev. William McSherry, S. J., 1837-40; Rev. Joseph A. Lopez, 1840; Rev. James Ryder, S. J., 1840-45; Rev. Samuel A. Mulledy, S. J., 1845; Rev. Thomas F. Mulledy, S. J., 1845-48; Rev. James Ryder, S. J., 1848-51; Rev. Charles H. Stonestreet, S. J., 1851-52; Rev. Bernard A. Maguire, S. J., 1852-58; Rev. John Early, S. J., 1858-65; ·Rev. Bernard A. Maguire, S. J., 1866-70; Rev. John Early, S. J., 1870-73; Rev. Patrick F. Healy, S. J., 1873-82; Rev. James A. Doonan, S. J., 1882-88; Rev. Joseph Havens Richards, S. J., 1888-—.

The institution is in a prosperous condition, its various departments having a liberal patronage.

The Columbian College was incorporated by an act of Congress in February, 1821. The movement resulting in this incorporation was started early in 1817, by a returned missionary from India, Rev. Luther Rice, who conceived the idea of founding such a college in Washington, for the education of ministers of the Gospel in the special service of the Baptist denomination of Christians. Around this college, he projected schools of philosophical, scientific, and classical culture, which were to be national in their aims and nonsectarian in their discipline.

A "Literary Association," formed of Rev. Mr. Rice, Rev. Obadiah B. Brown, Rev. Spencer H. Cone, and Enoch Reynolds, purchased a piece of ground containing forty-six and one-half acres adjoining the city of Washington, paying therefor $7,000. This was in 1819. Among the contributors to this sum were John Quincy Adams, William H. Crawford, and John C. Calhoun, members of President Monroe's Cabinet, together with thirty-two members of Congress and many of the citizens of Washington. The trustees named in the act of incorporation were Obadiah B. Brown, Luther Rice, Enoch Reynolds, Josiah Meigs, Spencer H. Cone, Daniel Brown, Return J. Meigs, Jr., Joseph Gibson, Joseph Cone, Thomas Corcoran, Burgiss Allison, Thomas Sewall, and Joseph Thaw. The first meeting of this board of trustees was held March 5, 1821, and on the 6th Rev. Obadiah B. Brown was elected president of the board, Enoch Reynolds secretary, and Luther Rice treasurer.

The erection of a college edifice had been commenced in 1820, and it was completed in 1822, at a cost of $35,000. This building was one hundred and seventeen feet by forty-six feet in size, and four stories high. There were also erected a Philosophical Hall, and two dwelling houses for the professors. Rev. William Staughton, D. D., a native of England, and an eminent pulpit orator, was the first president of the institution. The first circular of the college was issued June 27, 1821; the theological department opened on September 5, 1821, and the classical department on January 9, 1822. For admission to the freshman class, it was necessary to be able to write Latin correctly, and to read with facility Cæsar's Commentaries, Virgil, Sallust, Cicero's Select Orations, the Greek of the New Testament, and the *Græca Minora*, and to have an acquaintance with common arithmetic, English grammar, and the elements of geography.

The expenses of those who only attended the preparatory school during the day were less than $50 per annum; while of those who boarded in the institution, the expenses were $2.65 per week for board, lights, fuel, and incidentals; for library, room rent, and furniture, $20 per annum. Tuition in the college classes was $50 per annum, and in the preparatory school, $32 per annum.

As early as November 15, 1821, the project of establishing a school of medicine was discussed, and but a short period afterward it was decided that a law school should be instituted "at no distant day."

The following year, Luther Rice agitated the founding of a philosophical department, and the scheme was practically adopted in 1823, a circular being addressed by the college authorities to military and naval authorities in the United States to secure their coöperation in collecting illustrative material for the institution. From these indications it will be seen that the institution was rapidly assuming the scope and character of a university.

The first college commencement occurred on the 15th of December, 1824, its exercises being witnessed by the President of the United States, certain members of the Cabinet, prominent members of Congress, and General Lafayette.

The opening of the college was auspicious. The attendance was quite good; but the heavy expense attending the erection and equipment of buildings and the paying of salaries had the effect, in the face of small tuition receipts and the absence of an endowment fund, to produce a financial panic. The crash came in 1827, when the faculty resigned, and threw a pall over the enterprise. The following year the doors were reopened, and the institution entered upon a more prosperous career. Like other institutions of a similar character, the college had to struggle for existence and growth. The sacrifices of trustees, presidents, and professors ultimately prevailed, and guaranteed a more prosperous future.

Dr. Staughton resigned the presidency of the college in 1827, and was succeeded, in 1828, by Rev. Stephen Chapin, D. D., who held the position until he resigned, in 1841. During his administration, the college was freed from the distrust and debt which encumbered it when his career began.

In 1843, Rev. Joel S. Bacon, D. D., the third president, began the establishment of an endowment fund, which has been accumulating ever since. Among the early contributors to the fund of the college were John Quincy Adams, who at one time loaned it $18,000, and subsequently remitted a part of the sum; and John Withers, of Virginia, who, between 1835 and 1861, made gifts for various purposes to the amount of $70,000. In 1865, William W. Corcoran presented to the college a building for the medical school, valued at $30,000. Seven years later, he proffered an estate near the city on condition that $100,000 additional should be obtained for a permanent endowment. This amount was obtained, and the college realized from his estate, in 1885, the sum of $85,000. In 1883, he gave $30,000 for the new university building, and three years later, $25,000 for the permanent endowment fund.

In 1873, Mrs. Elizabeth J. Stone, of Washington, bequeathed some valuable works of art which are now in the museum of the university.

It has been previously stated that a medical department was projected in 1821. Thomas Sewall, M. D., and James M. Staughton, M. D., were chosen professors. The school, however, did not formally commence operations until March 30, 1825, when a three-months' course, with twenty-two students, was begun. The school was continued without interruption until 1834, when a suspension began that continued for five years, no well-defined cause being known for the suspension.

The medical department held its sessions in a building at the corner of Tenth and E streets until 1844, when Congress authorized the use of a building on Judiciary Square. This building, enlarged and remodeled in 1853, was occupied for school and hospital purposes until the breaking out of the War, when the Government took possession again. For several years, temporary quarters were occupied. This condition was interrupted in 1866, when the Corcoran building on H Street was secured, and has been used ever since.

The law department was not opened until February 3, 1826, when a faculty, consisting of Hon. William Cranch, LL. D., Chief Justice of the Circuit Court of the United States, and Hon. Thomas Carroll, clerk of the Supreme Court, was chosen. Owing to financial and other embarrassments, it was discontinued from 1827 to 1865. At the latter date, it was reorganized in a building on Fifth Street, and has become one of the leading institutions of its kind in this country. The Corcoran Scientific School was established in 1884. It has been very successful in its work. In 1887, the dental school was established, and is rapidly growing in numbers and influence.

By act of Congress, dated March 3, 1873, the corporation was changed to that of "The Columbian University." In 1883-84, a new university building was erected on the corner of Fifteenth and H streets at a cost of $75,000. The university buildings are worth half a million of dollars.

The presidents of the institution have been the following: Rev. William Staughton, D. D., 1821-27; Rev. Stephen Chapin, D. D., 1828-41; Rev. Joel Smith Bacon, D. D., 1843-54; Rev. Joseph G. Binney, D. D., 1855-58; Rev. George W. Samson, D. D., 1859-71; James Clark Welling, LL. D., 1871—.

The university is in a prosperous condition, and well patronized, as will be seen from the accompanying statistics taken from the report of the attendance during the session of 1890–91:   Preparatory school, 95; college proper, 66; Corcoran Scientific School, 110; medical school, 155; school of dentistry, 17; law school, 312; total, 755.

Howard University was chartered by Congress March 2, 1867. The preparatory department was opened in May, 1868, on Seventh Street, in a leased structure near the site of the university building. The number of students with which the university opened was 5; but it soon increased to 60. The entire number enrolled the first year was 127. The first teacher employed was a failure, but finding this to be the case, he resigned. Then A. L. Barber, a graduate of Oberlin College, took charge, with Miss Julia A. Lord, of Maine, as assistant. At the close of the first term of this school, there were 32 male students in attendance, and 4 females; but as there were then 5,000 colored pupils in the District of Columbia, it seemed certain that these numbers must be greatly increased.

November, 24, 1868, the pupils moved into the new university building. About this time the law department of this university was put in operation by the election of John M. Langston, on October 12, and A. G. Riddle, December 29, as professors. The department opened January 1, 1869. It was considered then that the opening of this department was of great historical significance, as it was the only law school ever established for the especial benefit of the colored race. The original members of this class were as follows: From the District of Columbia, C. H. W. Stokely, W. H. Lewis, L. A. Bell; from Pennsylvania, George D. Johnson; from North Carolina, G. L. Mabson; from Ohio, Solomon Johnson, Henry Thomas, O. G. B. Wall, and John H. Cook. Subsequently, seven other members joined the class. The work of the session closed March 31, 1869, the lecture room being filled with those interested in the question of the education of the negro.

The medical department of this university was opened in 1869, with the following faculty: Major-General O. O. Howard, LL. D., president; Silas L. Loomis, M. D., dean, and professor of chemistry and toxicology; Robert Reyburn, M. D., professor of the principles and practice of medicine; Joseph Taber Johnson, secretary, and professor of obstetrics and diseases of women and children; Edwin Bently, professor of descriptive and pathological anatomy; Phineas H. Strong, professor of the principles and practice of medicine; Charles B. Purvis, professor of the *materia medica* and therapeutics; Robert Reyburn, professor of practical and operative surgery; Alexander T. Augusta, practical anatomy. Lectures began October 6, 1869. The fees were as follows: Matriculation, $5; course of . lectures, $135; graduation, $30; single tickets, $20, and clinical instruction, free.

The originators of Howard University were all Northern men, and all of them connected with the new Congregational church of Washington. The prime mover in the enterprise was Rev. B. F. Morris, of Cincinnati, Ohio, who was, at the time, in Government service, and who subsequently, in a fit of melancholy, committed suicide at Springfield, Ohio. His father, Thomas Morris, a Senator from Ohio from 1833 to 1839, was a native of Virginia, but a strong anti-slavery man and champion of freedom.

Two of Morris's able coadjutors were Rev. Charles B. Boynton, pastor of the Congregational church, and Mr. H. A. Brewster, who had also philanthropic impulses. The first design was to organize an institution for the preparation of colored men for the ministry. This was modified to include the qualifying of persons for teaching. It was originally intended to admit only colored students, but this was changed to embrace white students, thus reversing the order established at Oberlin College.

The university site, one hundred and fifty acres, was purchased of John A. Smith, for $147,500, the deed being delivered May 25, 1866. The sum of $5,000 additional was paid Thomas Coyle for the surrender of a lease for a term of years to take sand from the ground. The university structure is a four-story building of commanding appearance.. It and the dormitory structure cost in the aggregate about $100,000. The funds were furnished by the Freedmen's Bureau.

The presidents of the university include the following: Rev. Charles B. Boynton, D. D., Rev. Byron Sunderland, D. D., Rev. William W. Patton, and Rev. James E. Rankin, D. D., LL. D., present incumbent.

The idea of a national university is much older than a national university. President Washington, on January 8, 1796, warmly urged upon Congress the establishment of such a university, and again on December 7, 1796, as well also as the establishment of a military academy. A few days afterward, the commissioners of the city of Washington, Gustavus Scott, William Thornton, and Alexander White, presented a memorial to Congress asking for authority to accept donations for such an institution, and stated that President Washington had donated a square of land in the new city containing nearly twenty acres, and that he had offered to donate fifty shares of stock in the Potomac Company. December 21, 1796, Mr. Madison reported that it was expedient that authority be given, in accordance with the memorial, to proper persons to receive and hold in trust pecuniary donations in aid of appropriations already made toward the establishment of a national university.

When Mr. Madison, the father of the Constitution, became President of the United States, he also earnestly recommended to Congress the establishment of such a university, which was referred to a committee; while this committee admitted that Congress had exclusive jurisdiction over the District of Columbia, and although it said there was no constitutional impediment to the incorporation of such a university, yet the money of the people seemed to them reserved for other uses, etc. Mr. Madison, again on December 5, 1816, urged upon Congress the establishment of a national university, which recommendation was referred to a committee consisting of Mr. Wilde, of Georgia; Mr. Sergeant, of Pennsylvania; Mr. Calhoun, of South Carolina; Mr. Sheffen, of Virginia; Mr. Herbert, of Maryland; Mr. Savage, of New York, and Mr. Ormsby, of Kentucky. On February 20, 1817, Mr. Wilde reported a bill "For the Establishment of a National University," which provided that such an institution should be established in the District of Columbia, by means of any money in the treasury not otherwise appropriated. This bill was not taken up for discussion until March 3, 1817, when on account of the pending adjournment of Congress, it was indefinitely postponed.

Though various efforts were made, from time to time, for the realization of this iridescent project, nothing really tangible was accomplished until 1879, when the National University, undenominational in purpose and composition, was incorporated under the general laws of the District, by the following gentlemen: Hon. Arthur MacArthur, Hon. M. G. Emery, Hon. Thomas Wilson, Hon. Samuel F. Miller, S. S. Baker, Esq., Dr. H. H. Barker, Dr. G. Wythe Cook, Hon. Henry Strong, Hon. H. O. Claughton, Eugene Carusi, Esq., and William C. Wittemore, Esq.

The law department was the first division to organize, that occurring at the time of the incorporation. A two-years' course, with a one-year post-graduate annex, was established. Its sessions were held and are now held at night, for the accommodation of the large army of clerks in Government service who avail themselves of this means of development.

The medical and dental departments were established in 1884, and are both in a flourishing condition, being located in a comfortable building on the corner of Eighth and K streets Northwest.

Prior to 1890, the President of the United States was *ex officio* chancellor of the university. In that year, however, a change occurred, and Hon. S. F. Miller, Associate Justice of the Supreme Court, was selected. This position he held until the time of his death, in the autumn of 1890, since which time Hon. Arthur MacArthur has held the position.

Of the medical and dental departments, John T. Winter, M. D., is president, and Howard H. Barker, M. D., is dean.

Of the law department, Hon. Arthur MacArthur, LL. D., is president, and Eugene D. Carusi, Esq., is secretary and treasurer.

The institution is in need of a suitable building for general purposes. The law school occupies a comfortable building of its own, on Thirteenth Street, near New York Avenue. It was erected in 1890.

The Catholic University of America, one of the prominent educational institutions of the National Capital and of the country, is pleasantly and advantageously located at the corner of Lincoln Avenue and Fourth Street East Extension. It was incorporated on the 21st of April, 1887, and is, therefore, but a young institution. In addition to its original commodious buildings, it is securing such means as will enable it greatly to increase its facilities for accommodating all departments of work.

At a meeting of the board of directors on the 8th of April, 1891, it was determined to erect, at once, a new building for the Hall of Philosophy. The means therefor were obtained from a bequest by Rev. James McMahon, rector of St. Andrew's Church, City Hall Place, New York City, amounting to some $400,000.

Dr. McMahon's generosity is a fine supplement to the bequest made by Miss Caldwell, which furnished the magnificent building now occupied for theological and other purposes.

Of the board of directors, Cardinal Gibbons, of Baltimore, is chancellor. The rector of the university is the Rt. Rev. John J. Keane, D. D.; vice-rector, Rev. P. J. Garrigan, D. D.; academic secretary, Rev. Joseph Pohl, D. D., Ph. D.; secretary to the rector, Merwin-Marie Snell, Esq.

The officers of the Divinity College are: President, V. Rev. John B. Hogan, S. S., D. D.; librarian, Rev. Alexis Julius Orban, S. S., D. D.; assistant librarian, Mr. W. A. Willyams; dean, V. Rev. Monsignor Joseph Schroeder; director of the observatory, Rev. George M. Searle, C. S. P.; superintendent of the grounds, Nicholas Crook. Liberal plans for the development of the university are in contemplation.

On the 29th of May, 1891, the American University, an educa-

33

tional institution of national importance and commanding the support and confidence of all Protestant people, was regularly organized by the following persons, at the parlors of the Arlington Hotel: Governor R. E. Pattison, of Pennsylvania; Mark Hoyt, Colonel John A. Wright, Senator James McMillan, Representative William M. Springer, Rev. Charles W. Buoy, Hon. Julian S. Carr, Bishop John F. Hurst, Mrs. John A. Logan, Miss Elizabeth J. Somers, Hon. M. G. Emery, B. H. Warner, Andrew B. Duvall, B. F. Leighton, H. B. Moulton, Benjamin Charlton, John E. Beall, S. W. Woodward, John E. Andrus, and Rev. David H. Carroll.

Mark Hoyt, of New York, was chosen president of the board; Bishop John F. Hurst, D. D., LL. D., chancellor of the university; Rev. Charles W. Baldwin, of Washington, secretary, and Rev. Albert Osborn, of Buffalo, registrar.

Bishop Hurst announced that the sum of $100,000, which was to be raised by the people of Washington to secure a site for the university, had nearly all been subscribed. It was determined, also, to take early steps for making an appeal to the people of the country of America for $10,000,000, with which to found and endow the university.

The certificate of incorporation was filed in the office of the recorder of deeds on the 3d of June, 1891. The institution is to be under the auspices of the Methodist Episcopal Church, under the title of "The American University," and two-thirds of its trustees and the chancellor are ever to be identified with that denomination.

The site purchased embraces ninety-two acres at the northwestern end of Massachusetts Avenue, and cost $100,000.

Gonzaga College, located on I Street Northwest, between North Capitol and First streets, was started as "The Washington Seminary" in 1826 (some say, 1816). It is a product of Georgetown College, and under the same order of the Church. When it began, the Catholic population was comparatively sparse and poor. Tuition charges were made in the seminary, which was contrary to the instructions of the order under which it was established. Shortly, an order came from headquarters to suspend the school. It was done, and the institution, for lack of support, was closed. In 1848, the order of suspension was revoked, and the seminary reopened. In 1858, it was chartered under the title of "Gonzaga College," "to have and to enjoy the power and faculty of conferring and confirming . . . such degrees in the liberal arts and sciences as are usually granted to colleges."

The course of study is divided into two departments: The college course proper, including Latin and Greek classics, and the non-classical, embracing English language, literature, mathematics, and natural science. The officers of the institution consist of Rev. Cornelius Gillespie, S. J., president and treasurer; Rev. Arthur J. MacAvoy, S. J., vice-president, prefect of schools; and Rev. Anthony M. Ciampi, S. J., chaplain.

Columbia Institution for the Deaf and Dumb, located on the grounds known as "Kendall Green," in the northeastern part of the city, is one of the eleemosynary institutions of the city in which is centered much interest. The site, embracing at first but a few acres and a small building, and later twenty-five acres, included, after the purchase made in 1872, the entire one hundred acres which constituted the estate of the Hon. Amos Kendall, Postmaster-General from 1835 to 1840.

The institution was regulary incorporated February 16, 1857, by Byron Sunderland, J. C. McGuire, David A. Hall, and George W. Riggs, of Washington City; Judson Mitchell, of Georgetown, and Amos Kendall and William Stickney, of the county of Washington. The title to grounds and buildings was vested in the United States. The Secretary of the Interior was authorized to pay $150 per year for the maintenance and tuition of such persons as were sent to the institution, viz., deaf-mute children of the District of Columbia, and of the army and navy. In 1864, a collegiate department was organized by act of Congress, and named the National Deaf-Mute College. The institution is accessible to both sexes. The president of the institution is Professor E. M. Gallaudet, who has been identified with it from its organization.

The Rittenhouse Academy was established on Indiana Avenue, near Third Street, in 1840, by Rev. C. H. Nourse, a citizen of Washington. After a time it passed into the hands of his brother, Professor J. E. Nourse, of the navy, from whom it was purchased at the opening of the year 1849 by Professor O. C. Wight, and continued in the same building. During the following summer, Mr. Wight took out the old-fashioned seats and furnished it with modern furniture from Boston, the first of the kind introduced into Washington. Though forty-three years of age, the furniture still looks comparatively new.

Mr. Wight is a native of Massachusetts, and a graduate of Dartmouth College, of the class of 1842. For the five years preceding his coming to Washington, he taught in Rockville, Maryland. He has been a teacher for nearly fifty-eight years; and during his last forty-nine years' continuous work in the Rittenhouse Academy, he has lost no time except during a month's illness from *la grippe* during the winter of ·1891–92.

The work of the academy has been the preparation of young men for college; and its students have been admitted to the classes of Harvard, Yale, Princeton, Brown, Lehigh, West Point, etc. Many of them occupy prominent positions in life; among them the Professor points with pleasure to Judge Bradley, C. C. Glover, of the firm of Riggs & Company, and various bank cashiers. The army, navy, and business men of Washington have given the academy a liberal patronage.

St. John's College, conducted by the Brothers of the Christian Schools, is an English, classical, and commercial day school for boys and young men. It is pleasantly located on Vermont Avenue, near Thomas Circle. It was founded in 1865, and incorporated under the general laws of the District. The first building was a two-story brick structure on K Street, near Fourteenth. In 1876, the site on Vermont Avenue was purchased by Brother Tobias, who erected the present handsome structure. The institution has had but two presidents, Brother Tobias, from 1865 to 1890, and Brother Fabrician, present incumbent, since the latter date.

The Academy of the Holy Cross, located at 1312 Massachusetts Avenue Northwest, is an institution of learning under the direction of the Sisters of the Holy Cross. It originated in a private house, on Fifteenth and H streets, in 1870, and was projected by Dr. Charles I. White, pastor of St. Matthew's Church. In 1879, the present commodious brick structure on Massachusetts Avenue was erected, and the academy removed.

St. Cecilia's Academy, corner of East Capitol and Sixth streets, was established on C Street, between First and Second, Southeast, in a private dwelling, in September, 1868, by Rev. Father Boyle, then in charge of St. Peter's Parish. In 1874, the present structure, a three-story brick with basement, sixty by seventy-five feet, was erected, and the academy removed. In July, 1877, it was regularly incorporated. It is under the control of the Sisters of the Holy Cross. Sister Ambrose was the first mother superior, and held the position for a number of years. She was succeeded by Sister M. Aquina, the present incumbent. The course of study is thorough, covering a period of eleven years. The attendance is large, the number of pupils in English branches being one hundred and sixty-eight, and the number in music seventy. In addition to these, there are pupils in other subjects.

The Spencerian Business College, in the National Bank of the Republic building, corner of Seventh and D streets Northwest, is the result of a consolidation of two business institutions. The National Union Business College was founded in 1866, by Professor Henry N. Copp, in the *Intelligencer* building, corner of Seventh and D streets. The same year, he extended to Mr. Henry C. Spencer, for some time connected with the chain of Bryant and Stratton Business colleges as superintendent, an invitation to become an associate with him. Shortly thereafter, the same request was given to Mrs. Sara A. Spencer.

In the autumn of 1867, Mr. Copp purchased the Bryant and Stratton College, and the resulting institution was known as the Consolidated Business College. It was fixed in the National Bank of the Republic building. On the 1st of October, 1870, this institution was purchased by H. C. Spencer, and the following summer was removed to Liberty Hall, corner of Seventh and L streets, where it remained ten years. In 1881, a tornado unroofing the building and destroying much property, the college was removed to Lincoln Hall building, corner of Ninth and D streets. In this location it remained and prospered until December 6, 1886, when fire destroyed the building, with the prosperous college. Recovering from the ashes, the college sought its present quarters and at once began to retrieve its losses and reassert itself as the exponent of a practical business education.

Its course of study is thorough and practical. Its college commencements, commanding the most distinguished speakers of the country, and its courses of lectures, are usually conducted in the most capacious halls to be had. Its enrollment of different students during the year 1891 was six hundred and twenty-five, representing the children of the most prominent families of the city.

Professor Henry C. Spencer, principal of the college, died August 30, 1891, honored and revered by student, neighbor, and friend. His wife and long pedagogical associate, Mrs. Sara A. Spencer, became his successor, and is now devoting her best energies to the work of practical education.

Glen Echo Chautauqua, a national summer school projected on the plan of the pioneer organization at Chautauqua, New York, was caused to materialize in the early summer of 1891. The organization embraced Edwin Baltzley, A. S. Pratt, Edward Baltzley, James B. Henderson, and A. H. Gillet, who constituted its first board of trustees. On the 20th of May, 1891, the corner stone of the arch in the main entrance of the stone amphitheater was laid with appropriate ceremonies. The first regular session, with full line of lectures and entertainments, was held during the summer of 1891, Rev. A. H. Gillet chancellor.

The National Bureau of Education, under the direction of the Department of the Interior, originated in a general demand of the educators of the country for a central agency to collect, preserve, and publish educational statistics. It was created by an act of Congress, March 2, 1867, General Garfield being chairman of the committee in Congress which reported the bill, and the most prominent supporter of the measure on the floor. Its functions are succinctly stated in the act: "For the purpose of collecting such statistics and facts as shall show the condition and progress of education in the several States and Territories, and of diffusing such information respecting the organization and management of school systems and methods of teaching as shall aid the people of the United States in the establishment and maintenance of efficient school systems, and otherwise promote the cause of education." The bureau is not administrative, and hence has no control over State systems. It is conducted by a Commissioner of Education appointed by the President. The first incumbent of the office was Hon. Henry Barnard, LL. D., of Connecticut, who held the position for three years from 1867. He was succeeded in 1870 by General John Eaton, LL. D., of Tennessee, who performed the duties of the position until he was followed, in 1886, by Dr. Nathaniel H. R. Dawson, of Alabama. A change of national administration occurring, Dr. Dawson was superseded in the summer of 1889 by Dr. William T. Harris, of Concord, Massachusetts, formerly superintendent of the schools of the city of St. Louis. The bureau, never endowed as fully as it deserves, occupies humble apartments on the corner of G and Eighth streets Northwest.

Norwood Institute, a select preparatory and classical school, is located at 1407 and 1409 Massachusetts Avenue and 1212 and 1214 Fourteenth Street Northwest. It was organized September 26, 1881, by Mr. and Mrs. William D.. Cabell, as principals, and is still under their management. The institution has a good course of study, and is supported by the patronage of leading citizens of the city.

Wood's Commercial College, located on East Capitol Street, was founded by Court F. Wood as a night school. In the latter part of 1891, it secured new quarters in Baum's Hall, and instituted day sessions. A little later in the season, the proprietor purchased Starin's Commercial School, conducted on E Street, between North Capitol and First, Northwest, and consolidated it with his own.

Wayland Seminary, on Meridian Hill, north of the city, was founded in 1865, by the Baptist Church, for the education of colored preachers and teachers. The building, a three-story brick with accommodations for two hundred students, was erected in 1873-74 at a cost of $35,000, voluntarily contributed by friends of the institution. The work on the structure was all done by colored labor.

The Ivy Institute is an institution specially devoted to private instruction, with a view to qualifying patrons for passing examinations in the Civil Service for various governmental positions. It began in 1876, under the direction of Professor Thomas Flynn, A. M., its present manager. The school is located on the corner of K and Eighth streets.

Miss Balch, on Tenth Street Northwest, has been for several years conducting a similar school. Her patronage has been quite extensive.

Mount Vernon Seminary, corner of M and Eleventh streets Northwest, is one of the largest and most popular schools for young ladies, not only in the city, but in the country. It began, in 1875, on F Street, with but two or three pupils; and under the energetic and skillful management of its founder and principal, Mrs. Elizabeth J. Somers, has reached its present prosperous and commanding position. The location is a pleasant one, and the view in all directions most gratifying. The buildings are convenient and commodious, affording every modern facility for both boarders and day pupils. The faculty embraces some twenty-five instructors, representing leading American colleges. The patronage comes from leading families in Washington and throughout the United States. The enrollment during the scholastic year of 1891-92 is upwards of sixty boarding pupils, and one hundred and fifteen day pupils. Extensive additions were made to the buildings during the year 1891; and all these buildings are neatly furnished, thoroughly heated and ventilated, and admirably adapted to their purpose.

Columbia College of Commerce, located at 623 Louisiana Avenue, opposite the post office, was founded in May, 1885, by Mr. C. K. Urner, for fifteen years preceding that time an instructor in the Eastman Business University, of Poughkeepsie, New York. It is a practical business school, with day and evening sessions to meet the wants of the large class of young people who must attend classes when they can find it suitable to do so. The organization consists of C. H. Urner, president; C. K. Urner, principal, and Mrs. M. N. Urner, secretary and treasurer.

Following is a list of the libraries in Washington, together with the number of volumes and pamphlets in each:

Academy of the Visitation, 1,000; American Medical Association, 7,000; Bar Association, 7,000; Bureau of Education, 17,500; Bureau of Medicine and Surgery, 16,000; Bureau of Ordnance, 3,000; Bureau of Statistics, 5,000, 6,500 pamphlets; Carroll Institute, 3,000; Coast and Geodetic Survey, 8,000, pamphlets, 7,000; Columbia Institution for Deaf and Dumb, 4,000; Columbian University, 6,000; Department of Agriculture, 24,000, pamphlets, 8,000; Department of Justice, 20,000; Department of State, 50,000, pamphlets, 3,000; Department of the Interior, 10,500; District of Columbia, 2,000; Executive Mansion, 4,000; General Land Office, 3,000; Geological Survey, 30,000, pamphlets, 42,-000; Georgetown College, 35,000; Gonzaga College, 10,000; Government Hospital for the Insane, 2,480; Health Department, District of Columbia, 2,000; House of Representatives, 125,000; Howard University, 15,000; Hydrographic Office, 3,000; Library of Congress, 650,000, pamphlets, 200,000; Library of Supreme Council 33, Southern Jurisdiction, United States of America, 15,000; Light Battery C, Third Artillery, 2,000; Light-house Board, Treasury Department, 3,500; Marine Hospital Bureau, 1,500, pamphlets, 1,000; Masonic Library, 3,000; Nautical Almanac Office, 1,600; Naval Observatory, 13,000, pamphlets, 3,000; Navy Department, 24,100, pamphlets, 1,000; Patent Office Scientific Library, 50,000; Post Office Department, 8,000; St. John's College, 4,000; Senate Library, 47,000; Soldiers' Home, 5,700; Solicitor of the Treasury, 7,000; Surgeon General's Office, 102,000; pamphlets, 152,225; Treasury Department, 18,000; War Department, 30,000; Weather Bureau, 12,000, pamphlets, 2,500; Young Men's Christian Association, 2,000. Total number of volumes, 1,412,880; pamphlets, 426,225.

CHAPTER XV.

EARLY in the century al E~. ' was written about the city of Washington, because it had then recently become the Capital of the Nation. Some articles were written for magazines and some were published in book form. One of the earliest of the books upon the District to attract attention was "The Chorographical and Statistical Description of the District of Columbia," published in 1816, the author being D. B. Warden. Jonathan Elliott, in 1830, published a book entitled "The Ten Miles Square," which contains much interesting original historical and documentary matter relating to Washington, and which is quoted to-day as the best authority upon the subject so far written.

In 1845, William Q. Force published "Force's Picture of the City of Washington," containing a brief historical sketch of the city, descriptions of the Government buildings, of the statuary, and of the public and educational institutions, etc., of Washington, and a sketch of Georgetown, of Alexandria, and of Bladensburg.

In 1848, Joseph B. Varnum, Jr., published a work called "The Seat of Government of the United States," which was a review of the discussions in and out of Congress on the site and plan of the Federal City. In 1854, a second edition of this work was published. It contains one hundred and twenty pages.

Colonel John S. Williams, in 1857, published a "History of the Invasion and Capture of Washington, and of the Events which Preceded and Followed." It was written with the view of removing the obloquy which, in his opinion, has been undeservedly cast upon the American troops in the battle of Bladensburg. According to Colonel Williams, the blame for the result of this battle properly lay with the Government itself and with the commanding general, and this he labors to prove.

There are many other books written thus early by Washington authors, but further particularization would perhaps be tedious.

Among those who have contributed to the fame of Washington as a literary center, the following may be referred to: Professor Joseph Henry, Ainsworth R. Spofford, Mrs. Southworth, George Alfred Townsend, Don Piatt, Ben: Perley Poore, Albert Pike, Walt Whitman, Mrs. Lippincott ("Grace Greenwood"), Harriet Prescott Spofford, and Dr. J. M. Toner. Some of these and several others are specially mentioned below.

John Burroughs was a contributor to the *Atlantic Monthly*, his articles being mainly on natural history. Walt Whitman was for a time a clerk in the office of the general library, and was pronounced by the *Westminster Review* "the only real representative of art of the American Democracy"; which criticism indicates that while this good gray poet may not have been universally admired by his own countrymen, yet he had warm admirers in Europe.

Mrs. Helen C. Weeks was one of the first of the story writers for children, surpassed only, perhaps, by Miss Alcott.

George Alfred Townsend is at least one of the most prolific of American writers, and while he occasionally repeats the mistakes of his authorities, yet he is always exceedingly entertaining, and usually instructive. He has been in all parts of the civilized world, and has contributed to numerous papers and magazines in both Europe and the United States. He came to Washington in 1868, and resided here several years. The Chicago *Tribune* paid him $20,000 for one thousand columns of preferred matter, furnished at the rate of three hundred columns per year. Since then, he has been a regular and invaluable correspondent of the Cincinnati *Enquirer*, giving that paper its chief value to the general reader. His local work on Washington, entitled "Washington, Outside and Inside," partly historical, partly descriptive, and partly discursive, is very entertaining, and in the discursive portion is an excellent illustration of a marked characteristic of human nature,—that of excessive severity against former friends, having, on account of their faults and imperfections, become their enemy.

Ben: Perley Poore was educated for the law, but always lived the life of a Bohemian, because that life was free and unrestrained. He early became European correspondent of the Boston *Atlas,* and afterward married in Georgetown, which city was the birthplace of his mother.

He became a newspaper correspondent in Washington in 1838, but did not become a regular correspondent until his return from France in 1847, and then for the Boston *Journal*. Besides this paper, he corresponded for the New York *Commercial Advertiser*, the New Orleans *Times*, and *Harper's Weekly*. He was also the author of several books, among them "The Rise and Fall of Louis Philippe"; but his greatest work was probably his "Personal Reminiscences." Every one consults, and every one is dissatisfied with, his index of Government publications; but could any of his critics have prepared a better one?

The career of Mrs. E. D. E. N. Southworth as an author, while a most remarkable one, is well known to most readers. She was born in Washington in 1819. Her first story was entitled the "Irish Emigrant," and was published in the *Saturday Visitor*, of Baltimore. Her "Wife's Victory" was begun in 1846, in the *Visitor*, but was completed in the *National Era*, of Washington. She afterward became a contributor to the Philadelphia *Saturday Evening Post*, and then to the New York *Ledger*, and was perhaps the most popular of its contributors.

Professor Spencer F. Baird wrote many monographs on natural history. Dr. Albert G. Mackay was the author of several standard works on Freemasonry. Judge Charles G. Nott wrote "Sketches of the War." Theodore N. Gill wrote numerous papers for scientific journals, his specialty being ichthyology. General A. A. Humphreys wrote "The Physics and Hydraulics of the Mississippi River"; Miss Martha Thomas, the novel, "Life's Lessons"; Professor Benjamin Peirce, many works on physics and mathematics. Edward McPherson wrote a "Political History of the United States during the Rebellion," and a "History of Reconstruction," and has since published a political manual every two years. Professor J. E. Hilgard is the author of numerous scientific papers. Nathan Sargent, or "Oliver Oldschool," was one of the Nestors of Washington journalism, Mr. E. Kingman being another. J. R. Dodge wrote "The Red Men of the Ohio Valley," and other works. Dr. N. C. Towle wrote "History and Analysis of the Constitution." Joseph J. Woodward, M. D., wrote a volume of poems. Rev. Charles B. Boynton, D. D., wrote "The Four Great Powers," and several other works. Samuel Tyler wrote several books and reviews of poetry, philosophy, etc. Charles D. Drake was the author of a learned treatise on the law of suits by attachment. Mrs. Mary Clemmer wrote many letters for the New York *Independent*, "Ten Years in Washington," novels, and other works. D. W. Bartlett was a voluminous writer, and Rev. J. P. Newman wrote

"From Dan to Beersheba"; Professor S. M. Shute, "A Manual of Anglo-Saxon"; and George Taylor, "Indications of Creation."

Ben: Perley Poore has already been mentioned. He died in 1887. He was succeeded as the "Dean of the Press" by General H. V. Boynton, who has been a prominent newspaper correspondent since 1866. For many years he was the special correspondent of the Cincinnati *Commercial Gazette*, but within the last year or two he has severed his connection with that paper and is now one of the special writers for the Washington *Post*.

Dr. J. M. Toner is the author of "The Medical Men of the Revolution, with a Brief History of the Medical Department of the Continental Army"; "Wills of the American Ancestors of George Washington, in the Line of the Original Owner and the Inheritors of Mount Vernon"; "Contributions to the Study of Yellow Fever"; "The Toner Lectures," instituted to encourage the discovery of new truths for the advancement of medicine; "Address before the Rocky Mountain Medical Association, Containing Some Observations upon the Geological Age of the World"; "The Appearance of Animal Life upon the Globe," and numerous other works of value.

George Bancroft, the eminent historian, wrote a volume of poems, and published translations of Heeren's "Politics of Ancient Greece" and Heeren's "History of the Political System of Europe." His "History of the United States," which placed him among the great writers of the age, was issued in ten volumes from 1834 to 1874. The first three volumes are devoted to the Colonization, and the next seven to the Revolutionary, period. "A History of the Formation of the Constitution of the United States" was afterward written. He was also the author of numerous other works. Dr. Bancroft was born at Worcester, Massachusetts, in 1800, and died in Washington, 1891.

Alexander Graham Bell has written "Facts and Opinions Relating to the Deaf," "Memoir upon the Formation of a Deaf Variety of the Human Race," "Upon the Method of Teaching Language to a Very Young Congenital Deaf Child," "Upon the Electrical Experiments to Determine the Location of the Bullet in the Body of the Late President Garfield," "Upon the Production of Sound by Radiant Energy," and other works.

John Shaw Billings, M. D., besides other works, wrote "Bibliography of Cholera," "Hospital Construction and Organization," "A Treatise on Public Health and Hygiene," "The National Medical Dictionary, Including English, French, German, Italian, and Latin Technical Terms used in Medicine and the Collateral Sciences"; but his great work is the "Index Catalogue of the Library of the Surgeon General's Office."

Swan Moses Burnett has written "A Case of Choroiditis Exsudation, Accompanied with Partial Micropsia, Metamorphopsia, and Chromatopsie Scotomata of Singularly Regular Forms," "A Case of Diplacusis Binauratis, with Remarks," "A Case of Restricted Range of Audition," "How We See," and other works.

James C. Welling, M. D., president of Columbia University, has written "Connecticut Federalism, or Aristocratic Politics in a Social Democracy," and "The Fundamental Elements of Intellectual Education."

Robert Fletcher, M. D., has written "On Prehistoric Trephining and Cranial Amulets," "Paul Broca and the French School of Anthropology," "A Study of Some Recent Experiments on Serpent Venom," "Tattooing among Civilized People," and other works.

Frances Hodgson Burnett, wife of Dr. S. M. Burnett, came with her husband to Washington in 1875. She wrote "That Lass o' Lowrie's," "Kathleen Mavourneen," "Pretty Polly Pemberton," "Theo," and other stories, for a Philadelphia paper. Afterward came "Haworth's," her second novel; "A Fair Barbarian"; "Through One Administration," and "Little Lord Fauntleroy," the latter of which has been frequently dramatized.

Edward Miner Gallaudet has written "Manual of International Law," "A Life of Thomas Hopkins Gallaudet," "The Combined System of Educating the Deaf," and "International Ethics." Dr. Gallaudet came to Washington in 1857, and took charge of the Columbian Institution for the Deaf, Dumb, and Blind.

Madam M. V. Dahlgren wrote a "Memoir of John A. Dahlgren," and several novels.

Clarence E. Dutton wrote "On the Chemistry of the Bessemer Process," "The Geology of the High Plateaus of Utah," "Tertiary History of the Grand Cañon District," and a large number of articles on scientific subjects.

Henry Gannett is the author of "Boundaries of the United States and the Several States and Territories, with a Sketch of Territorial Changes"; "Meteorological Observations during 1872, in Utah, Idaho, and Montana"; "Modern History and Present Distribution of the North American Indians," and other works.

Theodore Nicholas Gill has written "Arrangement of the Families of Fishes, or, Classes Pisces, Marsipobranchii, and Leptocardii"; "Arrangement of the Family of Mammals, with Analytical Tables";

"Arrangement of Families of Mollusks"; "The Doctrine of Darwin," and many other valuable scientific works and articles.

George Brown Goode has written "American Fisheries: A History of Menhaden"; "Bibliographies of American Naturalists"; "The Origin of the National Scientific and Educational Institutions of the United States"; "Contributions to the Natural History of the Bermudas," etc.

Gardner Greene Hubbard is the author of "American Railroads"; "The Education of Deaf-Mutes: Shall it be by Signs, or Articulation?" etc.

Garrick Mallery is the author of "Customs of Courtesy"; "Introduction to the Study of Sign Language among the North American Indians, as Illustrating the Gesture Speech of Mankind"; "The Relations of President Garfield to Science," etc.

Thomas Corwin Mendenhall is the author of "A Century of Electricity," and other valuable scientific works.

Professor Simon Newcomb is the author of many able and valuable works, among them "The A B C of Finance"; "A Critical Examination of Our Financial Policy during the Southern Rebellion"; "Discussion and Results of Observations on the Transits of Mercury from 1677 to 1881"; "Elementary Theorems Relating to the Geometry of a Space of Three Dimensions, and of Uniformity Curvature in the Fourth Dimension"; "Measures of the Velocity of Light Made under the Direction of the Secretary in 1882"; "Newcomb's Mathematical Course"; "Popular Astronomy," and others.

Charles Valentine Riley has written a great deal on the subject of Entomology, among his works being "The Cotton Worm of the United States," "Darwin's Work in Entomology," "Little Known Facts about Well-Known Animals," "The Periodical Cicada," etc.

Lester F. Ward has written "Dynamic Sociology," "Haeckel's Genesis of Man," "Mind as a Social Factor," "Politico-social Functions," "Types of the Laramie Flora," "Botany of the District of Columbia," etc.

William B. Webb is the author of "A Digest of the Laws of the Corporation of Washington City, and of the Charter and Other Acts of Congress Concerning the Same," and of a part of Fortes' "Economic Legislation Relating to Incorporated Companies."

William Torrey Harris has contributed largely to magazines on art, education, and philosophy, and has published numerous works, among them "A Statement of American Education," "On the Function of the Study of Latin and Greek in Education," "Emerson's Orientalism," "Hegel's Logic," "The Idea of the State and its Necessity," etc.

Samuel Clagett Busey, M. D., has written numerous treatises on medical subjects, some of them being the following: "Congenital Occlusion and Dilatation of Lymph Channels"; "The Mortality of Young Children: Its Causes and Prevention"; and also on other subjects, as "Immigration: Its Evils and Consequences."

Charles Daniel Drake, recently deceased, wrote "Camp Jackson: Its History and Significance"; "Christianity, the Friend of the Working Classes"; "The Duties of American Citizens"; "The Veto Power: Its Nature and History."

Stephen Johnson Field is the author of "Personal Reminiscences of Early Days in California, and Other States," "Remarks on the Electoral Commission on the Florida Case," etc.

Olive Risley Seward wrote "Around the World Stories," and edited William Henry Seward's "Travels around the World."

Anna Laurens Dawes, daughter of Senator Dawes, of Massachusetts, has written "How We are Governed," "The Modern Jew, His Present and Future," and other works, and a "Life of Charles Sumner."

A. W. Greely is the author of "American Weather," "Isothermal Lines of the United States," "Three Years of Arctic Service; an Account of the Lady Franklin Bay Expedition of 1881-84," etc.

Samuel Pierpont Langley has written "The New Astronomy," "Researches on Solar Heat and its Absorption by the Earth's Atmosphere," "The Temperature of the Moon," etc.

John George Nicolay is the author, in conjunction with John Hay, of "Abraham Lincoln: A History," published in the *Century Magazine*, and afterward in book form.

Charles Nordhoff is the author of "America for Free Workingmen," "How Slavery Injures the Free Workingman," "California for Health, Pleasure, and Residence," "God and the Future Life," "Politics for Young Americans," etc.

Ainsworth Rand Spofford, Librarian of Congress, is the author of "Annual Report of the Librarian of Congress," "The American Almanac," "The Binding and Preservation of Books," "The Founding of Washington City, with Some Considerations on the Origin of Cities and Location of National Capitals," "The Higher Law Tried by Reason and Authority," etc.

John Hay was editor-in-chief for several months of the New York *Tribune*, and has published "Pike County Ballads," "Castilian Days," and with John G. Nicolay, wrote "Abraham Lincoln: A History."

Anna Hanson Dorsey is a native of Georgetown, District of Columbia. She is the author of a great many works of fiction, one of which, "May Brooke," is remarkable for having been republished in Scotland, and for being the first Catholic book issued in Scotland since the Reformation. She has also writen, among other works, "The Student of Blenheim Forest"; "Flowers of Love and Memory"; "Oriental Pearls"; "Coaina, the Rose of the Algonquins"; "Gun, the Leper"; "The Fate of the Dane, and Other Stories."

Miss E. Ruhamah Scidmore is the author of "Alaska, Its Southern Coast, and the Sitka Archipelago"; "The Berkeleys and Their Neighbors,' etc.

Molly Elliott Seawell is the author of a number of popular novels. Among them is "Hale Weston, a Novel"; "Little Jarvis"; "Midshipman Paulding," and others.

Henry Adams, grandson of John Quincy Adams, is an historical and biographical writer, among his works being "Historical Essays," "History of the United States of America," "John Randolph," "The Life of Albert Gallatin," and other works.

Major J. W. Powell, Director of the Geological Survey, is one of the most voluminous of Washington writers. His public reports, as well as his private writings, are so numerous that not even a complete list of them can be presented. Some of the more important of his public works are: "Report of Special Commissioners, J. W. Powell and G. W. Ingalls, on the Condition of the Ute Indians in Utah, and Other Tribes"; "Exploration of the Colorado River of the West and its Tributaries"; "Report on the Geology of the Uinta Mountains"; "Introduction to the Study of Indian Languages"; "Report on the Lands of the Arid Regions of the United States"; "Report on the Method of Surveying the Public Domain"; Annual Reports, 1 to 12, inclusive, of the Bureau of Ethnology, the seventh annual report containing one of this author's most important papers, entitled, "Indian Linguistic Families of America North of Mexico," being a classification of these tribes on a linguistic basis; Annual Reports, 2 to 12, inclusive, of the United States Geological Survey, 10, 11, and 12 in two parts, the second parts of each relating to irrigation. No attempt is made to present a partial list even of his private publications, for the reason that justice could not be done him in such an attempt. In addition to his many books, he has written many articles which have been published in the principal periodicals of the day, and now has in press a most interesting work called "The Cañons of the Colorado."

Professor W. J. McGee is also a voluminous writer of scientific works. Those that are mentioned here pertain either directly or indirectly to the geology of the District of Columbia: "Geologic Formations of the District of Columbia," "The Columbian Formation," "The Geology of the Head of Chesapeake Bay," "Three Formations of the Middle Atlantic Slope," "Paleolithic Man in America," "The Geologic Antecedents of Man in the Potomac Valley," and numerous other works of a similar nature, some of which have been quoted from in former chapters of this work.

Alexander D. Anderson is the author of numerous important works, the principal one being entitled "The Silver Country of the Great Southwest," published in 1877. It is a review of the mineral and other wealth, the attractions and material development, of the former kingdom of New Spain, comprising Mexico and the Mexican cessions to the United States in 1848 and 1853. He is also the author of "Tehuantepec Inter-Ocean Railroad," 1881; "Mexico from the Material Standpoint," 1884; "The Tehuantepec Ship Railway," 1884; "Our Foreign Commerce of the Second Century," 1884; "The Mississippi River and its Forty-four Navigable Tributaries," published by resolution of the United States Senate, 1890. It is, however, only proper to state that Mr. Anderson's literary work has all been performed with some ulterior object in view other than literature; his main object having been to promote the success and closer union of the Three Americas.

Richard P. Jackson, in 1878, published "The Chronicles of Georgetown, District of Columbia," a book of three hundred and fifty 12mo pages, divided into nine chapters, on various features of the history of the city of Georgetown. It is a valuable work, containing much information about Georgetown not to be found in other works.

James Wood Davidson is the author of "The Living Writers of the South"; "School History of South Carolina"; "The Correspondent"; "The Poetry of the Future," in which is advanced a new theory of beauty, and the poetical; and "The Florida of To-day," pronounced by the New York *Sun* the best book on Florida that has ever appeared.

George E. Harris, formerly of Mississippi, has written and published the following works: "Chronological Register of Decisions, with Abbreviations, of English, American, and Scotch-Irish Law Books"; "Contracts by Married Women"; "Law of Subrogation"; "Damages by Corporations"; "Law of Certiorari," and other books upon different features of the law.

The architects of the Capitol have been mentioned in connection with the history of that building. Stephen L. Hallett appears to have been the architect of no building in Washington, except so far as he was the architect of the Capitol. George Hadfield was the successor

34

of Hallett, and besides his work on the Capitol, has left evidences of his ability and genius in the City Hall. James Hoban came next as the architect of the Capitol. He was also the architect of the President's House, and of the first post office in Washington, as well as of many other good buildings. After its destruction by fire, in 1814, he rebuilt the President's House. Succeeding James Hoban, came Benjamin H. Latrobe, who was undoubtedly a man of genius. He was the builder of the wings of the old Capitol. After the destruction of the Capitol by the British, he returned to Washington and took charge of its reconstruction. He designed what Madison named the American order of architecture. Besides his work on the Capitol, he erected St. John's Church, and the Van Ness and Brentwood mansions, remaining in the city until 1817, when he removed to Baltimore. He was the preceptor of Strickland, as Strickland was of Walter, and Walter of Clark, the present architect of the Capitol.

Charles Bulfinch came next after Latrobe, in 1817. He had erected numerous buildings in New England, and was architect of the Capitol thirteen years. He also built in Washington the church for the Unitarians, and the old penitentiary at Greenleaf's Point, in which the conspirators and assassins were imprisoned, tried, and hanged in 1865. Robert Mills succeeded Bulfinch, but had very little to do with the Capitol. He designed the Washington Monument, the center building of the Treasury Department, with its colonnade, and the First Presbyterian Church. He was also architect of the Patent Office until 1852, when he was succeeded by Thomas U. Walter. After Mr. Mills came perhaps the greatest genius of all the architects of the Capitol, Thomas U. Walter, of Philadelphia, mentioned above as the pupil of Strickland. He was architect of the wings of the Capitol from 1851 to 1865, and designed the great dome. During this time he assisted in the erection of the Treasury building, the Patent Office and the General Post Office extensions. In 1865, he was succeeded by the present architect, Edward Clark, his pupil, who, besides his work at the Capitol, has designed numerous houses in Washington.

Besides these architects of the Capitol, there have been many meritorious artists in this line in Washington, especially since 1871, when the era of improvement began. Mr. Adolph Cluss is a German, whose designs are peculiarly his own. He designed the Center Market House and several of the public schoolhouses, among them the Wallach, the Franklin, and the Jefferson; private residences too numerous to mention; the National Museum, and the Army Medical

Museum. Paul Schulze has been his partner for many years. Walter S. West came from Virginia, and evidences of his skill are visible in the changes made in the old Crawford property on Highland Place, and in several private residences. On the Treasury building the architect next succeeding Robert Mills was A. B. Young, who superintended the work for several years. Following him was Supervising Architect A. B. Mullett, who, up to the time of his death, was at the head of the firm of A. B. Mullett & Sons. He was the architect of the noble pile known as the State, War, and Navy Departments building, and of many buildings erected by the Government in various parts of the country. Mr. Mullett also designed the new National Theater and the *Sun* building, on F Street, the first of the high buildings erected in Washington.

James G. Hill succeeded Mr. Mullett as Supervising Architect of the Treasury. His principal works in Washington are the National Bank of Washington and the Washington Loan and Trust Company's building. Harvey L. Page was the architect of Albaugh's Theater and of many private buildings. William M. Poindexter has designed many private residences, but his principal work is the new Columbia University building. Charles E. Frazier is the architect of the Blaine mansion and the Cameron mansion, besides numerous other buildings. There are, of course, many other meritorious architects in Washington, but further detail would doubtless be tedious to the general reader.

The Corcoran Gallery of Art, including ground, building, its contents, and endowment fund, is the gift of William Wilson Corcoran[1] to the public. The building stands on Pennsylvania Avenue, opposite the

---

[1] William Wilson Corcoran was the fifth child and third son of Thomas Corcoran, a native of Limerick, Ireland, who came to Baltimore in 1754. He was born December 27, 1798, and commenced his school days in 1803, and in 1805 he entered a school kept by Thomas Kirk, a highly educated Irish gentleman, remaining therein until 1810. He then studied the languages one year with Rev. William Allen, a graduate of Aberdeen. In 1811, he entered Georgetown College, remaining there one year, and then studied with Rev. Addison Belt, a graduate of Princeton. In 1815, contrary to the desires of his father that he should have a classical education, he entered the dry-goods store of his brothers, James and Thomas, and in 1817 they established him in business under the firm name of W. W. Corcoran & Company. In 1819, this firm purchased the two-story brick building at the corner of Bridge and Congress streets, to which they added a third story, and commenced the wholesale auction and commission business, carrying on a very extensive and prosperous business until 1823, when, on account of the financial crisis of that year, they were compelled to suspend, being only able to pay their confidential debts, consisting of endorsements, commission accounts, and borrowed money, compromising all other debts at fifty per centum. Then for some years, Mr.

War and Navy Departments building. It has a front of one hundred and six feet, and a depth of one hundred and twenty-five feet. It is of brick, with brown-stone facings and ornaments, mansard roof, and large central pavilion, with two smaller ones at the corners, and it is in the Renaissance style of architecture. The cost of the building and ground was $250,000, and the original collection of pictures and statuary was worth $100,000. The institution is maintained by an endowment fund of $900,000, the income of which is managed by a board of trustees consisting of nine members, who are empowered to fill vacancies in their number by election.

The first story in the building is devoted mainly to statuary, the second to paintings and to selections from the choicest sculpture, including the Greek Slave and other fine works. The first story is twenty feet high and the second twenty-four, with an arched ceiling thirty-eight feet high in the center. In the second story are displayed many of the choice works of art of American and European painters, which form one of the most valuable collections on the continent.

The building was designed by Mr. James Renwick, architect, and was begun in 1859; but before completion, it was taken possession·of by the Quartermaster-General's Department, and occupied from early in 1861 to 1869. May 10, 1869, Mr. Corcoran placed it in the hands of nine trustees for the purposes already named, and the institution was incorporated by Congress May 24, 1870. By the act of incorporation, the building and its contents were declared free from all taxation. After the incorporation, the work of reconstruction and adaptation of the building to its original design was begun, and carried to comple-

Corcoran devoted himself to the interests of his father, collecting his rents and super-intending his property. In 1828, he took charge of the real estate and suspended debt of the Bank of the United States, with which and with the affairs of the Bank of Columbia he was occupied until 1836.

In 1824, Mr. Corcoran was appointed a first lieutenant of volunteers by President Monroe, and in 1825 he was appointed to a captaincy by President John Quincy Adams; and in 1827 he was appointed a captain of artillery by the same President. In 1830, he was appointed a lieutenant-colonel by President Jackson, and a colonel in 1832.

December 23, 1835, he was married to Louise Amory Morris, daughter of Commodore Charles Morris, and by her he had the following children: Harriet Louise, born September 22, 1836, died September 5, 1837; Louise Morris, born March 20, 1838, died December 4, 1867; and Charles Morris, born July 16, 1840, died August 11, 1841.

In 1837, Mr. Corcoran commenced the brokerage business in Washington, in a small store ten by sixteen feet, on Pennsylvania Avenue, near Fifteenth Street. Here his business was eminently successful, and in 1839 he removed to the old Bank of the Metropolis building, at the corner of Fifteenth and F streets. Having taken into part-nership George W. Riggs, under the firm name of Corcoran & Riggs, this firm, in

tion in 1871. The gentlemen named in the act of incorporation were James M. Carlisle, James C. Hall, George W. Riggs, Anthony Hyde, James G. Berrett, James C. Kennedy, Henry D. Cooke, and James C. McGuire, of the city of Washington and of Georgetown, District of Columbia, and William T. Walters, of Baltimore, Maryland. They were styled "The Trustees of the Corcoran Gallery of Art."

On the 22d of February, 1871, Mr. Corcoran gave a grand ball and reception in the building in honor of the day, the proceeds of which he presented to the fund of the Washington Monument Society. In 1873, a trustee went to Europe, empowered to purchase works of art for the gallery, and Mr. Corcoran's private collection of paintings and statuary was placed in it. November 6, 1873, the board of trustees completed the organization of the institution. January 19, 1874, the picture galleries, the octagon room, and the hall of bronzes were thrown open for private exhibition by day and night, Mr. Corcoran receiving the congratulations of his friends on the occasion. April 29, 1874, the halls of sculpture and of bronzes were opened to the public, and in December, 1874, the two side galleries of sculpture adjoining the main hall; so that all the rooms of the institution for exhibition purposes were then opened to the public.

The front of the building under the main and corner pavilions is divided by pilasters into recesses, and is ornamented with wreaths and with the monogram of the founder, and over the central pavilion is the inscription, "Dedicated to Art." On the front of the building are four niches with statues seven feet high — of Phidias, Raphael, Michael Angelo, and Albert Dürer; and on the side are seven niches

1845, bought the old United States Bank building, at the corner of Fifteenth Street and New York Avenue, together with all its property and effects uncollected. In 1847, Mr. Corcoran settled with all his old creditors of 1823, paying them in the aggregate about $46,000, including principal and interest. In 1848, the firm of Corcoran & Riggs (Mr. George W. Riggs having been succeeded by his brother, Elisha Riggs), having on hand about twelve millions of the six per cent. loan of 1848, the demand for which had fallen off, and which was at a discount, Mr. Corcoran determined to try the European markets, and after a short time spent in negotiation, sold five millions to six of the most prominent houses of London, England. This success brought great relief to the money market, and secured that amount of exchange for the United States. The stock then gradually advanced until it reached one hundred and nineteen and a half, enabling the firm to realize a handsome profit, instead of suffering a great loss, which would otherwise have been the result. April 1, 1854, Mr. Corcoran retired from the firm of Riggs & Company, and for the rest of his life devoted himself to his private interests, and in dispensing the immense wealth he had so honorably acquired. His benefactions are very numerous, and his magnificent munificence is his proudest monument. His death occurred February 24, 1888.

containing statues of Titian, Da Vinci, Rubens, Rembrandt, Murillo, Canova, and Crawford. These were all executed by M. Ezekiel, a native artist. In the central pediment is a large bronze medalion profile portrait of Mr. Corcoran, with foliage decorations, and on the tops of the two columns are bronze groups of children holding garlands, and the emblems of architecture and music. These were also the work of M. Ezekiel.

On either side, resting on the stone coping of the steps at the entrance to the building, are a pair of colossal bronze lions. They were cast from molds made over the famous lions by Canova, at the tomb of Clement XIII., in St. Peter's, at Rome.

In the rear of the gallery, facing on Seventeenth Street, is a building twenty-four feet wide, and extending back one hundred and six feet, erected during the summer of 1889 for the accommodation of the Corcoran School of Art. This building is one story high in front, this portion containing three class rooms, each lighted by an ample skylight. In the rear, on the first floor, is a room forty-four by twenty-four feet, communicating with the sculpture hall of the gallery, and containing the Tayloe collection, bequeathed to the gallery by Mrs. B. O. Tayloe, of Washington, District of Columbia. Over this is a room of the same size, for the life class of the school.

The chief interest attaching to this gallery of art is, of course, in the interior of the building. The main hall is ninety-five feet by twenty-four feet, is lighted by windows on the north side, and opens into two adjoining galleries of sculpture on the east side of the building, and into the room containing the Tayloe collection. On the west, it opens into the hall of bronzes, sixty-two feet by nineteen feet. The central portion of the ceiling of this hall is supported by four Corinthian columns with gilt capitals.

The picture galleries are in the second story. The main picture gallery is ninety-five feet by forty-four feet, twenty-four feet in height to the corner of the arched ceiling, and thirty-eight feet to the inner skylight. This room is handsomely decorated, by Mr. Vincenzo Stiepevitch. On the east and west sides of the main hall are smaller galleries, which open into two corner ones in the front of the building. Between these corner galleries, and immediately opposite to the entrance to the main gallery, is the octagon room, containing the Greek Slave as the chief ornament.

The board of trustees at the present time is as follows: Charles M. Matthews, James C. Welling, Edward Clark, Samuel H. Kauffman, Frederick B. McGuire, Walter S. Cox, Charles C. Glover, Calderon

Carlisle, and W. M. Galt. James C. Welling is president; Charles M. Matthews, vice-president, and ——————, secretary and treasurer. The curator is Dr. F. Sinclair Barbarin, and the teacher of the art school E. F. Andrews.

The artists in Washington, aside from architects, who have contributed to the fame of the city as an art center, are Harold McDonald, Robert C. Hinckley, Edmund C. Messer, Eleazer H. Miller, Richard Brooke, Max Weyl, S. J. Uhl, and E. F. Andrews, all painters in oil; William H. Holmes and Delancy Gill, painters in water colors, and U. S. Dunbar and Clarke Mills, sculptors.

CHAPTER XVI.

CHURCH HISTORY.

Trinity Catholic Church—St. Patrick's Church—St. Peter's Church—St. Matthew's Church—St. Mary's Church—St. Dominic's Church—St. Aloysius' Church—Other Catholic Churches—St. Paul's Episcopal Church—Christ Church—St. John's Church, Georgetown—St. John's Church, Washington—Other Episcopal Churches—Dunbarton Avenue Methodist Episcopal Church, Georgetown—Fourth Street Church—Foundry Church—Wesley Chapel—Ryland Chapel—Other Methodist Episcopal Churches—Methodist Protestant Churches—West Street Presbyterian Church, Georgetown—First Church—F Street Church—Second Church—New York Avenue Church—Fourth Church—Other Presbyterian Churches—Congregational Churches—First Baptist Church—Second Church—E Street Church—Other Baptist Churches—German Evangelical Lutheran Church—St. Paul's English Lutheran Church—Trinity Church—St. John's (Johannes'), Church—Other Lutheran Churches—The Reformed Churches—United Brethren Church—Unitarian Churches—Vermont Avenue Christian Church—Ninth Street Church—The Washington Hebrew Congregation—The Adams Israel Congregation—The Church of the Holy City.

TRINITY CATHOLIC CHURCH, of Georgetown, was established prior to 1795; for on April 6 of that year, according to the church records, a marriage was solemnized, and on the 14th of May a baptism. These records were signed by Rev. Francis Neale, S. J., the first pastor. The lot had been purchased some years before by Bishop Carroll, and the church edifice was paid for by contributions from the people of the adjoining counties. It was erected at least no later than 1797, by Andrew Boyle, who contributed of his own means, —according to some, donating the lot. On this lot stood a blacksmith shop, in which mass was said until the means for the erection of the church could be collected. The donation of the lot appears to have been upon the condition that two of Mr. Boyle's sons should be educated in Georgetown College; for when the last son left that institution, there still remained an unexpired term of tuition due the estate, which was paid by the college in money.

Rev. Father Neale was succeeded in 1818 by Rev. C. de Thoux, a Belgian preacher, who conducted the first confession in the church. During his charge, accessions were numerous, rendering the enlargement of the church a necessity. Arches were opened through the side walls and sheds were erected, and galleries were reached from the outside by means of staircases. The next pastor was Rev. Stephen Duboison, formerly private treasurer to Napoleon. He was succeeded by Rev. James F. M. Lucas, the founder of St. Peter's Church. Next came Rev. Philip A. Sacchi, an exile from Russia on account of his religion. He was, in turn, succeeded by Rev. Peter P. Kroes, and he by Rev. Peter O'Flannagan, whose pastorate of eleven years closed with 1852. In 1852, Rev. Joseph Aschwanden became pastor, taking charge of the new church erected in 1849-50. The church was dedicated on Sunday, June 15, 1851.

The next pastor was Rev. Anthony Ciampi, who remained one year. He was followed by Rev. Thomas Mulledy, who remained until 1858. Rev. Aschwänden returned and remained until the time of his death, in 1868. In this year Hippolyte Gache, becoming pastor, erected a pastoral residence near the church. After two years, he was succeeded by Rev. Charles H. Stonestreet, who continued until 1874. Rev. John S. DeWolf, the next pastor, made an addition to the church for the benefit of the parochial school for boys, which for several years had occupied a building on the opposite side of the street. In 1877, Rev. J. J. Murphy, S. J., became pastor again, but continued only one year, when Rev. Anthony Ciampi returned. Subsequent pastors have been Rev. Julius Maitrugrees, Rev. S. A. Kelley, Rev. Robert W. Brady, and Rev. William J. Scanlan, S. J., the present incumbent. The membership of the church is now about three thousand.

St. Patrick's Catholic Church was organized in 1797, some of the original members being . Thomas Carberry, Ennis Casenaves, and families by the name of Young and Clarke. The first pastor was Rev. Andrew Caffrayes, and the second the Rev. William Matthews, from 1800 to 1854, fifty-four years,—one of the longest pastorates in the history of this country.

The first church building erected by this congregation stood on F Street, near Tenth Street, and was erected in 1810. It was one hundred and twenty by eighty-five feet in size, and was a plain brick building in the form of a Latin cross. It was furnished with a handsome pulpit of rich foreign wood, presented to the church organization by Mr. Ribello, then representative in Washington of the Empire of Brazil. This church was used until near the beginning of the War of the Rebellion, when a new and much larger church was erected and completed. Its erection was provided for at a meeting held May 10, 1857, upon a lot received as a bequest from Rev. William Matthews, located on Tenth Street, between F and G streets. This church has cost up to the present time $120,000, and though not completed, it was dedicated in 1884. After the death of Rev. Mr. Matthews, which occui.ed in April, 1854, the pastor was Rev. Timothy J. O'Toole, who, on April 8, 1860, severing his connection with the church, was succeeded by Rev. J. A. Walter, of Baltimore, who is still the pastor.

St. Peter's Roman Catholic Church was organized May 10, 1820, some of the original members being as follows: Rev. William Matthews, Daniel Carroll of Duddington, William Brent, James Hoban, Nicholas L. Queen, James Scallan, Ed. Mattingly, James Spratt, and James Barry. The church building, erected in 1821, after being enlarged from time to time, was torn down in 1889, and the present marble building erected on the site of the old church, at the corner of Second and C streets Southeast, and it was dedicated November 23, 1890. It cost over $100,000. Out of the territory assigned originally to St. Peter's Church, two other parishes have been formed. The present membership of the church is four thousand. The pastors of this church have been: Revs. James F. M. Lucas, first pastor; M. P. Deagle, James Hoener, S. Shreiber, Joseph Van Horseigh, Edmund H. Knight, F. E. Boyle, Desederius DeWulf, J. O. Sullivan, George W. Devine, and J. M. O'Brien, the present pastor. An event of unusual interest to this congregation occurred in October, 1885, in the elevation of its pastor, Rev. J. O. Sullivan, to the vacant See of the Diocese of Mobile, and his consecration in the venerable sanctuary.

St. Matthew's Catholic Church was established in 1841 or 1842, the church building being consecrated May 15, 1842. The first pastor was Rev. John P. Donelan, who was succeeded by John B. Byrne. Afterward, Rev. James B. Donelan became pastor of the church. September 28, 1856, an addition was made to the church building, upon which occasion high mass was said by Rev. E. Lyman, of Baltimore, who had formerly been an Episcopal clergyman, Mrs. C. Young, of Baltimore, being the singer. In 1858, Rev. Charles J. White, D. D., was pastor, with Rev. E. Q. S. Waldner as assistant. Since then the pastors have been Rev. Francis Boyle, Rev. P. L. Chapelle, D. D., and Rev. Thomas L. Lee.

St. Mary's Catholic Church, Fifth Street, near H, Northwest, was organized in October, 1844, with some twenty families. The ground on which the church stands was furnished by General Van Ness. The corner stone of the first house — a brick structure — was laid March 25, 1846, and the house was completed early in 1847, the first services being held August 15. The structure cost $45,000. The present commodious brick edifice was erected in 1891, at a cost of $81,000. On the grounds are a fine brick parsonage and a good, two-story brick building, the lower story of which is used for school, and the upper for ladies' dwelling, purposes. The last-named building was erected in 1866. The membership of the congregation includes one hundred and fifty families.

St. Dominic's Church was organized in 1856, and was situated on F Street, between Sixth and Seventh streets. Rev. J. A. Wilson was pastor. In 1858 Rev. N. D. Young was pastor, and in 1862 Rev. Father Sherman who died that year. In April, 1865, this church erected a great bell weighing 3,145 pounds, which was then by far the largest bell in the District of Columbia. The fine church edifice belonging to this congregation was destroyed by fire March 12, 1885, a sad blow to the members and friends of the parish. The great bell met its doom just before the walls fell in. Scarcely had the smoke ceased to rise from the ruins when plans were matured for the erection of another church edifice, which within a short time stood in place of the old one. Nearly all the Catholics of southwest Washington belong to St. Dominic's, and hence its membership is very large. The pastor at the present time is V. Rev. P. A. Dinahan.

St. Aloysius Catholic Church is located at the corner of North Capitol Avenue and I Street. It was organized in 1859, and its fine church edifice erected during that year. It was so far completed as to be dedicated on Sunday, October 16. The introductory services were conducted by Rev. Mr. Villager, S. J., and the sermon of the occasion was delivered by the V. Rev. John Hughes, Archbishop of New York. The dimensions of the church building were one hundred and sixty by eighty feet, and the height of the interior of the audience room was fifty-seven feet. Over the main altar there was hung a portrait representing the first communion of St. Aloysius, by Mr. Brimidi, who had done so much of the decorative work of the Capitol building. There were also busts of St. Ignatius Loyola and St. Francis Xavier. The seating capacity of the audience room was about one thousand two hundred. The building was planned and the plan carried out by Rev. B. Sestini, S. J., the cost of it when completed being about $50,000. The pastor of the church at that time was the Rev. C. H. Stonestreet, S. J.

St. Aloysius, the patron saint of this church, was born in March,

1568, in the Castle of Castiglione, in Lombardy, very near the spot upon which was fought the great battle of Solferino, in June, 1859, and died in Rome, June 21, 1591.

In connection with the church, and under direction of its pastor, Rev. C. Gillespie, is Gonzaga College, a brief sketch of which is given elsewhere.

The Church of the Immaculate Conception, located at the corner of Eighth and N streets Northwest, was begun in 1864. The edifice erected in 1865 was a two-story structure, forty-three by seventy-five feet in size, and was dedicated Sunday, July 2, 1865, by Archbishop Spaulding. A schoolhouse was erected at the same time, and a second one for girls within the last few years, the latter building being a fine brick structure four stories in height, on P Street. The present pastor is Rev. S. F. Ryan.

St. Stephen's Catholic Church, located on the corner of Pennsylvania Avenue and Twenty-fifth Street Northwest, was organized October 22, 1865, at which time it was decided to erect a church worth $30,000. The corner stone of this new structure, built in the Byzantine style of architecture, of pressed brick, and fifty-three by one hundred and fifteen feet in size, was laid June 3, 1866, by Rev. C. L. White, and on December 29, 1867, the basement story was completed and dedicated. The church edifice, finished at a cost of $60,000, was dedicated December 27, 1868, by V. Rev. Thomas Foley. The membership of the church is now about three thousand three hundred. The pastors of this church have been Revs. John McNally and John Gloyd.

St. Augustine's Catholic Church commenced in a two-story brick building erected for school purposes, with less than one hundred communicants, in the year 1866. Their new church building was erected in 1874. The building is sixty-five by one hundred and thirty-five feet, and the ceiling is fifty-five feet in the clear from the floor. There were placed high up around the altar likenesses of three of the patrons of the church, the most prominent of which is St. Augustine, after whom the church was named. On the right is the portrait of Martin de Porras, after whom the church was originally named, the change of name being made according to the necessities of canon law, which declares that only saints can be patrons of the churches. On the left is the portrait of Peter Claver, whose memory is revered by all good Catholics. The seating capacity of the church is one thousand five hundred. The building was dedicated June 11, 1874. This has been a prosperous church organization, and its pastor at the present time is Rev. Michael J. Walsh.

St. Joseph's Roman Catholic Church is located at the corner of C and Second streets Northeast. The parish was organized by Rev. B. Wiget, October 25, 1868, and the corner stone of the church building was laid the same day by Bishop Gibbons, of North Carolina, who also delivered an address in English, after which an address was delivered in German by Rev. F. X. Weininger, S. J. The church, which was designed only as a temporary structure, was partly of brick and partly of wood, and was of the Gothic style of architecture. The projector of this enterprise was Rev. Mr. Wiget, president of Gonzaga College. The plan of the building was copied from the Cathedral of Cologne. There were also erected a parochial schoolhouse and a pastoral residence. Rev. V. F. Schmitt, who had been pastor at Frostburg, Maryland, for over eighteen years, was appointed to St. Joseph's Church October 1886. To aid him in the reorganization of this parish, which from a German congregation had become an English one, the Rev. ... Hue, of St. Peter's Church, was assigned as his assistant. A new parochial schoolhouse, forty feet by one hundred feet in size, two stories high, was erected in 1887. In the spring of 1888 the present fine brown-stone church edifice was begun, finished in January, 1891, and dedicated on the 18th of that month by Cardinal Gibbons, the Rev. J. J. Keane, rector of the Catholic University, preaching the dedicatory sermon, and Rev. Dr. Chappelle, the present coadjutor Bishop of Sante Fe, New Mexico, celebrating the first solemn high mass. The present fine Gothic church building, with its elegant interior finish, new marble altars, and a large three-manual organ, is second to none in the city of Washington. The building is seventy-five feet by one hundred and fifty-six feet in size, has a seating capacity of twelve hundred persons, and cost $80,000. The church is at the present time very prosperous.

St. Paul's Roman Catholic Church, located at the corner of Fifteenth and V streets Northwest, was organized December 25, 1886. The first pastor, who is still pastor of the church, was Rev. James F. Mackin. The brick chapel cost $15,000, and was dedicated May 19, 1887, by Cardinal Gibbons, Archbishop of Baltimore. The original membership was about six hundred, and the membership in February, 1892, was about one thousand, nine hundred and fifty. The church was begun as a mission of St. Matthew's Church in 1886, and became an independent church September 1, 1889.

The Holy Name Catholic Church was organized in a private house, 716 H Street Northwest, February 1, 1891, by Rev. J. T. Delaney. It is a colony from St. Aloysius' Church, and the membership at this time is one thousand. A two-story brick church edifice was erected in 1891 on a lot on the corner of Eleventh and K streets. The dedication of this new building took place June 12, 1892.

St. Paul's Episcopal Church, Rock Creek Parish, is the pioneer Episcopal church of this region. Its origin is traced to 1719, when Rev. John Frazier, rector of St. John's Parish, was instrumental in erecting a small chapel on the site of the present structure. One of the contributors to this enterprise was John Bradford, of Prince George's County, Maryland, who gave one hundred acres of land and one thousand pounds of tobacco for the purpose. In 1729, St. Paul's Parish was formally separated from St. John's, and Rev. George Murdock was chosen rector. The second rector was Rev. Alexander Williamson, who served from 1761 to 1776. About this time, or prior (perhaps 1775), the present edifice was begun, the size being forty by sixty feet.

The succeeding pastors were: Rev. Thomas Reed, 1776-1814; Rev. C. C. Austin, 1820; Rev. William McCormick, 1828; Rev. R. Ash, 1830; Rev. Christian Wiltburger, 1831; Rev. B. M. Miller, 1837; Rev. K. J. Stewart, 1839; Rev. W. A. Harris, 1841; Rev. Wood, 1849; Rev. Kerr, 1851; and Rev. James A. Buck, present incumbent, since 1853.

The original building was decided, in 1820, to be too large, and walls were erected within the walls; in 1850, however, the interior walls were removed, and the house restored to its original size. During the rectorship of Mr. Buck, many changes and improvements have been made to the property, adding artistic to historic interest.

Christ Church, Protestant Episcopal, of Washington Parish, was organized in 1794; or, stated more precisely, Washington Parish was then organized, and covered the entire territory of the city. During the continuance of the Revolutionary War, there was a modest frame building standing on what is now New Jersey Avenue, near D Street Southeast, which had been used as a barn. In this frame building religious services were held, and the little congregation was attached to St. John's Parish, in Prince George's County, Maryland. It was known as Christ's Church, and many of the prominent men of this part of the country worshiped therein. This little building was used for nearly thirty years, and Rev. A. T. McCormick held services in it as late as 1807, the year in which the present Christ Church was organized. The church on the present site, however, was not used until August, 1809, nor formally dedicated until October 7, following, the building being dedicated by Rt. Rev. Thomas John Clagget, Bishop of Maryland.

On May 25, 1795, the first vestry was elected, and the Rev. George Ralph chosen rector. In electing Mr. Ralph rector, the vestry reserved the right to elect a rector for that portion of the parish within the limits of Georgetown, and subsequently elected Rev. Edward Gant to that position.

In 1795, James Greenleaf presented the vestry with a lot on Square 456, east of the post office, and Samuel Blodgett presented the church with the timber necessary for the erection of its building.

On May 11, 1806, Mr. William Prout gave the land on which the present church is situated,—Nos. 6 and 7, Square 877, on the north side of G Street, between Sixth and Seventh streets, Southeast, the condition being that the church should be erected within a year. On May 4 Rev. A. T. McCormick was elected rector, and the church was opened for services on Sunday, August 9, 1807. The name was then changed from Christ's to Christ Church, the old one on New Jersey Avenue being known by the former name. Square 1,026, on H Street, between Thirteenth and Fourteenth streets, Southeast, was purchased for a burial ground; but proving too low for such purpose, its use was abandoned, and in March, 1808, Square 1,115, between E and G, and Eighteenth and Nineteenth streets, Southeast, purchased for $200, and named "Washington Parish Burial Ground." According to the original rules, no person of color, nor anyone "known to deny a belief in the Christian religion," is allowed to be buried therein. In 1816, the vestry set apart one hundred grave sites for members of Congress, and subsequently three hundred more, and the privilege was extended to heads of departments and their families, and to the families of members of Congress.

Rev. Mr. McCormick officiated as pastor until 1823, when he was succeeded by Rev. Ethan Allen, who resigned in 1830. Since then the rectors have been Rev. Henry H. Bean, who resigned in 1835; Rev. W. Hodges, who resigned in 1855; Rev. Joshua Morsell, Rev. Mark Olds, 1865; Rev. C. H. Shield, to 1869; Rev. William McGuire, until 1872; Rev. C. D. Andrews, until 1887, and then Rev. Gilbert F. Williams, until the present time. The church is in a very prosperous condition. It has one general society, called "Christ Church Guild," and the Sunday-school is remarkably large and active in its work.

St. John's Protestant Episcopal Church, of Georgetown, was organized as early as 1796, through the efforts of Rev. Walter D. Addison, assisted by Rev. Dr. Balch, a Presbyterian divine. Rev. Mr. Addison was then settled in the parish of Broad Creek, Prince George's County, opposite Alexandria. Upon visiting some Episco-

palians living in Georgetown, he was invited to hold services in Dr.
Balch's church, and was by him assisted to organize this church.
Colonel William Deakins donated a lot for the, church edifice to stand
upon, and $1,500 was collected toward its erection. This sum carried
up the walls to the first range of windows, and it remained in an
unfinished condition for six or seven years, and it was not until 1803
that a meeting of the citizens of Georgetown was held to take
measures for completing the building, which resulted in sufficiently
finishing the building to allow of public worship therein. Early in
1804 the trustees advertised for a rector, and in April Rev. Mr. Sayres
was chosen rector, and at once entered upon his duties. The church was
in excellent condition until 1809, when Rev. Mr. Sayres died. It was
attended through his ministry by the fashionable people of the place.

In January, 1809, Rev. Walter D. Addison became rector of this
church, at which time it was as largely attended from Washington
as from Georgetown, there being at that time no church in Washington except Christ Church, at the Navy Yard. In 1811, owing to
the large congregations, it was deemed necessary to enlarge the
building. The plan failed, however, because of the difficulty of raising
the necessary means, and because the pew holders would not consent
to retain their pews at the same price as they had been paying and
at the same time be at a greater distance from the pulpit, as would
be the case in consequence of the enlargement of the church. From
this period until 1817, the church continued in operation, but with a
moderate measure of prosperity. Rev. Mr. Addison was furnished
with an assistant in May, 1817, in the person of Rev. Ruel Keith, who
remained in this position until the organization of Christ Church,
Georgetown, when he was chosen rector of the new organization.
From this time, St. John's was in a feeble condition, and in
1821 Mr. Addison resigned, and took charge of Rock Creek Church
and Addison Chapel, near Bladensburg, and was succeeded in the
rectorship of St. John's by Rev. Stephen S. Tyng, who remained until
1823, and then removed to Queen's Parish, Anne Arundel County,
Maryland. Rev. Mr. Addison was then recalled and remained rector
until 1827, when, owing to the complete failure, he again resigned. He
was succeeded by the Rev. Mr. James, who remained with the church
between one and two years. Then came, for a short time, Rev.
Sutherland Douglass, who was succeeded by Rev. Mr. Addison, who,
though totally blind, held an occasional service until 1831, when the
church was finally abandoned to the possession of a sculptor and
the birds, and thus acquired the name of "The Swallow Barn."

In 1838, the property was sold for taxes, $50 being paid; it was repurchased and refitted for church purposes. Rev. Dr. Alexander M. Marbury was chosen rector, remaining until 1841, when he was succeeded by Rev. C. M. Butler. Governor Cooke and his brother, Jay Cooke, contributed largely toward the rebuilding of the church, the organ being a present from the Governor. Rev. Mr. Butler's successor was Dr. John S. Lindsey, who officiated until 1888, when he was succeeded by the present rector, Rev. J. A. Regerter.

St. John's Protestant Episcopal Church, of Washington, was proposed in 1814 or 1815, the corner stone of the building laid with public ceremonies February 16, 1816, the parish organized and set off from that of Christ Church, Washington, July 17, 1816, and the first wardens, W. W. Seaton and David Easton, were elected August 5, 1816. The original edifice was erected from designs furnished by Benjamin H. Latrobe, one of the architects of the Capitol, in the form of a Greek cross, but so arranged as to admit of enlargement on the plan of a Roman cross. This building cost $25,000, and was opened for religious services in December, 1816. This church was lighted by means of a lantern on the dome, and by means of semi-circular windows in each arm of the cross, and by windows above and below on each side of each arm. In 1821, the west transept was added, and also a portico and steeple; and in 1883, the building was enlarged and improved. The church as originally erected was consecrated December 27, 1816, by Rt. Rev. James Kemp, D. D., Bishop of the Diocese of Maryland. Rev. William H. Wilmer was the first rector, serving until April, 1817, when he was succeeded by Rev. William Hawley, who remained rector until his death, which occurred January 23, 1845. He was succeeded by Rev. Smith Pyne, who had been his assistant rector, and who was rector until November, 1864, when Rev. John Vaughn Lewis succeeded him. He, in turn, was succeeded by Rev. William A. Leonard, who resigned when elected bishop, and was succeeded by Rev. George William Douglass, who entered upon his duties November 1, 1889. He was assistant rector of Trinity Church, New York City, when called to this rectorship. This church is very prosperous, and contributes annually for all purposes about $50,000. The President's pew, set apart December 7, 1816, was occupied by every President of the United States down to the time of President Lincoln, and subsequently by President Arthur.

Trinity Protestant Episcopal Church, at the northeast corner of Third and C streets Northwest, was established in 1828, and its church edifice erected the same year. It was located on Fifth Street,

35

between D and E streets, facing Judiciary Square, and was dedicated
in 1829. Rev. Henry Vandyke Johns was the first rector. As time
passed, the membership of the church grew to large proportions; the
church on Fifth Street became too small, and it was decided to erect
a new building. In the meantime, however, there had been several
rectors, succeeding Rev. Mr. Johns, who, on February 16, 1832, accepted a call to a church in Rochester, New York. He was succeeded
by Rev. Chauncey Cotton; and on December 1, 1833, Rev. William F.
Chesley, the successor of Rev. Mr. Cotton, preached here for the first
time. Rev. John Owens was rector of this church in 1839, and Rev.
H. Stringfellow in 1844 and 1846. At the time the present site of
Trinity Church was chosen, the rector was Rev. Clement Butler. The
corner stone of the new building at this location was laid April 2,
1850, by the rector, and interesting addresses were delivered by Rev.
Mr. Tillinghast, Rev. Mr. Gilliss, and others. An address was also
delivered by Hon. Mr. Berrien. The new building was opened for
religious services March 9, 1851, Rev. Dr. Butler preaching the sermon.
Rev. Dr. Butler remained with this church until September, 1854, his
rectorship having lasted seven years. He was succeeded by Rev. G.
D. Cummins, who remained until July, 1858. After Dr. Cummins
left, Rev. Henry J. Kershaw acted as rector for several months. About
January 1, 1859, Rev. Dr. Butler was recalled, and was succeeded by
Rev. R. J. Keeling, who was rector during the War. He was succeeded
May 12, 1867, by the present rector, Rev. J. G. Addison, D. D. There
are about four hundred communicants in this church, and it has a
large and flourishing Sunday-school, of which Dr. Hickling is the
superintendent. Henry Clay and Daniel Webster were both communicants of this church.

The Church of the Epiphany originated in a mission enterprise
in 1841, under charge of Rev. John W. French, formerly chaplain
to the House of Representatives, and afterward city missionary. On
January 6, 1842, the day of the Feast of the Epiphany, at a meeting
of about thirty persons held at the house of Mrs. Easton, on the
corner of I and Nineteenth streets, it was decided to organize a
new congregation and to adopt the name of Epiphany Church. A
vestry was elected August 10, 1842, and the new parish admitted by
the Convention of the Diocese of Maryland in May, 1844. The corner
stone of this church building was laid August 12, 1843. The edifice
erected was a plain, rectangular structure, with low ceiling and
pointed windows, upon a lot given by Miss Harrison, and dedicated
in June, 1852. After the retirement of Rev. Mr. French, in 1856, he

having been appointed chaplain to the military academy at West Point, various ministers preached occasionally for this church, among them Rev. Dr. Harold, acting missionary of the Protestant Episcopal Church in Washington; but on Christmas day of that year, Rev. C. H. Hall began his ministry as the regular successor of Rev. Mr. French. He remained until 1869, when he left to take charge of Holy Trinity Church, Brooklyn. In 1857 and 1858, the transepts, tower, and a chancel were erected, and a new altar and a new font provided. In 1869, Rev. Dr. Hall was succeeded by Rev. Thomas A. Starkey, D. D., now Bishop of Northern New Jersey, who remained until 1871. During his ministry, a recessed chancel was erected. Rev. Wilbur F. Watkins succeeded Dr. Starkey, being installed January 5, 1873, and remained until 1875. During his ministry, the building was so rebuilt and remodeled that but little of the original structure remained, the cost of the improvements being more than $50,000. In 1875, Rev. William Paret, D. D., became rector, remaining until 1884, when he was consecrated Bishop of Maryland, but during his ministry here the remainder of an old building debt was paid off, and his first act as bishop was to consecrate the reconstructed church, January 14, 1885. Rev. Dr. Samuel H. Giesy then became rector, and remained until his death, in 1888, when he was succeeded by the present rector, Rev. R. H. McKim, D. D., who was called from Trinity Church, New Orleans. A mission house and chapel was erected in 1891 at the corner of Twelfth and C streets, at a cost of $30,000.

The Church of the Ascension, standing at the corner of Massachusetts Avenue and Twelfth Street, was organized in May, 1844, Rev. L. J. Gilliss, then acting as missionary in that part of the city, being called to the rectorship. The trustees at the time were T. H. Gilliss, William J. Darden, John M. Duncanson, William A. Bradley, A. Holmead, James Reeves, and Samuel Butt. This organization was given a site for its building by General and Mrs. John P. Van Ness, a short time previous to the death of Mrs. Van Ness, but until able to build, they occupied Mr. McLeod's academy, on Ninth Street. The corner stone of the new church building was laid September 5, 1844, on H Street, near the Orphans' Asylum, by Rt. Rev. Bishop W. R. Whittingham. The edifice erected here was fifty-four by eighty-five feet in size, and of the Gothic style of architecture. The church was opened for public worship December 14, 1845, many distinguished persons being present, among them Major-General Scott. Rev. Dr. Stanley, after being associated with Dr. Gilliss, succeeded him to the rectorship, and was himself followed by Rev. William Pinckney, who began his ministry here October 11, 1857. Upon the resignation of Dr. Pinckney, Rev. Orlando Hutton, D. D., became rector, and at the close of his ministry, Rev. Dr. Pinckney returned on the condition that he should have an assistant. In 1873, Rev. John H. Elliott, D. D., became associate rector.

In 1874, the corner stone of a new church building was laid on Massachusetts Avenue and Twelfth Street. In December, 1875, the congregation took possession of the new building. The entire cost of this building was $205,000, of which sum Mr. Corcoran gave $100,000. Improvements, including a new pipe organ, have recently been added. On the death of Bishop Pinckney, Dr. Elliott became rector, and is still in the position. This church has two missions, one for colored people near the Freedmen's Hospital, and the other for Chinamen.

Grace Episcopal Church was established in 1851, in the Seventh Ward, a separate parish having been laid off by the Convention of the State of Maryland. A Sunday-school has been maintained for several years by the exertions of ladies of the vicinity, but church services had been only occasionally enjoyed. Rev. Alfred Holmead was elected pastor, and regular services held. Measures were then taken looking to the erection of a new church building, and the corner stone was laid October 7, 1851, Rev. Smith Pyne being the principal actor in the ceremonies, assisted by Rev. Mr. Holmead. The church was erected at the corner of D and Ninth streets Southwest, and was seventy by thirty feet. The present rector is Rev. J. W. Phillips.

St. Alban's Protestant Episcopal Church, on the turnpike leading from Georgetown to Rockville, was established in 1854. Its present pastor is Rev. Neilson Falls.

St. Andrew's Episcopal Church, on the corner of Fourteenth and Corcoran streets, was established as a parish in 1857, and began to erect an edifice on the site of the Lutheran Memorial Church, on Fourteenth Street, near Thomas Circle. The War coming on, the parish became demoralized, and the site, which had been donated by Hon. Caleb Cushing, was sold for taxes. By decree of court, the property reverted to Mr. Cushing, who sold it and divided the proceeds between several parishes.

For a number of years after this loss of site, St. Andrew's was maintained as a mission station by the Rev. Harris. In 1881, the present site was acquired, and Rev. Josiah B. Perry became rector. The chapel was erected at the time, and has been enlarged several times since. The church has over four hundred communicants, and is in a prosperous condition.

The Church of the Incarnation (Episcopal), at Twelfth and N streets Northwest, was founded in 1865. The corner stone of the present church edifice was laid June 18, 1866, and on December 24, 1867, the first service was held in the completed building, Rev. Charles Hall delivering the discourse. The church cost $21,000. The first rector was Rev. James R. Hubbard, who served from July 16, 1871, to May 31, 1874. He was succeeded by the present rector, Rev. I. L. Townsend, on October 18, 1874. The present membership is three hundred and twenty-five.

St. Paul's Episcopal Church, located on Twenty-third Street, between Pennsylvania Avenue and I Street, Northwest, was organized in 1866, when it was separated from the parish of St. John's. The St. Paul Parish is geographically small, extending from Twenty-second Street to the boundary, thence around on the borders of Rock Creek to Twenty-fifth Street, to H, and thence to Twenty-third again. The number of its communicants is over four hundred and fifty.

Immediately after the founding of the church, work began on the edifice, which is one of the neatest and coziest in the city. The first rector of the parish was Rev. Augustus Jackson, who retained his position fourteen years. His successor was Rev. William Barker, who, in 1887, was followed by the present rector, Rev. Alfred Harding. This congregation has given special attention to music, it being the first in the city, it is alleged, to introduce the choral service.

St. Mark's Protestant Episcopal Church, located on Third Street, near A, Southeast, was organized in May, 1869, with thirty-five members, by Rev. A. Floridus Steele, the only rector. The first building was a wooden one, standing in the rear of the present structure, and was thirty-five by sixty-five feet. In 1889, the present brick edifice was erected, at a cost of $21,000. The new house has not yet been consecrated.

This congregation is a colony from Christ's Church. It is sustaining the Mission of the Good Shepherd, with forty attendants, at 312 K Street Northeast. The congregation has grown to two hundred and forty.

St. James' Episcopal Church, on Eighth Street, near Massachusetts Avenue, Northeast, was organized June 26, 1873, from Washington Parish. The building, not yet finished, is constructed of Potomac blue stone, with interior lining of brick. The part first built was occupied March 2, 1884. Thus far the structure has cost $15,000.

The membership at the date of organization numbered twenty-seven; at present, two hundred and ten. The rectors from the first have been Revs. James A. Harrold, J. M. E. McKee, F. W. Winslow, I. L. Townsend, and J. W. Clark, the present incumbent.

The Dunbarton Avenue Methodist Episcopal Church, of Georgetown, was founded in 1792, and was the first church of this denomination established in the District of Columbia. The doctrines of this Church were preached in Georgetown as early as 1772, and it is reasonably certain that the first sermon was preached here by Robert Williams, an Englishman, who came to the United States in 1769, and that this first sermon was preached in October, 1772, when Mr. Williams was *en route* to Norfolk, Virginia, accompanied by William Walters, a young native preacher, who was received into the regular ministry the following year, 1773, and who became the first native American itinerant, "having honor never to be shared, never impaired."[1] This first apostle of Methodism was also the founder of the same denomination in Virginia and North Carolina.

Three of the most prominent pioneer preachers — Robert Strawbridge, who built the first Methodist chapel in America; Richard Owings, the first American local preacher, and William Walters, the first native American itinerant, were all connected with Methodism in Georgetown. They were followed by Philip Gatch, who was born in Baltimore County, Maryland, and was the second native American itinerant. Philip Gatch suffered much persecution. At one of his appointments near Bladensburg, he was seized by a mob and tarred. The last stroke made with the paddle with which the tar was applied, was drawn across his naked eye-ball, causing severe pain, and from the effects of which he never fully recovered. Of this event Mr. Gatch wrote: "If I ever felt for the souls of men, I did for theirs. When I got to my appointment, the spirit of the Lord so overpowered me that I fell prostrate in prayer before him for my enemies. The Lord, no doubt, granted my request, for the man who put the tar on, and several others, were afterward converted."

It is not certain where the first place of public worship of this denomination in Georgetown was located, but it is considered tolerably safe to say that the first meetings were held in a cooper shop belonging to a Mr. Williams, and standing near the intersection of Gay and Congress streets. It is probable that the first house built especially for religious purposes by this organization was erected on

[1] Abel Stevens.

Montgomery Street in the early part of 1795. Bishop Asbury speaks of this building under date of November 2, 1795, as a "new chapel." The building was a small brick one, and the ground upon which it stood was conveyed to the society March 22, 1800, for five shillings. In 1806 the building was enlarged, and in 1849 it was sold for a school building. In 1849, during the pastorate of Rev. Henry Slicer, the present edifice was erected. Funds from abroad to the amount of $2,500, and from the home field to the extent of $7,000, were collected. In 1868 the church was thoroughly repaired and refurnished; and in 1882 it was refrescoed, repainted, and provided with new doors, carpets, and cushions. The site of the present church edifice was purchased from David English for $500, the deed bearing date of May 16, 1849.

From this congregation a number of colonies have sprung. In 1828, forty-four members withdrew and organized the "Associate Methodist Church," now known as the Protestant Methodist Church, elsewhere described.

In 1854, a mission school was established in West Georgetown by Edward H. Brown and James A. White. In 1855, a church was built, of which the first pastor was Rev. William F. Speake, now pastor of Fourth (Ebenezer) Church, Southeast. This congregation is now known as the "Calvary Methodist Episcopal Church."

A colored church was in existence at a very early date. It was, until 1855, under the control of the white congregation, the junior preacher of the charge usually looking after the interests of the colored congregation.

Inasmuch as this is the parent congregation of the Methodist Episcopal Church in the District, the list of preachers from the first is appended: Robert Strawbridge, Richard Owings, Philip Ebert, Edward Drumgole, Philip Gatch, Robert Strawbridge, William Walters, Freeborn Garrettson, Martin Rodda, Samuel Spraggs, Caleb Peddicord, Richard Garrettson, William Glendenning, William Walters, Thomas Foster, Charles Scott, Jonathan Forrest, Reuben Ellis, Philip Cox, Michael Ellis, Ignatius Pigman, William Phœbus, John Magary, Isaac Smith, Jonathan Forrest, William Ringgold, Samuel Breeve, Michael Ellis, Joseph O. Cromwell, Jonathan Forrest, Benton Riggin, Benjamin Roberts, Robert Green, John Allen, James Wilson, John Childs, George Haggerty, John Regan, John Rowen, Aquilla Garrettson, Joshua Wells, Thomas Bell, Morris Howe, Rezin Simpson, F. Garrettson, Jr., Edmund Wayman, John Chalmers, William Bishop, John Bloodgood, D. Martin, Aquilla Garrettson, Thomas Lucas, Lasley Matthews, Joseph Rowen, Wilson Lee, and John Potts, to 1800;

Thomas Lyell, William Walters, John Potts, Seely Bunn. From 1801 to 1804, the society in Washington at the "Point" was supplied by the preachers stationed in Georgetown. In 1805, the pastor in Georgetown, after the first quarter, changed every other Sabbath with William Walters, stationed in Washington. John Bloodgood, Enoch George, Thomas F. Sargent, Stephen George Roszel, Nicholas Snethen, Robert R. Roberts, Asa Shinn, Stephen G. Roszel, William Ryland, Thomas Burch, John Davis, Beverly Waugh, James McCann, Job Guest, to 1825–26; Norval Wilson, Robert S. Vinton, John L. Amiss, Henry Furlong, James M. Hanson, Charles B. Tippitt, Henry Slicer, William Hamilton, William B. Edwards, Littleton F. Morgan, James S. Hansberger,[1] Stephen Asbury Roszel,[1] Stephen George Roszel,[1] Alfred Griffith, William Wicks,[1] Henry Tarring, William Taylor,[1] Thomas Sewell, Henry Slicer, William H. Wilson,[1] Charles McElfresh,[1] John Lanahan, Samuel Rodgers,[1] to 1850; Andrew J. Myers,[1] Samuel Brison, John C. Dice,[1] John Landstreet,[1] Benjamin F. Brooke, B. Newton Brown, William B. Edwards, N. J. B. Morgan, William H. Chapman, William B. Edwards, James A. McCauley, John H. Dashiell, B. Peyton Brown, to 1875; Richard Norris, J. McKendree Reiley, J. J. G. Webster, William I. McKenney, W. S. Edwards, M. F. B. Rice, J. Edwin Ames, and George Elliott. Of this long line of esteemed pastors, four were elected bishops: Enoch George, Robert R. Roberts, Beverly Waugh, and William Taylor.

The Fourth Street Methodist Episcopal Church, on Fourth Street, between South Carolina Avenue and G Street Southeast, is the pioneer organization of this denomination in the city.

All Methodist history connected with Washington prior to 1802 is largely inferential. At the Baltimore Conference, held that year, William Walters was appointed pastor at Georgetown and Washington. At that time the nucleus of Methodism was Greenleaf's Point, in the southern part of the city. At the corner of what is now South Capitol and N streets, stood the "Twenty Buildings," in one of which the Methodists, under the direction of Mr. Walters, held their first services. Of the attendants at the Point may be mentioned Mrs. Elizabeth Lipscomb, Joseph Wheat, Peter Miller, and George Collard. Mention is made of these members in connection with a church meeting at Georgetown, April 7, 1803, in which it was stipulated that the "friends at the Point" agreed to pay one-third of the salary and one-fourth of the board of the preacher in charge, Rev. John Potts.

---

[1] Junior preachers in charge of the colored church.

About 1807, the congregation changed from "the Point" to Dudley Carroll's barn, which stood on New Jersey Avenue, south of E Street. It was the home of the Methodist congregation from 1807 to 1811. During this period (1807–11), the membership increased from one hundred and two to one hundred and fifty-nine.

On the 5th of October, 1810, the trustees, consisting of Henry Foxall, John Brashears, Electius Middleton, Ambrose White, James Vauzenette, John A. Chambers, Leonard Machall, John Eliason, and Jacob Hoffman, bought a lot of William Prout, for the sum of $227.64. Under the pastorate of Rev. Beverly Waugh, they began the erection of the first church edifice owned by the Methodists in Washington. It was a brick structure of modest pretensions, and was dedicated in November, 1811. A chapel was erected by its side for school purposes a few years later. The church was not supplied at first with benches or chairs, and the sexes were separated by a partition. This church was called Ebenezer.

In 1830, a number of members, seceding, established what is now called the First Methodist Protestant Church, on the corner of Fifth Street and Virginia Avenue Southeast.

The present house of worship was erected in 1857, under the pastorate of Rev. W. H. Chapman.

Foundry Methodist Episcopal Church was established in 1814 and organized in 1815. The man who above all others was deserving of credit for its establishment was Rev. Henry Foxall, whose foundry is mentioned in the "Manufacturing" chapter. In 1814, Mr. Foxall purchased a lot at the corner of Fourteenth and G streets, erected a church edifice upon it, and presented it to the society. The first trustees of this church were Isaac Owen, Leonard Machall, John Eliason, William Doughty, Joel Brown, John Lutz, and Samuel McKinney. This first church building was dedicated September 10, 1815. Soon after building the church, Mr. Foxall went to England, and in his absence the congregation built a parsonage, a two-story frame building, which displeased Mr. Foxall, as it was his intention to erect a fine parsonage for the church at his own expense. He died near his native village in England in 1823. With regard to the name of the church, it was supposed to have been adopted from the fact that John Wesley and his associates, when driven out of the English church, first occupied an old foundry, and to the additional fact that Mr. Foxall established this church with money made in his own foundry.

The building at the corner of Fourteenth and G streets was used

Thomas Lyell, William W.... John Potts, Seely Bunn. From 1801
to 1804, the society in W.... ton at the "Point" was supplied by
the preachers stationed i.... town. In 1805, the pastor in George-
town, after the first quart.... changed every other Sabbath with
William Walters, stationed i.... Washington. John Bloodgood, Enoch
George, Thomas F. Sargent, ... George Roszel, Nicholas Snethen,
Robert R. Roberts, Asa Shi.... Stephen G. Roszel, William Ryland,
Thomas Burch, John Davi.... Beverly Waugh, James McCann, Job
Guest, to 1825–26; Norval .... Robert S. Vinton, John L. Amiss,
Henry Furlong, James M. I.... Charles B. Tippitt, Henry Slicer,
William Hamilton, William .... Edwards, Littleton F. Morgan, James
S. Hansberger,¹ Stephen A.... Roszel,¹ Stephen George Roszel,¹ Alfred
Griffith, William Wicks,¹ H.... Torring, William Taylor,¹ Thomas
Sewell, Henry Slicer, Willia.... H. Wilson, Charles McElfresh,¹ John
Lanahan, Samuel Rodgers, ... 1860; Andrew J. Myers,¹ Samuel
Brison, John C. Dice,¹ Jo.... Lanahan,¹ Benjamin F. Brooke, B.
Newton Brown, William B.... Edwards, N. J. B. Morgan, William
H. Chapman, William B. E.... James A. McCauley, John H.
Dashiell, B. Peyton Brow.... 1875; Richard Norris, J. McKendre
Reiley, J. J. G. Webster .... William I. McKenney, W. S. Edward,
M. F. B. Rice, J. Edwin A.... and George Elliott. Of this long lis
of esteemed pastors, four w.... elected bishops: Enoch George, Robe
R. Roberts, Beverly W..... and William Taylor.

The Fourth Street M.... st Episcopal Church, on Fourth str
between South Carolina Av.... and G Street Southeast, is the p
organization of this deno.... tion in the city.

All Methodist history .... nected with Washington prior to
is largely inferential. A.... Baltimore Conference, held that
William Walters was ap.... d pastor at Georgetown and W
ton. At that time the .... of Methodism was Greenleaf's
the southern part of th.... Point, corner of what is n
Capitol and N streets, ... "Buildings."
the Methodists, under .... M.
services. Of the atten....
Elizabeth Lipscomb, Joseph....
lard. Mention is made of th....
meeting at Georgetown. Ap....
the "friends at the Point"....
one-fourth of the board of....

About 1807, the congregation hanged from "the man were:
Dudley Carroll's barn, which stood on New Jersey A son, 1844–
of E Street. It was the home of te Methodist congres The first
1807 to 1811. During this period (187–11), the members tion of the
from one hundred and two to one hadred and fifty-nine down and

On the 5th of October, 1810, t trustees, consist ncity of two
Foxall, John Brashears, Electius Midleton, Ambro l was dedi-
Vauzenette, John A. Chambers, Leoard Machall, J Mr. Krebs. In
Jacob Hoffman, bought a lot of illiam Prout, Its present
$227.64. Under the pastorate of Rv. Beverly W pastorate of
the erection of the first church edice owned
Washington. It was a brick strucre of thwest. It was
was dedicated in November, 1811. chap ompleted for a
for school purposes a few years late. T The conference
at first with benches or chairs, a the and a church
partition. This church was called as pastor.

In 1830, a number of member achusetts Ave-
called the First Methodist Protes house was
Street and Virginia Avenue Sout iam G. Eggle-
The present house of wor Rev. George
pastorate of Rev. W. H. Cha liam Hamilton;
Foundry Methodist Epi p 1868, Rev. Mr.
and organized in 1815. The m enomination. Its
of edit for it establishment and thirty-one.
is mentioned in the "Man
purchased a lot at the organized in 1846.
a church edifice up ue and Twentieth
trustees of this and eighteen, and
Eliason, Willia
McKinney. T rch was organized in
1815. Soon ent for the District of
and in his ment was that it should
ting the metropolis, and
seat plan. The trustees
T. H. Havenner, W. G.
ler, F. Howard, S. Nor-
f the Methodist Episcopal
l issued a circular strongly
pliance with a request from
ted Rev. Henry Slicer agent

without repair until 1835, when it was repaired. It was again repaired in 1849, when the galleries, till then occupied by the colored members, were taken down, and the floor of the church raised so as to make a basement, which was then used for a Sunday-school. A separate church was erected for the accommodation of the colored members on Eleventh Street, named Asbury Methodist Episcopal Church, organized, at that time, with about three hundred members. The Foundry Church, as improved according to the plan last mentioned, was used until May, 1864, when it was torn down and a new building erected in its place, the corner stone being laid July 20, 1864, with Masonic ceremonies. This church edifice was dedicated November 4, 1866, Rev. D. W. Bartine, D. D., of Philadelphia, delivering the address.

The first pastor of this church was Rev. Thomas Burch, an Irishman, and the second was Rev. William Ryland, in 1816; Rev. Mr. Burch in 1817; Rev. John Emery, 1818-19; Rev. William Ryland, 1820-21; Rev. Samuel Davis, until September, 1822, when he died, and then Rev. Joseph Baer; Rev. William Hamilton, 1823-24; Rev. William Ryland, 1825-26; Rev. John Davis, 1827-28; Rev. Stephen Roszell, 1829-30; Rev. James M. Hanson and Rev. George Nildt, 1831-32; Rev. John Baer, 1833; Rev. Samuel Brayson and Rev. Thomas B. Sargent, 1834-35; Rev. William Hamilton and Rev. Charles B. Tippet, 1836-37; Rev. Henry Slicer, 1838-39; Rev. Thomas C. Thornton, 1840 and half of 1841; Rev. John A. Robb, remainder of 1841; Rev. John Davis, 1842-43; Rev. Henry Tarring, 1844-45; Rev. Nicholas J. B. Morgan, 1846-47; Rev. John Lanahan, 1848-49; Rev. Littleton F. Morgan, 1850-51; Rev. Jesse T. Peek, D. D., 1852-53; Rev. Elisha P. Phelps, 1854-55; Rev. Samuel Register, 1856-57; Rev. B. H. Nadal, D. D., 1858-59; Rev. William B. Edwards, D. D., 1860-61; Rev. William Hearst, to August, 1862; Rev. J. R. Effinger and Rev. Joseph B. Stitt, remainder of 1862; Rev. W. M. D. Ryan, 1863-65; Rev. B. Peyton Brown, 1866-68; Rev. Alexander Gibson, D. D., 1869-71; Rev. Samuel A. Wilson, 1872; Rev. Horace A. Cleveland, 1873-75; Rev. B. Peyton Brown, 1876-77; Rev. John Lanahan, D. D., 1878-80; Rev. Frank Ward, 1881-83; Rev. Henry R. Naylor, D. D., 1884-86; Rev. George Elliott, 1887-1891.

Wesley Chapel, of the Methodist Episcopal Church, located at the southwest corner of Fifth and F streets Northwest, was organized in 1823. In its earlier years, it was visited, at times, by the prominent members of the denomination. Rev. Bishop McKendree occupied its pulpit on the 17th of May, 1829. In 1838, Rev. G. S. Cookman became pastor, and remained until 1841.

Some of the pastors who came after Rev. Mr. Cookman were: John Davis, 1841-43; W. B. Edwards, 1843-44; Norval Wilson, 1844-48; H. Slicer, 1848; Dashiell, 1855; W. Krebs, 1856-58. The first house of worship, erected about the time of the organization of the church, served its purposes until 1856, when it was taken down and replaced by a new and larger one, with a seating capacity of two thousand five hundred, and at a cost of $16,000, which was dedicated December 26, 1856, during the pastorate of Rev. Mr. Krebs. In March, 1858, Rev. E. D. Morgan, D. D., became pastor. Its present membership is four hundred and thirty-four, under the pastorate of Rev. L. B. Wilson.

Ryland Chapel is on D and Tenth streets Southwest. It was organized in 1843. Its house of worship was not completed for a year or two later. Rev. F. S. Evans was pastor. The conference report for 1891 shows four hundred and seven members, and a church property valued at $25,000. Rev. J. A. Price is serving as pastor.

McKendree Methodist Episcopal Church is on Massachusetts Avenue, near Ninth Street, and was organized in 1844. A house was begun, but not finished, that year. In 1845, Rev. William G. Eggleston was pastor; in 1847, Rev. T. M. Reese; in 1856, Rev. George Hildt; in 1857, Rev. Dabney Bale; in 1859, Rev. William Hamilton; in 1861, Rev. Dr. Ryan; in 1863, Rev. J. Thrush; in 1868, Rev. Mr. Krebs. It is now one of the large churches of the denomination. Its membership for 1891 was reported as four hundred and thirty-one. The pastor is Rev. L. T. Widerman.

Union Chapel Methodist Episcopal Church was organized in 1846. It is situated at the corner of Pennsylvania Avenue and Twentieth Street. It has a membership of two hundred and eighteen, and Rev. Joel Brown is pastor.

The Metropolitan Methodist Episcopal Church was organized in 1853, at a time when Rev. R. L. Dashiell was agent for the District of Columbia. The idea connected with its establishment was that it should give increased accommodations to strangers visiting the metropolis, and hence it was intended to build it on the free-seat plan. The trustees of the church were C. W. Boteler, Sr., T. H. Havenner, W. G. Deale, T. Pursell, C. H. Lane, Samuel Fowler, F. Howard, S. Norment, and Z. W. McKnew. The bishops of the Methodist Episcopal Church, under date of March 16, 1853, had issued a circular strongly recommending the enterprise, and in compliance with a request from the Baltimore Annual Conference, appointed Rev. Henry Slicer agent for the new church.

The church building which it was then designed to erect, was to be situated on the corner of C and Four and a Half streets, and was to be seventy-five feet front on C Street, and one hundred and eight feet deep on Four and a Half Street. The corner stone was laid October 23, 1854, the address of the occasion being made by Bishop Simpson. The walls of this building were erected to a height of a few feet above the surface of the ground, and then, on account of want of funds, caused by the impractibility of making collections in the Southern States because of the breaking out of the War, were permitted to remain in that condition until 1868, when a determined effort was made to complete the edifice. Rev. Francis S. De Hass was appointed general agent, and he succeeded in raising over $100,-000 toward its completion. The church erected in part with this money is a brown-stone structure in the Gothic style of architecture. At the time of the dedication, March 7, 1869, it had cost $225,000, the tower and steeple not then being completed nor the chimes put in. To do this would cost, as was then supposed, $25,000 more, bringing the entire cost of the church up to $250,000. The main entrance to the building is on C Street, and from the vestibule rise commodious stairways to the galleries, besides which three doors admit to the main audience room. This room is sixty-four by eighty-five feet in size, seating comfortably one thousand two hundred persons, and being at that time considered the finest room in the District. In the gallery is a superb organ, manufactured by Johnson, of Westfield, Massachusetts, and presented to the church by Carlos Pierce of that State, at an expense to him of $15,000. In the auditorium there were set apart pews for each State and Territory, the President, and the Cabinet officers. The rest of the pews were rented, except those in the gallery, which were free. The fountain in bronze was designed by Clarke Mills. It represented Hagar in the Wilderness. The trustees at that time were President U. S. Grant, S. P. Chase, M. G. Emery, S. Norment, S. Fowler, F. A. Lutz, F. Howard, T. L. Tullock, and D. A. Burr. The dedicatory exercises were of a most interesting nature. The morning address was delivered by Bishop Simpson, the afternoon address by Rev. W. Morley Punshon, one of the greatest pulpit orators of England, and the evening address by Rev. Dr. T. M. Eddy, of the *Northwestern Christian Advocate*. Fifteen thousand dollars were raised on the day of the dedication.

Subsequently to this time, the steeple was erected, carried to a height of two hundred and twenty-five feet, and a chime of bells, sixteen in number, put in. On the wall west of the pulpit, beneath the gallery, are two mural tablets, erected respectively to the memory of General U. S. Grant and General John A. Logan, both of whom were regular attendants at this church. Since this time, the ministers of this church have been: Rev. J. P. Newman, D. D., elected bishop in the midst of his term; Rev. T. M. Eddy, D. D., elected missionary secretary at the beginning of his term; Rev. O. H. Tiffany, D. D.; Rev. H. R. Naylor, afterward presiding elder of this district; Rev. R. N. Baer, D. D., Rev. E. D. Huntley, D. D., and Rev. George H. Corey, D. D., the present pastor.

Fletcher Chapel Methodist Episcopal Church was established in 1853. It is situated at the corner of Fourth Street and New York Avenue Northwest. At first it was a mission in charge of McKendree Chapel. Its membership is ninety-nine, and Rev. W. C. Griffin is pastor.

Waugh Chapel, corner Third and A streets Northeast, was first known as Capitol Hill Methodist Episcopal Church. It was organized in 1853, and September 5, 1854, the corner stone was laid, Rev. Beverly Waugh, bishop of the Methodist Episcopal Church, and Revs. N. Wilson and A. Griffith officiating. In March, 1857, Rev. R. R. S. Hough became pastor, during whose ministry the structure was completed. The dedication occurred February 7, 1858. At this time, the indebtedness on the church was $2,000, steps for the liquidation of which were taken. It was on this occasion, too, that the name was changed from Capitol Hill to that of Waugh Chapel.

In March, 1858, Mr. Hough was succeeded by Rev. Theodore Carson. Without attempting to give the full list of intervening pastors, it may be stated that the present pastor is Rev. Alexander J. Gibson. The church has a comfortable parsonage attached, and is in a flourishing condition, its membership being five hundred and sixteen.

Grace Methodist Episcopal Church is located at the corner of Ninth and S streets Northwest. It had its origin in a mission Sunday-school in 1863, sustained by teachers from Wesley Chapel. George W. Riggs gave the ground for a building site, and a temporary frame structure was erected, and a mission church organized. At the session of the Baltimore Annual Conference for 1871, this mission church was erected into a station, and Rev. M. F. B. Rice appointed pastor. He desired a new church building, and, the membership endorsing the suggestion, raised $4,000 for the purpose. The corner stone of this new church was laid October 14, 1872, the building when complete costing about $20,000. Its present membership is reported at one hundred and sixty-two. Rev. Samuel Shannon is the pastor.

Fifteenth Street Methodist Episcopal Church is located at the corner of Fifteenth and R streets Northwest. It was organized in 1872. According to the conference report of 1891, it has two hundred and nineteen members, and the pastor is Rev. L. A. Threlkeld.

North Capitol Methodist Episcopal Church was organized in 1876, with seventy-seven members. The first church building was a frame one, standing at the corner of North Capitol and K streets Northeast, and cost about $1,000. This building served the purposes of the congregation until 1891, when a new brick building was erected on the same site, costing $18,000. This new church has not as yet been dedicated, but will be sometime during the year 1892. The pastors of this church have been as follows: Revs. D. M. Browning, Charles T. Wiede, Harry Boggs, James McLaren, F. H. Havenner, W. H. Reed, J. Clarke Hagey, Charles T. Wiede, and Charles O. Cook, present pastor. The membership in 1878 was eighty-one, and in 1891 one hundred and forty-six.

Hamline Methodist Episcopal Church, corner of Ninth and P streets Northwest, was organized in 1867. It is the largest church of the denomination in the city. Its membership is eight hundred and thirty-seven, and the property of the church is worth $75,000. The pastor is Rev. Henry R. Naylor.

Independent Methodist Episcopal Church, located on Eleventh Street, between G and I, Southeast, was organized in 1887, by Rev. Jacob D. Wilson. The congregation is not under the jurisdiction of any conference, but is guided and guarded by its pastor, Rev. Wilson.

Douglas Memorial Methodist Episcopal Church, corner of Eleventh and H streets Northeast, was organized with a few scattered members in 1878, and named in honor of Miss Flora Douglas, who subsequently married the Rev. George Markham. It was then a mission chapel. It has grown rapidly in consequence of the growth of the city in that vicinity, and its membership is now more than four hundred, with a Sunday-school enrolling over six hundred. The little brick chapel is consequently too small to accommodate the congregations that attend, and steps have been taken to erect a commodious building. The pastorate has been filled by W. H. Reed, W. M. Hammack, Charles T. House, William Rogers, D. M. Browning, and E. O. Eldridge. The latter has just entered upon his work.

Twelfth Street Methodist Church, corner of Twelfth and E streets Southeast, is a small congregation, having, in 1891, seventy-four members, with a church property valued at $9,000. Rev. Henry Baker is pastor.

Mount Vernon Place Methodist Episcopal Church, South, corner of Ninth and K streets Northwest, was organized in 1869. The pastor is Rev. J. D. Weightman.

Grace Methodist Episcopal Church, South, was organized in 1886. The first services were held in the Odd Fellows' Hall, on Pennsylvania Avenue Southeast. Not long afterward, the church at the corner of Seventh and A streets Northeast was purchased, and has ever since been used as a place of worship. At the time of the organization of the church, there were twenty-seven members, while at the present time there are one hundred and twenty. Its first pastor, Rev. J. C. Jones, was appointed in 1887, and served four years. He was succeeded by Rev. Harry C. Febrey in March, 1891.

Mount Olivet Methodist Episcopal Church, South, is at the corner of Seventh and C streets Southwest, and the pastor is Rev. John K. White.

Congress Street Methodist Protestant Church, located on Thirty-first Street Northwest (Georgetown), was organized in 1828. In 1829, the lot on which the church structure stands was purchased for $1,035. The first edifice was erected in 1830, during the pastorate of Rev. W. W. Wallace. In 1857, it was replaced by another, which in 1867 was enlarged and improved, and in February, 1868, dedicated, the sermon being preached by Rev. Augustus Webster. The parsonage was built in 1841, during the pastorate of Rev. L. H. Reese, at a cost of $4,000, on a lot purchased in 1839 for $615.

The list of ministers includes the following: Revs. W. W. Wallace, Dennis B. Dorsey, Frederick Styer, Thomas H. Stockton, John W. Porter, Josiah Varden, Augustus Webster, Bignal Appleby, Levi R. Reese, John G. Wilson, Joseph Warden, William Collier, John Everest, J. J. Murray, S. R. Cox, J. B. Sutherland, Dr. Murray, David Wilson, Washington Roby, Daniel E. Reese, Daniel Bowers, D. A. Shermer, Dr. Bates, T. D. Valiant, J. T. Murray. This list extends to 1878. The present pastor is Rev. W. R. Graham.

The Central Methodist Protestant Church was organized April 3, 1829, with members from the Foundry Methodist Episcopal Church who joined the movement resulting in the Methodist Protestant Church. Its first class leader was Rev. W. C. Lipscomb.

On April 14, 1836, at the annual session of this denomination held in Washington, the number of members reported as belonging thereto was about four thousand, with eight hundred children in the Sunday-schools. The appointments for Washington and Georgetown were: Georgetown, Rev. Josiah Varden; Ninth Street, Rev. Levi R. Reese, and East Washington, Rev. Thomas G. Clayton. In 1838, there was no regular minister in the pulpit of this church, but Rev. William Lanphier preached occasionally. Rev. A. Webster became pastor April 14, 1839, and in 1844 it was Rev. U Ward. Following is a list of the pastors from that time to the present: Rev. William Mitchell, 1845–46; Rev. S. K. Cox, 1846–47; Rev. L. R. Reese, 1847–49; Rev. William Collier, 1849–50; Rev. William T. Eva, 1850–52; Rev. Daniel E. Reese, 1852–55; Rev. T. Light Wilson, 1855–57; Rev. F. Swentzel, 1857-59; Rev. L. W. Bates, 1859–60; Rev. P. Light· Wilson, 1860-62; Revs. W. Roby and W. M. Strayer, 1862–63; Rev. C. T. Cochol, 1863–64; Rev. J. T. Ward, 1864–66; Rev. Dr. E. J. Drinkhouse, 1868–74; Rev. Dr. W. S. Hammond, 1875–76; Rev. Dr. David Wilson, 1877–80; Rev. P. T. Hall, 1880–81; Rev. J. T. Smith, 1882; Rev. Dr. J. T. Mills, 1883–87; Rev. S. Reese Murray, 1887 to the present time.

The first building erected by this church was a frame structure, called "The Tabernacle," at Twelfth and H streets, forty-nine by twenty-one feet in size, with a seating capacity of two hundred and fifty, and dedicated by Rev. Levi R. Reese, December 23, 1832. In April, 1835, a new brick church on Ninth Street, between E and F streets, was erected, sixty-five by fifty feet in size, and dedicated July 9 by Rev. Josiah Varden. In 1879, this church was remodeled and enlarged by Rev. Dr. Wilson, at a cost of $11,000. In 1887, under the pastorate of Rev. S. Reese Murray, the congregation erected a chapel at Twelfth and M streets Northwest, paying for the ground $33,000, and for the erection of the chapel $10,000.

This church differs from other Methodist churches in many particulars: It has no titled bishops; it admits laymen in equal numbers with clergymen in the annual and general conferences; it elects its officers annually; and it has no time limit to pastoral appointments.

The First Methodist Protestant Church, corner Fifth Street and Virginia Avenue Southeast, was organized in 1830. It was a colony of the Fourth (Ebenezer) Methodist Episcopal Church. The house of worship is a frame structure of good dimensions. A frame parsonage adjoins the building. The property is valued at $17,000. The pastor, Rev. J. E. Nicholson, has recently removed to New Jersey, and his successor has not been installed.

The North Carolina Avenue Methodist Protestant Church was organized in 1872, with seventeen members. It is located at the corner of North Carolina Avenue and Eighth Street, on Capitol Hill. Its pastors have been Revs. S. G. Valiant, J. Shreve, J. W. Trust, P. T. Hall, W. J. Neepier, J. W. Tomb, A. W. Mather, and David

Wilson, the present pastor. For the last four years, the membership has been about one hundred.

Mt. Tabor Methodist Protestant Church, on Thirty-second Street Northwest, was organized in 1874. Rev. H. C. Cushing is pastor.

The first presbytery organized for this region was the Presbytery of Baltimore, in 1786. In 1823, the Presbytery of the District of Columbia was formed by the Synod of Philadelphia, on the petition of the Presbytery of Baltimore, and the new presbytery held its first meeting at Alexandria, May 11, 1824, with Rev. J. Breckenridge as moderator, the churches represented having at that time a membership of two hundred and seventy-seven. The General Assembly of 1836 transferred this presbytery from the Synod of Philadelphia to that of Virginia, the membership of the churches being then one thousand, two hundred and fifty-nine. In 1837 and 1838, the Presbyterian Church was separated into two branches,—the Old and New schools, and in 1839, when a vote was taken on receiving a mandate from the Synod of Virginia, requiring adherence to the acts of the Assembly of 1838 exscinding several of the Northern synods from the Church, the Presbytery of the District of Columbia divided,— Messrs. Laurie, Harrison, Bosworth, and Breckenridge representing their churches, and Revs. I. L. Skinner and J. McVean, without pastoral charges, withdrawing from the body, and declining to recognize its further jurisdiction. The Presbytery of the District of Columbia thereupon dropped their names from the rolls, the General Assembly, Old School, recognizing them, however, as the true body of that name. They retained this name until 1841, when they were merged into the Presbytery of Baltimore. In 1858, they were set off from this presbytery to form the Presbytery of the Potomac.

From 1839 to 1870, therefore, the condition of the churches in the District of Columbia with reference to the two schools into which the Presbyterian Church was divided, was as follows: From 1839 to 1841, some of them were under the Presbytery of the District of Columbia, Old School, while the others were under the Presbytery of the District of Columbia, New School; from 1841 to 1858, some were under the Presbytery of Baltimore, Old School, while the others were under the Presbytery of the District of Columbia, New School; and from 1858 to 1870, some were under the Presbytery of the Potomac, Old School, while the others were under the Presbytery of the District of Columbia, New School.

In 1870, when the union of the two schools was effected, these two presbyteries were united in one, the union being effected June 20

36

of that year, under the name of the Presbytery of Washington City. At this time, the membership of the churches belonging to the two presbyteries was two thousand, eight hundred and ninety-three, and in 1888 it had increased to four thousand, seven hundred and seventy-six. In 1892, the membership of the churches belonging to the Presbytery of Washington is about six thousand.

The West Street Presbyterian Church, Georgetown, was the result of a movement begun in 1780, when Rev. Stephen B. Balch, a native of Maryland, and a licentiate of the old Donegal Presbytery, of Pennsylvania, on his way to make a missionary tour of the Carolinas, preached to a few persons in Georgetown, who were of Scotch and New England descent. Some of them were descendants of Colonel Ninian Beall, who, at an earlier date, had liberally befriended the old Marlborough Church in Maryland. The next year Rev. Mr. Balch, under his commission as an evangelist, organized a church. This congregation worshiped for two years on the site of the present Presbyterian mission on Market Street, and then built a small church edifice, thirty feet square, at the corner of Washington and Bridge streets, a location fitly chosen to accommodate those who desired to attend. In 1821, this building was replaced by one of much larger dimensions. Toward the latter part of Rev. Mr. Balch's pastorate, he had as an assistant Rev. John C. Smith, who, upon the death of Dr. Balch, September 7, 1833, became pastor, and remained in this position until called to the pastorate of the Fourth Presbyterian Church of Washington, April 9, 1839. He was succeeded by Rev. R. T. Berry, October 3, 1841, to August 28, 1849; Rev. J. M. P. Atkinson, March 12, 1850, to February 12, 1856; Rev. J. H. Bocock, D. D., February 17, 1857, to May 27, 1861; Rev. F. T. Brown, June 9, 1861, to February 6, 1865; Rev. A. A. E. Taylor, June 21, 1865, to May 3, 1869; Rev. D. W. Moffat, May 6, 1870, to April 10, 1872; Rev. S. H. Howe, May, 1872, to 1883; Rev. T. S. Childs, a short time that year, and then Rev. Thomas Fullerton, D. D., the present pastor.

In 1871, the question of a removal became a question for discussion, and the present site, on P Street, near Thirty-first Street, was selected. The new edifice was dedicated June 8, 1879, and Rev. Dr. Howe installed pastor. The roll of membership in 1887 contained the names of two hundred and ninety individuals, and numerous additions have since been made. The membership of the Sunday-school is upward of four hundred. The church properties, the building, chapel, manse, and mission, are worth $60,000, and they are free from debt. The chapel, with its lot and that of the church, was the gift of Messrs. Darby and Cissel, when residents of Georgetown.

The First Presbyterian Church, located at the present time on Four and a Half Street, had its origin as early as 1795; for the records of Baltimore Presbytery for April 29, that year, show that a call was presented "from the churches in Washington for the services of Rev. John Breckenridge"; and on the 24th of June of the same year, at a called meeting at Bladensburg, on the report of "a committee respecting the churches in said town and its vicinity," measures were taken for the future installation of Rev. Mr. Breckenridge. The first services of this new congregation were held in a carpenter shop erected for the use of the workmen engaged in building the Presidential Mansion, and when this shop was taken down, a frame chapel was erected on F Street, near St. Patrick's Church. In 1803, this small congregation was weakened by the withdrawal of several of the members to form F Street Presbyterian Church by those who had previously belonged to the Associate Reformed Presbyterian Church in Philadelphia, who had removed to Washington when it became the seat of government of the United States; but for a time, the services of Rev. Mr. Breckenridge were continued with what remained of the congregation under his appointment from the General Assembly, and he also preached to the Presbyterians at Bladensburg, the Washington services being held in the Eastern Academy building.

In 1810, George Blagden, Elias B. Caldwell, John Coyle, Daniel Rapine, and John McClelland formed themselves into a committee to attempt the building of a house of worship; but until this church edifice was completed, religious services were held in the basement of the north wing of the Capitol. On June 25, 1812, the church erected by this building committee was entered for the first time, and its dedicatory sermon preached by Rev. Mr. Breckenridge. It was situated on South Capitol Street, and among the contributors toward its erection were President Madison, Hon. James Munroe, William R. King, John Lambert, and Josiah Quincy. Its first cost was $4,000, but it was afterward enlarged at a cost of $3,000. Rev. Mr. Breckenridge was installed July 4, 1813, and was pastor of the church until May, 1818. After his resignation, the pulpit was supplied by John McKnight, Andrew Hunter, and John Clark, until the call, in 1819, to Rev. Reuben Post, who was installed June 24 of that year.

On account of the persistent growth of the city toward the west, the congregation did not grow as it had been hoped. The site of the present building on Four and a Half Street was selected and a contract for a new church thereon entered into for $8,000. The corner stone of this church was laid April 10, 1827, and the building was dedicated December 9 of the same year. Rev. Dr. Post remained pastor until June 24, 1836. The next regular pastor was Rev. W. McLain, who was installed January 11, 1837, and remained with the church until failing health compelled him to resign, in 1840. He, however, remained in the service of the presbytery as stated clerk, and also held the office of secretary of the American Colonization Society until his death, February 13, 1873.

Rev. Charles Rich was installed pastor of this church November 30, 1840, and remained three years, when he resigned on account of ill health. Rev. William T. Sprole was called to this church in the fall of 1843, and was succeeded March 1, 1848, by Rev. Elisha Ballentyne, who remained until 1851, resigning on account of ill health. The next regular pastor was the present one, Rev. Byron Sunderland, D. D., who was installed April 21, 1853. Soon after Dr. Sunderland became pastor, it became necessary to enlarge the church building, which was accomplished by raising it and extending it over the rear portion of its grounds, increasing the seating capacity to one thousand. The building, as thus enlarged, was dedicated December 9, 1860, the services being by the Rev. Dr. Spring in the morning, Rev. C. H. Read in the afternoon, and Rev. J. Jenkins in the evening. These three ministers represented the Old School, the New School, and the Southern School of the Presbyterian Church as it existed at that day.

Dr. Sunderland's pastorate has been a remarkable one, extending from April, 1853, almost continuously to the present time, a period of thirty-nine years, the only intermission or break in it being while the Doctor was abroad in Paris during a portion of the years 1864 and 1865, as pastor of the American Chapel in that city. It could not be expected that perfect harmony should exist in such a church during its entire existence. On several occasions there has been misunderstanding, which has tended to weaken the church by a withdrawal of a portion of its members. In 1866, one of these occasions occurred, because of dissatisfaction on the part of some that Frederick Douglass was permitted to deliver a lecture in the church for the benefit of the National Home Association of colored orphans, the lecture being upon "The Assassination and its Lessons." Chief Justice Chase presided, and the audience was a very large one, part of whom being negroes. The use of the church for this purpose was very distasteful to many of the members, and they protested against it in vigorous terms. But the lecture having been delivered in spite of the protest, many of the members withdrew, and even some of those who insisted on its delivery.

Numerous other embarrassments have been encountered, but, notwithstanding all of them, the First Presbyterian Church has continued to grow, and it is strong and active in all directions to-day.

The F Street Presbyterian Church, as has been stated in the sketch of the First Church, was organized in 1803, from members retiring from that church. At a meeting of the Synod of Philadelphia in 1823, this church was ordered to be enrolled in the Presbytery of the District of Columbia. At the time of the organization of this church, Rev. James Laurie, of Edinburgh, then visiting here, was invited to assist in the collection of a congregation, and he was installed pastor in 1804. A church building was erected in 1808, and Mr. Laurie remained the sole pastor until 1841. He was then affected with a protracted illness, and was assisted in his duties by Rev. Dr. Van Rensselaer, then by Rev. Dr. Septimus Tustin, then by Rev. Ninian Bennatyne, then by Rev. L. H. Christian, and by Rev. D. X. Junkin, who remained until after Dr. Laurie's death, which occurred April 17, 1853. March 2, 1854, Rev. Phineas D. Gurley was installed pastor as the successor of Rev. Dr. Laurie, and remained the pastor until the consolidation of this church with the Second Presbyterian Church in 1859.

Second Presbyterian Church was organized May 9, 1820, with forty-one members, and constituted October 13, following. June 6, 1821, Rev. Daniel Baker was elected pastor, who remained until called, in 1828, to the Independent Presbyterian Church of Savannah, Georgia. Rev. Luther Halsey, of Princeton, having declined a call to this church, Rev. J. N. Campbell served as stated supply until the fall of 1830, from which time to 1845 the church was supplied by the pastors, Revs. E. H. Smith, P. H. Fowler, George Wood, R. W. Clark, W. W. Eels, and J. Knox. Then there were temporary supplies until 1849, when Rev. James R. Eckard became the pastor, remaining until 1853. A short supply followed, by Rev. J. D. Matthews, and then the church was supplied by Rev. Dr. James G. Hamner until the union with the F Street Church, above referred to.

New York Avenue Presbyterian Church resulted from the above consolidation. Rev. Dr. Gurley, who had been largely instrumental in securing the union, merged his pastorate of F Street Church into that of the united congregations. The building of the F Street Church was sold for something more than $12,000 to the Messrs. Willard, and is now known as Willard Hall. Rev. Dr. Gurley died September 30,

1868, and in November, 1869, was succeeded in the ministry of this church by Rev. S. S. Mitchell, of Harrisburg, Pennsylvania, who remained until 1878, when he accepted a call to the Reformed church in Brooklyn, and was followed here by Rev. J. R. Paxton, who remained until February 19, 1882, when he was succeeded by the present pastor, Rev. Dr. William Alvin Bartlett, who was installed October 24, 1882. The estimated value of all the property held by the trustees of this church is in excess of $100,000. The new building on New York Avenue was dedicated on Sunday, October 14, 1860, the discourse of the occasion being delivered by Rev. Dr. Boardman, of Philadelphia.

The Fourth Presbyterian Church was established in 1828. In November of that year, the "Central Presbyterian Society of Washington" was formed by twenty members at a meeting held at Jacob Gideon's house, on Seventh Street, and Rev. J. N. Danforth was invited to take charge of the congregation. November 24, the "Fourth Presbyterian Church of Washington" was organized at the same place, D. M. Wilson being the presiding elder. At first the new organization worshiped in Z. D. Brashear's schoolroom, on the southeast corner of Ninth and H streets. A woman's prayer-meeting was organized under the guidance of Mrs. Jacob Gideon, and was held in her house every week for twenty-five years, until her death, in 1853. The first church edifice erected by this church was a one-story structure, and was without seats or chimneys. It was erected on a lot purchased of John P. Van Ness, and was dedicated March 1, 1829, by Rev. John Breckenridge, D. D. Great success attended the ministry of Rev. Mr. Danforth, the number of communicants being sixty-three at the time of the dedication of this building. In 1832 Mr. Danforth was succeeded in his pulpit by Rev. Mason Noble, from Troy, New York. He was succeeded September 27, 1839, by Rev. J. C. Smith, who had preached in Georgetown seven years. On March 1, 1840, Dr. Smith preached from Nehemiah 2:18, "And they said, Let us rise up and build," the result of which sermon was that the corner stone of a new structure was laid June 24, 1840. The building was sixty-one feet by eighty feet in size, the largest church edifice then in the city. It was dedicated June 20, 1841, the dedicatory sermon being preached by Rev. E. N. Kirk, D. D., of Boston, Massachusetts. Rev. Dr. Smith, on September 10, 1864, preached the twenty-fifth anniversary sermon, stating that at that date there were three hundred and thirty-seven names on the rolls, and that he had baptized six hundred and twenty-one persons. Dr. Smith was succeeded by Rev. J. T. Kelly January 23, 1878, who remains pastor at the present time.

The Fifteenth Street Presbyterian Church was organized May 14, 1842, as the "First Colored Presbyterian Church of Washington." Forty communicants of this organization worshiped in Cook's school-house, at H and Fourteenth streets, until they were enabled, by the assistance of the First, Second, and Fourth churches, to erect a small frame building on the site of their present church, on Fifteenth Street, between I and K streets, in 1853. Rev. John F. Cook was the pastor. Rev. W. Catto was installed pastor in 1858, and Rev. B. F. Tanner in .1861. In 1864, the pulpit became vacant, and was thereafter sup-plied by Rev. W. B. Evans and others, until the installation of Rev. H. H. Garnett, who remained until October 3, 1866, when he was followed by Rev. J. H. Muse. Rev. Sella Martin was pastor from December 27, 1868, until February 18, 1870. From this time until the settlement of Rev. G. Van Deurs, in 1874, the pulpit was supplied by Rev. Septimus Tustin. Rev. Mr. Van Deurs was succeeded in 1875 by Rev. J. Brown, and he, in 1878, by Rev. F. J. Grimke, who remained until 1885. From this time until 1887, the pulpit was filled by Rev. C. H. A. Buckley, D. D., one of the professors of Howard University. Rev. J. R. Riley was installed pastor January 18, 1887, and is the present pastor. The building is worth $55,000, and was erected and furnished largely by other Presbyterian churches in Wash-ington.

Assembly's Presbyterian Church was organized March 1, 1853, as the Fifth Presbyterian Church, and was the result of work done by Rev. John C. Smith, D. D., pastor at the time of the Fourth Presby-terian Church, by Rev. A. G. Carothers, and George S. Gideon. The corner stone of the building was laid September 1, 1852, at the corner of Fifth and I streets, and the church edifice was dedicated November 6, 1853. Rev. Mr. Carothers preached January 30, 1853, and accepted the call to the pastorate in March following, being installed on the 20th of that month. After the completion of the dedicatory cere-monies, Rev. John C. Smith gave a short history of the church, and stated that it had received assistance from twenty-three States, and the Choctaw nation of Indians, besides being substantially assisted by the heroine of Tampico. The land was donated by Silas H. Hill and Joseph D. Varnum. The edifice cost $13,000, being turned over to the church free from debt. In 1860 Rev. Mr. Collins became pastor of this church, and in 1861 Rev. T. B. McFalls, remaining until 1868, when he was succeeded by Rev. William Hart.

As a result of the War, and of the withdrawal of members to form a Southern Presbyterian Church (Central Presbyterian), this church in

1870 had become greatly reduced in numbers and strength. The Central Congregational Church, which had been formed from the First Congregational Church by those who had withdrawn therefrom some two years before, together with their pastor, Rev. Dr. Boynton, were without a building. They dissolved their organization, and joined Assembly's Presbyterian Church by letter in August, 1870. The present pastor, Rev. Mr. Little, was called in 1873. Since the consolidation above mentioned, the church has been most prosperous and united, and has shown a steady and encouraging growth.

The Sixth Presbyterian Church was the result of the labors of Rev. Mason Noble, who, in 1851, held a series of prayer-meetings in private residences in South Washington. The first public services were held August 28, 1852, in "Island Hall." On January 23, 1853, at a meeting presided over by Dr. Noble, thirty-two members were enrolled and John Knight elected ruling elder. Dr. Noble served the church from the date of its organization until 1855, and again from 1858 to 1862, and also from 1870 to the time of his death, October 24, 1881. During his first absence, the pulpit was filled by Rev. B. F. Morris. Rev. George H. Smyth was pastor from 1864 to 1869, and Rev. George P. Noble was stated supply from 1869 to 1870. On September 27, 1882, Rev. Frank H. Burdick was elected pastor, and served until 1887. Rev. Scott F. Hershey, Ph. D., the present pastor, was installed October 5, 1887. The membership of the church is about one hundred and seventy-five.

The Western Presbyterian Church was organized in 1853, and worshiped temporarily at the corner of E and Twenty-second streets. On July 3, 1854, Rev. C. Smith, the pastor, purchased of Silas B. Hill and Joseph B. Varnum, Jr., a lot on H Street, near Nineteenth Street, and received from them a donation of $600 toward the payment therefor. Rev. T. N. Haskell was the pastor of this church at the time. A church building was erected on this lot which was dedicated June 7, 1857, Rev. Mr. Haskell preaching the dedicatory sermon. At night Rev. Byron Sunderland, D. D., preached the closing sermon of the day.

At the time of the dedication of the church there had been expended $16,000, and all debts had been paid but about $2,000. The church was built in the Elizabethan style of architecture.

On May 18, 1858, an important meeting was held in this church, the Presbytery of the District of Columbia convening on that day to pass upon the dissolution of the pastoral relations of Rev. Mr. Haskell with the church, and the authorization of his acceptance of the ministry of the Congregational Society of Boston, Massachusetts. The presbytery also reported favorably upon the attainments of Dr. James M. Wilson, M. D., of Washington, and declared him qualified to preach. Rev. J. R. Bartlett was installed pastor August 31, 1859, but removed to the South at the beginning of the War of the Rebellion. In March, 1862, Rev. J. N. Coombs, formerly a Methodist minister, was received and installed, and remained pastor until December 27, 1874. Rev. David Wills became pastor March 1, 1875, and remained until January 28, 1878, and was succeeded by the present pastor, Rev. T. S. Wynkoop, who was installed October 23, 1878. The membership of this church is about three hundred.

Westminster Presbyterian Church was organized June 14, 1853, by the name of the Seventh Street Presbyterian Church of Washington. The site on Seventh Street was donated to the church by Charles Stott. In December, 1873, by a vote of the congregation, the name was changed to "Westminster." Rev. John M. Henry, installed in 1853, remained pastor until 1855, when he was succeeded by Rev. E. B. Cleghorn. Rev. Dr. B. F. Bittinger was installed pastor March 12, 1857, and remained until 1863, when Rev. William Y. Brown became stated supply, followed by Rev. W. W. Campbell, the latter being installed pastor in 1865. Dr. Bittinger succeeded him, being installed January 5, 1868, and remains pastor at the present time.

Capitol Hill Presbyterian Church was, at the time of its organization, the only church of that denomination in its section of the city, including the Capitol and the Navy Yard, the territory under consideration comprising more than a third of the area of the city and a population of more than fifteen thousand. The initial steps toward this organization were taken in the fall of 1863. Rev. John Chester, son of Rev. William Chester, secretary of the Presbyterian Board of Education, by invitation came to Washington to labor in this promising field. In February, 1864, a small number of persons met in a small building known as the mission schoolhouse, in which on the 28th of that month Rev. Mr. Chester preached to them his first sermon. This mission schoolhouse stood on First Street East. The Capitol Hill Presbyterian Church was organized April 11, 1864, under the sanction of the Presbytery of Potomac, with thirty-two members of other churches and two by profession of faith, Rev. Mr. Chester being installed pastor on the same day. A lot was purchased and a chapel was completed so as to be dedicated February 12, 1865, the new society having been assisted in its efforts to raise the money by other Presbyterian churches in Washington and by the

Board of Church Extension, which contributed $1,000 toward the result. When the little chapel was dedicated, it was entirely free from debt. It stood on Fourth Street East, near Pennsylvania Avenue.

In February, 1866, the corner stone of the present building was laid, and then the Presbytery of Potomac proposed to the General Assembly to incorporate with the church the proceeds of the property on E Street Northwest, which had been held for a long time with the view of establishing there a Metropolitan church, and the transfer was accordingly ordered by the General Assembly in 1868. After considerable delay, the property was transferred and the church erected, and the name changed to the Metropolitan Presbyterian Church. The church edifice, which stands at the corner of Fourth and B streets Southeast, was dedicated December 8, 1872, and by the spring of 1878 it was entirely free from debt. Rev. John Chester is still pastor of this church, which, a few years since, spared a colony for the establishment of a mission in the eastern part of the city.

The North Presbyterian Church was organized December 10, 1865. Under the care of Rev. L. R. Fox, the church was organized with twenty-three members, and Mr. Fox was installed pastor December 31, 1865. The church edifice had been dedicated on the 3d of the same month. Rev. Mr. Fox was succeeded by Rev. Charles B. Ramsdell, who was installed December 13, 1875. In 1878, the original building was enlarged, and at the present time the estimated value of the church property is about $30,000. The seating capacity of the church is about five hundred, and the membership about two hundred.

The Central Presbyterian Church was organized May 31, 1868, with twenty-nine members. The movement resulting in this organization began in the preceding January, when twelve individuals favoring it held a meeting in the old Trinity Church, then the Columbia Law building, the rent of which was guaranteed by General Thomas Ewing. The members present at once inaugurated plans for the selection of a site for a church edifice, one of the leading members being Mrs. Ellen Adair, who contributed nearly $2,000 toward the enterprise, and another being Miss Mary E. Coyle. By November, 1871, a lot was selected, and in December, 1871, it was purchased. It has a front of fifty-eight feet on I Street and one hundred and forty feet on Third Street. The chapel erected thereon was completed January 1, 1873, and dedicated January 19, 1874. The main edifice was completed November 14, 1885, and dedicated December 6, 1885. The seating capacity of the audience room is seven hundred, and with the chapel thrown into it, which can readily be done, it is one thousand two hundred. The architecture of the building is Gothic. Rev. A..W. Pitzer, D. D., the founder of the church, is still its pastor, and the membership is at the present time about two hundred. This is the only Presbyterian church in Washington connected with the Southern General Assembly.

The Eastern Presbyterian Church was organized May 9, 1875. The lots on Eighth Street, upon which a frame chapel was erected, were donated to the enterprise by Moses Kelly. Rev. J. T. Kelly supplied the pulpit for a time, and then Rev. George B. Patch was installed, November 1, 1875. Rev. Mr. Patch resigned in 1881, and Rev. S. S. Wallen was installed his successor April 10, 1882, and remained pastor until the fall of 1883, when he was succeeded by Rev. Eugene Peck, who was installed February 13, 1884. The present pastor, Rev. M. N. Cornelius, D. D., succeeded Rev. Mr. Peck. The present membership is about one hundred.

Unity Presbyterian Church was organized with fifty members, March 15, 1882. Rev. G. B. Patch was the first, and has been so far the only, pastor of the church. The first place of worship was Clabaugh Hall, located on Fourteenth Street, between Corcoran and Riggs streets, which was rented for religious services until such time as a church building could be erected. The second and present place of worship was and is the brick chapel located on the corner of Fourteenth and R streets, which cost $8,000, and was dedicated November 15, 1884. At this time, the membership was one hundred and ten, and on April 1, 1891, it was two hundred and seventy-four. This church organization is out of debt, and owns the edifice and grounds upon which it stands and the vacant lot on the corner of Fourteenth and R streets.

The origin of the Church of the Covenant was as follows: In the spring of 1883, a meeting was held at the house of Justice Strong, who had interested himself in the apparent necessity for the building of a Presbyterian church in the northwestern portion of the city, for the purpose of discussing the feasibility of organizing such a church. Those present at this meeting were, besides Justice Strong, Justice Matthews, James G. Blaine, Gardiner G. Hubbard, M. W. Galt, William M. Galt, Admiral Colhoun, Admiral Carter, Samuel Shellabarger, James Fitch, Otis Bigelow, and William Ballantyne. Soon after this meeting was held, the site now occupied by the church, at the corner of Connecticut Avenue and Eighteenth Street, was selected. At a subsequent meeting, a committee, composed of Justice Strong, James G. Blaine, Gardiner G. Hubbard, William M. Galt, William Ballantyne, and James E. Fitch, was appointed to solicit subscriptions and secure the lot by making a payment. Among the early subscribers to the fund for the purchase of this lot were Senator Cameron, James G. Blaine, William Walter Phelps, Colonel John Hay, Ex-Senator Yulee, Judge Strong, and Gardiner G. Hubbard.

The Covenant Presbyterian Church was organized October 13, 1885, with fifty-three members. The church building is one of the largest and most unique of the church edifices of Washington. The walls are of stone, but the main feature of the exterior is the tower or campanile, which is twenty feet square and rises to a height of one hundred and forty-eight feet to the top of the finial. The body of the church forms a parallelogram. The front is on Connecticut Avenue. It is flanked on one side by the tower, and on the other by a low projection, forming the vestibule for one of the main entrances, the other entrance being in the tower. The interior of the church is very handsome. Semicircular arches, springing from four large pillars, support the lantern with its domed roof. The walls and ceilings are decorated in plaster in low relief, from cartoon designs, in the Italian style. The pillars are bronzed. The windows are filled with cathedral glass, with the exception of the large double window on the north side, which is filled with stained glass. The design represents the extreme scenes in the life of Christ — the annunciation to the shepherds and the appearance after resurrection. This window was the gift of Mrs. Martha M. Read as a memorial to her father, Admiral Dahlgren.

The organ made for this church is enclosed in an oak case, enriched with carving. It has three manuals and has thirty-nine stops. It is one of the best organs made. The pulpit and communion table are of unique design, and were the gift of the pastor, Rev. Tennis S. Hamlin, D. D., the first and only pastor of this church, who had the wood of which they are made imported in the log from the Holy Land. In both pulpit and table there are three varieties of wood — olive, oak, and cedar. The top of each is a solid piece of olive, which is susceptible of a high polish. The chandelier, which was presented by the children of the Sunday-school, cost $800. It is a copy of the chandelier in the mosque of St. Sophia in Constantinople. The chapel was occupied for public worship October 11, 1885, and the principal edifice about a year afterward, but it has not yet been dedicated. The membership of the church when organized was fifty-three; January, 1892, it was four hundred and thirty-five.

This church supports the Peck Memorial Chapel, located at the corner of Twenty-eighth and M streets, besides Sunday-school, industrial school, reading room, etc., Rev. Charles Alvin Smith being in charge.

The First Congregational Church of Washington, corner of Tenth and G streets Northwest, was organized November 12, 1865, and recognized by council November 15. Long before this time, however, there had been made several attempts to establish a church of this denomination. The first of these attempts was on August 3, 1847, when a few gentlemen met in the law office of Bigelow & Peugh, on the corner of E and Seventh streets, and resolved to organize a Congregational church essentially on the plan of the Cambridge platform, whose standard of piety should be high, whose doctrines should be evangelical, and which should favor the leading reforms of the day, including Bible, missionary, tract, anti-slavery, Sunday-school, and temperance efforts. It has been stated by some that this was the first religious body in the city, and indeed in the entire South, to insert an anti-slavery plank in its creed, though anti-slavery work had been done by the Methodists in Tennessee at least forty years before.

Meetings were held in many different places, and there was occasional preaching and a Sunday-school. At length, one of their members offered to build a church and rent it to them. This offer of Mr. Cookman was accepted and the first Congregational church building was erected, and afterward twice enlarged. It was on Eighth Street, is still standing, and is now, and for many years has been, used as the Jewish synagogue. The church, however, was not popular in Washington, as it was not always easy to distinguish between anti-slavery principles and abolitionism. Besides this, there was a still greater difficulty in their way — division among themselves on the slavery question; some being extreme in their convictions as to the sin of slavery, and at the same time intolerant of opposite opinion. On account of these internal quarrels, the council refused to constitute them a church, and gradually thinning off in numbers, they quietly dissolved, and as an organization have never been heard of since.

The next attempt to organize a Congregational church was made in 1852. This organization was to be both anti-slavery and Congregational. The difficulty still was abolition. Rev. Dr. Charles B. Boynton, of Cincinnati, twice declined to fill the pulpit. J. B. Grinnell, who had just graduated from an orthodox theological school, and who was warranted sound on the slavery question, came and preached a short time, but could not hold the congregation. Then came the Rev. Alexander Duncanson, who had just arrived in the United States from Scotland. At this time the old Trinity Church property came into

market, and Mr. Grinnell went to New York and New England to raise the money with which to buy it, and came back to Washington with money enough to make the first payment, and with this payment secured the possession of the premises. Thus the Congregationalists of Washington again had a building in which to hold religious services. Then upon the invitation of Mr. Grinnell, in behalf of this church, a council of three hundred pastors and delegates came from all parts of the country to visit the church. Of this council Professor Calvin E. Stowe was chosen moderator. Before this large council the young Scotch preacher had to state his theological views, which he succeeded in doing to the satisfaction of the council until he came to the doctrine of the perseverance of the saints. Here, unfortunately for his hope of becoming pastor of this new church, he stated his belief that Christians sometimes fall from grace, which so shocked the learned gentlemen composing the council that he was rejected. The council adjourned on Saturday. It had, during the week, heard one Congregational sermon, from Henry Ward Beecher, one of its members, but only one of the council was invited to preach in any of the Washington churches on Sunday, this one being the Rev. Dr. Sweetser, of Worcester, Massachusetts, a special friend of Mrs. President Pierce, who was invited by Rev. Dr. Gurley, at the request of Mrs. Pierce, to preach in the New York Avenue Presbyterian Church.

Scarcely had the council adjourned, when every Department clerk who belonged to this church received a notice that he must choose between his anti-slavery church and his position under the Government, and every one of them gave up his connection with the church. Rev. Mr. Duncanson having been rejected, the little church began looking round for another pastor. An invitation was extended to Rev. Henry Ward Beecher, but he declined. Rev. Horace James, of Worcester, Massachusetts, was then invited to the pulpit, but he also declined. In August, 1856, Rev. E. H. Nevins, D. D., of Massachusetts, accepted a call, but remained only a short time, and then Rev. George W. Bassett became the pastor and remained until 1858, when, on account of financial reverses, he could no longer serve without pay, as he had been voluntarily doing, and the church was too feeble to pay him, so he left the pulpit; and after a brave struggle against numerous difficulties, the little church gave up the ghost.

The third attempt to found a Congregational church in Washington was made in 1865, and was this time a success. A society having been formed, a meeting was held, September 17, in the Unitarian church on the corner of D and Sixth streets, Rev. Charles B. Boynton, D. D., for twenty years previously a popular pastor in Cincinnati, officiating twice that day. After remaining here a short time, Metzerott's Hall, on Pennsylvania Avenue, was secured and occupied for some time. Afterward, finding that old Trinity Church had been purchased by Columbia College, and that its lecture room would be an excellent place for Sunday service, the congregation moved into it, remaining through the summer, and then, by arrangement, into the hall of the House of Representatives, the pastor of the church having been elected chaplain of the House.

At the first informal meeting of the members of this church, October 11, 1865, fifty-six persons agreed to join the proposed new church. At the time of the organization of the church, one hundred and four joined, and two weeks later nineteen more were added. A council was held October 2, 1866, to install the newly elected pastor, Rev. Dr. Boynton. The question of a site for a church building soon began to agitate the membership, and at length a lot on the corner of Tenth and G streets was purchased, and the corner stone of a new church building was laid October 2, 1866, at which time Major-General O. O. Howard was introduced by Dr. Boynton, and Rev. Edwin Johnson, of Baltimore, delivered an address. The building erected on this site had a full seating capacity of two thousand five hundred persons. In the erection of this building, assistance was received from the Church of the Pilgrims, in Brooklyn, which contributed over $7,000 toward the building fund, and suggested that the church be named the "Howard Monumental Church."

November 18, 1868, a council from the different Congregational churches throughout the North and Northwest convened in Washington, in response to an invitation sent out October 24, to consult as to the best method of adjusting difficulties then existing in this church, which had arisen through their pastor's ministrations. This council was called by a minority of the church, and when it met in the church on Tenth and G streets, the proposition was made to the majority that they should consent to consider it a mutual council. To this proposition the majority declined to accede, saying that a mutual council had been called to meet January 13, 1869, and that any member of the minority of the church would have the same right to be heard in the mutual council as any other member. On the next day, the council listened to the charges against the pastor made by the minority, as likewise to Dr. Boynton's reply; but the charges and the reply would occupy more space than can be granted to them in this work, except to say that Dr. Boynton took exceptions to being tried by an *ex parte* council, especially when a mutual council had been called, and to say, also, that a statement was published, signed by over one hundred members, to the effect that, in their opinion, the difficulties then existing had been caused, not by the course pursued by the pastor, but by the determined efforts of the minority, by whom the *ex parte* council had been called. One of the principal difficulties seems to have been in reference to what was termed "amalgamation," the pastor having charged that General Howard was an "amalgamationist," meaning by this term the commingling of both white and black people in the same church and the same school. "Some time since, Dr. Boynton preached a sermon on the subject of colored people entering the church, just at a time when colored children were introduced, a noticeable feature of which was that not one word was in it to encourage the intermingling of colored with white children in the schools."

The mutual council referred to above convened in Washington January 13, 1869. Dr. Boynton presented his preliminary statement. He said that it was a fundamental principle of the Congregational Church that the majority must rule, and that if, after a full discussion of questions at issue, the minority could not be reconciled to the government of a majority, they must withdraw. He was quite willing there should be a full investigation of every charge. Wednesday and Thursday were consumed in the discussion, and on Friday General Howard made a statement as to the financial condition of the church, showing that the building had cost about $100,000, of which $60,000 had been subscribed. It became evident, through the discussion, that General Howard and Dr. Boynton could only settle personal differences personally, and that church troubles must be settled by the council. On Saturday morning, the 16th, the committee to which had been referred the troubles in the church made a report, stating that the attitude of the church toward the colored people had excited painful interest throughout the country, and that the council was not surprised that the controversy had arisen, yet they did not believe either the pastor or the majority of the church was opposed to the colored people; notwithstanding this, however, they believed that the blacks could best work out their own salvation apart from the whites.

April 22, a meeting was held to consider the question that agitated and disturbed the church, at which time, in order to open up a way for a reconciliation, Dr. Boynton resigned, and his resignation was at once accepted. James S. Delano then presented a petition, signed by a large number of the members, asking letters of dismission for the purpose of forming a new church, and on motion of General Howard, the letters asked for were granted. The meeting then adjourned, and a meeting of the seceding members was immediately organized, at which Dr. Boynton was chosen moderator. The name suggested at that time for this new organization was the "People's Church," of which, by April 25, there were about one hundred and twenty-five members. The Young Men's Christian Association rooms were secured, and Rev. Dr. Boynton was elected pastor. The church thus organized held its meetings for a time in the Thirteenth Street Baptist Church, until the Young Men's Christian Association rooms were completed.

The First Church occupies its own fine edifice on the corner of Tenth and G streets, and its present pastor is Rev. S. M. Newman.

The People's Congregational Church, located on O Street, between Seventh and Eighth, Northwest, was organized in 1869, and its first pastor was Rev. Charles B. Boynton, D. D. The causes leading to its organization are detailed in the sketch of the First Church, and need only to be referred to. The congregation is in good condition. The pastor is Rev. J. H. Dailey, residing at 2028 Vermont Avenue.

The Tabernacle Congregational Church was organized in 1881. It is located on Ninth Street, between B Street and Virginia Avenue, and is under the pastoral supervision of Rev. G. J. Jones, Ph. D.

Lincoln Memorial Congregational Church, corner of Eleventh and R streets Northwest, was organized in 1881. Its pastor is Rev. George W. Moore.

Plymouth Congregational, corner Seventeenth and P streets Northwest, was organized also in 1881. Rev. Sterling N. Brown is serving as its pastor.

The Fifth Congregational Church was organized May 13, 1886, with fifteen members. The first and present pastor is Rev. B. N. Seymour, who began September 17, 1887, and was ordained in November, 1887. Services are held in Milford Hall, at the corner of Eighth and I streets Northeast, which was purchased in May, 1888, for $5,000. The membership of this church on January 1, 1892, was seventy-five.

The First Baptist Church was organized March 7, 1802, with six members, in a private house, by Rev. William Parkinson, at that time and for some years afterward chaplain of one of the Houses of Congress. The six members of this church at the time of its organization were Charles P. Polk, Cephas Fox, Charles Rogers, John Buchan, Joseph Borrows, and Sarah Borrows. They proceeded at once to

37

secure a church building, and purchased a lot on the southwest corner of Nineteenth and I streets. Upon this lot they erected a brick church building, and occupied it for the first time in the following November. The building thus early begun was not finished, however, until 1809. The church was without a regular pastor until 1807, though it had had services by Rev. Mr. Parkinson and others from time to time. In 1807 Rev. Obadiah B. Brown became the pastor, and remained until 1850. At the beginning of his pastorate, the congregation consisted of twenty-seven members, while at its close the membership was composed of one hundred and fifty persons. He was succeeded by Rev. Stephen P. Hill, D. D., from Baltimore.

Under Rev. Mr. Brown's ministry, the church building was from time to time improved. In 1809 wide galleries were put in, so wide indeed that an old member, presumably an old salt, remarked that the church reminded him of the hatchway of a ship. At this time the system of pew renting was adopted, and forty-four pews were rented for the aggregate sum of $300 per annum. A converted actor, named Spencer H. Cone, of Baltimore, removed to Washington, joined this church, and was ordained to preach, becoming pastor of the Baptist church at Alexandria. Oliver C. Comstock, a member of Congress from New York, was also converted and ordained to the ministry. In addition to these two, the following were ordained ministers of the Gospel: Joseph H. Jones, William Sedgwick, Robert W. Cushman, Luther Rice, James D. Knowles, Baron Stow, George F. Adams, John Pratt, Joseph T. Robert, Robert B. C. Howell, Stephen Chapin, and Henry W. Dodge.

Previous to 1826, the question had been discussed of erecting a church in the central portion of the city. A lot was purchased on D Street, between Eighth and Ninth streets, Northwest, for $100, but the financial condition of the congregation was so low that no action could be taken for several years. In 1833, the question was again taken up as to a change in the location of the church, and this time it was pushed to completion. Lot No. 10, in Square 377, on the east side of Tenth Street, between E and F streets, Northwest, was secured, and the erection of a new church building begun in July, 1833. This building was of brick, sixty-five feet long and forty-five feet wide, with a Sunday-school room and lecture room in the rear, twenty-two by thirty feet, and a tower in the front. The cost of the church was somewhat upward of $8,000. This church was located on the site subsequently made historic from the assassination of President Lincoln in Ford's Theater, built upon the spot.

Soon after the removal to the new church building, a large portion of the colored members of the church were formed into a separate organization and granted the use of the old church building, and this colored Baptist church is still in existence.

In 1840, the new church building was damaged by fire, and in 1843 there was a revival of religion, as there had been in 1816 and in 1839. As has been stated above, Rev. Stephen P. Hill, D. D., succeeded Rev. Mr. Brown, and during the pastorate of Dr. Hill, the church property on Tenth Street was sold. This was on account of a consolidation of this church with the Fourth Baptist, and the removal of the First Church to the property of the Fourth Church on Thirteenth Street. The proceeds of the sale of the Tenth Street church property were used in paying off a portion of the debt of the Fourth Church. At the time of the consolidation, Rev. Isaac Cole was pastor of the Fourth Church, and he became joint pastor of the new congregation with Dr. Hill. In February, 1862, the church building was greatly damaged by a hurricane. The steeple was blown down, and, falling on the roof of the church, crushed through, completely wrecking the interior. The damage having been repaired, the building was taken for a hospital by the Government, the congregation meeting in the meantime in the New York Avenue Presbyterian Church, the use of which was tendered them; and thus the New York Avenue Church reciprocated a similar favor conferred upon it some years before by this church. The joint pastorate terminated in 1860, when the Rev. Dr. Samson, president of Columbia College, accepted the pastorate of this church, and served without pay for three years, for the purpose of assisting the church. He was succeeded by Rev. A. D. Gillettee, D. D., who remained five years. Rev. J. H. Cuthbert, D. D., then became the pastor, and remained seventeen years. The Rev. Charles A. Stakely succeeded Dr. Cuthbert, and was installed pastor in December, 1887. He is still the pastor.

The Second Baptist Church, corner of Fourth Street and Virginia Avenue Southeast, was organized June 1, 1810, with five members dismissed from the First Baptist Church. The first house of worship stood near the Navy Yard, for which reason it was sometimes called the Navy Yard Baptist Church. The congregation belonged to the Columbia Baptist Association, composed principally of churches in Virginia. In 1826, it had about one hundred and sixty members. The first regular pastor was Rev. Osborn. Some of his successors were: Rev. Barton, Rev. Lynd, Rev. Rollin Neale, Rev. Leland (1839), Rev. G. W. Samson (1844), Rev. J. W. Greer (1871), Rev. P.

Warren (died March 12, 1871). One of the most conspicuous men in the list of early pastors was Rev. Stephen Cone, at one time chaplain of the House of Representatives. He had, also, pastorates in several of the leading Eastern cities. The present pastor is E. Hez Swem, under whom the congregation has reached a membership of five hundred and seventy-eight.

The present house of worship, a brick structure, was erected some thirty-five or forty years ago. Funds are being raised for the erection of a new and enlarged edifice during the year 1892.

The E Street Baptist Church, located on E Street, between Sixth and Seventh, Northwest, was organized in 1842. One of the early pastors was Rev. G. W. Samson. He was finally chosen president of Columbia College and was succeeded by Rev. J. Spencer Kennard, who entered upon his duties October 23, 1859. This congregation has a comfortable brick structure, and is one of the active Baptist churches of the city. It reported in 1891 a membership of three hundred and seventy-four souls, and held property estimated to be worth $90,000. Its total receipts for the year were $5,836.88. Its pastor is the Rev. J. J. Muir.

Fifth Baptist Church, located on D Street, between Four and a Half and Sixth, Southwest, was formerly known as Island Baptist Church. It was founded in June, 1857. In September of that year, a site was purchased on Virginia Avenue, between Four and a Half and Sixth streets, and on the 23d of said month a committee of delegates from the various Baptist churches of the city met to examine Mr. C. C. Meader as to his fitness, and to prepare for his ordination. The day selected was September 27, when he was ordained to the work. He has remained pastor ever since. The congregation enrolls four hundred and fifty-two members.

Calvary Baptist Church was organized June 2, 1862, with thirty-five constituent members. Services were at first held in "Old Trinity Church," on Fifth Street, between D and E streets, Rev. T. R. Howlett, D. D., being the first pastor. The corner stone of the first church building erected by this organization was laid September 6, 1863, Rev. Mr. Howlett, Rev. G. W. Samson, and Rev. Dr. Gillettee taking part in the ceremonies. The lot upon which this church was erected was on the corner of H and Eighth streets Northwest, and was purchased for the church by Hon. Amos Kendall, at a cost of $8,000. Mr. Kendall also placed at the disposal of the church a building fund of $13,000, and donated the income of $25,000, which, besides paying the pastor's salary, gave a handsome sum for other purposes. The church building thus erected was a fine specimen of the Gothic style of architecture, and cost $50,000. It was seventy-five by ninety-five feet in size, and the tower terminated in an octagonal open-work iron spire, bearing a cruciform flower, and was one hundred and sixty feet high. The spire was sixty feet high, and beneath it was suspended a bell weighing four thousand pounds. Under the bell was a clock with a face eight feet square. The entire cost of the church, ground, and furniture was more than $115,000, more than half of which was contributed by Hon. Amos Kendall, who was then more than seventy-six years of age. This church was dedicated June 3, 1866. When completed, it had one of the finest auditoriums in the city. This church organization has also erected Kendall Chapel, on Thirteen and a Half and D streets Southwest, at a cost of $8,000, and Memorial Chapel, of brick, at Fifth and P streets, at a cost of $15,000. In 1872 the membership of this church was three hundred and five, and in 1892, one thousand and one hundred.

Since Rev. Dr. Howlett's pastorate closed, the pastors have been Rev. J. W. Parker, D. D., Rev. A. F. Mason, D. D., and the present pastor, Rev. S. H. Greene, D. D., whose pastorate began in 1880. During this time, more than one thousand two hundred persons have united with the church. In 1867 the church edifice was destroyed by fire, and a new edifice was erected in 1869.

Gay Street Baptist Church, corner of Thirty-first and N streets, Georgetown, was organized June 19, 1866, by Rev. James Nelson, now of the Richmond Female Seminary, with eleven members. For two years, the congregation was permitted to use the Presbyterian chapel on Market (now Thirty-third) Street. It then secured grounds and an edifice, through the generosity, largely, of Mr. James S. Welch, and a legacy from John McCutchen, deceased. The house of worship, a frame structure, was erected during the pastorate of Dr. Nelson, the dedication occurring October 11, 1868. The seating capacity is for six hundred persons. The list of pastors includes the following: Revs. James Nelson, A. J. Huntington, George W. Beale, George E. Truitt, Joseph Walker, —— Lodge, George W. McCullough, W. S. O. Thomas. The present membership is one hundred and seventy-one. In this number is Mrs. James S. Welch, widow of the late James S. Welch. She was the first person baptized after the church was organized, and is recognized now as a true mother in Israel.

The Metropolitan Baptist Church was organized February 27, 1878, with thirty-one members, there having been a society in existence for some time, but no regular church organization. The first building erected by them was a chapel built in the fall and winter of 1875–76, which was intended as the rear portion of a larger church to be erected subsequently, the foundation of which was laid in the fall of 1886, at the corner of A and Sixth streets Northeast, the superstructure of which was erected in 1887 and 1888. The pastors of the church have been the following: Rev. Stephen H. Mirick, Rev. Dr. Joseph W. Parker, Rev. William M. Ingersoll, Rev. William H. Young, B. D., and Rev. Green Clay Smith, the present pastor. The membership, at first thirty-one, has gradually increased to two hundred and forty-four.

The Grace Baptist Church, located on South Carolina Avenue and Ninth Street Southeast, until May 7, 1891, known as "The East Capitol Street Baptist Church," was organized December 28, 1884, with some thirty members. For over six years, the congregation met in a hall on the corner of Fourth and East Capitol streets. Finally, without a pastor, it bought a site, and erected in 1890–91 a brick edifice with stone trimmings. It was first occupied in June, 1891, but was not dedicated until October 25th of that year. Its membership is one hundred and five. The pastorate has been filled in succession by Revs. Owen McVey Miller, Frank Gardner, and James D. Smith.

Maryland Avenue Baptist Church, corner of Maryland Avenue and Fourteenth Street Northeast, was organized in 1891. It reported fifty-seven members in 1891, and property valued at $8,000. Its pastor is Rev. S. R. White.

Concordia Lutheran Church is located on the corner of Twentieth and G streets Northwest, and in 1833 was organized by a small band of Germans under the name of the German Evangelical Lutheran Church, worshiping for a time in the City Hall. They then erected a church at the above location, which, in 1853, was enlarged. On December 27, 1846, Rev. Samuel D. Finkle entered upon the active duties of his ministry, and as the church grew and prospered, a parsonage was built, a school established, and a society organized having for its object the assistance of the congregation in pecuniary and other affairs. The pastor now is Rev. Ernest Drewitz.

St. Paul's English Lutheran Church was started in 1842, the Synod of the Evangelical Lutheran Church of Maryland, at its session in October, that year, appointing Rev. Albert A. Muller to the station at Washington and Georgetown, with a view of establishing such a church at one or both of these places. Services were held for a time in Mr. Todd's new hall on Pennsylvania Avenue. June 18, 1844, the corner stone of the new church building was laid at the intersection of H and Eleventh streets Northwest, with imposing ceremonies, the address being delivered by Rev. Dr. Morris, of Baltimore. Rev. A. A. Muller was followed by Rev. J. G Butler, who, August 14, 1859, preached his tenth anniversary sermon. A neat church building was then possessed by the congregation, and the burden of debt had been removed. In May, 1861, Rev. Mr. Butler accepted the chaplaincy of the Fifth Pennsylvania Regiment. The present pastor is Rev. S. Domer, D. D.

Trinity German Evangelical Lutheran Church was organized in 1851. The church is located at the corner of Fourth and E streets Northwest, is of brick, and cost $12,000. It was dedicated November 22, 1857, by Rev. Wilhelm Nordmann, then pastor of the church. The pastors have been, since Rev. Mr. Nordmann, Revs. Ernst Burger, Peter Brand, Wilhelm Lubkert, and Heinrich Christian, the latter since November, 1876. At the present time, there are ninety-five voting members, and nearly four hundred confirmed members. There is a parochial school connected with the church, with two teachers and sixty-eight pupils.

St. John's (Johannes') German Evangelical Lutheran Church, located at No. 318 Four and a Half Street Southwest, was organized in 1853. The church edifice is a brick structure, and the present membership includes one hundred and forty-four families. There are several organizations within the church, viz.: St. John's Benefit Association, with 24 members; St. John's Woman's Society, with 26 members; St. John's Young People's Society, with 38 members. In the list of pastors there have been the following: Rev. Meister, the first; Rev. Schloegel, Rev. F. P. H. Henninghausen, Rev. A. Frey, Dr. Keitz, Rev. Diehl, Rev. John H. Mengert, Rev. Kurtz, Rev. Selinger, Rev. E. Lehnert, and Rev. H. K. Müller.

Zion's Lutheran Church, at the corner of Sixth and P streets Northwest, was established in 1867, and erected a frame building, which was dedicated March 30, 1873. The first pastor was Rev. William A. Frey, and those succeeding him have been Revs. Emil Henckell, Mr. Steihauer, A. Eisenhauer, G. W. S. Landau, H. Unglaub, and the present pastor, A. Homrighaus. The present membership is about one hundred and fifty. English preaching has become a main feature of the service.

Memorial Lutheran Church is situated at the corner of Fourteenth and Vermont Avenue Northwest. The lot upon which this church stands was purchased in March, 1866, from Hon. Caleb Cushing for $8,000, by the people of St. Paul's English Lutheran Church, the subscription for the entire amount being secured from them on a single Sunday morning. The memorial chapel in the rear of the present church was dedicated February 5, 1868. The foundation of the new church was begun in the summer of 1870, the corner stone being laid October 31, that year. The present pastor is Rev. J. G. Butler.

The Church of the Reformation (Lutheran) was organized in April, 1870, in a frame chapel which stood on First Street, near C, Southeast, by Rev. W. E. Parson, with twenty-three charter members. The little chapel was used until 1881, when a site was purchased on the corner of Pennsylvania Avenue and Second Street Southeast, and a commodious two-story brick edifice, with lecture room in basement, was erected. The church has a membership of two hundred and fifty communicants. The pastors, in regular order, have been: W. E. Parson, 1870-72; Philip Graif, 1872-75; Louis Hay, 1776-79; W. E. Parson, 1879, present incumbent.

The Evangelical Lutheran Church, corner of Thirty-second and Q streets, Georgetown, is comparatively new as to its organization, but old as respects the title to church property. Colonel Charles Beatty, one of the founders of Georgetown, had, in 1769, set apart for the sole benefit of the Lutheran Church a plat of ground containing from one-half to three-quarters of an acre, and caused the same to be so entered and designated in the town plat. Subsequently, the site was used by the Lutherans for school purposes, and for a burial ground. Their title to the property has been affirmed by the Supreme Court. About 1865, the Germans raised funds under the direction of Rev. S. Finkle, D. D., to erect the present neat brick Gothic structure. The dedication of the house occurred June 5, 1870, and in the autumn of the same year an organization with some twelve members was consummated. The first pastor was Rev. J. J. Suman. He was succeeded in the spring of 1871 by Rev. George A. Nixdorff, of Frederick, Maryland, who has canceled the debt that hung over the church.

Grace Lutheran Church, situated at the corner of Thirteenth and Corcoran streets Northwest, was organized in 1876. Rev. Emanuel G. Tressel has the spiritual supervision of its membership.

Our Redeemer Lutheran Church is located on Eighth Street, above Florida Avenue, Northwest. It was organized in 1885, and is now under the pastoral oversight of Rev. D. E. Wiseman.

St. Mark's Lutheran Church was organized in 1889, in Potomac

Hall, with fifteen members. Its church edifice stands on C Street, between Twelfth and Thirteenth streets, Southwest, is a brick structure, and cost $12,000. It has not yet been dedicated. Rev. W. H. Gotwald was the first, and is the present, pastor. The membership is now about sixty. It is the only Lutheran church in the city in connection with the General Synod where the pastor wears the robe and the full Common Service is regularly used.

Keller Memorial Lutheran Church, corner of Ninth Street and Maryland Avenue Northeast, has but a recent origin. The beautiful edifice was erected during 1891–92. The main audience room has a seating capacity for six hundred.

The First German Reformed Trinity Church was organized December 8, 1867. Of the original membership, only one now remains alive, Charles Schroth, of this city. The first pastor of this church was Rev. J. W. Ebbinghaus. A frame church was erected at the corner of N and Sixth streets Northwest, and a new brick building was dedicated October 25, 1891. The church has a membership now of about one hundred families, and works in connection with the Reformed Church of the United States. The pastors who have succeeded the first one mentioned above have been Rev. Robert Reitzel, Rev. Mr. Schild, Rev. M. Treiber, Rev. Mr. Wetterstrom, Rev. M. G. J. Stern, Rev. R. A. Guenther, Rev. H. A. Maier, Rev. W. L. Elterich, and Rev. Gustav Facius, the present pastor.

The Grace Reformed Church of the United States, located on Fifteenth Street, between P Street and Rhode Island Avenue, was organized in 1877, through the labors of Dr. Thomas G. Apple, of Lancaster, Pennsylvania; Dr. Staley, of Baltimore, and Dr. Eschbach, of Frederick. The present house of worship is a brick chapel, which was erected in 1881. The congregation has about one hundred members. The first pastor was Rev. C. F. Sontag, who officiated some eight years. He was succeeded by Rev. A. T. G. Apple, the present incumbent.

In the summer of 1891, a movement was made toward the erection of a church by the United Brethren in Christ. A lot one hundred by one hundred and twelve feet, on the northwest corner of North Capitol and R streets, was purchased for the sum of $11,200. Arrangements are now being perfected for the construction of a building during the coming year. The congregation is receiving financial assistance from the Church-Erection Society of the United Brethren Church. The pastor is Rev. C. I. B. Brane, A. M., for many years the Washington correspondent of the *Religious Telescope*, of Dayton, Ohio.

The Church of Our Father, Universalist, stands at the corner of Thirteenth and L streets Northwest. The first movement toward the organization of a Universalist church in Washington was made in 1867, by the General Convention of this denomination. Rev. E. G. Brooks preached two Sundays, and Rev. A. A. Miner, D. D., of Boston, Massachusetts, also preached two Sundays. The first services were held in Union League Hall, on Ninth Street. Meetings were held afterward in Masonic Temple, and in Metzerott Hall, on Pennsylvania Avenue, services being conducted by different ministers. The society, named Murray Universalist Society, was organized in May, 1869.

When the charter for the church organization was secured, in 1874, the name given to the organization was "The First Universalist Church in Washington, District of Columbia." This charter was obtained during the ministry of Rev. C. H. Fay, who came here from Middletown, Connecticut, in 1873. About the time of the organization of the church, the services were transferred to Talmage Hall, and were held there and at Masonic Hall, and at Lincoln Hall, until the present church building was ready for occupancy. Rev. Mr. Fay remained pastor until May, 1877, when he resigned, and in the following fall he was succeeded by Rev. Alexander Kent, who had previously preached at Baltimore, Maryland. At the beginning of Rev. Kent's ministry, there were fifty-six members in the church, and as their numbers increased, Mr. Kent, with the consent of the General Convention, inaugurated a movement looking toward the erection of a new church building. This was begun in 1879, the larger portion of the contributions being from friends outside of Washington. This church building was completed and occupied for the first time in May, 1883. It was dedicated in October following, under its present name, "The Church of Our Father." The dedicatory sermon was preached by Rev. A. A. Miner, D. D., of Boston, Massachusetts. Rev. Mr. Kent remained pastor of the church until 1890, with the exception of about one year, resigning in October, 1888, being recalled in June, 1889, and entering upon the second portion of his pastorate in September, 1889. At the time of his retirement, there were about one hundred and twenty members in the church. He was succeeded by Professor S. A Whitcomb. The Optimist Club of the Universalist Church was organized October 13, 1874.

All Souls' Unitarian Church was established in 1820. Early in the spring of 1821, active measures were taken to erect a church building, which was dedicated Thursday, June 9, 1822, Rev. Mr. Little preaching the dedicatory sermon in the morning, and Mr. Ralph Eddowes, of Philadelphia, preaching in the afternoon. The bell erected upon this church was the first church bell in the city. It was cast at the foundry established near Boston by the famous Paul Revere, and was purchased with subscriptions by John Quincy Adams, John C. Calhoun, and other distinguished men. This bell was rung for public purposes until 1861, but then its use was discontinued, because it had on the day of the death of old John Brown rung a requiem for him.

The precise date of Mr. Little's retirement from this church does not appear, but it must have been in 1826, for in the file of the papers of that year (the papers then and for many years afterward being almost devoid of reference to local events) there were occasional notices of ministers of this denomination preaching in the First Unitarian Church. Of these occasional supplies may be mentioned Rev. Darnelle; Rev. Mr. Walls, of Cambridge, Massachusetts; Rev. Mr. Motte, of Charleston, South Carolina, and Rev. Mr. Green, of Lynn, Massachusetts. For the most of 1828 and 1829, Rev. Andrew Bigelow was pastor of this church. During the winter of 1829–30, the church was looking for a minister, and at length secured Rev. Cazneau Palfrey, who was ordained October 5, 1830, sermon and charge by Rev. Francis Parkman, of Boston, his ministry continuing until January, 1836. During the time of his pastorate, in the winter of 1833–34, Rev. Mr. Palfrey delivered a series of lectures on the doctrines of the Unitarian Church, the titles being "The Person, Character, and Office of Christ," "The Holy Spirit," "Total Depravity," and "The Paternal Character of God." In 1839, Rev. Stephen G. Bulfinch, son of the architect of the Capitol, became the pastor, and remained six years. Rev. Edward Everett Hale next became the pastor, from October, 1844, to March, 1845.

Rev. J. Angier preached for this church a short time in 1846, and then Rev. Orville Dewey became pastor of this church. Dr. Dewey preached during the succeeding winter, and in the spring of 1847 Rev. Samuel Longfellow preached for one month. For the next three years the minister was Rev. Joseph Henry Allen, who was succeeded by Dr. Orville Dewey in the winter of 1851–52. During this year, Dr. Dewey, who was one of the matchless orators of Unitarianism, delivered to the Lowell Institute, of Boston, a course of lectures upon Natural Theology, enlarging its scope, however, to include the entire problem of human destiny. This course of lectures was repeated in Washington by request. Dr. Dewey remained with this church until July, 1853, with a short intermission in 1852. Then came Moncure

Daniel Conway. He was installed minister February 28, 1855, and remained until the close of 1856. For a short time the minister was Rev. W. D. Haley, who was followed by Rev. William Henry Channing. At this time the city was full of sick and wounded soldiers, and, under the lead of Mr. Channing, the congregation promptly offered the use of the church for hospital purposes — the first church in the city to manifest its patriotism. The officers of the Government soon offered the Senate chamber to the church for Sunday worship, and in December, 1863, Mr. Channing was elected chaplain of Congress. During the two winters of his chaplaincy, the American Unitarian Association sent to Washington many of the ablest ministers of the denomination, and services were held simultaneously every Sunday at the church and at the hall of the House of Representatives. February 12, 1865, Mr. Channing invited Rev. Mr. Garnet to preach for him in the House of Representatives, "the first colored preacher ever heard in the National Capitol."

Rev. Dr. Rufus P. Stebbins preached during the winter of 1867–68 for six months. Then, for a short time, came Rev. William Shargan, and for five years, from December, 1870, to December, 1875, the minister was Rev. Frederick Hinckley. Soon after 1870, when the center of population was moving rapidly toward the northwest, it was felt that, the old church building becoming, as it was, dilapidated, ill-placed, and inaccessible, a new church building, more eligible in location, larger, and more attractive, was essential to the continued prosperity of the congregation. At the Saratoga Conference of 1876, an appeal for assistance was made to the denomination at large, and the delegates present pledged their several charges for $25,000, which amount was collected the next year. The bequest of Mr. Winn, of Woburn, Massachusetts, of $100,000 was made about this time, and of this amount $10,000 was granted for the purpose of the erection of the new church. The old church property was sold to the city for a police court for $20,000, and additional contributions in the city brought the amount up to $65,000. With this sum, the present lot was purchased for $20,000, the building was erected for $40,000, and the organ was purchased for $5,000, thus completing the purchase and payment for the entire property for the sum secured, and without incurring any debt.

While the new church building was being erected, the society was reorganized in accordance with the laws of the District of Columbia, and changed its name to "All Souls' Church," and adopted, June 4, 1877, a bond of union, constitution, and by-laws. Sunday,

July 2, Rev. Clay MacCauley was invited to settle as minister, and was installed January 30, 1878. The new church building was dedicated January 29, 1878, Rev. Henry W. Bellows preaching the dedicatory sermon. Rev. Mr. MacCauley remained until the summer of 1880, and is now a missionary of the Unitarian Association in Japan. The next and present minister was the Rev. Rush R. Shippen, who was installed April 13, 1881, Rev. Robert Collyer preaching the installation sermon. His first sermon was preached on the next Sunday, which was Easter Sunday. The membership at the present time, January 1, 1892, is two hundred and twenty.

The Twentieth Century Club was organized in April, 1890, by the women of the church. The "Lend-a-Hand" was organized by twenty-two young women of the congregation in October, 1890. The Channing Club was organized January 20, 1891. The above, together with the Parish Union, constitute the working forces of the church outside of its own organization, and all perform efficient and acceptable labor.

The People's Church is the name of an organization which began in this city in the autumn of 1891. Its first meetings, conducted by Rev. Alexander Kent, the originator, were held in Union Hall, afterward changed to the Academy of Music, and still later to the Builders' Exchange, on Thirteenth Street Northwest. The fatherhood of God, the brotherhood of man, and the oneness of the life divine and human were announced as fundamental principles. The acceptance of this announcement was not made a condition of membership; but sympathy with the purpose and a desire to work for the attainment of these ends were all that was required.

Vermont Avenue Christian Church was organized in 1843, by Dr. Barclay, subsequently a missionary to Jerusalem and author of a large work entitled "The City of the Great King." The organization occurred in the southwest part of the city, in a small frame schoolhouse which stood on Maryland Avenue.

The first house of worship owned by the congregation was a frame structure purchased from the Southern Methodist Church, and removed from M Street to the site on Vermont Avenue, the dedication being conducted by Elder J. Z. Taylor in 1869. Owing to the fact that President Garfield was a member of this congregation, an appeal was made shortly after his assassination to the organization throughout the United States for means to erect a structure which would be a Memorial Church. The appeal was successful. A fine structure was secured, which, including site, cost about $67,000. In this new structure is preserved the old family seat of President Garfield. The new edifice was dedicated January 20, 1884, by President W. K. Pendleton, of Bethany College, West Virginia.

Much of the preaching was at first done by supplies. Protracted meetings were held, from time to time, by such men as D. P. Henderson, of Missouri; Knowles Shaw, of Indiana, and others. The regular pastors have been Dr. J. T. Barclay, Henry T. Anderson, O. A. Bartholomew, and F. D. Power. During Mr. Bartholomew's pastorate, the membership reached two hundred. Under the efficient labors of Mr. Power, it has grown to five hundred and fifty; and in April, 1891, it sent to the corner of Ninth and D streets Northwest a colony of eighty-five, called "Ninth Street Christian Church," which has grown to three hundred and eighty-five under the charge of E. B. Bagley.

The Washington Hebrew Congregation was organized in 1854. Its synagogue is located on Eighth Street, between H and I streets, Northwest. The building was erected by the First Congregational Church, and twice enlarged by them. The Hebrew Congregation took possession of this building May 20, 1859, Rev. Landsberg being the rabbi at the time. In March, 1863, steps were inaugurated to secure funds with which to acquire a larger and better building. The result was the present commodious brick structure. It had been used by the United States Government for hospital purposes. It has been twice renovated and enlarged, viz., in 1877 and 1886. The list of pastors has embraced Revs: Mela, Jacobi, Landsberg, Weil, Jacobson, Stemple, Goldberg, and L. Stern, present incumbent. He was installed in 1872. The present membership is two hundred and eight families.

The Adams Israel Congregation (Orthodox), whose synagogue is situated on the corner of Sixth and G streets Northwest, was organized in 1875. Its present pastor is Rev. Leopold Heiman.

The Church of the Holy City is situated on Dupont Circle, Northwest. Rev. Jabez Fox was the first regular pastor of the congregation. The present pastor is Rev. Frank Sewall.

CHAPTER XVII.

MEDICAL HISTORY.

Introduction of Vaccination in the District of Columbia — Early Physicians — Healthfulness of Washington — Board of Health — Cholera Epidemic — Its Prevention by the Board of Health — Deaths from Cholera — Sketches of Physicians — Medical Societies.

VACCINATION was introduced in Washington during the summer of 1801, the President receiving some *aura vaccina* from Dr. Waterhouse, Cambridge, with a view of having its effects tried here. This first virus was given to Dr. Grant, of Georgetown, and was used by him.

December 14, 1801, Dr. Tongue informed the citizens of Washington through the public prints, as was then the custom everywhere, that he practiced physic, and particularly surgery. He had been, he said, a private pupil of Dr. Rush, to whom he referred.

T. Bruff, dentist, and inventor of the perpendicular extracting instruments, notified the public December 28, 1801, that he had arrived in Georgetown, and that he offered his services to the ladies and gentlemen of the District.

In September, 1803, it became known to the satisfaction of the authorities of the city of Alexandria that a malignant fever prevailed in a portion of Alexandria, and the authorities of the city of Washington were officially notified of the fact. The Council immediately passed "An Act for the Relief of Certain Persons," and authorized the Mayor to borrow money for the purpose of assisting such of those from Alexandria who might temporarily take up their residence in Washington in order to escape the fever. The trustees of the poor were authorized to render assistance to any of the inhabitants of Alexandria that might stand in need. Three hundred dollars were appropriated, and the Mayor was authorized to borrow $2,000 if the money in the treasury should prove insufficient for the emergency. While it was not thought possible for the fever to spread in Washington, yet every precaution was taken to prevent it. According to the health department of Alexandria, the greater number of deaths and the increase in sickness were in great measure owing to the "uncommon drouth" of the season. In order to more effectually assist the distressed in Alexandria, a subscription paper was placed in the hands of Daniel C. Brent, and the public were requested to subscribe to the extent of their ability.

October 2, 1805, Dr. Benson announced that he had removed to the house opposite Mr. Morin's tavern.

April 21, 1806, Dr. Starling Archer, then late of the navy, died on account of a wound received in a duel on the 17th of the same month. He was universally esteemed, and his death was lamented by all who knew him.

Dr. Briscoe, in 1806, was located a few doors west of the "Seven Buildings," on Pennsylvania Avenue, and kept at his house a supply of useful medicines and other articles needed by physicians.

In January, 1808, Dr. Lancaster located in Washington, on Pennsylvania Avenue, and announced that he had had several years' experience.

In the following September, Dr. William Grayson began the practice of medicine in Washington, locating two doors from Semmes's Tavern, in Georgetown.

Dr. Robert French began the practice of medicine and surgery in Georgetown about May 1, 1809, and had his "shop" in the house then lately occupied by Dr. John Weems, deceased.

Dr. John Willis had been in the city some time in 1809, and was then located on Pennsylvania Avenue. He died April 4, 1811. He was a wealthy man and a valuable member of society. At the time of his death, his home was in Orange County, Virginia.

The precise time when Dr. George A. Carroll first established himself in the city cannot be positively stated, but he resumed the practice of physic here in 1813, in the corner house next door to General Van Ness.

In 1815, Dr. William Gardner was a great advertiser, curing cancers, tumors, etc.

Dr. John Ott, of Georgetown, died April 8, 1818. He was spoken of at the time as having had no superior in every relation of life. He was a father to the poor, a friend to the distressed, and an example to others in the performance of every civil and social duty.

In December, 1816, Dr. Henderson came to Georgetown, and established himself in the practice of medicine, surgery, and midwifery.

Dr. E. Harrison came in April, 1817, and located near Timmon's Hotel. He died about August 25, 1819.

Dr. James H. Blake was one of the most prominent and most highly respected of the physicians and citizens of early Washington.

He was a native of Calvert County, Maryland, dwelt several years in Virginia, and came to Washington in 1807, where he lived the rest of his life. As a public man he was successively magistrate in Virginia and in Washington, District of Columbia. He was a member of the Legislature of Virginia, and was several times elected Mayor of Washington, and was for a time collector of internal revenue. At the time of his death, which occurred July 29, 1819, he was register of wills for Washington County. He died after a long and painful illness, sincerely mourned by the entire community.

Mrs. Edward Davis, "niece of the late Mrs. Whitewood," established herself in Washington and Georgetown, as a midwife, in March, 1823. She came highly recommended by Jonathan Barber, lecturer on anatomy and physiology, and Fellow of the Medical Society of London and Royal College of Surgery.

Dr. Richard Randall began the practice of medicine and surgery here in June, 1825. Dr. John Sinnott, A. M., M. D., commenced the practice of medicine, surgery, and midwifery in Washington in December, 1825, with his office at Mrs. Sinnott's Academy, in Varnum's Row, on D Street. He had had fifteen years' experience in the various branches of his profession. Dr. Sinnott advertised in French as well as in English.

Dr. Gilroy commenced the practice here about July, 1826, as also did Dr. Adam B. Hooe, Jr. Dr. Thomas began here in August, 1827, having his office next door to Dr. Huntt, on Fourteenth Street. About the same time, Dr. A. B. Hayden, dentist, having determined to settle permanently in Washington, offered his services to the people of the District of Columbia.

Reports of the number of deaths in the city began to be made in 1819, and they were for the next few years as follows: For 1819, 279; for 1820, 327; for 1821, 355; for 1823, 356; for 1824, 290. The greatest number of deaths were caused by cholera infantum and consumption. From the former in 1819 there were 15; in 1820, 43; in 1821, 31; and from consumption, in 1819, 101; in 1820, 42; and in 1821, 37.

As always has been the case, the people of Washington in the early day were sensitive over the question of the comparative healthfulness of their city, and to show that cities further north had nothing to boast of over Washington in this respect, the following table was prepared and published, showing the proportion of deaths to the entire population:

38

Year.	Washington.	Boston.	Baltimore.	New York.	Philadelphia.
1820	40.51	39.83	38.60	35.16	33.90
1821	38.72	32.73	32.07	37.01	36.82
1822	48.13	40.88	28.71	43.04	33.21
1823	41.40	45.10	32.54	42.85	26.46
1824	52.57	42.30	48.14	36.05	28.26
1825	70.00	40.19	47.12	33.09	33.29
1826	57.41	49.13	39.01	35.42	31.22
Average......	49.82	41.45	38.02	37.12	31.89

From the facts brought to light in the above table, it was suggested to the Philadelphia and New York insurers of lives that it would be expedient for them to omit from their policies the stipulation that the persons insured by them should not go so far south as the Potomac River.

In 1824, the members of the Board of Health were Drs. Thomas Sim, Henry Huntt, Thomas Sewall, Frederick May, and C. B. Hamilton. In January, 1828, there was a case of varioloid at Greenleaf's Point, in the city of Washington, and as it was easy of communication to others and was occasionally fatal to human life, it became the duty of the Board of Health to do what they could to prevent its spread. They therefore issued rules and regulations for the government of the people in respect to the case. They were not to have any intercourse with the patient, and those attending upon the patient were not to mingle with society until all danger was passed. Vaccination was urged upon all who had not been vaccinated, the poor to be vaccinated free of expense by calling upon the physician of their ward. Henry Huntt was president of the Board of Health, and Andrew Coyle secretary.

The Board of Health was provided for by an act of the corporation passed March 30, 1822. It was by this act invested with the power to form a code of regulations with reference to the health of the city, especially with respect to contagious diseases, which, however, were not to be repugnant to the act of incorporation or charter of the city. It was given power to declare what in its opinion were nuisances or sources of disease, such opinion to be published, and thereupon each member of the board was required to give notice to the ward commissioner of any nuisances in his ward, and upon receipt of such notice the commissioner was required to have the same removed. The board had conferred upon it such other powers as are common to such organizations.

The first great necessity that came upon the board for the exercise of what were considered by many extraordinary powers was in connection with the cholera epidemic of 1832. The cholera appears to have first been noticed in this country that year in New York City, June 26, 1832, and but twelve deaths occurred up to the 7th of July; but during that month it rapidly increased in severity. About August 10, the disease first made its appearance in Washington, several deaths occurring from other causes, however, being thought by some to have been caused by cholera, but which the physicians said were from typhus fever. But one man, named John Nally, a printer, aged about twenty-one, after having been afflicted with diarrhea for several weeks, was suddenly seized with cholera, and died in twenty-five hours. "This unfortunate young man had been an habitual drunkard for four years, and for six weeks prior to his death had indulged in all manner of excesses, and had scarcely been sober during that time." It was commonly observed that the intemperate man was by far the greatest sufferer. A full report of this case was published by the attending physician, Dr. Alexander McD. Davis, in the *National Intelligencer* of August 17, 1832.

In order to prevent the spread of this "great epidemic of the world," as it was then called, the Board of Aldermen and Board of Common Council of the city of Washington appointed six persons for the First, Second, and Third wards, and four persons for the Fourth, Fifth, and Sixth wards, to serve as police commissioners, and to be associated with the Board of Health for four months; and the Mayor was authorized to appoint such additional number of scavengers as he might think proper. The Board of Health recommended that religious bodies refrain from holding night meetings, and resolved that the vending of ardent spirits in whatever quantity was a nuisance; and inasmuch as they had the authority to do any and everything necessary to preserve the health of the city, directed the discontinuance of the sale of such spirits for ninety days from August 14, 1832.

On August 16, the board, "after due deliberation, have resolved and do now declare that the following articles are in their opinion highly prejudicial to health at the present season. Believing them in the light of nuisances, they hereby direct that the sale of them, or their introduction within the limits of the city, be prohibited from and after the 22d instant, for the space of ninety days.

"Cabbage, green corn, cucumbers, peas, beans, parsnips, carrots, eggplant, simblins or squashes, pumpkins, turnips, watermelons, cantaloupes, muskmelons, apples, pears, peaches, plums, damsons, cherries, apricots, pineapples, oranges, lemons, limes, cocoanuts, ice creams, fish, crabs, oysters, clams, lobsters, and crawfish."

"The board also recommend that the city authorities prohibit for ninety days all theatrical performances or other exhibitions which be calculated to produce large collections of persons." The board opposed quarantine regulations, "as tending to create a false confidence in such provisions to the neglect of more important preservatives from the disease." They also recommended that the heads of families make rigid daily inquiries into the health of all those committed to their charge.

On August 17, 1832, physicians were appointed to the several hospitals in the city, as follows: Western Hospital — Attending physicians, Drs. Waters and Briscoe; consulting physicians, Drs. Sim, Thomas, and Johnson. Central Hospital — Attending physicians, Drs. A. McD. Davis, Thomas R. Miller, James Waring, and B. Miller; consulting physicians, Drs. Huntt, Causin, and Sewall. Eastern Hospital — Attending physicians, Drs. Young and Boyd; consulting physicians, Drs. May and McWilliams.

Thus were preparations perfected for warfare with the dread disease. But it was scarcely to be expected that such sweeping regulations as those adopted by the Board of Health should fail to give much dissatisfaction to those who had the articles for sale that were prohibited entrance into the city. A certain writer, in a lengthy article published in the papers at the time, which was written with considerable force and intelligence but with little confidence in the wisdom of the physicians, objected to the regulations, because, as he said, neither the Board of Health nor the corporate authorities of the city possessed the legal authority to prohibit the sale of watermelons in the city. "It would be right for you to exclude this article of trade if it were certain, or even if good reasons existed to induce the belief, created by facts, that watermelons produce cholera. None such do, or can, or have been shown to exist, except in the speculating honesty and contradictory theories of physicians. Before physicians can, with safety, say what is or what is not proper to be eaten during the prevalence of cholera, they must first know the disease and its cause. This they are perfectly ignorant of, and every opinion expressed by them is speculation and conjecture."

Many others had the same opinion as to the wisdom of the course then pursued by the Board of Health, and also as to its authority to impose such restrictions. A public meeting was therefore called, of the citizens, at the City Hall for the evening of August 21, "at half past seven o'clock, to take into consideration the restrictions attempted to be imposed upon the productions of the earth and of honest industry by the despotic proceedings of the Board of Health of the 16th instant. A full meeting on this occasion is obviously important to every citizen, as well as to the cultivators of the soil, and to the caterers of our markets; and a free discussion of the merits of the subject, so deeply involving the reserved and inalienable rights of freemen, is particularly invited. Among other matters of moment which will doubtless be developed, it will be easy to show that the Board of Health have either turned their eyes aside from the real nuisances that abound in the city, or have overlooked them, or connived at them; if not in open and agreed expressions of purpose, at least in effect, as the real nuisances have not been subdued; and have substituted for their denunciations the wholesome and seasonable productions of the earth, with the obvious tendency to paralyze industry and superinduce famine, which is as bad as the plague. It will be equally easy to show that the moderate use of the productions of the season is eminently conducive to health, and that total abstinence from them is highly injurious to digestion, and invites disease. It will be easy to convince every intelligent man that tomatoes, beets, potatoes, and onions, the only articles that find favor in the eyes of the sage Board of Health, are not produced in sufficient quantity to substitute for twenty or thirty other vegetables which they have proscribed, nor, indeed, are they more wholesome than most of those which their sapient heads have forbid," etc.

The editors of the *National Intelligencer* were careful to have it distinctly understood that they took no part in the controversy, because it was not in their line.

At the meeting thus called, at the City Hall, Dr. Mayo was called to the chair, and John H. Beale made secretary. Dr. Mayo, having prepared some resolutions to present to the meeting, asked leave to call some one to the chair while he read his resolutions. Being permitted to do so, he called upon Mr. Moulder to preside while the resolutions were being read and discussed. After reciting the sanative regulations as adopted by the Board of Health, the resolutions were presented, as follows:

"*Resolved,* That we, the citizens of Washington, in general town meeting assembled, do hereby enter our solemn protest against the authority above assumed, and positively forbid any attempt to execute the edict above quoted.

"*Resolved,* That we will contribute our individual and united aid to abate nuisances in masses of putrid matter and stagnant water.

"*Resolved,* That we request the Mayor and corporate authorities of the city to interpose in behalf of the citizens in vindicating the freedom of the markets."

A public meeting of other citizens was also held at the City Hall to approve the regulations of the Board of Health.

On the 21st, the board reported on four cases of cholera that had been found during the preceding three days; one white man, convalescent; one colored man, intemperate, dead; one colored woman, dead; one colored man, intemperate, dangerously ill.

On the 22d, the Board of Health published an address to the citizens of Washington, in which they said that they had been appointed by the constituted authorities of the city without solicitation; they were aware that ignorance and selfish cupidity and vicious propensities would find themselves thwarted and opposed, and from these sources opposition was to have been anticipated to any measure which might be prescribed. Measures were being taken calculated to cast odium upon the action of the board, which, if successful, would render the exertions of the board fruitless and unavailing, and, left without the support of public opinion, the consequences would be chargeable to others, not to them.

On August 23, there were 2 deaths from cholera; August 24, 1; August 26, 6; August 27, 1; August 28, 2; August 29, 1; August 30, 1; August 31, 3; September 1 and 2, 8. It was stated in the papers, that up to the 1st of September about half of the cases that had occurred had been reported. The greatest number of cases had occurred in the square southwest of the General Post Office. On September 1, Drs. Nathaniel P. Causin and Alexander McWilliams made a solemn appeal to the people to neglect no symptom which indicated an attack of the disease, stating that they had learned from experience that the preliminary symptoms, when taken in time, uniformly yielded to treatment by calomel and opium, followed by a gentle dose of castor oil, or rhubarb, or magnesia; but if the preliminary symptoms were neglected, and a sudden and severe attack of the disease should supervene, more than nineteen-twentieths of those thus stricken must surely die.

On September 3, there were 13 deaths, besides several among the colored people of which there was no report. September 4, there were 10 deaths. The *Intelligencer* said it had the names of 12 persons who had died between noon of Sunday, the 1st of September, and noon of Monday, the 2d, none of whom had been reported. It was believed that the number between noon of Monday and noon of Tuesday was fully as great, 25. September 5, the number reported was 11; on the 6th, 10; the 7th, 8; the 9th, 15; 10th, 13; 11th, 6; 12th, 8; 13th, 6; 14th, 10; 15th, 4; 16th, 3; 17th, 6; 18th, 5; 19th, 9; 20th and 21st, 1; 22d and 23d, 2; 24th, 2; 25th, 1; 26th, 1.

By October 1, the cholera was believed to have disappeared. On January 1, 1833, the official report of the cholera epidemic of 1832 was made to the Board of Health by Dr. Henry Huntt, Thomas Sewall, and Nathaniel P. Causin. As to the number of deaths from cholera, the report gave: Males, 269; females, 190; total, 459. Whites, 251; blacks, free, 162; slaves, 46. As to age—Under ten, 45; from ten to twenty, 51; from twenty to thirty, 93; from thirty to forty, 108; from forty to fifty, 59; from fifty to sixty, 48; over sixty, 55.

Frederick May, M. D., was a native of Boston, Massachusetts, born November 16, 1773. He studied medicine with Dr. John Warren, and came to Washington in 1795. He was for many years the chief physician and surgeon of the place. He was professor of obstetrics in Columbia College from 1823 to 1839, at which time he resigned. At the time of his death, which occurred January 23, 1847, he was president of the Medical Society of the District of Columbia. Dr. May was always one of the most prominent citizens of Washington while he lived in the place.

Henry Huntt, M. D., one of the most prominent of the early physicians of Washington, was a native of Calvert County, Maryland. When about eighteen years of age, he went to live with an uncle, Dr. Clement Smith, a most respectable and learned physician, in Prince George's County. Here he became a student of the healing art. In 1805–06, he attended a course of lectures in the University of Pennsylvania. Returning to Maryland in the spring of 1806, he became a partner with his uncle, and soon became distinguished by his attention and kindness to his patients. In 1808 and 1809, he was led to make observations on the nature and treatment of diarrhea and dysentery, more especially upon the chronic forms of those diseases, and the result of his investigations was that he substituted in their treatment an acid for a mercurial and alkaline treatment.

A country practice affording too limited a field for professional preferment for one of Dr. Huntt's ambition, he abandoned his practice in Prince George's County, and came to Washington City in the fall of 1810, with the intention of applying for the position of surgeon's mate in the United States Navy. He received the desired appointment June 2, 1811, and performed the duties of that station for more than two years. Considerations of a private nature caused him to resign this appointment May 31, 1813, with the determination to enter into private practice; but in 1814 a greater demand than usual existed for hospital surgeons in the army, and applying for one of these positions, he was appointed by the Secretary of War to Burlington Hospital, Vermont. Here he soon attained rank in the highest grade of surgeons, performing many notable operations.

At the close of the War of 1815, he returned to Washington, and became permanently established here in private practice. With the view of attaining greater efficiency, he abandoned surgery and obstetrics. The prevalence of pneumonia in this section of the country at that time led him to publish his views of the pathology and treatment of the disease.

In 1820 he was connected with the health office in Washington, and was for several years the acting officer. Afterward he succeeded in having organized a more efficient Board of Health, of which in 1824 he was elected the first president, serving in this position until 1833, when he retired. His death occurred when he was in the fifty-sixth year of his age.

Dr. Huntt was especially noted for his success in the treatment of diseases of children, fevers, scarlatina, and pneumonia, and his judgment and discernment were of a high order. His mind was a storehouse of facts, and he never lost a useful hint in his profession from want of careful observation. He did not receive the degree of doctor of medicine in regular course, but it was conferred on him in consequence of his eminence as a physician, by the University of Maryland, in 1824. He was a member of the celebrated Ph. K. B. Society, was one of the founders of the Columbian Institute, of the Medical Society of the District of Columbia, and of the Medical Association in Washington, and was a zealous supporter of scientific medicine.

Benjamin Schenkmyer Bohrer, M. D., was born in Georgetown, District of Columbia, April 6, 1788, and died of paralysis, at his home in Georgetown, December 19, 1862. Finishing his preliminary education at a private academy, he began the study of medicine in the office of Dr. Charles Worthington, then a prominent practitioner of the District of Columbia, and graduated from the University of Pennsylvania in 1810. He practiced for some time in Georgetown, and in 1822 moved to Cincinnati, Ohio, where he had been appointed to fill the chair of *materia medica* in the Ohio Medical College. After serving in that position for several sessions, he returned to Georgetown, where he acquired a highly lucrative practice. He was one of the charter members of the Medical Society of the District of Columbia, and was a member of the Medical Association of the District of Columbia, and one of the early visitors appointed by the President of the United States to inspect the United States Hospital for the Insane. He was buried in Oak Hill Cemetery, Georgetown, District of Columbia.

Thomas Sewall, M. D., was born in Augusta, Maine, in 1786. He studied medicine and took his professional degree in Boston. He was engaged in the practice of medicine at Essex, Massachusetts, for several years, and removed to Washington in 1820. He was instrumental in organizing the medical department of Columbia College, was a member of the first faculty, and was appointed professor of anatomy in 1825, from which time, up to the time of his death, he was punctual in the delivery of his course of lectures. He was a fine scholar, a lifelong student, and published a number of papers on phrenology, medicine, and temperance, his essay on temperance being translated into German, and having a large circulation in Europe. He died in Washington, April 10, 1845.

John B. Blake, M. D., was a son of James H. Blake, who was prominent in Washington for many years, and who was Mayor of the city during the administration of President Madison. He was born at Colchester, Maryland, August 12, 1800, and received his education at Charlotte Hall Academy, St. Mary's County, Maryland, and at Georgetown College, where he graduated. Having graduated in medicine at the University of Maryland, in Baltimore, he began the practice of medicine in Washington with Dr. William Jones, and was in partnership with him for several years. He was appointed by President Jackson to a clerkship in the office of the Register of the Treasury, filling this position until 1855, when he was appointed by President Pierce to the office of Commissioner of Public Buildings, in which position he remained until after the election of Mr. Lincoln to the Presidency. He served as president of the National Metropolitan Bank about ten years, and he was for a long time secretary of the Washington National Monument Society. Toward the close of his life he was president of the Metropolitan Fire Insurance Company.

He was a communicant of Trinity Episcopal Church for more than fifty years, and at the time of his death was president of the Oldest Inhabitant Association. He died October 26, 1881, and was buried in Oak Hill Cemetery.

Joshua Riley, M. D., was born in Baltimore, Maryland, January 19, 1800, and died in Georgetown, February 11, 1875. He came to Georgetown at the age of eighteen, and was employed in the drug store of John Little for some time. He graduated from the University of Maryland in 1824, and immediately afterward began the practice of medicine in Georgetown. He soon acquired, and enjoyed during his professional life, a large and lucrative practice, and won the esteem and confidence of all with whom he came in contact. From 1844 to 1859, he was engaged as professor of *materia medica* in the National Medical College, and was active in founding the Washington Infirmary, the first clinical school in the District. He was president of the Medical Association of the District of Columbia for several years. He died of paralysis, in Georgetown, February 11, 1875, having been an active practitioner for more than fifty years. He was a man of marked ability, genial manners, and unspotted reputation.

Harvey Lindsly, M. D., was descended on both sides of his family from English parentage. He was born in Morris County, New Jersey, January 11, 1804. He prepared for college at the classical academy in Somerset County, New Jersey, conducted by Rev. Dr. Finley, afterward president of the University of Georgia; graduated at Princeton, and studied medicine at New York and Washington, taking his medical degree in 1828. He immediately began the practice of medicine in Washington, and resided here until his death, but for the last twelve or fifteen years of his life he was not in active practice. He was a member of the Medical Society of Washington, of the American Medical Association, and of numerous other medical societies in different parts of the country. For several years he was professor of obstetrics, and afterward professor of the principles and practice of medicine, in the National Medical College of the District of Columbia. He contributed a number of valuable papers to the *North American Review*, the *American Journal of Medical Science*, and the *Southern Literary Messenger*. His death occurred April 28, 1889.

Noble Young, M. D., was of Scotch-Irish descent, and was born in Baltimore, Maryland, June 26, 1808. He prepared for college at the Catholic seminary in Washington, and graduated from the .medical department of Columbia College, District of Columbia, in 1828, and immediately began the practice of medicine in Washington. At the

Eng by E. G. Wil ams b Bro NY

time of h death, he was the oldest practitioner in the city. He was a man of extensive acquirements, and a most entertaining conversationalist. He was one of the chief promoters and founders of the medical department of the University of Georgetown, and held the chair of principles and practice of medicine until 1876, when he resigned and was elected *emeritus* professor He was one of the charter members of the Medical Society of the District of Columbia, and was an original member of the Medical Association of the District. His death occurred April 11, 1883.

Thomas Miller, M. D. was born in Port Royal, Virginia, February 18, 1806, and died at his residence, in Washington, September 29, 1873. His father was Major Miller, who came to Washington and became attached to the Navy Department during the administration of President Madison. He received his early education under the care of the Jesuits at the old Washington Seminary, now known as Gonzaga College, and began the study of medicine under Henry Boteler, M. D. In 1827 he went to Philadelphia graduated in 1829 he began the practice of medicine in Washington the same year. From that time on, for forty years, he was connected with every movement looking to the advancement of the profession. In 1830, Dr. Miller, with others, formed the Washington Medical Institute for the purpose of giving instruction to students, and in 1832 he began a course of lectures in practical anatomy. In the same year he was one of the physicians to the Central Cholera Hospital, and in 1833 he was one of the originators of the Medical Association of the District of Columbia. In this year he was married to the daughter of General Walter Jones. In 1839 he became professor of anatomy in the National Medical College. On his retirement, he was made *emeritus* professor and president of the faculty. Dr. Miller was the first president of the Botanical Society organized in 1841; for many years he was a member of the Board of Health and of the Board of Aldermen. He was one of the consulting staff of Providence Hospital and of the Children's

f James Crowling who was formerly the son of William Hall, a native of England a Georgetown Scotch and a successful merchant of Alexandria, Virginia. He was born September 10, 1808, and his father died in 1810. His mother afterward married Rev. James Laurie, a popular and eloquent Presbyterian divine of Washington. James C. Hall was sent to the classical academy of Rev. James Carnahan, of Georgetown, District of Columbia who was afterward the distinguished president of Princeton College for many years. When sufficiently

time of his death, he was the oldest practitioner in the city. He was a man of extensive acquirements, and a most entertaining conversationalist. He was one of the chief promoters and founders of the medical department of the University of Georgetown, and held the chair of principles and practice of medicine until 1876, when he resigned and was elected *emeritus* professor. He was one of the charter members of the Medical Society of the District of Columbia, and was an original member of the Medical Association of the District. His death occurred April 11, 1883.

Thomas Miller, M. D., was born in Port Royal, Virginia, February 18, 1806, and died at his residence, in Washington, September 20, 1873. His father was Major Miller, who came to Washington and became attached to the Navy Department during the administration of President Madison. He received his early education under the care of the Jesuits at the old Washington Seminary, now known as Gonzaga College, and began the study of medicine under Henry Huntt, M. D. In 1827 he went to Philadelphia, graduated in 1829, and began the practice of medicine in Washington the same year. From that time on, for forty years, he was connected with every movement looking to the advancement of the profession. In 1830, Dr. Miller, with a few others, formed the Washington Medical Institute for the purpose of giving instruction to students, and in 1832 he began a course of lectures in practical anatomy. In the same year he was one of the physicians to the Central Cholera Hospital, and in 1833 he was one of the originators of the Medical Association of the District of Columbia. In this year he was married to the daughter of General Walter Jones. In 1839 he became professor of anatomy in the National Medical College. On his retirement, he was made *emeritus* professor and president of the faculty. Dr. Miller was the first president of the Pathological Society organized in 1841; for many years he was a member of the Board of Health and of the Board of Aldermen. He was one of the consulting staff of Providence Hospital and of the Children's Hospital.

James Crowdhill Hall, M. D., was the son of William Hall, a native of England, a prominent citizen, and a successful merchant of Alexandria, Virginia. He was born October 10, 1805, and his father died in 1810. His mother afterward married Rev. James Laurie, a popular and eloquent Presbyterian minister of Washington. James C. Hall was sent to the classical academy of Rev. James Carnahan, of Georgetown, District of Columbia, who was afterward the distinguished president of Princeton College for thirty years. When sufficiently advanced, young Hall was sent to Jefferson College, Pennsylvania. Returning home, he selected medicine as his profession, beginning its study with Dr. Thomas Henderson, at that time professor in the medical department of Columbia College. In 1825, he went to Philadelphia to attend lectures, and became a student of the University of Pennsylvania, graduating in 1827, taking a special course in both anatomy and chemistry. He then spent a year in Blockley Hospital, and after an extensive clinical experience returned to Washington, "undoubtedly the most accomplished and highly educated physician in the place." In the sick room, Dr. Hall was the model physician; quick of perception, sympathetic in manner, kind and assuring in disposition, he speedily won the confidence of his patients, and was thus the more easily successful in the treatment of disease. He acquired a considerable estate. He never married, but gave liberally to a half-sister and her children, and made a handsome bequest to the Washington City Orphan Asylum in memory of his mother, known as the "Laurie Fund." He was interested in the Children's Hospital; was one of the trustees of the Corcoran Art Gallery, and was connected in an official capacity with many other associations and societies in Washington. He attended professionally all the Presidents of the United States from John Quincy Adams down to Abraham Lincoln. He died, highly respected by all who knew him, June 7, 1880.

William B. Magruder, M. D., was the son of James A. and Milicent Magruder. He was born February 11, 1810, and studied medicine with Dr. Benjamin S. Bohrer, of Georgetown, District of Columbia, graduating from the University of Maryland in 1831. He began the practice of his profession the same year, remaining in Georgetown until 1832, when the cholera epidemic having driven away the resident physicians of that part of the city known as the West End, First Ward, he took charge of the cholera hospital, and was for a time the only physician in that section of the city. He was connected with the city government for nearly thirty years, and was Mayor from 1856 to 1858. On March 2, 1843, he was made a Mason by Hiram Lodge, and was afterward elected worshipful master. In 1854, he was elevated to the position of most worshipful grand master. He died May 30, 1869, and was buried in Oak Hill Cemetery.

Louis Mackall, M. D., was the son of Benjamin and Christiana (Beall) Mackall, and was born in Georgetown, District of Columbia, January 1, 1801. He was educated at Dr. Carnahan's classical institute in Georgetown, and graduated in medicine from the University of Maryland in 1824. He first actively engaged in the practice of his profession

in Prince George's County, Maryland, and returned to Georgetown in 1840. He wrote an essay on "Physical Force," and also one on "The Law of Muscular Action." He was married twice, the first time to Sarah Somerwell, and the second time to Mary Bruce.

William P. Johnston, M. D., was born in Savannah, Georgia, June 11, 1811, and died in Washington October 24, 1876. He was the son of Colonel James and Ann Marion Johnston, and grandson of Dr. Andrew Johnston, a native of Scotland, and a graduate of the University of Edinburgh. Dr. Johnston's early education was completed at Round Hill School, in Northampton, Massachusetts, at the head of which was the distinguished George Bancroft. He then entered the sophomore class at Yale College, graduating in 1833. After spending the winter of 1833–34 in Georgia, he repaired to Philadelphia and began the study of medicine under the direction of Professor William Horner, attending lectures at the University of Pennsylvania and at the summer school of medicine at the Philadelphia Medical Institute. He graduated in 1836, and was appointed one of the resident physicians at the Blockley Hospital, serving there one year.

In the spring of 1837, he became physician to the Philadelphia Dispensary, taking charge of the southwestern district. In the autumn of 1837, he went to Europe, where he remained three years, spending most of the time in Paris in attendance upon hospitals and in acquiring knowledge of special diseases, one year being spent in travel on the Continent and in England.

Dr. Johnston's intention, on returning, was to commence the practice of his profession in Philadelphia, but a visit to Alexandria and his marriage to Miss Hooe induced him to settle in Washington, in December, 1840. In coming to this determination he was aided by Dr. James C. Hall. In 1842 Dr. Johnston was elected professor of surgery in the National Medical College, but in 1845 he was at his own request transferred to the chair of obstetrics and diseases of women and children, lecturing almost uninterruptedly from this time until 1871. He was concerned with other members of the faculty in establishing the Washington Infirmary, where clinical lectures were given in connection with the didactic course. This hospital remained in successful operation up to the beginning of the War, when it was taken by the Government for use as a hospital, and was afterward burned.

Dr. Johnston was one of the originators of the Pathological Society in Washington in 1841, and he was an active member of the Clinical Society of the District of Columbia, being elected to all its offices. He was also a member of the Medical Association of the District of Columbia and of the American Medical Association, being vice-president of the latter in 1888. He conceived the idea of establishing an association for the young and active members of the profession, in which they might acquire greater freedom of debate than in the older body, suggesting the founding of the "Clinico-Pathological Society," which for some years was a successful working organization. It has recently been revived, and is now a thriving body.

For many years, Dr. Johnston was a member of the advisory and consulting board of Providence Hospital, and gave clinical lectures in its wards. He was an active participant in the founding of the Children's Hospital, and to the furthering of the prosperity of this charity devoted a great deal of time and energy. At the time of his death, he was president of the medical board. He was devoted to his profession and its interests, giving his entire time to the most laborious work, and rarely seeking rest and recreation. He was also actively interested in the development of the material prosperity of Washington, and was one of the founders and original directors of the Arlington Fire Insurance Company.

Dr. Johnston's genial and courteous manners, together with the regard he always had for the feelings of others, gained for him the esteem of the profession and of the public; and his kindness of heart and sympathy for distress and affliction endeared him to all who ever solicited his advice. It was this feeling that prompted him to aid the imprisoned Confederates in the Old Capitol Prison, for which purpose he obtained the permission of Secretary Stanton for Dr. J. C. Hall, F. B. McGuire, and himself to visit the prisoners, and for a long time he ministered to their urgent material necessities. It was only when reports came of the maltreatment of the Union soldiers in Southern prisons that this permission was taken away.

During the thirty-five years of his professional career, Dr. Johnston enjoyed the most uninterrupted good health, being noted for his vigor and untiring energy. But in time, the organ that had borne the brunt of great physical exertion began to show signs of disturbance, and after a few months' illness, with marked symptoms of cardiac disease, he passed away.

Grafton Tyler, M. D., was descended from a family of Tylers that came from England and settled in Maryland in 1660. He was born November 21, 1811, and was the second son of Grafton and Ann H. (Plummer) Tyler, and brother of Professor Samuel Tyler, of Columbia College, Washington. Dr. Tyler began the study of medi-

James E. Morgan M.D

cine with Dr. Richard Hockett, and attended lectures at the University of Maryland, and was an office student of Samuel Baker, Sr., of Baltimore. He graduated from the University of Maryland in 1833. Although at first inclined to surgery, he gradually settled down to general family practice. In 1843 he removed to Georgetown, where he acquired a good business and was for many years physician to Georgetown College. In 1846 he was elected to the chair of pathology and practice of medicine in the Medical Department of the Columbian University, and a few years later to that of clinical medicine in the Washington Infirmary. In 1859 he resigned both positions, but was immediately elected *emeritus* professor. For six years he served as a member of the board of visitors to the Government hospital for the insane. He was a member of all the medical societies and associations of Washington, and was consulting physician to Providence Hospital and president of its medical board from its opening in 1863. He also contributed largely to the medical literature of his day. He died August 26, 1884, and was buried in Oak Hill Cemetery.

James Ethelbert Morgan, M. D., an eminently successful physician of Washington, was a descendant of the Morgans of Monmouthshire, in Wales, and of the Cecils of Kent, England. The Morgans, being Catholics and adherents of James I., were, upon a change of rulers, compelled to leave Great Britain and seek an asylum with Lord Baltimore in Maryland. James E. Morgan was the son of George and Maria (Cecil) Morgan, and was born in St. Mary's County, Maryland, September 25, 1822, and received his education at St. John's College, at Frederick, Maryland. In 1845, he graduated in medicine from the Columbia Medical College, and settled in Washington as a practitioner, soon securing a large and lucrative practice in all branches of his profession. He also collected around him a considerable number of young students, to whom he gave clinical lectures in his office. In 1848 he was appointed demonstrator of anatomy in the National Medical College, and in 1852 he accepted the chair of physiology in the medical department of the University of Georgetown. In 1858, he was transferred to the chair of *materia medica* and therapeutics, which he continued to fill until 1876, when he retired from active duties, but continued as *emeritus* professor. He took charge of the Soldiers' Rest, an institution for the reception of sick and disabled soldiers on their way from the Union armies in the South. He was appointed, in connection with Robert King Stone, to investigate the National Hotel disease, which, while it lasted, caused such an excitement throughout the United States. He was president of the Medical Society of the

District of Columbia, and was one of the earlier members of the American Medical Association. He filled numerous offices; civil and professioual, all of which serves to indicate the character of the man. He died June 2, 1889.

Robert King Stone, M. D., was a native of Washington, and one of its most distinguished physicians. He was born in 1822, and died from apoplexy April 23, 1872. At an early age he entered Princeton College, and ranked among its brightest students, graduating with the bachelor's degree in 1842. Returning to Washington, he entered the office of Dr. Thomas Miller, by whom he was selected as assistant in the dissecting room. After attending a course of lectures at the National Medical College, he entered the University of Pennsylvania, graduating therefrom in 1845. He then attended the hopitals of London, Edinburgh, Vienna, and Paris, making a special study of ophthalmic surgery and the diseases of the eye and ear. His favorite studies, however, were comparative anatomy and operative surgery, in both of which he acquired more than ordinary distinction. Returning to Washington in 1847, he began a course of lectures on general practice, and became assistant to the chair of anatomy in the National Medical College, and in 1848 was appointed adjunct professor to the chair of anatomy and physiology. His brilliant career was suddenly cut short by a painful accident, being thrown from his carriage and having his thigh fractured in such a way that recovery was extremely slow, and he never again engaged in active practice. In 1849 Dr. Stone married a daughter of Thomas Ritchie, founder of the Richmond *Enquirer*, and in 1845 of the Washington *Union*.

Alexander Yelverton Peyton Garnett, M. D., was a son of Muscoe and Maria Willis (Battaile) Garnett, and was born in Essex County, Virginia, September 19, 1820. He graduated from the University of Pennsylvania in the spring of 1841, and entered the United States naval service as assistant and past assistant surgeon, serving until 1848, when he resigned and located in Washington, where he began the practice of medicine, and continued thus engaged here until the time of his death, with the exception of the period when he was in the service of the Confederate States. During this time he was in charge of the two hospitals at Richmond, and he was a member of the board of medical examiners for the Confederate Army. From 1858 to 1861, and again from 1867 to 1870, he was professor of clinical medicine in the National Medical College, and was afterward *emeritus* professor of the same institution. He married, June 13, 1848, Mary E. Wise, daughter of the Hon. Henry A. Wise, of Virginia.

Louis Mackall, Jr., son of Louis Mackall preceding, by his first wife, was born in Prince George's County, Maryland, April 10, 1831. He was educated in Georgetown, District of Columbia, at W. R. Abbott's classical seminary, and at Georgetown College. He graduated in medicine from the University of Maryland in 1851, and began the practice of medicine in Georgetown. For some time he held the chair of clinical medicine in Georgetown College, and was subsequently professor of physiology in the same institution. He was married in 1851 to Margaret W. McVeam, of Georgetown.

Daniel Randall Hagner, M. D., is the son of Peter Hagner, who for nearly fifty years held the position of Third Auditor of the Treasury. He was born in Washington July 19, 1830; was educated at St. James College, in the medical department of Columbia College, and in the medical department of the University of Pennsylvania, graduating from the latter institution in 1851. In the same year, he established himself in Washington, paying special attention to diseases of the chest. He was a member of the Medical Society of the District of Columbia, and published an important work entitled "Vaccination and Revaccination," which was published by order of the Medical Society of the District of Columbia. For ten years he was attending physician at Providence Hospital, a member of the advisory and consulting board, and also attending physician to St. Anne's Infant Asylum, and also a member of the advisory and consulting board.

John C. Riley, M. D., son of Joshua Riley, M. D., was born in Georgetown, District of Columbia, December 15, 1828, and died at his residence February 22, 1879. He studied and graduated at Georgetown College, and became a student in the National Medical College in Washington, graduating in ·1851, and immediately entered upon the practice of medicine. In 1859, he succeeded his father in the chair of *materia medica*, pharmacy, and therapeutics in the medical department of the Columbian University, and occupied the chair until within a few years of his death. He was a member of the various medical associations in Washington, and was consulting physician to Providence Hospital, to the Central Free Dispensary, and to the Washington Eye and Ear Infirmary, and it is believed that his assiduous devotion to his duties caused his early death.

William Gray Palmer, M. D., was the son of W. P. Palmer, of Montgomery County, Maryland, and was born in that county February 22, 1824. He graduated from the University of Pennsylvania in 1844, and removed to Washington in 1852. He was a member of the Medical Society and of the Medical Association of the District

39

of Columbia, in 1863 being made secretary of the former, and in 1872 its president. He was also a member of the city Council. In 1847 he married Miss Jackson, of Washington, a member of the Lowndes family of Maryland.

Nathan Smith Lincoln, M. D., LL. D., was born at Gardner, Massachusetts, and is the eldest son of Gracia Eliza Smith and the Rev. Increase Sumner Lincoln. His ancestors on both sides are English, his father being a descendant of the famous Lincolns of Hingham, Massachusetts, who emigrated to this country in 1635, to which family President Lincoln also belonged. On the maternal side, Dr. Lincoln is descended from the Rev. Peter Bulkley, of Bulkley Manor, England. His great-grandfather was General Jonathan Chase, of Revolutionary fame, and it is a curious coincidence that while, on the one side, General Chase drew up the articles of surrender for Burgoyne's army at Saratoga, General Benjamin Lincoln received the sword of Cornwallis, when he surrendered to Washington at Yorktown.

Dr. Lincoln belongs to a family distinguished not only in war, but in the ranks of science and learning. His grandfather, Dr. Nathan Smith, was the most celebrated surgeon of his day, having founded the medical schools of Yale and Dartmouth, occupying the surgical chair of Yale at the time of his death in 1829. He was also professor of surgery at Bowdoin College and the University of Vermont.

At the time of Dr. Lincoln's birth, and for many years after, his father, the Rev. Increase Sumner Lincoln, held the pastorate of the First Congregational Church of Gardner, Massachusetts, until he became a Unitarian. He was widely known as a scholar, and associated himself with the Abolition Party at an early stage of its existence, being a warm friend of Wendell Phillips and William Lloyd Garrison. He died in 1890, at the advanced age of ninety-one, at that time being the oldest Unitarian minister in the United States, and having been actively engaged in the ministry for sixty-five years.

Dr. Lincoln was graduated from Dartmouth College in 1850, receiving at that time the degrees of Bachelor of Arts and Master of Arts, and since then that of Doctor of Laws from his *alma mater.* He studied medicine under his uncle, Dr. Nathan R. Smith, of Baltimore, at the same time attending medical lectures at the University of Maryland, and received his degree of Doctor of Medicine from that institution in 1852. Until January, 1854, he practiced his profession in Baltimore, and since that date has been established in Washington, holding many offices of distinction. In 1857 he was elected professor of chemistry in Columbian University; in 1859, was made professor of theory and

Eng by E.G.Williams & Bro. N.Y.

practice of medicine; in 1860, professor of anatomy and physiology, and in 1861, professor of surgery. The latter chair was retained until 1874, when he resigned it on account of the pressure of private practice. After serving for several years as one of the surgeons to the Washington Infirmary, he was appointed by President Lincoln, in 1861, surgeon to the District of Columbia volunteers, and having served three months, was then made surgeon-in-chief of the hospitals established in Washington by the Quartermaster's Department of the army, a position which he held during the War of the Rebellion and for some months after its close. In 1866 he was elected one of the surgeons to the Providence Hospital, an appointment that he resigned in 1875. He was, for a number of years, physician to the Deaf-Mute College and to several other institutions. Having made a specialty of surgery, he has performed successfully a large number of important operations, including amputations at the hip joint, lithotomy, removing tumors from the region of the head and neck, ligation of the large arteries, etc. He is a member of the District of Columbia Medical Society, was its vice-president in 1872, and its president in 1875–76; a member of the American Medical Society, and of the Archæological Society of the United States; president of the Alumni Association of the University of Maryland, and a member of the Philosophical Society of Washington.

Joseph Meredith Toner, M. D., was born in Pittsburgh, Pennsylvania, April 30, 1825. He received his classical education at Western Pennsylvania University and at Mount St. Mary's College, and graduated at Vermont Medical College in 1850, and at Jefferson Medical College in 1853. After a short residence at Summitville, Allegheny County, Pennsylvania, and at Harper's Ferry, Virginia, he settled at Washington, District of Columbia, in 1855. He was one of the founders of Providence Hospital and of St. Anne's Infant Asylum, to both of which he was for some years visiting physician. Since 1856 he has been attending physician to St. Joseph's Orphan Asylum.

Being aware of the perishable nature of the early medical literature of this country, he devised a plan for a repository of medical works by the American Medical Association, that should be under the control of the medical profession and located at Washington. This collection now contains six thousand volumes, and is deposited in the Smithsonian Institution. In 1871 he founded the Toner Lectures, placing $3,000, which has now increased to $5,000, in the hands of trustees who are charged with the duties of procuring two lectures annually containing some new fact valuable to medical science. The interest of

this fund, except ten per cent., which is annually added to the principal, is paid to the authors of the lectures, which are included in the
regular Smithsonian publications. This was the first course of lectures
endowed in this country on these conditions. In 1875, and for three
subsequent years, he gave the Toner medal at Jefferson Medical College to the person presenting the best thesis embodying the results of
original investigation, and for many years he has given a medal to
the University of Georgetown to encourage original observations.

He was president of the American Medical Association in 1873,
and of the American Health Association in 1874. He was a vice-
president of the International Medical Congress in 1876, and a vice-
president and registrar of the Ninth International Congress in 1887.
He has devoted much time and research to early American medical
literature, and has collected more than one thousand treatises published
before 1800, and has in preparation a "Biographical Dictionary of
Deceased American Physicians." In 1882, he gave his entire library,
consisting of twenty-eight thousand books and eighteen thousand
pamphlets, to the Government of the United States, to be known as
"The Toner Collection," and this library is now a portion of the
Congressional Library, though it is required by law to be kept separate, and treated as rare books. He has contributed largely to medical
literature, a number of his works being named in another chapter in
this volume.

Thomas Antisell, M. D., was the son of a lawyer, and his ancestry
is traced back to the last English crusaders. He was born in Dublin,
Ireland, January 16, 1817, and was educated at Trinity College, Dublin, at the Dublin School of Medicine, at the Irish Apothecaries' Hall
School, and graduated from the Royal College of Surgeons, London,
in November, 1839. He practiced in Dublin until 1848, in New York
until 1854, and came to Washington in 1856. During most of his
medical career, he was a teacher of medicine, his specialties being
analytical and technical chemistry. He was a member of the various
medical and scientific societies of the District of Columbia, and contributed liberally to medical literature. During the War of the
Rebellion, he had charge of the military hospital at Charlottesville,
from July, 1861, to May, 1862, and from September, 1862, to the
close of the War. In the interval, he had charge of the hospital in
Danville, Virginia.

W. W. Johnston, M. D., son of Dr. William P. Johnston, was
born in Washington December 28, 1843, and graduated from the
University of Pennsylvania in March, 1865. He was one year resident

J. M. Toner M.D.

in Bellevue Hospital, New York, and for six months in Charity and other hospitals on Blackwell's Island. Going to Edinburgh, he became clinical assistant to Professor J. Hughes Bennett, and also assistant to Dr. T. Granger Stewart, pathologist to the Royal Infirmary. Afterward he pursued his studies in Paris. In 1858, he returned to Washington, and has since been engaged in general medical practice. Since 1871, he has been professor of the theory and practice of medicine in the medical department of Columbian University; is consulting physician to the Children's Hospital, and has served as president of the Medical Society of the District of Columbia, of the Medical Association, and of the Washington Obstetrical and Gynecological Society.

Armistead Peter, M. D., was a son of Major George Peter, who entered the army of the United States in 1799, and who was a member of Congress from Maryland. He was born in Montgomery County, Maryland, February 23, 1840. He studied medicine at the National Medical College of the District of Columbia, and in the medical department of the Columbian University, graduating in 1861. Immediately afterward, he settled in Georgetown in the practice of medicine. He was a member of the medical societies of the District of Columbia, was a member of the Georgetown board of health, and during the War was acting assistant surgeon of the United States Army. He married in 1867 Martha C. Kennon, daughter of Commodore Beverly Kennon, of the United States Navy.

Charles Mason Ford, M. D., was the son of John N. Ford, of Troy, New York, and was born May 15, 1840. He died of rheumatic fever in Washington, February 15, 1884. He began the study of medicine with Dr. Alfred Watkins, of Troy, and graduated from the University of Pennsylvania in 1861. He was soon afterward appointed assistant surgeon of the navy, and assigned to duty with the Huntsville blockading squadron under Captain Cicero Price. Contracting rheumatism, he resigned and came to Washington, where he was appointed assistant surgeon and assigned to duty at Clifton Hospital, and afterward to special duty at the Old Capitol Prison. As soon as he determined to settle permanently in Washington, he became connected with Providence Hospital, and for more than fourteen years was on the medical staff of that institution. For some years he was physician at the Washington Almshouse, and at the time of his death, which occurred February 15, 1884, he was surgeon to the Baltimore and Potomac Railroad Company. Dr. Ford stood high in his profession, as he did in Masonry, and was greatly beloved by both his professional and Masonic brethren.

Gideon Stinson Palmer, M. D., was born in Gardiner, Maine, June 14, 1813. He graduated from Bowdoin College in 1838, and afterward studied medicine and graduated at the Maine Medical School in 1841. At the beginning of the War, he enlisted as a volunteer surgeon, and served as brigade surgeon on General Howard's staff in the Army of the Potomac until the close of the War. He was in charge of Lincoln Hospital, and of the army hospital at Annapolis, retiring with rank of brevet lieutenant-colonel. In 1869, at the request of General Howard, he took the chair of physiology and hygiene in the medical department of Howard University, and was for many years dean of the university faculty, and surgeon in charge of the Freedmen's Hospital. He died December 8, 1891, in the seventy-ninth year of his age.

Daniel Webster Prentiss, M. D., was born in Washington, District of Columbia, May 21, 1843, as were his parents before him. His father, William Henry Prentiss, was born in 1796. The father of William Henry Prentis was William Prentiss, a son of Caleb Prentiss, of Cambridge, Massachusetts. William Prentiss was a merchant, and was associated with Joseph Greenleaf in building a row of brick houses on Greenleaf's Point about the year 1797, in one of which houses William Henry Prentiss was born. William Henry Prentiss married Miss Sarah A. Cooper, daughter of Isaac Cooper, a merchant in Washington. Dr. D. W. Prentiss's grandmother, on the father's side, was Eunice Payne (Greenleaf) Prentiss, a niece of Robert Treat Payne, and a cousin of John Howard Payne, author of "Home, Sweet Home"; so that William Henry Prentiss was grandnephew to Robert Treat Payne and second cousin to John Howard Payne. The general education of Dr. Prentiss was obtained in the schools of Washington and at Columbian University, from which institution he received, in 1861, the degree of Bachelor of Philosophy, and the degree of Master of Arts in 1864. He received the degree of Doctor of Medicine from the University of Pennsylvania in 1864. He was married to Emilie A. Schmidt, daughter of Frederick Schmidt, of Rhenish Bavaria, October 12, 1864. Their children are Louise, married to Frederick W. True, of the United States National Museum; Eunice, who died at the age of seventeen, and three sons—Spencer Baird, Daniel Webster, Jr., and Elliott. In 1864, he became engaged in the general practice of medicine in Washington, and has since then continuously held a prominent position in the profession. Since 1879, he has been professor of *materia medica* and therapeutics in the medical department of Columbian University. He was a member of the Board of Health in 1864; lecturer on dietetics and administration of medicines in the Nurses' Training School, and dean of the

D. Webster Prentiss

medical faculty of the Training School in 1878-83; a trustee in that school in 1880-84, and president of the board in 1884; physician in charge of the eye and ear service of Columbian Dispensary, 1874-78; visiting physician to Providence Hospital in 1882, and a commissioner of pharmacy of the District of Columbia since its organization, and president of the board since 1888. Dr. Prentiss is a member of the Medical Society, Medical Association, Obstetrical and Gynecological Society, Clinico-Pathological Society, the Philosophical, the Biological, Geographical, and Anthropological societies of the District of Columbia; is a member of the American Medical Association, the American Association for the Advancement of Science, the Association of American Physicians, and was a delegate to the International Medical Congress at Copenhagen, in 1884, and to Berlin in 1890. He has delivered numerous lectures under various auspices in his native city. "Hypnotism in Animals," given in a popular course at the National Museum, appeared in the *American Naturalist*, September, 1882. By invitation of Spencer F. Baird, he delivered a course of lectures on *materia medica* at the National Museum in 1883. Some of the leading papers which Dr. Prentiss has contributed to medical literature are the following:

"Report on Disinfectants to the Board of Health of the District of Columbia," 1867, in the *Journal of American Medical Science;* "G. S. W. through the Pelvis," October, 1865; "Case of Morphine Poisoning," 1867; "Diphtheria and Tracheotomy, Membranous Croup, and Operations for Radical Cure of Hernia," 1868; "Case of Inflammation of Fibrous Capsule of Eyeball," 1868; "Case of Spurious Labor Pains at Fifth Month"; "Convulsions after Profuse Hemorrhage from Abortion at the Sixth Week"; "Obstruction of Bowels in an Infant, with Autopsy," 1870; "Hysterical Tetanus," 1879; "Case of Mastoid Abscess Opening into Lateral Sinus, and Death from Pyæmia," 1882; "Is Croupous Pneumonia a Zymotic Disease?" "Chorea in Pregnancy, and Abscess of the Liver," 1874; "Case of Double Hydronephrosis, with Specimen, and Remarkable Case of Hysteria with Paralysis and Aphasia," 1883; "Cases of Poisoning by Atropia, by Opium, and by Quinine," 1890; "On Revision of Pharmacopœia of 1880"; "Death from Diphtheretic Paralysis"; "Remarkable Change in the Color of the Hair from Light Blonde to Almost Black in a Patient while under Treatment by Hypodermic Injections of Pilocarpine"; "Case of Prolonged Anuria," 1881; "Membranous Croup Treated with Pilocarpine"; "Change in the Color of the Hair," 1881; "Overdose of Podophyllin," 1882; "Maternal Impressions — Effect on Fœtus," 1882; "Answer to a Protest Against the Use of the Metric System in Prescribing," 1883; Croupous

Pneumonia," report of eleven cases occurring in private practice from February to June, 1878, read before the Medical Society of the District of Columbia; a "Report of the Pharmacopœia Convention of 1880," as a delegate from the National Medical College, 1880; a "Review of the Sixth Decennial Revision of the Pharmacopœia of 1880"; "Avi-Fauna Columbiana," being a list of the birds of the District of Columbia, revised and rewritten by Dr. Elliott Coues and Dr. D. W. Prentiss, 1883; "Gall Stones or Soap," 1889; a "Report of Five Hundred Consecutive Cases of Labor in Private Practice," 1888; "Case of Change of Color of Hair of Old Age to Black, Produced by Jaborandi," 1889; "Three Cases of Poisoning by Japanese Lacquer, by Pellets Labeled 'Rhus,' and by Cashew Nuts," 1889; "Report of a Remarkable Case of Slow Pulse," 1889; "Purpura Hemorrhage Rheumatica," 1890; "Apoplexy Following La Grippe," in the Philadelphia *Medical News,* August 29, 1891.

John R. Piper, M. D., the first physician to introduce homeopathy into Washington, was born in Baltimore in 1811, and was educated in his native city, studying medicine at, and graduating from, the University of Maryland in 1839. After living in the South and West for some years, he returned to Baltimore, and embraced the principles of homeopathy. He located permanently in Washington, District of Columbia, in 1849, and, during a period of thirty years, was a most successful practitioner, despite the opposition which the new system of practice encountered here, as elsewhere, in the United States. During the latter years of his life, he was afflicted with cancer in the face, and went to Europe with the hope of obtaining relief, if not absolute cure, being treated there by the most eminent homeopathic physician in Europe next to Hahnemann. Upon his return to America, he consulted a celebrated cancer physician in Philadelphia, but the treatment of this physician, if followed, failed to effect a cure, and on account of his disease Dr. Piper was compelled to confine himself to office practice after his return to Washington. His death occurred March 16, 1871. Dr. Piper was one of the first members of the American Institute of Homeopathy, and it is due to him that this system of practice was first recognized as a success in Washington.

Dr. Green was one of the earliest of the homeopathic physicians to settle in Washington, but the precise year of his coming could not be ascertained. His office was on Four and a Half Street, and he remained in practice here about seven years.

Dr. Appleton came next after Dr. Green, remaining about four years.

Gustavus William Pope, M. D., is the eldest son of Dr. G. W. Pope, Sr., and was born in December, 1829. His early education was received at Whitesborough Institute. Matriculating at the University of New York in 1847, remaining there three years, and graduating at Albany in 1851, he became assistant physician to the New York State Lunatic Asylum in 1852; but the close confinement of his position affecting his health, he resigned, returned to his father, and assisted him in his practice. For two years he was physician to the Oneida Almshouse, and while thus engaged his attention was directed to the claims of Homeopathy, and after giving the subject thorough attention for three successive years, he became convinced of its superiority over the allopathic system of practice. He removed to Washington in 1856, where he soon secured an extensive practice. · At that time there were but two homeopathic physicians in Washington, Dr. Piper and Dr. Green, and upon the death of these two physicians Dr. Pope became the senior homeopathic physician in Washington. Dr. Pope has made notable discoveries in medicine, one of them being the antidotive action of belladonna and opium, fully twenty years before the subject was mentioned in medical journals. He was the first to introduce into homeopathic practice in Washington the *Veratrum viride* and *Gilsemium*. In 1856 Dr. Pope treated the first case of diphtheria that ever appeared in Washington, and during that year and 1857 he treated about one hundred cases, losing only three. It is probably just to say that to Dr. Pope is due the firm establishment of homeopathy in Washington.

Tullio Suzzara Verdi, M. D., is a native of Italy, having been born in Mantua in 1829. He was educated at the Mantuan Gymnasium of Science and Literature, and entered the Sardinian army in 1848, under King Charles Albert, who was then moving into Lombardy against the Austrians, and after the defeat of the Piedmontese army at Novarara, in 1849, by Marshal Radetsky, young Verdi escaped into Switzerland, thence to Paris, thence to England, and from England he came to the United States. In Brown University, he familiarized himself with the English language while teaching the Italian and French. Three years later, he succeeded Professor G. W. Greene as professor of modern languages, and while engaged with the duties of this professorship, devoted all his spare time to the study of medicine under Dr. Okie. In 1854 he attended medical lectures in Philadelphia, graduating from both the allopathic and homeopathic schools. For some time he practiced in Rhode Island, but removed to Washington in 1857, where he has since been engaged in the practice of medicine according to the principles of homeopathy. In 1871, he was appointed by the President of the United States a member of the only board of health of the District of Columbia created by Congress. On April 15, 1873, Governor Cooke appointed him sanitary commissioner to visit the principal European cities with the view of perfecting a sanitary system for the city of Washington. Dr. Verdi still continues in practice in this city.

Dr. Simon I. Groot was born in Glenville, New York, March 16, 1820, graduated from the Berkshire Medical College, Pittsfield, Massachusetts, in 1846, and commenced practice in Virginia, remaining there until 1861, when he came to Washington, and has been engaged here in the practice of medicine according to homeopathic principles most of the time since then; though in May, 1888, he sold his practice to Dr. James A. Freer, who thus became his regular successor. Dr. Groot is probably the only homeopathic physician licensed by the Medical Society of the District of Columbia, but this was mainly, if not wholly, on the ground of his having graduated from a regular school of medicine.

Dr. Charles Waldemar Sonnenschmidt, a native of Suhl, Prussia, was born January 2, 1832. Both his father and grandfather were Lutheran ministers. He was educated by his father and in various institutions until old enough to be subject to military service in his own country, and then he emigrated to the United States. He graduated at Georgetown College, District of Columbia, and commenced the practice of medicine in Washington in 1867. He has ever enjoyed a quiet and comfortable practice. Dr. Sonnenschmidt is a member of the American Institute of Homeopathy, and served for some years as secretary of the Homeopathic Medical Society of Washington.

The Medical Society of the District of Columbia was organized September 26, 1817, and was subsequently chartered by Congress, by an act approved by the President of the United States February 16, 1819. By this charter the society was authorized to license duly qualified physicians to practice medicine within the District of Columbia. The first officers were: Dr. Charles Worthington, president; Drs. Arnold Elzey and James H. Blake, vice-presidents; Dr. Henry Huntt, corresponding secretary; Dr. Thomas Henderson, recording secretary; Dr. W. Jones, treasurer, and Dr. R. Weightman, librarian.

A new hall for this society was commenced in 1867, and it was completed and dedicated in 1869, the ceremony occurring January 27. This hall is located on the south side of F Street, west of Tenth Street. It is three stories high, with a handsome pressed-brick front.

At the time of the erection of this hall, Dr. Thomas Miller was president of the society, Dr. F. Howard first vice-president, Dr. Louis Mackall second vice-president, Dr. J. W. Lovejoy corresponding secretary, Dr. William Lee recording secretary, Dr. William Marbury treasurer, and Dr. J. M. Toner librarian.

At the present time, the officers are as follows; D. W. Prentiss, president; J. B. Hamilton and J. T. Winter vice-presidents; Thomas C. Smith, corresponding secretary; S. S. Adams, recording secretary; C. W. Franzoni, treasurer; J. H. Mundell, librarian.

The Medical Association of the District of Columbia was formed January 4, 1833, under the name of the "Washington Medical Association." The physicians of Georgetown were admitted to membership June 6, 1848, and the present name of the association adopted. The object of this association is the elevation of the medical profession, the establishment of a code of ethics and a fee bill, and the promotion of harmony and good fellowship among its members. The membership consists of the regular practitioners of medicine of the District of Columbia. Frederick May, M. D., was the first president of the society. The present officers are: C. W. Franzoni, president; G. B. Harrison and C. W. Richardson, vice-presidents; J. Dudley Morgan, secretary; and S. S. Adams, treasurer.

The Homeopathic Medical Society was organized in 1870, under a charter granted by Congress. At first there were seven members, which number has increased to about forty. The society holds regular monthly meetings in the rooms of the Washington Homeopathic Medical Dispensary. The officers of the society at the present time are as follows: Dr. L. B. Swormstedt, president, and Dr. Z. B. Babbitt, secretary.

Besides the above societies there are in Washington the Medical and Surgical Society of the District of Columbia, the Medico-chirurgical Society, the Woman's Clinic, and the Washington Obstetrical and Gynecological Society.

CHAPTER XVIII.

THE Smithsonian Institution, the name of which is now familiar to every intelligent individual in Christendom, is situated on the Mall, between Seventh and Twelfth streets, in the southwest part of Washington. It is on "the Smithsonian Grounds," which cover fifty-two acres, finely laid out with fine driveways, handsome lawns, and beautiful groves of luxurious trees. The laying out of the grounds was designed and partially executed by the distinguished landscape gardener and horticulturist, Andrew J. Downing, but he died in 1852, before his work was completed. To his memory the American Pomological Society erected a monumental vase in the eastern part of the grounds. The building of the institution was constructed of red sandstone, from quarries near Washington, on the upper Potomac. The style of architecture is the Byzantine. The front of the building is four hundred and twenty-six feet in width. The center is two hundred by fifty feet, and there are two wings, the eastern one having a vestibule and porch attached, and the western one a semicircular projection. It was designed by James Renwick, Jr., and was the first building, not an ecclesiastical edifice, of this order of architecture erected in this country. The interior is substantially constructed, and conveniently arranged for the purposes for which it was designed. The center of the building is used mainly for the exhibition of objects of natural history, and the wings are utilized for the apartments of the officials and employees. The building is surmounted by nine towers, of different designs and altitudes, the highest one being one hundred and forty-five feet above the ground.

The history of this institution, and especially of the bequest by means of which it was founded, is extremely interesting, and it is given somewhat in detail in this work, for the benefit of those readers thereof who may not be familiar therewith. It was made by an Englishman, named James Smithson, who died at Genoa, Italy, June 27, 1829, having made a will disposing of his estate, a copy of which is here inserted in full.

"I, James Smithson, son of Hugh, first Duke of Northumberland, and Elizabeth, heiress of the Hungerfords, of Audley, and niece of Charles the Proud, Duke of Somerset, now residing in Bentick Street, Cavendish Square, do, this 23d day of October, 1826, make this, my last, will and testament.

"I bequeath the whole of my property, of every nature and kind soever, to my bankers, Messrs. Drummond, of Charing Cross, in trust, to be disposed of in the following manner, and desire of my said executors to put my property under the management of the Court of Chancery:

"To John Fitall, formerly my servant, but now employed in the London docks, and residing at No. 27 Jubilee Place, North, Mile End Old Town, in consideration of his attachment and fidelity to me, and the long and great care he has taken of my effects, and my having done but little for him, I give or bequeath the annuity or annual sum of £100 sterling, for his life, to be paid to him quarterly, free from legacy, duty, and all other deductions; the first payment to be paid to him at the expiration of three months after my death. I have at divers times lent sums of money to Henry Honore Juilly, formerly my servant, but now keeping the Hungerford, in the Rue Caumartin, at Paris, and for which sums of money I have undated bills or bonds signed by him. Now I will and direct that if he desires it, these sums of money be let remain in his hands at an interest of five per cent. for five years after the date of the present will.

"To Henry James Hungerford, my nephew, heretofore called Henry James Dickinson, son of my late brother, Lieutenant-Colonel Henry Lewis Dickinson, now residing with Mr. Auboin, at Bourg la Reine, near Paris, I give and bequeath for his life the whole of the income arising from my property of every nature and kind whatever, after the payment of the above annuity; and after the death of John Fitall, that annuity also, the payments to be made at the time the interest or dividends become due on the stocks or other property from which the income arises.

"Should the said Henry James Hungerford have a child, legitimate or illegitimate, I leave to said child or children, his or their heirs, executors, or assigns, after the death of his or their father, the whole of my property of every kind, absolutely and forever, to be divided between them, if there are more than one, in the manner their father shall judge proper; and in case of his omitting to decide this, as the Lord Chancellor shall judge proper.

"Should my nephew, Henry James Hungerford, marry, I empower him to make a jointure.

"In case of the death of my said nephew, without leaving a child or children, or in case of the death of the child or children he may have, under the age of twenty-one years, or intestate, I then bequeath the whole of my property, subject to the annuity of £100 to John Fitall, and for the security of the payment of which I mean stock to remain in this country, to the United States of America, to found at Washington, under the name of the Smithsonian Institution, an establishment for the increase and diffusion of knowledge among men.

"I think it proper here to state that all the money which will be standing in the present five per cents., at my death, in the name of the father of my above-mentioned nephew, Henry James Hungerford, and all of that in my name, is the property of my said nephew, being what he inherited from his father, or what I have laid up for him from the savings of his income.

"James Smithson."

The following letter to Hon. Aaron Vail, *Chargé d'Affaires* of the United States at London, was the first intimation that the fund mentioned in the will of Mr. Smithson was at the disposal of the United States, when the proper steps should be taken to secure legal possession of the same:

"Craven Street, Strand, July 21, 1835.

"Sir: We send you enclosed the copy of the will of Mr. Smithson, on the subject of which we yesterday did ourselves the pleasure of waiting upon you; and we avail ourselves of the opportunity to repeat in writing what we verbally communicated.

"Pursuant to the instructions contained in the will, an amicable suit was, on the death of the testator, instituted in chancery by Mr. Hungerford against Messrs. Drummond, the executors; under which suit the assets were realized. They were very considerable; and there is now standing in the name of the accountant-general of the Court of Chancery, as the trustees of the will, stock amounting to about £100,000. During Mr. Hungerford's life he received the income arising from this property; but news has just reached England that Mr. Hungerford has died abroad, leaving no child to survive him.

"It now becomes necessary that measures be taken for the purpose of causing the decision of the Court of Chancery, as to the further disposition of the property. On reference to the will, it will appear that it is not very clearly defined to whom, on behalf of the United States, the property should be paid or transferred; indeed, there is so much doubt that we apprehend that the Attorney-General must, on behalf of the Crown of England, be joined in the proceedings which it is requisite that the United States should institute.

"We act in this matter for Messrs. Drummond, the bankers, who are mere stockholders, and who are ready to do all in their power to facilitate getting the decision and carrying into effect the testator's intentions. We shall therefore be happy to communicate with such professional advisers as your Government may think fit to appoint to act for them in this country. In the meantime, we may perhaps be permitted to add that it is perfectly competent for us to carry on the proceedings on behalf the United States, and possibly some expense and delay may be avoided by our so doing.

"Having thus briefly stated the nature of the business, we at present abstain from making any suggestions as to the party in whose name proceedings should be adopted, considering the point should be determined by our counsel here after the opinion of the proper law officers in the United States has been taken on the subject.

"Any further information you may require we shall be happy to give you, and are, sir,

"Your most obedient servants,

"CLARKE, FYNMORE, & FLADGATE.

"A. VAIL, ESQ., 49 York Terrace."

Soon after receiving this communication, Hon. Mr. Vail wrote to Hon. John Forsyth, Secretary of State of the United States, at Washington, as follows:

"LEGATION OF THE UNITED STATES, LONDON, July 28, 1835.

"SIR: The papers which I have the honor herewith to communicate to you will acquaint you with the particulars of a bequest of property to a large amount left to the United States by Mr. James Smithson, for the purpose, as stated in the will, of founding at Washington an institution for the increase and diffusion of knowledge among men. The letter of Messrs. Clarke, Fynmore, & Fladgate, the solicitors by whom I was apprised of the existence of the will, together with the inquiries I have made, leave no doubt of its having been established, and its disposition recognized by the Court of Chancery; the first legatee under it having for several years, and to the time of his death, received the income of the property, which is stated to have amounted to upward of £4,000 per annum.

"According to the view taken of the case by the solicitors, it is now for the United States, in the event of their accepting the bequest and the trust coupled with it, to come foward by their representative and make themselves parties to an amicable suit before the Lord Chancellor, for the purpose of legally establishing the fact of the demise of the first legatee without children and intestate; prove their claim to the benefit of the will, and obtain a decree in chancery awarding them the proceeds of the estate. Messrs. Clarke, Fynmore, & Fladgate are willing to undertake the management of the suit on the part of the United States, and from what I have learned of their standing, may safely be confided in. Not being acquainted with the exact structure of our institutions, they are unable to point out the exact manner in which the United States should be represented in the contemplated suit; but they believe that their diplomatic agent here, if constituted for that purpose the legal representative of the President, would be recognized by the Court of Chancery as the proper organ of the United States for all the purposes of the will.

"Should it be thought necessary to await the action of Congress to authorize the institution of the requisite legal proceedings, and should the course suggested by the solicitors meet the views of the President, his power of attorney authorizing the diplomatic agent here to act in his name will, I apprehend, be necessary; and as the suit will involve some expense not connected with the contingent fund of the legation, your instructions upon this branch of the subject will likewise be desirable.

"I am, with great respect, your obedient servant,

"A. Vail.

"John Forsyth, Esq.,

"Secretary of State of the United States, Washington."

To this letter the following reply was sent:

"Department of State, Washington, September 26, 1835.

"Sir: I have the honor to acknowledge the receipt of your dispatch of the 28th of July last (No. 197) relative to the bequest of property to a large amount left to the United States by Mr. James Smithson, for the purpose of founding an institution for the increase and diffusion of knowledge among men, and to inform you that your letter and the papers which accompanied it have been submitted to the President, who has determined to lay the subject before Congress at its next session. The result of its deliberations, when obtained, shall be communicated to you, with the necessary instructions.

"Of the course intended to be pursued in relation to this matter, as above explained, you will take occasion to acquaint the solicitors who apprized you of the existence of Mr. Smithson's will.

"I am, Sir, your obedient servant,

"JOHN FORSYTH.

"AARON VAIL,

"*Chargé d'Affaires* of the United States, London."

On the 17th of December, 1835, President Jackson transmitted to Congress all the correspondence and information in his possession in reference to the subject, and said: "The Executive having no authority to take any steps for accepting the trust and obtaining the funds, the papers are communicated with a view to such measures as Congress may deem necessary."

The select committee appointed by the House of Representatives to consider this matter, consisted of the following members: Hon. John Quincy Adams; Mr. Thomas, of Maryland; Mr. Garland, of Virginia; Mr. Pearce, of Rhode Island; Mr. Speight, of North Carolina; Mr. McKennan, of Pennsylvania; Mr. Hannegan, of Indiana; Mr. Garland, of Louisiana, and Mr. Chapin, of New York. This committee submitted the question to Congress whether it was competent to the United States, whether it comported with their dignity, whether it was expedient and proper, that the United States should appear as suitors in a court of justice in England to assert their claim to the legacy in question as trustees for the intended charitable institution to be founded at Washington. The conclusion arrived at was that the United States must be regarded as the *Parens Patriæ* of the District of Columbia, and that in that character they had a right and were in duty bound to assert a claim to any property given to them for the purpose of founding a charitable institution of any kind within the District of Columbia, and concluded with recommending the adoption of a joint resolution authorizing the President to take measures for the recovery of the said legacy.

On the 5th of January, 1836, Mr. Leigh, from the Judiciary Committee, made a report to the Senate, informing that body of the fact of the bequest having been made, and also giving a succinct history of the proceedings so far taken, including the correspondence presented above.

40

In the House of Representatives, on January 14, Mr. Adams, from the House select committee, made a report in which he stated that Congress, in its representative capacity, was alone competent to accept the bequest, and added some interesting historical reflections.

"The testator, James Smithson, a subject of Great Britain, declares himself, in the caption of the will, a descendant in blood from the Percys and the Seymours, two of the most illustrious historical names in the British Isles. Nearly two centuries since, immediately after the restoration of the royal family of the Stuarts, in 1660, an ancestor of his own name, Hugh Smithson, received from Charles the Second, as a reward for his eminent services to that house during the civil wars, the dignity of a barony of England, a dignity still held by the Dukes of Northumberland, as descendants from the same Hugh Smithson. The father of the testator, by his marriage with the lady Elizabeth Seymour, who was descendant by a famous line from the ancient Percys, and by subsequent creation of George the Third, in 1766 became the first Duke of Northumberland. His son and successor, the brother of the testator, was known in the history of the Revolutionary War by the name of Lord Percy, was present as the British officer at the sanguinary opening scene of our Revolutionary War at Lexington, and at the battle of Bunker Hill, and was the bearer to the British Government of the dispatches from the commander-in-chief of the royal forces announcing the event of said memorable day; and the present Duke of Northumberland, the testator's nephew, was the ambassador extraordinary of Great Britain, sent to assist in the coronation of the late King of France, Charles the Tenth, a few months only before the date of this bequest from his relative to the United States of America. . . . The father of the testator, upon forming his alliance with the heir of the Percys, assumed, by an act of the British Parliament, that name, and under it became Duke of Northumberland. But, renowned as is the name of Percy in the historical annals of England; resounding as it does from the summit of the Cheviot Hills to the ears of our generation in the ballad of Chevy Chase, with the classical commentary of Addison; freshened and renovated in our memory, as it has recently been, from the purest fountain of poetical inspiration, in the loftier strain of Alnwick Castle, by a bard of our own native land; doubly immortalized as it is in the deathless dramas of Shakespeare; "confident against the world in arms," as it must have been in long ages past, and may still be in the virtues of its present possessors by inheritance, let the trust of James Smithson to the United States of America be faithfully executed by their

Representatives in Congress; let the result accomplish his object; and a wreath of more unfading virtue shall entwine itself in the lapse of future ages around the name of Smithson, than the united hands of tradition, history, and poetry have braided round the name of Percy, through the long perspective of a thousand years," etc.

As a conclusion to the report, the committee submitted the following bill:

"A BILL to Authorize the President of the United States to Assert and Prosecute with Effect the Right of the United States to the Bequest of James Smithson, late of London, Deceased, to Found at Washington, under the Name of the Smithsonian Institution, an Establishment for the Increase and Diffusion of Knowledge among Men:

"*Be it enacted, etc.*, That the President of the United States be, and is hereby, authorized to constitute and appoint an agent or agents to assert and prosecute, for and in behalf of the United States, and in their authority, as may be advisable, in the Court of Chancery or orther tribunal in England, the right of the United States to the legacy bequeathed to them by the last will and testament of James Smithson, late of London, deceased, for the purpose of founding at Washington, under the name of the Smithsonian Institution, an institution for the increase and diffusion of knowledge among men; and to empower such agent or agents to receive and grant acquittance for all such sums of money or other funds as may or shall be decreed or adjudged to the United States for or on account of said legacy.

"SEC. 2. That said agent or agents shall, before receiving any part of said legacy, give a bond or bonds in the penal sum of $500,-000 to the Treasurer of the United States and his successors in office, with good and sufficient security to the Secretary, for the faithful performance of the duties of the said agency, and for the faithful remittance to the Treasurer of the United States of all and every sum or sums of money, or other funds, which he or they may receive in payment in whole or in part of said legacy, and the Treasurer of the United States is hereby authorized and required to keep safely all sums of money or other funds which may be received by him in virtue of the said bequest, and to account therefor separately from all other funds of his office, and subject to such further disposal thereof as may be hereafter provided by Congress.

"SEC. 3. That any and all sums of money or other funds which shall be received for and on account of said legacy, shall be applied in such manner as Congress may hereafter direct, to the purpose of founding and endowing at Washington, under the name of the Smithsonian Institution, an establishment for the increase and diffusion of knowledge among men, to which application of the said moneys and other funds the faith of the United States is hereby pledged.

"SEC. 4. To the end that the claim to the said bequest may be prosecuted with effect, and the necessary expenses of prosecuting the same be defrayed, the President of the United States be, and he is hereby, authorized to apply to that purpose any sum not exceeding $10,000 out of any money in the treasury not otherwise appropriated."

This act was approved by the President July 1, 1836. And under its authority the President appointed Richard Rush, of Pennsylvania, the agent to recover the funds in England; who, having arrived in England, notified Messrs. Clarke, Fynmore, & Fladgate of that fact September 14, 1836. The work was begun as soon as practicable, but had not progressed far when a complication arose with reference to the interest of Henry James Dickinson, named in the will. It then transpired that Henry James Dickinson was the son of Lieutenant-Colonel Henry Lewis Dickinson by a Mrs. Coates, who was still living, and was married to a Frenchman named De la Batut. During the lifetime of young Dickinson he had made his mother ample allowance for her support, but at his death this allowance ceased. Mr. Rush was satisfied that under the will of Mr. Smithson she had no claim against the fund bequeathed to the United States, and stated that her claim was under the will of Henry Lewis Dickinson, made at Paris in 1819, by which he left all his property in trust to his brother, Mr. Smithson, for his (Dickinson's) son, Dickinson, or Henry James Hungerford. Half of the interest of it, however, was to go to Mrs. Coates while she lived, and it thus appeared to Mr. Rush that the fee of the French attorney, which had been presented for payment out of the Smithson bequest, could not be charged to this fund. During the progress of the suit, however, Mr. Rush consented to a certain amount being allowed to Madam De la Batut for the sake of preventing delay, and at length the Chancery Court decided to retain for her benefit a sum which should produce an annuity of £150 9s., which, together with arrears, as she had received nothing since 1834, amounted to £5,542. On May 9, 1838, after numerous and vexatious delays, the court decreed that the Smithson bequest belonged to the United States. On the 5th of June, the attorneys, Clarke, Fynmore, & Fladgate, informed Mr. Rush that everything was completed, and the following sums had been transferred to his name, and that they were entirely at his disposal, free from the control of the Court of Chancery. These sums were as follows: £64,535 18*s.* 9*d.* consols; £12,000 reduced annuities; £16,100 bank stock. On the 9th of the month, Mr. Rush shipped to the United States by the ship *Mediator*, in gold, the net proceeds of this amount, which was £105,565 12*s.* 5*d.*, the gross amount being £106,- 370 7*s.* 3*d.* Upon its arrival in the United States, it was, by the direction of the Secretary of the Treasury, deposited in the mint at Philadelphia, and amounted in dollars to $508,318.46.

In the meantime, on July 7, 1838, an act was passed by Congress to provide for the support of the military academy of the United States at West Point for the year 1838. The sixth section of this act was as follows:

"That all money arising from the bequest of the late James Smithson, of London, for the purpose of founding at Washington, in this District, an institution to be denominated the Smithsonian Institution, which may be paid into the treasury, is hereby appropriated, and shall be invested by the Secretary, with the approval of the President of the United States, in stocks of States, bearing interest at not less than five per cent. per annum, which said stocks shall be held by the Secretary in trust for the uses specified in the last will and testament of said Smithson, until provision is made by law for carrying the purpose into effect; and that the annual interest accruing on the stock aforesaid shall be in like manner invested for the benefit of said institution."

Under authority of this act, granted as will be seen before the money was received in the treasury, the Secretary of the Treasury, on the 4th of September,. 1838, invested $499,500 of the money in the purchase of five hundred $1,000 bonds of the State of Arkansas, bearing six per cent. interest, payable semiannually, on the 1st of January and July of each year after September 4, 1838; and the further sum of $8,270.67 in the purchase of eight bonds of the State of Michigan, bearing six per cent. interest, payable semiannually on the first Monday in January and July in each year after the 1st of May, 1838. The remainder of the money was left in the treasury. Thus the United States became pledged for the faithful application of the purpose of the testator — the increase and diffusion of knowledge among men.

On December 6, 1838, the President invited the attention of Congress to the obligation resting upon the United States to fulfill the object of the bequest, and on the next day transmitted to Congress reports from the Secretary of the State and of the Treasury in compliance with a resolution of the House of Representatives of the 9th of July preceding, requesting all such documents, communications, etc., as might be in the possession of the Executive, or which could be obtained, as should illustrate the origin, progress, and consummation of the process by which the Smithsonian bequest had been recovered, etc.

A variety of projects had been presented by individuals, which were referred to the committee for consideration; but as they all contemplated the establishment of a school, college, or university, the committee did not consider them suitable for carrying out the purposes of the testator. The committee agreed from the first that no part of the fund should be applied to the establishment of any such institution or ecclesiastical establishment, and they also agreed that they would recommend that the capital of the fund should be preserved entire and unimpaired, and so invested as to yield an income of six per cent. per annum, which income only should be annually applied by Congress, and that the capital itself should be increased, rather than diminished.

While the committee was deliberating upon the means of carrying into effect these objects by special enactments, the Senate, on January 12, 1839, adopted a joint resolution to the effect that a joint committee of seven members of the Senate, and as many members of the House as the House should think proper to appoint, should be appointed to consider the entire question of establishing an institution for the application of the legacy of James Smithson, of a charter for the institution, etc., and to consider the expediency of ways and means to be provided by Congress other than said legacy, but in addition thereto, and in aid of said benevolent intention, and to report by bill, or otherwise. Thus two widely divergent plans were suggested by the House and Senate respectively, and after considerable discussion it became apparent that further joint deliberation would offer no prospect of concurrence.

February 6, 1839, a series of resolutions was presented to the joint committee for consideration, which were to the effect that no part of the Smithsonian Fund ought to be applied to the education of children or youth of the United States, nor to any school, college, university, or institute of education. These resolutions were adopted on the 13th of that month. The report of the committee of the House, drawn up by a master mind, one fully alive to the value of the increase of knowledge,—that of no less a personage than the venerable John Quincy Adams,—strongly urged the establishment of an astronomical observatory at Washington, and gave in a most lucid and comprehen-

sive manner the history of astronomy, and presented in the clearest
language an estimate of the immense importance to the world, especially to commerce and navigation, of the Royal Observatory of
England and of France. In Europe, at that time, according to the
able and interesting report, there were one hundred and twenty
astronomical observatories, while in the United States there was not
one. With such observations, the committee submitted the following bill:

"A Bill for the Disposal and Management of the Fund Bequeathed
    by James Smithson to the United States, for the Establishment
    of an Institution for the Increase and Diffusion of Knowledge
    among Men:

    "*Be it enacted*, etc., That the Vice-President of the United States,
the Chief Justice of the United States, the Secretary of State, of the
Treasury, of War, of the Navy, the Attorney-General, and the Mayor
of the city of Washington, all during the time for which they shall
hold their respective offices, together with three members of the Senate
and four members of the House, to be annually elected by their respective Houses on the second Wednesday of December, and to continue
in office until others are elected in their stead, shall be and hereby are
constituted a body politic and corporate by the style and title of the
'Trustees of the Smithsonian Institution for the Increase and Diffusion
of Knowledge among Men,' with perpetual succession and the usual
powers, duties, and liabilities incident to corporations.

Section 2 gave the corporation thus constituted power to appoint
a secretary and treasurer, and to prescribe their duties. Section 3
provided that the sum of $508,318.46, placed in the treasury of the
United States September 1, 1838, as the proceeds, in part, of the
bequest of James Smithson to the United States, together with all
the sums which had been or might be thereafter realized, should be
placed to the credit of the fund to be denominated the Smithson
Fund in the treasury of the United States, and the faith of the United
States was pledged for the preservation of said fund, undiminished
and unimpaired, to bear interest at the rate of six per cent. a year,
payable on the first days of January and July, to the treasurer of
the board of trustees of the Smithson Fund, to be applied to the purposes of the fund, conformably to the laws, and subject to the rules
and regulations of the board of trustees.

Section 4 provided that no part of the said Smithsonian Fund,
principal or interest, should be applied to any school, college, univer-

sity, institute of education, or ecclesiastical establishment. Section 5 provided that the appropriations made from time to time by Congress should be for the accruing interest, and not for principal of the fund, etc. Section 6 provided that the sum of $30,000, part of the first year's interest, be applied toward the erection, at the city of Washington, of an astronomical observatory, adapted to the most effective and continual observations of the phenomena of the heavens, etc. Section 7 provided that the site should be in the city of Washington, on land belonging to the United States, etc.

There were five other sections to the bill, the 12th setting apart from the second and third years' interest the sum of $60,000, which was to be invested, and the interest arising from such investment was to be applied to the payment of the salary of an astronomical observer, and to the incidental and contingent expenses and repairs upon the building.

February 25, 1839, the Senate having taken up the bill introduced by Mr. Robbins, of Rhode Island, providing for the appointment of nine commissioners annually — three by the Senate, three by the House, and three by the President, to take charge of the Smithsonian Fund, to draw up an act of incorporation for the institution, and to constitute a portion of its board of trustees, when incorporated, Hon. John C. Calhoun then made the following remarkable speech:

"This is a bill making provision for the common benefit of mankind; but we are restricted in our powers. The question whether we have the power to establish a university or not, was the subject of consideration at an early stage of our Government, and President Washington decided that Congress had the power; but the question was voted down, and never revived. And now what would we do? We accept a fund from a foreigner, and would do what we are not authorized to do by the Constitution. We would enlarge our grant of power direct from the States of the Union. Sir, can you show me a word that goes to invest us with such a power? I not only regard the measure proposed as unconstitutional, but to me it appears to involve a species of meanness which I cannot describe, a want of dignity wholly unworthy of this Government. Some years ago, we accepted a statue of Mr. Jefferson, which is no more like him than I am, and we made a tacit admission, by its acceptance, that we were too stingy to purchase one worthy of the man and the Nation; and now what would we do by this? We would accept a donation from a foreigner, to do with it what we have no right to do, and just as if we were not rich enough ourselves to do what it proposed, or too mean to do it if it were in our power. Sir, we are rich enough our-selves, and if we are not, this bequest cannot give us the power."

Hon. Thomas H. Benton spoke in a similar strain to this of Mr. Calhoun, that "it was a violation of the Constitution," as did also Mr. Niles, of Connecticut; while Robert J. Walker of Mississippi, Ambrose H. Sevier of Arkansas, Mr. Wright and Richard A. Bayard of Delaware, were strongly in favor of the resolution. The bill was laid on the table by a vote of 20 to 15.

March 16, 1840, the Secretary of the Treasury, in obedience to a resolution of Congress, submitted the following statement of the moneys of the United States invested in State stocks: In bonds of the State of Arkansas, $523,000; in bonds of the State of Michigan, $8,000; and in bonds of the State of Illinois, $26,000. September 8, 1841, the Senate passed a bill to amend so much of the sixth sec-tion of the act for the support of the military academy at West Point, of 1838, referred to above, as required the Secretary of the Treasury to invest the annual interest accruing on the investment of the money arising from the bequest of James Smithson in the stocks of the States, and required him instead to invest the money or interest so accruing in any stock of the United States bearing interest not less than five per cent., and on the 10th of the month the House concurred in this amendment. On the 9th of September, a statement was sent to Congress by Hon. Thomas Ewing, Secretary of the Treasury, showing the following investments of the Smithsonian Fund. In bond of the State of Arkansas, $538,000; in Illinois bonds, $56,000; in Ohio bonds, $18,000, and in Michigan bonds, $8,000; total, $620,000.

In the debate upon the amendment to the sixth section of the act-to support the military academy, adopted as above narrated, Hon. Lewis F. Linn, of Missouri, in the Senate, called attention to the fact that the Democratic Party, during the Presidential campaign of 1840, had been slandered, vilified, and abused with the most unfounded charges of designs to discredit the States of the Union. The Dem-ocratic Party had been denounced from one end of the Union to the other, for having prostrated the whole credit system; yet now what spectacle do we behold? What but that to be expected from the Whig Party, which had so notoriously proved to the world that their professions out of power were one thing, while their per-formance in power were quite another thing? Now they have the first opportunity, they offer the most outrageous, treacherous, and fatal stab to the State stock credit system that was ever attempted by any of the representatives of the people or of the States, etc.

Hon. Henry Clay, in his usual clear and intelligent manner, replied, that the relation between the Government of the United States and those of the separate States, of the latter being debtor to the former, ought always to be avoided; for what means could be used to coerce the States if they should refuse to pay the bonds? The Government had stocks of its own in which the trust fund could be invested, and he preferred the adoption of this principle, that in all cases of trust funds an account should be kept with the United States. He regarded the Smithsonian Fund as a sacred trust, which the Government would be bound to restore if it should be lost. The Government had assumed the responsibility for the money, and it should remain in the treasury under the control of the Government so long as the Government was responsible.

Future events showed in the clearest possible manner that what Mr. Clay said might at least have been prompted by the commonest principles of business sagacity, as it was certainly the clearest of common sense.

President Tyler, in his message to Congress, of the 6th of December, 1841, made the following recommendation: "I suggest for your consideration the propriety of making, without further delay, some specific application of the funds derived under the will of Mr. Smithson, of England, for the diffusion of knowledge, and which have heretofore been vested in public stocks until such time as Congress should think proper to give them a specific direction. Nor will you, I feel confident, permit any abatement of the principal of the legacy to be made, should it turn out that the stocks in which the investments have been made have undergone a depreciation.'

The select committee of the House to carry into effect this recommendation of the President, was composed of Hon. John Quincy Adams; Hon. Richard W. Habersham, of Georgia; Hon. Truman Smith, of Connecticut; Hon. Joseph R. Underwood, of Kentucky; Hon. Benjamin Randall, of Maine; Hon. Charles J. Ingersoll, of Pennsylvania; Hon. R. M. T. Hunter, of Virginia; Hon. George S. Houston, of Alabama; and Hon. Samuel S. Bowne, of New York.

December 10, 1841, Mr. Adams, from this committee, reported to the House that the $500,000 loaned to the State of Arkansas was not payable before the 26th of October, 1860, and the $38,000 subsequently loaned to that State was not payable before January 1, 1861. The bonds of the other States in which this fund had been invested did not mature until about the same time, and some of them were not redeemable until 1870, and many of them were payable only at the pleasure of the State! The account with the several States then stood as follows: Arkansas, $538,000; Michigan, $8,000; Illinois, $46,000; Ohio, $18,000; the United States, $1,291.86.

June 7, 1844, Mr. Adams, from the select committee of the House, submitted a report in which he showed from documents submitted likewise that the Government had invested in bonds of the State of Arkansas the sum of $538,000, upon which up to December 31, 1843, that State had paid $93,591.73 interest, and that there remained due at the same date the sum of $75,687.84, and that the interest was accumulating at the rate of $32,000 per year. Michigan owed at the same time $480 in interest; Illinois owed $3,360, and Ohio owed nothing. The interest due from the three States amounted to $79,-527.84, which, added to the principal, $620,000, made a total sum of $699,527.84. And if the fund should continue to be invested in this manner, for which there was no remedy, the aggregate amount would be, by December 31, 1846, more than $800,000. None of the bonds were payable before 1850, and some of them not before 1870, and all payable at the pleasure of the States, and yet Congress, on July 1, 1836, in accepting the bequest, solemnly pledged the faith of the Government of the United States that all the sums of money and other funds received from and on account of this legacy should be applied to the humane and generous purpose of the testator. For the redemption of this pledge it was absolutely necessary that the funds then locked up in the bonds of the States, and the accruing interest on the same, should be made available for the disposal of Congress, in order that Congress might execute the trust which it had assumed. For this purpose the committee reported a bill for the appropriation of the sum of $800,000, to be invested in certificates of stock of the United States bearing interest at the rate of six per cent., payable semiannually, and redeemable at the pleasure of Congress by the substitution of other funds of equal value, which sum of $800,000 was to be constituted permanent funds, as follows: To replace the $508,318.46 deposited in the mint at Philadelphia September 1, 1838, and invested as already narrated, and $300,000 to supply the place of the interest that would have accrued by December 31, 1846.

This bill thus introduced by Mr. Adams provided for the erection, at the city of Washington, of an astronomical observatory, adapted to the most effectual and continual observation of the phenomena of the heavens, and providing the necessary machinery for carrying out the intention and will of Mr. Smithson; but it was not acted upon during that session of Congress.

December 12, 1844, Benjamin Tappan, of Ohio, introduced a bill into the Senate to establish the Smithsonian Institution, providing for the appointment of a board of managers who should select the location of the institution from that part of the Mall west of Seventh Street, and providing also that the institution to be established should be devoted to agriculture, horticulture, rural economy, chemistry, natural history, geology, architecture, domestic science, astronomy, and navigation. In other words, according to this bill, the institution was to be a school or college. This plan was discussed in a most able manner from the day it was introduced until January, 1845, by Rufus Choate, of Massachusetts; James A. Pearce, of Maryland; Mr. Tappan; John J. Crittenden, of Kentucky; William Allen, of Ohio; Robert J. Walker, of Mississippi, and was finally passed January 23, 1845.

The idea of the House of Representatives was somewhat different from that embodied in the above bill. The question came up early in the session of 1845–46, and on February 28, 1846, Robert Dale Owen, chairman of the select committee, made an earnest appeal to the House to dispose of the subject, and presented for the consideration of the House the condition of the Smithsonian Fund; Arkansas was then behind in the payment of interest due up to December 31, 1845, $132,841.52; Illinois, $1,680; Michigan, $180.07; total interest in arrears, $134,701.59. The question came up April 22, 1846, as the special order of the day, and Mr. Owen made another most earnest and able appeal to the House to dispose of the subject. He said it was then sixteen years since Mr. Smithson died; it was nearly ten years since Congress accepted the trust; it was nearly eight years since the money arrived in this country, and yet though distinguished men, notably the Hon. John Quincy Adams, from Massachusetts, had made noble efforts to accomplish something, yet nothing had been done. He said that he knew that there were some strict constructionists in the House who would, even at this late day, vote to return the money to the British Court of Chancery; and immediately upon the making of this remark, George W. Jones, of Tennessee, distinguished himself by saying that he most certainly would. Upon the conclusion of Mr. Owen's speech, Mr. Jones moved to strike out all after the word "be" in the sixth line of the first section, and insert the following:

"Paid by the Secretary of the Treasury to the heirs-at-law, or next of kin, of the said James Smithson, or their authorized agents, whenever they shall demand the same; provided that the Secretary of the Treasury shall, in paying over said money as herein directed, deliver to said heirs all State bonds or other stocks of every kind which have been purchased with said money, or any part thereof, in lieu of so much of said money as shall have been invested in said bonds or other stocks. And the balance of said sum of money, if any, not so invested, shall be paid out of any money in the treasury not otherwise appropriated."

If the above amendment should be rejected, then Mr. Jones said he was in favor of turning over to the Smithsonian Institution the same said bonds and stocks, and let that institution get what it could out of them. John S. Chipman, of Michigan, supported the dishonest and dishonorable plan of Mr. Jones. Mr. Owen's speech in reply to all the objections to the bill was most able and just; showing their flimsy and unreasonable character, and the essential injustice and lack of principle which the most of them involved. Notwithstanding Mr. Owen's convincing arguments and statements, Andrew Johnson could not be made to understand them, and he, like his colleague, Mr. Jones, and Mr. Chipman, favored sending the money back to England, and moved to add to the substitute of Mr. Jones the following words: "Not actually paid into the treasury by the States which have borrowed and used the fund." But to the everlasting honor of the House of Representatives, when the substitute of Mr. Jones came to be voted upon it was overwhelmingly defeated by a vote of 8 yeas to 115 nays. Finally, after numerous attempts to amend the bill, some of which were successful, the bill was passed by a vote of 85 yeas to 76 nays.

In the Senate, the bill passed August 10, 1846, by a vote of 26 to 13. It was signed by the President on the same day, and regents were appointed by both Houses of Congress. The chancellors of the institution have been the Justices of the Supreme Court of the United States since that time, and the Secretaries. By far the most important officers connected with the institution have been the following: Professor Joseph Henry, elected in December, 1846, and who served until May 13, 1878, the date of his death; his successor, Professor Spencer Fulton Baird, who had been assistant to Professor Henry since 1850, and who served until his death, August 19, 1887; and Professor Baird's successor, the present incumbent, Professor S. P. Langley, who had been assistant to Professor Baird. Dr. G. Brown Goode is the assistant at the present time, and is in charge of the National Museum. William J. Rhees was chief clerk of the institution from the time of his appointment in 1853 until October, 1891, when he was succeeded by William C. Winlock, son of the celebrated astronomer Winlock, though now the title of Mr. Winlock is not chief clerk, but assistant in charge of office.

Professor Henry was a most eminent physicist. He was especially successful in his researches into the phenomena of electricity, and
it is perhaps not too much to say that to him are we really indebted
for the electric telegraph. He also instituted a great many elaborate
experiments upon illuminating materials, and made many discoveries
with reference to the burning of different kinds of oils. He also
made valuable discoveries with reference to the laws of sound as
applied to the construction of public buildings and lecture halls, and
also as applied to the production of fog signals. One of his first
administrative acts as secretary of the Smithsonian Institution, was to
organize a large and widespread corps of observers of meteorological
conditions, and to make arrangements for simultaneous reports by
means of the telegraph. That is, he was the first to apply the
telegraph to meteorological research and to utilize the generalizations
made in weather forecasts, embracing the entire North American
Continent under a single system.

Professor Baird, the successor of Professor Henry, was an eminent
naturalist, and had been connected with the great surveys of the West.
He had contributed valuable reports relating to the products of the
West, which are yet standard authority. After he became secretary
of the Smithsonian Institution, he was made Fish Commissioner, and
instituted many valuable researches into the habits and food of fishes,
resulting in a great extension of knowledge of such matters.

Professor Langley, the present secretary, was selected as an eminent
astronomer and solar physicist. He had made important contributions
to solar physics, and has continued his experiments since he became
secretary. He has also taken great interest and expended considerable
time in researches into the laws and conditions of aerial flight. An
astro-physical observatory has recently been established in connection
with the institution, in which the professor is engaged in making
observations on the solar atmosphere.

To close this history of the Smithsonian Institution, it may be
proper to note the present amount of its funds. Besides the sum
mentioned above, as the Smithsonian bequest, Mr. Smithson left what
is known as a residuary bequest, amounting to £5,015, which was
retained for the use of Madam de la Batut, who died in 1861. This
sum was turned over to George Peabody & Company, in 1864. In
their hands it had increased by March 3, 1865, to $26,210.63 in gold.
Different portions of this amount were sold at different premiums,
and when all was thus sold it netted to the fund $54,165.38.

With reference to the sums invested in State bonds, it should be stated that no State defaulted but Arkansas, and also that nothing was lost even by the investment of the $500,000 in Arkansas bonds; for in adjusting accounts between that State and the United States the debt of Arkansas to the Smithsonian Fund had been retained in the United States Treasury. In 1891 the fund was increased by a donation thereto by Thomas G. Hodgkins, of Setauket, Long Island, of $200,000, and at the present time the fund amounts to $903,000, authority being granted by Congress February 8, 1867, to increase it to $1,000,000.

The United States Naval Observatory was authorized by an act of Congress approved by President Tyler August 18, 1842. This institution, though not the finest, is yet one of the finest and most useful to science, navigation, and commerce in the world. When its usefulness and the dignity it confers upon the Nation are taken into consideration, it is a remarkable, if not a surprising, circumstance that so long a time should have elapsed before the establishment of any institution in the United States claiming the name of an astronomical observatory, excepting a few temporary structures erected during colonial times for special purposes.

Efforts had before been made, all looking in this direction. Action for the establishment of such an observatory originated in the earliest movements for the finding of a first meridian of the United States, a history of which may be found elsewhere in this volume. Memorials toward this object by **Mr.** William Lambert, of Virginia, were presented to the House of Representatives in 1810, 1815, and 1818. These memorials were approved by the House, and Mr. Lambert was appointed to make the necessary astronomical observations for determining the longitude of the Capitol from Greenwich, England.

The first superintendent of the Coast Survey, Mr. F. R. Hassler, in his report made on returning from the purchase of his instruments in London, England, in 1816, recommended the establishment of an astronomical observatory in Washington, "as a national object, a scientific ornament, and a means for encouraging an interest for science in general." Among the eminent men who supported Mr. Hassler's views were President Madison and Secretary of State A. J. Dallas. Mr. Hassler submitted a detailed plan for an observatory, and selected a site for it north of the Capitol.

Most prominent, however, among those who early advocated and persistently urged upon the Nation the founding of an astronomical observatory, was John Quincy Adams. In October, 1823, while Secretary of State to President Monroe, in a letter to a member of the corporation of Harvard College, Mr. Adams urged the establishment of such an observatory at Cambridge, offering to contribute $1,000 toward this object, provided the requisite sum should be raised within two years. At the expiration of that time, the amount not having been raised, Mr. Adams renewed his offer. But these efforts failed, the scientific spirit not having been sufficiently developed even in Harvard at that time.

In 1825, in his first message to Congress, he earnestly urged upon that body the establishment of a national observatory, the adoption of a uniform standard of weights and measures, the establishment of a naval academy, a nautical almanac, and a national university. Congress, however, treated all of these wise and patriotic recommendations with indifference and neglect. The reason, in part at least, for this neglect on the part of Congress, was the prevalence at that time among the dominant political party in that body, not only of an intense party rancor, but also of a bitter personal hatred of Mr. Adams himself, which made it impracticable for the intellectual vision of those members of Congress, influenced by those feelings, to perceive the great and permanent value of the recommendations to the country.

There were some members, however, who were not thus prejudiced and blind. Hon. C. F. Mercer, of Virginia, as chairman of the select committee of the House of Representatives to which, in the order of regular routine, the subject had been referred, strongly advocated the views of President Adams, and reported to the House, on March 18, 1826, a bill for the erection of a national observatory at the city of Washington, together with sundry documents containing estimates of the cost of erecting the necessary buildings for such an establishment, for the instruments and books which it would require, and for the compensation of a principal astronomer, two assistants, and two attendants. These estimates were based upon the principle of providing the establishment at the smallest possible expense, to which end it was provided that the observatory should be attached to the engineer's office in the Department of War, and that the mathematical and astronomical instruments then belonging to that department should be transferred to the observatory. But the recommendations of the President and of the committee were permitted to lie on the tables of both Houses unnoticed, and it was reserved for the Emperor Nicholas, of Russia, to make the capital of his nation what the Capital of the United States should have been — the center of astronomical science, by the establishment of Pulkowa Observatory, the noblest observatory in the world.

The first structure in Washington which may be properly termed a fixed astronomical observatory was erected on Capitol Hill in 1834, by Lieutenant Wilkes, for the naval depot of charts. It was equipped with a three and three-quarter inch transit instrument, made in 1815 for the Coast Survey, and loaned to the Navy Department on applicacation of Lieutenant Wilkes, and with some portable instruments made for the use of an exploring expedition contemplated by the Government in 1828.

In June, 1838, information was received in this country that Mr. Smithson's bequest had been received for the founding of an institution at Washington, and Mr. Adams again made strenuous exertion for the establishment of an astronomical observatory as a part of that institution. Mr. Adams waited upon President Van Buren, and urged his views upon the subject, and a few months later, at the request of the Secretary of State, reduced his views to writing, advocating the appropriation of a part of the Smithsonian Fund to the establishment of an astronomical observatory. Although concurring in the views of Mr. Adams, President Van Buren took no action in the matter. Recommendations for the establishment of an observatory had been made by Mr. Branch, Secretary of the Navy, in 1830; by his successor, Mr. Dickerson, in 1835, and by Mr. Paulding in 1838. In this year a series of observations was commenced in the small observatory connected with the depot of charts, under charge of Lieutenant James M. Gilliss, of the United States Navy, near the Capitol. These observations were continued until 1842, and aided materially in bringing about the establishment of the present observatory. Hon. A. P. Upshur directed Lieutenant Gilliss to prepare a plan for an observatory, and the report of Lieutenant Gilliss, presented November 23, 1843, was accepted by the department, and the construction of a building, with its equipment for astronomical work, was placed in his charge.

Thus it is seen that there were many eminent men in high positions in the Government who favored the establishment of such an institution. The reason for President Van Buren's inaction is perhaps to be found in the fact that the dominant political party, to which he belonged, and from which he expected future honors, was so filled with and actuated by animosity toward Mr. Adams, that whatever he favored they most necessarily opposed. Of this feeling Mr. Adams's biographer used the following language: "Opposition to the design became identified with party spirit, and to defeat it no language of contempt or of ridicule was omitted by the partisans of General Jack-

41

son. In every appropriation which it was apprehended might be converted to its accomplishment, the restriction, 'and no other,' was carefully inserted." An illustration of this careful opposition is presented in the second section of an act passed July 10, 1832, providing for the survey of the coast of the United States, by the following insertion:

"*Provided*, That nothing in this act, or in the act hereby revived, shall be construed to authorize the construction or maintenance of a permanent astronomical observatory.'

In August, 1838, the United States Exploration Expedition having been organized, Lieutenant Gilliss was directed to take charge of the apparatus at the little observatory erected by Lieutenant Wilkes, and to observe moon-culminating stars as often as possible for use in determining differences of longitude in connection with the expedition. The building being found unsuitable for the purpose designed, it was remodeled by Lieutenant Gilliss, who procured two good clocks,—one for mean time, the other for sidereal time,—a three and one-fourth inch achromatic telescope, and a meridian circle. The observatory thus equipped was the first working observatory in the United States.

On March 5, 1840, (?) Mr. Adams, as chairman of the select committee on the Smithsonian Fund, made a report again advocating the views which he had so often urged before. While the question was pending, the Senate passed a joint resolution providing for a joint committee on the Smithsonian Fund. The House, concurring, appointed as its portion of this committee the members of the select committee. The two portions of the committee failed to agree, and presented to their respective Houses separate reports. Mr. Adams, for his portion of the committee, made a report favoring the application of a portion of the income from the Smithsonian Fund toward the erection of an astronomical observatory; and Mr. Preston, of South Carolina, for the Senate portion of the committee, presented a directly contrary report.

On April 12, 1842, Mr. Adams, as chairman of the committee on the Smithsonian Fund, presented a third report, in the form of a bill, for the disposal of the Smithsonian Fund, including in his plan the construction and maintenance of an astronomical observatory, and while Mr. Adams's plan was rejected, yet that very Congress, at that very session, established an astronomical observatory under a fictitious name, through a bill authorizing the construction of a depot for charts and instruments of the Navy of the United States, and this bill finally became a law August 31, 1842, in the following form:

"*Be it enacted, etc.*, That the Secretary of the Navy be and he is hereby authorized to contract for the building of a suitable house for a depot of charts and instruments of the Navy of the United States, on a plan not exceeding in cost the sum of $25,000.

"2. That the sum of $10,000 be and is hereby appropriated out of any money in the treasury not otherwise appropriated, toward carrying this law into effect.

"3. That the said establishment may be located on any portion of the public lands in the District of Columbia which the President of the United States may deem suited to the purpose."

Upon the recommendation of Lieutenant Gilliss, who was appointed by the Secretary of the Navy to prepare plans for the construction of the depot of charts provided for by this law, Reservation No. 4, as marked on the original plan of the city of Washington, was selected by President Tyler as the site of the proposed observatory. This reservation had been designated by President Washington in a letter written by him October 21, 1796, to the commissioners to lay out the city of Washington, as the site of a scientific institution, and had long been known in Washington as "University Square." This square lies on the north bank of the Potomac River, in the southwest part of the city of Washington; the north fronting on E Street, 810 feet; the east, on Twenty-third Street, 1,103 feet; the west, on Twenty-fifth Street, 620 feet, and the south fronting on the Potomac River. The area of the square is somewhat more than seventeen acres.

The site of the main building erected on this square is ninety-five feet above high water in the Potomac. Its elevation gives a horizontal range of one and a quarter miles to the north, and of eight miles to the south.

The central building of the observatory is fifty feet and eight inches square, on the outside, from the foundation to a height of two feet and six inches above the ground. All the foundations to the ground line are of blue rock, and two feet thick; the remainder of the outside walls is of brick, and eighteen inches thick, finished in the best manner; the partition walls are of brick, and fourteen inches thick. The building is two stories high above the basement, with a parapet and balustrade of wood surrounding the top. It is surmounted by a revolving dome twenty-three feet in diameter, resting on a circular wall built up to a height of seven feet above the roof. To the east, west, and south of this central building, wings were erected by Lieutenant Gilliss, the eastern and western wings being twenty-six feet in length and twenty-one feet wide, and the south wing being twenty-one feet in length and the same width as the others.

After consulting Americans most conversant with subjects of this kind, Lieutenant Gilliss went to Europe to consult with foreign astronomers. In March, 1843, he returned home, and began the erection of the observatory as described above. The building was completed, the instruments mounted and adjusted, and the library procured within eighteen months, and all was ready for occupancy and use by September, 1844. On October 1, 1844, Lieutenant M. F. Maury was assigned to the charge of the institution, and directed to remove thereto the nautical books, charts, and instruments of the depot of charts. A corps of three lieutenants, six midshipmen, and one other assistant were assigned him, and soon afterward four more lieutenants were assigned to the observatory. Within the year, three professors were assigned to the corps, and the assistance of Mr. Sears C. Walker was procured, who was doubtless then one of the most practical and accomplished astronomers that the United States had produced. Mr. Walker, however, on account of difficulties with Lieutenant Maury, remained at the observatory only until March, 1847, when he resigned; but during the time of his stay, he fixed the latitude of the dome of the observatory at thirty-eight degrees, fifty-three minutes, and thirty-nine and twenty-five hundredths seconds.

In 1847 quarters were erected east of the main building, for the superintendent. In 1848 the east wing was extended twenty-four feet, connecting these quarters with the main building, and furnishing a store room for chronometers. In 1868 the observing-room for the transit circle was erected, and the large dome for the twenty-six inch equatorial was completed in 1873.

As has been already stated, the latitude of the observatory, deduced from observations made with the mural circle by Sears C. Walker in 1845 and 1846, is thirty-eight degrees, fifty-three minutes, and thirty-nine and twenty-five hundredths seconds. From observations made with the same instrument in 1861 and 1864, inclusive, the latitude was found to be thirty-eight degrees, fifty-three minutes, and thirty-eight and eight-tenths seconds. The point to which all differences of longitude measured from the observatory are referred, is the center of the dome, and the most probable value of its latitude is that last given above. For the determination of its longitude from Greenwich, by telegraph, the following data were communicated in an official letter of the Superintendent of the Coast Survey, August 10, 1872:

	Hours.	Minutes.	Seconds.
Determined in 1867	5	8	12.11
Determined in 1870	5	8	12.16
Determined in 1872	5	8	12.10
Mean Difference of time	5	8	12.125

This gives for the longitude of the dome of the observatory seventy-seven degrees, three minutes, and one and eight hundred and seventy-five thousandths. The instruments in use in this observatory are as follows:

The mural circle, 5 feet in diameter, mounted in 1844; the transit instrument, a 7-foot achromatic, with a clear aperture of 5.35 inches, mounted in 1844; the prime vertical transit instrument, with an object glass of 4.86 inches aperture, and a focal length of 6 feet and 5 inches, mounted in 1845; the 9.6-inch equatorial, with an object glass having a clear aperture of 9.62 inches, and a focal length of 14 feet 4.5 inches, mounted in 1845; the transit circle, having telescope with clear aperture of 8.52 inches, and focal length of 12 feet .7 inches, mounted in 1865; the 26-inch equatorial, which was provided for by act of Congress approved July 15, 1870, and cost $46,000, with a 32-foot tube, a clear aperture of 28 inches, and the principal focal distance of nearly 390 inches, mounted in 1873; a chronometer, with barrel 6 inches in diameter and 13.5 inches long; a comet seeker, with an object glass 3.9 inches in diameter and 32.4 inches focal length, and 5 eyepieces magnifying from 13.6 to 41.6 diameters; a standard sidereal clock, a counting clock, a standard mean time clock, a barometer of the cistern form, a thermometer with Fahrenheit scale graduated from — 36 degrees to + 157 degrees, a spectroscope, a dynameter, a sidereal clock, a driving clock, and a chronograph.

Following is a list of the superintendents of the observatory: Commander M. F. Maury, from October 1, 1844, to April 20, 1861; Captain J. M. Gilliss, from April 22, 1861, to February 9, 1865; Rear Admiral C. H. Davis, from April 28, 1865, to May 8, 1867; Rear Admiral B. F. Sands, from May 8, 1867, to February 23, 1874; Rear Admiral C. H. Davis, from February 23, 1874, to May 1, 1877; Rear Admiral John Rodgers, May 1, 1877, to May 5, 1882; Commander William T. Sampson, temporarily, June 3, 1882, to July 1, 1882; Vice-Admiral S. C. Rowan, July 1, 1882, to May 2, 1883; Rear Admiral R. W. Shufeldt, May 2, 1883, to February 21, 1884; Rear Admiral S. R. Franklin, February 21, 1884, to March 31, 1885; Commander A. D. Brown, temporarily, April 2, 1885, to May 31, 1885; Captain (now Rear Admiral) George E. Belknap, June 1, 1885, to June 7, 1886;

Commander A. D. Brown, temporarily, June 7, 1886, to November 15, 1886; Captain R. L. Phythian, November 15, 1886, to June 28, 1890; Captain F. V. McNair, June 28, 1890, to the present time.

The nucleus of a library was formed in 1843 by Lieutenant Gilliss, when in Europe, by the receipt of donations of books amounting to nearly three hundred volumes, on astronomical and other scientific subjects. The donors were the Royal Astronomical Society, the Royal Society, the Admiralty, the East India Company, and the directors of the observatories at Greenwich, Berlin, Brussels, and Munich. Besides these donations there were upward of seven hundred volumes purchased by Lieutenant Gilliss. Up to 1874 the number of volumes had increased to about six thousand volumes, by an annual exchange of publications made by the observatory with most of the scientific institutions in the world, of scientific treatises. The number of volumes contained in the library in 1891 was about thirteen thousand, besides about three thousand unbound pamphlets.

Following is a list of those who have acted as librarians of the Naval Observatory since its foundation:

J. S. Hubbard, professor of mathematics, from May, 1845, to August, 1863; William Harkness, professor of mathematics, from August, 1863, to October, 1865; J. E. Nourse, professor of mathematics, from October, 1865, to February, 1879; E. S. Holden, professor of mathematics, from February, 1879, to February, 1881; E. F. Qualtrough, lieutenant United States Navy, from February, 1881, to June, 1882; G. E. Yardley, lieutenant United States Navy, from June, 1882, to July, 1883; J. C. Wilson, lieutenant United States Navy, from July, 1883, to August, 1885; L. L. Reamey, lieutenant United States Navy, from August, 1885, to May, 1887; W. D. Horigan,[1] assistant in library (acting librarian), from May, 1887, to May, 1889; H. M. Paul, assistant astronomer, from May, 1889, to date.

[1] During the interval from May, 1887, to May, 1889, no one was formally assigned to the charge of the library; but Mr. W. D. Horigan, who had been an assistant in the library for several years, performed all the duties of an acting librarian. Beginning with July 1, 1891, a regular position of assistant librarian has been provided for by Congress, and Mr. Horigan has been appointed to that position. No salary for a librarian has ever been provided by Congress, and at present it is necessary to take one of the assistant astronomers entirely from astronomical work to perform this duty. The library is the most complete and important in the literature of astronomy and mathematics to be found in this country, and Congress should provide for its proper care and growth by providing a salary adequate to secure the services of a librarian not only trained in modern library methods, but also thoroughly familiar with the literature and history of mathematics and astronomy.

A new observatory building has recently been erected in George-town, to which the instruments are at the present time' (1892) being removed.

The Congressional Library was established in 1800, with a number of books obtained from London by Albert Gallatin, Dr. Mitchell, and others. The following is the list thus obtained: "212 folios, 164 quartos, 581 octavos, 7 duodecimos, and 9 magazines," — 973 volumes in all. It was then the only library of reference possessed by the Government. In 1804 the number of volumes had increased to nearly 1,500, of different languages. During the session of Congress of 1805–06, an appropriation was made for the purchase of books, and placed in the hands of a joint committee of the two Houses, consisting of Messrs. Mitchell and Baldwin of the Senate, and J. Clay, T. M. Rudolph, and Dana of the House. Mr. Beckley was at this time librarian. The library was then beginning to attract the attention of the country, and the suggestion was frequently made to authors that they leave a copy of each of their works to it, "as it would be a better advertisement than could be secured otherwise."

December 6, 1811, an act was passed by Congress appropriating $1,000 per year for five years, which was to be added to what remained on hand from former appropriations, for the purchase of books. Pre-vious to the War of 1812–15 the number of books had increased to three thousand, but during the invasion of the city by the British in August, 1814, they were all destroyed. Thereupon, Mr. Jefferson offered his valuable collection to Congress, consisting of about seven thousand volumes, considered then the finest in the country, and this, purchased for $23,950, became the nucleus for the new library. To its purchase, however, objections were made, on account of the great number of Bibles it contained, as well as the infidel character of some of the other volumes. George Watterston was appointed libra-rian by President Madison in 1815, and superintended the removal of the library three times. His successor was appointed by President Jackson in 1829.

The room for the library was finished in 1824. It is entered from the gallery of the principal stairway west of the rotunda. As first ocen-pied, it was ninety-two feet long, thirty-four feet wide, and thirty-five feet high. This was the main room, and in addition there was a room adjoining, making the whole in the form of an L, the wing portion being of the same width and height as the main room. This main room was divided into twelve arched alcoves, ornamented with pilas-ters copied from the pillars of the celebrated octagonal tower at

Athens. On the roof, which was ten feet above the ceiling, were the skylights, through which, and also through the windows on the west, the room was lighted. The principal room, as well as the reading-room on the north, attached to it, was furnished with sofas, mahogany tables, desks, brussels carpets, etc. At each corner of the apartment was a staircase leading to the galleries above, of which there were three extending all round the room, and which were calculated to hold several thousand volumes. These galleries were so arranged that anyone could read or write in them with comfort and convenience.

The Congressional Library was destroyed by fire December 24, 1851. Immediately afterward, Mr. T. U. Walter, at that time architect of the public buildings, in obedience to a request, made an investigation as to the extent of the injury, and made plans and estimates for repairing the damage. On the 27th of February, 1852, Mr. Walter submitted a design for the reconstruction of the principal apartment of the library within its original limits, and an act was passed by Congress appropriating $72,500 for carrying out Mr. Walter's design. A contract for supplying the iron needed in this work was entered into June 21, 1852, with Messrs. Janes, Beebe, & Company, of New York. The work went on as rapidly as possible, and when complete it may be described as follows:

It embraced the entire western projection of the Capitol as it then was. The main room occupying the center of this western projection is ninety-one feet long, thirty-five feet wide, and thirty-eight feet high. At each end it connects with a room of corresponding height, twenty-nine feet and six inches wide, and seventy feet long. The three rooms are fitted up with iron cases and iron ceilings. They are roofed with copper laid on iron rafters, and lighted by ornamental skylights. There are also two additional apartments, each eighteen feet and six inches by thirty-five feet in size, thus forming a suite of five rooms, embracing an extent of three hundred and two feet.

The main library room occupies the space of the old library before the fire. On each side of the room are three stories of iron cases, each nine feet and six inches in height. The lower story consists of alcoves projecting eight feet and six inches into the room, with cases on each side of the projections. The second story has similar alcoves, excepting that their extension into the room is but five feet, leaving a platform three feet and six inches in width resting on the cases below, which constitutes a commodious gallery. A similar platform is constructed on the alcoves of the second story, forming a gallery to approach the upper cases; thus making three stories, receding as they ascend, and the galleries are continued across the ends of the room. The galleries are all floored with cast-iron plates, and are protected by pedestals and railings. They are approached by two semicircular staircases of cast iron, recessed in the end of the walls of the room.

At the time of the fire of December 24, 1851, there were in the library fifty-five thousand volumes, of which thirty-five thousand were destroyed, besides a number of valuable paintings, including Gilbert Stuart's portraits of the first five Presidents. Since then, as the value of such an institution has been more and more appreciated, the library has constantly grown. In 1866, through the efforts of Rutherford B. Hayes, then a member of Congress from the second Ohio district, who was chairman of the committee on the library, the invaluable collections belonging to Peter Force of Washington were purchased for $100,000, and deposited in the library. These collections of books, pamphlets, etc., pertaining to early American history, are of inestimable value. In 1866 the Smithsonian Library was added to the Library of Congress. In 1882 this library was enriched by the addition of the Toner Library, mentioned in the sketch of Dr. J. M. Toner in the "Medical" chapter of this volume. According to the latest published report of the librarian, that for the year ending December 31, 1890, the aggregate number of volumes in the library was then six hundred and forty-eight thousand, nine hundred and twenty-eight, and of pamphlets about two hundred and seven thousand. Two copies of all copyright publications are required to be deposited in this library.

John S. Meehan was appointed librarian May 28, 1839; John G. Stephenson, May 24, 1861; and Ainsworth R. Spofford, December 31, 1864, retaining the position up to the present time.

The Navy Yard at the city of Washington was established by an act of Congress approved March 27, 1804. It contains within its limits about twenty-eight acres of land on the right bank of the Eastern Branch. All the vessels that were afloat at the beginning of the War of 1812-$_{15}$ had been thoroughly repaired at this yard. Before the war, there had been built here the following vessels: Ships, the *Wasp* and the *Argus;* the brig *Viper*, the frigate *Essex*, and twelve gunboats. After the war, and previous to 1830, there were built the *Columbus*, of 74 guns; the frigates *Potomac* and *Brandywine*, each of 44 guns; the schooners *Shark* and *Grampus*, each of 12 guns; the sloop of war *St. Louis*, of 24 guns; and the frigate *Columbia*, of 44 guns. In

1830 there were employed in the Navy Yard about two hundred men, and when ships were being built, the number of men employed was increased according to the necessities of the case. The manufactures about the Navy Yard were such as main anchors, chain cables, cambooses, blocks, ordnance fixtures, and all kinds of stores, brass and other castings. A great deal of labor-saving machinery was erected to carry on operations in the yard, the most important of which, previous to 1830, was a fourteen horse-power steam engine, by which there were kept in motion nearly five hundred feet of shafting. There had also been erected a gang saw, by which a log of any dimensions could be cut into lumber by one passage through it. There were 2 hammers for forging hammers, 2 hydraulic pulleys, 2 circular saws, 1 turning and boring lathe, which was capable of being converted into a machine for boring steam-engine cylinders; 9 turning lathes, 5 grindstones, and four drill lathes for boring sheaves, and other machinery.

There is in the yard a beautiful monument erected by the officers of the navy to the memory of their associates who fell in the Tripolitan War. It is a small Doric column with emblematical designs, and is crowned with an eagle in the attitude of flight. The base is sculptured in basso-relievo, representing Tripoli, its forts, the Mediterranean Sea, and the American fleet in the foreground, and on each angle stands an appropriate marble figure. One represents Columbia, directing the attention of her children to History, who is recording the daring deeds of American heroes; the third represents Fame, with a wreath of laurel in one hand and a pen in the other; while the fourth represents Mercury, or the god of commerce, with his cornucopia and caduceus.

In 1850 a new foundry was put in operation, which made brass cannon, shells, shot, and machinery necessary for the various shops of the yard itself, and there were numerous shops for anchors, cables, tanks, etc., in full operation. An improvement was made in 1851, in the erection of a building two hundred by sixty feet in size, in which machinery was erected for rolling copper, etc.

On April 21, 1861, the commandant of the Navy Yard, Captain Franklin Buchanan, received an order from the Secretary of the Navy to have the steamers *Baltimore, Mount Vernon, Philadelphia,* and *Powhatan* equipped for service forthwith. Upon its receipt, he resigned his commission and joined the Confederate forces. All the officers of the yard at that time who were of Southern birth, with one shining exception in the person of John Rainbow, followed the example of Captain Buchanan. The next day Commander John A. Dahlgren was appointed commandant of the yard.

It is manifestly impracticable to go into details with reference to the history of the Navy Yard during the whole period of its existence. Suffice it to say that, in accordance with an order issued April 14, 1886, the Navy Yard was changed into an ordnance yard. It is now utilized for the manufacture of all kinds of ordnance, the largest guns so far made being twelve-inch guns, weighing 101,300 pounds, and of a total length of 36 feet 8 inches. The greatest diameter of these guns is 45 inches, and the charge is 425 pounds. The projectile weighs 850 pounds, and the distance to which it is thrown is 12 miles. The yard has just commenced to build thirteen-inch guns, the weight of which is 135,500 pounds, or $67\frac{1}{2}$ tons. The length of these guns is 40 feet; the greatest diameter, 49 inches; the charge, 550 pounds; and the projectile weighs 1,100 pounds. The penetrating power is 26.5 inches of steel, and the distance to which the projectile is thrown is 13 miles.

The Soldiers' Home, formerly called the Military Asylum, occupies a site once the property of George W. Riggs, from whom it was purchased by the Government. At the time of the purchase there were two hundred and eighty-five acres in the tract, but since that time it has been increased to five hundred acres. It is situated about three miles north of the Capitol, and a mile north of Florida Avenue. A large edifice of native marble, whose white tower may be seen for miles in all directions, was first erected, and was ready for occupancy January 1, 1857. It contains spacious sleeping-rooms, sufficient to accommodate two hundred and fifty inmates. While this building was in process of erection, the inmates, numbering seventy-four, occupied the mansion built by Mr. Riggs. In 1856, besides the main building, two large mansions were upon the property, one occupied by Colonel M. M. Payne as governor of the home, the other by Dr. Benjamin King, secretary and treasurer, and who was then also in temporary charge of the sick. Major Larkin Smith was deputy governor.

In the early history of the home, the old soldiers could do pretty much as they pleased, yet they were subject to certain wholesome regulations, and there were workshops provided where they could work at their trades, and the products of their industry were purchased by the Ordnance and Quartermaster's departments at fair prices. Those who were then entitled to the benefits of the asylum or home were the following:

1. Those who had served faithfully in the United States Army for twenty years.

2. Soldiers and members of the Marine Corps wounded or disabled by disease in the Mexican War.

3. Soldiers who had contributed to the funds of the asylum, under certain conditions.

The commissioners in charge of the asylum in 1856, by virtue of their offices, were General Winfield Scott, General George Gibson, and General Thomas S. Jesup, the Surgeon-General of the United States Army, and Colonels Cooper and Larned. The funds of the asylum were supplied from a monthly contribution by the rank and file of the army, added to the proceeds of a large sum of money brought from Mexico by General Scott at the close of the war with that country. Upon his return from Mexico, General Scott labored assiduously with Congress to procure the passage of a law authorizing the establishment of this home, and at length his efforts were successful. In the spring of 1852, the War Department detailed as architect of the buildings, Captain B. S. Alexander, of the corps of engineers of the United States Army who had constructed a lighthouse at Minot's Lodge, below Boston Harbor. The work of construction was given to Mr. Gilbert Cameron, then late of New York. The day upon which the building was required to be completed was December 1, 1855, but on account of changes in the plan made and determined upon while the work was in progress, the building was not completed on time, and about that time the contractor and his men were expelled from the building and he was informed that if he again appeared upon the ground he would be arrested as a trespasser. The work was then transferred to other persons, the building being completed at the expense of the institution. The building was constructed of white marble from quarries in New York, as were also the General Post Office and Brown's Hotel. After the expulsion of the contractor, other changes were made, involving a large expenditure of the funds proper of the institution.

There are five public entrances to the grounds of the Soldiers' Home — Whitney Avenue Gate, on the west side; Ivy and Scott gates, on the north side; by way of Rock Creek Church road, and East Gate, by Sherman and Harewood roads, on the east side. The grounds, which are very beautiful, are open every day in the year. This was the first home of the kind ever established, and is used exclusively for soldiers of the regular army.

The main building is the one already mentioned, and stands in the northern end of the grounds. It is named the Scott building. The south front of this building was first erected of marble, and in the Norman style of architecture. This portion has recently undergone important improvements, an additional story having been added at a cost of $80,000. The ornamental capstones have cut into them emblems of different arms of the service. A fine view of the surrounding country and the city of Washington is presented from the large square tower, which rises to a height of one hundred and twenty feet, and was designed by W. M. Poindexter, the well-known Washington architect.

The Sherman building connects with this addition on the north. It was named in honor of General W. T. Sherman, the first president of the board of commissioners after the reorganization in 1883. This building contains one of the handsomest military mess halls in the world. A billiard room is in the northwest corner of the building. The dormitory contains accommodations for one hundred and twenty-five inmates. The Scott and Sherman buildings, as will readily be seen, are in reality but one structure, though its parts were erected at different times. The entire structure, when viewed from the east or west, resembles the outlines of a capital H.

The King dormitory stands immediately east of the Scott building, and is a plain brick edifice. It was named in honor of Captain Benjamin King, the first secretary and treasurer of the asylum. Next to the Scott building it is the oldest structure on the grounds. Ninety-five inmates are accommodated in this building, among them the colored veterans.

The Anderson building, named in honor of General Robert Anderson, of Fort Sumter fame, is west of the Scott building. This building is also known as the "President's Cottage," having been the summer home of some of the Presidents of the United States. It was once the country residence of the Riggs family, and was erected nearly eighty years ago. Thirty-five inmates and the band of the Home are accommodated in this building.

The Library building is immediately north of the Sherman building. It contains reading-rooms and other appropriate conveniences. The library has five thousand volumes, and the reading-room is well supplied with periodicals and papers.

West of the Library building stands the Sheridan building, named after General P. H. Sheridan, who was president of the managers of the home when the building was erected. This is the most popular of the dormitories connected with the home, all its appointments being first-class. It contains accommodations for one hundred and twenty-five inmates, besides the Temperance Hall and theater. This is a square brick building, surrounded by three tiers of balconies.

The gardener's cottage and the chapel are south of the Scott building. From the front of the former is obtained a view of the Capitol, by means of what is called the Capitol Vista. The chapel is of Seneca freestone, and has two vestry rooms and a movable altar. Services are held on Sundays, under the auspices of three different denominations—the Roman Catholics in the morning, Lutherans in the afternoon, and the Episcopalians in the evening. At the southeast corner of the chapel is a granite monument, erected to the memory of Henry Wilson, of Massachussetts, and bearing the following inscription: "Henry Wilson, the soldiers' friend, died, Vice President of the United States, November 22, 1875. Erected by the enlisted men of the army."

In the distance directly south are Barnes' Hospital, ambulance, and carriage houses, and hospital steward's cottage, pump house, and dead house. The hospital is a model institution, and has accommodations for eighty-five patients. Its annual expenses amount to $20,000. A pretty summer house stands on the high ground west of the hospital. The lodges at the different gates and two other buildings, one of these being the old farm house on what was formerly the Wood farm, the other a small house north of the mansion, are the only ones provided for the families of inmates of the home.

In the southern portion of the grounds is the dairy farm, once the property of W. W. Corcoran, containing two hundred and fifty acres. The Corcoran cottage was erected on this tract about 1850. Directly south of it is a fine spring and spring house, and just beyond is the southern limit of the home grounds. The proposed new city reservoir is outside the fence, and in the middle of this reservoir is the famous Capitol spring, which formerly supplied the Capitol building with water.

Following is a list of the governors of the home: I. B. Crane, colonel First Artillery, December 20, 1851, to September 13, 1852; Larkin Smith, brevet major, September 13, 1852, to November 5, 1855; M. M. Payne, brevet colonel, November 5, 1855, to July 4, 1857; J. A. Haskins, brevet major, July 4, 1857, to November 7, 1857; M. M. Payne, colonel Second Artillery, November 7, 1857, to February 10, 1858; J. A. Haskins, February 10, 1858, to May 6, 1858; I. L. Alexander, major Eighth Infantry, deputy governor, May 8, 1858, to November 23, 1863; Justin Dimick, colonel United States Army, November 23, 1863, to April 1, 1868; I. B. McIntosh, brevet major-general, April 1, 1868, to July 1, 1868; A. Cady, colonel and brevet brigadier-general, July 1, 1868, to January 29, 1869; A. S.

Lee, brevet lieutenant-colonel, January 29, 1869, to October 5, 1871; T. G. Pitcher, brevet brigadier-general United States Army, October 5, 1871, to July 1, 1877. J. H. Potter, colonel Twenty-fourth Infantry, July 1, 1877, to July 2, 1881; S. D. Sturgis, colonel First Cavalry, brevet major-general United States Army, July 2, 1881, to May 15, 1885; Henry I. Hunt, brevet major-general United States Army, May 15, 1885, to September 23, 1885; R. Catlin, captain United States Army, deputy governor, September 23, 1885, to May 26, 1886; Henry I. Hunt, brevet major-general United States Army, May 26, 1886, to February 28, 1889; Orlando B. Willcox, brigadier-general, retired, February 28, 1889, to the present time.

The home has an excellent brass band, organized in 1886. Its members are inmates of the home, and they receive extra compensation. The band plays every afternoon, except Saturday, on the parade ground or in the hall, and every Wednesday afternoon between four and five o'clock it plays in front of Barnes' Hospital. The band also attends all funerals of inmates.

General Scott levied on the city of Mexico $300,000 for the violation of a truce. Of this money Congress appropriated $118,719 toward the erection of the Scott building. Since then the expenses of the institution have been paid out of its own funds. The revenues of the home are derived from the interest on a sinking fund, a tax of twelve and a half cents each month on each enlisted man in the army, from money due deserters, from fines, court-martial forfeitures, and from the proceeds of the unclaimed effects of deceased inmates. The amount realized annually is near $200,000, the regular annual expenses being about $200,000. The permanent surplus fund now amounts to $2,348,529.43, which draws interest at the rate of three per cent. per annum. The treasurer of the home is Major Richard C. Parker, who of course, has charge of the financial interests of the institution.

The first inmate was William Daily, admitted in May, 1851. The total number of inmates admitted to date is 7,097. There were on the rolls January 25, 1892, 1,228, of whom twenty-five are colored. The number steadily increases from year to year.

The movement resulting in the establishment of a national asylum for the insane commenced at least as early as 1841, on the 5th of January of that year the Hon. William Cost Johnson, of Maryland, asking unanimous consent to consider a bill making temporary provision for the lunatics of the District of Columbia. The bill was taken up on a suspension of the rules, and after considerable discussion it was defeated by a vote of 72 to 82. On January 7, on motion of Mr. Fillmore, the vote was reconsidered, and the bill passed the House by a vote of 110 to 59. Those opposing the bill did so on constitutional grounds; those favoring it favored it from motives of right, justice, and charity.

At that time the corporation of Washington was allowing $2 per week for the care of each insane person, and asked the assistance of Congress only in case of persons requiring restraint. The insane were then kept in the old jail.

The District of Columbia, in appealing to Congress for aid, justified herself by the consideration that many of the insane whom she had to support belonged in distant parts of the country. Some of them were old men who came to Washington to secure pensions, which were in many cases refused, and in many of these cases the applicant became insane. Others came to Washington as inventors of many a crazy scheme, and failed to obtain a patent, and then became insane. Still others came to seek office under the Government, and being in many cases disappointed, became insane, like the applicants for pensions and patents. Hence, it was not just that the care of all the insane in the District should be taken care of by the District.

February 2, 1841, an act was approved making an appropriation of $3,000 to this object, and on August 3, 1841, another act was approved appropriating $3,500 to the same purpose, and authorizing the marshal of the District to provide for the pauper lunatics at any public asylum in the United States, consulting economy in the selection.

During the session of 1851–52, Congress appropriated $100,000 for the purpose of founding in the District a hospital for the insane of the District, and of the army and navy, to be erected on the beautiful place of Mr. Blagden, south of the Anacostia River. This result was brought about chiefly through the labors of Miss Dix, widely known for her philanthropic efforts in favor of the insane. Its erection was commenced in 1855 or 1856, and was about one-third completed in October of that year. At that time there were 95 patients in the institution; white males, 47; white females, 36; black males, 8; black females, 4. Dr. Nichols had charge of the hospital, and was assisted by Dr. William Young. The matron was Mrs. Montgomery.

This asylum is situated on Nichols Avenue. It is a national institution, and receives all the insane of the army and navy and the revenue marine service, and also the indigent insane of the District of Columbia. United States convicts, becoming insane, are also sent to this hospital by order of the Secretary of the Interior, on the request of the Attorney-General. W. W. Godding, M. D., is at this time superintendent of the hospital.

Providence Hospital is situated at the corner of Second and D streets Southeast. It was for several years in the old "infirmary," until that was destroyed by fire in 1859, and then a new building becoming an absolute necessity, the present building was provided for. It was commenced in June, 1861. All classes of patients were received, except those afflicted with contagious diseases. From the first, it has been in charge of Sisters of Charity, who, in 1866, on account of the limited accommodations at their command compared with their field of usefulness, commenced the erection of a new building, the corner stone of which was laid July 5, 1866. The building then erected is one hundred and eighty-one feet in length and ninety-nine feet in depth, and it cost $110,000. The resident physicians are W. Don Cannon and Henry L. Hayes, and the medical and surgical staff is composed of some of the most distinguished physicians of the city.

The Columbia Hospital for Women was established in 1866. The first meeting of its incorporators was held June 21, 1866, at which A. D. Gillette, D. D., was elected president; C. H. Hall, D. D., and P. D. Gurley, D. D., vice-presidents; Rev. J. Coombs, secretary; Moses Kelly, treasurer. J. H. Thompson, M. D., was the physician in charge. Dr. Nictols and W. B. Matchett were appointed a committee to apply to Congress for an appropriation of $10,000 to defray the current expenses for that year. There were at first forty beds in the hospital which were supported by voluntary contributions, and fifty to be supported by popular subscription. Charles Knapp and H. D. Cooke had been the chief contributors to the support of the hospital up to this time. This hospital is finely situated at the corner of Pennsylvania Avenue and Twenty-fifth Street.

The Washington Orphan Asylum was established October 10, 1815, and during its earlier history it was managed by an association of benevolent ladies of the city. Mrs. Madison, wife of President Madison, was its first directress; Mrs. John P. Van Ness was her successor, and for many years she devoted herself to the interests of the asylum with a zeal and liberality both helpful to the society having the institution in charge and highly honorable to herself. The asylum was first opened for girls, in a house on Seventh Street, between H and I streets, and afterward a large building was erected for its use on what was known as Mausoleum Square, fronting on H Street, between Ninth and Tenth streets. The corner stone of this building

42

was laid by Mrs. Van Ness, in the presence of a large number of people. The institution was incorporated by Congress in May, 1828, by the name of the "Washington City Orphan Asylum." This new building was occupied from 1826 to September, 1866, and from the time this house was occupied, orphans of both sexes were admitted. In 1848 Mr. Matthew Wright, then late of Washington, bequeathed the interest of $10,000 to aid in the support of the institution. Congress had previously donated lots in the city to the institution, valued at $10,000.

St. Vincent's Female Orphan Asylum was established by Rev. William Mathews and the Catholics of Washington about 1825, and it was chartered by Congress in 1831. It is situated on Tenth and G streets Northwest, and its management is entrusted to the Sisters of Charity. It is supported by private charity and voluntary contributions. In 1834 it received from Congress a donation of lots in Washington worth $10,000. It is one of the most prominent of the public charities in the city.

Garfield Memorial Hospital is situated at the head of Tenth Street Northwest, and owes its origin to a philanthropic movement begun within a month after President Garfield's death. Those interested in the establishment of this institution were some of them of national prominence—James G. Blaine, W. T. Sherman, S. F. Miller, William Windom, and Mrs. John A. Logan. It was incorporated in 1882, with Hon. S. F. Miller, president; B. G. Lovejoy, secretary, and Edward Temple, treasurer. Upon the death of Judge Miller, Justice John M. Harlan became president. The Ladies' Aid Society has always done efficient service in sustaining the claims of the hospital. The entire property of this hospital, including its five acres of ground and five buildings, is valued at $250,000. The medical staff has always been exceedingly efficient. Congress makes an appropriation annually of about $15,000 for the current expenses of free wards, the general expenses, amounting to some $20,000 per annum, being met by the efforts of the Ladies' Aid Society. The capacity of the institution has increased from ten beds, in 1883, to one hundred and twenty at the present time. The number of patients admitted in 1891 was four hundred and ninety-five.

Besides the above-mentioned public institutions, there are also the following: The National Homeopathic Hospital, at the corner of N and Second streets Northwest; the Homeopathic Dispensary and Emergency Hospital, on Massachusetts Avenue, near Seventh Street; the Aged Women's Home, of which Mrs. B. Kennon is president and

Mrs. J. B. Nourse secretary, and which is situated at 1255 Thirty-second Street Northwest; the Children's Hospital, on W Street, near Thirteenth Street, Northwest, of which M. W. Galt is president and W. S. Thompson secretary; the Church Orphanage Association, St. John's Parish, at 525 Twentieth Street Northwest; the Colored Women's Home, St. Matthew's Parish, at 1909 R Street Northwest; the Emergency Hospital, at the corner of Fifteenth and D streets Northwest; the Epiphany Church Home for Aged Women, at 1319 II Street Northwest; the Freedman's Hospital, at the corner of Pomeroy and Fifth streets Northwest, supported by the General Government; the German Orphan Asylum, on Good Hope road; the Home for Friendless Colored Girls, on Erie Street, between Seventeenth and Eighteenth streets, Northwest; the Home for the Aged, of the Little Sisters of the Poor, at the corner of H and Third streets Northeast; the House of the Good Shepherd, at the corner of Thirty-sixth and T streets Northwest; the House of Mercy, 2408 K Street Northwest; the Lenthall Home for Widows, at the corner of Nineteenth and G streets Northwest; the Methodist Home for Aged Women, at the corner of Twelfth and N streets Northwest; the National Association for the Relief of Colored Women and Children, on Eighth Street, near Grant Avenue, Northwest; the National Temperance Home, 218 Four and a Half Street Northwest; St. Ann's Infant Orphan Asylum, at 2300 K Street Northwest, founded in August, 1860, and under the care of the Sisters of Charity; St. Joseph's Male Orphan Asylum, on H Street, near Tenth Street, Northwest, in charge of the Sisters of the Holy Cross; the Washington Home for Incurables, on Meridian Avenue, Mount Pleasant; the Washington Hospital for Foundlings, at 1715 Fifteenth Street Northwest; the Women's Christian Association Home, at 1719 Thirteenth Street Northwest; and the Young Women's Christian Home, at 404 Sixth Street Northwest.

CHAPTER XIX.

GOVERNMENT BUILDINGS AND PUBLIC MONUMENTS.

THE Capitol, in which Congress holds its sessions, is located on Capitol Hill. It consisted originally of two wings and a rotunda in the center. It is of the Corinthian order of architecture, and was built of freestone from the quarries of Acquia Creek, Virginia. The commissioners appointed to lay out the city of Washington were directed to procure suitable buildings for the accommodation of Congress and of the President, and for the public use of the Government of the United States. Shortly after the city was surveyed, they entered upon this portion of their duties. The Federal House of Congress was designated on Major L'Enfant's plan of the city as "The Capitol," and this name was adopted on the approval of President Washington. From the surveys it was ascertained that the hill in the eastern section of the city was nearly in the center of the District, and it was for this reason that the Capitol was erected upon it, facing eastward, in which direction a spacious plateau extends about two miles, upon which plateau it was believed and expected that the best houses would be erected. Hence the Capitol was built facing eastward, but for reasons given in another part of this history, the growth of the city was almost entirely toward the west, and so to-day the Capitol stands with its back toward the most populous part of the Capital.

A premium of $500 and a building lot was offered by the commissioners in an advertisement for the best design of a Capitol building, and in response to this advertisement sixteen designs were submitted to the commissioners by architects in different parts of the country. But upon a careful examination of these designs by Mr. Jefferson, then Secretary of State, who really possessed nearly all the taste and ability in this direction that was possessed by the Government officials, they were promptly rejected. Mr. Jefferson preferred the adoption of the models of antiquity, which had the approval of thousands of years. In July, 1792, a French architect living in New York, named Stephen L. Hallett, sent a sketch of a design to the commissioners which met with favor, and he was invited to Washington to examine the locality chosen for the Capitol, in order that he might perfect his designs, which in some particulars were satisfactory.

About the same time, an amateur draughtsman, named Dr. William Thornton, an Englishman who had resided some years in the West Indies, and had then come to the United States, presented to President Washington an elaborate and highly colored design, which greatly pleased the President, and he wrote to the commissioners suggesting the substitution of Dr. Thornton's plan in place of Mr. Hallett's, and that Mr. Hallett be engaged as supervising architect, as Dr. Thornton had no practical knowledge of architecture.

This letter of President Washington's was written January 31, 1793. In it he said that he had under consideration the two plans mentioned above. He said that he thought Mr. Hallett's had a great deal of merit; but he preferred Dr. Thornton's for grandeur, simplicity, and beauty, the propriety with which the apartments were distributed, and the economy in the mass of the whole structure. He therefore thought it best to give the Doctor time to finish his plan, and for this purpose to delay, until the next meeting of the commissioners of the District, a final decision. He said some difficulty arose with reference to Mr. Hallett, who was led into his plan by ideas "we all expressed to him"; but that ought not to induce the acceptance of his plan in preference to a better, and that it would be best to liberally requite him for the time he had expended upon it, that his feelings should be soothed as much as possible, and left it to the commissioners to prepare him for the possibility of the Doctor's plan being preferred to his.

On March 3, 1793, the President wrote a letter introducing Dr. Thornton to the commissioners, and he came down to Washington from Philadelphia to show them his design. July 23, 1793, the President wrote again to the commissioners in favor of a plan of the Capitol by Judge Turner, and said: "The dome which is suggested as an addition to the center of the edifice, would, in my opinion, give a beauty and grandeur to the pile; and might be useful for the reception of a bell, clock, etc. . . . Could such a plan as Judge Turner's be surrounded with columns and a colonnade like that which was presented by Mr. Hallett, without departing from the principles of architecture, and yet not to be too expensive for our means, it would, in my judgment, be a noble and desirable structure; but I would have it understood in *this* instance and always that I profess to have no knowledge of architecture, and think we should be governed by the established rules laid down by the professors of this art."

July 25, 1793, President Washington again wrote the commissioners on the same subject from Philadelphia, stating that objections to the plan of Dr. Thornton for the Capitol building had been made by both the persons, Mr. Carstairs and Mr. Williams, chosen by Dr. Thornton as practical architects and competent judges of such things; that Mr. Hallett's plan was free from the objections of Dr. Thornton's, and would not cost more than half as much. Mr. Hoban was therefore informed that the foundation would be begun according to Mr. Hallett's plan, "leaving the recess in the east front open for further consideration. But it was the wish that the portico of the east front, which was in Dr. Thornton's plan, should be preserved in that of Mr. Hallett's, the recess which Mr. Hallett proposed striking every one unpleasantly, as the space between the two wings was too contracted to give it the noble appearance of the buildings of which it was an imitation; but whether the portico or the recess should be finally decided upon, would make no difference in the commencement of the foundation, except in that particular part."

The question of plan continued to give the commissioners trouble for a considerable time, and for several weeks the different aspirants for the distinguished honor of furnishing the plans for the Capitol building of the new American nation worked with intense rivalry and bitter feelings. At length, however, Dr. Thornton's plan was in the main adopted, at which Mr. Hallett felt greatly aggrieved, and in order "to soothe his feelings," as President Washington had expressed it, he was made supervising architect of the Capitol, with a salary of $400 per year, and at once began work on the edifice.[1]

The corner stone of this building was laid in the southeast corner

[1] See Dr. Thornton's address "To the Members of the House of Representatives of the United States," of January 1, 1805. It is there clearly shown that Mr. Hallett, as supervising architect of the Capitol, worked in the main according to Dr. Thornton's plan.

of the north wing September 18, 1793, in the presence of President Washington and a large assemblage of citizens. A grand Masonic, military, and civic procession was formed on the square in front of the President's grounds, whence it marched to the Capitol square with martial music and flying banners. The ceremony was both imposing and grand, large numbers from various portions of the country being in attendance. On the corner stone was placed a large silver plate inscribed with the following words:

"This southeast corner stone of the Capitol of the United States of America, in the city of Washington, was laid on the 18th day of September, 1793, in the eighteenth year of American independence, in the first year of the second term of the presidency of George Washington, whose virtues in the civil administration of his country have been as conspicuous and beneficial as his military valor and prudence have been useful in establishing her liberties, and in the year of Masonry 5793, by the President of the United States, in concert with the Grand Lodge of Maryland, several lodges under its jurisdiction, and Lodge No. 22, from Alexandria, Virginia." ·

A few months after the corner stone had been laid, a difficulty sprang up between Mr. Hallett as architect and Dr. Thornton, who had been appointed one of the commissioners. Mr. Hallett was requested to furnish the commissioners with his various drawings and designs, which he refused to do, and was in consequence dismissed from the public service. George Hadfield, from England, coming highly recommended by Benjamin West and by James Hoban, architect of the President's House, was then appointed to the place, and Mr. Hadfield and Mr. Hoban were associated most, or all, of the time during which the north wing was in progress. It was completed in 1800.

In 1803 the construction of the south wing of the Capitol was placed in charge of Benjamin Henry Latrobe, who had come from London, England, to the United States in 1796. He had studied architecture in London with Mr. Cockrell, one of the leading architects of his day. He was introduced to Judge Bushrod Washington, a nephew of President Washington, at Norfolk, Virginia, and was taken to Mount Vernon to be introduced to General Washington by Judge Washington. General Washington was favorably impressed with Mr. Latrobe, and afterward frequently consulted him in reference to the public buildings. Mr. Latrobe was given by the commissioners full power to construct the south wing of the Capitol, and to remodel the north wing according to his own plans. Mr. Latrobe finished his work in 1811, completing the hall for the reception of Congress, and connecting the two wings by a large wooden building or bridge which occupied the place of the present rotunda. Such portions of the building as were necessary for the public use being completed, work upon it was suspended during the War of 1812–15. The walls of the wings were constructed of sandstone from quarries at Acquia Creek, and the bricks used in the interior were made by Andrew Hoke at the site on the Capitol Hill, selected by Captain Elisha Williams. The commissioners made the contract for three hundred thousand brick for this purpose with Mr. Hoke, May 1, 1792, agreeing to give him fifteen shillings per thousand for good merchantable brick, 9 inches long, 4¼ inches wide, and 2½ inches thick. Congress commenced to occupy this building in 1800, and continued to occupy it until it was partially demolished by the British troops August 24, 1814. It cost the Government previous to that war $789,070.98 — the north wing, completed in 1800, $480,262.57, and the south wing, completed in 1811, $308,808.41. The hall of the House of Representatives was in the second story of the south wing, and was sixty feet high to the highest point in the ceiling. The Senate chamber was in the north wing of the building and was seventy-four feet in its greatest length and forty-two feet in height.

In the evening of August 24, 1814, "the British army, commanded jointly by General Ross and Admiral Cockburn, reached Capitol Hill, flushed and excited by their victory at Bladensburg. As General Ross rode toward the Capitol, his horse was killed by a shot fired from a house in the vicinity. The shot was apparently aimed at the British general, and it so enraged the troops that, after setting fire to the house containing the sharpshooter, they marched quickly to the Capitol, and fired several volleys into its windows. A regiment then marched into the hall of the House of Representatives, the drums and fifes playing 'The British Grenadiers,' and the soldiers were formed around the Speaker's chair. Admiral Cockburn was escorted to the post of honor, and, seating himself, derisively called the excited assemblage to order. 'Shall this harbor of Yankee democracy be burned? All for it say, Aye!' he shouted. There was a tumultuous cry of affirmation, and then the order was given to burn the building. The pitch-pine boards were torn from the passageway between the wings; the books and papers of the Library of Congress were pulled from their shelves and scattered over the floor; valuable paintings in a room adjoining the Senate chamber were cut from their frames, and the torch applied to the combustible mass. Presently clouds of smoke and columns of fire ascended from the Capitol, and it seemed doomed to destruction. The soldiers discharged army rockets through the roof of each wing, and when the fire was burning furiously, left the building and marched up Pennsylvania Avenue to fire the other public edifices. The wooden passageway and the roofs and exterior of the wings were burned, but the walls were saved, as the flames were extinguished in time by a severe rain, which set in within half an hour after the fire had begun, and continued all the evening."

After the British invasion, Congress held its first session in Blodgett's Hotel, which occupied the site of the present post office building. Afterward, while the Capitol was being rebuilt, Congress assembled in a building erected for the purpose by the patriotic citizens of Washington, near the eastern grounds of the Capitol. Here it held its session for several years. The building has always been known as the "Old Capitol Building." At the time of the burning of the Capitol, Mr. Latrobe was in Pittsburgh, engaged in the construction of a steamboat for Robert Fulton; but he was immediately recalled to Washington to superintend the reconstruction of the Capitol, which, after a thorough examination, he reported as capable of easy restoration, the foundations and walls remaining for the most part unimpaired. To him is due the credit of the old hall of the House of Representatives, now the national statuary hall; the old Senate chamber, now the hall of the Supreme Court; the Law Library, and the old lobbies. He remained in charge until 1817, when he resigned and was succeeded by Mr. Charles Bulfinch, who was entrusted with the further prosecution of the work with the understanding that the Capitol should be completed according to the designs of Mr. Latrobe.

Mr. Bulfinch was a native of Massachusetts, and had constructed the old statehouse at Boston, besides other notable buildings. He remained at work on the Capitol building ten years, and for the most part followed the designs of Mr. Latrobe, executing under these designs the Senate chamber and the hall of Representatives, and completing what were then called the wings. He also connected these wings by the central rotunda, which for many years was called the "Rotundo," and completed it with a low dome. He also built the main hall of the Library of Congress, etc., and in 1827 reported to Congress that the Capitol was complete. When finished, it was declared by every one majestic, and perfect in all its adaptations. It stood on a commanding situation on Capitol Hill, was imposing in its appearance, and was admirably adapted to the uses for which it was designed. It covered 1½ acres of ground, and was surrounded by 22½ acres. It was in length 352 feet 4 inches; the depth of the wings was 121 feet 6 inches; the eastern projection of the steps was 65 feet, and the western projection of steps 83 feet. The height of the wings to the top of the balustrade was 70 feet; the height to the top of the center of the dome, 145 feet; the diameter of the rotunda was 96 feet, and the height of the rotunda 96 feet; the greatest length of the Representatives' hall was 95 feet, and the greatest width 60 feet; the greatest length of the Senate chamber was 74 feet, and the greatest width 42 feet. The cost of the center building, which was commenced in 1818 and completed in 1827, was $957,647.35; and the entire cost of the building up to that time, including what Mr. Bulfinch had done on the wings, was $2,433,814.

From this time until 1850 the Capitol was large enough for the uses of the Nation, and during this period it was in charge of Robert Mills, a Washington architect, who made several small improvements as suggested by the necessities of the occasion. But in 1850, the number of members of both branches of Congress having been largely increased, the necessity for ampler and better accommodations became evident. The mode of enlargement decided upon was the extension of the wings by greater wings or extensions, to be constructed of marble and to be connected with the original Capitol by wide corridors. The architect engaged for this work was Thomas U. Walter, of Philadelphia, who had constructed Girard College. Mr. Walter immediately began the work of construction according to plans designed by himself, General Montgomery C. Meigs, an accomplished engineer, being appointed as general superintendent and inspector.

The corner stone of the House of Representatives extension, on the south wing, was laid by President Fillmore, assisted by the Grand Lodge of Masons of the District of Columbia, the Grand Master wearing the regalia worn by President Washington as Master Mason when he laid the corner stone of the original edifice. On this latter occasion an eloquent oration was delivered by Daniel Webster, Secretary of State, which was listened to by a vast assemblage of people. Beneath this corner stone was deposited the following record:

"On the morning of the first day of the seventy-sixth year of the independence of the United States of America, in the city of Washington, being the 4th day of July, 1851, this stone, designated as the corner stone of the extension of the Capitol, according to a plan approved by the President, in pursuance of an act of Congress, was laid by Millard Fillmore, President of the United States, assisted by the Grand Master of the Masonic Lodges, in the presence of many members of Congress; of officers of the Executive and Judiciary Departments, National, State, and District; of officers of the Army and Navy; the corporate authorities of this and neighboring cities; many associations, civil, military, and masonic; officers of the Smithsonian Institution, and National Institute; professors of colleges and teachers of schools of the District of Columbia, with their students and pupils; and a vast concourse of people from places near and remote, including a few surviving gentlemen who witnessed the laying of the corner stone of the Capitol by President Washington on the 18th day of September, 1793. If, therefore, it shall hereafter be the will of God that this structure shall fall from its base, that its foundations be upturned, and this deposit brought to the eyes of men, be it known that, on this day, the Union of the United States of America stands firm; that their constitution still exists unimpaired, and with all its original usefulness and glory, growing every day stronger and stronger in the affections of the great body of the American people, and attracting more and more the admiration of the world. And all here assembled, whether belonging to public or to private life, with hearts devoutly thankful to Almighty God for the preservation of the liberty and happiness of the country, unite in sincere and fervent prayers that this deposit, and the walls and arches, the domes and towers, the columns and entablatures, now to be erected over it, may endure forever! God save the United States of America!

"DANIEL WEBSTER,

"Secretary of State of the United States."

The old Capitol building was surmounted by three domes, the middle one, standing where stands the present one, being of wood and extending to a height one hundred and forty-two feet lower than the one that supplanted it. This wooden dome was removed in 1856, when the construction of the present magnificent one was commenced. In order to support so vast an additional weight the Capitol building was trussed up, and strengthened, so that it might be able to bear it. This new dome is divided into four sections, the first occupied by thirty-six columns of cast iron, twenty-seven feet high, and three feet in diameter, and decreasing to two and a half feet at the top. The columns rest on a cast-iron foundation, which again rests on a circular wall, bolted, girded, clamped, and compacted by every imaginable contrivance into a mass of solid matter, forming, as it were, but a single body. On these thirty-six columns, which are hollow, fluted, and about an inch thick, is placed a ring to form the foundation for a superimposed section of pilasters smaller than the columns but equal in number, on which is placed strong panel work constituting a third section. The fourth section is the dome proper, which differs from other domes by having an elliptical section instead of a circular one. To be more specific, the external contour is approximately elliptical from the top of the columns; the main ribs are in the form of a pointed arch, and the ceiling is approximately circular. The whole is surmounted by circular plates of iron, of considerable thickness, bearing an altar-like structure girded with fasces, all in iron, and supporting a globe, around which is a belt with the inscription "E pluribus unum." Upon this globe stands the Goddess of Liberty, capped with eagle feathers, and holding in her right hand a sheathed sword, and in her left a wreath and shield. Around her forehead is a fillet studded with thirteen stars.

This dome rests on a continuous wall of masonry, while most of the domes of the old world rest on piers. According to the calculations of the architect, the weight of the dome completed is **13,477** pounds on each square foot, while the stone sustaining it is capable of sustaining a weight of 755,280 pounds per square foot. The pressure of the new dome upon the foundation walls at the level of the cellar floor is 51,292,253 pounds, while the pressure of the old dome was only 48,756,221 pounds, and the weight of the statue of Liberty is 15,000 pounds.

The most remarkable feature of this Goddess of Liberty is its headdress. As it is not generally known how this peculiar feature came to be selected, the explanation is here inserted, as given by Hon. Jefferson Davis, who was Secretary of War at the time of the selection of the figure to grace the dome. To aid in the execution of the work, he appointed Captain M. C. Meigs superintendent of construction. Several of the most distinguished American statuaries were invited to accept orders, among them Hiram Powers, who submitted for the dome of the Capitol a colossal female figure, on the head of which was the liberty cap. To this cap Mr. Davis objected, because it was among the Romans the badge of an emancipated slave; and as the people of the United States were born freemen, he considered it inappropriate to them. Mr. Powers yielded to the objection, and designed a headdress of feathers for the figure, which was accepted, because feathers seemed to him, in view of the aboriginal inhabitants, appropriate to a statue typical of America, leaving the question of taste to the critics, which we also do. Crawford received $3,000 for the plaster model of the statue, and Clarke Mills received $9,800 for the casting in bronze. The additional expense for labor and metal ran the entire expense up to $23,796.82.

The new hall of the House of Representatives was lighted up for the first time December 2, 1857, and the lighting was considered a great success. There were forty-five open squares in the ceiling, in five rows of nine in each row. Each square has within it a smaller square, surrounding which were arranged twenty-eight burners, making twelve hundred and sixty burners in all, and all were lighted in twenty seconds. The method of lighting used was the invention of Captain M. C. Meigs, who was in charge of the Capitol extension. The entire number of jets used in the lighting was forty-five thousand, and the quantity of pipe laid in the skylight was nearly three-fourths of a mile.

The heating apparatus was, at the time it was put into the Capitol, thought to be superior to anything of the kind ever invented. Pure air was brought into a large rapidly revolving wheel or fan, the hollow circumference of which was divided into pockets, and was thrown thence into a chamber cummunicating with some seven or eight miles of iron pipes coiling about each other, and about one inch apart, in which pipes it was warmed by steam. Passing through this mass of iron pipes the heated air goes into a closed well, whence it arises and enters into the Senate chamber, the committee rooms, and other rooms.

On Tuesday, January 4, 1859, the Senate met in the old chamber for the last time, and on motion of Senator Crittenden, moved into their new hall, the one they have ever since occupied. The occasion was one of great interest to the people of Washington, and notwithstanding the inclemency of the weather and the bad walking, for there were then no street cars, there were present more people than could get into either the old hall or the new one. It was generally considered that the new Senate chamber was in stricter taste than the hall of the House of Representatives, that it was less heavily embellished, but this was perhaps owing to the smallness of the hall, and the small number of the Senators to be accommodated. The President of the Senate sits directly opposite the Speaker of the House, and each is visible to the other when the doors of the two halls are open, and distant from each other about eight hundred feet.

The columns surrounding the two wings of the Capitol, as erected

from 1851 to 1865, were from the marble quarry of John F. Connolly,
about a mile west of Cockeysville, on the line of the Northern Central
Railroad. The number required for the fronts of the Capitol extension
was 100, each weighing 23 tons. The contract price for them was
$1,550 for each column. These columns are 25¼ feet long, 3 feet
8 inches in diameter at the base, 3 feet in diameter at the top, and
are fluted. In June, 1860, the first of these columns was taken from
the quarry to the Bolton depot, and thence over the Howard Street
track to the Camden station. By December 1, 1860, twenty of them
had been delivered, and three of them were finished and placed in
the building with their beautiful capitals, which are in the ornate
Corinthian order.

The dome of the Capitol was finished on Friday, August 26,
1864, and there were at that time about thirty marble workers at
work on the marble columns in front of the edifice. By November
1, 1864, the eastern portico of the north wing was finished. The
shafts of the columns were all monoliths, and the pedestals also were
each wrought out of a single block of marble. The capitals were
executed in two courses, with the foliage sculptured out of the solid
marble. The architrave over each center columniation is also mono-
lithic, and the ceilings are entirely composed of massive blocks of
marble deeply paneled and richly ornamented. The eastern portion
of the south wing, however, was not then finished.

The rotunda, mentioned above, occupies the center of the Capitol
building, and is ninety-six feet in diameter and ninety-six feet high.
It is divided in its circuit into panels by lofty Grecian pilasters or
antæ, which support a bold entablature ornamented with wreaths,
with an hemispherical dome rising above filled with large plain cais-
sons. The panels of the circular walls are appropriated to paintings
and basso-relievos of historical subjects. Panel No. 1 contains a
painting of the "Signing of the Declaration of Independence"; Panel
No. 2, the "Capitulation of Saratoga"; Panel No. 3, the "Capitulation
of Yorktown"; Panel No. 4, "Washington Crossing the Delaware,"
by Trumbull; Panel No. 5, the "Baptism of Pocahontas," by
Chapman; Panel No. 6, the "Embarkation of the Pilgrims at Delft
Haven," by Weir; Panel No. 7, the "Landing of Columbus," by
Vanderlyn, and Panel No. 8, the "Discovery of the Mississippi by De
Soto," by Powell.

The bronze folding doors hanging at the east front of the Capitol
were cast at Munich, Bavaria, in the latter part of 1861, by the artist
Rogers, who had been commissioned some years previously by the

Government of the United States for that purpose. The doors were designed and modeled at Rome, but cast at the Royal Foundry at Munich. The workmanship is admirable, there being a sharpness in the lines and a finish in the details which are seldom seen. Each door is divided into four panels, and these, with the semicircular space above, make nine divisions. In each of these divisions is represented an important epoch in the life of Columbus. The figures stand out in full relief. The crowning event in his career occupies the space above the doors. Standing on a mound, Columbus here forms the central figure, having just landed from a boat, and with the standard of Aragon and Castile planted upon the virgin soil of a new continent, and with sword upraised in his right hand, he takes possession of the land in the name of his sovereign. In one compartment is represented the triumphal entry of Columbus into Madrid on his first return from America. Another shows Columbus in chains about to embark for Europe. Another shows him on his deathbed, attended only by some priests and a nun. In the thickness of the doors niches are formed at certain intervals, in which are small whole length figures of contemporaries of Columbus. The large bosses so often seen in doors are in this case supplied by the heads of the most prominent of the historians who have written about Columbus, and the ornaments below each niche are the heads of animals indigenous to the country, with fruits and flowers entwined which are also characteristic of the New World. The cost of the Capitol up to July 15, 1870, was $12,256,150.69.

Statuary Hall, the old hall of the House of Representatives, contains statues of many of the prominent statesmen of the Nation's history, and the east portico of the Capitol is ornamented with statuary suggestive of epochs in the history of the United States and the world.

The President's Mansion, or White House, as it is usually called, is situated at the upper end of Pennsylvania Avenue. It was erected in accordance with plans presented by Captain James Hoban, an Irishman, and one of the early architects of the Capital City. This plan was presented because of the offer by the commissioners of premiums for competitive plans, Captain Hoban being the successful competitor. The corner stone was laid October 13, 1792, and the building, which was modeled after the palace of the Duke of Leinster, although not completed was yet so far advanced as to be occupied by President John Adams upon his arrival in the new Capital, November 1, 1800. It is one hundred and seventy feet front by eighty-six feet deep, and has the appearance of being built of white marble, but is in reality of freestone painted white. It has a rectangular Ionic portico in front, and a semicircular Ionic portico in the rear. It is two stories high, each story being twenty-two feet. It stands at the intersection of Pennsylvania, New York, Connecticut, and Vermont avenues, the entrance fronting to the north upon an open square. From the south side is presented a fine view of the Potomac River, the Washington Monument, and a portion of Virginia. In 1814 it was almost destroyed by the British, nothing but the walls being left standing, and it was rebuilt upon plans furnished by Captain Hoban.

From the rectangular portico at the north front a spacious vestibule is entered, and from this to the east is the East Room, the one public apartment in the White House. On this floor are three other apartments — the Green Room, the Blue Room, and the Red Room, and also an apartment called the State Dining Room, all of which are closed to visitors during the day, except that occasionally a party is conducted through them during the morning hours by an usher. State receptions are held in the Blue Room. The upper story of the mansion is devoted to business offices and the private apartments of the President. Those of public interest are the Library Room, where the President receives callers during the day, and the Cabinet Room, where Cabinet meetings are held on Tuesdays and Fridays. The Library Room is a very interesting apartment. The numerous book-cases are filled with a fine library, the nucleus of which was established in 1851, soon after Congress had made an appropriation of $2,000 for that purpose. When this was done, it was thought strange that it had not been done before. Almost immediately after the passage of the appropriation act, however, C. Lanman, who was at the time librarian of the War Department, purchased nine hundred volumes upon law, history, science, and general literature. Duplicate copies of public documents being found in the War Department, the Secretary of War immediately transferred them to the President's library, and thus an excellent nucleus of a library was collected. Since then, the library has grown so that it now numbers five thousand volumes.

The City Hall is one of the oldest buildings in the city. It is situated on the south portion of Judiciary Square, and fronts on Four and a Half Street. Its corner stone was laid August 22, 1820, with Masonic ceremonies, in the presence of a large number of people. The plans were by Architect George Hadfield, and it was claimed for the building that when it should be completed it would be the finest specimen of chaste architecture in the United States. The history of this building, if written in detail, might be made exceedingly interesting. It was erected by the corporation of Washington; but a few years since, it was sold to the Government of the United States for $75,000.

The Treasury Department of the Government was established by an act passed by the first Congress in 1789. When the Government removed to Washington in 1800, a small wooden building was erected for the use of the Treasury Department, which served its purposes until burned down by the British in August, 1814. Another building was speedily constructed, which served until March 31, 1833, when it was destroyed by fire. There was then some delay in reference to the construction of a new Treasury building. An act was at length passed by Congress, providing for the erection of a new building, in July, 1836. According to this act, the President was authorized to have erected a fireproof building upon such a plan and of such materials as he might deem most advantageous. It was then proposed by those entrusted with the work of constructing this proposed building to locate it further down the tract on which the other buildings had been erected, in order that there might be a clear and unobstructed view all along Pennsylvania Avenue from the Capitol and from the President's House; but Robert Mills, the architect, was so long in selecting a location (?) that the President became impatient, and, walking over the ground one morning, planted his cane in the extreme northeastern corner, and said: "Here, right here, I want the corner stone," and the corner stone was laid in obedience to his commands. The huge building for this reason stands on Pennsylvania Avenue, breaking the continuity of this magnificent avenue, and preventing the President from seeing the Capitol from the windows of his residence. But in determining upon the plan of the building, President Jackson called upon his Secretary of the Treasury, Hon. Levi Woodbury, for the number of rooms the Treasury Department would need. Mr. Woodbury informed the President that it would require one hundred and eight rooms, thirty-six in the center building and thirty-six in each of the wings. The President thereupon endorsed upon the note, "Let the foundation be laid accordingly, for center, and north and south wings." In December, 1837, when the foundation of the entire building had been laid more than a year, when more than $145,800 had been expended upon it, and when the work had progressed so far that it was impossible to construct the rooms according to such a plan without great loss, Mr. Woodbury gave notice that the business of the department would need one hundred and thirty-two rooms instead of one hundred and eight. Up to this time, or a little later, there seems to have been no estimate of what the cost of the building would be, and so far as plan is concerned there appears to have been a design to erect a magnificent building without regard to cost. July 6, 1836, Mr. Mills, the architect, submitted a plan to the President which the President approved. The diagram had one entire front, with a center building running back, to correspond in appearance with the State Department building, which, by being altered somewhat in appearance, was to form the north wing. On the south there was a building projected and referred to as the general building of the department.

According to the report of the architect, the style of architecture adopted in this building was the Grecian Ionic, with its richest ornamentations. The granite approaches were from Pennsylvania and New York avenues, and the gateways opposite these approaches would show the drive up to the portico, etc. The first appropriation for this building was $100,000. In June, 1838, the plan of the building was exhibited to Congress, and the estimate of its cost was then $500,000. By August, 1839, the building was so far completed that it was occupied by the following officers: The Secretary of the Treasury, the Treasurer, the Register, the First Comptroller, the Attorney-General, the Solicitor, and the Commissioner of the General Land Office. The floors of the corridors of the two principal stories were paved with black and white marble tiles, and the attic corridors were paved with German white and red flagstones, and the basement corridor floor was paved with Seneca freestone. The main corridor running north and south was three hundred and forty feet long, and that running east and west was one hundred and seventy feet long. The grand staircase of white marble, when thrown into connection with the hall studded with massive Doric columns supporting a fretted ceiling, was at once striking and picturesque. There are three main approaches, upon the colonnade level, to the interior of the building, leading to the same number of marble stairways, which lead to different stories of the building and down to the basement. The building contains one hundred and fifty rooms of different dimensions.

By January, 1842, there had been expended on the building $608,867.84, and $53,000 more was asked for, making $661,867.84. If the entire building were to be completed according to the original plan of the architect under the date of May 26, 1841, the cost would be as follows: South wing would require $265,000; the north wing,

$245,000, out buildings and grading, $50,000; to finish the building already erected, $40,000; total, $600,000, which added to the amount already expended, the sum was $1,208,867.84. And if the actual cost of the wings should exceed the estimate as much as had the cost of the main building, the entire cost would reach $1,500,000. The committee on public expenditures severely criticised the executive officers of the Government for their extravagant plans, and for their having kept these plans secret as long as possible, so as actually to lead Congress into an extravagant expenditure of the public money.

Notwithstanding the great cost of the building, it was found necessary, in 1855, to add extensions, designs for which were furnished by Thomas U. Walter. The building so far had been constructed of Virginia freestone, and the extensions were constructed of Maine granite. These were finished in 1869. The total cost of the building up to this time was nearly $7,000,000, and since then large sums have been expended in alterations and interior decorations. At the present time the building extends four hundred and sixty feet on Fifteenth Street and two hundred and sixty-four feet on Pennsylvania Avenue. There are four façades, those on the north, west, and south having massive porticos with Ionic columns. Each portico has a broad flight of steps descending to a spacious platform. The north side is ornamented with a fountain, and the superb architectural design of the entire building gives it a majestic appearance. It would seem as though this building were large enough for any business the Treasury Department would ever have to transact, but this is far from being the case, as at present some of the bureaus have to find accommodations elsewhere.

The Patent Office was established by an act of Congress passed April 10, 1790, "to promote the progress of the useful arts by securing for limited times to authors and inventors the exclusive right to their respective writings and discoveries." Under this law the Secretary of State, the Secretary of War, and the Attorney-General, or any two of them, were, on application, to grant patents for an invention, provided they thought it sufficiently useful and important. From the passage of the act until July 31, 1790, these three officials awaited a successful applicant for a patent. Upon that day appeared Samuel Hopkins, who had discovered a new method of making pot and pearl ashes, for which he was granted a patent, the first issued by the Government of the United States, and the first of nearly a half million of patents of inventions and discoveries more or less useful. The act of signing that patent to Samuel Hopkins is called by the present Commissioner of Patents "an act of historic grandeur," when the wonderful transformations of a century are taken into contemplation. Fifty-seven patents in all were granted under the law of 1790, and in the determination of the question as to the advisability of granting a patent in these cases, so much labor, research, study, and scientific learning were required that it was at length an impossibility for the officers of the Government, having other important duties to perform, to give to this study and research the time necessary to an efficient performance of their duties as patent commissioners. A new law was therefore passed in 1793, making it the duty of the Secretary of State to issue patents, subject to the revision of the Attorney-General. This law prevailed until the great law of 1836 was enacted. Under the law of 1793 there were issued upward of nine thousand patents, no other condition being imposed upon the applicant for a patent than that the fees be paid, the oath to the invention be made, and other unimportant forms be complied with. But under this law there was not, as there had been under the law of 1790, any power to refuse to grant a patent, if the conditions just recited were complied with, and as a consequence, many useless inventions were patented, and, as many were infringements on public and private rights, the evil was increasing every day, until 1836, when a new law was passed on the subject of patents.

The first superintendent of the Patent Office was Dr. W. Thornton, a gentleman of great and varied attainments, who continued to officiate for many years. In 1836 the office was destroyed by fire, and likewise nearly all the records, models, etc., as well as the post office and General Post Office. This was considered, as it really was, an appalling disaster, as, after the smoke of the fire had blown away, there lay in ashes and ruin all of the accumulations of the previous thirty-six years, including the extensive correspondence of Dr. Thornton with the ingenious and scientific men of the United States and Europe, carried on for a period of upward of twenty-three years. The Patent Office was then moved into the City Hall, and the new Patent Office building was begun soon afterward, and was completed, except as to the additions made in later years, toward the latter part of 1839. This colossal structure stands on a Government reservation of four acres, extending from Seventh to Ninth streets, and from F to G streets, Northwest, the reservation being the one set apart by Major L'Enfant in his plan of Washington for a great national church. It is four hundred and ten feet from east to west, and two hundred and seventy-five feet from north to south.

The basement story of this building contains one long room

232 by 62 feet in size; two other rooms 30 by 20 feet; eight rooms each 20 by 22; besides a spacious wing for storage, 86 by 38, a corridor 15 feet wide, and four small rooms 20 by 10 feet in size. The second floor is similarly divided into rooms. The basement is of split granite, except the base of the portico, which is of dressed granite. The superstructure is of freestone. The main building is two hundred and seventy feet long and seventy feet wide. After the wings were added, the façades were two hundred and forty feet. The east wing was added in 1853, and the north and west wings some years later. The east and west wings were constructed of Maryland marble, and the north wing of granite. The building is of the Doric style of architecture. The main entrance is on F Street, through a massive portico of two rows of large columns, designed after the entrance of the Parthenon in Athens, and is precisely of the same dimensions. The portico is reached by a lofty flight of broad granite steps. On the Seventh Street side is another great portico, and there are smaller ones on the other two sides. The entire number of compartments is nearly two hundred, besides the extensive halls of the museum of models. The architects were Robert Mills, who constructed the original portion, Thomas U. Walter, and Edward Clark, who constructed the extensions.

Originally, Congress authorized the erection of a building that should cost $108,000, to be borne by the Patent Office Fund. This sum, however, did not suffice to complete the front, which was only about one-fourth of the edifice according to the original plan, and it fell short of the actual cost of that portion of the building by about $309,550, which was supplied by the public treasury. By authority of an act of Congress passed March 3, 1849, the erection of the wings was carried on. The south front was then erected at a cost of $417,550, the Patent Fund contributing $108,000. For the east wing there was appropriated $250,000, of which the Patent Fund furnished $211,000 and the public treasury $39,000. In 1850 it was estimated that to complete the east wing it would require $200,000 more, which would make the contribution from the public treasury $239,000, so that when the east wing should be completed, the cost of the entire building would be $867,550, of which the public treasury would contribute $548,550 and the Patent Fund the rest.

The Department of Agriculture building is situated in South Washington, just north of B Street Southwest, and opposite Thirteenth Street. It was erected in 1868, and is three full stories in height above a basement, and has a mansard roof. It is 170 by 61 feet in size, and cost $140,420.

The Pension building is located on the north portion of Judiciary Square. It is an immense brick structure, 400 by 200 feet in size, and 75 feet high. It covers 1.84 acres of ground, and is fireproof throughout. The noticeable feature of the exterior is the frieze over the first story, consisting of a terra cotta sculptured band three feet wide extending all round the building, representing military and naval subjects. This building required 15,000,000 brick in its construction, and cost $1,000,000. The interior court will accommodate 18,000 persons at an inauguration ball, and will hold 59,000 persons. It is used, of course, for the headquarters of the Pension Department of the Government. General Montgomery C. Meigs was the architect and builder, and modeled it after the Farnese Palace at Florence, Italy.

The Bureau of Engraving and Printing stands on the corner of B and Fourteenth streets Southwest. The building was erected in 1878–80, and is 220 by 135 feet in size. Its cost was $300,000. It is used by the Government for the manufacture of paper money and bonds.

The new State, War, and Navy building is situated at the corner of Pennsylvania Avenue and Seventeenth Street, west of the Executive Mansion. It was designed by A. B. Mullett, late supervising architect of the Treasury Department. It consists of four buildings harmonizing with each other, and united by connecting wings, which constitute altogether one of the finest buildings, if not the finest building, in the world. From north to south it is five hundred and sixty-seven feet, and from east to west it is three hundred and forty-two feet, thus covering an area of four and nine-twentieths acres. The Department of State occupies the south wing of this building; the Department of the Navy, the east wing; and the Department of War, the north wing. The height of the building is one hundred and forty-five feet, and it contains five hundred and sixty-six rooms and two miles of corridor. The cost of the building was nearly $11,000,000, and it is of what is called the Renaissance style of architecture.

The new Congressional Library building, now in process of erection, occupies the center of a site of ten and a half acres, between First and Second streets East, and East Capitol and B streets South, and is about nine hundred feet east of the south wing of the Capitol. The ground was purchased in 1887 for $585,000. The ground plan of the building is four hundred and seventy feet from north to south and three hundred and sixty-five feet from east to west, thus covering a trifle more than three and three-tenths acres of ground, and being surrounded by an esplanade of somewhat more than six acres. The building is constructed of granite and marble, and consists of a cellar and two stories, aggregating sixty-nine feet from the ground. It is in the Renaissance style of architecture. The reading-room in the central rotunda is one hundred feet in diameter, and opens into the book repositories, which radiate from the center, and of which there are nine stories. The capacity of this library is eight million volumes, and the building is estimated to cost $6,000,000.

The Washington Monument is situated on the Government reservation bounded by Fourteenth Street West and the Potomac River. The site was designated by Congress in 1848, and is said to have been selected by Washington himself, when he was President of the United States. The monument is a plain obeliscal shaft, rising to a height of 555 feet above its base, and stands upon a mound having an elevation of 17 feet above the general level of the surrounding surface, so that the top of the monument is 572 feet higher than the same general level. The base of this mound extends out from the base of the monument to a distance of 350 to 450 feet, gradually sloping down to the general level. The foundation of the shaft is 126 feet square and 37 feet below the base of the shaft. The shaft is 55 feet square at the base, 30 feet square at the top, and is surmounted by a pyramid 55 feet high. The lower portion of the monument is constructed of blue gneiss, and is faced with large crystal marble, the upper portion being of the same marble cut with granite backing. In the interior lining are set 82 blocks of stone presented by the States and cities of the Union, by various societies, and by foreign countries, all of which are appropriately inscribed, and can be easily read in ascending the monument, this ascension being provided for by an elevator and a staircase around the elevator shaft in the interior. The shaft is lighted by electricity, the only openings being the doorway at the bottom and small windows at the top.

This monument is the highest artificial structure in the world, with the exception of the Eiffel Tower at Paris. It rises many feet above the Capitol, and above any of the cathedral spires in Europe and the East. It is fifteen feet higher than the main tower of the new city hall at Philadelphia, thirty feet higher than the great cathedral at Cologne, and ninety-five feet higher than St. Peter's at Rome. The prospect from the summit of the monument is very fine. It extends from the Allegheny Mountains on the west to the Atlantic Ocean; and covers the city of Washington on the north and east, and extends beyond into Maryland, and south far into Virginia.

The question of a national memorial to the Hero of the Revolution began to be discussed at an early day. In **1783** the Continental Congress adopted a resolution for the erection of a statue "in honor of George Washington, the illustrious Commander-in-Chief of the United States Army during the war which vindicated and secured their liberty, sovereignty, and independence"; but the resolution was not carried into effect, as it was understood that Washington did not desire a statue to be erected while he was living. In the House of Representatives, December 21, **1799**, Mr. Marshall, of Virginia, submitted the following resolution, which passed *nemine contradicente:*

"*Resolved, by the Senate and House of Representatives of the United States, in Congress assembled*, That a marble monument be erected by the United States at the Capitol in the city of Washington, and that the family of General Washington be requested to permit his body to be deposited under it; and that the monument be so designed as to commemorate the great events of his military and political life."

On January 8, 1800, the President sent the following letters to Congress:

"*Gentlemen of the Senate and Gentlemen of the House of Representatives:*

"In compliance with the request in one of the resolutions of Congress of the 21st of December last, I transmitted a copy of those resolutions, by my secretary, Mr. Shaw, to Mrs. Washington, assuring her of the profound respect Congress will ever bear to her person and character, of their condolence in the late afflicting dispensation of Providence, and entreating her assent to the interment of the remains of General Washington in the manner expressed in the resolution. As the sentiments of that virtuous lady, not less beloved by this Nation than she is at present greatly afflicted, can never be so well expressed as in her own words, I transmit to Congress her original letter.

"It would be an attempt of too much delicacy to make any comments upon it, but there can be no doubt that the Nation at large, as well as all branches of the Government, will be highly gratified by an arrangement which will diminish the sacrifices she makes in her individual feelings.

"JOHN ADAMS.

"United States, 8th January, 1800."

Following is Mrs. Washington's letter, referred to by President Adams:

"Mount Vernon, 31st December, 1799.

"Sir: While I feel, with the keenest anguish, the late dispensation of Divine Providence, I cannot be insensible to the mournful tributes of respect and veneration which are paid to the memory of my dear deceased husband; and as his best services and most anxious wishes were always devoted to the welfare and happiness of his country, to know that they were truly appreciated and gratefully remembered, affords no inconsiderable consolation.

"Taught by the great example which I have so long had before me, never to oppose my private wishes to the public welfare, I must consent· to the request made by Congress, which you have had the goodness to transmit to me, and in doing this I need not, and I cannot, say what sacrifice of individual feeling I make to a sense of public duty.

"With grateful acknowledgments and unfeigned thanks for the personal respect and evidences of condolence expressed by Congress and yourself, I remain

"Very respectfully, Sir,

"Your most obedient and humble servant,

"Martha Washington.

"To the President of the United States."

Notwithstanding the consent of Mrs. Washington was thus obtained to the depositing of the remains of General Washington in the Capitol building, and the early recognition of the duty of the Government to appropriately remember the services of the first General and the first President of the Nation, the subject was postponed in the Senate until the next session, and then postponed again from year to year, for about twenty years, nothing being done by Congress except to pass resolutions upon the propriety of carrying out the early designs of Congress, and again postpone action. In the meantime, many people throughout the Union felt deeply mortified and chagrined at the neglect of Congress to fittingly express its appreciation of the great services of the first soldier and the first President of the Republic, and as a consequence a popular movement was attempted by which it was hoped to raise the money necessary to carry out the design of erecting a suitable monument to the memory of Washington. The plan was to raise if possible a popular subscription of $1 from each family throughout the United States, and by 1812 about $35,000 was thus raised. It is to be noticed, however, that during all these first years, and first efforts, the design was to deposit the remains of General Washington under the monument to be erected to his memory in the Capitol building at Washington, to erect a mausoleum, or to establish a national university. The popular movement here mentioned was in view of such a university, Washington himself having left a portion of his property to be devoted to such an institution.

At length, on the 15th of January, 1824, Mr. Buchanan, of Pennsylvania, introduced a resolution into the House of Representatives to the effect that a committee be appointed whose duty it should be to inquire in what manner the resolution of Congress of December 21, 1799, relative to the erection of a monument in the Capitol at the city of Washington to commemorate the great events in the military and political life of General Washington, might best be accomplished, and that the committee be permitted to report by bill or otherwise. Mr. Buchanan made an able speech in favor of Congress doing something to show that they honored the memory of the founder of the Nation. There was, however, some opposition even to the performance of this act of justice to the memory of the great Washington, and it is only surprising that the objections to the erection of the proposed monument were not based on constitutional grounds. Mr. Carey, of Georgia, made a speech in opposition to the movement, deprecating the practice of erecting monuments of this kind to the memory of illustrious men. He said it was a principle of vanity which had given existence to the practice. Classical enthusiasm beclouded the judgment, and persuaded us to bring associations derived from the venerable sculpture of ancient times to times of a wholly different character, and to a country in wholly different circumstances. Mr. Trimble opposed "the present consideration of the question," and upon a vote being taken, the subject was laid on the table by a vote of 97 to 67.

February 22, 1830, on motion of Mr. Mitchell, of Maryland, the resolution adopted by Congress in 1799, together with the correspondence between President Adams and Mrs. Washington, was referred to a committee, with power to report by bill or otherwise, and on motion of Mr. Clay this committee was composed of one member from each State in the Union. Here the matter rested until 1832, when, on the 13th of February, a joint committee of the two Houses was appointed for the purpose of making preparations to celebrate in an appropriate matter the one hundredth anniversary of the birth of General Washington, and to revive the project, which had so frequently been postponed, of erecting a monument to his memory.

It was the design to have, as a part of the celebration, an oration on the character of Washington delivered by John Marshall, Chief Justice of the United States; but Justice Marshall was compelled to decline the part assigned to him on account of enfeebled health. It was also a part of the design for that celebration to have the body of General Washington removed to the vault in the Capitol prepared years before to receive it, and also to remove the remains of Mrs. Washington to the same vault at the same time; to have the President, James Madison, Charles Carroll of Carrollton, besides most of the high functionaries of the Government, participate in the celebration, and to make it one of the most imposing ceremonies ever witnessed. But the intention of Congress to remove the remains of General and Mrs. Washington at this time was frustrated by the refusal of the proprietor of Mount Vernon to permit them to be removed; but, notwithstanding this failure, Congress by its attempt to remove the remains, redeemed its pledge from discredit; the wisdom of President Washington's maxims of republican policy was revered in the debate on the subject of their removal, and full gratitude for his services in the Revolutionary War was feelingly and abundantly expressed. The day was however fittingly celebrated in Washington.

October 31, 1833, at a meeting held for the purpose, the Washington National Monument Society was organized, Daniel Brent being chairman of the meeting and Peter Force secretary. The following persons were elected as the officers of the society: President, Chief Justice of the United States; vice-presidents, William Cranch, Joseph Gales, Jr., and W. W. Seaton; treasurer, Samuel H. Smith; secretary, George Watterston; managers, General T. S. Jesup, Colonel George Bomford, Colonel James Kearney, R. C. Weightman, Colonel N. Towson, William Brent, Peter Force, Colonel A. Henderson, Thomas Carbery, Thomas Munroe, M. St. Clair Clarke, W. A. Bradley, and J. McClelland. The *ex officio* members of the board of managers were the President and Vice-President of the United States and all the members of the Cabinet.

A constitution for the society was at the same time adopted. The name adopted and incorporated into the constitution was "The Washington National Monument Society," and the object for which the society was organized was stated to be the erection of a great national monument to the memory of Washington at the seat of the Federal Government. Section 2 provided for the above-named officers and four general collectors. Section 6 divided the United States into four general collection districts; the first embracing that portion of the country containing Maine, New Hampshire, Vermont, Massachusetts, Connecticut, and New York; the second, the other middle States, the District of Columbia and Virginia; the third, the other Southern States, except as below; and the fourth, the Western States, Tennessee, Arkansas, Mississippi, and Alabama.

The duty of these general collectors was to call in person, or by deputy, upon every one in their respective districts, and receive such sums of money as they might be disposed to contribute, retaining ten per cent. for their services. The regular officers of the society were to be elected at each annual meeting of the society on February 22.

By the death of Chief Justice John Marshall, the presidency of this society became vacant, and Ex-President James Madison accepted the appointment to the position July 25, 1835.

State after State was visited by the agents of this society, Ohio and Maine being the first to manifest an encouraging interest in the movement. February 1, 1837, Mr. Watterston, to satisfy inquirers that some progress was being made, published a report of what had been accomplished up to that time. This report showed that Ohio had contributed $5,834.45; Maryland, $3,030.94; Pennsylvania, $2,000; Mississippi, $2,120; New Jersey, $1,251.74; New York, $1,000, and other States smaller amounts, the total amount collected being $22,-238.64. There were several of the States in which no attempt had then been made to collect money for this object.

The board of managers wishing to lay the foundation stone as soon as practicable, made application to Congress for a portion of the Mall as a site for the proposed monument. The bill passed the House, but was overlooked in the Senate. June 10, 1837, several designs having been presented to the board of managers, the following resolution was passed:

"That the thanks of the board of managers be presented to Robert Mills, of Washington; S. M. Stone, and Benne & Platt, of New Haven; Thomas McClelland, of New York; E. Barasius, of Baltimore; George Hadfield, William Elliott, and others, for the handsome designs submitted by them respectively to the board, which, in the opinion of the board, indicate a genius and skill highly creditable to the artists."

Progress in the collection of money was still slow, and on June 20, 1838, representations derogatory to the character of the board of managers having appeared in the public prints, a detailed statement of the receipts and expenditures of the board was published by Secretary Watterston, as follows: Receipts—From Maine, $1,600; Vermont, \$31.95; Connecticut, \$1,438.61; New York, \$1,167.21; New Jersey, \$1,419.61; Pennsylvania, \$2,102.85; Delaware, \$361.98; Maryland, \$3,057.99; Virginia, \$1,500; South Carolina, \$570; Kentucky, \$1,610; Ohio, \$6,391; Louisiana, \$701.25; Indiana, \$340; Illinois, \$700; Mississippi, \$2,120; District of Columbia, \$836.36; Florida, \$227; officers and sailors of the army, \$565.89; of the navy, \$228.25; total, \$26,970.14; interest on so much as had been invested, \$1,608.73, making in all \$28,578.87. The expenses had been inconsiderable.

In December, 1840, impatience with the progress of the work became again so manifest that the secretary, or some one on his authority, replied to a complaining correspondent from Warren County, Ohio, that about \$40,000 had been collected, adding that "your noble State of Ohio has contributed nearly one-fourth of that sum." Desiring to make a commencement of the proposed work, the board again made application to Congress for a portion of the public Mall for a site; but, to the astonishment of every one, it was not only refused in the Senate, but the members of the board were grossly calumniated by the two Senators from Ohio,[1] the State from which the largest collection had been made. This wanton attack upon the characters of men who had devoted gratuitously their time and services to the accomplishment of an object which it was believed every patriotic American sincerely desired to have accomplished, and the refusal of the Senate to grant a portion of the Mall for a site for the monument, put a stop for a time, and to a considerable degree, to further collections. The board of managers then sought to enlist the services of the marshals and the deputy marshals throughout the country who were engaged in taking the census to obtain additional subscriptions; but in this they met with another disappointment, the Secretary of State[2] forbidding the enumerators to engage in that kind of work.

February 27, 1841, Samuel H. Smith, treasurer of the society, published a report showing that since 1835 the total receipts for the erection of the monument up to January 10, 1841, had been \$39,-700.47. On March 29, 1841, Mr. Smith published a statement to the effect that Dr. James Hagan, collector of funds for the society in Mississippi, had collected \$3,213.36, which he had sent in, except his commission. On January 17, 1842, Mr. Smith made his annual report, showing a total amount collected of \$41,370. February 26, 1844, according to Mr. Smith's annual report for the previous year, there had been raised \$47,061.85.

[1] William Allen and Thomas Morris.
[2] John Forsyth, of Georgia.

November 30, 1844, at a meeting of the board of managers it was

"*Resolved*, That a committee of three members be appointed to procure a suitable design for the monument of Washington, with authority to confer with the Committee on Public Buildings and Grounds, or other persons, in relation to a proper site for said monument, and that said committee report to the board before any final action thereon."

The committee appointed consisted of W. W. Seaton, Peter Force, and George Watterston. January 30, 1845, the amount of money on hand was $49,783.70. November 18 of that year, Samuel H. Smith, the treasurer of this society, died, and he was succeeded by his son, J. B. H. Smith. November 21, 1846, the amount of money on hand was $55,359.66.

About this time the board of managers decided to resume collections of money throughout the United States, with which to carry forward their great design, and in order to systematize the work and thus guarantee its success, they appointed Hon. Elisha Whittlesey, of Ohio, as general agent, with power to appoint subagents according to his own judgment. They said that the delay in commencing the work of erecting the monument was occasioned by the want of a proper site upon which to erect it. They had long hoped that a site would be granted by Congress, and they then hoped that such a site would be given at the next session. The board of managers then consisted of the following gentlemen: Major-General Winfield Scott, General N. Towson, Colonel J. J. Abert, Colonel James Kearney, General Walter Jones, Thomas Munroe, Thomas Carberry, Peter Force, W. A. Bradley, P. R. Fendall, and John P. Ingle. The officers of the society were as follows: The President of the United States, president *ex officio;* William Brent, W. W. Seaton, and General A. Henderson, vice-presidents; treasurer, J. B. H. Smith; secretary, George Watterston. About this time an offer of a site was made by George W. P. Custis, on the Arlington estate, and of another near the canal, one hundred feet above tide water. To these generous offers Mr. Watterston replied that the constitution of the society limited the location to the city of Washington, and that therefore it was impossible to accept either of the valuable proffers.

January 26, 1848, a joint resolution granting a site for the monument was passed by the House of Representatives, as it had come down to them from the Senate, and the board of managers, thereupon, with the approval of the President of the United States, selected the ground lying west of Fifteenth Street, where the monument now stands. At that time it was the intention of the society to erect the monument six hundred feet high, but this design was subsequently changed. Excavations for its foundation were at once commenced, and they were completed by June 1 following. The corner stone of the monument reached the railroad depot June 5, and on the next day it was removed to its destined location, attended by a large procession of the citizens, preceded by the Marine Band and a body of marines under command of Major Pulizzi. The American flag was hoisted on the car which conveyed the stone from the depot, and a live eagle was placed on the corner stone itself. After a delay at the Fourteenth Street bridge, caused by the wheels of the car getting off the track, the stone was safely deposited in the afternoon of Wednesday, June 7, where it was permanently to remain. It is a block of white marble, weighing twenty-four thousand five hundred pounds. It is six feet eight inches square, and nearly three feet thick. It came from the marble quarries of Mr. Symington, fourteen miles from Baltimore, Mr. Symington having presented it to the city, together with a cover two feet six inches thick. It was transported by the Susquehanna, and the Baltimore and Ohio Railroad Company, free of charge, to the depot in Washington. The wagon on which it was conveyed from the depot in Washington to the place on the monument was furnished by Mr. Philip Ennis.

The laying of this corner stone was an imposing affair, and was participated in by the military and by a large number of citizens, including all kinds of civic organizations. Joseph H. Bradley was the marshal of the day. The oration on the occasion was delivered by one of the most eloquent orators in the country, Hon. Robert C. Winthrop, of Massachusetts. The prayer was by Rev. Mr. McJilton, of Baltimore, and the Masonic address was delivered by B. B. French, Grand Master of the District of Columbia. Robert Mills was the architect of the monument. The American eagle, which was so conspicuous on this occasion, with its dark plumage, piercing eye, and snowy head and tail, was the same that surmounted the arch of welcome erected at Alexandria to Lafayette, and was afterward presented to M. Vattemare for the National Museum at Paris, France.

January 1, 1849, the funds of the society amounted to $56,289.66. About May 1, 1849, an offer was received from Mr. D. Sayre, of Alabama, proposing on the part of some of the citizens of that State to quarry and prepare a block of marble from the quarries of Talladega County, to be placed in the monument. The marble was very beautiful, finely grained, and susceptible of a high polish. The offer of Mr. Sayre was accepted, and the suggestion published by Mr. Watterston that, if any other State or any public institution should be disposed to furnish a stone to be placed in the monument, the board of managers would take pleasure in having it placed therein in an appropriate position, that of Alabama to be placed first. The dimensions given out by Mr. Watterston for these memorial marbles were as follows: Four feet long, two feet high, and one foot six inches broad, with a front bevel of one-fourth of an inch to a foot. By June 30, besides Alabama, Georgia, South Carolina, North Carolina, Virginia, and Delaware had reported their intention of complying with the suggestion thus thrown out. Next came Maine and Mississippi.

The first, however, to be inserted in the monument was one from the Franklin Fire Company of Washington, District of Columbia, inscribed with the name of the company and "Initiated, 1827. We Strive to Save." The second stone inserted was of freestone, three feet long, two feet high, and two feet wide, and bore this inscription: "Presented by George Watterston, Secretary of the Washington National Monument Society, as a Testimonial of his Gratitude and Veneration, A. D. 1849." This was in October of that year, at which time the structure had risen forty-four feet above the ground. The army and navy furnished contributions to aid in the construction of the monument, and the Choctaw Indians sent a stone to be inserted similar to those of the States. The forty children of the Washington City Orphan Asylum, accompanied by Miss Latimer, on November 1 marched to the monument, and tendered their monthly donation of one cent each. This was in accordance with a plan then recently adopted, which it was hoped would be adopted by every school in the country.

December 5, 1849, among other subscriptions received, was one from Mr. James Lenox, of New York City, of $500. January 15, 1850, the thanks of the society were tendered to the Bank of the Metropolis for its subscription of $100, and shortly afterward also to the Bank of Washington for a subscription of the same amount. On this same day a resolution was introduced into the Kentucky Senate by Hon. J. Speed Smith, as follows:

"*Resolved, by the General Assembly of the State of Kentucky,* That the Governor be, and he is hereby, authorized and requested to cause a suitable block of native marble to be conveyed to Washington City to take its proper place in the monument now being erected to the memory of the Father of his Country, and that the following words be engraved thereon: 'Under the auspices of Heaven, and the precepts of Washington, Kentucky will be the last to give up the Union.'"

The National Greys contributed a block of white marble. The Legislature of Indiana made provision for a block of marble for the monument to bear this inscription: "Indiana; Knows no North, no South; nothing but the Union." The council of the Chickasaw Indians appropriated $200 to the monument fund in February, 1850. Louisiana passed an act to provide a stone for the monument, to bear the following inscription: "The State of Louisiana, Ever Loyal to the Constitution and the Union." Massachusetts, on March 1, 1850, directed a stone to be prepared for the same purpose with the following inscription: "Massachusetts; Our Country is safe while the memory of Washington is revered." Maryland directed the following inscription to be placed on the stone contributed by her: "Maryland; the Memorial of her regard for the Federal Constitution, and of her 'cordial, habitual, and immovable attachment to the American Union.'" California, February 2, 1850, passed a joint resolution providing for a block of marble or granite from her own quarries to be placed in the monument. Thus the States, one by one, and rapidly succeeding each other, adopted resolutions, or passed acts, providing for the placing of an emblem in the monument, and by April 12, 1850, all of them had taken action but two. The memento of Michigan was a block of native copper, the exposed surface of which was to be three by one and one-half feet, and to bear the following inscription in letters of native silver: "From Michigan; an Emblem of her trust in the Union." May 31, 1850, the city of Washington appropriated $2,500 to the monument fund, to be paid in five annual installments. Professor Francis Lieber, of South Carolina, contributed a box of sand from the mound erected at Cracow to the memory of Kosciusko.

July 4, 1850, was celebrated at the monument in an appropriate manner. Prayer was offered by Rev. Dr. Butler; the Declaration of Independence was read by Walter Lenox, Mayor of Washington; the oration of the day was delivered by Hon. H. S. Foote, of Mississippi; General Walter Jones presented the Washington block of marble in the name of the city; George W. P. Custis delivered a patriotic address, and the benediction was pronounced by the Rev. Mr. Morgan, of the Methodist Episcopal Church. At this time there was a wide-spread interest in the enterprise, and contributions kept coming in from all parts of the country. From January 1 to November 1, 1850, the contributions averaged $2,800 per month.

During the first ten months of 1850, the contributions amounted to $28,000, and by the 1st of January the monument had attained

44

a height of eighty feet from the base. December 27, 1850, a committee appointed by a convention of subordinate lodges of the Odd Fellows of the county and city of Philadelphia addressed a letter to Hon. Millard Fillmore, President of the United States, informing him that they had performed a duty imposed upon them by seventy-two contributary lodges of that order, of preparing and presenting a block of marble for the monument. December 30, the President acknowledged receipt of the letter, and said in reply that we were bound by every consideration, human and divine, to transmit the union unimpaired to our posterity. The block of marble was a beautiful piece of fine-grained marble, six feet long, by four feet wide, and two feet thick, weighing about four tons. It was appropriately inscribed with the names of the seventy-two lodges referred to above, together with the three links of the order.

A number of Indian tribes of the West contributed a block from the far famed "Starved Rock," near Ottawa, Illinois, upon which the last surviving remnant of the Illinois Indians gathered, where they were beseiged on every side, and when at last, compelled by hunger and in desperation, they attempted to force a passage through the ranks of their enemies, they were slain almost to a man, leaving scarcely enough to tell the tale. The Indians, having no land of their own, had inscribed on their contribution the following: "This step the red man gives to the pale face to build him a path to the better hunting ground."

Wheatland, in Monroe County, New York, set a good example to the rest of the country, several of her citizens subscribing sums varying from $50 down to fifty cents, in the aggregate more than $1,200. July 4, 1851, W. W. Corcoran subscribed to the monument fund $50, and announced his intention of subscribing the same amount each year, on the 4th of July, until the monument should be completed. December 24, 1851, Lewis Cass, Jr., of the United States Legation at Rome, wrote to Mr. George Watterston informing him that it was the intention of the Pope, through Cardinal Antonelli, Secretary of State of the Roman Government, to contribute a block of marble toward the erection of the monument, which Mr. Watterston acknowledged in suitable terms. Some time afterward a passionate, but not wise, address was published in opposition to the placing of this stone in the monument by Mr. J. T. Weishampel, of Baltimore, who thought he could see in the proposition the purpose of the Pope to remove to America, and that this was indicated by the proposed inscription, "Rome to America."

By March 1, 1852, there had been collected about $130,000, and the monument had risen to a height of somewhat more than one hundred feet. June 3, 1852, an ordinance was adopted by the corporation of Savannah, Georgia, making an annual appropriation of $100, from that time until the monument should be completed. This fitting and patriotic action was appropriately acknowledged by the society, as was also the receipt of $60 from the family of Francis A. Evans, of Louisiana. August 13, J. Y. Hendrick, pastor of the Presbyterian church at Clarksville, Tennessee, sent forward a contribution from his church of $50, and about the same time Joel M. Smith, of Nashville, Tennessee, sent $78 as a contribution from McKendree Church of that city. September 9, J. W. Jones, of Augusta, Georgia, sent a contribution of $425 from various churches and citizens of his city, and about the same time Mr. Cardigan, of Baton Rouge, Louisiana, sent $280 collected by Richard Wall.

A movement was made in the fall of 1852 to secure contributions to the national monument at the time of voting for President, November 2, the first response being from Cincinnati, Ohio, which city sent forward $177.76. Returns from this attempt kept coming in all the fall and winter, and it is probable that in this way nearly, if not quite, $20,000 was raised. In October, 1852, the Swiss Republic presented a block of marble for the monument, which was received in November, and suitably acknowledged by the Hon. Edward Everett, Secretary of State. February 22, 1853, the Sansome Hook and Ladder Company contributed $1,000 toward the monument, and Madam Biscaccianti contributed the proceeds of a concert, $500, toward the same object.

George Watterston, secretary of the society charged with the erection of this monument, died February 4, 1854, and on the 14th of the same month John Carroll Brent was elected to the vacancy thus caused. Contributions continued to be made, but in decreasing amounts, and at length, in 1856, when the monument had attained a height of one hundred and seventy-four feet and had cost $230,000, all that had been contributed, the work upon it was discontinued until 1876, when Congress took charge of the work and appropriated money for its completion. In August, 1884, the monument reached a height of five hundred feet, from which elevation the square pyramidal roof begins, and rises to an additional height of fifty-five feet. The cap stone was placed in position December 6, 1884. It was formally opened to the public in 1888, since which time aseensions have been made free, by means of the elevator or the iron stairway, on week days from 9:00 A. M. to 5:30 P. M. The amount of money appropriated by Congress to complete this noble monument was $1,000,000, so that its entire cost was $1,230,000.

The Washington Statue, by Greenough, was sculptured in Florence, Italy, and was received at the Navy Yard, in Washington, in October, 1841, and removed to its appointed place, in the rotunda of the Capitol, in December following, where it was raised to its lofty pedestal. Here it remained until August, 1843, when it was removed, and in September following was elevated to its present position, east of and facing the Capitol. This statue was described, at the time, in the following language:

"Nothing can be more human, and at the same time more God-like, than this colossal statue of Washington. It is a sort of a domestic Jupiter. The sublime repose and simplicity of the whole figure, united as it is with exceeding energy of expression, so perfectly classical without the slightest abstract imitation, for the artist seems to have embodied Seneca's admirable advice as to style, 'Similem esse te volo, quomodo filium, non quomodo imaginem,' as there is no mistaking the pure lineage of this statue, being intended to fill the central position of the Capitol, he has addressed his statue of Washington to a distant posterity, and made it a physical abstract of his whole career, rather than the chronicle of any one deed, or any one leading feature of his life. He is therefore seated as a first magistrate, and extends with his left hand a sword, the emblem of his military command, toward the people; as a sovereign he points heavenward with his right hand. By this double gesture is conveyed the idea of an entire abrogation of self, and making the patriot a conductor between God and man.

"The chair in which he is seated tells also its history. The superior part is richly ornamented with acanthus and garlands of flowers, while the base is solid, simple, and massive, which plainly indicates that high cultivation is the proper result of sound government, and that nations, when well planned and well tilled, must flourish as well as grow. Upon the picture of Columbus, which leans against the back of the chair on the left side, is connected the history of America with that of Europe; while that of an Indian chief, on the right, is emblematic of the state America was in when civilization dawned upon it. The bas-relief on the right side of the chair, which was the first crest of the American national arms, is the rising sun, under which is inscribed, 'Magnus ab integro sectorum nascitur ordo.' The relievo on the left side represents the genii of North and South

America, under the infants Hercules and Iphicles, the latter shrinking in dread, while the former struggles successfully with the obstacles and dangers of an incipient political existence. The motto for this relief is 'Incipe posse puer cui non risere parentes.' In this statue Greenough has achieved a glorious work, and one that cannot fail to reach its destination,—the distant posterity to which it is addressed."

The motto on the back of the chair in which Washington is represented as sitting is as follows: "Simulacrum istud ad magnum libertatis extemplum, nec sine ipsa duraturum."

The famous Jackson Statue was cast in the latter part of 1852 by Clarke Mills. As soon as the pedestal was prepared to receive it, it was placed thereon, and inaugurated or dedicated January 8, 1853. The procession formed in front of the City Hall at about eleven o'clock in the morning, passed down Four and a Half Street to Pennsylvania Avenue, and thence to Lafayette Square. Most of the executive officers of the Government were present. Rev. Dr. Butler opened the ceremonies with prayer, and then Hon. Stephen A. Douglas delivered an address. Mr. Mills was then introduced and enthusiastically cheered. Mr. Mills was a native of New York, but had settled in Charleston, South Carolina, had become a citizen of that State, and had there, to the astonishment of all, when only a mere plasterer, executed a fine marble cast of Hon. John C. Calhoun. While on his way to Italy to prosecute his studies, at the time when the Jackson Statue committee was in search of an artist, in 1848, Mr. Mills became acquainted with some of the members of the committee in Washington, whose names were as follows: Hon. Cave Johnson, Hon. Amos Kendall, General John P. Van Ness, James Hoban, John W. Maury, Charles K. Gardner, Jesse E. Dow, William A. Harris, Charles P. Sengstack, Francis P. Blair, John C. Rives, Thomas Ritchie, and B. B. French. Afterward, in consequence of the death of John P. Van Ness, James Hoban, and Jesse E. Dow, and the resignation of William A. Harris, John M. Mc-Calla, George W. Hughes, Andrew J. Donelson, and George Parker were chosen to fill their places. This committee collected $12,000, for which, after some doubts as to Mr. Mills's ability to make a satisfactory equestrian statue were removed, it was decided to give him the contract. After surmounting great difficulties in the erection of his foundry, and making his own cast of the statue, he succeeded in the accomplishment of his task, the entire cost of the statue being $19,000, including the five years of labor of Mr. Mills.

The foundations of the equestrian statue of General Washington were laid in 1859, within the circle at the intersection of Pennsylvania Avenue, K Street, New Hampshire Avenue, and Twenty-third Street. In January, 1860, the greater part of the casting was taken from Clarke Mills's foundry, near Bladensburg, to this position, and the completed statue was dedicated February 22, 1860, the oration of the occasion being delivered by Hon. Thomas S. Bocock, of Virginia. Mr. Bocock said it was the tardy completion of a work resolved upon by the Continental Congress immediately after the Revolution, the delay being caused perhaps by the failure to find sooner a suitable artist. He then proceeded to give a history of the event in the battle of Princeton which the pose of the statue was designed to commemorate, and which was the turning point in the War of the Revolution. After the oration the President of the United States dedicated the statue, and in his remarks said: "I accept the auspicious omen which the heavens at this moment present to us —a calm sunset almost without a cloud, after a boisterous and tempestuous day," and at the conclusion of the President's address there was an address by Mr. Mills, who said that the statue was intended for a greater elevation than that upon which it stood, but the appropriation was inadequate to carry out the original design.

The Farragut Statue, by Mrs. Vinnie Ream Hoxie, was the first monument erected in the National Capital to commemorate the services of one of the country's naval heroes. Twenty years before this time, there were but three monuments in the city dedicated to the memory of distinguished men. Greenough's Statue of Washington, variously estimated, was the first, unveiled in 1843; the bronze equestrian statue of Washington, erected in Lafayette Square, was the second, and the equestrian statue of Washington, at the intersection of Pennsylvania Avenue and New Hampshire Avenue, was the third. Next as a work of art came the Statue of Liberty, designed by Thomas Crawford, and cast by Clarke Mills, completed in 1865.

The Lincoln Statue, in front of the City Hall, came next. This was the work of Flannery Brothers, sculptors, Washington, and was paid for by funds raised from voluntary subscriptions by friends and admirers of the martyr President. The business part of the work connected with the erection of this monument was conducted by the Lincoln National Monument Association, organized April 25, 1865. The president of this association was Richard Wallach; vice-president, Joseph F. Brown; secretary, Crosby S. Noyes; treasurer, George W. Riggs. There were fifty directors, of whom the following belonged in Washington: Joseph F. Brown, Asbury Lloyd, John B. Turton,

Dr. W. G. H. Newman, George II. Plant, Z. Richards, N. D. Larner, E. C. Carrington, John P. Pepper, S. J. Bowen, George F. Gulick, B. B. French, George R. Ruff, C. V. Morris, John G. Dudley, John H. Semmes, James Kelly, William P. Ferguson; from Georgetown, Henry Addison, William H. Tenney; from Washington County, S. P. Brown and Dr. C. H. Nichols.

The monument was dedicated April 16, 1868, in the presence of an immense concourse of people, the arrangements being in charge of Mayor Wallach. An address was made by Hon. B. B. French, and E. B. Olmstead read a poem written for the occasion. The monument was then unveiled by President Andrew Johnson.

The bronze equestrian statue of General Winfield Scott, at the intersection of Massachusetts and Rhode Island avenues with Sixteenth Street, was ordered by Congress, and cast from cannon captured by the General in Mexico. The model was designed by H. K. Browne, the sculptor, and the statue was cast in the foundry of Wood & Company, of Philadelphia. The pedestal on which stands the statue is a marvel of skillful work, and is formed of blocks of New England granite, the largest ever successfully quarried and carried to a great distance. They weigh four hundred tons.

The bronze statue of General John A. Rawlins, adjutant-general of General Grant's staff, and also his Secretary of War when President, was ordered by Congress, and unveiled in 1874. It was first erected in Rawlins Square, between New York Avenue and Potomac Flats, above Eighteenth Street. It was designed by Bailey, and cast in Wood & Company's foundry. The General is represented in the uniform of his rank, and is of heroic size. The statue of General Rawlins was afterward moved to its present location, on Pennsylvania Avenue and Ninth Street, in accordance with a resolution of Congress.

The bronze statue of Lincoln in Lincoln Park, called "Emancipation," was designed by Ball, the sculptor, and cast in Munich. It was unveiled April 14, 1876, an anniversary of his assassination. This monument is the result of the labors of the emancipated citizens of the United States. The first contribution therefor came from Charlotte Scott, of Virginia, formerly a slave, the amount being $5, and being the first earned by her as a free woman. At the unveiling, Frederick Douglass was the orator, the entire ceremonies being conducted by the people of the race President Lincoln had made free.

The Statue of Peace, standing on Pennsylvania Avenue and First Street, was designed by Admiral Porter, and the work was done in

Rome by the sculptor Franklin Simmons, of Maine. It is made of beautiful Carrara marble, and was erected to the memory of those officers, sailors, and marines who died in defense of their country during the War of the Rebellion. Architect Clark designed the foundation, for which Congress made an appropriation. It is composed of a circular base, steps, and platform; but many persons think the location is illy adapted to such a beautiful work of art.

The bronze statue of General McPherson stands in McPherson Square. It was unveiled in October, 1876, with appropriate ceremonies, General John A. Logan being the orator of the day, who delivered a most impressive and impassioned tribute to the young Major-General who came to such an untimely end in the battle of Atlanta. The monument was erected by the Society of the Army of the Tennessee, the statue being the work of Louis T. Rebasso. The pedestal was built with money appropriated by Congress, and contains a tomb designed for the remains of General McPherson, but as the citizens of Clyde, Ohio, his native city, objected to their removal, they were not placed in this receptacle.

The bronze equestrian statue of General Nathaniel Greene, one of the great soldiers of the Revolutionary War, was erected in Greene Square, at the intersection of Massachusetts and Maryland avenues, Capitol Hill, in 1877. It was designed by H. K. Browne, and cast in the foundry of Wood & Company, of Philadelphia. The General is represented as wearing the uniform of his rank in the Continental Army, riding rapidly and pointing forward with the most intense purpose, and at the same time looking backward as if urging his troops to follow.

The bronze equestrian statue of Major-General George H. Thomas was unveiled November 19, 1879. It adorns the circle named after him, at the intersection of Massachusetts and Vermont avenues. It was erected by the Society of the Army of the Cumberland, in honor of the General. The oration on the occasion of the unveiling was delivered by Hon. Stanley Matthews.

The marble statue of Benjamin Franklin, designed by Ernest Plassman, standing on Pennsylvania Avenue and Tenth Street, presented to the city in 1889 by Stillson Hutchins, stands on a granite pedestal eleven feet high, and is eight feet six inches high. The philosopher is represented in the costume of the days of his diplomatic residence at Versailles, France.

The heroic bronze statue of Chief Justice John Marshall is situated at the foot of the terrace on the west side of the Capitol. It was erected in 1884 by Congress and the Bar of the United States, and cost $40,000.

The bronze statue of James A. Garfield is at the Maryland Avenue entrance to the Capitol grounds. It was erected by the Army of the Cumberland in 1887, at a cost of $33,500, upon a pedestal erected by Congress at a cost of $31,500. The recumbent figures represent the student, warrior, and statesman.

The semi-heroic bronze statue of Professor Joseph Henry, first secretary of the Smithsonian Institution, erected on the Smithsonian grounds, was unveiled in 1881. It was erected by Congress at a cost of $15,000.

The heroic bronze statue of Rear Admiral Samuel F. Dupont stands on Connecticut Avenue, one square from the British Legation. It was ordered by Congress in 1882, and was erected in 1884 at a cost of $14,000.

The heroic bronze statue of Martin Luther is immediately north of the Thomas Statue, in front of the Memorial Lutheran Church. It was erected in 1884, in commemoration of the birth of Luther, November 10, 1483, and cost, with pedestal, $10,000.

The statue of Lafayette and his compatriots, Count de Rochambeau and Chevalier Duportail, and Counts D'Estaing and DeGrasse, is in the southeast corner of Lafayette Square, opposite the Presidential Mansion. It was ordered by Congress in 1884, and erected in 1890. The total elevation to the top of the surmounting statue is forty-five feet. The female figure in front represents America offering the sword of liberty to Lafayette. The juvenile figures in the rear of the monument are the "The Children of Liberty." The entire cost of this monument was nearly $60,000. The sculptors were Antoine Falquiere and Antonin Mercie, of France.

CHAPTER XX.

First Burying Ground—Congressional Cemetery—Oak Hill Cemetery—Rock Creek Cemetery—Glenwood Cemetery—Arlington Cemetery—Other Cemeteries.

THE first burying ground in the city of Washington was Square No. 109, situated between Eighth and Boundary streets, and Nineteenth and Twentieth streets, Northwest. Prior to 1796, this property was owned by Anthony Holmead, and was part of a large estate, but in that year, when the division of the city into squares occurred between the commissioners and the proprietors, Square No. 109 was allotted to the commissioners.

On February 28, 1798, this square was set aside as a cemetery, and public notice was given to that effect. By an act of May 15, 1802, the corporation of Washington was authorized to take care of and regulate burial grounds, and these grounds were fitted up as a suitable place for the burial of the dead. Up to 1816, this was the most popular burying ground in Washington. The last interment made therein occurred in 1859 or 1860.

An act of Congress of March 3, 1879, granted to the District of Columbia the right and title of the United States in and to Square 109, to be used for public schools, and authorized the commissioners to sell any part or the whole of the square. The proceeds of the sale were directed to be used exclusively for the purchase of sites for public schoolhouses. The same act also authorized the commissioners to remove all bodies and tombstones. Subsequently an act was passed appropriating $3,000 for the exhumation and removal of such bodies as were identified to such cemeteries as the relatives or friends might select. This was done in 1880, with the exception of about two thousand bodies, which afterward, in accordance with arrangements made with the proper authorities, were removed to Graceland and Rock Creek cemeteries. The old burying ground, Square No. 109, was subsequently sold.

The Congressional Cemetery was established early in the history of the city. The project was carried out April 4, 1807, by a few of the most prominent inhabitants of the place, belonging to different denominations of Christians in the eastern part of the city. These projectors of this celebrated repository for the dead, in a most commendable spirit, placed the prices of the lots so low that individuals in humble circumstances could avail themselves of equal advantages with their more prosperous neighbors. It was agreed by the association that as soon as they should be reimbursed for the money expended in the purchase of the ground and in its improvement, the entire property should be placed under the direction of the Protestant Episcopal church, the vestry of which was an incorporated body.

Among the original signers to the subscription paper were Henry Ingle, George Blagden, Griffith Coombs, S. N. Smallwood, Dr. Frederick May, Peter Miller, John T. Frost, and Commodore Thomas Tingey. It is believed that the first interment was that of Hon. Uriah Tracey, a member of the United States Congress from Connecticut. The site, as described in 1841, was four hundred and seventy-eight feet by four hundred and thirteen feet, with a gentle slope toward the south. The ranges of lots are designated north and south by letters, and east and west by numbers. One of the most conspicuous monuments in this cemetery is that to the Hon. George Clinton, a pyramid of freestone about twelve feet high and reared on a broad base. One side presents a bold relief profile likeness, cut in marble, beneath which appears the following inscription:

"To the Memory of George Clinton. He was born in the State of New York on the 26th of July, 1739, and died at the city of Washington, 20th of April, 1811, in the seventy-third year of his age. He was a soldier and statesman of the Revolution, eminent in counsel, distinguished in war. He filled with unexampled usefulness, purity, and ability, among many other high offices, those of governor of his native State, and of Vice-President of the United States. While he lived, his virtue, wisdom, and valor were the pride, the ornament, and the security of his country; and when he died, he left an illustrious example of a well-spent life, worthy of all imitation. "This monument is affectionately dedicated by his children."

There is also a splendid pyramidal monument erected to the memory of Elbridge Gerry, of Massachusetts, Vice-President of the United States at the time of his death. He died suddenly on his way to the Capitol to preside in the Senate, November 23, 1814, at the age of seventy years, thus fulfilling his own injunction, "It is the duty of every citizen, though he have but one day to live, to devote that day to the service of his country."

There is also a monument to the memory of Major-General Jacob Brown, who died in 1828, at the age of fifty-three years. In 1839 it was under the care of Christ Episcopal Church. A general receiving vault stands on one of the main avenues, erected by Congress for those for whom no graves had been prepared. It is of freestone, has an iron door, and is surrounded by a neat iron paling which encloses an area devoted to trees and shrubs. The rule with reference to this vault is that bodies may remain therein for two months, when they must be removed and interred. In early days, however, this rule was not rigidly enforced, as the remains of the author of the "British Spy" were permitted to remain in the vault ten months. To him his friends and the members of the bar had promised to erect a suitable monument, provided his burial was permitted in the cemetery; but the pledge was not redeemed, and the remains of the illustrious Wirt were, after a long delay, at length thrown into an obscure grave to molder with the common and undistinguished dead. William Pinkney, of Maryland, the most eminent orator of his age, also lies buried here.

Besides the above-named distinguished dead, many others are buried in this cemetery, to present a complete list of whom is manifestly impracticable. The cemetery is well worth a visit from the stranger.

Oak Hill Cemetery is located on the heights of Georgetown and bordering on Rock Creek. It was previously known as "Parrott's Woods." It owes its origin to W. W. Corcoran, who purchased fifteen acres of land of Lewis Washington, and when the charter for Oak Hill Cemetery Company was obtained from Congress, March 3, 1849, he conveyed this land to the company for the purposes of a cemetery. The size of the cemetery has since been increased, until now it contains nearly forty acres. The incorporators were Lorenzo Thomas, John Marbury, Edward M. Linthicum, and George Poe.

There have been buried in this cemetery a great many distinguished personages. One of these was Edwin M. Stanton, the great War Secretary of President Lincoln. To his memory there has been erected a gray granite monument about twenty feet high, tapering from base to top like a slender pyramid. It bears the inscription: "Edwin M. Stanton. Born December 19, 1814. Died December 24, 1869."

There is also a monument to General Jesse Lee Reno, who was killed at the battle of South Mountain, September 14, 1862. There is one to the memory of Hon. Samuel Hooper, a Representative in Congress from Massachusetts, who died February 14, 1875, and also one to Alexander de Bisco **Bodisco**, Russian minister to the United States, who died November 23, 1854. Charles B. Fisk, chief engineer of the Chesapeake and Ohio Canal, is also remembered by a monument. There are two mausoleums — one erected by **W. W.** Corcoran, the other being that of the Van Ness family, transferred from its former position on H Street. This latter is said to be a copy of the Temple of Vesta. Professor Joseph Henry has a monument in this cemetery. He was born December 17, 1797, and died January 13, 1878. This cemetery is also the last resting place of John Howard Payne, author of "Home, Sweet Home." He was born June 9, 1791, and died at Tunis, Algiers, April 9, 1852. Others of more or less note lie within these sacred precincts, but further mention is forborne.

Rock Creek Cemetery lies immediately north of the Soldiers' Home. It contains one hundred acres, upon which is also St. Paul's Church, Rock Creek Parish. In colonial times the land was given to this parish to be held in perpetuity for church purposes. A portion of the ground has long been used for burying purposes. The cemetery was staked in in 1852, by the rector and vestry of Rock Creek Parish, ten or more acres being inclosed in a substantial manner. It was then highly ornamented by nature, and regularly appropriated to the purposes above mentioned. At that time Rev. David Kerr was rector, and the vestry consisted of John Agg, James M. Carlisle, William H. Dundas, Darius Clagett, George McCeney, Erasmus J. Middleton, C. H. Wiltberger, and Hezekiah Davis. Since then, part of the "Glebe," as the whole piece of ground has long been known, was surveyed and laid out for cemetery purposes. It is for the most part shaded by forest trees of great age, and being secure from the encroachments of the city, it is a favorite place for the sepulture of the dead. At the present time, the cemetery committee is composed of Rev. James A. Buck, John Miller, and General Thomas I. Pitcher; the secretary and treasurer is J. B. Wiltberger, and the superintendent, M. L. Moudy.

Glenwood Cemetery is located on Lincoln Avenue, about half a mile from Florida Avenue, on high ground overlooking the city, and is about one and a half miles north of the Capitol building. It contains about ninety acres of ground, and is laid out on the plan of Greenwood Cemetery, New York. It was incorporated July 27, 1854, and dedicated by Rev. Dr. Butler, August 1, 1854. The act of incorporation was amended February 27, 1877, the control and direction of the cemetery by this amendment being committed to a board of trustees, annually elected by the lot owners.

Arlington Cemetery is one of the principal national cemeteries in which repose so many of the dead soldiers of the Union. It lies across the Potomac, in Virginia, directly west of South Washington and directly south of the Aqueduct bridge at Georgetown. It is elevated more than two hundred feet above the Potomac, and the old estate of which the famous Arlington Mansion was the homestead originally contained eleven hundred acres. It was the property of Daniel Parke Custis, the first husband of Mrs. George Washington. Washington left it to his wife's grandson, his own adopted son, George Washington Parke Custis, who died in 1857, leaving the estate to his daughter, Mrs. Robert E. Lee, during her lifetime, and then to his grandsons, Custis and Fitzhugh Lee. As it was not the property of General Robert E. Lee, it could not be confiscated; but because of the large accumulation of taxes upon it, Virginia ordered it to be sold, and it was bought in 1864 by the Government of the United States for $23,000. In May, 1865, it was established as the first of the eighty-two national cemeteries for the remains of the Nation's dead. Some years afterward George W. Lee, the eldest son of General Lee, brought suit to recover the estate, upon the ground that it had been illegally sold, and after a long litigation established his claim. He then conveyed it to the Government for $150,000. The cemetery contains two hundred acres of land enclosed by a low wall of masonry. The ground is shaded by oaks of two hundred years' growth, and the drives and walks wind around and through beautiful green lawns, and parterres of flowers and variegated plants. There are some fifty or sixty acres of graves, the soldiers buried here numbering sixteen thousand, two hundred and sixty-four, the graves being arranged in regular rows, the natural level of the grass rolling over all. Each grave is marked by a white marble headstone, bearing the name of the soldier buried beneath, so far as the names were known. There are also buried in the cemetery the remains of a few of the soldiers of the Confederacy.

Perhaps the most interesting monument in this cemetery is the tomb erected to the memory of the dead soldiers, two thousand, one hundred and eleven in number, who could not be identified. They were gathered mostly from the battlefields of Bull Run and the road to the Rappahannock. The inscription upon this tomb reads as follows:

"Beneath this stone repose the bones of two thousand, one hundred and eleven unknown soldiers, gathered after the War from the fields of Bull Run and the Route to the Rappahannock. Their remains could not be identified, but their names and deaths are recorded in the archives of their country, and its grateful citizens honor them as of their noble army of martyrs. May they rest in peace. September, A. D. 1866."

The effect of the entire cemetery is to suggest neatness, coolness, and rest. A visit to the cemetery can scarcely fail to awaken or to enliven the spirit of patriotism, over which the varied forest trees, the oak, the chestnut, the walnut, the hickory, the elm, cast no shadows of mourning. While they laid down their lives, their country has survived.

Other cemeteries in or near Washington are the following: Battle Ground, Brightwood Avenue; Graceland, Fifteenth and H streets North-east; Harmonia Burial Ground, Brentwood road, two miles from the city; Mount Olivet, Bladensburg road; Prospect Hill, Lincoln Avenue; and Soldiers' Home, National.

CHAPTER XXI.

SOCIETIES.

FREEMASONRY has passed through two stages of development,
and is in its third stage. For several centuries it was a mere
operative body; then for some hundreds of years it was both operative
and speculative, and finally it became wholly speculative. The last
change in its nature occurred soon after the death of Sir Christopher
Wren, by the formation of the Grand Lodge of England in 1717, by
the four lodges then in active work in the south part of England
at the celebrated Apple Tree Tavern; and having now dropped its
operative feature and become wholly speculative, it rapidly spread
throughout the world. In its new form it was introduced into France
in 1725; into Ireland, in 1729; into Holland, Russia, and Spain, in
1731; into Italy, in 1733, and into Scotland, in 1736 — the Grand
Lodge being organized in Scotland in 1736 on the same principles as
in England in 1717.

In 1730 an attempt was made to introduce the organization into
the English colonies in America by the appointment of a provincial
grand master for New Jersey, but it is not known whether the incumbent established many lodges. However, a lodge was organized in
Boston, Massachusetts, in 1733, and others then speedily followed in
other colonies. After the establishment of independence by the colonies, the lodges of this country availed themselves of the privileges
possessed by similar bodies in all independent countries, and ceased to
derive their warrants from the grand lodges of England or of Scotland, as had previously been the case.

702

Masonry is of ancient date in Georgetown. What was known for many years as Potomac Lodge, No. 5, Free and Accepted Masons, was reorganized in 1806. At the time of this reorganization its membership was composed mainly of Scotchmen. One of its ancient relics of which it came into possession at this time is a Bible, having on the flyleaf the following inscription: "A present from Mr. Colin Campbell to St. Andrews Lodge, 1773, Bladensburg." This Bible was used by this lodge until 1818. The lodge from which Potomac Lodge was the regular descendant was known as Lodge No. 9, and it belonged to the Grand Lodge of the State of Maryland. Little is known of this Lodge No. 9, except that on August 21, 1789, a petition was presented to the Grand Lodge of Maryland praying for a warrant authorizing them to convene as a regular lodge, which petition was granted, authorizing the lodge to meet at Georgetown, in Maryland. It is also known that Lodge No. 9 and Lodge No. 22 of Virginia assisted in the ceremonies of the laying of the corner stone of the Capitol building, at Washington, September 18, 1793, and that the marble gavel used at that time by President Washington, and which was manufactured for that express purpose, was presented to Lodge No. 9 of Maryland, being received by Valentine Reintzel from the hands of the President himself. Valentine Reintzel was master of Lodge No. 9 at that time, and was made grand master of the Grand Lodge of the District of Columbia, when that lodge was formed in 1811. Soon after 1793 Lodge No. 9 ceased to exist, and if annalists are to be believed, from a most remarkable cause, the great accession to its membership.

Federal City Lodge, No. 15, the first lodge formed in Washington, was chartered by the Grand Lodge of Maryland, September 12, 1793, precisely six days previous to the laying of the corner stone of the Capitol. Columbia Lodge, No. 19, was chartered October 22, 1795, but had only a brief existence, suspending prior to 1806.

Potomac Lodge, No. 43, was organized December 19, 1806, and retained this name until the Grand Lodge of the District of Columbia was formed, in 1811, when it became Potomac Lodge, No. 5, of the jurisdiction of the District of Columbia Grand Lodge. This grand lodge was formed by delegates from five lodges, January 8, 1811, and as has been before stated, Valentine Reintzel was the first grand master.

An incident worthy of note in the history of Masonry in the District of Columbia is this: That during the anti-Masonic frenzy which swept over the country from 1827 to 1836, Lorenzo Dow, on

45

May 10, 1830, delivered an address to the members of Lodge No. 5, in which he avowed himself a Mason, and gave some wholesome advice to the lodge. Dow died in 1834, in Georgetown, at the house of George W. Haller, and was buried therefrom February 4, in Holmead's burying ground.

A new Masonic Hall was completed in Georgetown in July, 1859, and was opened on the 25th of that month. It then surpassed any room in the District of Columbia devoted to similar purposes. The lodge principally concerned in the erection of this hall then owned the marble gavel used by General Washington, when he laid the foundation stone of the Capitol of the United States, September 18, 1793. It passed to Columbia Lodge, No. 19, of Maryland; then to Potomac Lodge, No. 43, and at length it became the property of Potomac Lodge, No. 5. The hall opened as above mentioned cost $12,000, and it was looked upon as a real ornament to the town. This hall was dedicated October 18, 1859, the Knights Templar, Royal Arch Masons, and Master Masons meeting to the number of two thousand, and being addressed by Grand High Priest Mackay, of Charleston, South Carolina.

After several preliminary meetings, the Masonic Hall Association was organized March 14, 1865, with B. B. French president, E. L. Stevens secretary, and W. S. Huntington treasurer. B. B. French served as president until December, 1870; J. Purdy, until December, 1875; N. Acker, until December, 1877; P. H. Hooe, until December, 1885; R. B. Donaldson, until March 8, 1887, and I. L. Johnson, until the present time. E. L. Stevens served as secretary until December, 1866; Noble D. Larner, from that time to December, 1875; R. Ball, until December, 1877; and Noble D. Larner, again, from December, 1877, until the present time. W. S. Huntington served as treasurer until December, 1871; the office was then vacant one year; N. Acker, from December, 1872, to December, 1875; A. T. Longley, until December, 1877; W. H. Goods, until the present time.

This association, in March, 1865, purchased property at the northwest corner of Ninth and F streets from Gonzaga College for $20,000, upon which they erected the Masonic Temple now standing there, at a cost of about $200,000, war prices accounting for its great cost. It is a four-story building, with a front on Ninth Street of 51 feet 5 inches, and on F Street of 131 feet 5 inches, and on the west end an L extends to the north 92 feet 10 inches. The corner stone of this building was laid May 30, 1868, by B. B. French, grand master; Andrew Johnson, then President of the United States, not only

Eng by E G Williams & Bro NY

taking part in the ceremonies, but marching in the procession over the entire route. The address was delivered by Past Grand Master H. P. H. Bromwell, of Illinois, then a member of the House of Representatives. The temple was finished and dedicated May 20, 1870, the address being delivered by Ben: Perley Poore, of Massachusetts. Noble D. Larner was grand secretary on both occasions.

Following is a list of the grand masters of the District of Columbia from 1811 to 1892: Valentine Reintzel, 1811; A. McCormick, 1812-13; Amos Alexander, 1814; John Davidson, 1815-16; Amos Alexander, 1817; Daniel Kurtz, 1818-19; William Hewitt, 1820-21; W. W. Seaton, 1822-24; Samuel Birch, 1825; John N. Moulder, 1826-27; William Hewitt, 1828-29; John N. Moulder, 1830-32; R. C. Weightman, 1833; Clement T. Coote, 1834; William W. Billing, 1835-37; John N. Moulder, 1838; M. Dove, 1839; Robert Keyworth, 1840-41; John Mason, 1842; William M. Ellis, 1844; W. B. Magruder, 1845-46; B. B. French, 1847-53; W. B. Magruder, 1854; Charles S. Frailey, 1855-56; George C. Whiting, 1857-61; C. F. Stansbury, 1862; Y. P. Page, 1863; J. E. F. Holmead, 1864; George C. Whiting, 1865-67; B. B. French, 1868; R. B. Donaldson, 1869-70; C. F. Stansbury, 1871-74; I. L. Johnson, 1875-76; Eldred G. Davis, 1877-78; H. A. Whitney, 1879; Joseph S. McCoy, 1880; Noble D. Larner, 1881-82; E. H. Chamberlin, 1883; M. M. Parker,[1] 1884-85; T. P. Chiffelle, 1886; J. M. Yznaga, 1887; J. W. Lee, Jr., 1888; H. Dingman, 1889; James A. Sample, 1890; Thomas F. Gibbs, 1891, and Fred G. Alexander, 1892.

The number of Masonic lodges in the District of Columbia on the 1st of January, 1867, was sixteen, fourteen of which were in

---

[1] Myron M. Parker was born in Fairfax, Vermont, in 1843. He was preparing for college at the breaking out of the War, when he left school and enlisted in the First Vermont Cavalry, with which command he served until the close of the War. In 1865 he received an appointment in the War Department, where he served several years, holding positions of trust and responsibility.

He graduated from the law department of the Columbian University in 1876, and has since taken a lively interest in that institution, donating annually to the post-graduate class the "Myron M. Parker" prize.

In 1879 he was appointed assistant postmaster of the city. He was secretary of the Washington committee on the ceremonies incident to the laying of the corner stone of the Yorktown Monument. In Masonic circles he has been very prominent. He was Grand Master of Masons in 1884-85, and officiated as such at the dedication of the Washington Monument. He was chairman of the Triennial Committee to receive and entertain the Grand Encampment, Knights Templar of the United States, at its twenty-fourth conclave, held in Washington in 1889, and is at present an officer of the Grand Encampment.

Washington and Georgetown, as follows: Federal Lodge, No. 1; Naval Lodge, No. 4; Potomac Lodge, No. 5; Lebanon Lodge, No. 7; New Jerusalem Lodge, No. 9; Hiram Lodge, No. 10; St. John's Lodge, No. 11; National Lodge, No. 12; Washington Centennial Lodge, No. 14; B. B. French Lodge, No. 15; Dawson Lodge, No. 16; Harmony Lodge, No. 17; Acacia Lodge, No. 18, and Lafayette Lodge, No. 19. There were then also three chapters and two commanderies.

At the present time, besides the above, there are the following: Columbia, No. 3; Hope, No. 20; Anacostia, No. 21; George C. Whiting, No. 22; Pentalpha, No. 23; Stansbury, No. 24; Arminius, No. 25, and Osiris, No. 26.

The Grand Chapter, Royal Arch Masons, meets in Masonic Temple on the second Wednesdays of June and December.

There are the following chapters of Royal Arch Masons: Columbia, No. 1; Washington, No. 2; Mount Vernon, No. 3; Eureka, No. 4; Lafayette, No. 5; Washington Naval, No. 6; Mount Horeb, No. 7; and Potomac, No. 8.

Of Knights Templar there are the following commanderies: Washington, No. 1; Columbia, No. 2; Potomac, No. 3, and DeMolay Mounted Commandery, No. 4.

Of Scottish Rite Masons there are the following: Supreme Council, 33, Southern Jurisdiction of the United States; Mithras Lodge of Perfection; Evangelist Chapter; Robert De Bruce Council of Kadosh; Albert Pike Consistory, and Orient Lodge of Perfection.

Of the Royal Order of Scotland there is the Provincial Grand Lodge of the United States.

In addition to the above, there are the following: The Masonic

In 1882 Mr. Parker actively engaged in the real estate business, in which he has been very successful, his transactions running into the millions.

He has always been interested in the advancement of Washington, and has taken a leading part in all public enterprises, contributing largely of his time and means. He was one of the promoters of the proposed Constitutional Convention in 1889, the World's Columbian Exposition in 1892, and was one of the three selected to present the claims of Washington before the committee of Congress.

Mr. Parker has been closely identified with the growth and prosperity of Washington, and is connected with many of her leading financial institutions, being a director in the American Security and Trust Company, the Columbia National Bank, the Columbia Fire Insurance Company, the Columbia Title Company, Eckington and Soldiers' Home Railroad, and other financial institutions. Mr. Parker also takes interest in charitable institutions, being a director in the Emergency Hospital, Washington Hospital for Foundlings, and Training School for Nurses.

He was one of the organizers of the Washington Board of Trade, and for the past three years has been its president.

Veteran Association; the Masonic Mutual Relief Association; St. John's Mite Association, and the District of Columbia Association of Fraternal Beneficial Societies.

Of colored Masonic organizations there are the following: The Grand Lodge, which meets on the second Wednesdays of June and December, and on December 27; ten lodges; the Grand Royal Arch Chapter, and four subordinate chapters; the Grand Commandery of Knights Templar and four subordinate commanderies; the Scottish Rite Supreme Council, 33, Southern Jurisdiction of the United States; Galahad Lodge of Perfection, 14, Buddah Chapter of Rose Cross, 18, Loraster Council of Kadosh, 30, and Jonathan Daviss Consistory, 32.

In the latter part of the eighteenth century, societies of mechanics and laborers existed in London, England, calling themselves "Ancient and Honorable Loyal Odd Fellows." From them the "Union Order of Odd Fellows" sprang, and spread rapidly throughout England. The order was at this time convivial in its nature, and attempts were made to abolish that feature. From these attempts a new system arose in 1813, and several seceding lodges formed the "Manchester Unity." This Unity now embraces most of the Odd Fellows in England.

The first lodge of Independent Odd Fellows formed in the United States was the Washington Lodge, in Baltimore, Maryland, April 26, 1819. At this time there were but five persons duly instructed in the principles of the order, but as only five members were required for the incipient structure of a lodge, arrangements were made to secure a charter from the Manchester Unity in England, for which purpose Thomas Wildey proceeded to the mother country for the charter, and procured a charter for the Grand Lodge of Maryland and the United States. Upon his return to Baltimore, the lodge above named was organized by Mr. Wildey and four others. At this time there were a few lodges in the United States, in New York City and Boston; but they were in no way national in their character. The second lodge of the Independent Order of Odd Fellows was organized in Boston March 26, 1820, and another was organized in Philadelphia December 26, 1821. Both of these lodges received their charters from Baltimore in 1823, Maryland being regarded as the headquarters by virtue of the charter brought over from England. Maryland, however, shortly afterward relinquished this right to a body formed of representatives from different States, the name of which was "The Grand Lodge of the United States."

The first lodge established in Washington was named Central

Lodge, No. —, and was instituted November 26, 1827. The Grand Lodge of the District of Columbia was instituted November 28, 1828. In the following October, Concord Lodge, No. —, was formed in this city, and soon afterward a lodge was established in Alexandria and also in Georgetown. All of these lodges, with the exception of Central Lodge, surrendered their charters, but previously to the surrender a portion of the members of Central Lodge had branched to form Washington Lodge in 1833, so that they were entitled to maintain their District Grand Lodge, which prevented them from reverting to the jurisdiction of the Grand Lodge of the United States.

In 1839, Central Lodge having passed through a period of depression and again revived, lost a portion of her members residing in the eastern part of the city, in the vicinity of the Navy Yard, who formed Eastern Lodge, No. 7. About the same time Potomac Lodge, No. 8, was formed at Alexandria. In 1841 and 1842, two other lodges were organized, namely, Harmony Lodge, No. 9, and Union Lodge, No. 11, both in the vicinity of the Navy Yard.

A new Odd Fellows' Hall was erected in 1845, on Seventh Street, fronting on that street sixty-five feet, eighty feet in depth, and three stories high. The first story was of granite, and the other stories of brick. This hall was dedicated May 25, with most interesting ceremonies, in the presence of a large concourse of people from various States. In the procession that was formed there were one thousand Odd Fellows, and the line was three-fourths of a mile long. The lodges in the procession were as follows: Central Lodge, No. 1; Washington Lodge, No. 6; Eastern Lodge, No. 7; Harmony Lodge, No. 9; Columbia Lodge, No. 10; Union Lodge, No. 11; Friendship Lodge, No. 12; Beacon Lodge, No. 15; Metropolis Lodge, No. 16; Excelsior Lodge, No. 17; and Columbia and Magenenu Encampments, all of Washington; Covenant Lodge, No. 13; Mechanics' Lodge, No. 18, and Mount Pisgah Encampment, all of Georgetown; Potomac Lodge, No. 8; Mount Vernon Lodge, No. 14, and Marley Encampment, all of Alexandria; besides several encampments from Richmond and Baltimore. Among the distinguished Odd Fellows present were Thomas Wildey, founder of the order in the United States, and James L. Ridgely, corresponding secretary of the Grand Lodge of the United States. The procession was under command of Cranston Laurie, grand master, assisted by his aids, William M. Randolph and John Waters. An address was delivered from a temporary rostrum, and an ode to Odd Fellowship was sung by the Harmoneons, who volunteered their services. Rev. Dr. Muller read a portion of Scrip-ture; Rev. S. K. Cox offered prayer. An introductory address was delivered by Walter Lenox, vice grand, and an eloquent and powerful oration was delivered by William F. Giles, of Baltimore. The exercises closed in the evening with a levee in their new, spacious, and elegant saloon.

Of lodges of Odd Fellows, in addition to those mentioned above as taking part in the dedication of the new hall, there are now the following: Oriental, No. 19; Federal City, No. 20, and Golden Rule, No. 21.

There are the following lodges of the Degree of Rebekah: Naomi, No. 1; Ruth, No. 2, and Martha Washington, No. 3.

There are the following encampments: Columbian, No. 1; Magenenu, No. 4; Mount Nebo, No. 6; and Fred D. Stuart, No. 7.

There is also the Independent Order of Odd Fellows Relief Association, and the Odd Fellows Veteran Association.

The Grand United Order of Odd Fellows opened a new lodge room at the corner of Eleventh Street and Pennsylvania Avenue September 1, 1870. This room was occupied jointly by the following lodges: Union Friendship, No. 891, with 90 members; Eastern Star, No. 1,028, with 120 members; John F. Cook, No. 1,195, with 70 members; Mount Olive, No. 1,333, with 60 members; J. F. N. Wilkinson, No. 1,343, with 62 members; Bloom of Youth, No. 1,368, with 68 members; Rising Sun, No. 1,365, with 60 members; Star of the West, No. 1,369, with 90 members; Peter Ogden, No. 1,374, with 75 members; James McCrumill, No. 1,437, with 58 members. These were all the lodges there were then in Washington, but there were three in Georgetown which had a place of meeting in that city. This order is similar in its objects, organization, etc., to the Independent Order of Odd Fellows, but its name is different, and it also differs in this, that it receives its charters from the parent body in England.

Of this order of Odd Fellows there are the District Grand Lodge, No. 20, which meets annually on the second Monday in September; the Washington Patriarchie, No. 18, which meets on the second Monday in each month; Georgetown Patriarchie, No. 42, which meets on the fourth Wednesday in each month; Past Grand Masters' Council, No. 4, and Past Grand Masters' Council, No. 44. There are also twenty-four lodges of this order in Washington and Georgetown, and two associations, Relief Association and Hall Association.

Of the Knights of Pythias there are the Grand Lodge and fifteen subordinate lodges; the supreme section and four other sections of endowment rank; six divisions of uniform rank.

Of the Knights of the Golden Eagle there are the Grand Castle and six subordinate castles.

Of the Knights of Honor there are the Grand Lodge and five subordinate lodges, and Columbia Lodge, No. 509.

Of the National Union there are the Cabinet and twenty-one councils.

Of the order of Chosen Friends there are six councils.

Of the Order of United American Mechanics there are the American Guard Council, No. 1, and Liberty Council, No. 2.

The Order of United American Mechanics, Junior, has nine councils.

The Royal Arcanum has four councils, and Iron Hall Branch, No. 340.

The Sons of Jonadab have ten councils.

The Royal Templars of Temperance have Capitol Council, No. 1. The Sons of Temperance have Friendship Division, No. 14. The Independent Order of Good Templars has the Grand Lodge, which meets annually in the fourth week in November, and fifteen subordinate lodges.

The American Legion of Honor has the Grand Council, which meets on the third Thursday in February, and it also has nine subordinate councils.

The Ancient Order of Druids has the Washington Grove, No. 1, which meets on the first and third Sundays of each month.

The Independent Order of Rechabites has twenty-six tents.

The Improved Order of Red Men has the Great Council, which meets on the second Monday of January, April, July, and October, and six tribes.

The Independent Order of Sons of Benjamin has two lodges, Columbia Lodge, No. 101, and District Lodge, No. 124.

The Washington Library Company was formed in March, 1811, and a constitution was adopted the same month, each share being fixed at $12. At an election held April 1, 1811, directors were chosen as follows: Buckner Thruston, Samuel H. Smith, James Laurie, William James, John Hewitt, Abraham Bradley, Jr., and Joseph Stretch. On April 5, 1813, the following were chosen directors: James Laurie, Thomas H. Gillis, Jonathan S. Findlay, George Way, William Parker, and Joseph Stretch. James Laurie was elected president, William Parker treasurer, and John C. Steiner librarian.

April 3, 1816, Josiah Meigs was elected president; William Parker, treasurer, and John Sessford, librarian. Josiah Meigs was elected president annually for several years. Under a joint resolution of Congress passed March 3, 1823, the company became entitled to any surplus copies of books in the Department of State and a copy of the laws of the United States, the journals of Congress, documents, and state reports previously published, and state papers which might be published after that date. At that time the collection of books in the Congressional Library was the private library of members of Congress and of a few privileged individuals, the citizens of Washington and citizens in general deriving no benefit from it, as they do at the present time. This fact made it necessary to do what could be done then to provide library facilities for the people. But it was seen that in order to make this library of the use to the public that such an institution ought to be, it was necessary that it should be better sustained than it had been so far. The company had a lot and a building on Eleventh Street, south of Pennsylvania Avenue, opposite Carusi's saloon, and the rooms were open from 2:00 P. M. to sunset. By 1857 the number of volumes in the library reached six thousand, and the institution was patronized by the best men in Washington. Soon after this time it was suffered to become of little use to the public, but in February, 1858, the rooms were enlarged and the building put in complete repair. The library was increased and the number of shareholders was also increased and the rooms were kept open afternoon and evening. A meeting was held February 11, 1858, to determine what the future of the library should be, at which it was resolved to appoint a committee to place the claims of the library before the public. This committee consisted of twenty of the leading citizens of Washington. Soon afterward it was made public that the library had recently received several valuable donations, among them the magnificent library of the then late Dr. James Laurie, consisting of more than one thousand volumes, the donor being Dr. J. C. Hall. Other donations had been made by Mrs. Dr. Thornton, Charles B. King, and J. F. Haliday. The committee of twenty citizens, on the 27th of February, published an address to the citizens of Washington, earnestly commending the library to them and hoping they would enable the managers to make it a "People's Library and Reading-room." This company continued in existence for several years after this period, and then turned its library over to the high school of Washington and disbanded.

On July 21, 1828, a meeting was held at the City Hall for the purpose of organizing a society for the promotion of temperance. The president of the meeting was Hon. William Cranch, and the meeting was opened with prayer by the Rev. J. L. Skinner. A constitution previously drafted was presented, and unanimously adopted. This society was named the Washington City Temperance Society, and when organized, the president was Hon. William Cranch; vice-president, Rev. Dr. Robert B. Semple; treasurer, James L. Edwards; secretary, John Coyle, Jr., and directors, Revs. John Davis, Reuben Post, Obadiah B. Brown, Andrew Coyle, and James H. Handy.

The first temperance society organized in the United States was in 1808, at a small town in New York State, with forty-seven members. The second was in Massachusetts in 1813, called the Massachusetts Society for the Suppression of Intemperance. Next came the American Temperance Society, of Boston, in 1826, under the direction of which State, county, and town associations rapidly formed, and in 1831 there were in existence nineteen States and three thousand local societies, with a membership of three hundred thousand. It is believed that the first temperance address in Washington was by Rev. Justin Edwards.

On December 31, 1831, there was held a large temperance meeting in the House of Representatives, presided over by the Hon. Lewis Cass, and addressed by Hon. Daniel Webster, Hon. Felix Grundy, Hon. Theodore Frelinghuysen, and others. The first Congressional Temperance Society was organized in 1833, with Hon. Lewis Cass as president. This society was revived in 1837, in 1842, in 1844, and in 1866.

The Washington Temperance Society was organized by six men who were accustomed to meet nightly for the purpose of drinking, while sitting in a tavern in Baltimore. They then signed the pledge of total abstinence. Three days after, William Mitchell and his five associates formed the Washington Temperance Society, which in 1841 had a membership of over one hundred thousand. This movement proved, however, to be but a great spasm of virtue, and soon passed away, but it led to the organization of the Sons of Temperance, the first meeting of which was held in New York September 29, 1842. The first division of this order in the District of Columbia was formed in 1844, and by 1858 every division of this jurisdiction had surrendered their charters. On October 22, 1855, Good Samaritan Division, No. 1, was instituted, and in July, 1862, Federal City, No. 2, was formed. Equal Division, No. 3, was formed January 1, 1863; Armory Square, No. 4, soon afterward, and then Columbia, No. 5. Both of these last two were formed of soldiers in the hospitals. Within two years from the organization of Armory Square Division, No. 4, a branch of the order was formed and in successful operation in every hospital in the city but one, and from April, 1863, to April, 1865, more than seven thousand soldiers took up the cause of the Sons of Temperance in the District of Columbia. From January, 1863, to October 1, 1867, thirty-nine divisions were instituted in the District, and at the end of this time there were nineteen of them in successful operation, with four thousand five hundred members.

The first annual meeting of the Congressional Temperance Society was held Sunday evening, January 26, 1868, in the House of Representatives, Senator Wilson presiding. Hon. William Plants, of Ohio, Horace Greeley, Hon. Samuel F. Carey and Hon. Thomas H. Ford, both of Ohio, and General Hurlbut, of Illinois, made speeches in favor of temperance. Mr. Greeley's speech was very radical. This society is still in existence.

The Washington Bible Society was organized in 1836. Its fifteenth anniversary was celebrated in the F Street Presbyterian Church, May 26, 1851. M. St. Clarke was the president. A resolution was adopted in favor of supplying the parlors of hotels each with a copy of the Bible, and recommending that the board of managers supply a copy to such hotels as had proprietors willing it should be done. A resolution was then adopted, on motion of Rev. Dr. Junkin, that, recognizing the Bible as the book of religion, the book of liberty, the infallible exponent of human duty and of human rights, the society regarded the free and universal circulation of the Sacred Volume as a most important means of maintaining and propagating among men the true religion and the principles and institutions of regulated liberty, etc.

The eighteenth anniversary of this society was celebrated May 29, 1854, John P. Ingle, president, in the chair. During the year then closing, the receipts of the society from the sale of Bibles and Testaments amounted to $1,426.13. Since the last previous report the entire number of volumes in the depository had been 3,992 — 1,512 Bibles and 2,480 Testaments. The total issue from the depository during the same period had been 1,196 Bibles and 1,801 Testaments. The agent of the society had visited during the year 8,459 families and places of business, finding 862 of them without either a Bible or Testament, and supplying by sale or by gift 647, while 215 of them refused to receive a copy of either. John P. Ingle was again elected president, together with six vice-presidents, and Mitchell H. Miller was elected secretary, Michael Nourse treasurer, and there were elected twelve directors.

Without attempting to trace the history of this society minutely, suffice it to say that at present it meets at No. 1409 New York Avenue Northwest. The managers are the pastors of the several churches of the city, *ex officio;* life directors, and ministers of the Gospel who are life members. Rev. A. W. Pitzer is president at the present time, and William Ballantyne treasurer and depositary.

The Young Men's Christian Association was organized June 9, 1852, at a meeting held in Masonic Hall. At the beginning, this association addressed itself to the work of perfecting theories of universal application, and in order to carry out its work it excluded sectarianism and denominational theology. Two well-lighted and pleasant rooms were rented on Seventh Street, near the post office, where the stranger was always welcome, and where a large number of papers and periodicals were always to be found. During the first six months of its existence, a library of several hundred volumes was collected — all donations, and nearly all from persons in New York, Philadelphia, and Washington. At the end of the first year, there were 350 volumes in the library; at the end of the second year, 1,040, 900 of which had been donated and 140 purchased. William J. Rhees was the first recording secretary.

The association is located at 1409 and 1411 New York Avenue, and its rooms are open daily from 9:00 A. M. to 10:00 P. M. The president is William B. Gurley; treasurer, J. C. Pratt; recording secretary, J. H. Lichliter; general secretary, James E. Pugh.

The Women's Christian Association meets at 1719 Thirteenth Street Northwest. The president of this association is Mrs. Justice Harlan; vice-presidents, Mrs. Chief Justice Fuller, Mrs. S. C. Pomeroy, Mrs. John Rodgers, Mrs. William Stickney, Mrs. J. G. Ames, Mrs. D. W. Mahon, and Mrs. G. O. Little; secretary, Mrs. Thomas Wilson; treasurer, Mrs. D. A. Freeman, and register, Mrs. C. B. Jewell.

The patriotic orders of the District of Columbia are the following:

The Associated Veterans of 1846 and the various organizations coming under the general head of the Grand Army of the Republic. All of these organizations belong to the Department of the Potomac, having its headquarters at No. 1412 Pennsylvania Avenue Northwest. The several Grand Army posts are as follows:

John A. Rawlins Post, No. 1; Kit Carson, No. 2; Lincoln Post, No. 3; O. P. Morton Post, No. 4; George G. Meade, No. 5; John F. Reynolds, No. 6; James A. Garfield, No. 7; Burnside Post, No. 8; Charles Sumner Post, No. 9; Farragut Post, No. 10; Charles P. Stone

Post, No. 11; U. S. Grant Post, No. 12; John A. Logan Post, No. 13; Phil. A. Sheridan Post, No. 14; George H. Thomas Post, No. 15; W. T. Sherman Post, No. 16. The Union Veterans' Union has three commands — Hancock Command, No. 1; John A. Logan Command, No. 2; and Phil. A. Sheridan Command, No. 3.

Besides these, there are the District Commandery of the Military Order of the Loyal Legion, the National Association Veterans of the Mexican War, the Society of Loyal Volunteers, the National American Woman Suffrage Association, the District Woman Suffrage Association, the National Society of the Daughters of the American Revolution, and St. George's Society — a benevolent society founded in 1870, for the relief of English-born people in distress.

There are six scientific societies in Washington, having an aggregate membership of about one thousand, two hundred and fifty. These societies are as follows:

The Anthropological Society, organized February 17, 1870, to encourage the study of the natural history of man, especially on the American Continent.

The Biological Society, organized December 3, 1880, to encourage the study of biological science.

The Chemical Society, organized January 31, 1884, for the study of chemical science, pure and applied.

The Entomological Society, organized February 29, 1884, for the study of entomological science in all its bearings.

The National Geographic Society, organized January 27, 1888, for the study and distribution of geographic knowledge.

The Philosophical Society, organized October 13, 1871, for the purpose of the free exchange of views on scientific subjects and the promotion of scientific inquiry among its members. This is one of the most important societies in Washington. It has published eleven volumes of bulletins. The annual dues are $5. It has a mathematical section, organized March 29, 1883.

A Joint Commission of the above societies was formed February 25, 1888, consisting of three delegates from each of the component societies, its functions being advisory, except that it may execute instructions on general subjects and in special cases from two or more of the societies.

The Blavatsky Branch of the Theosophical Society meets at No. 1006 F Street, Reavel Savage being the president, and J. Guilford White secretary.

CHAPTER XXII.

THE BENCH AND BAR.

NOTHING perhaps more significantly exhibits the abnormal character of the Territory of Columbia, as it was called by those who established it, than its peculiar judicial organization. From the very nature of the case, this Territory formed a community separate and distinct from every other portion of the Union. The constitutional provision that gave to Congress exclusive legislative authority in its affairs separated it from the States and gave it a distinct character. It was not a part of any State organization, and its government was committed to the care of the national legislature and not to that of the people who inhabited it. The very fact that a whole community was, by operation of law, taken from under the control of the government of the State to which it belonged and placed under an exclusive legislation in which it could have no part, was calculated to give to this Territory a character peculiarly its own. In nothing was this so remarkable as in the organization and history of the judicial system which was to regulate the most intimate relations of its citizens. In the very first act of Congress, passed July 16, 1790, establishing the temporary and permanent seat of the Government of the United States, provision was made by which the operation of the laws of the State from which the District was selected for the purpose mentioned in the act should continue in force until the time fixed for the removal of the Government to the territory so selected, and until the Congress of the United States should make further provision for its government. Congress in this way took care to provide against a sudden change in the law governing the territory selected, until the time should arrive when it could itself provide by positive and distinct legislation for the local necessities of the community. This state of things continued until **1801.** Congress then passed an act entitled "An Act Concerning the District of Columbia," by which the laws of the States of Maryland and Virginia, out of which States the Territory had been carved, were continued in force as the body of law by which the people of that Territory were to be governed. The District itself was divided into two counties, one of which, embracing that portion lying east of the Potomac River, was, together with the islands of that river, to be called and known as the County of Washington; the other part, embracing that part lying west of the Potomac River, was to be called the County of Alexandria. As by the subsequent retrocession of this last mentioned portion of the District of Columbia to Virginia, Alexandria County was incorporated into and became again a part of that State, it is not deemed necessary, in this history, to say anything more in reference to the laws and courts peculiar to it, and their jurisdiction therein, except that by this act it was made a part of the judicial system of the District.

Under the act from which we have quoted, a court was established in the District of Columbia which was called the Circuit Court of the District of Columbia, the judges of which were vested with all the powers conferred upon the judges of the Circuit Courts of the United States. This Circuit Court was to consist of one chief justice and two associate justices, who were to hold their offices during good behavior, and to be qualified by taking the oath provided by law to be taken by the justices of the Circuit Courts of the United States, and who were also to have power to appoint a clerk and such other officers as were necessary to the establishment of a complete judicial system.

The same act made provision for the terms of the court in the two counties of which the District was composed, and conferred upon it a wide jurisdiction over all crimes and offenses and all cases in law and equity. It is not necessary here to go into any more detail with respect to the powers of this court or into its peculiar organization.

At the outset, for the purpose of preserving the rights and relations existing between the citizens of the territory so selected for the seat of the Government, Congress enacted that in all cases where judgments or decrees had been obtained or should be obtained thereafter, in suits depending at the time of cession in any of the courts of Virginia or Maryland, where the defendant had property within the Territory of Columbia, the plaintiff might have execution for the purpose of enforcing his rights in those courts in such cases. It will thus be seen that while Congress was establishing a new system of judiciary for the Territory of Columbia, it took care to provide for all rights existing in the States by which the Territory had been ceded to the Government of the United States, before that cession took place. Under this condition of things the courts of the District of Columbia were established, and entered upon their duties as the judicial government of the Territory of Columbia. By the laws enacted to carry into effect this new judicial system, Congress gave to the citizens of this peculiar Territory the right of appeal to the Supreme Court of the United States. At first this right of appeal was given in all cases where the amount involved exceeded $100. Afterward, this amount was increased to $1,000, but when it was so increased the right of appeal was preserved to litigants in all cases where the amount exceeded $100 and was less than $1,000, in which it could be shown to a judge of the Supreme Court that the questions involved were of so serious a nature as to authorize the interposition of that court. Under this system, the appeal to the Supreme Court being direct, and not as in the States, in which courts of appeal exist, a great many cases which under ordinary circumstances would not have been carried to the Supreme Court at all were brought before it for consideration. This condition of things operated to bring a great many cases that had been decided by the courts of the District of Columbia to the Supreme Court for the final adjudication. In the course of time it was found essential to enlarge the sum necessary to authorize an appeal to the Supreme Court of the United States, until now no appeal can be had to this court, except in certain cases mentioned in the statute, unless the sum involved exceed $5,000.

Besides the Circuit Court, of which we have been speaking, provision was made for the appointment, in each of the counties of Washington and Alexandria, of a judge to be called the Judge of the Orphan's Court, and of a Register of Wills, who were authorized to

, perform all the duties incumbent upon officers of like character in the States from which this Territory had been taken. This separate Probate Court continued to exist until the change was made in the organization of the courts to which reference will be hereafter made, when the duties of the Probate Court were imposed upon one of the judges of the courts of the District of Columbia. The office of Register of Wills was not changed, and continues until the present time. It may be well to mention in this connection, that long subsequently to the time of which we are now speaking, Congress created another court in the District of Columbia, called the Police Court; but it is not deemed necessary to say anything further of these minor courts. In what is to be said hereafter, attention will be confined to those courts which compose the judicial system of the District of Columbia. We have said enough to show that, in 1801, when the territory set apart under the act of Congress had been selected, and the seat of government had been firmly established in that territory or district, Congress took immediate means to provide for it a permanent judicial system. It established a Circuit Court, organized as already described, with ample jurisdiction, and with all the officers required for such a court. Besides the officers already mentioned, provision was made for the appointment of a marshal of the District of Columbia, an officer similar to the marshal of the Circuit Courts of the United States.

It will appear from what has already been said that while Congress had taken care to establish within the Territory of Columbia the courts designated above, and had conferred upon those courts ample jurisdiction, and had provided for them the officers necessary for the proper conduct of their affairs, the law by which those tribunals was to be governed was the law as it existed in the States from which that Territory had been carved at the time of the cession. It is somewhat remarkable that through all the years that have since elapsed, Congress has found so little time to attend to the organic law of the District of Columbia that it remains to-day to a remarkable degree as it did in 1790, when the territory was ceded by the two States of Maryland and Virginia. This condition of things is not due to any want, on the part of the citizens of the District, or of Congress itself, of a desire that proper laws for the government of this Territory should be enacted, but more, perhaps entirely, to the fact that the special legislature of the District is at the same time the legislature of the Nation, and that this national legislature is occupied with matters so important as to render attention to the affairs of the District impracticable.

46

Congress in 1802, by an act passed April 29 of that year, authorized the chief judge of the Circuit Court of the District of Columbia to
hold a District Court of the United States in that District, and gave
to that court the same powers and jurisdiction which were by law
vested in the District Courts of the United States. This gave to this
chief judge, among other things, jurisdiction in admiralty and bankruptcy cases.

Enough has been said already about the history of these courts.
The jurisdiction of the courts in all its details has been established
by many decisions of the Supreme Court of the United States, which
can scarcely be said to form a part of the history of the city of
Washington. It may not be amiss, however, to call attention to one
case which went from the Circuit Court of the District of Columbia
to the Supreme Court of the United States, a case of great importance
and interest to all the citizens of the United States, and of special
interest to those of the District of Columbia, because it determined
in the most comprehensive and at the same time in the most precise
manner the jurisdiction of the Circuit Court of the District of
Columbia. The case referred to was that of Kendall *versus* the United
States *ex rel.* Stokes, *et al.*, decided in 1838, and reported in the twelfth
volume of Peter's Supreme Court Report on page 524. This case
came before the Supreme Court of the United States upon appeal
from the Circuit Court under these circumstances: Stockton & Stokes,
who were contractors for carrying the mails of the United States,
applied to the Circuit Court of the District of Columbia for a writ of
mandamus commanding the Postmaster-General of the United States,
Hon. Amos Kendall, to credit them (the said contractors) with money
which had been found to be due them upon a statement made by the
officers of the Treasury Department. The Postmaster-General refused
to obey the writ upon the ground that the officer of the Treasury who
had stated the account had transcended his authority in delaring the
balance due to the contractors. The questions which arose in the case
were, first, whether there was any cause for the writ of mandamus;
and second, whether the Circuit Court of the District of Columbia had
authority to issue the writ. The Supreme Court said that the act of
Congress of February 27, 1801, concerning the District of Columbia,
by which the Circuit Court was created and its powers and duties
defined, established the fact that in the District of Columbia there is no
division between the General and the State Governments. Congress
has entire control over the District for every purpose of government,
and it is reasonable to suppose that in organizing a judicial system

in that District, all powers necessary for the purposes of government were vested in the courts of justice. The Circuit Court is the highest court of original jurisdiction in that community, and if the power to issue a mandamus exists in any court it is vested in this Circuit Court of the District of Columbia. The first section of the act declares that the laws of Maryland as they then existed should continue in that part of the District which was ceded by Maryland, and it is admitted that at the date of this act the common law of England was in force in Maryland, and continued in force in that part ceded to the United States by Maryland, and that it had been determined that the power to issue a mandamus in a proper case is a branch of the common law. After arguing the constitutional question at considerable length, the distinguished Justice delivering the opinion of the court said:

"We are then to construe the third section of the act of February 27, 1801, as if the eleventh section of the act of February 13, 1801, had been incorporated at full length, and in this section it is declared that the Circuit Court of the District of Columbia shall have cognizance of all cases in law or equity arising under the Constitution and laws of the United States and treaties which shall be made under their authority, which are the very words of the Constitution, and which is, of course, a delegation of the whole judicial power in cases arising under the Constitution and laws, etc., which meets and supplies the precise wants of delegation of power which prevented the exercise of jurisdiction in other cases cited, and must, on the principles which governed the decisions of the courts in those cases, be sufficient to vest the power in the Circuit Court of the District of Columbia."

The court affirmed the decision of the court below, which had authorized the issuance of the writ prayed for, thus establishing this broad jurisdiction of the Circuit Court of the District of Columbia.

Having now seen how the courts of the District were established and their jurisdiction defined and determined, we will proceed to the pleasing task of rehearsing the history of the good and great men who presided over those tribunals. We shall find that in this singular community the judiciary has ever maintained a high character for the purity and integrity of its members.

The first chief justice appointed for the Circuit Court of the District of Columbia was Thomas Johnson, March 3, 1801. Thomas Johnson was a particular friend of President Washington, was a man of distinguished ability, and had held the position of commissioner to select the territory for the Federal District. He was a delegate to the Continental Congress, was Governor of Maryland, judge of the United

States District Court for the State of Maryland, and a Justice of the Supreme Court of the United States from 1791 to 1793, when he resigned. He declined the appointment of chief justice of the Circuit Court of the District of Columbia, and the position was then bestowed on William Kilty, who was appointed March 23, 1801.

William Kilty was born in London, England, in 1757, and was educated at the College of St. Omer's, in French Flanders. At the beginning of the Revolutionary War, he was residing on his father's plantation in Calvert County, Maryland. He joined the American army in 1776, and served as a surgeon until 1783, when he returned to Annapolis and studied law. He took a distinguished position at the bar, and was selected by the legislature of the State to prepare the work now so well known as "Kilty's Laws of Maryland." The position of chief justice of the Circuit Court of the District of Columbia he filled until January 20, 1806, when he was appointed chancellor of Maryland, serving in this position until his death, October 10, 1821. While he was chancellor of the State of Maryland, he prepared, under the orders of the legislature of the State, a report of the English statutes applicable to Maryland. The profound erudition and legal acumen displayed in this work gave it great authority throughout the State, and it became the foundation of the statute law of Maryland. Judge Kilty was a man of singular attractiveness of character and of great culture and erudition. His relations with his brethren of the bench and bar were of the most agreeable description. At his death, the bench and bar of the State of Maryland united in paying appropriate tribute to his memory. He is buried in the old cemetery at Annapolis, under a monument erected by his son, the late Rear Admiral Kilty, of the United States Navy.

The next chief justice of this court was William Cranch, who had been appointed an assistant justice in the same court March 3, 1801. He received his appointment as chief justice February 4, 1806. He was born in Weymouth, Massachusetts, July 17, 1769, graduated from Harvard College in 1787, commenced the study of law, and was admitted to the bar in 1790. After a few years spent in practice in Massachusetts, he removed to the District of Columbia in 1794, and here passed the remainder of his life. In 1800 he was appointed one of the commissioners of public buildings, and on February 27, 1801, was nominated assistant justice in the Circuit Court for the District of Columbia by President Adams. In 1805, upon the resignation of Chief Justice Kilty, he was appointed chief justice by President Jefferson, and he remained in this position until September

1, 1855, when he died, having been for fifty-five years a judge of the United States Circuit Court and for fifty years chief justice. His biographer says of him that in all this period, notwithstanding the facility of appeal to the United States Supreme Court, appeal from the Circuit Court being for smaller amounts than from the Circuit and District Courts in the States, only two of his own decisions were overruled and sent back for amendment by the highest court in the country. During the time when he filled the office of assistant justice and chief justice of the Circuit Court of the District of Columbia, he also filled the office of reporter to the Supreme Court of the United States. Nine volumes of his reports were published, and are well known to the lawyers of the United States. In this office of reporter he was preceded by Mr. A. J. Dallas, and he was succeeded by Henry Wheaton and Richard Peters, all of whom were distinguished reporters. He also, during his occupancy of the office of assistant judge and chief justice, made accurate reports of the cases decided in the Circuit Court of the District of Columbia from 1801 to 1841, which were published in six volumes, and are known as "Cranch's Circuit Court Reports." In conformity with an act of Congress he prepared a code of laws for the District of Columbia, which, like many other codes prepared under the direction of that body, were afterward neglected.

Judge Cranch was remarkable in every particular in which a judge can be distinguished. He was a man of great learning, and was always a careful student of the cases entrusted to his charge. He was, from the very position he occupied, obliged to review the decisions of the executive departments bearing upon questions involving the rights of citizens; and in all the conflicts of the courts he maintained the character of a pure and upright judge. He was eminently a religious man, was a Unitarian · in faith, and an example of Christian charity in all the circumstances of life. His habits of life were singularly simple, his character childlike and confiding. During his long career he possessed the respect of all who knew his abilities and services, and of all who were acquainted with him as a man.

The next appointment of chief justice of this Circuit Court was that of George W. Hopkins, October 5, 1855. Mr. Hopkins was a Virginian by birth, had been a Representative in Congress and *chargé d'affaires* of the United States to Portugal, and having declined the office of chief justice to this court, served in the Thirty-fifth Congress.

James Dunlop was then appointed to this position, and was the last of the chief justices of this court. He was born March 28, 1793.

His father was a Scotchman by birth, and his mother was a daughter of Robert Peter, one of the original proprietors of the city of Washington. He was educated at a private school in Georgetown and at the College of New Jersey, at Princeton, graduating therefrom in 1811, delivering the valedictory of his class. Afterward, he entered upon the study of law in the office of Francis Scott Key, and became a partner of that gentleman soon after being admitted to the bar. This partnership continued until Mr. Key removed to Baltimore. He was for some time assistant district attorney for the United States for the District of Columbia, and was actively engaged in the prosecution of cases incident to that office. He was the recorder of Georgetown during the construction of the Chesapeake and Ohio Canal in 1832–37. In 1838 he was appointed a judge of the newly organized Criminal Court of the District of Columbia, being the first judge appointed to preside in that court. He continued to hold that position until 1845, when, upon the death of Judge Thruston, he was appointed to succeed him as one of the assistant justices of the Circuit Court of the District of Columbia. He held this position until 1857, when he was made chief justice, and continued in that position until the abolition of the court in 1863. Judge Dunlop survived his judgeship several years, dying May 6, 1872, at his farm in Montgomery County, Maryland. He was a courtly gentleman, dignified and elegant, and always maintained the amenities of the bench. During his entire career he was respected by the members of the bar and by the general public.

Following are sketches of the associate justices of the Circuit Court.

James Marshall was one of the earliest justices of the Circuit Court of the District of Columbia, having been appointed March 3, 1801. Very little is known of this gentleman except that he held the office but a few years.

Nicholas Fitzhugh was a native of Virginia, and became a resident of the District of Columbia soon after the removal of the seat of government thereto. He was appointed a justice of the Circuit Court, he also holding the office only for a few years.

Allen R. Duckett was born in Maryland, and became a resident of the District of Columbia soon after the removal of the seat of government. He was appointed a justice of the Circuit Court in 1806, and like the two gentlemen next preceding in this narrative, held the office for a short time only.

Buckner Thruston was appointed a justice of the Circuit Court of the District of Columbia December 14, 1809. He was a native of

Virginia, and in early life migrated to Kentucky. Being a man of superior ability, he was appointed a Federal judge of the Territory of Orleans in 1805, and in the same year was elected one of the United States Senators from Kentucky for six years. Being selected in 1809 as one of the justices of the Circuit Court of the District of Columbia, he held that office until his death, August 30, 1845, a period of thirty-six years. He was a man of remarkable ability, and during the long years of his occupancy of this position, he was most highly respected, not only as a justice, but also as a man of great learning, and remarkable for his strict adherence to what he believed to be right. While he was a man of great eccentricity of character, he never sought to pander in any way to personal friendship, but always pursued the strict path of duty.

James L. Morsell was born in Calvert County, Maryland, in January, 1775. He received a good education, studied law, and came to the bar in Georgetown early in the present century. He served in the War of 1812, and in 1816 was appointed one of the judges of the Circuit Court of the District of Columbia by President Madison, and continued to hold that office until 1863, when the Circuit Court was by an act of Congress abolished. He died in 1870, having attained the age of ninety-five years. For forty-seven years he held the position of a justice of the Circuit Court, and his term of that office was only terminated finally by the act of Congress that abolished the court. During all that time there was no breath upon his purity, no question about his integrity and honor as a man. He lived a simple, unostentatious life, and was beloved and esteemed by all who knew him. At one time in his career, desiring to retire, he determined to resign his office, and so signified to the members of the bar; but such was the expression of regret from all who knew him that he changed his determination and continued to hold his position to the last.

William M. Merrick was appointed one of the justices of the Circuit Court of the District of Columbia December 14, 1855, and served until this court was superseded by the Supreme Court of the District, established by an act of Congress in 1863. Mr. Merrick was born in Charles County, Maryland, in 1818, and received his education in that State. He studied law and was admitted to the bar in Baltimore in 1839. He settled in Frederick in 1844, and was deputy attorney-general for Frederick County in 1845. In 1854 he removed to Washington, and was appointed one of the justices of the Circuit Court for the District. After the abolishment of this court and the establishment of the Supreme Court, Judge Merrick retired to Maryland

and resumed the practice of law. His biographer states of him that
from 1866 to 1867 he was senior professor of law in the Columbian
University of the District of Columbia. He was a member of the
State Constitutional Convention in 1867, was elected to the State legislature in 1870, and was elected a member of the Forty-second Congress. In 1885 he was appointed by President Cleveland an associate
justice of the Supreme Court of the District of Columbia. Through
all his judicial life Judge Merrick was recognized as a learned, careful, and most excellent judge. He was a man of great ability, and a
patient, careful student of the cases coming before him. His sole
aim in this responsible position was to see that justice was done
between man and man.

The *personnel* of the court continued unchanged from the date
of the appointment of Judge Merrick until it ceased to exist in the
manner hereafter described. During this period those great events
occurred which more than once threatened the very existence of the
country and its institutions. It is useless to relate how in the District of Columbia the vicissitudes of the War and the remarkable
events that followed in its tracks were more seriously felt than in
any other portion the Union. All forms of business felt the baleful
effects of the condition of things in the country, and the courts were
never more sorely tried in their efforts to preserve order and maintain
the supremacy of the law. It is not too much to say that the Circuit
Court of the District of Columbia was distinguished in these disastrous times, not only for the good work it did in keeping free from
all taint the dispensation of justice and the enforcement of law, but
in maintaining as it did at all times and under all circumstances the
respect of the entire community in which it exercised its power.

In 1863 Congress determined to make a radical change in the
judicial system that for so many years had existed in the District of
Columbia, and to that end a bill was reported from the Senate
Judiciary Committee, and was with little delay considered in that
body. It will be interesting as part of the history of the courts of
the District to make something more than a mere allusion to the
debate upon the bill, and with that view a brief account of that debate
is here given.

The bill by means of which the change in the courts was to be
effected was introduced into the Senate in February, 1863, was known
as Senate Bill No. 359, and was entitled "An Act to Reorganize the
Courts in the District of Columbia, and for Other Purposes." The
debate upon this bill was exceedingly interesting. The motives of

those favoring the measure were called in question, and the bill was opposed on constitutional grounds.

Mr. Saulsbury, of Delaware, opposed the bill upon the ground that no petition for the substitution of the new court for the old one had been presented by the people of the District, and because he had been informed that the bill met with opposition from every respectable member of the bar of the District. He thought that in the times of change through which the country was then passing, something should be left unchanged, and if anything should be left unchanged, it should be the judiciary system of the country. He could see nothing to be gained from the change, for the new court was to have the same powers as the old, except that the Orphans' Court was to be abolished. The only·object he could see in the attempt to pass the bill was the expulsion of the judges then on the bench.

Mr. Ira Harris, of New York, who had charge of the bill, disclaimed the imputation of being influenced by such motives as had been suggested by Mr. Saulsbury, not only for himself but also for the Judiciary Committee. He said that the judicial system of the District of Columbia was established in 1801, and ever since that time Congress had been patching it until it had made it exceedingly complicated and incongruous; that whenever the change should be made the incumbents of the judgeships would be displaced, and he thought the time most opportune for making the change, as there was then one vacancy, the Criminal Court being without a judge, and one of the other judges was practically superannuated. Besides, if there was a judge of the Circuit Court worthy of being retained, let him be retained. He also said that so far as his knowledge extended, the bar of the District was in favor of the change, and certainly one of the judges to be legislated out of office had, at a public meeting held a year or two before, made a speech advocating the very change then in process of accomplishment. This was all on February 18. On the 20th Mr. Harris had learned that the bar of the District was inclined to acquiesce in the proposed change, provided the Orphans' Court was left undisturbed, and therefore made an amendment providing for this object, which, upon being submitted to the Senate, was rejected.

Mr. Powell, of Kentucky, could see no motive for the proposed change except to get rid of the judges and to substitute partisan judges in their place. He therefore proposed to amend the bill by striking out the first section of the bill, after the enacting clause, and inserting: "That an additional judge be added to the Circuit Court of the District of Columbia," which he thought would test the sincerity of those proposing to establish a Supreme Court.

Mr. Davis, of Kentucky, ventured to assert that if the incumbents of the court proposed to be abolished were Republicans, and a Democrat were in the Presidential chair, the majority of the Republicans in the Senate would never pass the bill to remove, by a mode different from impeachment, but more certain, the incumbents of the offices, and thus open a way for a Democratic President to fill their places. Mr. Davis objected to the removal of these judges on constitutional grounds, and referred to Webster, Calhoun, and Clay as supporting the .position that where an office is filled by a President by and with the consent of the Senate, the President has no power of removal except with the concurrence of the Senate.

Mr. Sumner quoted Chief Justice Marshall in favor of the position that the Circuit Court of the District of Columbia was a legislative court in contradistinction to a constitutional court, that the jurisdiction with which that court was invested was not a part of that judicial power which is defined in the third article of the Constitution, but it was conferred by Congress in the exercise of those general powers which that body possesses over Territorial courts; and that therefore, so far as authority was concerned, Congress had authority to abolish the Circuit Court, and to establish the Supreme Court, as it proposed to do.

Mr. Davis presented a petition against the proposed change, signed by forty-nine of the leading members of the bar of the District of Columbia.

Mr. Harris maintained the same position as that of Mr. Sumner, that the Congress had ample authority to abolish the Circuit Court; that court was not made immortal, as Mr. Davis, of Kentucky, sought to establish.

The bill became a law, by the signature of the President, March 3, 1863. By force of this act the old Circuit Court was abolished, and its judges ceased to hold the offices occupied by them so long and with so much honor. The present Supreme Court of the District of Columbia was also established by this act, and it is deemed best for the proper understanding of its powers and jurisdiction to quote here a few of its sections, as follows:

"There shall be established in the District of Columbia a court to be called the Supreme Court of the District of Columbia, which shall have general jurisdiction in law and equity. It shall consist of four justices, one of whom shall be denominated as chief justice. These justices shall be appointed by the President by and with the advice and consent of the Senate, and shall hold their offices during good behavior. Each justice, before entering upon the duties of his office, shall take the oath prescribed to be taken by judges of the courts of the United States. Any three of said justices may hold a general term, and any one of them may hold a special term or circuit court. The court shall have power to appoint a clerk, and shall possess the same powers and exercise the same jurisdiction as are possessed and exercised by the Circuit Court of the District of Columbia. Any one of said justices may hold a District Court of the United States for the District of Columbia in the same manner and with the same powers and jurisdiction possessed and exercised by other District Courts of the United States. Any one of the justices may hold a criminal court for the trial of all criminals and offenses arising within said District, and such court shall possess the same powers and exercise the same jurisdiction now possessed and exercised by the Criminal Court of the District of Columbia."

Special provisions are made for the regulation of the general and special terms of the court, and for the hearing and trial of causes therein; and an appeal is given from the decision of the special term, where the judgments and orders made at the special terms are to be reviewed and affirmed, revised or modified, as shall be just. The act also confers upon the court power to make rules regulating the time and manner of taking appeals, and authorizes it to establish such other rules as may be deemed necessary for the regulation of the practice in the several courts of the District. The right to have all final judgments, orders, or decrees of the court reëxamined and revised or affirmed in the Supreme Court of the United States is reserved, under certain regulations and conditions, in the same manner as is provided concerning the final judgments, etc., of the Circuit Court of the District of Columbia. By subsequent enactments, this organic act is modified and amended, and the jurisdiction of the court is somewhat enlarged; but for the purposes of this work, the synopsis given seems sufficient.

It will be seen that by this legislation a most radical change was made in the character of the courts, and it will appear presently that an equally radical change was made in the *personnel* of the court.

The President did not retain either of the judges of the old Circuit Court, but appointed David K. Cartter, of Ohio, chief justice, and Abraham B. Olin of New York, Andrew Wylie of the District of Columbia, and George P. Fisher of Delaware, associate justices of the new court.

David K. Cartter was the first chief justice appointed under the act of Congress establishing the Supreme Court of the District of

Columbia. He was born in Ohio, and from 1849 to 1853 was a Representative in Congress from the eighteenth district of that State. He was appointed by President Lincoln minister to Bolivia in 1861, and in 1863 was appointed chief justice of the Supreme Court of the District of Columbia. This office he held until his death, in 1887, a period of twenty-four years.

Chief Justice Cartter was a man of the most remarkable intellectual capacity. His memory was phenomenal. His aim in the trial of cases that came before him was to accomplish what he called substantial justice, and he u-ed his wonderful ability always with the view of bringing about a complete settlement of the causes that he tried. Personally, he was a man of singular attractiveness. His wit and his peculiar methods in the treatment of the causes that came before him will long be remembered by the bench and bar of the District of Columbia, and while it is fairly questionable whether his place in the community was exactly in the judicial line, yet there can be no question that his abilities were such as to fit him for any place he might be called to occupy. He was singularly individual in his character, and not at all times apparently amiable, but even when at times he seemed to be rude and unfriendly, he was eminently kind-hearted.

The successor of Judge Cartter, and the present chief justice of the Supreme Court of the District of Columbia, is Edward F. Bingham, who was appointed by President Cleveland, April 22, 1887. Judge Bingham was one of the State judges of Ohio, and had been for fourteen years when he was selected from that bench to fill the position he now holds. He has been for so short a time chief justice of this court that little can be said except that he has shown himself to be a strictly correct and upright judge. His decisions are manifestly fair, and show a great deal of ability and learning, and there is every reason to apprehend that his career on the bench will be honorable to himself as well as eminently useful to his fellow-citizens.

Abraham B. Olin was born in Shaftesbury, Bennington County, Vermont, in 1812. He graduated from Williams College in 1835' and soon afterward was admitted to the bar and emigrated to the State of New York, spending the rest of his professional life in Troy, in that State. He was for several years recorder of the city of Troy, and was elected to the House of Representatives of the Thirty-fifth, Thirty-sixth, and Thirty-seventh Congresses from the thirteenth district. Upon the organization of the Supreme Court of the District of Columbia, in 1863, he was appointed one of the first justices of that court, and as an evidence of his fitness for the position the degree of Doctor of

Laws was conferred upon him by Union College, at Schenectady, New York. He was a man of great learning and an educated and cultivated lawyer. Personally, Judge Olin was the kindest and most sympathetic of men. He was at all times companionable, and won the affection of all who knew him.

George P. Fisher was born in Milford, Kent County, Delaware, in 1817, and graduated at Dickinson College in 1838. In 1843 and 1844 he was elected to the Delaware House of Representatives, and in 1849 was the confidential clerk of John M. Clayton, then Secretary of State. From 1857 to 1860 he was attorney-general of Delaware, and he was elected to the Thirty-seventh Congress from that State. He was appointed, March 1, 1863, one of the associate justices of the Supreme Court of the District of Columbia, which place he resigned to accept that of district attorney for the District of Columbia, from which position he was removed in 1875.

Andrew Wylie, who was also one of the associate justices of the Supreme Court of the District, was born in Washington County, Pennsylvania, February 25, 1814. His father was president successively of Jefferson and Washington colleges in that county, and Andrew Wylie attended the latter college until he was fifteen years of age. In 1829 his father moved to Bloomington, Indiana, and became president of the State university there, in which institution his son Andrew continued until 1832. For a year or two after this he lived upon his father's farm, and in 1834 entered the Transylvania University, at Lexington, Kentucky, graduating therefrom in 1836. He entered the law office of Walter Forward, who then resided at Pittsburgh, and was afterward Secretary of the Treasury, remaining there a couple of years. About 1840 he was admitted to the bar at Pittsburgh, and practiced law until 1845, most of the time being city solicitor. In 1845 he was married to Miss Caroline Bryan, of Alexandria, Virginia, and in December, 1848, he removed to Washington City, and there began the practice of the law. In January, 1863, Judge Crawford having resigned, he was appointed judge of the Criminal Court, but before he could be confirmed the Supreme Court of the District of Columbia was established, and he was appointed by Mr. Lincoln one of the associate justices of that court, which position he held until 1885, when he retired, as he was entitled under the law to do, and he still lives in the city of Washington in great comfort and elegance, highly respected by all who know him.

David C. Humphreys was born in the State of Tennessee, and received his early education in that State. Upon his arrival at maturity, he pursued the study of law at Nashville, in the office of his uncle, Hon. T. J. Campbell, at one time a Representative in Congress from Tennessee, and the clerk of the House of Representatives from 1847 to 1850. Soon after the completion of his law studies, Mr. Humphreys emigrated to the State of Alabama, and commenced the practice of law in the town of Elyville, now Birmingham, in that State. He was appointed an associate justice of the Supreme Court of the District of Columbia May 13, 1870, and held that position until his death, in June, 1879.

Arthur McArthur was born in Glasgow, Scotland, in 1815, and is a descendant of noble ancestry. He came to this country when very young, and was educated at Amherst, Massachusetts, and at the Wesleyan University, Middletown, Connecticut. He studied law in New York, and was admitted to the bar in 1840. He practiced in New York and in Springfield, Massachusetts, for nine years with marked success. In 1849 he removed to Milwaukee, Wisconsin, commencing the practice of the law in that city, and in a short time attained a high position at the bar. He was elected city attorney, and in 1855 was elected Lieutenant-Governor of the State, and by reason of some defect in the title of the Governor, he served as Governor of Wisconsin for a short time. While he was Lieutenant-Governor he was elected judge of the second judicial circuit of Wisconsin, holding the position six years, and at the end of his term was reëlected, thus serving two terms in that office with honor to himself and to the satisfaction of the people. In 1870 he was appointed by President Grant associate justice of the Supreme Court of the District of Columbia, which position he filled for seventeen years, thus rounding out a period of nearly thirty years upon the bench.

Judge McArthur was recognized as an active, fearless, and consistent judge, and in the performance of the duties of his office was at all times impartial, kind, and considerate. It is owing to his industry that the cases decided in the courts of the District of Columbia are reported in such a way as to be available to the profession. For more than thirty years before Judge McArthur undertook to report the decisions of the courts, no public report had been made of them, whereas now there is only an interval of twenty-two years, from 1841 to 1863, for which there are no reports. During his entire career Judge McArthur has shown great interest in the charitable and educational institutions of the community, having been for many years president of the Humane Society, and having written a work entitled "Education in Relation to Manual Industry." He is also the author of the following works: "A Biography of the English Language from the Earliest Times, with Notices of its Authors, Ancient and Modern"; "An Historical Study of Mary Stuart, Commonly Called Mary, Queen of Scotts, Recounting the Principal Events of Her Life, and Illustrating the Injustice that has been done Her Memory and Character"; "A Series of Twelve Lectures on the Law as Applicable to a Business Education"; and a volume of "Addresses and Papers on Various Subjects." All of these are works of great research, and bear witness to the scholarship and industry of their author. Judge McArthur still lives in the city of Washington, his remarkable vigor and active energy giving promise of many years of usefulness. His family consists of his wife and one son by a former marriage, and he is spending the evening of his days in great comfort, surrounded by a host of friends and in the possession of the esteem of the entire community.

A. B. Hagner was born in the District of Columbia, being a son of Peter Hagner, the first Third Auditor of the Treasury, was graduated from Princeton College in 1845, and was admitted to the bar in Maryland and settled at Annapolis. He was, on one occasion, judge advocate-general of a naval court-martial, and was a special judge in Prince George's County, Maryland, in 1864. He was twice a candidate for Congress, but failed to be elected. He was a Presidential elector in 1871, and in 1879 was appointed, and is to-day, one of the associate justices of the Supreme Court of the District of Columbia.

Walter S. Cox, the son of a lawyer of distinguished ability, was born in Georgetown, and received his education at Georgetown College, taking a degree at that institution in 1843. He studied law at Harvard College, where he graduated in 1847, and was admitted to the bar of the District of Columbia the same year. He commenced practice in the office of his father, and in 1848, his father having died, he succeeded to the entire practice. He was a very successful practitioner, being always distinguished by his great familiarity with the abstruse doctrines of the law relating to real estate. In 1879 he was appointed one of the associate justices of the Supreme Court of the District of Columbia, which position he still holds.

Charles P. James was appointed on the District Bench July 29, 1879, and holds a commission as one of the judges of the Supreme Court of the District of Columbia dating from December 10, 1879, the date of the confirmation of his appointment by the United States Senate. Judge James, in addition to his duties upon the bench, was for four years a professor in the law school of Georgetown College, performing the duties of that position with entire satisfaction. He was born in Ohio, graduated at Harvard University, and commenced the practice of the law in the city of Cincinnati. After several years of successful practice at the bar, he was appointed a judge of the Superior Court of Cincinnati and held that office for several years with great credit to himself and satisfaction to the community. In January, 1864, he came to the city of Washington and entered upon the practice of his profession in the city. He was successful as a practitioner, was engaged in several cases of importance, and was distinguished for those sterling qualities of patience and unassuming industry that are the best guaranties of professional distinction. When Congress determined to create a commission to make a complete revision of the statute law of the United States, Mr. James was appointed one of the commissioners. With that energy and strict attention to the appointed duty before him which has always distinguished him, he entered upon the work of the office to which he was assigned, and the result shows how faithful and industrious he was.

Martin V. Montgomery was born in Eaton Rapids, Michigan, in 1840. He was in the Union Army in 1861, serving in the Second Michigan Cavalry. In 1862 he studied law, and in 1863 was elected clerk of his township. In 1866 he commenced the practice of the law, and was elected a representative in the legislature of his State in 1870. In 1874 he was an unsuccessful candidate for the attorney-generalship of the State, and in 1885 was appointed by President Cleveland Commissioner of Patents at Washington. In 1887 he was appointed one of the associate justices of the Supreme Court of the District of Columbia. He has recently announced to the bar his intention to resign his position on the bench and return to the practice of his profession. This step is sincerely and universally regretted by the bar and the citizens of the District, notwithstanding that it is considered wise on his part. Judge Montgomery will carry with him wherever he goes the kindest wishes of all who know him.

Andrew C. Bradley is a native of the District of Columbia, and belongs to the family of Bradleys which has been for so many years prominently identified with the history of the District. He is a descendant of Phineas Bradley, who was appointed Assistant Post-master-General in 1818. He was educated at the schools of the District, studied law, was admitted to the bar, and for several years was a successful practitioner in its courts. While still a young man he was appointed by President Harrison an associate justice of the Supreme Court of the District of Columbia, which position he still retains.

The Criminal Court of the District of Columbia was established in 1838, previous to which time criminal jurisdiction had been exercised by the Circuit Court. Thomas F. Mason was the first judge of the Criminal Court, holding the position, however, only a short time. James Dunlop was the second judge of this court, serving in this capacity from 1839 to 1845. He was succeeded by Thomas Hartley Crawford, who was born in Chambersburg, Pennsylvania, in 1786, and graduated in 1804, studied law and was admitted to the bar in 1807. He served as a Representative in Congress from Pennsylvania from 1829 to 1833. In 1836 he was a commissioner to investigate certain alleged frauds in the purchase of lands from the Creek Indians, and in 1838 was appointed by President Van Buren Commissioner of Indian Affairs, and took up his residence in Washington, holding the office for seven years. In 1845 he was appointed by President Polk judge of the Criminal Court of the District of Columbia, which position he held until his death. He was a man of distinguished ability, and during his occupancy of the position of judge of the Criminal Court of the District tried several of the most important cases that ever came before any criminal court in the United States. He was a patient, careful, consistent judge, and was distinguished for his devotion to the work imposed upon him by the position he held.

In addition to these two courts already mentioned, there was created by Congress the Police Court for the District of Columbia, consisting of one judge. This court, under the act creating it, was restricted in its jurisdiction, but was clothed with power to hear and determine a large number of cases that otherwise would have had to be tried in the Supreme Court of the District. Within the past few years the business of this court has increased to such an extent that Congress has authorized another judge, so that now there are two judges of this court. One of these judges is Thomas F. Miller, the other being Irving G. Kimball.

The courts of the District of Columbia have been the arena of so many remarkable trials that any history of these courts will be incomplete without some account of the great causes that have been considered and adjudicated before them. It will not be out of place, therefore, to give a brief account of the trials referred to as a part of this history.

Richard Lawrence made an attack, January 30, 1835, upon the life of Andrew Jackson, President of the United States, snapping two pistols at him, both of which failed to explode. President Jackson was at the time coming out of the rotunda of the Capitol, having attended

47

the funeral of Warren R. Davis, a member of Congress. Lawrence was arrested and put upon trial for his crime, the punishment for which could only extend to fine and imprisonment, if found guilty. An attempt was made before the grand jury to prove his insanity, to which the District attorney objected. The jury therefore asked for the opinion and instructions of the court, Judge Cranch being then chief justice of the Circuit Court. Judge Cranch delivered the opinion of the court on this question, to the effect that every person was presumed in law to be sane until the contrary was proved, and hence it was unnecessary to summon witnesses to prove the sanity of the accused. The prisoner should wait for that until he should be put upon his trial. Quoting from Chief Justice McKean, in Schaffer's case, he said: "If, then, you undertake to inquire, not only upon what ground the charge is made, but also upon what it is denied, you will in effect usurp the jurisdiction of the petit jury. You will supersede the legal authority of the court in judging of the competency and inadmissibility of witnesses, and having thus undertaken to try the question, that question may be determined upon by a bare majority, or by a much greater number of your body than twelve peers prescribed by the law of the land," etc.

W. L. Brent & Son were the attorneys for the defense. February 5, 1835, they made application to the court for the issuance of a writ of *habeas corpus* upon the ground of the prisoner's insanity, and on the 14th of the month the petition was refused, because the judge was of the opinion that a writ of *habeas corpus* was not to be granted upon application merely; it was not to be awarded without some reasonable ground shown by affidavit, and that if a prisoner were a dangerous maniac the only way in which he could insure the safety of the public was to remand him to the prison in which he was confined; and were that done, his imprisonment would be interminable; he would have no day in court, no means to compel a trial, etc.

The case came on for trial April 11, 1835, before Judge Cranch, of the Circuit Court, the indictment being for an assault upon Andrew Jackson, President of the United States, with intent to kill and murder him. It was shown to the satisfaction of the jury that the defendant was really insane, in that he supposed himself to be the King of England and also of the United States, the United States being in his view an appendage of England, and that Andrew Jackson was in his way in the enjoyment of his right; and that the assault upon the President was done under that delusion. The jury, after five minutes' deliberation, brought in the following verdict: "We find the prisoner not guilty, he being under the influence of insanity at the time he committed the act." The court remanded the prisoner, being of the opinion from the evidence that it would be extremely dangerous for him to be at large while under such mental illusion.

Richard H. White was accused of setting fire to the Treasury building March 30, 1833, and was indicted and tried for this crime March 30, 1836. Brent & Brent were his attorneys, the attorney for the prosecution being J. R. Key. White's attorneys moved that the indictment be quashed, on the ground that more than two years had elapsed between the burning of the Treasury and the finding of the indictment, and pleaded the act of Congress of April 30, 1790, to the effect that no person should be prosecuted, tried, or punished for any offense not capital, nor for any fine or forfeiture under any penal statute, unless the indictment or information for the same should be found or instituted within two years from the time of the committing of the offense or incurring the fine or forfeiture; "*Provided*, that nothing in said statute contained should extend to any person fleeing from justice."

The court refused to quash the indictment, because, until the fact should appear upon the trial, it could not be certain that the person was not one fleeing from justice, and the case came before the court and jury for trial.

After a pretty full hearing of the case, the jury retired on Saturday, December 24, 1836, and were kept in their room until the 27th, when they were discharged because they could not agree.

A second trial commenced on January 6, 1837, and the case was given to the jury on the 13th of that month. The verdict this time was that the defendant was guilty of burning the Treasury, but that he was acquitted on the plea of limitation. This not being a formal verdict, it was agreed that the District attorney and the counsel for the defense should each submit to the jury such form of verdict as they supposed would be conformable to the intention of the jury. This was done, and the jury then returned their verdict in the following form: "We, the jury, are of the opinion that the offense as charged was committed by the prisoner, and we find him not guilty upon the plea of limitations, more than two years having elapsed from the committing of the offense to the finding of the indictment."

J. R. Key, for the United States, then moved for a *venire de novo*, which, after argument, was awarded by Chief Justice Cranch.

The cause then came up for trial at the March term, 1837, with the same counsel as before. The jury, on April 29, failed to agree and were discharged. At the November term, 1837, the court quashed the indictment. Mr. Key, for the United States, sent up another indictment to the grand jury, the prisoner not being discharged, but being permitted to go at large on the old recognizance. The case was continued until the next term, when it was argued by Key for the United States, and by the Messrs. Brent for the defense, from the 8th to the 13th of June, and on the 14th the jury gave the following verdict: "We find for the defendant on the plea of limitations, not guilty," and he was discharged.

The Gardiner case, as it is called, was in substance as follows: It is well known that by the treaty of Gaudalupe Hidalgo a board of commissioners was provided for which had for its duty the adjudication of claims of citizens of the United States against Mexico. Dr. George A. Gardiner brought a claim against the United States on the ground that he had purchased a valuable mine in the State of San Luis Potosi, paying therefor $330,392, which he was working, and making in gross $20,000 per month, his expenses being from $10,000 to $12,000 per month, and that on the 21st of October, 1846, he was ordered out of Mexico by the Mexican authorities, and thus the value of his property, which he placed at $500,000, was entirely destroyed. He presented evidence to the board of commissioners in the shape of authenticated documents showing his ownership of the mines, and in November, 1850, presented additional testimony at the request of the board, this additional testimony consisting of a copy of his mining title taken from the book of registry of mines in the office of the prefect of Rio Verde, sustained by affidavits.

It was subsequently discovered that all of his alleged testimony was manufactured, and he was indicted for perjury on July 19, 1851. Dr. Gardiner fled to England, but returned, in accordance with an arrangement that he should be admitted to bail in the sum of $20,000, this money to be a part of that which he had obtained from the Government on his alleged title to money from the Government on his claim. The indictment was in accordance with an act of Congress passed March 1, 1823, section 3 of that act being as follows:

"That if any person shall swear or affirm falsely touching the expenditure of public money, or in support of any claim against the United States, he or she shall, upon conviction therefor, suffer as for wilful and corrupt perjury."

The United States District attorney at that time was Philip R. Fendall, and in the prosecution he was assisted by Henry May. The attorneys for the defense were Joseph H. Bradley and J. M. Carlisle.

The District attorney said that the evidence presented was designed to establish four points:

1. That Dr. Gardiner had large mines.

2. That he was personally present at his alleged mines in Lagunillas through the term of his mining operations.

3. That the alleged mines existed, and were of great value.

4. That he was the owner of these mines.

And that if the falsity of any one of these propositions was proven, then the defendant was guilty. The District attorney then went on to prove that every one of the four propositions was false.

The case or trial commenced on March 11, 1853, and was given to the jury May 20, following. The jury came into court on the 28th of the month unable to agree, and were discharged.

The original award to Dr. Gardiner was $428,000. Gardiner paid his counsel one-fourth of this sum, and sold one-fourth for $22,000. Thus $214,000 of the award remained, together with the $22,000 received for one-fourth, making in all $236,000, as the net amount received by Dr. Gardiner. The Government attached $220,000 or $230,000 of this amount, leaving him only $16,000 or $6,000 as his share, according to which amount the Government attached.

After the disagreement of the jury, a new trial was ordered and a commission appointed to visit Mexico. Henry May was placed at the head of the commission, and nearly a year elapsed before the second trial commenced. During the progress of the second trial, and just before the cross-examination of J. Charles Gardiner, or I. Carlos Gardiner, as he was called, began, Henry May left the court room and soon returned with a tin box, and, opening it, produced a letter from I. Carlos Gardiner to his brother, George A. Gardiner, containing the most conclusive evidence of the fraud. The witness, though admitting that the handwriting looked like his, would not admit that it was his. Mr. May then proceeded to unfold the most extraordinary story of fraud, forgery, and perjury that was ever heard in any court, astonishing every one who heard it, and at the same time also completely establishing the guilt of the accused. The case being given to the jury, they soon returned with a verdict of "Guilty." Dr. Gardiner thereupon took something out of his vest pocket, put it in his mouth, and asked for a drink of water, and upon reaching the rail, fell in a fit at the entrance. While stoutly denying that he had taken poison, he died in about an hour's time. This act of suicide was in accord with the determination frequently expressed on his part never to suffer any sentence the court might pronounce.

Philemon T. Herbert, Representative in Congress from California, shot and killed Thomas Keating, a waiter in Willard's Hotel, May 8, 1856. Mr. Herbert was arrested and placed in jail. Philip Barton Key was District attorney at the time, and the counsel for the prisoner were Joseph H. Bradley, Hon. John B. Weller, Hon. Percy Walker, and Hon. Philip Phillips. His counsel immediately procured a writ of *habeas corpus*, and brought the prisoner before Judge Crawford on Saturday, the judge withholding his decision as to the granting of the writ until Monday, when he decided "that a conviction for murder should not take place," and that the prisoner should be admitted to bail in the sum of $10,000 to answer to a charge of manslaughter. July 2, the grand jury made a presentment for murder against the accused, and he was forthwith arrested and placed in jail, the trial being set for July 9. The trial commenced on the 10th, with Bradley and Walker, assisted by Daniel Ratcliffe, for the defense. After a careful trial the jury failed to agree, and a new trial was had, occupying from the 17th to the 25th of that month. In this second trial the prosecution was assisted by William P. Preston, of Baltimore, the counsel for the defense being the same as before. The evidence showed that Herbert came into the dining-room of the hotel late, and in a rough manner ordered a servant to get his breakfast, which order was executed only in part; and that he thereupon ordered Keating to assist the other waiter in getting his breakfast, which Keating refused to do, as one waiter was enough. This made Herbert very angry, and he drew his pistol and advanced upon Keating with the apparent intention of shooting him, but withdrew without doing so. Immediately after, a quarrel arose over the matter, and a number of persons made an attack upon Herbert, who then fired, killing Keating. The instructions to the jury were to this effect: That "if the jury believed from the evidence that at the time the pistol was fired Herbert was being pressed by superior numbers, and was in danger of death or of serious bodily harm, from which he could not safely escape, he was justified in taking life." The jury retired at 8:00 P. M., and in an hour returned with a verdict of acquittal.

February 27, 1859, Philip Barton Key, United States District attorney for the District of Columbia, was shot by the Hon. Daniel E. Sickles, a Representative in Congress from New York City, at the corner of Pennsylvania Avenue and Lafayette Square. Sickles charged a criminal intimacy between Key and his wife, Mrs. Sickles, and meeting Key at the place indicated, in broad day, and without warning to Key, shot and killed him. Sickles was immediately committed to prison to await the action of the grand jury. On the 7th of March the death of Key was announced to the Criminal Court, of which Thomas H. Crawford was judge, by Robert Ould, who had been appointed by the President to succeed Key as attorney for the District. On March 24, 1859, the indictment was presented to the court, it being for murder. The attorneys for Mr. Sickles were E. M. Stanton, since Secretary of War, Chilton & Magruder, and Daniel Ratcliffe. The trial was set for Monday, April 4, and commenced that day, the prosecution being assisted by J. M. Carlisle. After a trial lasting twenty days, closing April 26, the jury, after being out one hour and ten minutes, brought in a verdict of "Not guilty." Sickles afterward became distinguished as an officer of the army, and held many places of trust and honor. He still lives, and is highly esteemed by those who know him best.

Every incident connected with the assassination of President Lincoln has passed into history, and has become familiar to every American citizen. John H. Surratt was charged with being an accomplice of Booth, the assassin, and an aider and abetter in his infamous crime. It was known that he had been in the city during all the day of the murder; that the conspiracy, of which the crime was the result, was concocted in the house of Mrs. Surratt, his mother; and that he, John H. Surratt, was with Booth up to the very moment before the fatal shot. Again, it appeared that immediately after the murder of the President, Surratt had fled the city. He was traced to Canada, and again to Italy, where he was found enlisted among the soldiers of the Pope. Here he was arrested, but escaped to Egypt; was again arrested, finally brought to this country, and an indictment for murder was found against him by the grand jury for the District of Columbia. On the 10th of June, 1867, his trial commenced before the Criminal Court (the Supreme Court of the District of Columbia in special term as a criminal court) of the District of Columbia, with Justice George P. Fisher presiding. The United States was represented by E. C. Cunington, the District attorney, and Nathaniel P. Wilson, his assistant, and associate counsel Messrs. Edwards Pierrepont and A. G. Riddle, and the prisoner by Joseph H. Bradley, R. T. Merrick, and Joseph H. Bradley, Jr. A jury was finally obtained on the 18th of June, 1867, and the trial was proceeded with. A great many witnesses were examined on both sides, and many interesting questions were discussed. On Wednesday, August 7, 1867, the case was given to the jury, and on Saturday, August 10, the jury, being unable to agree upon a verdict, were discharged.

Hallet Kilbourn, a gentleman engaged in business in the city of Washington, was submitted to an experience in the courts so remarkable as to make his case one of the most noted in our judicial history.

In the month of January, 1876, a committee was appointed by the House of Representatives to investigate certain matters growing out of the failure of Jay Cooke & Company, in which it was alleged that Jay Cooke, McCulloch, & Company, of London, were indebted to the country on account of some advances made by the Secretary of the Navy just prior to their failure. It was alleged by the committee that Kilbourn & Latta, real-estate brokers of Washington, had invested money for Jay Cooke & Company and others in real estate, in Washington, in what was designated as the "real-estate pool," and the committee subpœnaed Mr. Hallet Kilbourn, of that firm, to come before it, and bring with him the books and papers of that firm for the inspection of the committee, and to testify in relation to the same. Mr. Kilbourn appeared before the committee, but declined to testify or produce the books and papers of the firm for the committee's inspection, asserting under oath that the business of their firm was in no way connected with the Government; that their transactions with Jay Cooke & Company had been fully settled, and maintaining that the committee had no right to investigate and publish their private business affairs to the world.

The committee thereupon reported Mr. Kilbourn to the House as in contempt, and on the 14th of March, 1876, the House ordered the sergeant-at-arms, John G. Thompson, to arrest and bring him before the bar of the House. This order was promptly executed, and in response to the Speaker, asking him if he still declined to comply with the commands of the committee, Mr. Kilbourn answered affirmatively, whereupon the House passed a resolution directing the sergeant-at-arms to confine Mr. Kilbourn in the common jail of the District of Columbia until he should purge himself of contempt by agreeing to comply with the demands of the investigating committee.

Mr. Kilbourn remained in jail five weeks, when he was brought before Chief Justice Cartter, of the District Court, on a writ of *habeas corpus* (the sergeant-at-arms having been directed by the House, after three days' discussion in that body, by a vote of 165 to 75, to obey the writ), and after several days' argument by attorneys for the Government and Mr. Kilbourn, he was discharged from custody by the order of the Chief Justice, April 28.

In August, 1876, Mr. Kilbourn brought suit against Sergeant-at-arms Thompson and others for false imprisonment. A majority of the court of the District in March, 1877, decided against Mr. Kilbourn's right of action, from which decision he appealed to the Supreme Court of the United States.

The Supreme Court, in January, 1881, by a unanimous opinion, decided that the action of the House of Representatives, in ordering the arrest and imprisonment of Mr. Kilbourn, was without law, and void, and sustained his action against Sergeant-at-arms Thompson, and remanded the case back to the court of the District for trial by jury to assess the amount of damages.

The first jury trial was had in April, 1882, before Judge McArthur, in which a verdict of $100,000 was rendered, which was set aside by the judge as excessive.

The second jury trial took place in November, 1883, before Judge Cox, the jury returning a verdict of $60,000 damages, which the judge set aside as excessive.

The third jury trial was held in March, 1884, before Judge Hagner, the jury rendering a verdict for $37,500 damages, which the judge reduced to $20,000, and this latter sum, with interest, was appropriated by Congress on March 4, 1885.

The attorneys who at different periods represented the Government in this long contested case were S. S. Shellabarger, Robert I. Christy, Judge William Merrick, W. H. Trescott, H. W. Garnett, Hon. Frank Hurd, Walter E. Smith, District Attorney Corkhill and Assistant Coyle, District Attorney Worthington, and Shellabarger & Wilson.

Those appearing for Mr. Kilbourn were Judge Jeremiah S. Black, Matthew H. Carpenter, General N. L. Jeffries, Hon. D. W. Voorhees, Enoch Totten, C. A. Eldridge, and W. D. Davidge.

On Saturday, July 2, 1881, as President Garfield was passing through the ladies' room of the Baltimore and Potomac Depot, at the corner of B and Sixth streets, in Washington City, Charles J. Guiteau, without provocation of any kind, fired two shots at him from a heavy revolver, the last proving fatal. The President lingered in great suffering, and died September 19, 1881. October 8, the grand jury found a true bill against Guiteau for the murder of James A. Garfield, President of the United States, and on the 11th of the month a copy of the indictment was served upon him. On the 14th of October Guiteau was brought into court and arraigned for the murder of the President, and pleaded not guilty, his defense being threefold:

1. Insanity, in that it was God's act, and not his; the divine

pressure on him to remove the President being so great that it destroyed his free agency, and therefore he was not legally responsible for his act.

2. The President died from malpractice. If he had been well treated, he would have recovered.

3. The President died in New Jersey, beyond the jurisdiction of the court. The malpractice and the President's death in New Jersey were special providences, and he was bound to avail himself of them in justice to the Lord and himself.

The trial commenced November 14, 1881, the District attorney, Hon. George B. Corkhill, Judge Porter of New York, and Mr. Walter D. Davidge of Washington representing the Government in the prosecution; Mr. Leigh Robinson,[1] of Washington, assigned by the court, and George Scoville and Charles Reed, of Chicago, being the counsel for the defense; Judge Walter S. Cox, of Washington, upon the bench. The defense of the prisoner was that he was insane, he contending that if he had shot the President on his own personal account, no punishment could be too severe, or could come too quickly; but that he was acting as the agent of the Deity, which put an entirely different construction upon the matter, and that he wished to put to the court, to the jury, and to the opposing counsel this condition of things. That was the idea he wanted them to entertain, and not to settle down on the cold-blooded idea that it was murder, because he never had the first conception of murder in the matter. He had killed the President because he had proved a traitor to the men that had made him President, etc.

After a long trial, the incidents of which are most remarkable and well known, on January 20, 1882, Mr. Scoville having finished his speech, which had consumed five days, the case went to the jury, who in a short time returned with a verdict of "Guilty, as charged in the indictment." A new trial was refused, and the prisoner was sentenced to be hanged June 30, 1882.

The Star Route cases, as they are called, were in many respects more worthy of notice than any that have ever taken place in the courts of our country. There was, in fact, but one case, except that there were a number of defendants, the charges against whom were several and distinct in their character, involving the consideration of different facts and requiring different verdicts, but they all proceeded at one time and were submitted to and decided by one jury.

---

[1] Mr. Robinson, finding it impossible to attend to the case, withdrew almost at the outset of the trial.

George Bliss, Esq., in his opening address to the jury, speaking of the importance of the case, uses the following language:

"In the view of the Government, by the fraudulent action of the defendants, more than $600,000 have been fraudulently taken from the treasury of the United States without any adequate return being made for it, and without any necessity for its being so taken on public grounds. It [the case] is important, too, from the former position of the parties involved. One of the parties was formerly Second Assistant Postmaster-General of the United States, and as such, was by virtue of his office charged with the reputation, and the management, and the control of the entire mail service of the United States so far as it relates to the transportation of the mails, and having under his care practically the disbursement of, I think, about $16,-000,000 a year. Another of the defendants was an Ex-United States Senator from the State of Arkansas."

Mr. Bliss, speaking further, and by way of explaining the term "star route," says:

"Section 3949 of the Revised Statutes provides that 'all contracts for carrying the mail shall be in the name of the United States,' and shall be awarded to the lowest bidder tendering sufficient guaranty for faithful performances, without other reference to the mode of transportation than may be necessary to provide for the due *celerity, certainty, and security* thereof.

"And here let me say, gentlemen, you hear a great deal of star route prosecution and of star routes. It is in this section, which is a reënactment of an act passed in 1845, that that phraseology has its origin. The phrase as used was 'celerity, certainty, and security.' This statute made a change from a practice which prevailed before, authorizing regard to be had to the conveyances in which the mails were to be transported, etc., and it declared that the only element was celerity, certainty, and security, and on the post-office records, when they came to designate the routes under the statute, they put three stars against them instead of writing out the orders, as representing the words 'celerity, certainty, and security.' That is the origin of the phrase 'star routes,' as I understand it."

In these cases the defendants were John W. Dorsey, John R. Miner, John M. Peck, Stephen W. Dorsey, Harvey M. Vaile, Montfort C. Reredell, Thomas J. Bradley, and William H. Turner. The first proceeding in the case was by information which was quashed by the court. Indictments were then found against the several defendants for conspiracy to defraud the Government in certain mail contracts. The United States was represented by George B. Cork-hill, United States attorney for the District of Columbia, who had associated with him George Bliss, of New York, R. T. Merrick, and W. W. Ker. The defense had for their counsel Messrs. Shellabarger & Wilson, Jeff Chandler, Enoch Totten, A. B. Williams, Robert G. Ingersoll, Judge Carpenter, C. C. Cole, Mr. Wiltshire, John McSweeney, L. G. Hine, S. S. Henkle, and Walter D. Davidge. The first trial commenced June 1, 1882, Mr. Justice Wylie presiding, and terminated September 11, 1882. The jury by their verdict found M. C. Reredell and John R. Miner guilty, John M. Peck and William H. Turner not guilty, and as to J. W. and S. W. Dorsey, Harvey M. Vaile, and Thomas H. Brady they could not agree. The case was tried again by the same justice, commencing December 7, 1882, the same counsel appearing, with one or two exceptions, and a verdict was rendered June 14, 1883, by which all the defendants were acquitted.

It will appear from a glance at the history of the courts of the District of Columbia that, while those courts have been, during the whole period of that history, presided over by judges eminent for their ability, fidelity, and learning, the lawyers who have practiced therein, and have formed the bar of those courts, have been equally distinguished for that talent and industry at all times so essential as an aid to the courts. The bar of the District of Columbia (and in this connection reference is made to the local bar, and not to that large number of eminent lawyers who come to the courts of the District in special cases) has always been distinguished for the high character and great learning of the men who composed it. It will not be amiss to mention a few of the men who, in past times, have admittedly held the highest places at the District bar, and who have illustrated the character heretofore claimed for that bar. In making this mention, which necessarily must be confined to a comparative few, no discrimination against any whose names are omitted is intended, and there can be no room for the feeling that anyone has been forgotten. The necessity of the case and the need of brevity in the mention made of men who, if properly treated, were worthy each of a full biography must be carefully considered and acknowledged.

Preëminent among the members of the early bar, and unequaled throughout its whole history, was Walter Jones. While he was in fact a member of the local bar of the District, he ranked among the greatest lawyers in the whole country and was the peer of any who adorned the day in which he lived, among them Binney, Sargeant, Pinckney, Wirt, Taney, Webster, and Reverdy Johnson. Except that he was born in Virginia and secured his education in that State, commenced the practice of law in Alexandria, and from there came to the city of Washington, the writer knows very little concerning the early life of the great lawyer. He was an omnivorous reader, and had the faculty of so assimilating what he read that his acquirements were always at his command and ever ready for use. In every branch of the profession he was most accomplished. So remarkable was his knowledge of the rules of common law pleading that the papers prepared by him in some of the cases in which he was engaged as counsel are bodily copied into reports as examples of excellence. Unequaled in the close reasoning which distinguished his argument at the bar, he was at the same time so powerful in his use of facts as to be a most formidable adversary before a jury, and in his examination of witnesses his knowledge of men was manifested in a manner most wonderful. Somehow he managed to throw an interest about the case which he tried most peculiar in its kind and not always observable. Perhaps his most distinguishing characteristic was his power of statement. It could be said of him, as it has been said of other great lawyers, that his statement of a case was worth the argument of twenty other men. Every lawyer knows how to appreciate and value the possessor of this power to state a case so clearly.

The only public office he is known to have held was that of general in the militia of the District of Columbia, and he was always addressed as General Jones. Like many other men of his character, he lacked the faculty of taking care of the money that he made by his professional labors, and though his fees must have been at times quite large, he lived and died comparatively poor. Such a man could not fail to be eccentric, and this, combined with his constant occupation in the great cases in which he was engaged, made him somewhat of a recluse and kept him away from familiar intercourse with his fellow-men. He was so warmly admired and esteemed, however, that his memory is cherished by all who knew him with a feeling akin to affection.

Francis S. Key, whose fame would seem to rest most upon his authorship of the famous patriotic song so dear to every American heart, was nevertheless a very distinguished lawyer, and for many years held the very highest positions at the bar of the District of Columbia. He was a man of great brilliancy of intellect, and was a ready and powerful debater. For many years he was the attorney for the United States for the District of Columbia, and as such was engaged in several cases of the greatest importance. President Jackson manifested for him at all times the sincerest respect and esteem, and gave freely to him of his confidence and friendship. After living for many years in the District, he removed to Baltimore, but while he became a leading member of the Maryland bar, he gained his earliest laurels at the bar of the District of Columbia, where he was long and well remembered.

William L. Brent was born in Maryland, from which State he emigrated to Louisiana, and from there was sent to the Congress of the United States, serving in the House of Representatives from 1823 to 1829. At the end of his service in Congress he settled in the city of Washington, and commenced the practice of the law. The records of the the courts and the reports of the cases tried before them show that his practice was extensive and important. At one time his name appeared in almost every case of importance, and it is concluded that he bore himself so as to merit the favor shown him.

It is impossible in the brief space allotted in this work to do justice to the abilities, character, and acquirements of such a man as Philip Richard Fendall. He was born in Alexandria, Virginia, in 1794, after the cession of the part of the State in which that city was situated to the General Government for the purposes of the Capital City, and so he can be well considered a native of the District of Columbia. In 1815 he graduated at Princeton, in New Jersey, and in 1820 was admitted to the bar of Alexandria, and a few years later came to the city of Washington to live. Mr. Fendall, from the beginning of his career, was distinguished for that intellectual excellence which comes from faithful mental training and culture. No man was more exact in his knowledge, more careful and reliable in his statement about every subject to which he addressed himself. He first attracted attention by his writings on literary and political topics, and several of his essays were recognized as deserving of great distinction for the beauty of the style in which they were clothed and the depth of thought and power of reason which they displayed.

But though Mr. Fendall, through his long life, always manifested a love for the charms of literary culture, he was seriously devoted to the sterner duties of his profession with his whole mind and soul. Professional distinction came more slowly, but it came all the more truly. He was a painstaking, most careful, laborious, and industrious lawyer, and it was not long before those who knew how to value such qualities sought his counsel and professional assistance. We do not mean to dwell upon the professional career of Mr. Fendall. The best evidence of his success as a lawyer is to be found in the fact that he filled the office of United States attorney for the District of

Columbia from 1841 to 1845, and again from 1849 to 1853, and that during the period in which he held that office he prosecuted successfully some of the most important cases that ever came before the courts of the United States. It was somewhat remarkable that in all and through all the active scenes of his professional career Mr. Fendall should have preserved his scholarly character as completely as he did. In all of his arguments to the court, in all of his speeches to the jury, this peculiar characteristic was ever a striking feature, and he was at all times remarkable not only for the beauty and completeness of the style of his efforts, but for the charm of his manner as an orator. After a most honorable career, he died in 1868. The city manifested its grief for his loss in a pronounced demonstration, and the courts and the bar paid his memory the fullest honors. He was preëminently devoted to his family, some of whom survive to-day, and it is manifest that his talents, his excellencies, and his virtues have been inherited by those who are now treading in his footsteps.

Richard S. Coxe, who came to the city of Washington from the State of New Jersey, brought with him from that State a reputation for considerable eminence already acquired. He had reported some of the decisions of the courts of that State, and had compiled and published a general digest, which was recognized as authority of the very highest character. Nothing more was wanted than these achievements to show that he was thoroughly equipped for the work of an active practitioner of the profession of his choice. But his studies were not confined to the law; he had devoted himself so assiduously to the study of the literature of our language that he had become the author of a work called "A Dictionary of the English Language, by an American Gentleman," which at the time of its publication, and long afterward, was esteemed authority of the very highest character. Those who remember him, and who associated with him in his best days, cannot fail to recall his wonderful familiarity with the writings of the best of our English classics. But these were merely accomplishments; the reputation of Mr. Coxe was based upon more substantial acquirements. No one excelled him in his excellence as a lawyer in any way, and the best proof of this is to be found in the fact that it was said of him, at one time, that he was employed in more cases upon the docket of the Supreme Court of the United States than any other lawyer in the United States. It was in such a forum as the Supreme Court that his talents were best exhibited and appreciated. The very facility which his early training had given him in the use of the English language, served him a great purpose in the court, and his arguments gained new strength from the fact that they were always clothed in such pure and beautiful English. Through a long life Mr. Coxe was always distinguished as a lawyer, and died in Washington greatly esteemed and respected.

For nearly fifty years Joseph H. Bradley was engaged in the active practice of law in the courts of the District of Columbia, and was most of that time admittedly one of the leading members of the bar. It would have been difficult at any time during his attention to active practice to have found anywhere in the country a better trial lawyer than Mr. Bradley. What distinguished Mr. Bradley in his practice was his entire devotion to the interest of the client whose cause he undertook. Everything else was forgotten by him for the time being, and every energy, talent, and capacity he possessed were devoted to the matter in hand. He worked and toiled early and late for his client; he left nothing undone that could be done in his cause; no expedient was left untried. Indeed, so earnest was he always that, if need be, he was ready to make his client's case his own personal quarrel, and it took very little to make him fight for him, if need be.

Fortunately, he was a man of wonderful physical capacity, else the constant strain upon him of an immense practice, so full of toil and care as he made it, would have insured an early death. It was very fortunate, too, that Mr. Bradley was blessed with a fund of good spirits, a buoyant disposition, and a self-reliance that always stood him in good stead through the changes of a life full of activity and never-ending variety. He never held a public office, but was more than once urged by the members of the bar and his fellow-citizens for a position upon the bench, and at one time he probably would have accepted it, but he was not selected by the power having the appointment, and he died as he had lived, in private station. During his whole life he was an idol of the public, and his death was most seriously mourned.

James Mandeville Carlisle was the contemporary of Mr. Bradley, and the two not only stood for many years side by side in their position at the bar, but for many years their names appeared upon one side or the other of every case of importance that came before the courts of the District. Born in Alexandria while it was a part of the District of Columbia, he came to the city of Washington when a mere boy and really had no other home. Mr. Carlisle may be said to have been a self-made man, and all that he was and all that he became were the results of his own application and determination. He made himself an excellent classical scholar, and was always noted

for his familiarity with the Latin authors, he acquired the French and Spanish languages so that he not only spoke them with ease, but what is very rare, wrote them with great facility and correctness. His education as a lawyer was acquired in the offices of William Wirt and Richard A. Coxe, and he came to the bar at a very early age. It is rare to find so many of the good qualities of a lawyer combined as presented themselves in Mr. Carlisle's character. Everything he touched he adorned. Bright, witty, magnetic, he won the hearts of all with whom he came in contact. Before the court, dealing with nice questions and construing the authorities that sustained and strengthened his arguments, and before the jury, demonstrating the strength of the facts that he arrayed before them, he was alike excellent. For many years his practice was almost confined to the Supreme Court, and it is not saying too much to say that no lawyer ever more completely won and held the esteem, confidence, and respect of that great court than did Mr. Carlisle. Through nearly the whole of his professional career he was the retained counsel of several of the embassies to this country from foreign courts, and was thoroughly competent for the service required of him in that department of his practice. As a man he had those manners and qualities that always win friendship and admiration. To young men he was particularly gracious and kind, and many a tyro has gained courage and consolation at a kind word from him at a moment when it seemed as if he must resign all expectation of professional success. Of course such a man must be popular, and he was, until the latest hour of his life, beloved by his fellow-citizens of all classes.[1]

---

[1] Mr. Carlisle was particularly clever in clothing in prose or verse some witty thought that occurred to him in the course of an argument or trial at the bar, and not unfrequently he created great amusement by giving to what was else very grave and uninteresting an amusing aspect. As an example of this happy talent, the following may be given by way of illustration. One day, in the Supreme Court of the United States, a case involving in some way the Cliquot champagne was under argument. A Mr. Eaton being of counsel, and it is presumed rather uninteresting in his presentation of his case, Mr. Carlisle wrote upon a slip of paper the following amusing epigram:

> "The widow Cliquot, oh ho! oh ho!
> The widow Cliquot, oh! ho!
> We're all of us thinkin'
> Right good is your drinkin',
> But really your Eatin' so! so! so! so!
> But really your Eatin' so! so!"

The slip of paper upon which this was written was afterwards found among some papers sent to the clerk of the court by Chief Justice Taney, who had evidently taken it home with him to enjoy it at his leisure.

48

Henry May, son of Dr. Frederick May, was born in Washington, and received a classical education. He studied law in the office of General Walter Jones, was admitted to the bar, and attained a high rank in the profession. Among the important cases in which he appeared was the trial of George Gardiner for forging a Mexican mine claim. In this case he was employed for the Government by Daniel Webster, then Secretary of State. He removed to Baltimore in 1850, was elected to Congress as a Democrat in 1854, and was reëlected in 1860. Although he was a Union man, he advocated compromise measures on the prospect of civil war, and in 1861, with the sanction of President Lincoln, left his seat in Congress and visited Richmond, to confer with Confederate authorities on peace measures. During his absence an effort was made to expel him from the House on the charge of disloyalty, and on his return he was for several weeks imprisoned in Fort Lafayette. He was subsequently released on parole, and completed his term in the House of Representatives. He died September 25, 1866, in the city of Baltimore, which he had adopted as his home, leaving many friends in the city of Washington who remember his many excellent qualities as a man and his brilliancy as a lawyer and advocate.

William B. Webb was born in the city of Washington September 17, 1825; received his early education at the private schools of Washington and at a boarding-school near Baltimore; in 1840 he entered the freshman class at Columbia College, now Columbian University, at Washington, and graduated in 1844, taking the degree of Bachelor of Arts from that institution, which afterward bestowed upon him the degree of Master of Arts. He studied law and was admitted to the bar of the District of Columbia in 1847, and commenced the practice of his chosen profession in his native city. On the breaking out of the War in 1861, he was elected captain of a company of volunteers, and offered the services of himself and his company to the Government, but there being no organization of troops at the time to which his company could be assigned, his offer was not accepted. In the fall of 1861, upon the formation of the metropolitan police for the District of Columbia, he was elected by the board of police superintendent of the force, which office he accepted. After successfully organizing the force, he resigned his position in 1863, and resumed the practice of his profession, which he quietly pursued until 1885, when he was appointed by President Cleveland the Republican commissioner of the District of Columbia under the law creating a permanent government for that District. He was, at the expiration of his term of

Wm. F. Mattingly

service, reappointed by the President, but the Senate failing to act upon his nomination, he again, in 1889, returned to the practice of his profession.

William F. Mattingly, one of the prominent lawyers of the city of Washington, was born in Washington May 30, 1837. His education was received in the public schools of the city, and at Columbia College, from which institution he graduated in 1857. He has occupied numerous positions of trust in his native city, having been one of the trustees of Columbian University since 1872; and since 1888 he has been lecturer in the law school of the same university, on practical commercial law. He studied law in the office of William J. Stone, Jr., on leaving college, and was admitted to the bar of the old Circuit Court in October, 1860, since which time he has been constantly and successfully engaged in the practice of law in Washington.

What has been said of the members of the bar of the District of Columbia in the foregoing pages has been said only of men of the past. It must not be supposed, however, from this that the worth and excellence of the bar of the District are things of the past. On the contrary, it may be safely said that the bar of to-day loses nothing by comparison with its former history. The men of to-day have no occasion to hang their heads; they are worthy successors of those who have preceded them. It would be out of place to attempt sketches of men whose future is yet before them. The present day accords to them, not only in its applause, but in ways that are of much greater present value, the rewards that come from the possession of talent, industry, and ability. The future will crown their record in the praise accorded them by some future historian.

CHAPTER XXIII.

CLAIMS.

THE business of the prosecution of claims against the United States
for amounts due because of services, civil, military, or naval, for
balances unsettled on contracts, and for property impressed and used
for the Government during the wars that have occurred, has become
one of the professions of the country. As such cases must be prosecuted at the Capital, before the departments and the courts and
commissions established for their adjudication, and as many of them
must be argued before the Supreme Court of the United States, this
profession is not only one of the largest in the city of Washington,
but its members have a standing second only, if not in every way
equal, to that of the regular profession of the law. There are many
members of this profession who are exclusively devoted to its demands,
while others are connected also with the regular practice of the law
in the courts of general jurisdiction. Some of these are men who
have occupied the highest positions in the service of the country as
officers of the military, naval, judicial, and executive departments, as
bureau officers, or as members of either branch of Congress.

From the very beginning of the history of the country these
claims have existed, arising in greater numbers after the prosecution
of the wars in which the Government has from time to time been
engaged. The War of the Revolution gave rise to a very large
amount of these claims, many of which required for their proper
prosecution the aid of men competent to construe the acts of Congress
under which the claims arose, and to understand and present the
principles governing contracts in all their various forms. Prominent
among the claims were those for half pay granted by Congress to
the men who had fought in the Revolutionary armies, and the various
methods of commutation of that half pay. It is not worth while to

dwell upon this matter, as it is a part of the history of the country with which every well-read American citizen is familiar.

Following the course of the history of the country, we find that from time to time every class of claims that has arisen has been prosecuted by men specially fitted for such duty. The French spoliation claims, as they are familiarly known, which from the beginning of the present century have been presented to the Government, have recently been presented (to the Government) in such form as to gain a settlement, the act providing for such payment being approved March 3, 1891. During all these years of struggle to secure justice at the hands of the Government in the matter of these claims, they have had in their prosecution men of the highest character and ability. Besides these there were the Florida claims, the claims arising out of the various Indian wars, and the occupation of the Indian Territory, the settlement of the public lands, of the Virginia military bounty lands, and the claims arising out of them, involving large interests in what was known as the Northwest Territory, now occupied by great and flourishing States,— all of these may be mentioned in connection with this business of the profession of the prosecution of claims against the Government. After the conclusion of the Mexican War a commission was created before which claims for the adjudication of large sums were presented. And again after the conclusion of the War of the Rebellion the Government constituted a commission, called the Southern Claims Commission, which held its sessions in every respect as if it were a court, and heard arguments of counsel and adjudged the cases that came before it in the most careful and judicial manner conceivable. In this connection reference may be made to the Alabama Claims Commission, before which came a multitude of claims arising out of depredations upon the commerce of the United States during the War of the Rebellion. This commission was composed of lawyers of the highest standing, one or more of them having been judges in the States from which they were appointed. It was assisted in its investigations by a lawyer of the very highest standing, who had been a Senator of the United States and at one time Postmaster-General. Before this commission came many of the most distinguished lawyers of the country, and the cases in court were heard upon records and briefs as carefully drawn as those of the highest court in the land.

In recognition of the importance of the proper prosecution of claims against the Government, Congress, in August, 1856, established the Court of Claims, a court as well known throughout the country as the Supreme Court itself. This tribunal is presided over by judges of the very highest ability, and so dignified and important is the position of judge upon this bench that it is sought after by the best lawyers in the land. Before it appear at each term of its sessions lawyers of the highest position from every part of the country, and especially from the District of Columbia, to argue cases embracing within their scope and requiring for their settlement a construction of the most abstruse principles of law, and requiring at the hands of the lawyers managing them the most careful study and investigation. Cases from this court go to the Supreme Court of the United States upon appeal, and their argument in that court is attended with as much necessity for ability as the argument of any cases that come before it. The Government is represented before this Court of Claims by the Solicitor-General and by one of the assistant attorney-generals. The great advantage of this court is, that by its organization the Government is protected against a multitude of cases or claims that would otherwise be presented, having no real foundation either in law or in equity. Persons coming before this court are obliged to support their claims by the strictest proof, and with witnesses and depositions, all of which are submitted to the closest scrutiny. Therefore, educated and experienced lawyers, within a comparatively recent period, have become a greater necessity than in earlier times.

Within the last few years, Congress has made the most ample provision for the reward of those men who imperiled life and limb in the defense of their country during the War of the Rebellion, having created pensions to so great an extent that the amount appropriated each year for their payment amounts to many millions of dollars. In these acts, too, for the better protection of those to whom these pensions are donated, Congress has thought best to limit the compensation to be paid to agents for the prosecution of such claims. This of itself is the highest recognition of the necessity and value of the services of these practitioners. The extent to which the prosecution of these claims has grown in the past few years is a matter of sufficient interest to enlist the attention of every citizen, and it must be in every way best for the Government and the claimant that this multitude of claims should be presented in such a way as to effectuate their proper and speedy determination. That this is accomplished best by a class of men who have given their attention to the law under which these claims arise, and who, from their experience and education, have the facilities for preparing the papers necessary in presenting the claims in the proper form, no one can reasonably doubt.

Everything seems to indicate that this profession will increase in importance as time progresses. There can never come a period in the history of our country when claims against the Government will cease. The very fact that Congress is, year after year, making larger and larger appropriations of public moneys for the purpose of satisfying these demands of the citizens of the country, serves to render the existence of the profession of which we are treating a necessity.

The largest private claim agency in Washington is doubtless that of George E. Lemon, whose magnificent building, at 1729 New York Avenue, has the appearance of a Government department building.

It has been stated above that the lawyers engaged in the practice before the Court of Claims and before the departments are, many of them, exceptionally able men. The following list, though selected in a semi-random manner, is, notwithstanding, believed to contain the names of a considerable proportion of the ablest lawyers who have been, and are now, engaged in this practice:

Charles Alert, Robert J. Atkinson, Clifford Arrick, Lewis Abraham, Oliver D. Barrett, John S. Blair, William Birney, A. C. Bradley, A. T. Britton, George S. Boutwell, Richard S. Coxe, James M. Carlisle, Samuel Chilton, John A. J. Creswell, N. P. Chipman, Joseph Casey, James Coleman, C. C. Cole, Jeff Chandler, Charles Alphonse de Chambrun, W. D. Davidge, T. J. Durant, J. W. Douglass, W. W. Dudley, Thomas Ewing, Jr., George Earle, W. E. Earle, C. J. Ellis, P. R. Fendall, F. J. D. Fuller, John E. Fay, R. H. Gillett, John B. Goode, L. G. Hine, George E. Lemon, C. P. Lincoln, James E. Padgett, J. Randolph Tucker, Theodore W. Tallmadge,[1] Eppa Hunton, Frank A. Carpenter, Arthur S. Denver, S. J. Fague & Son, Allen C. Clark, Harvey Spaulding & Sons, and James Tanner.

---

[1] There is a tradition that the name of Tallmadge originated in Wales in the following manner: Persons of a tall stature living on the border of a marsh were called *talle-muche* (*muche* in the Welsh language meaning marsh). In the progress of the language, *muche* changed to *madge*; hence the name *Tallmadge*.

Britton's Journal of Spiritual Science, Literature, and Art published in January, 1873, an article noticing the death of Nathaniel Potter Tallmadge, of Columbia County, New York, containing the following from the history of the Tallmadge family in England:

"All the Tallmadges in the United States are descendants from one of two brothers, Thomas and William, who emigrated from England in 1631, on a vessel named *The Plow.* William died without issue. Thomas, with his two sons, in 1639, located in Southampton, Long Island. These two sons were named Thomas and Robert. Some of the later generations have moved to the Western States. Nathaniel P. Tallmadge, who served two terms as a Senator from New York, became distinguished when Henry Clay, Daniel Webster, and other great men were likewise in the Senate of the United States. Major Tallmadge has a conspicuous place in the history of the

Revolutionary War, from having charge of Major André after his arrest. General James Tallmadge has a prominent place in the history of New York City. The famous Brooklyn divine, T. De Witt Talmage is a descendant from Thomas, aforesaid, who dropped one of the *l*'s and the *d* from the family name, which spelling has been adopted by all his descendants. Robert's descendants have retained the original spelling of the name."

It will be clear, therefore, from the spelling of the family name, that Theodore W. Tallmadge is a descendant of Robert Tallmadge. He was born in Maysville, Kentucky, January 25, 1827, and received a liberal education through the generous heart of his father, Darius Tallmadge, who, from his own experience, realized the necessity of the education of the young. He at first attended Howe's Academy, at Lancaster, Ohio, and for two years, 1841 and 1842, he attended the college of Augusta, Kentucky. He passed his freshman year, 1843, in the Ohio University, at Athens, and the remaining three years of his college life were spent at Princeton College, graduating therefrom in 1846. He studied law at Columbus, Ohio, in the office of Henry Stanbery, and was admitted to practice in the Supreme Court of Ohio and the Circuit Court of the United States in 1848. In 1849 he commenced the practice of law with Hon. John T. Brasee, and in January, 1852, he opened a private banking house in Lancaster, Ohio, pursuing the banking business for several years, during which time he was president of the Wabash Bank, at Wabash, Indiana, which had a note circulation of $200,000, and he was also a director in the Hocking Valley Bank, at Lancaster.

He became engaged in the real estate business at Columbus, Ohio, to which place he moved in April, 1859.

On April 18, 1861, when the Governor of Ohio, William Dennison, called for volunteers under the proclamation of President Abraham Lincoln, Mr. Tallmadge was placed as quartermaster on the staff of Henry Wilson, major-general of the Ohio militia, and at once commenced active duty in receiving and placing into quarters the troops arriving at the general rendezvous, Columbus, Ohio, designated by the Governor. The following May, when the militia of the State was reorganized under act of the legislature, Mr. Tallmadge was commissioned for five years assistant quartermaster and commissary of subsistence by the Governor of Ohio, with the rank of captain in the Ohio volunteer militia, being first sent to the camp of the Seventeenth Regiment Ohio Volunteer Infantry at Lancaster. When that regiment was ordered into active service, Captain Tallmadge was placed in charge of a steamboat with supplies and arms sent by the Governor of Ohio for the use of the Ohio troops under General McClellan, who was preparing to make an advance into West Virginia. Arriving at Parkersburg, and delivering said supplies to General W. S. Rosecrans, then in command of thirteen regiments of three months' volunteers, Captain Tallmadge was detailed to serve on the staff of that general as quartermaster, marching with the brigade *via* Clarksburg, until the battle at Rich Mountain, July 11, 1861, the first battle of the War. He continued on active duty as assistant quartermaster and commissary for one year, having been ordered to various points where Ohio troops were in rendezvous and in service needing arms and supplies. He accompanied the hospital boats sent by the Governor of Ohio with physicians and nurses for taking care of the wounded at the battle of Shiloh, arriving two days after the battle, and was placed in charge of the detail which conveyed the wounded to the boats. In July, 1863, Governor Tod ordered the State militia to Camp Chase, four miles from the Capitol, and Captain Tallmadge was placed on duty as the quartermaster. This call was occasioned by the raid then being made through Indiana and Ohio by the Confederate General Morgan.

In March, 1862, Mr. Tallmadge established the business of prosecuting soldiers' claims at Columbus, Ohio, which proved so successful as to render necessary several

branch offices and the employment of a large force of clerks. Having advertised extensively, and being found adapted to the business as well as successful in the prosecuting of cases, he became, at the close of the War, the most prominent claim agent in the State of Ohio. In October, 1878, he moved his main office to Washington, District of Columbia, still retaining one in Columbus, Ohio, and in other places throughout the United States.

He is a member of the Federal Bar Association of Washington, District of Columbia, practicing in the Court of Claims and all the Government departments. He is a member of Burnside Post No. 8 of the Department of the Potomac of the Grand Army of the Republic, having been elected for three terms as chaplain, and has served as aid-de-camp on the staff of Colonel Charles P. Lincoln, department commander, also in that capacity on the staff of Commander-in-chief William Warner and Wheelock G. Veazey. During most of his life he has been a member of the Methodist Episcopal Church, serving for ten years as trustee of the Wesley Chapel, in Columbus, Ohio, and in the past nine years leader of the strangers' class meeting in the Metropolitan Methodist Episcopal Church, Washington City.

In October, 1849, he married Ellen E., daughter of Hon. John T. Brasee, in Lancaster, Ohio, who died in Columbus, Ohio, February 2, 1865. By that marriage he had six children: Mary, born August 29, 1850; died February 11, 1851, at Lancaster, Ohio. Sarah, born January 9, 1852; married to Harry A. Stephens, residing in Cleveland, Ohio. Frank, born January 9, 1854; resides at Columbus, Ohio. James, born June 6, 1857; died August 14, 1858. Darius, born May 9, 1859. Theodore, born November 18, 1862.

Theodore W. Tallmadge was married June 27, 1867, to Harriet Washington, daughter of Major Andrew Parks, of Charleston, Kanawha County, West Virginia. By this second marriage Mr. Tallmadge has two children — Flora, born October 1, 1868; and Andrew, born January 16, 1870.

49

INDEX.